CW00926811

THE LEGAL SKILLS BOOK
A STUDENT'S GUIDE TO PROFESSIONAL SKILLS

THE LEGAL SKILLS BOOK

A STUDENT'S GUIDE TO PROFESSIONAL SKILLS

Professor Hugh Brayne

University of Sunderland

Professor Richard Grimes

University of Derby

BUTTERWORTHS

London, Edinburgh, Dublin

1998

United Kingdom	Butterworths, a Division of Reed Elsevier (UK) Ltd, Halsbury House, 35 Chancery Lane, LONDON WC2A 1EL and 4 Hill Street, EDINBURGH EH2 3JZ
Australia	Butterworths, a Division of Reed International Books Australia Pty Ltd, CHATSWOOD, New South Wales
Canada	Butterworths Canada Ltd, MARKHAM, Ontario
Hong Kong	Butterworths Asia (Hong Kong), HONG KONG
India	Butterworths India, NEW DELHI
Ireland	Butterworth (Ireland) Ltd, DUBLIN
Malaysia	Malayan Law Journal Sdn Bhd, KUALA LUMPUR
New Zealand	Butterworths of New Zealand Ltd, WELLINGTON
Singapore	Butterworths Asia, SINGAPORE
South Africa	Butterworths Publishers (Pty) Ltd, DURBAN
USA	Lexis Law Publishing, CHARLOTTESVILLE, Virginia

© Reed Elsevier (UK) Ltd 1998

All rights reserved. No part of this publication may be reproduced in any material form (including photocopying or storing it in any medium by electronic means and whether or not transiently or incidentally to some other use of this publication) without the written permission of the copyright owner except in accordance with the provisions of the Copyright, Designs and Patents Act 1988 or under the terms of a licence issued by the Copyright Licensing Agency Ltd, 90 Tottenham Court Road, London, England W1P 0LP. Applications for the copyright owner's written permission to reproduce any part of this publication should be addressed to the publisher.

Warning: The doing of an unauthorised act in relation to a copyright work may result in both a civil claim for damages and criminal prosecution.

Any Crown copyright material is reproduced with the permission of the Controller of Her Majesty's Stationery Office.

A CIP Catalogue record for this book is available from the British Library.

First edition 1994

ISBN 0 406 90415 4

Typeset by Columns Design Ltd, Reading
Printed by Cromwell Press, Trowbridge, Wiltshire

Visit us at our website: http://www.butterworths.co.uk

PREFACE TO SECOND EDITION

We have been pleasantly surprised that a book aimed at Legal Practice Course (LPC) students has been used just as much by degree students, bar students and training managers. Perhaps this proves one of our most important claims – that skills are not things you bolt on to your study or practice of law. They are a part of it, and without them it is hard to make sense of the law and impossible to apply it.

The skills for becoming a competent solicitor are hardly different from those of becoming a competent barrister. So with a little adjustment we have tried to widen the audience and address the needs of the Bar Vocational Course (BVC) student as well. Perhaps more controversially, we have decided to make the book expressly relevant to undergraduate law students too. We cannot do justice to the debate here about whether skills belong in the undergraduate curriculum, but events in the real world seem to be overtaking the purists who don't want skills to taint their academic law. The second edition comes out at a time when the National Committee of Inquiry into Higher Education ('Dearing'), and the government's plans for lifelong learning in higher education have put skills and vocational relevance ahead of knowledge. Anyway, we have yet to find a serious degree student who is not interested in the skills which connect theory to practice, whatever their own career plan. Skills will give you a handle on law – at least we think that our integrated approach will.

What will you get out of this book? Whatever your reason for being interested in skills, we think you will gain an increased understanding of how law works, and a practical philosophy for achieving high standards of competence in all legal work. We place great emphasis on the core skills of legal research and communication. We use concrete examples, and we metaphorically hold your hand as you work through the elements of the skills. We hope you will see there is no need to be frightened.

At the level required of an LPC student, this book is enough to pass the skill assessments. A BVC student will gain understanding of the practical philosophy of lawyering skills, which will enhance assessment performance. But we do not seek to tell you all you need to know about BVC skills, so much as to turbo charge the other guidance you will receive. The same goes for undergraduate law students: what we demonstrate is not how to pass tests, but how to understand how law really works. That will help you pass tests.

We have changed the title of the book since we wrote the first edition. We always preferred the title 'The Legal Skills Book'. Now that we are addressing a wider audience than just students training for professional practice we have been able to persuade our publishers to agree to this title for the second edition.

We debated, in the light of this realignment, whether to retain a chapter on negotiation, which is no longer an assessed LPC skill. We kept it in because resolving disputes and reaching agreement is a core function of the law. It is also an assessed area in the bar course, and an area of growing interest to undergraduates, who are responding enthusiastically to the national negotiating competition. So as far as this book is concerned, the core professional skills remain DRAIN – drafting, research, advocacy, interviewing, and negotiation – rather than ARID. We prefer to call 'negotiation' dispute resolution, and we have added the skill of communication, which we deal with first. But that does spoil the acronym.

We have removed our wills probate case study, and beefed up our business law case study, in response to the new LPC standards. We have added a little material on opinion writing to appeal to bar students, though the foundation of the skill is already there in research and communication. The other change we made, getting closer to the real world of real clients, is that we have given our characters more realistic names. Clients are real people – how could we have even hinted otherwise? You meet them at the end of the first chapter, and we use them to guide you through the skills.

Who wrote what bit? We worked extensively on each other's draft chapters, in both editions, so we both accept responsibility for the whole of the book. The division of labour was approximately:

Chapter 1: Introduction: mostly Hugh Brayne
Chapter 2: Communication for Lawyers: Hugh Brayne
Chapter 3: Interviewing: Hugh Brayne
Chapter 4: Research Skills: Both
Chapter 5: Writing and Drafting in a Legal Context: Richard Grimes
Chapter 6: Reaching Agreements and Resolving Disputes: Mostly Richard Grimes
Chapter 7: Advocacy: Richard Grimes
Chapter 8: Conclusion: Both

We have had a great deal of help with this second edition. Our editors from Butterworths have been a delight to work with, and have enabled us to access much of the legal research software we talk about in chapter 4. Butterworths and Lexis-Nexis generously provided us with access at home to CD and LEXIS research materials. We both have had two new jobs since the first edition came out. Hugh has had great support from Professor Graham Henderson, Director of Sunderland Business School, and during his two years as Head of the Law School at Kingston University, from Professor David Miles, Dean of the Faculty of Business and Law. Richard is grateful to Keith Harrison, Director, School of Financial Studies and Law at Sheffield Hallam University and Sue Wall, Dean of School of European and International Studies, University of Derby. Mark Findlay, Foundation Professor of Law at the University of the South Pacific (Fiji), Jeff Giddings, Senior Lecturer at the Faculty of Law, Griffith University, Australia, and Libby Taylor, Bond University, Australia, also warrant mention for their insight, enthusiasm and support.

PREFACE TO FIRST EDITION

We had a lot of fun writing this book. Legal skills offer a fantastic insight into people, problem-solving, legal method, legal research and the role of the lawyer. Much of this only became clear as we researched and wrote the book. We quickly found there was a deeper level to legal skills than we could find in any existing books. We found a wealth of good material dealing with the components of discrete skills, in fact a marketplace awash with books riding the LPC skills wave. Everyone is able to tell you what to do.

But where can you find out the how and the why of legal skills? Why people turn to lawyers, and what lawyers should be doing for them? How lawyers should relate to clients in a professional environment? We have found answers. The answers are that you communicate with people as if they really matter, and you research each client's problem as if you really care about finding the best possible solution.

The answers are not difficult to understand. It will take a lifetime and a day to put them into practice, but we are sure that by reading this book you can give yourself a grasp of the essential skills of good lawyering that no previous generation of trainees ever had. To make sure you do read this book we have gone out of our way to speak to you as if you are a human being rather than a jargon machine. We are happy to state opinions, admit faults, use colloquial language and breach writing conventions. What would make us unhappy is if you found the book hard to read. What we want above all is that you enjoy reading this book, enjoy training in legal skills, and get excited about the career you are about to embark on.

We are two authors with our own ideas. We agree on the basic ideas, but do not wish to hide our differences from view. Usually we say 'we' in the text, but sometimes we say 'I', where one of us wishes to share a quirky opinion or a personal experience.

We use a lot of examples. Sometimes the client is male, sometimes female: that's easy enough. Sometimes we are talking about no particular client, or solicitor, or witness, in which case we sometimes say 'she or he', sometimes 'he or she', sometimes just 'he' and sometimes just 'she' – yes, we are very flexible. If we say he more than she it is because we are men, for which we half-heartedly apologise.

Much of the final shaping of this book took place at Old Thrang, a farmhouse in the Lake District. We are grateful to David Brayshaw for making this available just when we needed a retreat. Thanks are also due to Paulene Collins from the Law Society for permission to reproduce the skills standards for the LPC; Professor Phil Kenny from Northumbria University and Keith Harrison of Sheffield Hallam University who supported the project throughout; Tessa Green, on whose work our self-assessment checklists are modelled; hundreds of students at both universities who have gone through our clinical skills, LSF and LPC programmes and sharpened our ideas and reminded us of how much fun law can (sometimes) be, and many others including colleagues, medics, counsellors, solicitors, friends, neighbours and our families for support and inspiration.

But ...

If it all gets too much, maybe the case of *Rolph v Zolan* reported in the *Independent* in May 1993 can inspire you. The defendant was a solicitor who was being sued for not paying a builder. The report starts:

> '[The plaintiff] issued a county court summons on 25 July 1991, shortly before the end of the six year limitation period, and it was served at the defendant's house. But unbeknown to the plaintiff, the defendant had, in October 1986, emigrated to Spain to start a new career as a guitarist and flamenco dancer.'

There is more to life than the law!

Hugh Brayne

Richard Grimes

June 1994

CONTENTS

TABLE OF STATUTES

LIST OF CASES

xx · **List of cases**

Chapter 1

INTRODUCTION

Legal skills

You think legal skills matter? We presume that's why you've opened this book.

You may want to develop your legal skills because you are heading for a career in law. In that case you will be using this book to help get through the skills exercises on the Legal Practice Course or Bar Vocational Course.

You may wish to understand and acquire the foundations of the skills of legal practice because you have realised that they will improve your insight into your academic studies of law.

And you are probably motivated by employability – what employers increasingly want, in whatever field you go into, is not just academic knowledge. They want clear evidence of ability to get on and do things – relate to people, communicate in clear English, listen to others, find things out, solve problems constructively, and present ideas persuasively. If you can do this with legal problems you can do it in other areas. That is why people with good legal training tend to be successful in fields such as management and politics as well as in law. They can think, communicate and act.

This book does not just describe the skills from the outside; we attempt to provide you with the experience of using them. But the value of skills is in the doing. If you apply some of the methods we advocate, and if you get systematic feedback from yourself, from colleagues, and from tutors, then this becomes a book about doing. We'll come back later in this introduction to methods of working on your own skills and getting feedback.

We do not apologise for looking at skills from a practice perspective. Even if you are an undergraduate, if you are trying to understand law, why not understand it as it is practised by real lawyers? Law degrees based solely on academic knowledge are going to become a thing of the past, if the recommendations of the Lord Chancellor's Advisory Committee on Legal Education and Conduct are implemented. In their 1996 report they make quite clear that law is to be studied in context, and that the acquisition of skills and values is the top priority. So even if your institution does not require you personally to practise the skills of the lawyer, your ability to understand and use law in this real perspective is educating you according to the future standards for law degrees. For the degree student wondering about taking on skills as well as knowledge, I wonder if the following quote will help convince you are going to be rewarded with a better educational experience by understanding the legal skills context of your studies:

> 'Nearly every student finds that large portions of the curriculum are meaningless. Thus, education becomes a futile attempt to learn material that has no personal meaning. Such learning involves the mind only: it is learning that takes place "from the neck up". It does not involve feelings or meanings; it has no relevance for the whole person. In contrast, there is such a thing as significant, meaningful, experiential learning.' (Rogers and Freiberg, 1994 quoted in Thompson 1997 at page 4).

How good should you be at these skills?

Why should you aim for high standards in developing your skills? The answer is carrots and sticks. If you exercise any of the skills in this book in real life, your work will be judged by the standards of a tightly regulated profession. The sticks are the penalties for bad conduct. Let's get them out of the way, so we can then concentrate on the carrots, which are far more satisfying.

The sticks are all to do with discipline. Here are some that apply to solicitors:

- The Solicitor's Disciplinary Tribunal can strike you off, suspend you from practice, or fine you, for breach of professional standards (Solicitors Act 1974, section 47).

- The Office for the Supervision of Solicitors can make you compensate a client for 'inadequate professional services' (section 43).

- You can be ordered to reduce or forfeit your costs or pay those of your opponent (Rules of the Supreme Court, Order 62).

- You can be sued by a client, or an aggrieved non-client, for breach of contract or negligence if your work is below standard.

For barristers the penalties for rotten work look quite harsh too, though you can mess up in court without being sued:

- You can be made to apologise, return your fee, pay compensation (only £200 though), be disbarred or suspended, reprimanded or fined (Disciplinary Tribunal Regulations 1996, rule 19).

- You can pay the costs of the other side wasted by your shoddy work (Prosecution of Offences Act 1985, Courts and Legal Services Act 1990, section 19A).

Those are powerful sticks. However, the carrots of self-motivation are far more important in securing quality service, because few solicitors actually are disciplined for shoddy work. In 1997 out of almost 25,000 complaints about solicitors, only 207 reached the Solicitor's Disciplinary Tribunal, with 45 being struck off – Office for the Supervision of Solicitors

First Annual Report. Complaints that year were up by 30%, which many solicitors writing to the Law Society Gazette blame on the client. If *you* think the client responsible for poor performance by lawyers, you really do need to read the rest of this book now!

Far less formal complaints are made about barristers – around 360 a year (one for every 30 barristers, compared to one for every three solicitors).

Enough of sticks. It is more encouraging to look at the carrots: the satisfaction of providing a professional service to people who will appreciate your efforts; the achievement of personal financial security, even wealth; the fulfilment of being in control of your work; and, not to be understated, you can avoid a life of panic and overwork. Those are the rewards of being good at it.

What is good quality service?

If you are on the Legal Practice Course or Bar Vocational Course (from now on we will use the initials LPC and BVC) you will be immersed in the Solicitors' Practice Rules 1990 and the Code of Conduct of the Bar of England and Wales 1990. We have set out some of the rules telling you how good your work must be in two columns, for solicitors and barristers. The standards for barristers are more explicit, but there is no conflict between the two.

Solicitors must, under rule 1:

- act in the best interests of your client, and in accordance with your instructions;

- never compromise your independence or integrity;

- maintain a proper standard of service;

- comply with your duty to the court.

Barristers must

- promote and protect fearlessly and by all proper and lawful means your lay client's best interests (para 5.1);

- act promptly, conscientiously, diligently and with reasonable competence, and not take on work you have not time or expertise to handle (para 5.3);

- give advice which is practical, appropriate and clear (para 5.7) and without too much delay (para 5.6);

- not knowingly or recklessly mislead the court (para 5.2).

To these stated rules, we would add two possible rules of our own: to practise in a manner which is socially useful (something you will define for yourself), and in accordance with the economic realities of what your client can afford.

The duty to the court means you should place the interests of justice above those of the individual client. You cannot lie for the client, or mislead the court. We will look at this more closely in Chapter 7 on Advocacy.

The other rule 1 standards we will take together as the obligation to provide a proper standard of work. We postpone defining this until we have had a brief overview of professional lawyering skills. We believe you will then be able to see that the use of the skills is a fundamental component of providing a proper standard.

You cannot apply the law without understanding and using each of what are known as the DRAIN skills. DRAIN? The acronym has already been discussed in the preface, and it will crop up a few more times, so we will explain it here. The LPC was set up by the Law Society as a practical skills-based course. It is delivered and assessed in each teaching institution in a different way. So in order to ensure some uniformity of standard, the Law Society determined a minimum set of standards which each student has to achieve. When the BVC was set up beyond the Inns of Court, similar standards were published.

There are, of course, many opinions on what the important legal skills consist of. Communication, legal critique, opinion writing, mooting, for example, are categories of skill activities. The Law Society decided the emphasis should be on five broad categories: Drafting; Research; Advocacy; Interviewing; Negotiation. They have now taken out Negotiation, but we have kept it in because handling disputes is too important to omit. Everything you do within the other skills is carried out in the shadow of an eventual negotiation.

Each skill is separately identified, in this book and on the vocational courses. There is no way of avoiding this. Through shortage of time, and pressure to assess knowledge as well as skill on the vocational courses, each skill is usually treated as a free standing competence when it is assessed.

So can you pick them off one by one? 'OK, we've done interviewing, now we'll do research', like the tourist who 'did' Scotland on Thursday, and is 'doing' the Lake District on Friday.

You don't 'do' skills so much as absorb them. They become part of you, an approach to law, unlike knowledge which can be used and discarded. You will find that your legal understanding increases as you practise the skills.

You will never be 'done' with any of these skills. The danger on a vocational course which purports to test you on your competences in each of the skill areas is that you will come to believe that interviewing, say, stands alone from advocacy; that research and drafting are two different things. If you can achieve a pass in the tests that your institution sets you by adopting this approach, we will not advise you against it. But it is unlikely that you will, and that approach will not help you to be the good practitioner you are striving to become. If your interest is not the vocational qualification but a better understanding of law, picking off the skills as freestanding competences is, first, a waste of time and, secondly, not likely to advance your competence even in that individual skill. Remember always that competence in a skill is a means to a more important end, and not the end in itself (unless you are facing an assessment).

If there is no integration you are likely to find that competence is measured by a checklist approach: if you shake hands and ask the client about their journey, you have shown the skill of 'putting the client at ease' in an interview. If you have put a particular series of clauses in a property transfer, you have shown drafting skill. But remember the comment of the otherwise brilliant surgeon: 'the operation was a success, but unfortunately the patient died'. What matters is the result that you achieve for your client through the application of the skills. For assessment purposes we can't deny that it is the student at the centre of the process. In real life the process becomes client centred, and the skills matter only in terms of what they deliver.

The conveyance is not a success if the client does not want to move to that house on that date at that price: your drafting must be informed by what your client says he or she wants in your interviewing (guided by your advice). You do not build rapport in interviews as an end in itself: your interviewing must be informed by your strategy for identifying and dealing with the client's legal needs. So to interview you have to know law and procedure in the relevant area, which comes from research; you have to give advice in the light of choices, which can only be informed by your abilities as a negotiator and as an advocate.

Few clients come to you knowing exactly the outcome they want: if client A knew she wanted a High Court writ followed by Order 14 summary judgment and enforcement by an attachment of earnings order, you, the lawyer could be by-passed. Instead she comes to you saying, for example, 'X hasn't paid me for the widgets, it's not fair, help me'. Your task is to supply advice and services that enable the client to achieve the best result in her circumstances.

Let us stick with this litigation example, and look at each of the DRAIN skills. Your client arrives at your office wanting you to do something to get the money *now*. You immediately have to enquire about the details of why she thinks the debt is owing, the evidence available to prove it, and the tactics for recovering it. What skill are you exercising?

In the first interview you are, self-evidently, interviewing: in the interview you must also demonstrate an appreciation of negotiation (she wants the money now; that can only be achieved by quick settlement; even summary judgment is weeks away at best). You must employ your research skill to get at all the relevant facts. You tell her that, if the negotiation fails, you will advise her to issue proceedings; you are already anticipating using your drafting and advocacy skills, and viewing the option of going to court as part of a negotiation tactic. You make plain from the start that there are going to be times when you do not know the answer to legal or factual questions, that you are going to have to carry out research all the way through the case.

We have only touched on the first interview, and every skill is in mind as you take a note of the facts and offer your preliminary advice. There is one other point which this example demonstrates: all the skills, however well integrated, could not be exercised without you knowing something about litigation. You were unable even to ask for the relevant facts if you did not know that there are procedures for recovering debts in the county and High courts; you had to understand causes of action, and defences, which are matters of law (contract and perhaps sale of goods in the example). Skills are inseparable from law and procedure, and useless in their absence.

The example we chose was from the core subject of litigation – contentious work. Surely in non-contentious work, we hear you say, this interrelationship of all the skills is not required? To draft a lease, or a partnership agreement, all you need is interviewing to take instructions, drafting, and research on unfamiliar points. Where is the advocacy? Why do you need negotiation?

Let's approach this question first in relation to advocacy. Non-contentious work, almost by definition, should not require advocacy. Where is that element of dispute that makes this skill relevant? And if there is no dispute, there need be no negotiation.

In one sense, the answer is that the non-contentious lawyer does not need these skills, if by advocacy skills we mean simply the art of standing up in court and presenting evidence and argument. That can be delegated to a colleague or (for a solicitor) counsel; or avoided by negotiation. But that is to compartmentalise advocacy in a dangerous sense. What we have just described – courtroom advocacy – is the tip of the advocacy iceberg; the full scope of the art of advocacy covers preparation of a case, its fact, its law, its evidence, its tactics, its arguments.

These skills are of course required in a contentious matter, because any contentious matter, by definition, is a dispute which will end up being litigated if not settled or abandoned. So in the contentious matter you start out preparing the case in the shadow of the court: you cannot research the facts or the law if you do not know how the court will interpret those facts, or whether they will be ruled admissible in evidence. You cannot negotiate from strength if you do not understand your alternatives, one of which is to take the matter to court.

If drafting a conveyance, a contract, a will or a partnership deed was truly non-contentious, there would be no need to do it carefully; the work would never have to be tested. Every bit of a lawyer's work can ultimately be tested in court. That's why the non-contentious practitioner reads the law reports. It's like an innoculation: to avoid catching the thing you fear (smallpox/litigation) you deliberately introduce some of the culture inside your system (to create antibodies/effective anti-litigation documents). The better you draft it the less likely it is that you will catch the disease (get taken to court over the meaning of the document). The parties to any potential dispute will take advice; the adviser will tell each party that the agreement means exactly what you intended it to mean. The advice will be: there is no point in litigating.

But ultimately a person can litigate over anything they wish, including well drafted documents. The quality of your work – whether you like it or not – is then tested in the courtroom. You carry out your non-contentious work, therefore, with that spectre hanging over you. If non-contentious work were really litigation-proof, lawyers would go out of business.

A better term is 'rarely contentious', or, even more accurately, 'dispute avoidance' work. And if the non-contentious lawyer really wants to avoid litigation, the answer is: know the enemy. The enemy here is disputes and litigation, the court case, where all your carefully constructed wills or conveyances or contracts will be put under the court's and the advocates' microscope.

A proper standard of work

At this point, we want to remind you of where we started: the overriding need for a 'proper standard'. Your degree (or postgraduate conversion course) may not yet have prepared you for this. On many undergraduate courses you have been used to a diet of far-fetched legal problems cloaked around improbable characters with ridiculous names. Removing the real life detail is thought to help you focus on precise legal details. But it is a long way from the problems of real people: this approach did not teach you that facts are obtained, not given; that 'facts' are actually at best working hypotheses, that all parties to any matter have different hypotheses as to what the facts really are; that there are dimensions to a problem more important to the client than the legal solution, such as:

■ Can I afford this?

■ Can I wait?

■ Why does this problem make me feel so angry?

■ Can I bear the upset of using the law/not using the law?

■ Will my evidence stand up in the event of a dispute?

■ Do I need to retain a good relationship with the other party rather than 'win'?

■ Do I want money? Do I want victory? Do I want to recover some control over my life?

■ What risks am I prepared to take to obtain the best result?

■ Can I get on with my solicitor?

You did not learn, in solving knotty academic problems, that a relationship with a client develops over time; the client brings new facts, new problems, modifies his or her opinion and instructions to you in the light of your advice, or in defiance of your advice.

On a vocational course, and for evermore after that, you have to think about real problems, not pre-packaged ones. Your client, even the role-playing stooge, is briefed to be concerned about costs, risks, alternatives; to display emotions, to be coy about revealing certain facts: to be human in a fraught situation. This applies equally to the corporate client; your instructions are coming from a human representative of the client company. A good quality of service means putting your skills at the service of the client; your client is your boss. You have the task of interpreting the wishes of this boss – to recover a debt, to avoid a criminal penalty, to obtain a property, to form a business. The client is boss and buying your services. Nevertheless, you are like Jeeves with Wooster; only one of you is in control – you – whatever the other is encouraged to think.

The service you are selling is a skill, not a product. It cannot be taken from the store and offered on a take it or leave it basis: serving this boss means ascertaining his, her or its wishes; identifying the possibilities for achieving them; advising on how to modify these wishes in the light of what is possible; then using the skills at your disposal to go for it.

Quality work means not cutting corners; not settling for less than the client is entitled to or content with; getting things done quickly, if that is what the client wants; and finding alternatives to conflict if appropriate.

Your best professional service must survive any personal tensions of the lawyer–client relationship, and anticipate them. And at the end of the process, unless your client is asking you to do something unprofessional or has decided to terminate the retainer, the client remains your boss.

A working definition of a proper standard might now be: to deal accurately, promptly, efficiently, confidentially and creatively with your client's affairs, and to take all steps that are legitimate and affordable to achieve the agreed objectives set by the client.

Professional relationship with the client

To demonstrate your competence in the DRAIN skills, and to deliver a quality service, you must understand the nature of your relationship with the client.

Nothing you do serves any other purpose than the client's. (Your overriding duty to the court and the profession is within the context of serving clients; it is not freestanding.) The skill of, for example, drafting or advocacy or negotiation is one that is to be put at the client's disposal, not yours. There may be circumstances when it would save you from serious embarrassment to settle a matter and get your costs quickly, in order to hide a mistake you have made; there may be times when you do not have the expertise or time to handle the task. You may prefer to advise a client to plead guilty because you believe criminal legal aid rates make a trial uneconomic. You may prefer to push under the carpet the possibility that two clients seeking business advice may have conflicting interests.

Your client is entitled to know that you have a problem. Your own convenience is of no relevance. It is a serious breach of professional standards to compromise your client's interests without express instructions: for example, to get a good deal on costs; to turn away from litigation which you prefer to avoid; to compromise one client's interests in favour of another's interests.

The professional relationship with the client is most visible when you are face to face, in the interview; but it does not only take place there. The file is the property of the client; all drafts and memoranda are the client's, subject to any lien on unpaid costs. All interview notes, statements, attendances, are drafted with the client's needs in mind, not the solicitor's.

DRAIN skills – demonstrating your competence

You were probably told that one of the goals of your degree or CPE is to teach you to 'think like a lawyer'.

We suspect, in fact, that you have hardly started to think like a lawyer yet. You have become familiar with legal concepts, statutes, cases, primary sources, databases, and textbooks; you have learned to take a given set of facts, analyse the legal situation, and construct legal arguments.

The use of professional skills is some way removed from this world. You will, at last, begin to get a real taste of thinking like a lawyer.

What is it that you will now start doing, that you have not done before? The key difference is that you will be making decisions in the face of uncertainty: before now you have, more or less, been handed all the facts you need for the legal analysis: 'X, who has an eggshell skull', 'Y has for twenty years used a path over Blackacre' etc. Now you will have to evaluate X's medical condition in the light of conflicting – or inadequate – information, before you can even start to advise on the legal position or start to take decisions; you will have to consider how you are going to prove that Y has used that path, and which conflicting stories the other witnesses may put forward (if they can be traced), before advising on the covenants.

The nearest you will get to the facts now is probabilities. In the real world, facts are not given, and every person has their own view as to what reality is. You are going to have to develop strategies for finding out what the facts probably are – you are going to have to make predictions about what will be believed if there is a dispute. There is no truth: everyone is peddling their own model of it. Which model will a court prefer, which model will other parties be influenced by?

Thinking like a lawyer is the art of making decisions in a world of uncertainty. You will learn to break the habit that has served you so well in traditional law school problem solving exercises, the habit of advising your client in certainties – 'you will recover damages' or 'this agreement will achieve this result'. You will learn to say 'if X is true then Y may follow, assuming the following doesn't happen ... '. For example: '*If* we can get a surety in your bail application then bail *may* be granted, *if* the prosecution does not come up with new information, and so long as Mrs X is not sitting on the bench that day.' The nearest you can get to certainties will be a confident opinion, based on your analysis of fact and law, rather than definitive answers to questions.

The fundamental skill, in this new world you are entering, is not the analysis that comes after establishing the relevant facts and law; it is establishing those facts and principles in the first place, evaluating their reliability, checking the facts against the law and then producing choices and advice for the client.

How are you going to learn to achieve this?

The old method of learning skills for practice, in so far as anyone gave it systematic thought, was watching other lawyers and copying them. And even now, in textbooks on subjects like advocacy and drafting, the advice often found is: 'Here are examples of how the greatest lawyers have in the past carried out their skill – now off you go and copy them.'

But how many of you could learn to play the violin, dance rock and roll, ride a bike, ski, speak Russian, or argue before a judge, just by watching other people do it brilliantly. The excellent performance you are seeing or hearing is the tip of an iceberg; you are not seeing the training, the research, the patient analysis and the practice, that support those few brilliant moments of superb performance. Try to copy the form without the content, and your efforts will almost certainly come to nothing.

We do not suggest that watching the best performers is unhelpful – far from it. You can see what the best performance looks like, and set your sights accordingly, by listening to Menuhin, watching the Tour de France, or sitting in the High Court. But that is their performance, not yours, achieved by means that you do not yet know. Why, for example, was the particular question put to the witness at that moment so effective? You could copy by asking the same question in a similar case and fall flat on your face. It would be like delivering the punchline to the wrong joke. The same would apply if you always use the same will clauses, because you once obtained a precedent that you liked: it may have been perfect for that client, but slavishly using it for other clients is mindless and potentially dangerous, because you have failed to understand why that particular will was so good for that particular testator.

A recent radio story, apparently true, illustrates the point. A three-year-old girl had passed two happy weeks pretending to be a building worker while an extension was built at her home. She was even given her own wage packet. As she blew her earnings in the sweet shop, she was asked if she planned to carry on building the following week, to which she replied: 'I don't know; it depends if the f'ing bricks are delayed again.' Copying does not always impress, even if exact and in context, if you don't know what you are saying and why.

The skills requirements for a vocational course, together with a practice-orientated approach to teaching the subjects, means most of your work goes on the bit of the iceberg below the water line. When you come to demonstrate your competence, the examiner is looking above the water line; but he or she knows that the bulk below supports what is on top.

Assessment of professional skills on LPC/BVC courses

This section is mainly relevant to students on a vocational course. Some good news for some: very few LPC students fail their course as a sole result of failing a skill assessment. But on the BVC these assessments carry higher priority.

Unless on an exempting degree, you will not be assessed while conducting a real case. Facts and tasks will come to you either on paper/computer, through interview simulation, or through video. Material will be realistic, but tasks often will be free standing, so that when a skill assignment is set, it is likely to focus on that single skill.

For example, you will prepare for your interview performance probably knowing that you will not be assessed on how you follow it up: you can safely say to the 'client' (the person playing the role) 'I'll look up that point of law; I'll talk to that witness, and see you next week to discuss things further. Please make an appointment with my secretary on the way out.' You and the assessor will know that there is no secretary, no witness, and no follow-up. Your ability to interview will be assessed in that short isolated performance.

So some of what we have said about integration of the skills will now seem superfluous, something that does not need to be considered outside real legal practice. But we hope that you will agree, when we have dealt with each DRAIN skill in turn, that demonstration of the interrelationships does maximise your chance of demonstrating competence.

For vocational students both the Law Society and the Bar have set out outcome standards for the skills. We will set these out in each of the five skill chapters, and describe ways in which you can demonstrate your competence in relation to each. At the end of each chapter we have given you a self assessment checklist, since teaching staff have less time to give you feedback, then you and your peers will have to do this for yourselves. (There is more on self and peer assessment later in this chapter.)

What is a pass standard for a lawyer about to enter a training contract or pupillage?

The standard of a good solicitor or barrister in practice would be too high – though when you read the outcome standards you might think that this is what you are expected to achieve. The standard of measuring whether you are intelligent enough to be thrown in at the deep end (which was the level of skills training many of your predecessors were given) is too low. In this book we are aiming somewhere in between.

Perhaps your approach can be influenced by the following analysis of skills. Imagine you are going to start to learn to drive a car. Before you get in to the driving seat you have

- unconscious incompetence – you don't know anything, you don't even know what you don't know. Perhaps you can say 'vroom vroom' and turn the wheel like a child copying his or her mum. Then you get some instruction and you have moved into

- conscious incompetence – you know you have to lift the clutch as you nudge the accelerator and steer between the pavement and the oncoming traffic, and you know that you don't know how to do it. You practise, you get further guidance, you move to

- conscious competence – with a lot of effort you are moving the car forward, thinking and fretting about each stage, each new challenge. It is enormously tiring and stressful.

- unconscious competence – you just do it; you can even do it while having a phone conversation and thinking about what to cook tonight. You may even make mistakes because you have stopped thinking about it.

We suggest a very good outcome will be conscious competence. You must demonstrate that you understand the qualities exhibited by the good lawyer that you have a foundation on which to build and evaluate your later experience. The foundations on which you are building must be apparent. Please try to distinguish between foundations and superficialities. Foundations are clear communication in good English; understanding of human relationships; ability to identify problems and to ask the right questions before conducting your research. Superficialities are using legal jargon; 'meeting seating and greeting' or other formulaic/checklist approaches to getting to know your client. Superficialities are the things you can imitate – the 'vroom vroom' approach to demonstrating your skill – whereas foundations are those you have done a lot of work on.

Unlike the deep-end trainee, you must show that you know what you are trying to achieve, that you are working to a conceptual framework in everything you do. What you don't know you don't pretend to know. If you can demonstrate that you know that standards exist, and that your performance is modelled on them, you will not be expected to meet each and every standard with a high level of competence, which only comes about when you have absorbed aspects of them into unconscious competence.

Each institution will have its own approach. There may be a temptation to expect a standard too close to that of the good practitioner. In judging student performance the assessors, particularly those fresh from practice, sometimes do not always know how to look for the underlying strength, and too easily identify the faults: 'I wouldn't have done it that way myself'. A commonly accepted culture of acceptable performance at LPC level is not yet established, unlike the standard acceptable for degree classification.

Despite all the 'objective' criteria for measuring various components of your skills, we believe the common culture for assessment is based around the subjective question: is this performance good enough? Good enough for what? Good enough to start working under the supervision of an experienced practitioner? Good enough to start building on these skills in the real world of practice? You will be demonstrating an attitude of enquiry and problem solving, rather than the 'right' way to tackle a particular task. To look for excellence will lead to disappointment and failure: while excellence will be the goal, good enough at this stage in your career will be the foundation for later excellence.

How will you know if you are 'good enough'?

Every institution teaching a vocational course has its own criteria for assessment of competence. You must make sure that you have understood the assessment regime that operates as soon as you start the course. Find out when and how each skill is assessed; what practice opportunities you will have, what feedback you can expect on your performance, what video facilities are available for practising the oral skills.

Are there checklists of criteria which will be used for marking? Study them; practise and evaluate your own performance according to them; work with colleagues, as this helps not only the person being assessed, but the person doing the assessment. Study any demonstration material available that indicates the level of performance that your assessors are looking for.

Perhaps the definition of a skill is something you can only learn by doing. Reading this book will give you a foundation in each skill; it will guide you towards how to plan your performance, how to bring out the key features of your competence. You can use the guidance to look at how you and your colleagues are performing. But it will not do the work for you. 'I do and I understand' says Confucius; practise, practise and practise again, always spending time afterwards evaluating and learning from what you did. Spend time watching others; in court (most are open to the public) or by a placement in a legal environment, and critique what you see. Was it well done? Could it have been improved? Were there parts that show you how to tackle a similar problem?

Each skill has components which it is possible to look for. You will find after each of the DRAIN chapters a checklist of these components. They are set out on facing pages so that you (students, please, not lecturers) can, if you wish, photocopy them and use them to critique your own performance, and that of colleagues. These checklists may be more detailed than those used for the actual assessment, which typically cover about ten headings. We give this level of detail so that you can scrutinise your performance rather than merely arrive at a pass/fail judgment of competence.

You have not got the time to practise, because of the demands of the other subjects? We encourage you to think again. In practising the skill you are also getting to grips with the legal subject. Drafting, advocacy or research, for example, bring you face to face with the gaps in your knowledge and understanding; they give a new, perhaps more alive, context to the law and procedure that you will be assessed on. Learning about the Bail Act or the Partnership Act will become reinforced as you put it to the service of a client, even in a simulated exercise. Do a skills exercise instead of reading over your notes for the seventh time. You may learn more and enjoy yourself at the same time.

On your course you will be provided with opportunities and materials to practise all of these skills before assessment starts. But the onus is, in the end, on you; your lecturers already have a job, you are the ones who need to prove yourselves! Demand as much as you are able from those who can help, but they cannot do the job of becoming competent for you.

A word on self and peer assessment

Three words actually: be selective, be concrete and be constructive.

If you want feedback from someone else, there are two ways to ask.

Number 1: 'I've just done this mock interview – here's the video, tell me what you think' or 'Would you have a look at this research report for me?' Imagine you are presented with this request. Your heart sinks. You don't have the time and you don't know what you are looking for. The easiest things to spot will be mistakes, so that's how you feed back to your friend, who gets defensive and doesn't ask you again.

Number 2: you review your tape, your research report, and decide on maybe two key areas where you were having difficulty, or where you think you did something well but would like a second opinion. You say to your colleague: 'in this interview I was particularly troubled by my failure to show the client that I had understood how worried she was about the cost of losing the case; would you take a look at 6 min 32 sec through to 7 min 18 sec, and in particular pay attention to how you felt she was responding to what I said there? If you can offer concrete advice as to ways I might have handled it differently please tell me.'

By concrete we mean more than: 'you could have been more supportive/clear at 7 min 3 sec'. It means, for example, suggesting the exact words your friend might have considered using in the interview: 'I wonder if at that point you might have said instead of "well shall we move on to the question of costs?" something that allowed your client to go back over what seems to be preoccupying her and preventing her from understanding your explanation. How about: "Mrs Brown, I can tell this question is troubling you, but I am having some difficulty getting a clear picture in my head. Do you think perhaps you could tell me again why your husband said he doesn't want to take the case any further?" '

The same goes for the research report, the drafting exercise etc. 'Please look at whether I have identified the right question – see page 3 where I have highlighted the key questions – and suggest ways in which I might have rephrased the question to give a more precise identification of the research task'.

Constructive is the third word, and it must not be confused with nice, which just leads to bland and useless comment. 'That was very good' is fine, but what has been learned? 'I thought the way you said to your client at 19 minutes 54 seconds "Let's see if I've understood the issues clearly. You are very keen to get Mr X involved in your business venture; you need at least £50,000 to start the new production line; and you are undecided about whether you want to form a company or continue as a sole trader. Have I missed anything at this stage?" worked very well; how do you think your client felt when it became clear to him that you had got that clear sense of his priorities?'

Constructive criticism can be, by definition, critical. 'I do wonder at that point if you could have just paused a little longer to see if your client was thinking of anything else before you moved onto the question of suggesting that Mr X should see his own solicitor as soon as possible – which was a good point, but might have been delayed a little while'. This is not negative, compared for example with: 'I think you came in too soon with the point about Mr X's solicitor' or even 'Why didn't you deal with that later?' You can learn to send out signals that result in the person you are supporting not feeling he or she is put on the defensive.

Constructive criticism is a mixture of praise (with concrete reasons) and suggestions (with concrete suggestions). Do both. One rule of thumb is to start with praise, to end with praise, and to give more positive than negative comments overall. Have you heard of the 'mud sandwich'? (For 'mud' use a stronger word if you wish, at least between consenting adults in private.) If you are going to ask your friend to accept something potentially unpleasant, make sure it is surrounded by two nice chunks of something pleasant. 'Your statement of claim shows very clearly how the accident itself happened; I noticed that you identified the cause of action as "res ipsa loquitur", and I'm wondering if it should be negligence – perhaps we can look that up in a minute. The particulars of loss were very clear, and pleading the cost of nursing care from your client's mother is something I hadn't even thought of.'

Show that you know where you are going

Something we are surprised by when we mark undergraduate work is how little idea students have, after years of immersion in law, that it is not just what you say that wins the marks; it is how you organise it.

Whether it is the solution of one of the legal problems beloved of degree question setters, or the invitation to discuss some pithy quote, students perform best if they demonstrate, not implicitly but explicitly, a thought-out structure to what they write. A thread of logic and argument connecting all the points together, concluding with, yes, a conclusion, scores high marks; throw in some legal analysis and you hit a good degree standard. Identify the issues; explicitly analyse those that are important; write what is relevant to these, and why, rather than everything you know. In other words, you show that you can apply what you know rather than merely describe it.

The same approach applies to the demonstration of legal skills. You can rarely show competence on an impromptu basis; even the best stand-up comics, or those who deliver crushing answers at parliamentary question time, anticipate and plan for the occasion. In carrying out any skill task you must show that you are thinking and planning strategically.

How you go about devising and applying the strategy to solve problems is covered principally in Chapter 4 (Research). But to give you an overview, we offer you in the next two pages a series of steps spanning the entire relationship with the client; if you try to identify where your performance of a particular task fits into such a framework, you are en route to showing a strategic approach.

Stage 1: Taking initial instructions

1   *What* the client wants: find out the client's definition of what he or she wants from you and why.

2   *How* the client wants to get it: find out how the client would like to achieve these goals.

3   *When* the client wants it: find out how urgent it is for the client to get it.

4   *How badly* the client wants it: this includes how much the client is prepared to invest in getting it (money, energy and risk), and what is the alternative to getting it.

Stage 2: Exploring the instructions

5 *Get clarification from the client*: Are there any parts of stages 1–4 that do not make sense? Ask.

6 *Who else can help you get a full picture?* What information can you get from other sources? Who do you need to talk to? What documents could you ask for? How much will these enquiries cost? How much time will they take? Is it worth it or can you start acting now? Take instructions on these possibilities.

At this stage you have not advised. You have gathered information. Premature advice is bad advice.

When you now step into the arena, you will influence the answers you have obtained. Knowledge of law, procedure, experience of cost, timescales, and generation of your own strategies and goals will alter the client's own goals.

When you think you understand the problem and the goal, it is worth reminding yourself that solving problems is rarely static. New information constantly dictates altering the approach, and seeking yet further information and instructions. Bearing that in mind we go on to the next stage.

Stage 3: Generating solutions

7 List all the possible ways (strategies) you can think of to achieve what the client wants, including ways that you are unfamiliar with.

8 Take a good look at these strategies – abandon any that have zero chance of success.

9 Look at the rest. Make a list of everything you need to know or do before you have enough information to choose between the strategies. If you do not know where to start, talk to an expert or read a good textbook. Sleep on it.

10 Research what you need to research – fact, procedure and law.

11 Match the strategies to the client goals, advise the client and choose a preferred strategy.

You have now become involved; you have subjected the client's own analysis to a broadening investigation of the facts and potential facts; you have provided an increase in the range of solutions to be considered, and an initial analysis of feasibility.

Stage 4: Take stock

Look back over the previous steps; are any of the solutions proposed based on wishful thinking by the client or wrong assumptions by the lawyer? Sleep on it again if there is time, talk to colleagues (but do not mention confidential details to anyone outside the practice).

No irrevocable decisions have been made until you check:

12   Can it be done by the time the client wants?

13   Can it be done in the way the client wants?

14   Can it be done for a price (including effort and risk) the client will pay?

15   How certain is it that it can be done at all? Make a note of everything that could go wrong. Is this still a good strategy? If not, start again.

16   Will it achieve the client's objectives? (Have these changed in the meantime?)

Stage 5: Doing it

17   What information do you need – fact, law and procedure? Whose job is it to obtain it?

18   What are the steps to be taken? Who will take them, and when?

19   What will these steps cost? Will the client pay it? Do you have the resources and expertise to take them?

To carry out this process may become intuitive after a long period in practice. At this stage in your career, we wish to encourage you to make the process explicit rather than intuitive.

The case studies

In the remainder of this chapter we introduce you to the method used in this book for analysing and assimilating the skills.

Underpinning all five identified skills is the need for effective communication. The sharpest legal mind may be of little use if coupled with an inability to communicate with the client, the judge, or the other side. The following chapter will therefore look at oral and written communication skills.

With an understanding of skills generally, and communication in particular, attention can be turned to the individual identifiable skills. For reasons that will become apparent we have chosen to deal with them in the following order: Interviewing, Research, Drafting, Dispute Resolution and Advocacy. The acronym of IRDDRA may not roll off the tongue as readily as DRAIN but it will, we are confident, make more sense in the telling.

A lawyer can only be as good as the material he or she possesses. Interviewing is usually the first source of such material. Research – which means asking as well as answering questions – is a fundamental method of information gathering. The research may relate to the law or facts or both. Research is the basis for planning what you will do. Armed with the fruits of careful and skilful interviewing and research the lawyer is in a position to draft documentation relevant to that case. This may include letters to the client, or the opposition, court pleadings, a brief or instructions to counsel, or a document recording a formal transaction such as a conveyance or a will.

Once in possession of all the relevant material the lawyer can move towards the client's goals. Negotiation and advocacy may then arise, or other techniques of dispute resolution.

Throughout the life of a particular transaction you will need to review and evaluate progress. This will often require you to take further instructions (interviewing), pursue more research and perhaps negotiate again. The process of pursuing a solution to the problem at hand, or completing a transaction to the client's satisfaction, is therefore one that consistently requires the application of the whole range of DRAIN skills coupled with the ability to communicate effectively.

These skills are best understood in the context of legal practice. In order both to make sense of the skills and to give the content of the book interest and meaning, we have created a set of case studies taken from our collective experience in legal practice. Although inspired by real life, the characters in these studies are fictitious and their personal details entirely altered from those of the clients who gave us the original inspiration.

However, there will be sufficient character traits revealed for you to identify the sorts of people you may come into contact with in legal work. Hence, we will shortly meet the seemingly dependent meek and mild client who accepts without question the advice given to her. We will also encounter the forthright, confident client who appears to know what he wants and how he wants the lawyer to act for him. There is also the reluctant client from whom obtaining good instructions is difficult. For balance we have introduced a pair of relatively straightforward clients who want an uncomplicated transaction completing as soon as possible.

In all we use four case studies to illustrate the relevant skills. We have selected these to make them relevant to BVC students, who study Criminal and Civil Litigation in some detail, and LPC students, who study Litigation in less detail and also study Business Law and Practice and Conveyancing. Students on these course will therefore be able to gain insight into many of the legal issues arising in these subject areas throughout the progress of each case study. Other readers will, we hope, be able to relate to the realistic settings as a vehicle for the study of the professional skills. You do not need a detailed knowledge of these areas in order to read this book, as one of our main tasks is to show how to tackle problems through finding out. Once you have this skill you can transfer it to any area of law you like.

Our aim is therefore to give a practical and meaningful context for the analysis of the legal skills, and the objective is that you will develop a reflective understanding of the skills that lawyers use and need in practice. By reflective, we mean the process by which you can stand back and think systematically about the application of legal skills in real life situations.

The case studies will run throughout the chapters dealing with the DRAIN skills. Some will be more important at particular stages than others; for instance, the crime case will peak in the advocacy chapter; the conveyancing study will centre on drafting but will also appear elsewhere. The civil litigation dispute is used to illustrate dispute resolution. Sometimes the story has more than one ending – better than a novel! We promise to see each case to its conclusion.

We build and use research strategies in each case to give a basis for the eventual decision-making and for the various outcomes. Research may sound a very grand term for what is sometimes a simple, but always important, task. We establish a set of principles upon which a case or transaction is prepared and which is supported by the relevant law and facts. This approach will be particularly developed in the research chapter. You will not understand drafting, dispute resolution and advocacy unless you understand research techniques, and have followed the factual and legal development of our clients' cases in Chapter 4.

In each case study, in order to simplify matters, we have presumed the solicitor to be neutral in terms of gender, race, age, disability and class. Their names are A, B, C and D, and occasionally E. (Thought that would grab your interest!) While the clients and other characters are given life, the lawyers are not. This is simply a focusing technique. We appreciate – and so must you – that lawyers are no different from anyone else in that their own characteristics, preferences and even prejudices come into play. The lawyer needs to be aware of these in order to prevent them interfering with the client's interests. In an attempt to reinforce the principle of acting in the client's best interest, and in order to make this text manageable, the additional complications of the lawyer's personality will be left neutral. However, we do not ignore the personality issues entirely. In interviewing (Chapter 3) we look not only at how the client behaves, but at how the lawyer reacts. You may learn some psychology there.

Our solicitors are all diligent beyond belief, still learning their trade, and prefer to look everything up rather than rely on memory. They are like you should be when you start in practice. Although we usually use our five solicitors to illustrate the practice of the skills, where there is a difference in the task we will bring a barrister into the case study. The lawyer carrying out each task could of course, unless there is a question of rights of audience, be a trainee or pupil.

Let us look at the case studies and the characters concerned. Little will be said at this juncture of the facts of each case. These details will be drawn out of the client and through other factual investigation as the chapters progress.

Case studies

Case study 1: Litigation and advocacy – criminal procedure – solicitor A

Mr O'Connor runs a baker's shop in Sheffield. He employs two members of staff – Winifred Evans and Sharon Smith. Mr O'Connor claims that someone is taking money from the shop till, as he is regularly 'light' when the contents of the till are checked against the stock. He seeks advice from the police, who suggest that he carefully monitor the situation and, if it continues, they, the police, will arrange to purchase goods from the shop using marked coins. The following week, at Mr O'Connor's invitation, DC Regan and WPC Higgins call at the shop and buy sandwiches, using three pound coins, each apparently marked with a cross etched on it. Later that day the police are called and Mrs Evans is asked to reveal the contents of her pockets. She does so and three marked coins are found. Mrs Evans is eventually charged with theft. She leaves the police station having been bailed to attend the local magistrates' court in four weeks' time. Following discussions with her husband she decides to take legal advice and consults solicitor A.

Mrs Evans is very distressed by the whole affair. She is adamant that she is innocent (although can give no explanation as to how the coins came to be in her apron pocket). As an active and well known member of her local community she is desparate to get the whole matter over and done with whilst attracting the minimum of publicity.

Case study 2: Litigation and advocacy – civil procedure – solicitor B

Daniel McAuley is 14 years old. He is cycling along High Street, Jesmond when he is knocked off his bicycle, by a car driven by Mr Slater. As a result of the collision Daniel suffers a compound fracture to his left leg, concussion and minor abrasions to his arms, face and torso. His cycle is damaged beyond repair, as are his shoes, jeans, sweatshirt and trainers. He is admitted to Newcastle General Hospital where he is treated for his injuries. The police report shows that Mr Slater has been successfully prosecuted for drink-driving. Daniel's parents – Irene and Norman – take Daniel to see solicitor B, who has been recommended to them by the local advice agency.

Neither Daniel nor his parents have had previous dealings with lawyers. Daniel is a quiet unassuming youth, especially in the company of strangers. He does not create the impression of being very communicative. Irene and Norman feel that it is best to take the advice of the solicitor who after all is the expert in these things.

Case study 3: Conveyancing – solicitor C

Victoria Kennedy and Simon Mark Bennett are aged 23 and 25 respectively. They have made an offer through Harrisons, estate agents, of £55,000 to buy a house at 1 Paradise Road, Sheffield. The property is an end of terrace and is located in a residential area in the south west of the city. They are both first time buyers. They intend to set up home together and have no immediate plans to marry. Between them they have savings of £6,000 which they intend to use as a deposit for the house and to cover their legal and related expenses. Both work full-time for the local authority, one as a social worker and the other as welfare rights adviser. They approach the Hallam Building Society with whom they have their savings and who agree in principle to give them a mortgage. The vendors (sellers) are Paul and Janet Rigsby who have made an offer to buy another property in the local area. Victoria and Simon make an appointment to see C, a city based solicitor, having first telephoned a number of solicitors' firms for quotations for conveyancing fees. C's firm submits the lowest quotation.

Both Victoria and Simon want the conveyancing to be dealt with as quickly as possible. They are very conscious of their limited budget.

Case study 4: Business law and practice – solicitors D and E

Mohammed Kader is a Sheffield businessman who manufactures children's clothing. His business is relatively successful and he wishes to expand to increase his range and production by moving into more spacious factory and office accommodation. He is friends with Barkat Khan. Mr Khan (who is a university lecturer) has little business experience but is interested in investing in Mr Kader's business. Mr Kader's bankers are prepared to fund part of the expansion plan and Mr Khan is willing to provide the balance. The total investment is in excess of £100,000 and Mr Khan's contribution towards this is to be £30,000. Both Mr Kader and Mr Khan own their own homes which are subject to small mortgages. Mr Kader presently trades on his own account under the name of 'Kiddies Klothes'. Mr Kader consults solicitor D, who has acted for Mr Kader previously in other business and personal transactions, and suggests that D acts on behalf of both him and Mr Khan. Mr Kader has already looked at alternative venues for locating his business. He has discussed the possibility of a long term lease with a Mr Shearsby. Unfortunately Mr Shearsby has recently suffered a heart attack and has died. His widow Emily Shearsby stands to inherit the whole of her late husband's estate and although she has yet to take legal advice she is aware that Mr Shearsby had discussed the possible lease of his former business site to Mr Kader and is inclined to lease the factory to give herself a steady income. Mrs Shearsby consults solicitor E.

Mr Kader is a confident and forthright man who is very insistent on the way he wants his business affairs run. Mr Khan trusts Mr Kader's business judgement and is keen to make his investment in this venture. Mrs Shearsby was involved in the running of her late husband's business (he was a cutlery manufacturer) but mainly from the book-keeping side. She feels the need for guidance on the commercial sense of leasing the factory although she respects her late husband's views on this. Her involvement is complicated by a degree of hostility from her stepdaughter, who objects to what she sees as her own rightful inheritance being invested in this way.

Study skills – managing yourself and the case

While working through the case studies, you should bear in mind the need for organisational skills. These skills relate to both study and practice. They are not specific to law but are more in the nature of transferable skills. Nonetheless they are vitally important in the understanding and practice of law. What skills are we talking about?

Use of time

This consists to two elements – first, planning your time and, secondly, recording the time spent on any particular case.

Plan what you intend to do before you do it. Not only will this give greater efficiency in the use of time, but it ought to bring structure and order to your work. Time is also equated with money. If you are handling Legal Aid work, each minute taken on the case is liable to be scrutinised and payment will be made only if it can be justified. Similarly, time spent may be the subject of close examination at a hearing for the taxation of costs. Also, a private client is entitled to see how much time has been used as a base for fee charging. Practising lawyers need to keep a close record of time spent as a basis not only for assessing the appropriate charge but also in terms of the efficient use of their own time.

To this end mechanical and computerised recording systems can be used. While at first sight this may appear to be both onerous and unnecessarily overseeing – shades of big-brother – correctly done, it is an invaluable aid to case management. Be aware, therefore, of the time taken to interview, research, draft or represent.

However, we do not expect you to record time spent in the case studies contained in this book. It is unlikely that you will need to record time as part of your assessment. Awareness of time should not mean being hasty and cutting corners. For the next few years you will be spending more hours on a case than can be charged to the client. You are in the process of developing the right techniques. You must allow yourself time.

Use of time must also be understood as an integral part of study. Your study of skills must run alongside the core and optional subjects you may be taking. The efficient use of time is necessary as part of the overall study plan and required as a legal, if transferable, skill in itself. Set out what you have to do and how you intend to go about it, then monitor the time taken to do it. If you are taking an inordinate amount of time preparing, say, a plea in mitigation or drafting a letter to your client, you may be failing to focus your attention on the relevant material. You may not be spending time properly evaluating your work. Have a go at a task, complete it as soon as you can, then appraise it. Better still, let others do that for you. Join in the process of co-operative and mutual criticism. Practice, or at least good practice, can get you nearer to perfect, if the tools of analysis are used.

Brainstorming

Certain techniques may also assist you to carry out skill tasks, especially when you are a relative novice in the field. Sit down with a group of friends – students on the course, work colleagues – or if necessary on your own. Express the problem that you are trying to resolve. Ask yourself or the others, what questions, answers or solutions might be applied in this case. Allow all suggestions to be recorded without judgment or comment, until you have exhausted your ideas (this is called brainstorming). Try to build up a picture in the form of a task plan in which the elements generated by brainstorming appear to be relevant. Determine what priority should attach to each. Now you have at least started the task: you have a scheme and a set of ideas that focus your attention on preparation.

Keeping records

An accurate summary of everything done or said should be recorded. The time to do this is at the time it is said or done, or immediately afterwards. Not only is this essential as a tool of case management, but one day your client's file may be demanded by a court, or the Law Society, or a disgruntled client. It is therefore in the interest of both you and your client to make an accurate record of each development that has occurred during the conduct of the case. This means that all correspondence, telephone calls, faxes, draft documentation, statements, messages and research must be recorded and filed. Files should be kept in a legible form and the attendance notes and correspondence in chronological order.

Uniform systems assist in this respect. Standard forms for memoranda, and records of interview, or telephone messages should be used. When considering the progress in each of the case studies, be mindful of the need to construct a case file. Each file should be organised so that, at a glance, the current position can be ascertained. If you are, say, unwell, and a colleague has to deal with the case, it is essential that he or she can understand where the case is at and what now needs to be done. While you may not have to keep a file for the purposes of your course, you should know how and why this is done. As a matter of practice it might assist you to construct a file when you are given assignments. A lawyer in practice would have to, so why not you? The use of systems for recording case progress is explained in Chapter 5 (Drafting).

There are, in addition, professional rules relating to the maintenance and preservation of case files (Law Society, 1996) after the file is closed.

Conclusion

That's enough about the skills. Let's get on and work out how to actually do it. First, Chapter 2: how should lawyers communicate?

COMMUNICATION FOR LAWYERS

'Scintillate scintillate, globule aurific,
Fain would I fathom thy nature specific.
Loftily poised in the ether capacious;
Strongly resembling a gem carbonaceous.
Scintillate scintillate, globule aurific;
Fain would I fathom thy nature specific'.

('Twinkle twinkle little star', rewritten by a committee of legal drafters – source unknown.)

'This learned constable is too cunning to be understood'.

(Don Pedro about Dogberry, in *Much Ado About Nothing*.)

Communication – think about the word itself. Is it what you say, do or write that counts? No, by definition it is what gets communicated as a result. If you say, as did the general to the War Office: 'send reinforcements, we're going to advance', but the War Office hears: 'send three and fourpence, we're going to a dance', you are not going to get your troops.

Remember Strand cigarettes? Probably not, because they were killed off by an advertisement in the 1960s which ran 'You're never alone with a Strand'. Good, simple message, clearly expressed, yet sales plummeted and the brand was withdrawn; although the target audience was told to think one thing, they actually thought its opposite: Strand means loneliness. Advertisers rarely make that kind of mistake, because they know that the bottom line is changing behaviour. They are professional communicators, and you must be too.

The skill of communication is one of the most important building blocks in any field of work. You need this chapter if you are on a vocational course, if you are on a law degree, and even if you are an engineer who has bought the wrong book by mistake. Read on carefully.

The chapter is mainly about your communication, not your listening. (See the next chapter on meeting the client for help in listening.) Much, but not all, of this chapter is about your use of language. The chapter has three parts:

First, we look at general principles of communication which are of key importance for lawyers.

Second, we look at principles of good English.

Third, we look at oral communications.

1   Principles of communication for lawyers

We have divided our suggestions into eight key principles:

1   Work hard to make it sound effortless (it isn't, of course, but the audience doesn't have to know that).

2   Do not be pompous.

3   Decide what you want to say before you start.

4   Decide *who* you want to influence to do *what*.

5   Plan the communication.

6   Make it not too long, not too short, just right.

7   Use short sentences, short paragraphs and short sections.

8   Be assertive not abusive.

Principle 1: Work hard to make it sound effortless

> 'It usually takes me more than three weeks to prepare a good impromptu speech.'
>
> (Mark Twain, quoted in *A Feast of After Dinner Jokes* (Exley Publications, 1992).)

One of my favourite books is *Catch 22*. Even if it is not to your personal taste, you will probably accept that it has been a very successful book. It took Joseph Heller over ten years to write. Good writing takes time.

The Legal Skills Book, simple and self-evident as we hope its content may seem now that it is finished, took over a year to write, and even to revise for a second edition it took four months.

Yes, the result appears smooth, effortless and easy; this is the illusion Mark Twain, or any communicator, wants to create. But the truth is that it is a product which required painstaking preparation and refinement.

Good communication is like a juggling trick; it looks smooth and easy, until you try. But someone who is not a good juggler succeeds only in making it look very difficult. Here, for example, is a sentence from a letter drafted by one of our students:

> Further to our interview conducted on 3ʳᵈ December we are writing to inform you of our plans with regard to your case for the future. As regards proceedings in relation to your accident, these are underway. Although your employers propose to terminate your employment, we believe this is grounds for unfair dismissal and will commence proceedings forthwith on receiving instructions from yourself.

This is how students, and the public, often imagine lawyers communicate; and too often they are right. Complex, obscure language which in fact did not take any skill or insight to draft. In the previous chapter I referred to the 'Vroom Vroom' approach to learning to drive. You haven't learned how to do it but you think you can make the right noises. Examples such as this did not require any great legal knowledge either, as most of it is wrong! When the student rewrote this (after discussing what we were really trying to achieve), the rewrite took four drafts over four days. It ended up looking deceptively simple:

> There are, as we discussed last week, two issues arising out of your accident at work:
>
> 1   A claim against your employers for the injuries resulting. We agreed that we would have to take the case to court, as there is no likelihood of a settlement. We have now commenced court proceedings in the Newcastle county court. ...
>
> 2   You are worried that your employers will sack you while you are off work recovering from the accident. As we discussed, there is no need to take any action unless this actually happens. ...

Perhaps this extract from the letter looks less lawyerly than the first. It certainly looks less complicated.

We want you to develop communication skills that are simple, direct, and effective; in due course you will give people the impression that you communicate easily and effortlessly. They may even come to think you have a natural gift. You will know – and they do not need to know – how much work has gone into achieving this.

Part of the work you need to do to communicate well, as we will see, is knowing exactly what you wish to say. You need to do the research before you can say or write much of value.

Principle 2: Do not be pompous

> 'Sounding as if one is saying something important by using impressive sounding words and complex constructions does not necessarily mean that one is actually doing so.'
>
> (Fairbairn and Winch *Reading, Writing and Reasoning: A Guide for Students.*)

Lawyers too often like to think they are important people; some of them even deserve the esteem they expect. It is undeniably pleasant to be highly esteemed. One reason lay people think we lawyers – and student lawyers are included in the 'we' – are important is because we are ever-so-clever, and because we can understand the most complex and difficult material. Now if we want to remain esteemed (and paid accordingly) there has to be a lot of this difficult material around. (A conspiracy against the public interest, which is how George Bernard Shaw defined all professions.)

So you want to seem clever? One operational procedure for achieving satisfaction of the aforementioned objective of aggrandising the approbation received by members of the legal professions from persons untutored in legal procedures is to utilise prolixity and imperspicuity of sentence construction and to employ semantically challenging vocabulary.

One way lawyers inflate their egos is to use long, complicated sentences and obscure words.

(By the way – if you didn't see that the last two paragraphs said the same thing, you have proved one of the key points in this chapter: that communications are wasted if they are not understood.)

Do we really need to create this material to aid the client? Or are we doing it to bolster our own professional monopoly? The professional standards require a good quality of service to clients. Who should end up feeling good? If something makes you feel good, but does not help the client, it is probably unprofessional and probably pompous.

Let us look at a simple example of lawyers' use of language. A letter to a client is a good place to start. (Writing letters to clients is a topic we devote more attention to in Chapter 5 on Writing and Drafting in a Legal Context.) These clients, who we will meet again many times, wrote to their solicitor just before exchanging contracts on a sale and purchase, because the people who were going to buy their house were proposing a reduced deposit on exchange of contracts. Here is a badly planned, badly drafted letter in reply.

> Dear Sir and Madam,
>
> The writer acknowledges receipt of your letter of the 30th ult. received in this office on the 4th inst. The recent developments of which you appraised us in relation to your proposed sale of the property at 14, Clifton Villas are noted. The writer begs to advise that the vendor of a property must make up his own mind in relation to the suggestion by the purchaser of a reduced contractual deposit, but a vendor should take cognizance of the fact that a deposit in the region of five per centum of the contractually agreed purchase price is not, per se, a reason to discontinue with the proposed purchase.
>
> The writer most respectfully requests you to give consideration to the above and awaits your instructions thereon at your earliest convenience.
>
> Yours faithfully,
>
> Smythes

Over the top? It is based on many examples we have seen.

Let's have a try at simplifying the letter.

Dear Sir and Madam,

How about 'Dear Mr and Mrs Rigby', since those are their names? Or 'Dear Paul and Janet' - if first names were used in the interview.

The writer

Who is 'the writer'? Is it me? Change to 'I' in that case.

acknowledges receipt of your letter

Is there any good reason not to say 'thank you'? The avoidance of a thank you implies that the solicitor did not really like getting the letter; use of 'thank you' is gratifying for the recipient of any letter, costs nothing and concedes nothing.

of the 30th ult.

People who have not studied Latin, or who have forgotten it (people like me, most of you, most lawyers, almost everyone in fact), probably do not know what 'ult.' means (it refers in fact to the previous month).

received in this office on the 4th inst.

Same again – 'inst.' means this month, but is it actually necessary to refer to the date of receipt at all? If the date of receipt is important, for example because of a delay in replying to your client's request for advice, tackle the problem head on by admitting the lateness of your reply.

The recent developments

What are these recent developments? Why assume the reader knows without you explaining? If the developments need to be referred to, do it sooner rather than later.

of which you appraised us

How about 'that you told me about in your letter'?

in relation to your proposed sale of the property at 14, Clifton Villas

Is it necessary to identify the property, unless the client is known to be selling two?

are noted.

Noted by whom? An impersonal conveyancing department, a top of the range conveyancing software package, or a friendly supportive solicitor writing to a valued client?

The writer begs to advise

'My advice is' would do the job as well.

that the vendor of a property

Is the solicitor talking about this seller? in which case say 'you'; as a rule, avoid talking theory and abstraction if you can talk in concrete terms which the reader recognises.

> must make up his own mind

There are in fact two clients, and one is a woman. In any event 'you' is more appropriate than 'his' or 'her'.

> in relation to the suggestion by the purchaser of a reduced contractual deposit,

The actual question which the client needs to turn her mind to is not set out, which is unhelpful; the language is unnecessarily complex.

> but a vendor should take cognizance

Grand words meaning not much more than 'I am about to tell you something'.

> of the fact that a deposit in the region of

The client is unlikely to want to know about the range of deposits, but is particularly concerned with this one, which is 5%.

> five per centum

Say '5%' like the rest of the world.

> of the contractually agreed

Actually it is not yet agreed, and these last two words add nothing; even if they did, 'agreed' would be enough, the addition of 'contractually' is redundant (as well as being unnecessary, superfluous, and tautologous).

> purchase price is not, per se,

Hello! Who is this intruder 'Percy'? Does this Latinism mean anything more than 'in itself'? Does anything need to be said here at all?

> a reason to discontinue with the proposed purchase.

This is the very advice the client has been waiting for; is it clear enough? It has been phrased in an abstract way, and is poorly related to this client's need for advice.

> The writer

Still regrettably anonymous.

> most respectfully requests you

'Please' will convey enough respect.

> to give consideration to the above

What in particular does she need to think about? 'The above' is vague.

and awaits your instructions thereon

'Thereon' is a word beloved of lawyers. We hate it; it is not common English, adds no clarity to your meaning, and sounds pompous.

at your earliest convenience.

When, exactly, should the client reply? For all its apparent politeness and respect towards the client, it is nothing less than careless to fail to tell her exactly when her decision is needed, and how she should communicate it to you. (Or has the solicitor, in introducing this concept of her convenience, started to talk about the plumbing in the new flat?)

Yours faithfully,

Smythes

Your client may not know, still, who has written the letter; we see no reason to refuse to sign off with your own name, at least to a client.

So we re-draft this letter, minus the pompous language.

Dear Janet and Paul,

Thank you for your letter of 30th October.

I am sorry I did not reply sooner, but in fact the letter only reached me yesterday.

You asked about Mr Bennett and Ms Kennedy's sudden announcement that they will now only be able to pay a 5% deposit on exchange of contracts.

In fact deposits of only 5% are now quite common, and do not usually cause a problem; but it is entirely up to you whether you decide to continue with the sale on this basis.

We had planned to exchange contracts next Tuesday; please could you phone me as soon as possible, and no later than Monday at 5.00 pm to let me know your decision?

Yours sincerely,

(Your name)

How do you like this new version? It is much more accessible to the client. Have we already discovered the essence of good communications? End of chapter?

Sorry. This is going to be a long chapter, and the approach we have just taken – of translating pompous inscrutable English into simpler user-friendly style – is not the complete answer. We do not like the re-drafted letter much better than the original. Why? We can best answer this question under the next heading: decide what you want to say before you start to communicate.

Principle 3: Decide what you want to say before you start

'Poor writing is often the sign of muddled ideas; and once you have expressed your ideas in a form that other people can understand you usually find that the muddle has been sorted out.'

(John Adair *The Effective Communicator*.)

It is time to return to the letter to our conveyancing clients, Janet and Paul Rigby. We redrafted the complex pompous letter into plain English, but perhaps surprised you by saying we still did not like it. Why? The letter, in its original version, betrayed clear evidence of a solicitor who had not planned in advance what needed to be said. If all you do is to improve the style of a badly planned letter, all you get is user-friendly rubbish. Improving the English did not cure that fundamental flaw.

What was the essential point the solicitor needed to communicate?

The solicitor is trying to advise the client whether a 5% deposit from the buyer is acceptable as a security on exchange of contracts. Reading the original and the re-draft, you probably have the impression that the solicitor is sitting on the fence. In the first pompous draft the solicitor did not need to admit that she or he was uncertain what was best for the client; the uncertainty was swallowed up in the obscurity of the language. The writer allowed him or herself to be fooled into thinking the client was being advised, because, putting it at its cruellest, the solicitor was deceived by his or her own pomposity.

In the re-draft the fence-sitting is obvious. The client does not now need to go to an interpreter to ask 'What does my solicitor's letter mean?' That is one gain from banishing pompous language (unless you think it right for solicitors to hide their equivocation from their clients). Mark Adler, writing in *Law Society's Gazette* 90/40, 1 December 1993, at p 26, describes the process metaphorically: 'Most legal writing could be trimmed to a third of its length with no loss of meaning and some gain. As the water level falls ... previously hidden rocks appear.'

Before writing, decide therefore what you want to say. Read the file/case study material first, because there may be crucial information which your client expects you to know, and which informs the advice you give. Then, if you do not know what advice to give, the answer must be to find out by research.

What if your uncertainty is because there is no right answer to the problem? Say so. You can either say in the letter:

I am uncertain what you should do: here are the choices and the reasons.

Or you can say:

I am clear in my mind what to advise you: here are my reasons (here, if any, are my doubts).

If you know what you want to say, there is a good chance you will be able to say it; if you do not, there is no chance at all. The (imaginary) solicitor whose letter I just took to pieces did not start out by analysing the task ahead.

Let us approach the task again. The well-prepared solicitor has researched the facts and law as far as necessary before writing; here are his or her mental or written notes on the client's concerns and possible points of advice:

■ *Concern*:
What are the possible consequences of not agreeing to a 5% deposit on exchange of contracts?

Advice:
Buyer drops out (do I know how important that is to that client? if not, I had better find out); or
Buyer backs down and agrees to pay the higher deposit.

■ *Concern*:
If 5% is accepted, what is the risk that buyer drops out after exchange with only small deposit to lose?

Advice:
Is it likely? Many of my clients accept reduced deposits, this has not caused me a problem yet.

■ *Concern*:
What are the consequences if this unlikely event happens?

Advice:
Client keeps the deposit, loses the sale; probably loses the purchase of her new flat and the deposit she has paid on that.

■ *Background information*:
I know from earlier instructions that the Rigbys are extremely eager not to lose this sale and the purchase of their new house, and that they want to avoid delay because the move coincides with a new job. (Point that needs to be included.)

■ *Some points to raise*:
I haven't yet had any indication about reduced deposit from purchaser's solicitor – are they serious, or flying a kite?
Should my clients be thinking of paying a reduced deposit on their own purchase? (Perhaps this is the crucial issue.)

■ *Concluding advice*:
The client has to decide, but I am willing to talk further.

(For the sake of simplicity, we assume that no questions arise about whether the deposit would be held as stakeholder or agent, and whether it may be used towards the deposit on our client's purchase.)

I have used the word 'research' earlier. Isn't this rather a grand word for what is going on? All I mean here by research is that if ever you do not know what you have to say, you have to find out. That is what as a lawyer you are paid to do, and it is called factual and legal research. As you can see from the listing of the points, in this task of preparing to write a letter to a client it was not a huge research project, more a matter of ordering your thoughts in the light of what you know about conveyancing procedures and what you know, or can find out from a colleague, about the effect of various decisions the client might make. As you will see in the next chapter, research can at its simplest just be avoiding sloppiness, and knowing what questions to ask.

With the key points worked out, we are now able to write a letter that gives the clients the information they need.

Dear Janet and Paul,

Thank you for your letter of 30th October. I am sorry I did not reply sooner, but I only received it this morning.

Mr Bennett and Ms Kennedy have told you that they want to pay only a 5% deposit when we exchange contracts next Tuesday. As you point out in your letter, we had previously assumed a 10% deposit, and the draft contract which we went through last week confirms this.

They have left this announcement until the last minute, and this puts you into a difficult position.

You have to decide whether to insist on the normal 10% deposit, and risk losing the sale to Mr Bennett and Ms Kennedy, or to accept a 5% deposit, with the risk that Mr Bennett and Ms Kennedy may then refuse to complete the purchase.

I will look at each possibility in turn.

Insisting on 10%
They may be bluffing. You could refuse to exchange contracts without the usual 10% deposit. Mr Bennett and Ms Kennedy would either have to find the full 10%, or drop out of the purchase. If they drop out, this would leave you without a buyer, which would mean – at least in the short term – you would not be able to go ahead with buying the new flat.

I cannot judge as well as you can how likely they are to withdraw; you told me that they really like the flat, but, of course, that is no guarantee. We also know that they are trying to sell their own flat, and due to exchange contracts on that on Tuesday. Presumably if they pull out of buying your flat, they will have nowhere to move to and cannot proceed with the sale of their own. Also I have heard nothing from their solicitor about a reduced deposit; if this was a very important issue, I think they would have got their solicitor to negotiate the reduced deposit, rather than approach you personally at this late stage.

Accepting 5%
If you accept the 5% and go ahead with the exchange the worst possibility is that Mr Bennett and Ms Kennedy then fail to complete the purchase. If that happens you can keep their deposit. So the greater the deposit, the less likely they may be to back out, for the more they lose in doing so.

However, we have no reason to suspect that they are likely to pull out after exchange; 5% deposits are quite common, and I have not yet lost a sale where this has been the reason. In your case, the deposit will still be £3,750, which is a lot of money for them to throw away – even if it would not compensate you for wrecking your sale and purchase. If Mr Bennett and Ms Kennedy were having second thoughts about buying your house, I very much doubt if they would go ahead with an exchange of contracts at all.

My advice is that the risk of exchange not being followed by completion is very small, and that you should go ahead with exchange with a 5% deposit rather than lose the sale. But I must leave the decision to you. I will be happy to discuss my advice over the phone.

I do need to know your decision by Monday afternoon at the latest, as we are planning to exchange contracts on Tuesday, so that we can complete on Friday 21st.

A very important question which you may wish to discuss with me urgently is whether you want to consider trying to negotiate a reduced deposit on your own purchase? It is common practice for deposits to be passed on along the conveyancing chain. I would have to raise this with the seller's solicitor urgently, so please contact me as soon as you receive this letter if you want to take this possibility further.

Yours sincerely,

This letter will have taken a solicitor at least ten minutes to write. The conveyancing department might be looking unprofitable. Is this attention to working out what you want to say, and getting the style right, pie in the sky? No, for four reasons:

1 Until you are a qualified fee earner you have (or should have) the right to concentrate on quality learning rather than profit.

2 If what you say to your client is confusing, and the client makes an ill-informed decision, it may cost more time later to deal with her unhappiness (or the litigation, or the Office for the Supervision of Solicitors, or the remuneration certificate). At the least, if the Rigbys do not understand it, they will ring you up, and you will have to deal with their confusion (time wasted) before you can give them advice (duplication of effort).

   The Rigbys may join the club of your so-called difficult clients, who drive you crazy with their demands for explanations. You end up lying: 'Tell her I'm at court.' If you suffer from large numbers of such demanding clients, is there a message for you somewhere?

3 Confused clients often take their business elsewhere.

4 (The real 'right' answer.) You were right to say 'this letter is unprofitable to write', recognising the time and cost it takes to communicate the advice in such a long and carefully constructed letter. So, having worked out clearly what needs saying, you may decide that talking to the clients rather than writing is the best way to give the advice they want. Make a short checklist of key points and pick up the telephone. Make a detailed note of what each of you then says.

The task never was to write the perfectly sculpted letter. It was to convey information and advice to the client who needs it, in a manner which enables her to make a sensible choice. (However, if for assessments you are told to write a letter, you will fail if you write instead: 'This is stupid. I would phone!' Passing the course is head and shoulders above any other goal for now.)

Here is a further example demonstrating the need to work out what you have to say before you start to write. It comes from the case of *Donovan v Gwentoys* [1990] 1 All ER 1018.

The litigation was about solicitors' negligence. The client's affairs had been shockingly neglected. Eventually the limitation date was missed. Here is how it started, with a letter before action. (A 'letter before action' is customarily sent to a proposed defendant indicating the basis of the claim and the remedy sought. As you will learn in the Drafting chapter it must indicate brief details of the cause of action that the client will rely on, and what is being claimed.)

The errors are in the original.

Dear Sirs,

Re: Lorraine Elizabeth Donovan

We are instructed by the above name who was formerly in your employ in 1979 to 1980. Your records will reveal Mrs Donovan under her single name however, we do not have that name on record at present. Mrs Donovan suffered personal injuries as the result of your negligence and/or breach of statutory duty. In the near future we shall be issuing a Writ against yourselves for personal injuries arising out of the accident and should advise you to pass this letter to your insurers.

Yours Faithfully,

Imagine you are the recipient, a director of Gwentoys or the solicitor advising the company. How might you to respond to this letter? You will not have a clue what it is about, or probably even who it is about (unless you happen to have been informed that an ex-employee is now called Donovan).

This letter cannot be sensibly acted upon; it will probably be ignored, or at best result in a request for clarification of the name of the former employee, her employment record, and precise allegations of fault by the employer. If the solicitor acting for Mrs Donovan does not have this information, it is premature even to send a letter before action, because the hidden (no, on second thoughts, blatant!) message of the letter is 'we don't know much about this case'.

Again we are in the 'vroom vroom' school of motoring. The writer presumably knew that a letter before action was needed (that is what it says in the textbooks), but had no idea what to say because no research had been carried out.

■   Factual:
What was the client's name?
Between what dates was she employed?
What happened to her and when?
What was the extent of the injuries, and what were the consequences?
Was she off work?
How much did she lose?

■   And there were legal issues: What is the cause of action? Negligence? Breach of statutory duty? Which statute? Which regulations?

We should not be writing this letter before action until we have far more precise details of the incident, through, for example, interviewing our client and witnesses, inspecting places and things connected to the accident, obtaining reports of the accident and opinions of any experts. We should then have precise details of what, following on from the factual research, we are going to say is the cause of action (what duty we say the employer has breached).

Anything written before this investigation has been carried out is bad communication, not because it is badly expressed, but because there is nothing worth expressing.

My advice at this point can therefore be summarised: *it is not how you tell it that is most important; it is what you have to tell*. For, like all the skills, how you do it is important, but what you do is the core of the competence.

The fact that content is more important than style is not an excuse for carelessness about quality of communication. You cannot afford that, since on a communication assessment task the marking scheme will include style. But there is no incompatibility between the two aims, clear content and clear style; if you write and speak carefully and clearly, you will have to pay attention to content as well.

Imprecise use of language is often a smokescreen hiding the fact that the speaker does not know what she or he wants to say. Examiners and judges have seen enough smokescreens not to be fooled by them. They will probably see the confusion underneath, but will probably also feel annoyed at having to penetrate the smoke to see if there is anything underneath.

We think it is better – at least at this stage of your career, and preferably for ever – to speak or write clearly, even if that reveals that the content is rubbish. But, of course, once you have seen, through your clear style, that what you say is rubbish, you will work on the content. If, having hidden your lack of good content with obscure language, you cannot yourself recognise that it is rubbish, you will not improve. You may fail the course, or at best fail to become much of a lawyer.

Principle 4: Decide *who* you want to influence to do *what*

What you actually say or write does not, in the end, matter. What is received and acted on does. Imagine a radio broadcast – a party political broadcast, for example – sent out on the wrong frequency, so no-one hears it; or sent out during the televised World Cup football final between England and Scotland. There are no listeners, and there is no alteration of behaviour. There is no point even asking whether the broadcast itself was good.

That example is extreme. But a more relevant example to you is the party political broadcast that focuses on issues that the voters are not concerned with: for example, reform of the legal profession rather than unemployment. Political parties and advertising agencies spend large sums of money finding out what sort of things people will be receptive to, and they tailor their messages accordingly. You need to think about what sort of things your audiences are receptive to. Otherwise you too are broadcasting on the wrong frequency.

This principle is inextricably tied in with the rule of knowing what it is you want to say. Before you can know what you want to say you have to know what your objective is. Do not just send out a reply because you have received a letter; or cross-examine a witness just because he is standing there in front of you. The *Donovan v Gwentoys* letter before action is an example of how this approach results in poor quality drafting.

The only purpose of saying or writing something is to achieve a result. A result for the lawyer means influencing a person to behave in a way that legitimately furthers the lawful interests of your client. (We say 'legitimately' because you must not cheat or lie to influence behaviour.)

What is, after the event, a result started out life as an objective. In every matter you take on, you identify an overall aim (acquittal, an effective contract, or a workable business structure, for example) and a number of specific objectives (getting the jury to believe that your client was at a certain place at a certain time; getting an amendment to a draft contract agreed before exchange). Deciding on the aim will be a significant topic in the next chapter, so just for now, please assume that you know what the aim is.

Here are some overall aims from our case studies, and for each one a possible objective for a particular step we might plan to take:

■   *Aim:* To be acquitted.
     Objective: To obtain the co-operation of a particular witness who will give evidence even though it could put her employment at risk.

■   *Aim:* To win damages and costs..
     Objective: To set out in the letter before action a clear summary of the factual allegations which may induce the insurance company to accept liability and negotiate a settlement.

■   *Aim:* To create an appropriate legal framework for a business venture between my client and Mr Khan.
     Objective: To communicate the risks and advantages of not incorporating the business clearly so that my client can make an informed choice (and so that he cannot blame me if later the risks materialise).

■   *Aim:* To buy 1, Paradise Road on a suitable date and at an affordable price.
     Objective: To persuade the estate agent to talk seriously to her clients, the vendors, about a price reduction because of the poor condition of the house revealed in the survey.

There is always a receiver of your communication whose behaviour you are trying to influence. The completed partnership deed, for example, is not the aim in itself. It may sit in a cabinet, needing to persuade no-one for ten or more years, but when its time comes the disaffected partner, his solicitor, and if necessary the judge, are persuaded on reading the agreement that your client's wishes will prevail. The agreement to allow a right of access over a neighbour's property must persuade the solicitor of the next owner of the neighbouring property that the right can be exercised; and the owner after that and so on for evermore, or a judge if such a solicitor is not persuaded.

You therefore identify clearly, before you start, what objective you set for the communication. You identify the person, or range of people, you intend to influence, and the behaviour you desire from them. Make a virtue of this in your course. You are going to be marked, in most exercises, not only on the oral or written performance, but the apparent planning that went into it. Commonly you are asked to provide an outline plan. Make clear to yourself first, and the examiner second, that you understand who you have aimed this communication at (the audience), and what it is that you want them to do as a result (the objective).

Third, make clear to the person you are communicating with what you want them to do, or what they can expect to happen next. If you do not tell them, they may well decide for themselves without your clear guidance. For example: 'Please would you phone me by next Tuesday at midday at the latest with your instructions on whether to accept the offer. The best time to phone is before 10.00 every morning, except Monday when I shall be away.' Or: 'Your worships, I wish to submit that the evidence of confession obtained by the police is not admissible for the reasons set out in section 76 of the Police and Criminal Evidence Act, and I invite you to hold a trial within the trial on this matter.' Both of these are better than alternatives such as: 'Please contact me as soon as possible' (yes, but when? and for what purpose?), or 'Your worships, I submit that the confession was obtained by oppressive behaviour on the part of the police.' (That may or may not be true, but what exactly do you want us to do about it?)

It will help you in planning to be aware of the particular characteristics of your particular audience. Different audiences have different characteristics.

You can categorise audiences in several ways. For example:

Lawyer/lay person

Having made this distinction enables you to avoid mistakes like writing to a lay opponent saying, for example: 'This letter is of course to be treated as a Calderbank letter', or writing to your client to say: 'We will of course have to submit the usual requisitions on title before completion', or 'You will, of course, be aware that the statutory charge will attach to any property recovered or preserved'. (The latter is taken from a real letter which a client of another solicitor brought to the student law clinic to have interpreted.)

Our side/their side

Someone who is 'with us', such as a witness, may need, for example, regular signs of appreciation for the assistance they are giving; someone on 'their side' should be treated with a degree of formality, for example to avoid any suggestion that you are attempting to undermine their relationship with that other party.

Co-operative/unco-operative

A co-operative witness, for example, should not be threatened with a subpoena; an unco-operative witness may require the heavy hand.

Important/not important

Everyone you deal with is important. I mean here, of course, important as a means to achieving your client's goal. The more important a particular person is (for example a judge, a negotiator, a future business partner), the more significance for your client your communication will have. If the person is relatively unimportant for the client's affairs, you may (once you are experienced) decide to give the task less preparation.

People who have recognised status as important people (bank managers, counsel, magistrates, expert witnesses) may like to be reminded of their own importance and, having swallowed hard, you may be advised to use obsequious language if this really will help your client. You may not worship the bench, but that is – incredible as it sounds when you think about it – what they say they like to be called. You may find a particular barrister personally unpleasant, but you thank him or her courteously and sincerely – if not sincere you were daft to instruct them – for the advice; you are very grateful to the prison warder or court usher who has power over whether you are kept waiting or able to get on with your business.

Emotionally involved/emotionally disinterested

A person emotionally involved in the outcome or issue in which you are involved deserves, as a matter of common courtesy, to be treated with due sensitivity and, even though it is costing time, to be listened to for a few minutes. The blunt: 'and you'd better make sure your husband takes his toothbrush with him to the trial', or 'good news; the medical report says you'll probably have a reduced life expectancy; that'll be worth a few bob on the claim' belongs to the Fawlty Towers school of law.

Receptive/suspicious

The suspicious receiver of your communication needs to be reassured. 'Of course, you will want to know exactly what the consequences are of signing this contract; and rightly so … let me take you through the key terms one at a time, and please stop me at any stage if there is anything I have not made clear.' The receptive person too may be pretending to be confident, but we have enough experience of clients coming to advice sessions saying 'I didn't have a clue what my solicitor was saying, but I felt such a fool telling him, so I just said yes.'

Knowledgeable/unknowledgeable about this issue

It is probably unsafe to assume that people know much about the issues. Why should they? Even your client, who is the world's foremost expert on his or her own affairs, is fairly ignorant as soon as you start adding a legal dimension. 'What you clearly need here is a class F land charge to protect your interests in the matrimonial home.' 'Yes, but is there anything I can do to stop him selling the house; that's what I'm worried about, not charges?'

Empowered to make decisions/not so empowered

There is no point explaining everything succinctly to the telephonist or the court usher when it is a decision from the bank manager or the judge you are looking for. In negotiations with another party's solicitor, remember that the solicitor is not the party, and cannot make decisions.

Male/female

This may be of no relevance – for example, apart from calling the district judge 'Madam', you would expect a hearing in her court to be similar to a hearing before a male judge. (However, language can contain gender assumptions. If you explain your argument in terms of cricketing metaphors, perhaps fewer women than men will follow what you are saying.)

Gender might be highly relevant. A female client in an interview about her family life, for example, may be distressed by finding that her interviewer is a man. Rather than trying, and perhaps failing, to be 'right on' ('It's alright, I'm more of a feminist than most women' used to be the line) you might need to offer her a chance to be interviewed by a female colleague. (In your course assessment it is harder to make that offer realistically, but you can suggest 'I appreciate that you may prefer to deal with a woman solicitor, and if there is any further work to be done in this case, please tell me, so that I can arrange for you to see Mrs Jackson next time'.) The same problem can arise for male clients interviewed by women, of course: in any situation where you are of the opposite sex, ask yourself, if not the client, if this is appropriate.

Apparent disability/no apparent disability

Again, your perceptions of whether the audience, or members of it, have an apparent disability may make no difference. But if a person has, say, a hearing impediment, you may need to ensure that he or she can see your lips clearly. You will need good lighting. Unless you are assured of the good eyesight of your entire audience, use large and clear visual aids. Disability may therefore be a relevant consideration and you must be sensitive to this issue. Be careful when you use words metaphorically, like saying the business was 'crippled' – is there a better word?

Culturally or ethnically like me/from a different background

Whatever your good intentions, your upbringing may – I suggest will – have given you some prejudices about gender, sexual preference, race, cultural differences, age and disability. If you acknowledge their existence – to yourself, not in public – and accept that they are prejudice not fact, you can begin to override them.

You may otherwise react to a person you are communicating with (your audience) on the basis of stereotyping. We do not suggest the answer is equal treatment as such; rather it is for awareness of relevant differences, and refraining from judging people who are different. It is an issue of equality of opportunity.

Awareness of differing needs arising from people's backgrounds should give you some ability to respond appropriately. But unless a different response is called for in a way which assists the person to participate fully in whatever is happening, cultural or ethnic issues are otherwise immaterial.

This is a sensitive area, and two white male middle class politically correct-ish authors cannot presume to have more than limited insights. Making assumptions about people, just because they appear to be different from you, may be to label them inappropriately.

An awareness of 'colour' (the term used in the Race Relations Act), race, ethnic or cultural background is always necessary to avoid at best being insensitive and at worst offensive and unhelpful. A client may, for example, need translation facilities to follow and understand your advice or legal proceedings. In an interview your client may be reticent about their case because of cultural differences between you and them. Just because a client, say, does not look at you when you are giving advice does not mean he or she is not listening.

Take, as an example, the case study of Daniel McAuley. He is a teenager of Afro-Caribbean background, and at first sight he shows no apparent interest in the progress of his case. Should you be conscious of his colour? Of course 'colour' is relevant in that it may provide a clue to his cultural background. It is not a reason in itself for treating him in any particular way. A youth from a cultural background which is not the solicitor's may be reluctant, especially in front of a figure in authority, to participate readily. This particular young man may refrain from eye contact. He may well have been taught to do this as a mark of respect according to the norms of his culture. The white lawyer, used to a culture of teaching young people to look an authority figure in the eye, cannot expect to communicate in these circumstances unless at least aware of them. Providing the solicitor recognises these potential barriers, rather than labelling the client, there is a chance of mutual respect.

Beware of using words which can carry unintended racial or cultural messages, for example using black to mean negative ('blackleg', 'blacklist' 'things were looking black'). Do the words you use mean different things in different cultures or dialects.

> Question: Who did you visit then?

> Answer: My aunt.

For a British white person the word 'uncle' or 'aunt' has a clear meaning: the brother/sister of a parent. In cultures where extended families and friendship networks share childrearing tasks the aunt may not be a relative.

Ability, race, gender, class, power, age, profession – there are many ways of classifying your audience. Awareness is one thing; drawing wrong conclusions about other people is called stereotyping, and often hinders communication. Even if we take a politically neutral example, you may in any event be wrong in your categorisations. For example, you may write to a witness of an accident assuming them to be a disinterested non-lawyer, without knowing the witness is not only a judge but also married to the defendant's brother. But you are more likely to achieve your objective if you have at least had a try at identifying your audience's characteristics. You can then make an informed decision about what type of language, degree of formality, legal rules and conventions are appropriate. The point is to think about the audience before planning the communication. Awareness helps you avoid words like 'typical' and 'difficult' when talking about people who do not share your background or outlook.

Thinking in this way about the qualities of the target audience at least reminds you that the audience is not you. You are not communicating for your own benefit. Remember that the principle we are still exploring is that of deciding who it is you are targeting and what you want them to do as a result of your communication. For apart from a personal diary kept under lock and key, or your singing in the bath, what you say and write is directed towards someone else. You cannot use as your standard: 'well, it seems clear enough to me'. If you look at the categories we have listed, you are a lawyer, co-operative to this client, emotionally disinterested etc. But the person you are aiming to influence – perhaps a recalcitrant witness, a suspicious partner – may be a lay person, hostile, emotionally involved, and highly important.

You start from where this audience is. If the audience does not do what you intended them to do, it does not advance your client's interests to blame them. The magistrates were too prejudiced to understand my plea in mitigation; the buyer is pig-headed and will not listen to reason or come down in price; the witness is too stupid to answer my questions. Admit it if that happens – my communication failed. Look at it from a point of view you are very familiar with. You did not understand what the lecturer said, and the lecturer is saying to your face or behind your back: 'typical student, doesn't understand basic principles, in my day we were much better informed'. If you identify with that situation, would you agree that it is for the lecturer to adapt the teaching to your actual level of skill/knowledge/intelligence/somnolence, or to continue to lecture to an imaginary past generation of perfect students? The audience is unlikely to change its characteristics. Address them as they are. Otherwise they will fail to benefit from what is being said. Which means for the lawyer not getting the behaviour that is sought – the judicial decision, the co-operation or whatever.

It does not matter if you think your piece of work is brilliant, but the audience was just too stupid/out of touch/preoccupied/fuddy-duddy to realise. You may, of course, be right. You may even have a genius for attracting such people to yourself. But, true or not, you cannot change them into 'better' people.

The audience is not always who you think it is. Sometimes they are complete strangers to you, and if all goes well they may never realise that you had them in mind. We speak of the Office for the Supervision of Solicitors, the Chancery judge who presides over a contested will, the solicitor who your client's business partner shows the agreement to years after you have retired. Even a simple document like a letter or an attendance note in the file is addressed to this hidden audience, if the case goes haywire and your client blames you. These people should be saying of you when they read your file: 'Well at least it wasn't her fault that this matter has ended up before us.'

Example 1: The audience is a potential witness

How does this process work in practice? Solicitor A in the criminal case study is seeking information from a witness. What she knows of the witness from her client is that she is aged about 25, a part-time bakery worker, is on good terms with our client, but quite possibly anxious about getting involved because her employer is the chief prosecution witness. She knows about how the bakery operates, and so may be vitally important. The outcome that we want from the letter is for her to visit the office and tell us about the recent events at the bakery. (We will work out the questions we want to put to her – see Chapter 3.) Here is a slightly altered first draft of a letter originally drafted by one of my clinical students:

Dear Ms Smith

Re: Mrs Evans' theft

We understand from our client that you are a witness relevant to the above mentioned incident at O'Connor's bakery on 1st September 1998. We would therefore be much obliged if you could make an appointment to see [solicitor A] with a view to making a statement concerning the incident.

In doing so it may well be that there will be no need for you to appear in court, if the case goes that far. Obviously we appreciate the difficulty of your situation, as you still work for O'Connor's bakery. However, we must inform you failure to co-operate may result in a subpoena ordering your attendance at court.

Hoping for an early reply.

How would you, a reader well educated in the law, feel opening that letter over your toast and marmalade? Possibly sick with worry. And what do people do with worries? They fret, they repress them, they pretend bravado, they show anger. But they probably do not eagerly make appointments to see you.

Talk of 'above mentioned incidents' (which were in fact not mentioned above or below, or even at all), of 'obvious appreciation of difficulties', followed by the threats of court and wild creatures called subpoenas, is unlikely to succeed in obtaining the behaviour we want – for her to pick up the phone, or send us a letter.

Instead we suggest you try a simpler approach which takes into account that this reader is probably not familiar with legal procedures, and does not need to have them quoted at her; that she may actually want to help our client, but that she will be anxious about doing anything.

How can we get Ms Smith's co-operation? Appeal to her sense of justice? To her friendship with our client? (so find out from the client the nature of the relationship). At the very least we should avoid frightening her and make co-operation seem the easiest course.

How about:

We have recently been consulted by Mrs Winifred Evans. She tells us that until recently she worked with you at O'Connor's bakery.

She has come to see us because she has been accused of theft from the bakery. I imagine that you know some of the circumstances which led up to our client being accused. According to what she has told us, we have advised her that she is not guilty of any offence.

Mrs Evans tells me that you have worked together in the bakery for some years. We understand also that you were in the shop with her at the time she has been accused of putting coins from customers in her pocket (which was on 1st September).

I would very much like to talk to you to find out a little bit of background. I imagine I will need to talk to you for perhaps half an hour. I appreciate that this may not be something that you would choose to do; but I am sure that you will recognise that Mrs Evans faces a very serious charge, and it is important that we do what we can to prepare her case. Your co-operation would be very much appreciated.

I could talk to you at this office, or if that is difficult for you, I could visit you at home one evening. My daytime phone number is 123 4567, and if I am not there, my secretary, Kim Aynsley, will be able to make any arrangement for me.

I very much look forward to hearing from you.

The letter tries to address the likely concerns and reluctance of the witness. These concerns are acknowledged but not highlighted: for example, we do not say how difficult her position will be as she still works for Mr O'Connor. We try to convey confidence that she will co-operate. We do not 'hope that we may hear from you', we look forward to it.

The letter does not promise anything we cannot deliver, like confidentiality. (She would not be much of a witness in that case!) It is perhaps economical with the truth in that we tell her nothing about going to court, or witness orders, and you must judge for yourself if that is unethical.

Example 2: The audience is a customer of the client/a solicitor of the customer/a judge

Your client is Mr Kader, who makes children's clothes and, for this example, acts as a clothing distributor. You are drafting a clause to exclude liability for losses caused to any customer whose products are damaged, during distribution, by your client's negligence.

Who is your audience?

■ Your client, of course, who pays for the work – although of all potential readers Mr Kader is least likely to read it carefully, because he relies on you to get it right and may sue you if you fail.

■ Mr Kader's customers who bring Mr Kader their clothing for distribution and read your clause (perhaps hundreds of them every year, who you hope never to know by name).

■ Mr Kader's customer's solicitor, after your client has allegedly ruined a batch of valuable kiddies' clothes. You aim to earn that solicitor very little money, because he or she will read the clause, shrug their shoulders, and advise the customer that the exclusion clause is good. 'Next please.'

■ A judge – because the client's customer failed to take the sensible advice of their solicitor, and decided to litigate despite the plain legal effectiveness of the exclusion clause that you drafted. Will it stand up before a latter-day Lord Denning?

You draft a clause; you ensure that your client has it prominently displayed in all written terms of business, in all premises, that staff should be instructed to bring it to each and every customer's attention, and that they should be expressly advised of the need to obtain special insurance if they believe their clothes have particular value. You draft a clause which oozes plain English:

WARNING: exclusion of liability. We are a careful company and we do the best we can to produce good results. Before you decide to use our services for your precious kiddies' clothes we want you to be aware that we do not – repeat not – accept any liability whatsoever if our transportation, warehousing or packaging materials or procedures are faulty and damage your products. If your products are especially valuable please talk to our staff about arranging insurance cover. If you choose not to insure your products we will assume that you are happy to take the risk of anything going wrong. Please sign below to ensure that you have read and understood this.

Nothing could be plainer in intent to the target audience of your client's customer. Your client may well say to such a customer whose batch of clothing fell off one of Mr Kader's forklift trucks into a vat of used engine oil: 'Sorry, you read it, we discussed it, and you signed. It happens now and again, however careful we are.'

But is it plain to your ultimate target audience, the solicitor or the judge? It is not, because it will not influence their behaviour the way you intended. You wanted the solicitor to say to their client: 'sorry, no remedy'. Or at the least you wanted the judge to say to the solicitor at the end of a fruitless action for damages: 'I really cannot understand why you brought this action, and I am awarding a wasted costs order against you.' Instead the judge may well award damages against your client. And the reason? The clause did not take into account case law on the *contra proferentem* rule (eg *Hollier v Rambler Motors (AMC) Ltd* [1972] 2 QB 71). To make such a clause work liability for your client's *negligence* would have to be specifically excluded, for example using the words 'We don't even accept liability for this kind of damage if it is caused by the negligence of any of our staff': it makes the clause clumsier, and less accessible to the lay person. That is a sacrifice that you have to make, in order to achieve your goal.

Having drafted it you may advise your client that he would be better served by accepting liability, paying higher insurance premiums, and investing in staff training and improved handling procedures.

Are you getting the message? Goal first; research second; communication third.

Example 3: Different messages to different audiences

How do you write or speak when there is more than one audience? For example, you are preparing a speech in mitigation in a case which you have identified as hopeless. For the time being let us imagine that Mrs Evans has a long record of dishonesty offences, and committed the present offence in breach of a suspended sentence. The bench is bound to send your client to prison. 'What can I possibly say? My client will expect me to say something.' A lawyer may be tempted in this situation to make the client his or her target audience, not the court. 'I made the usual speech so the client would feel that something was being done, but I knew it would make no difference.'

Where does this fit in with the rules? Is this giving the client a good service?

No. The client is being deceived by what is being said, and therefore there is a failure of communication. There is indeed a breach of the professional practice rules: any knowledge you have which could be of relevance to your client must be put to him or her.

'A solicitor is usually under a duty to pass on to the client and use all information which is material to the client's business regardless of the source of that information.'

(Law Society *Guide to the Professional Conduct of Solicitors* Principle 16.07.)

Your audience – the client – believes you are saying something of assistance, which you are not. And what you are saying to the real audience is a charade: you are not trying to influence their behaviour. What you are trying to do is in your own interests – to make sure this client thinks you are a good lawyer and brings work back to you. If the decision-maker, the judge or magistrate, accepts this behaviour, the legal system is then colluding against the proper interests of the lay client.

We have therefore had to return to first principles of professional practice, rather than to first principles of communication.

You will need to address to the judge/magistrate points of argument on, say, fact and law which are effective in persuading the court to take a particular decision. In a mitigation speech, this requires understanding of the statutory requirements for the different types of sentence (see Chapter 6). The speech is structured around these, because only these factors should be taken into account by the court. Your client does not, of course, have a working knowledge of the Criminal Justice Act 1991 as amended, and cannot be expected to understand the mitigation speech as well as the magistrates. That is because the primary audience is the bench. You can and should go through what you plan to say, and why, with the client beforehand, and agree what you will be trying to achieve. That is when you address her as your audience.

Example 4: The audience is both the client and the court

You and your client are working in partnership; you are the expert, you hold the key to the legal process and you hold yourself out as able to unlock solutions that your client wants. Your client does not in fact have to know everything you do, but has to be given the opportunity to understand and approve the strategy, the risks, the aims, and the tools you will use. If you are going to be standing up in court using tools that your client cannot personally handle, you have to explain beforehand, in appropriate language, what you are doing and why. (It is not very different from informed consent to medical treatment.)

For example, you say to the court while defending Mrs Evans on a charge of theft:

> 'Your worships, s 76 of the Police and Criminal Evidence Act requires the prosecution to show beyond reasonable doubt that the confession contained in the document produced by WPC Higgins was not given in circumstances which make it likely to be unreliable.'

Until you have studied criminal evidence, that legal argument can make little sense to you. It makes no sense at all to Mrs Evans. Your client is not disinterested in the argument you use (disinterested, as correctly used, means unaffected by). Some clients may affect to be uninterested, out of bravado or fear or loss of trust in you and the system, but since their conviction is likely if your argument is unsuccessful, they are inevitably interested if you can reach them with a clear explanation of what is going to go on at court.

So we take as a basic premise of any communication that, whoever it is addressed to, the paying client must have the opportunity of understanding it. There are two ways to achieve this: by adapting the language you use at court, or explaining what you are going to say to the client before you do so.

By explaining to someone who cannot share your assumptions, you are playing something of the role of the teacher. One of the best ways of understanding something is to try to teach it. Explaining the process in simple terms in advance of the hearing gives you an opportunity to check that you have grasped what the task consists of.

Here is how you might have explained to your client what you were going to do at trial with the confession evidence (leaving out interruptions from the client which you would have dealt with as they arose):

> 'Mrs Evans. One of the problems we face at your trial is the fact that when you were interviewed by the police and they said to you: "It's obvious that you are the one who took this money from the bakery, and have been doing so since March" you replied "Yes, well, I suppose I must have".
>
> That is called a confession in law. It means that the police are allowed to give evidence of what you said to them when the case comes to court. It is obviously damaging to your case, because you appear to be agreeing with the police that you did steal money. It would be far better for the case if we were able to stop the court from hearing that evidence.
>
> From what you have told me you said that to the police because at the time you were feeling very confused. You had been in the police station for several hours; you had not had any refreshments; you felt the police were keeping you there until you said what they wanted to hear, and you were worried about your children, as you had been unable to contact your husband.
>
> What I want to discuss with you is the possibility of arguing at the trial that as a point of law this evidence is not admissible in the trial. That means, if I am successful, that the court cannot take it into account in deciding whether you did take any money and therefore commit an offence. It would not form part of the case against you.
>
> If I am successful in getting the magistrates to agree that what you said to the police should not be used in the trial, I will apply to the court to have the trial transferred to another set of magistrates who will know nothing about what you said or the decision to cut it out of any evidence.
>
> The law allows me to raise the possibility that your confession was obtained in the sort of circumstances you have told me about, when you were feeling under heavy pressure. The prosecution has to prove to the court that in all the circumstances the confession can be relied on, and we will have the opportunity to show everything that happened and which led to you saying what you did.
>
> So there will be legal argument on whether the confession can be put to the court; there will be evidence from the police about what happened while you were being detained for questioning. You will need to give evidence about the pressure you were under.'

This explanation takes some time. While giving it you would have to ask your client to interrupt at any time she wishes. You are giving a tutorial on a detail of the criminal justice system to someone with no previous experience. But if you bypass it, your client does not know what is going on.

Of course, this principle applies to any specialised communication on behalf of the lay client; there must be another explanatory communication to the client. You need to go over the key terms of, for example, a draft contract in terms that make sense to the client who you will ask to sign it. If you cannot give this explanation, are you sure you know what the original (difficult) one means yourself? Or are you falling into the imitation trap which we looked at in Chapter 1? In terms of communication, this means: do not copy what other people say or write if you do not understand it yourself.

Before finishing with the question of audience, in an assessment there is one further audience: the marker, who may have particular standards different from those of the target audiences we listed. Know those standards. If your lecturers supply you with samples of writing, advocacy or interviewing they call good, extract from those additional guidance. If they like a style that we would have you avoid, their standards are by definition right for this assessment task.

Principle 5: Plan the communication

In this part of the chapter we will be sparing on examples, as some fully worked examples are given in the relevant chapters, in particular Drafting and Advocacy. Research is not mentioned in the planning process. That is because there is no research stage as such – it will inform every stage, as Chapter 4 will make clearer.

Stage 1: The objective and the framework

Identifying the target audience, and the behaviour you want to influence, is the basis for the plan. Perhaps initially it helps to write this at the top of your blank piece of paper.

> As a result of this letter I want Mr Khan to appreciate the need to take independent legal advice as soon as possible.

(What follows? This is discussed in Chapter 5 – Writing and Drafting in a Legal Context.)

> As a result of this submission I want the District Judge to accept that I am entitled to see the maintenance records of Mr Slater's car.

(See chapter 7, Advocacy, for the follow up to this submission.)

You know what you want to achieve. You need to find out the procedural framework which dictates the content and style of your communication. For example:

■ *The rules say my application to set aside judgment must be supported by an affidavit. What do the rules say about how affidavits are prepared and what should be the contents of this one?* (Look in a book on civil procedure and either the *Supreme Court Practice* or the *County Court Practice*. See chapter 6 for more on this drafting task.)

■ *I want to issue proceedings against Mr Slater. What are the rules dictating the content of a Particulars of Claim?* (Again look it up, or turn to Chapter 6.)

■ *My client wants to be able get the woodwork treated before moving in. Am I free to draft my own conditions of sale for a contract to give her the right to do this?* (Is it the buyer's or the seller's task to draft the contract anyway? Look in a conveyancing procedure text or a practitioner work such as *Kenny*.)

■ *I intend to apply for bail for my client, but what are the circumstances in which bail can be granted or refused by a court?* (Look in *Stone's Justices' Manual, Blackstone's Criminal Practice* or *Archbold*. Turn to Chapter 7 of this book – Advocacy.)

This initial research on procedural requirements enables you to set out basic headings which will help you to group the different parts of the contents in a coherent way.

Assuming you are clear on your objective, your audience, and any procedural formalities, you can start to plan the content.

What comes next in planning?

Stage 2: The timescale

Start from the deadline: after carrying out the necessary research (such as court deadlines or client instructions) get out your diary and enter a few dates. It may help you to work backwards not forwards. For example:

24 October – planned start of Mr Kader's new business;

↕

17 October – meeting with Mr Khan's solicitors to execute partnership agreeement;

↕

12 October – make sure client has read and understood draft; post to other side;

↕

8 October – send off working draft with letter of explanation to client;

↕

1 October – first draft must be ready to go over with my principal;

↕

20 September – complete legal research and produce detailed contents outline for approval of principal;

↕

10 September – whoops, that's today – get started.

Stage 3: Jotting

List all the relevant material you will need to incorporate. On the first occasion, do not censor any idea. Add it to the list. This is called brainstorming; the idea is mentioned several times in this book. Brainstorming is best done with one or more colleagues. Do not start to criticise or to remove any material until you have entirely run out of ideas. Do that over more than one occasion, because the next time you do it, you will usually come up with further points, and also your mind will have been mulling over the task without conscious effort.

You now have a list of points. List them under various headings that you identified from the procedural requirements looked up in Stage 1 (or your own plan if there are no clear conventions or rules for this task). At this stage you can eliminate the ideas that are unhelpful, factually inaccurate, or irrelevant. (Store them somewhere accessible in case your judgment turns out to be wrong, though.)

Stage 4: Sifting, selecting, and spotting the gaps

Try next to put all this into a sensible order and comb through carefully to see if there are any gaps. Some more material may at this stage be discarded as not relevant to the structure and task. This stage includes trying to discover material that you should have put in at Stage 2, so do not move on to Stage 4 until you are sure you have identified the relevant gaps.

Stage 5: Allowing your genius time to work

If you have not already done so, take a break. Psychologists have long known through studying the lives of creative geniuses, and ordinary people too, that the mind does not stop working just because the centre of attention has gone elsewhere. On the contrary, it is when you have done a great deal of preparatory work and then started to relax that the creative rearrangement of the materials and the sudden flash of inspiration can occur. Plan time for your genius to come into play. Flashes of inspiration come unplanned – but plan your routine in such a way that you give them space.

EXAMPLE

Daniel McAuley has started proceedings following his cycle accident. The insurance company for Mr Slater has paid £5,000 into court. How might the previous four stages look?

- *Objective and framework*: To decide whether to advise an acceptance of the payment in. Having looked up CCR O 11, rules 1–3:

  - ☐ to advise Daniel on the cost implications of acceptance (costs as taxed or agreed will be met by Slater) or non-acceptance (costs met by Slater up to payment in; risk of paying own and his costs after that if payment in not beaten)

  - ☐ to advise Daniel on the likelihood of obtaining a higher award at trial or later higher offer

- *Timescale:* (having looked up the time limit for acceptance in the County Court Practice – see CCR O 11, rule 3(1))
  21 days from receipt of notice to accept payment – 23rd July
  If notice of acceptance to be sent – post 20th July
  If payment to be accepted – instructions in writing by 16th July
  Give client a week at least from receipt of letter to think and talk to me – send letter to arrive by 9th July
  Produce final draft by 6th July
  Research likely award by 4th July and produce first draft
  Start jotting 2nd July – today – and tell client by phone that letter on its way.

- *Jotting*
  The solicitor writes down everything that comes into his or her head that might be relevant in this letter. After ten minutes the list looks like this:

Costs – split order – value of claim – client wants new bike – firm's cashflow – parents' unrealistic expectations – deadline for answer – risks of litigation continuing – how long case will last – whose decision, Daniel or father – approval of court – investment of money – pain and suffering v compensation for actual losses – contributory negligence – uncertainty – anxiety – conditional fees – previous dealings with this insurance company – possibility of higher payment in – litigation always painful (for me as well as client) ...

■ *Sifting etc*
Some things in this list are irrelevant to Daniel's interests, and therefore to the solicitor's professional obligations: the firm's cashflow advantage in early settlement; the solicitor's dislike of litigation. Some things are, on reflection, omitted – why the insurers are making the payment in, for example, needs explaining, what they hope to gain.

Let's come back to this example after looking at the next stage – signposting.

Stage 6: Signposting

You have a number of ideas for your speech, meeting or document. What relationship can you build between these ideas? Having thought about your target audience, you predict that many of the points you are going to cover are unknown terrain. What signposts and map reading aids are you going to provide? In map reading, as in writing and speaking, try to take the simplest route between the start and finish of the journey; do not ask the reader to jump from one part to another, without showing where to find the bridges/signposts/slip roads (choose your own metaphor!).

One way of planning the route is to imagine your reader or listener is intelligent but very easily confused. (I tell students when preparing assignments to imagine the marker is an intelligent moron.) Markers will be capable of understanding exactly what you want of them, but only if they are taken through the material point by point. Otherwise they will drift off your path and miss your meaning.

If it is likely to be a long communication, decide in advance how to break it up. If you are likely to be talking for more than 20 minutes, which is (amongst everyone but university course designers) the generally accepted maximum span of uninterrupted concentration, divide your talk into different clearly identifiable areas, each not lasting very long. In your written work you can use headings to show the breaks and to guide the reader.

For example, you are writing to Daniel and his parents explaining the factors to take into account in accepting or rejecting the payment into court. Your headings might be the following – with the points from the brainstorming located under the relevant heading:

Why has a payment in been made?

Insurers pressuring you to take low but realistic payment now to avoid possible higher payment at trial.

What happens if you accept it?

Decision that of parents – best to ensure Daniel agrees at his age – Hearing before district judge on quantum and investment – final compensation, no later top up – costs will be paid (explain what costs means – not necessarily all my costs, mention success fee for conditional fee retainer)

What happens if you refuse it?

Costs up to date of payment in notice – after that risk of paying costs even if win, if fail to beat payment in (explain beating) – slight possibility of not winning case at all and paying all costs of both sides (insurance cover however) – litigation continues, perhaps another 12–18 months till trial – possibility of top up to payment in

How soon must you decide?

Explain deadline for telling me

How big is the risk of not accepting?

My advice on size of award (to be researched) – consider both actual losses and pain and suffering – medical condition not yet certain, will district judge approve acceptance yet? – failure to beat payment in could swallow up damages

Conclusion – my advice

Range of payment likely at trial (still to research) – insurers will have pitched it low but realistic – what contributory negligence? (to research) – this company hard negotiator, unlikely to increase payment in, trial likely if refusal – anxiety/risk/Daniel's desire for money now – relate to parents' expectations of level of award (explain how quantum calculated)

The brainstorming and singposting are creating a structure. The research is needed before this can be fleshed out into a letter of advice – in fact you will see it carried out in Chapter 4. As we have enough examples of completed letters in this chapter and Chapter 5, if you want to see how this one plus the Chapter 4 research on liability and quantum in Daniel's case can be turned into a letter, you will have to do it yourself.

Where else can headings be used in the planning? The answer is in almost any kind of document. They can help to break up the often dense prose of a contract or lease. For example:

■ *The parties*

■ *Obligations of the tenant*

■ *Obligations of the landlord*

■ *Termination*

■ *Disputes ...*

In your oral performances – advocacy and interviewing, and face to face negotiating – you can do the same thing. Everything you do can be signposted. In the example below the unspoken heading is underlined. At the start of the interview, you say (for example):

■ *The client's version of the problem:* 'Would you like to tell me in your own words what is the reason you have come to see me today?'

■ *The solicitor clarifies main issues:* 'Now I need to ask you a few specific questions just to clear up a few points in my mind. ... '

■ *The solicitor asks for detail and notes it down:* 'At this point we need to go a bit slower and I'll have to ask you very specific questions so I can take a few notes. ... '

■ *The need to reach some decisions during the interview:* 'Towards the end of the interview we are going to have to work out whether you think I can be of help to you, and if so, we'll have to work out exactly what we are each going to have to do next....'

This is the map of the terrain. During the interview, you can then refer to the signposts: 'Right, at this point I want to go over exactly what the police officer said to you in some detail ... '. 'Now we'll look specifically at the things you will do before we meet again next week.'

In the speech, for example to the district judge, the same principle will apply.

> 'Madam, in this application I intend first to explain the background facts of the case. I will then outline the nature of the discovery I seek, and the reasons why the documents are relevant to the issues in the case, and finally I will refer you to two cases which support my argument.'

Let us take a mitigation speech. You are going to have to cover certain topics: the seriousness of the offence, any mitigating factors, what is known about the offender, why a particular form of sentence is appropriate.

> 'Your worships, my client accepts that the offence is likely to be regarded as a serious one. I wish to deal with this aspect of the case first. ... Your worships, you are entitled to reduce the proposed sentence under s 28 of the Criminal Justice Act if what you know about the offender herself indicates that this is appropriate. I will start by outlining her present circumstances and then take you through her recent history. ... May I now turn to the question of what is a suitable sentencing option for this offender.'

(If the obsequious 'your worships' sticks a little in your throat, you can address the chair of the bench as 'Madam' or 'Sir'.)

If any particular area starts to grow too big, and you really cannot reduce it, break it down further. For example, you are drafting the letter to Mr McAuley's next friend advising him whether or not to accept a payment into court in respect of Daniel's claim for injuries after his cycle accident. One section begins to grow too big: divide it up into further discrete areas, with headings, such as:

■ *What happens if you refuse?*

☐ *The defendant may increase the offer*

☐ *The case may go to trial and beat the payment*

☐ *The case may go to trial and not beat it*

It may still be a difficult letter to draft in such clear terms that the client is completely informed. But the headings can only help.

Stage 7: Getting started – getting finished

After the planning comes the execution. What advice do we have? It is so easy to put the papers back in the in-tray, to decide 'I'll start that tomorrow'.

Are you really ready to start? Before you start to write (or plan the oral communication), you have decided your objectives, on paper or in your head. Do you now keep putting the papers to one side, because you think you cannot start unless you can do the whole task in one go? This is called procrastination.

On the other hand your excuse may be: *Oh, but I still have a bit more research to carry out; I'm not quite ready to start. But, but, but. ...*

We have emphasised the need to work out your goal, and your conclusion, before doing anything. Does it mean you cannot start writing until the blueprint is perfect?

That is also procrastination. In this book we emphasise research and preparation, and no doubt there will be criticisms that we expect more than a student can achieve. And here we are, when it comes to getting started, saying this can lead to procrastination. If we could, we would wave the magic wand and you would get the balance just right. We cannot. If you are procrastinating, either because of underpreparation or unwillingness to go beyond the preparation, only you can deal with it. At some point you are going to have to get started on preparing the letter, interview, speech etc.

For those who want to get finished before they have started – I am one of these – it can be hard to get started at all because the task is so daunting. The discipline of planning is necessary to rescue me from the tendency to get any old thing down on paper. For those who like to get everything well planned before starting, sometimes there is a need just to get something down on paper.

I suspect that whatever you are advised, you will use your own method.

But may I please offer a word of warning based on experience? If you start writing before you have finished the planning, sooner or later what you are doing must become subject to a rational plan. You cannot go on indefinitely without imposing a structure on your communication – unless you are willing to put your name to *Donovan v Gwentoys* style rubbish. You may already have the plan in your head, if what you are working on is a simple task. If not, as you write you are forming a plan. This can be an excellent way to proceed, for certain tasks, to see what it begins to look like and then revise it. We have written parts of this book on this basis.

I am willing to advise you to start writing as a way of getting ideas flowing, in the same way as you may have been jotting down key points. But never expect to complete the task without having identified your plan and ensuring that your communication fits it. Planning after the event is fine, so long as you demonstrate structure and lead the listener or reader to the conclusion via an ordered and legally relevant train of thought. You can even pretend to yourself that you planned it that way in advance.

But if you choose to write first, and plan later, your work will be a failure if at the time of completion you cannot discern or impose an underlying structure. The risk of writing too much before you have planned the order and content is that you fail to see the logical progression of the ideas, and become irrationally attached to the version that you have prepared.

But what if, when you have finished, you can see no plan or order, and none can be superimposed? Be willing to tear it up, press hard on the delete button, and start again. That is hard, and that is a reason why you should plan first.

And that brings us to the issue of length.

Principle 6: Make it not too long, not too short, just right

> 'President Theodore Roosevelt was asked how long it took him to prepare one of his speeches. His reply was that it depended on the length of the speech required; for a half-an-hour speech, two or three days, for five minutes, a week and if he had to speak for two hours then he could begin immediately.'

> 'A speech is like a love affair. Any fool can start it, but to end it requires considerable skill.' (Oscar Wilde)

> 'Never use a long speech when a short one would suffice.'

> (All quotes from *A Feast of After Dinner Jokes*.)

Law teachers sometimes have to lecture for hours on end (or do we? – that's not the issue here!). Of course, we address the students in informed, witty and exciting fashion. But when we see or hear what the students have taken in, we discover with amazement that they still do not understand some of the carefully explained material.

Of course we know why. It was drummed into me when I trained as a teacher, and countless psychology experiments have proved the point. People cannot pay attention for very long. They need a break, a change of pace, to get the blood flowing again. The human brain was not designed for long periods of passive learning, which is what listening to a talk or reading a book is about.

To overcome this problem, you have several complementary options:

1   Reduce the contents into brief sections, each easy to handle, with clear labels or signposts; I have made some suggestions already on signposting.

2 Give the reader/listener tasks that overcome the tendency of the attention to float away. Barristers addressing the jury become accomplished at this task.

> 'Members of the jury, I want you to imagine a perfect summer's day. The sun is shining, the birds are singing, in the background you can hear the occasional gentle knock of leather on willow as the village cricket game continues. Then, in the middle of this peaceful scene, ladies and gentlemen, you are interrupted by not one, not two, not three, but four loud motorbikes, the engines roaring, the riders clad in leather … , etc etc.'

They have taken the jury with them, and it was not difficult. You can do the same. The technique is not the clever imagery, but enlisting the listener on *your side*. The listener is transported from the tedium of listening to hour after hour of verbiage and invited to indulge in a bit of daydreaming. It works. And it improves the concentration of the listener.

Solicitors do not often have to engage a listener for such long periods. But they are often involved in prolonged interviews or court appearances. As well as inviting the listener to stroll in the realm of daydreams, the tedium and loss of concentration can be addressed by pauses: 'Should we take a short break now while I organise a cup of coffee?' 'I've got quite a good picture now, and perhaps we should stop the interview now, so that we can each collect our thoughts, and maybe you could come back for a further chat at the same time next week.'

The same applies if you are asked to make a presentation in class. Structure your presentation, use signposts, break what you say into sections that are easy to understand.

Summarise your key points as you go along – this is particularly important in interviewing and advocacy. Chapters 4 and 6 give you guidance.

Principle 7: Use short sentences, short paragraphs and short sections

96% of people can understand an 8 word sentence. Only 4% can understand a 27 word sentence at first reading (Adair, *The Effective Communicator*). OK, reviewers, I admit you can find sentences over these limits in this book, in this chapter or on this page. We did our best! Some writers do not try.

Information is easiest to absorb in reasonable-sized chunks. But lawyers have a terrible desire to be long-winded. An excellent book which we advise you to read is *Clarity for Lawyers*, by Mark Adler. It is a short book, but it is filled with examples of long-winded waffling stopped in its tracks and reformulated to express the writer's intentions economically and clearly. We need do no more than quote from p 1 to make Mr Adler's message clear:

> 'Lawyers with pens or dictating machines forget they are people; however amiable and unpretentious they may be at other times, when they compose the written word a strange personality emerges. Where a human being would say
>
> > The house is ready
>
> a solicitor employs a large staff to say

We hereby give you notice in accordance with clause 11 of the Contract dated 16th November 1987 the [sic] made between Miranda Homes Limited of 157 Bracknell Road South Farnham Hampshire (1) and East Hill Residents Association Limited of 157 Brackness Road, South Farnham, Hampshire SF4 5GR (2) and James Edward Brownlow & Katherine Elizabeth Brownlow of 81 Landfall Road South Farnham Hampshire (3) that the above property is now constructionally complete.'

There are actually two advantages to the brevity illustrated by this example:

- the reader or listener cannot pay attention to long-winded communications;

- brevity improves the clarity of what you have to say.

Actually, what we ask you to aim for is not brevity for its own sake, but conciseness. If you know what you have to say, or write, and it is all factually or legally relevant to the audience and behaviour you want to influence, be as long and detailed as you need – but not long-winded, continuing beyond the point where what you have to say is already likely to have been understood, and generally failing to recognise where you could have stopped speaking or writing or could indeed have said more briefly the things that for some reason you find yourself saying at too great a length, if you know what I mean.

In Adler's book, you will find that most of the examples of long and hard-to-understand writing become shorter as they become clearer. Just one more example – I would like to quote more but, after all, it is Adler's book, and he deserves the royalties – from pp 4 and 5 of *Clarity for Lawyers*.

It is a clause from a commercial lease, and sets out some of the tenant's obligations:

'Not to use or permit or suffer to be used the demised premises or any part thereof or any buildings or erections at any time hereafter erected thereon or on any part thereof as and for all or any of the purposes of a brewery or a club (whether proprietory or members) or a public house or other licensed premises or otherwise for the preparation manufacture supply distribution or sale whether wholesale or retail and whether for consumption on or off the premises of all or any alcoholic liquors of any description and not without the previous consent in writing of the Landlord to carry on or permit upon the demised premises any trade business or occupation other than that of a retail shop for the sale of X.'

Adler comments:

'This could only have been written by a man [sic] who thought that something terrible was going to happen when he stopped writing. He could have just said:

Not to make or sell alcoholic drinks in the shop or (without the landlord's written consent) to use it except for the retail sale of X.'

Clarity and brevity are raised again in Chapter 5 on Writing and Drafting.

Another reason why conciseness is valuable on your vocational course is that your work will be marked by examiners who will scroll through miles of video tapes of you talking to clients, negotiating with each other, and addressing imaginary judges; they will have piles of draft contracts, affidavits, pleadings or letters to mark. If you save their time by getting to the point they will reward you with what you want above all – a pass. If you really want a career as a waffler, save it until you get into practice, but with luck you will have lost the habit by then. At degree level a similar point applies. You may not be required to have your work videoed (although such methods are at last catching on) but being concise will be appreciated by tutors, colleagues and assessors).

Writing concisely is easier than speaking concisely. You can look at what you have written, and have another try at it. Redundant words and phrases can be removed. But once you have spoken, the words cannot be recalled for editing. You must know in advance exactly what the key points are that you will need to say.

That is why, in advocacy, an essentially oral activity, I have abandoned the cosy notion that thinking on my feet is all I need, and come round to writing out nearly all the questions I intend to ask, and, in advance, the outline of my summary speech. I prepare this in the knowledge that I expect certain answers to my questions, and that these will lead to the conclusion.

Are things different during an interview? This is one-to-one communication where you cannot prepare what you are going to say, only the structure. You still have objectives: most importantly to ascertain the information that is relevant to the task you identify. Brevity here – and there will be more on this in Chapter 3 on interviewing – is still a virtue. A long interview is unproductive and tiring, and, by and large, it is more important that you hear what the interviewee tells you than vice versa. Do not talk too much or too long.

Being brief actually takes up more time than being long-winded. Checking your language, pruning what is verbose, simplifying what is long-winded, takes more time than saying everything you can think of on the topic. It may appear that the short speech or letter was easy to produce. But anyone can let a hedge grow big. Pruning it into shape is the real discipline.

If you are still unpersuaded, you should listen to the hindsight of Neil Kinnock, interviewed in 1994 on BBC Television's 'The Downing Street Years'. Both he and Lady Thatcher agreed on one thing: in 1986, when the government was in serious difficulty over the leaks of a government letter connected with Westland Helicopters, if Neil Kinnock had made his parliamentary points more succinctly and less verbosely, he would probably have brought down the Conservative government.

Principle 8: Be assertive, not abusive

Your communications tell the world about your qualities and your organisation. People have nothing else to judge you on. However you may feel personally, you need to communicate in a way which shows preparation, consideration and understanding.

The public, including clients, often seem to love or hate their lawyer. Lawyers I suspect have the same emotions about their clients, their opponents and judges. It is unwise to let this emotion show through one way or the other in what you say or write. The lawyer's job is not to get involved. Please do not take this next analogy too far: but just to illustrate the point, you can see your role as that of a professional, cold, mercenary. You do what has to be done thoroughly, but dispassionately. You will be no good at the job if you get involved too deeply, and you will see your efficiency diminish. Mercenaries may get too keen on killing their opponents; lawyers may become discourteous and vindictive. Take a less hostile example – a therapist. Therapists are trained to be warm and supportive. But they achieve nothing for their client if they get personally involved, even to the extent of sharing their emotions or agendas with the client. It is the client's needs that dictate. The rest is distraction.

We have both been on the receiving end and, we regret to say, the giving end of discourtesy, especially in letters between solicitors. The tendency is not confined to lawyers, as Sir Ernest Gowers indicates in his excellent book *The Complete Plain Words* (p 12). Having stated that efficient performance of your task is the goal of good writing (in this case, replying to a letter), he continues:

> 'Be sure that you know what your correspondent is asking before you begin to answer him. Study his letter carefully. If he is obscure, spare no trouble in trying to get at his meaning. If you conclude that he means something different from what he says (as he well may) address yourself to his meaning not to his words, and do not be clever at his expense. Get into his skin, and adapt the atmosphere of your letter to suit that of his. If he is troubled, be sympathetic. If he is rude, be specially courteous. If he is muddle-headed, be specially lucid. If he is pig-headed, be patient. If he is helpful, be appreciative. If he convicts you of a mistake, acknowledge it freely and even with gratitude. But never let a flavour of the patronising creep in.'

I have worked on countless cases where the file is full of correspondence which breaches this rule. It is the hallmark of some practitioners to be rude to their opponent's lawyer. Why? They presumably believe that the intimidation gains advantage for their client. Or they have a warped view of the adversarial system, seeing it as all-out warfare rather than civilised dispute resolution. Does it in fact serve the client? And will it look good when you are being assessed?

The temptation to use charged language comes from three sources:

- over-identification with the client, and therefore personal animosity towards the opponent;

- belief that it will gain advantage to the client;

- misunderstanding of the professional role of the lawyer.

It is much easier to see when someone else has fallen into the trap than to avoid it yourself.

The outsider can not only spot that your language is over the top: being outside the case, he or she is likely to understand better than you how the person you wish to insult will react. Certainly judges reviewing the way the case has been conducted will be unimpressed with the passions aroused in the lawyers. Judges consistently say the same, that they are tired and bored by advocates or witnesses who are abusive to other parties, and over the top in their use of language.

I quote from a letter received in one of my law school clinical cases. The client was defending possession proceedings. Usually in cases like this the court grants possession orders against unrepresented defendants at the rate of one every two minutes on 'possession day'. Occasionally a party has obtained representation and the conveyor belt has to stop. That had happened in this case. The solicitor (and no doubt his clients, who could not get back into their house) was feeling personally aggrieved and wrote the following:

> We refer to this matter which has of course been adjourned.
>
> That your client, receiving professional advice, should persist in a Defence that has no merit. Mrs [name] knew full well the terms of the tenancy before she entered into it and of course completely understood that our Clients intended to return to the property, as owner occupiers, at some point after the commencement of the Tenancy. Notice was given and she signed an Agreement to that effect.
>
> Your client of course has the benefit of a Legal Aid certificate which our Client does not. It would appear that our Client is at a considerable costs disadvantage. We are concerned that this matter is being run as an academic exercise as we are advised by our Clients that not only did the Solicitor conducting the matter attend Court but also your Law Department's Professor and five undergraduate Law Students. If this particular Defence amounts to little more than an academic exercise, then of course we would be fully justified in seeking personal costs against your Law Centre. Such an Application will be made in any event on the grounds that it is entirely unreasonable for you to have advised your Client to defend this matter.

(The style of this letter leaves much to be desired. Please turn to p 81 for our 'Thoughts on Unnecessary Capital Letters'; and to p 68 on the advantages of separating the points you wish to make into separate paragraphs. But for now we are not concerned with style, but abusive content.)

Clearly the letter was intended to unsettle us. But what else did the writer intend, assuming the letter was a result of careful reflection, to say?

Here is what, I think, he intended to say:

- I hate you;

- I'll make you pay;

- It's not fair – you have legal aid and a professor;

- You have no defence;

- You are more interested in the academic interest than being proper solicitors.

If you agree that gratuitous insults are not desirable, they should be removed from the letter and only the substantive content should be written. Which of these points contain only personal feelings? Let us look one by one:

- *I hate you*: It is better that solicitors do not get this personally involved, but if that is how he really felt, it was best kept to himself. If he had a particular professional complaint, this should have been formulated.

- *I'll make you pay*: This is a legitimate threat if well-founded. However, research into the rules on costs should have been undertaken before making the threat. To make it without having the intention of carrying it out could only satisfy the writer's personal anger rather than advancing the interests of his clients. (How do I know this threat was not researched? It was never carried out. Research would have either shown the author how to carry out the threat, or that it was empty. As it was it was repeated almost weekly during the life of the case, with no action following the threat.)

■ *It's not fair – you have legal aid and a professor*: This is actually not a legitimate complaint. This part of the letter is pure whingeing abuse, focusing on the personal not the issue.

■ *You have no defence*: Instead of moaning, have it struck out.

■ *You are more interested in the academic interest than being proper solicitors*: True or false, it was irrelevant unless we had made a procedural mistake. (We could have written back: 'You are only in it for the money.')

Some solicitors believe that this kind of correspondence achieves results. They also think it impresses their client: look how fierce I am, look how I deserve my fee! While temporarily unsettling for the recipient, in the longer run the abuse is unproductive because:

■ it makes dispassionate exploration of compromise between lawyers difficult;

■ even worse, it clouds the judgment of the writer, who mistakes the force of the invective for the force of legal argument;

■ it is a sore waste of client money, likely to be disallowed on a taxation of costs.

If you have started to draft a letter containing personal abuse, I strongly advise you to take it apart into its main points, as we have done above. Break down what you wish to say into discrete points. Those that are merely the expression of personal feelings can be taken out. Can what is left be written courteously? If not, is it really saying anything after all? If replying to such a letter, take Gowers' advice and reply courteously to the points that are relevant.

The same approach must also go for verbal communication. Dispassionate politeness is the bedrock of an adversarial legal system; and one foundation for demonstrating that you can communicate as a practitioner is to keep your cool in the face of pressure, provocation, and your own feelings. Despite churning up in inner turmoil, do not call the chair of the bench an arrogant fool who doesn't know the Criminal Justice Act from a cornflake packet, even if he is and he doesn't; do not tell the person you are negotiating with that she is talking rubbish; do not use sarcasm ('We note that your client intends to claim public transport costs from now until doomsday', from a case I had at Northumbria's student clinic – for more on this case, and clinics in general, you may be interested to read Brayne H, Grimes R and Duncan N, *Clinical Legal Education: Active Learning in Your Law School*, Blackstone Press 1998).

There are always polite but assertive ways of saying things, and using them keeps you objective in your judgment and disinterested (not to be confused with uninterested).

■ To the foolish magistrate: 'With respect, your worships, I wonder if your decision is based on a reading of section 28 of the Criminal Justice Act which I disagree with; perhaps I can explain. … '

- To the negotiating opponent: 'You say you have evidence that my client Daniel is only pretending to be unfit to return to school; on the medical evidence we have from Dr Chang, that is incorrect, but if you have any evidence, I would very much like to see it. Can you send a copy of your report before Monday, so I can go over it with my client and then if you want to put a new offer, I'll be very interested to hear from you.'

Yes, you avoid rudeness. But politeness is not meekness. In practice, and in any assessment of your skill, you have to show that you will be able to stand firm in the face of a challenge or provocation. You will fight to put the interests of the client first, you will not submit to aggression aimed at you or the person whose interest you represent, nor will you rise to it.

What if someone is rude to you first? I see no advantage ever for rudeness to your client in return. (Of course you may have reason, such as provocation: what I mean is, looking back, was your behaviour in being rude helpful either to you or to your client? We look at 'difficult' clients in Chapter 3 on Interviewing.)

2   The use of good straightforward English

'There's no need to remind the world that you're a lawyer.'

('Symptoms of Bad Writing' 72 ABA J113 quoted in Barbara Child *Drafting Legal Documents*.)

There are two themes running through this part of the chapter: the advantages of plain English over legalese and guidance on problems with grammar and style.

Plain English v legalese

'A kind of folklore haunts the legal profession perpetuating a myth that judges prefer legalese and that the lawyer who does not use it will be laughed out of court. The myth is beginning to be exposed as such.'

(Barbara Child again.)

The claim that it is a myth is supported by several research studies Child cites, from California, Florida, Louisiana and Michigan. These studies show judges rate legalese less convincing than equivalent writing in plain English. And if the opinions of judges matter less to you than your reputation as a lawyer, these studies also found that the plain English versions were presumed to have come from the more prestigious law firms.

So one obstacle to good English is the cultural expectation that lawyers' English is somehow different. We will come back to some examples to help you overcome these expectations.

Problems with grammar and style

Better English by G H Vallins tells us that:

'[during] one comparatively short period there was a kind of autocracy – not absolute or authoritative – in English. ... That autocracy, as I have called it, was strongest in the first fifty years of compulsory education (1870–1920). The grammar taught in schools had to have its rights and wrongs, like arithmetic. And that tradition remains to this day. ... The formal rules of grammar can be taught, but not the indefinable spirit that underlies usage ... On the one side is the belief, fostered and developed through school and school examinations, that certain constructions are wrong – bad grammar, as the phrase was – and on the other the undoubted fact that eminent journalists, learned writers, and great literary men frequently used them.'

We are keen that you should use 'good' English, using 'correct' grammar and rules of punctuation. I will give you guidance and examples. But one obstacle to this is that you may have been taught artificial rules that hinder rather than aid understanding, and so we ask you to take the so-called rules of correct English with a pinch of salt; use them critically, as your servants not your masters. These 'rules' were often drummed into children without imparting understanding, and you may be applying them 'incorrectly'. I shall show some examples later.

What, then, is good English?

Books and books are written about using English well. Many of the authors love the English language above all others (see, for example, Melville *The Draftsman's Handbook*). They say the fantastic range of words from the Anglo Saxon, Viking, Norman, Latin and Celtic influence makes it the most versatile language available.

For a lawyer, these aesthetic judgments are unfortunately irrelevant. You have to use English, because that is the main language of the jurisdiction you have chosen to train for. So we do not need to convince you that English is versatile, poetic or persuasive. We have to convince you instead of something more basic, that:

'[T]here is no such thing as proper English: there is only good English. ... '

(Adair *The Effective Communicator*.)

In this part of the chapter we suggest you:

1 Demystify grammar

2 Adopt helpful conventions of punctuation

3 Cut paragraphs and sentences down to size

4 Choose the right level of formality

5 Go for precision

6 Cut legalese down to size

7 Keep it simple

8 Cut out unnecessary Latin

9 Use direct language

10 Use 'you' where appropriate

11 Avoid gender bias

12 Take care with negatives

13 Use emotive or persuasive words with care

14 Go Easy on Capital Letters

15 Do not be satisfied yet

Finally we look at some examples where redrafting can help.

Demystify grammar

English is a tool. Tools are not used for their own sake, but to achieve something. Whether in writing or in speaking, your use of English is about transferring information and influencing behaviour. (Isn't that a reasonable definition of legal work too?) The only worthwhile measure of how well you communicate is whether you are effective in getting your information understood in the way you want the target audience to understand it; and influencing their behaviour in the way you intend. There is, in that sense, no such thing even as 'good' English; there is English that succeeds, and English that does not.

There are of course rules of English that you should be aware of. But do not be a slave to them. For example, prepositions (of, with etc) at the end of a sentence are considered wrong by some grammarians, but something we are happy to put up with (but up with which others are not prepared to put). If it sounds better to sometimes split your infinitive, do it. If you decide always to avoid splitting the infinitive, the reader may not know if you are, in this sentence:

■   always deciding; or

■   always avoiding.

The rules of grammar were, as the quote from Vallins shows, artificially created. The English language already existed, and was quite well understood by people who used it (including people like Chaucer and Shakespeare) without the interference of grammarians. Do you remember the lament of the professor in 'My Fair Lady': 'Why can't a woman be more like a man?' These grammarians wanted English to be more like Latin, so they not only interfered with spellings (eg *det* became *debt*, because of the Latin *debitus*), but they also imported rules like avoiding split infinitives.

We have now become intimidated by these rules. Because people have been told in school: 'don't say "Johnnie and me", say "Johnnie and I"' or 'say "whom" if it is followed by a verb' it has become common to say things like:

■   'Are you coming out with Jane and I?' (try reversing the order of 'Jane and I' to realise the nonsense created: 'with I and Jane'); or

■   'James, whom I said was in court, was actually in his office' (take out 'I said' from the sentence and you realise that 'whom' is actually the subject of 'is' – 'whom was in court' can be recognised as rubbish).

So our first rule of good English is to run over the sound of what you are saying or writing in your head, and ask yourself if it sounds good. Then ask if the meaning is clear – that is, the meaning you intend to convey jumps out at you; and no other meanings.

> 'Christopher Price, Principal and Chief Executive, Leeds Metropolitan University told the conference 10 years ago, British education was so narrowly academic that it was failing to equip students. ... '

> (*Higher Education for Capability Bulletin*, February 1993)

This sentence may fall foul of the rules of punctuation. But what is really wrong is that its meaning is not clear. Was the speech made ten years ago, or was he saying that ten years ago British education was narrow?

Such ambiguities creep into even the best legal writing. Attempting to answer the question of whether taking abandoned property can be theft, Blackstone's *Criminal Practice 1997*, p 226 states: 'In *Small* (1988) 86 Cr App R 170 the Court of Appeal ... implicitly assumed that the proposition ... that one cannot steal abandoned property remains correct.'

'Cannot' in the sense of 'ought not' or in the sense of 'it does not count as stealing'?

Such ambiguities are inevitable. Look for them and aim to minimise them. This process of checking against unclear meaning is more important than the next stage, which is to see if your text complies with the rules of 'good' English.

You cannot always, or even usually, create clear English first time. You write a sentence or paragraph, or a complete affidavit, then you check it for meaning, ease of reading/listening, and then you check for compliance with the rules.

There are certain very useful guidelines in the use of English. You gain an advantage if you construct and punctuate sentences and spell words the way other people generally do. English is a code, and both the sender and receiver must use the same code if what the sender wants to convey is to be understood by the receiver.

Punctuation is often the greatest weakness of students (and others), so I will take you through the basic conventions. What I have to say is only a taster. If you need further help in the area of English usage, there are some wonderful books. I strongly recommend *Fowler's Modern English Usage* (Sir Ernest Gowers) and Sir Ernest Gowers' *The Complete Plain Words*. These books are not just about using plain English, but about working out what you want to say, and saying it effectively and economically, so that people will understand you.

The front cover of *The Complete Plain Words* contains my favourite example of why care should be taken in constructing sentences:

> 'If the baby does not thrive on raw milk, boil it.'

This is followed closely by the radio cricketing commentary ascribed to the late and great Brian Johnston: (*Guardian* 2 December 1993).

'The bowler's Holding; the batsman's Willey.'

Adopt helpful conventions of punctuation

I apologise to those who have no problems in this area. I hope you will enjoy some of the examples.

'When we arrived at the restaurant we met Alex and his brother Sam joined us later.'

How many were at the restaurant? Is Alex related to Sam? Only personal knowledge, or proper punctuation, can tell you. Here are two possibilities:

'When we arrived at the restaurant we met Alex; and his brother Sam joined us later.'

'When we arrived at the restaurant we met Alex and his brother. Sam joined us later.'

(This example is from Fairbairn and Winch *Reading, Writing and Reasoning: A Guide for Students.*)

Punctuation can therefore be vital to meaning.

The full stop (.)

This marks the end of an idea, and comes at the end of a complete sentence. Everyone knows this.

Not everyone knows that sentences need a verb. The following is not a sentence: 'Regarding your recent job application received at our office on 19th February'. Nothing is happening in the sentence. (Would 'Thank you for your application' fall foul of this rule? No, for it is short for 'I thank you'.)

So – a verb in every sentence? OK. Usually.

Full stops are also used to show a word has been shortened or abbreviated. You can write H.H.Judge A. Smythe for example. If the abbreviation is really well known, however, you do not need to add a full stop, such as MP, BBC, ACAS or LPC.

Semi colon (;)

This is used to separate one idea from another. You can use it where a full stop would be correct, but you wish to show a connection between the two ideas. For example: You can have coffee; you can have tea; you can have juice. Or you can have nothing.

Comma (,)

This is the one most frequently misused, not just by lawyers. Properly used it is an aid to understanding text, by separating connected ideas from each other within a sentence. A comma does not signify a fresh start, that would require a semi colon or full stop. (Re-read and repunctuate the last sentence, please, applying the rule it contains.)

Example: To issue a writ, send the court the fee, the writ, the correct number of copies and the Legal Aid Certificate.

In this example, why is there no comma between 'copies' and 'and'? A comma can be dispensed with in a list where the last item is preceded by 'and'. (But put a comma after 'the court' and your envelope will burst.)

As well as separating a list of nouns, a comma can separate a list of clauses (things with verbs in):

> 'Draft the summons, take it to the court, pay the fee, and the court staff will issue the summons.'

(For an example of commas helping you to make sense, in that last example try removing the last comma and you may be charged with attempting to bribe the court staff.)

If you have a list where the next idea is not so closely connected, try a semi colon instead:

> 'The court staff will issue the summons and give you a notice of issue; if it contains a mistake, they should tell you.'

Commas also separate out one part of an idea from the rest of the flow of the sentence:

> 'The advantage of a partnership, some people believe, is its informal structure. It can be formed, if all parties agree, on the spot.'

But do not separate different ideas with commas. The following sentence needs semi colons or full stops, not commas:

> 'I leave my personal belongings to my mother AB; I leave £500 to my neice CD.'

Commas are not neutral aids to punctuation. They do not just help the flow of the prose; they affect meaning. Look at the two sentences below.

> 'The new national conditions of sale are available.'

(There were some old national conditions.)

> 'The new, national, conditions of sale are available.'

(There is no such implication here; these conditions are new and they are national. If there were any old ones, they were not national.)

What is the difference between the two sentences below?

'Take the form of transfer which is in the top drawer.'

'Take the form of transfer, which is in the top drawer.'

Given the first instruction, you now know that of all the forms you could be looking for, the particular one you have been told to find is in the top drawer. Without the comma the clause 'which is in the top drawer' actually defines the thing you are talking about. But in the second instruction, you already know which form you want, and the information after the comma is additional. It does not *identify* the form, only where to find it.

A common mistake with commas is to use a single comma to separate a subject from its verb. For example:

'The plaintiff's long running case, eventually turned out to be a costly victory.'

Here you must either put commas on both sides of the word 'eventually', which interrupts the flow from subject to verb and emphasises 'eventually', or remove the single comma.

You should not, put commas in places, just because that is where you would pause, in speech.

Advice you may find helpful, if you have trouble getting to grips with commas, is to use them very sparingly. If you can use full stops, do so. That means keeping your sentences short. That may be good.

Now for a last example of how important a comma can be. You are advertising that your office is open every Saturday for advice. Which of these sentences will convey this accurately?

'Please drop in any Saturday, when our office is open.'

'Please drop in any Saturday when our office is open.'

Apostrophe (')

There are two main uses. First, an apostrophe shows that something belongs to something else, as in *The Law Society's Gazette*, or the assessors' standards.

Society's and *Assessors'* – why does the apostrophe sometimes go before the 's' and sometimes after? The convention is that if a word already has an 's' to make it a plural, the apostrophe goes after that 's'. Of course, you cannot hear this distinction (between *assessor's* and *assessors'*, and if it is important to show when you are speaking that the word remains singular or becomes plural, you can say 'the standards of the assessor' or 'the standards of the asessors'.

It is (it's) also used to show where a letter is left out of a word. 'It is' has become 'it's'. This does not (doesn't) usually cause too many problems, if you avoid confusing 'its' (meaning 'belonging to it) with 'it's' (meaning 'it is').

Can you see where an apostrophe is needed in the following sentence?

'Its vital to use grammar in its correct sense.'

Colon (:)

Colons are fun. They maintain a sense of anticipation and excitement in your writing, if used correctly. When you use a colon, you are indicating that something will follow which is connected to what has just been said:

> 'There are five kinds of legal aid: criminal, civil, green form, duty schemes and ABWOR.'

> 'The judge said: "This is the most scandalous case I have had the pleasure to hear in my forty years on the bench".'

We have not had space to say more on punctuation. If these rules do not trigger in you the sensation: 'of course, I just needed reminding', then we recommend closer scrutiny of the rules in *Fowler*, *Gowers*, or any other book on writing.

Cut paragraphs and sentences down to size

We are moving away from 'correct' writing into matters of preference. You are free to ignore this advice – but you had better have some good writing to show for your independence!

By and large, short sentences and short paragraphs are easier to understand than long ones. Lord Denning may have upset many cherished legal rules in his long career, but no-one has ever complained that they could not understand what he was saying. He achieved this through simple language and short sentences. Almost any case of his illustrates the point. For example – a case chosen at random from the shelves – *Gurtner v Circuit* [1968] 1 All ER at 333: The problem is about whether the Motor Insurers' Bureau can be joined as a party to an action where the defendant has not put in a defence. First, see how Lord Diplock introduces the issue:

> 'This appeal illustrates once again the legal anomalies which result from the method adopted by the Minister of Transport in 1946 to fill a gap in the protection of third parties injured by negligent driving of motor vehicles provided by the Road Traffic Acts 1930 and 1934. Under those Acts, although insurance against third party risks was made compulsory and insurers made directly liable to satisfy judgments against their assured, an injured person, although he had recovered judgment against a negligent defendant, could whistle for his money if (a) the defendant was not insured at the time of the accident or (b) his policy of insurance was avoided in the circumstances specified in s 10(3) of the Act of 1934 for non-disclosure or misrepresentation or (c) his insurer, too, was insolvent. To fill this gap, the insurers transacting compulsory motor vehicle insurance business in Great Britain, acting in agreement with the Minister of Transport, formed a company, the Motor Insurers' Bureau, to assume liability to satisfy judgments of these three kinds. Instead, however, of amending the legislation so as to impose on the Motor Insurers' Bureau a statutory liability to the unsatisfied judgment creditor as has been done by the Road Traffic Act 1934, in respect of the liability of insurers to satisfy judgments against defendants covered by a valid policy of insurance, the matter was dealt with by agreement of June 17, 1946, between the Minister of Transport and the Motor Insurers' Bureau.'

That sets the scene. He goes on to describe the problem of whether the Bureau can or should be joined as a party:

'Under cl 1 of its contract with the Minister and subject only to the conditions precedent in cl 5, the bureau give an unqualified undertaking to pay to the judgment creditor all sums remaining unpaid after seven days under a judgment against any person in respect of any liability for negligent driving of a motor vehicle. The existence and amount of the bureau's liability, of which the Minister can obtain an order for specific performance for the benefit of the unsatisfied judgment creditor, thus depends on the result of an action to which the bureau is not a necessary party. Although there may be a good defence to that action, judgment in it may be obtained by default either collusively – which is not the case in the present appeal – or because the defendant is unaware of the action or through impecuniosity or for some other reason is not concerned to resist it; and the damages may be assessed on such evidence as the plaintiff chooses to tender without being subjected to cross examination. Clearly the bureau have a lively interest, at any rate commercial, in seeing that all proper defences to the action as respects liability are raised and that all relevant material which tends to reduce the quantum of damages recoverable is adduced to the court. We have been informed that, in an attempt to mitigate the injustice to the bureau of allowing assessment of damages on judgments by default to proceed without critical scrutiny, it has been the practice of the Queen's Bench Masters, with the acquiescence of the plaintiffs, to allow the bureau to be represented at the hearing of the assessment to cross examine the plaintiff's witnesses and to adduce other evidence. Save, however, with the consent of the plaintiff, this sensible practice cannot be followed unless the bureau is entitled to be joined as a party to the action, and, even where the plaintiff does consent, it is desirable that this formality should be observed – if only to give the bureau a right to appeal or to resist an appeal by the plaintiff.'

Breathtakingly complex! There are up to five subclauses per sentence, and, when Lord Diplock gets a following wind, sentences reaching 86 words.

Here is Lord Denning covering some of the same ground.

'If the Motor Insurers' Bureau are not allowed to come in as a defendant, what will happen?

The order for substituted service will go unchallenged. The service on the defendant will be good, even though he knows nothing of the proceedings. He will not enter an appearance. The plaintiff will sign judgment in default of appearance. The judgment will be for damages to be assessed. The master will assess the judgment with no-one to oppose. The judgment will be completed for the ascertained sum.

The defendant will not pay it. Then the plaintiff will be able to come down on the Motor Insurers' Bureau and call on them to pay it because they have made a solemn agreement that they will pay. It is well known. It is set out in full in a note to *Hardy v Motor Insurers' Bureau* [citation given].

It is true that the injured person was not a party to that agreement between the bureau and the Minister of Transport and he cannot sue in his own name for the benefit of it; but the Minister of Transport can sue for specific performance of it. He can compel the bureau to honour their agreement by paying the injured person. ...

It is thus apparent that the Motor Insurers' Bureau are vitally concerned in the outcome of the action. They are directly affected, not only in their legal rights, but also in their pockets. They ought to be allowed to come in as defendants.'

Sentences are perhaps more critical than paragraphs. The extract from Lord Denning's judgment had no paragraphs in the original: I added them, as I thought his paragraph too long.

Of course, you can choose to write the occasional long sentence, or paragraph; readers like variety, and Denning's staccato prose can become a little breathless after a while.

But do not do this automatically – choose to do it, or not. Twenty-two words in a sentence is considered to be a safe maximum (Adair *The Effective Communicator*). Are you exceeding this regularly? If so, your sentences inevitably contain more than one idea, and, if it will help you to cure the habit of excess length, try cutting them down, at least until you have got the problem under control, to one idea per sentence. To practise what we preach, here is that last sentence again:

> 'If so, your sentences contain more than one idea. Try cutting them down to one idea per sentence. This will help cure the habit of excess length.'

Here is an example from *The Complete Plain Words*:

> 'Further to your letter of the above date and reference in connection with an allocation of ... , as already pointed out to you all the allocations for this period have been closed, and I therefore regret that it is not possible to add to the existing allocation which has been made to you and which covers in toto your requirements for this period when originally received, by virtue of the work on which you are engaged, a rather higher percentage has been given to you, namely 100 per cent of the original requirements and at this stage I am afraid it is not practicable for you to increase the requirement for the reasons already given.'

Hands up if you understand that.

Gowers reduces this verbiage to two simple sentences:

> 'Your original application was granted in full because of the importance of your work. I regret that the amount cannot now be increased, as no more allocations for this period will be made.'

Hands up if you understood this time – virtually everyone, we hope.

Paragraphs can also be cut down. Each cannot be expected to contain just one point, like a sentence, but paragraphs can be used to indicate a change of theme. One theme per paragraph is usually enough.

And please leave sufficient gaps between paragraphs – at least one extra line space. This is more pleasant to the eye and helps you understand.

An example of breaking long paragraphs into shorter ones is the solicitor's letter about the reduced deposit on pp 28–29.

Choose the right level of formality

My writing has occasionally been criticised for tending towards informality. (More often, though, I have been told it is a refreshing change.) We have, in fact, made a decision that the sort of book that students need will be easy to read, fast moving, relaxed and informal. That does not make it 'correct'. 'Correctness' doesn't matter. We hope it makes it effective.

But a highly informal style will not be appropriate in addressing a High Court judge – or even a new client. A decision to use relatively informal language does not give you the right to assume familiarity with the person you are communicating with. You risk alienating people if you address them in ways they do not expect. His lordship and their worships should be addressed according to the convention; and a new client who you do not know personally should, normally, be addressed as Mrs Shearsby, Ms Kennedy etc. Becoming more familiar requires permission, granted explicitly ('May I call you Victoria? Please call me Hugh.') or implicitly (use your own judgment).

It may be appropriate to say to a client in a criminal case: 'So this copper banged you up and wouldn't let you see your brief. I wonder what the beak will think about that.' (On the other hand your client may think your use of vernacular is patronising and wrong and therefore your language is ineffective.) In any event, in court you will have to say the same thing in words that the court finds appropriate: 'Your worships, the officer arrested the defendant and took him to the police station, where he was denied access to a solicitor in breach of the Police and Criminal Evidence Act, section 58.'

Here are three ways you might write to a client whose business partner, you have learned, has made a surprising announcement.

Dear Davey,

What a stunning bit of news. I was flabbergasted to learn that your old buddy has chucked it all in to play fast and loose on the stock market.

Dear Sir,

The writer was surprised to learn of the actions of your partner who has declared his intention of dissolving the partnership in order to avail himself of the opportunities of speculating in stocks and shares.

Dear Dave,

I was surprised to learn that Brian has decided to wind up the partnership, and that he intends to earn a living by trading in stocks and shares.

For me the last version creates the right balance. The point is to remember that you do have a choice; you can set the tone that you decide will work best.

Go for precision

Your language should avoid fudging. For example, you write 'a certain amount of money'. Are you communicating vagueness? Do you know know exactly how much money? If you do not, and it is relevant, find out the exact sum. (It is hard to imagine, unless you are telling an after-dinner anecdote or expounding a legal principle, how the actual amount could be irrelevant to a lawyer.) It is better to say 'I do not know how much' or to go and find out.

One of the worst tasks for a lawyer is taking over someone else's file. You open it and find attendance notes or client statements such as:

■ 'Advised client of his right to legal aid'; or

■ 'Discussed the defects in the draft partnership deed with other side'; or

■ 'I bought the flat in September with a 90% mortgage'; or

■ 'I agreed with Mr M that he would check the electrics before we bought the house'.

When trying to work out what actually happened there are too many questions unanswered:

■ What right to legal aid – green form? Civil? What was the client's response to the advice? Did the advice mention the statutory charge? Did the client accept the advice?

■ What were the defects in the draft deed? What decisions were made about altering the deed?

■ Which flat? When exactly? How much was borrowed? Who from? What was the purchase price?

■ Was this agreement made in conversation? In writing? When?

These are questions about interviewing technique and factual research, as well as about style of writing. But if you pay meticulous attention to writing, with full detail and without ambiguity, you will have to acquire the habit of asking the right questions in the interview.

But what about conciseness and brevity? Is there not a conflict between making sure every single relevant bit of information is recorded, and the need to avoid excessive length?

No. Precision is the art of including everything that is relevant for the particular purpose, and nothing that is irrelevant.

Taking this advice into account, here is an expanded note recording what the client told the solicitor in relation to the electrics problem:

> On 14 October last year I visited Mr M's premises at 7, Greenside Lane, and asked him to check the electrics of the house at 11, West Drive. He agreed to do this for a fee of £25, and said that he would carry out the inspection himself on Friday morning at 11.00. The conversation took place in the presence of my daughter, Samantha Jones, aged 19. At the time Mr M was wearing blue jeans and matching pullover. I think he looked quite attractive.

The last two sentences are probably irrelevant. They take us from precision into irrelevance.

However beware of snap decisions on relevance. Until you know what the case is about and have carried out any necessary research, you cannot judge. This case might be about an allegation that Mr M carried out the survey negligently. But if it were a criminal case where M's movements were crucial, what he was wearing is relevant and should be recorded.

Is the note otherwise complete? Look it over again – but remembering that it is only an extract from a more detailed document. Anything missing? Yes, the year of the conversation. It may be obvious now, but perhaps not when you blow the dust off the file in two years' time.

Cut legalese down to size

But don't cut down on the legal meaning of words; we are not saying you can use any English you fancy. You must pay attention not just to what you think the language means, but what other people think it means. Not for you the luxury of Humpty Dumpty in *Alice's Adventures in Wonderland*: ' "When I use a word", Humpty Dumpty said in a rather scornful tone, "it means just what I choose it to mean – neither more nor less".' (Humpty Dumpty goes on to state his philosophy of drafting: 'Impenetrability! That's what *I* say!')

Not, in most situations, a luxury afforded to the Parliamentary draftsman, who can declare that male means also female and vice versa (Interpretation Act 1978, section 6(a)).

We look at some words that have particular meanings in Chapter 5 on Drafting. There is nothing wrong with using complex language where that best conveys what you want to communicate. What becomes legalese is the use of complex words and structures that add nothing. Often legalese that has been used for generations has no legal meaning. Take the words 'Now this deed witnesseth that'. Lawyers use these words in vast numbers of contracts and conveyancing documents. But if you know your law, which is the background to any use of language, you will discover that the phrase is meaningless, it adds nothing. The formula is repeated because it once worked.

Not just lawyers are at fault here. Primo Levi, the late Italian author, tells a story of when he worked as a chemist in a paint factory, and had to find out why a batch of paint had congealed. He found it was caused by a contaminant which could be neutralised by the addition of a particular compound. Years after he had left this job, he writes in *The Periodic Table*, he found the factory was still adding the compound. No-one any longer knew why. The contaminant was no longer around.

There is a word for this: superstition.

You may think you have to copy legal language. Do so if you know what it means, and if you agree that the word or phrase used by previous lawyers is the best choice. Do not do so if you do not know what the word means, or why it was chosen. Find out, then choose.

You must use words which a judge will understand the same way as you intended. Within these constraints, you have choices about your use of language. You do not have to use words that lawyers for centuries have loved: 'said', 'hereunder', 'aforementioned' and so on. You do not have to make your sentences long. (Try again: sentences can be short. You do not have to follow precedents slavishly (in Chapter 5 we have more to say about the tyranny of precedents).)

A striking example of superstition is found sometimes in affidavits drafted to reply to the other side's affidavit. Solicitors often write: 'I have read what purports to be a true copy of the affidavit of So and So dated ... '. What on earth is this supposed to mean? Is the implication that the copy was a forgery, and access to the real one is being restricted to the judge and MI5?

This wording has been slavishly repeated since the days when copies had to be made by writing or typing them out again; in those days there was a real risk that the copy would be inaccurate, and unless you had read the original document sworn by the maker you were wise to state that you had only seen what, as far as you could tell, was a copy. But now? You have before you a photocopy, provided by a solicitor, with a copy of the signature of the deponent – and yet you still copy this outmoded clause?

Do not use a form of words just because other people do so. If you are uncertain about what something means, is it really right to copy it out? Then verbose, complex language is a smokescreen to hide your confusion. Your clients deserve better.

If you do know what it means, then you are free to use the best language available to make that meaning clear and effective.

Endeavour to ascertain the least circumlocutious mode of expression of content (*Keep It Simple, Stupid*: KISS)

If two words are equally good, use the commoner of the two, eg 'say' rather than 'state', 'tell' rather than 'advert'.

A few examples will make the point:

■   'with reference to the second paragraph thereof' can become 'in the second paragraph';

■   'kindly be good enough to advise me when you anticipate completion' becomes 'please tell me when you intend to complete', or 'when do you intend to complete?'

Redundant words can be cut out:

■   Just a few – a few

■   At this moment in time – now/presently

■   Final result – result

■   A certain amount of – some

■   True facts – facts

■   Make provision for – provide

■   In the majority of instances – usually

■   Give devise and bequeath – give

- Just and reasonable – reasonable

- I enclose herewith – I enclose

- The majority of – most

- Due to the fact that – because

Some well used clauses or phrases can sometimes be removed altogether, such as:

- It should be noted that

- I am writing to inform you

- It should be borne in mind that

- I feel that

(I am not saying these phrases are never appropriate. As with everything, say it if you decide it is the best way of communicating. Be self-critical, then go ahead.)

Why is it necessary to remove superfluous words? Everything you write or say costs time and money (and marks on an assessment). Anything superfluous distracts attention from what matters. And lawyers assume that every single word has meaning; a court may assume you meant something extra by using extra words.

'Said' is an example of a word that lawyers use without, usually, any increase in clairty of meaning: One of my favourite examples of overuse of the said word is the headnote to the case of *R v M'Naghten* [1843] X Clark & Finnelly 200:

> 'The prisoner had been indicted for that he, on the 20th day of January 1843, at the parish of Saint Martin in the Fields, in the county of Middlesex, and within the jurisdiction of the Central Criminal Court, in and upon one Edward Drummond, feloniously, wilfully, and of his malice aforethought, did make an assault; and that the said Daniel M'Naghten, a certain pistol of the value of 20s, loaded and charged with gunpowder and a leaden bullet (which pistol in his right hand he had and held), to, against and upon the said Edward Drummond, feloniously, wilfully and of his malice aforethought, did shoot and discharge; and that the said Daniel M'Naghten, with the leaden bullet aforesaid, out of the pistol aforesaid, by force of the gunpowder, etc, the said Edward Drummond, in and upon the back of him the said Edward Drummond, feloniously, etc did strike, penetrate and wound, giving to the said Edward Drummond, in and upon the back of the said Edward Drummond, one mortal wound, etc, of which mortal wound the said E Drummond languished until the 25th of April and then died; and that by means of the aforesaid, he the prisoner did kill and murder the said Edward Drummond. The prisoner pleaded Not guilty.'

There may have been good reasons in the early nineteenth century for this repetitive style. There are none now. In particular, there is no mention of any other Edward Drummond, and the use of 'said' every time the said Edward Drummond is mentioned in the said passage adds exactly nothing to our understanding. Nor is there more than one pistol, so 'aforesaid' can be removed.

(But look at the final sentence: what a wonderful contrast to the verbosity of the rest of the passage.)

In addition to the aforesaid said there are other abhorrent terms hereinafter mentioned. For example:

■ herewith

■ aforementioned

■ witnesseth

■ hereby

'I hereby agree to sell 5,000 widgets': The agreement is equally valid without 'hereby'. And the agreement gains no additional force with the addition of 'this agreement witnesseth that ... '.

Use simple words if you have a choice:

'Subsequent to her arrival, the Defendant made a telephonic communication in which she saw fit to appraise her husband of her involuntary incarceration by Her Majesty's Constabulary.'

This can be simplified to:

'After she arrived, she phoned her husband to tell him she had been arrested.'

Again, we lawyers are not the only guilty parties. An environmental scientist provided me with this gem from a report: 'The piscal life achieved 100% mortality.'

I hope the fish were alright!

Cut out unnecessary Latin

The *Supreme Court Practice 1996* offers advice about drafting witness statements (see 38/2A/8): 'The statement of the witness should be stated in a clear straightforward narrative form, and should use the language of the witness, his *ipsissima verba*.' Need we say any more?

Avoid Latinisms if you can. Sometimes a Latin phrase, like *res ipsa loquitur*, is a term of art, with a recognised legal meaning; then it has to be used in the precise context, such as the pleading or the submission to the judge. Everywhere else you can guarantee that such terms cause only confusion. (Several years ago a correspondent in the *Gazette* reported the phrase transcribed from the dictaphone as 'Ray's hips were locked together.') But when you have a choice as to whether to use words or phrases like: *inter alia* (among other things), *re* (about), *infra* (below), *mutatis mutandis* (with any necessary changes) then we think you should have a reason for choosing the Latin version.

For years the churches opposed making the Bible available in English. The reason historians give us is that the authorities feared that people who understood the Bible would challenge their authority. Lawyers must ask themselves if this is a justification for depriving the public of English.

Use direct language

Where possible use of the passive tense is to be avoided by students.

Yes, that means you: don't use the passive unless you have to.

When you use the passive in a sentence you make the object (the thing that something was done to) appear to be the subject: 'He was hit by a ball.' 'The letter was written by my secretary.'

The person who did it becomes less important than the thing that he or she did it to. Sometimes this is the best way to write. But often people use the passive out of carelessness.

There are three problems with the passive:

First: it allows you to leave out information without realising. For example: 'The letter was sent on 15th January after the matter had been fully reviewed.' Who wrote the letter, or did the reviewing?

The passive is great if you *intend* to omit such information. For example, in your letter to the Office for the Supervision of Solicitors: 'Regrettably the file was mislaid for several weeks' rather than 'The Senior Partner mislaid the file' ('but has instructed me not to tell you'). It is also fine if you intend to emphasise that the object of the action is more important in the context than the subject: 'The writ was returned by the Post Office' recognises that the writ being returned is more important than the Post Office's role as the doer. 'The Children Act 1989 is based on a philosophy of parental responsibility.' This sentence uses the passive, because it is not important, for the discussion, to say exactly who based it on that philosophy, the Government, Parliament, public opinion or whatever.

The passive – if used uncritically – allows vagueness to creep in. 'It is hoped that' … 'it is anticipated that' … 'a reply is expected by next week'. It is a great aid to sloppy thinking, as it allows you to ignore the question 'who is responsible for these sentiments and demands?' I have worn out several red pens with clinical students who write in file notes things like: 'An agreement was made whereby the carpets would be installed on 7th November.' This is no longer a question of stylistic preferences: the information that we need to conduct this client's case is simply lacking. A passive tense detector is one step towards prevention of this sloppiness.

Second: the passive tends to be more confusing than the active. Here is the wording of a parking ticket cited in *The Complete Plain Words* (the passive verbs are in italic):

> 'The vehicle *was left* in a parking place without payment of the charge *indicated* by a parking token duly *affixed* to a valid permit/parking card *displayed* on the vehicle/by the display on the vehicle of a valid season ticket/daily ticket.'

Who did, or omitted to do, all of these monstrous things? Off with his head.

Gowers rewrites this in the active voice:

> 'You left the vehicle in a parking place and did not show that you had paid the charge by displaying on the vehicle either a parking token fixed to a valid permit or parking card, or a valid season ticket or daily ticket.'

From a tenancy agreement: 'All rubbish must be removed by the tenant before the property is vacated' can become:

> 'The tenant must remove all rubbish before vacating the property.' (Or even more directly: 'You must remove all rubbish before you leave.')

Third: the passive voice is unnecessarily long-winded. 'This book was written by Hugh Brayne and Richard Grimes' is two words longer than necessary. (Unlike the book itself. Like Mozart defending his music in the film 'Amadeus', we believe it is neither too long, nor too short, but just right!)

As with all the rules, you have a choice. (A choice is to be had by students.)

Use 'you' where appropriate

This is particularly relevant in letter writing, and is something we touch on again in Chapter 5 on Writing and Drafting. The recipient of a letter is the most important person to have in mind. For example, in advising Mrs Evans about her prospects of getting legal aid: 'Courts are generally reluctant to grant legal aid to defendants unless there is a risk of prison' could be changed to 'The court is unlikely to grant you legal aid unless it thinks that you are at risk of going to prison'. (As I changed that sentence, I found myself wanting to expand on what I had said: for as soon as I put the word 'you' close to 'prison' I felt I owed this client a clearer explanation. This is a bonus of addressing the actual recipient of the information, not the generality of people affected by legal aid decisions (or whatever you are writing about).)

The use of 'you' may not seem appropriate for more formal documents. Business agreements, conveyances, are perhaps not yet ready for this informality. But it is becoming commonplace in tenancy agreements, consumer agreements, income tax forms, legal aid forms – in fact, almost any document you can think of that has been awarded a Plain English crystal mark. British Telecom recently sent customers a letter congratulating itself on its new, simple contract. This talks to you, the customer.

I have already advised against unthinking use of phrases like 'the writer' instead of 'I'. But the deliberate decision to use 'you' frequently (where appropriate, in particular in letters) reminds the reader/listener who is the most important person. Be careful to avoid excessive use of the word 'I'. If every paragraph starts with 'I' you are putting yourself first. 'I am in receipt of your letter' puts the writer first. 'Thank you for your letter' puts the reader first. 'I note your concerns that ... ' can be changed to 'You are concerned that ... '.

Avoid gender bias

The Interpretation Act 1978 and the Law of Property Act 1925 both say that masculine means feminine too. Therefore there is nothing technically incorrect, in formal drafting, to say he, his, him, meaning he or she, his or her, him or her. And even in less formal writing and speaking, there is a rearguard school of thought that gender neutral language is a modern affectation to be avoided. (I used the passive tense there because I deliberately wanted to remain vague – I do not identify myself with whoever these people are.)

It is a matter on which you should make a deliberate choice, rather than continuing to use male dominated language out of inertia. I personally believe that as times change, so does language. I prefer to be among those who aim to use language to include both genders rather than exclude the female. Most modern writing on drafting takes this line. Some legislation uses feminine pronouns, such as the Child Support Act 1991 – although in a stereotypical way, putting women in the position of the parent left behind looking after children.

There can be a degree of clumsiness in some gender neutral constructions. The reader may find his or her senses jarred. Sometimes, however, they cease to sound clumsy after your ear gets used to them. 'Spokesperson/spokeswoman' is now common. The BBC talks about 'firefighters' and 'police officers'.

There are other ways round jarring the ear. The word 'you' is gender neutral. We have chosen to address the reader as you throughout this book.

Your written and spoken communication fall into two categories. Things like pleadings, affidavits and letters are about actual people and events. Saying 'he' about a woman in that situation is careless and offensive. The barrister who I once observed calling a woman High Court judge 'my Lord' was repeatedly rebuked, but remained apparently unable to come to terms with seeing a woman in a wig and fancy dress.

But there is also writing/speaking about people who do not necessarily exist: hypothetical people, or future parties to an agreement. For example, in a court mitigation speech, the advocate talking about provocation says: 'a man can only take so much, and then he is tempted to take the law into his own hands'. Drafting an agreement to determine future behaviour – contracts, tenancy agreements, partnerships, where the gender of people affected cannot always be known – the drafter has to identify these people without knowing specifically which gender will apply.

You could decide to rely on the Interpretation Act and say 'he' throughout. For example, from the 1992 National Conditions of Sale, para 2.2.2:

> 'If before completion date the seller agrees to buy another property in England and Wales for *his* residence, *he* may use all or any part of the deposit. ... '

You are unlikely to be criticised or marked down for following the old convention of using the masculine in this situation. But if, like us, you choose to avoid saying he and meaning he or she, you have to redraft this kind of clause, and it is not always easy. One option is 'his or her' throughout. Another is to repeat the word 'seller' every time 'he' or 'his' is used; but this reads rather clumsily after a while. Another possibility is to reconstruct the sentence: 'The seller who agrees before completion date to buy another property in England or Wales may ....'

An interesting style is that used by Gwyneth Pitt in Employment Law (Sweet and Maxwell, 3rd edn, 1997). She sometimes says she and sometimes says he. The reader is left in no confusion and the text is readable.

Sometimes the plural can be used. It will not work in a contract about one seller and one buyer. But if it is a document describing the rights and duties of many people, who may not yet be involved, and whose gender is not fixed throughout the currency of the document, you can say instead of: 'Notice may be sent to a Director at his home address' – 'Notice may be sent to Directors at their home addresses'.

If what you are writing or saying is not to have specific legal effect – for example, it forms part of a persuasive argument – using the plural 'they' or 'their' instead of the singular 'he' or 'his' is also acceptable. For example, in the mitigation speech: 'People are entitled to say that they have had enough'; or in care proceedings: 'Children must have their views taken into account'.

A warning: this is a polarised issue; strong views are sometimes held by both the traditionalists and the reformers. The Law Society's *Guide to the Professional Conduct of Solicitors* has removed sexist language. The tide is turning. But for the purposes of a course assessment what is 'right' is what gets you through the assessments. After that, you are free to choose what we consider the right way – gender neutral language – or another way. Every man for herself, as one must make their own choice.

Take care with negatives

Negatives are harder to understand than positives. The reader or listener may lose the thread of what you are saying or writing while trying to work out the effect of the negatives. The reader is not at a disadvantage if you do not use too many negatives. (Got that?)

Negatives can include negative verbs, like deny, withhold or refuse. From a recent book review in the Gazette (quoted only from memory, unfortunately): 'It is impossible not to overstate the value of this book'. Translated, this is condemnation as saying 'you could easily overrate this book'. But the rest of the review was complimentary, so it was not improbable that the reviewer, by careless overuse of negatives, had failed to prevent his metaphorical knickers getting in a knot of nots.

In an affidavit dealing with finance on divorce: 'It was not uncommon in the later years of the marriage for the Respondent to refuse to stop withholding maintenance payments'. Did he pay, or not? 'Not uncommon' means – well, what does it mean? It is a fudge, and avoids saying anything precise. 'Refuse to stop withholding' – did he withhold? Refuse and desist cancel each other out, and he did withhold. After clarifying exactly what and when the respondent paid and did not pay the petitioner, the sentence can be rewritten (for example): 'The Respondent between April and September 1999 made only three payments towards the household expenses. *The Petitioner asked him to pay almost every week during that period, but the Respondent did not pay.*' By tightening up the language, and removing too many negatives, you also find yourself compelled towards greater precision.

Here are some more examples:

■ 'I am unable to disagree' (indicates a forceful argument) can change to 'I agree'; 'I am persuaded'; 'the argument is very convincing' etc.

■ 'A party shall not be prevented from commencing proceedings, notwithstanding the appointment of an arbitrator' (an example from *Gowers*) can become 'If an arbitrator is appointed a party may still commence legal proceedings'.

We are not saying all negatives are to be removed in favour of positives.

In *The Complete Plain Words* Gowers reminds us that 'Do not pull the pin out of this grenade' has more force than 'The pin must be left in the grenade'. 'He refused to pay maintenance for a whole year', or 'The Defendant failed to avoid the Plaintiff' are positive descriptions of things that did not happen – failures that you wish to pinpoint. The message is: choose the way you say things, and if a sentence looks in any way weak or confusing, removal of negatives and replacement with positives can be a not unhelpful way to avoid confusing the reader. It will also be a helpful way of making things clear for the reader.

Use emotive or persuasive words with care

You remember the poll tax 'riots' in 1990? Not one person was charged with the offence of riot under the Public Order Act 1986. There was technically no riot. A word like riot is emotive. What actually happened was a large demonstration with some outbreaks of violent disorder.

A Home Secretary recently spoke at a party conference about bail bandits – people committing offences while on bail. This may be the appropriate tone for a politician wishing to raise the temperature; it is not generally appropriate language for a lawyer.

Also, we advise against language that is purely persuasive. Your message should itself be persuasive, if that is your task. You do not need to use words like 'surely' or 'obviously', because if a thing is obvious, there is no need to say so. If it is not obvious, it does not become obvious by virtue of being described as obvious. In fact, as an informal criterion I use for gauging the experience and confidence of a student carrying out an interviewing or advocacy exercise, when the use of 'obviously' exceeds twice a minute I know I am obviously watching a real beginner.

Beware, then, of phrases that creep in, like 'it has to be admitted that' or 'no-one could doubt that'. We feel that no-one could possibly dispute that without a shadow of a doubt these phrases add little!

Go Easy On Capital Letters

Proper nouns have a capital letter. Hugh Brayne, Richard Grimes, Jane Beck, London, Aunt Frances, the Underground and the Law Society are all proper nouns – including the words aunt, underground, law and society because they are part of a name. If a word uniquely identifies someone, or thing, it becomes a proper noun: 'The Plaintiff sent a letter' is correct, if we know from the title to the document, for example, who this particular plaintiff is. We can equally say: 'All plaintiffs' (small case, no-one in particular identified) 'must be represented by the same solicitor, so the First Plaintiff' (in capitals – it is a proper noun, as if we had used the person's name) 'has instructed Dodds and Co'.

Many lawyers and their Typists seem to Love Capital Letters, as if it Helps Emphasise what they Believe to be Important. However, it is wrong and, to a snob, clearly uneducated.

Do not be satisfied yet

Are you satisfied with your first draft? The best advice I have read is that there is no such thing as good writing, only good rewriting. Put aside the techniques that got you through the exams; drafting in practice, and for assessments, is all about improving, refining, polishing your first attempt. That will take at least as much time as the first attempt. If you have time, draft a piece of work over several days. Sleep on it. Each time you come back to the writing – or to the prepared speech – you can bring a little more insight, a little more refinement.

How do you revise your work: what order do you take things in? Content first, I suggest. If you have time, sleep on it, so that you are not so wrapped up in what you have written that you cannot see its flaws and gaps. Then, after a break, read it right through trying to see it as the target reader will – a judge, a client, an opponent's solicitor. Try to see it from their angle: is there any part of what you need to say missing? confusing? misleading? are you conceding an advantage to an opponent that you do not need to? Is it clear what response or result is needed from the reader?

Are there any gaps in the material? Do you lack key information that means you cannot reach the conclusion? If you are asking the reader/listener to join you in the conclusion as an act of faith, without the material that shows how to get there, you create confusion. To be sure that you have searched for gaps, you have to be very critical of your own work: you have to look at your plan, and the final draft, more critically than any hostile opponent might. This takes time. At the time of preparing something, you are pleased with what you have done (or irrationally self-critical). You are not detached and objective, which is necessary. Step back, then on your own or with a colleague plan an assault from all angles on the material that will be contained in the communication that you are preparing.

Then look at style. Go through looking for:

■   anything redundant: prune it;

■   long paragraphs: divide them;

■   long sentences: divide them;

■   passages without headings: add them;

■   anything complex or jargonistic: simplify it.

(This may lead to a complete rethink – as was the case with the conveyancing letter to Ms Kennedy and Mr Green. After reorganising all the material we tore it up and phoned her.)

Now read it through again. Is it a good read (as far as this kind of document can be, of course)? Do you feel confused as you read it? Or is it easy to follow what you are trying to say? If you are finding it confusing, will any of the following help?

■   a table of contents?

■   an introduction setting out in brief what you are going to be talking about? a summary or conclusion?

■   some more signposts? headings? subheadings? connective phrases, such as 'The other issue I need to advise you on is ... '?

Finally, alway spoof read carfullly what you submit as your finl product. (Once when I was on holiday a letter was sent out to one of my clients which had been audio typed by a secretary who did not know my surname (Brayne). On the file on my return stood the following: 'In the absence of my brain on holiday ... '. Proofread carefully when you enter practice, because what you write becomes part of the record of what you have done. One mistake, or omission, in an affidavit, contract, conveyance etc can alter a transaction, and you may be called upon to defend your conduct on taxation of your costs or in disciplinary proceedings.

I have also learnt from experience to check not just the contents of letters but the address, not just against the last letter in the file, but against the original instructions. The client who was so rudely failing to reply to letter after letter was probably cursing you for not writing.

In the end, all the guidance and exhortations we can offer will not turn you into brilliant communicators. You and only you have to do that. I advise you to concentrate on one aspect at a time. For example, this week, think about use of negatives; next week concentrate on the passive tense; then go for sentence length. In due course you will have a lot of experience to consolidate.

Some simple examples to work on

Here are some examples of imprecise use of language. Can you improve on each one? First we use some short obvious examples. Then we look at some difficult drafting challenges, to gear you up for the Drafting chapter.

What is wrong with the following?

1   Please arrange an appointment to see Mr Smith and I.

2   The Defendant, whom the magistrates believed was lying, was convicted of perjury.

3   I have now discussed the suggestion of underpinning the property with the architect.

4   Any party to this agreement, who fails to pay the balance of the price within seven days, will pay an additional premium of £5.

5   After surveying the property, the fence is in need of repair.

6 'The practice of adjourning inquests judicially to review the coroner on a point of law was considered in [a case] which indicated that this should only be used in exceptional circumstances' (*Gazette* 16 February 1994).

7 Going through my files the other day, my secretary interrupted me.

8 A student who fails a skills assessment clearly can be made to repeat it.

Analysis of the examples

1 You would not say 'please see I', nor should you say 'please see Mr Smith and I'. 'Me' is correct.

2 If the magistrates had believed the Defendant, 'whom' is correct; clearly they did not. 'Who was convicted of perjury' is the clause; 'the magistrates believed' stands alone, between the commas, without an object.

3 The architect may have better things to do than being used to underpin the property. Say, for example, 'I have now discussed with the architect the ...'. This reminds me of the playground joke about the police looking for a man with one eye – how inefficient of them.

4 Remove the commas to achieve the result that is presumably the intention: only those parties who fail to pay are liable to the premium.The use of commas there means that the clause starting with 'who' does not define but merely describes. As written it means any party has to pay the additional premium, and the bit about failing to pay the balance is just a description of the party.

5 The meaning is not lost, but the language is sloppy, and suggests that the fence did the surveying. It could be ambiguous if, instead of the fence, which obviously could not do the survey, we wrote 'After surveying the property, the tenant must repair the fence.' This implies that the tenant surveyed the property. How about: 'It is clear from the survey that the tenant must repair the fence.' But clear to who? This is another issue, but really, having spotted this, I have to remind you to avoid such impersonal declarations. Try: 'I have read the survey. I believe the tenant must repair the fence.' Or 'It is clear to me that the tenant must repair the fence.'

6 By insisting on not splitting the infinitive, the author wrecked the meaning of this sentence. If 'judicially' and 'review' are not kept together, where they belong, you get the implication it was the adjournment that was judicially considered. So go ahead, split the infinitive just this once and write: 'The practice of adjourning inquests to judicially review the coroner ... '.

7 Who was going through the files? It appears to be the secretary. If it was you, a clearer way of saying so is: 'As I was going through my files, my secretary interrupted me'. (Or, less elegantly: 'Going through my files, I was interrupted by my secretary.' 'I' then refers to the person going through the files.)

8 The meaning could be that the failure is clear, or the need to repeat the assessment is clear; or the logic of the statement is thought to be clear.

Some more examples – reworking a draft

These are all real examples.

Here is a rule from the Rules of the Supreme Court, Order 81, rule 2. I have chosen this one because, while the language is not inaccessible, I think it has been constructed in a confusing way. The rule is designed to help parties to an action find out who the owners of a firm are. (Irrelevant parts of the rule are omitted.)

> '**2** (1) Any defendant to an action brought by partners in the name of a firm may serve on the plaintiffs or their solicitor a notice requiring them or him to furnish the defendant with a written statement of the names and places of residence of all the persons who were partners in the firm at the time when the cause of action accrued ...
>
> (3) Paragraph (1) shall have effect in relation to an action brought against partners in the name of a firm as it has effect in relation to an action brought by partners in the name of a firm but with the substitution for references to the defendant and the plaintiffs, of references to the plaintiffs and the defendants respectively. ... '

Read that rule, and try to work out if you can require a defendant firm to disclose full details of its partners.

The answer is that you can, and that is found by reading paragraph (3), then using this information to re-read paragraph (1) as if it was worded differently. (Are you still with us? On my first attempt to read this rule, I got lost, not only because of the mental gymnastics required in reading a paragraph as if it said something different from what it actually says, but also because there is in the original two inches of additional text between the two parts quoted, which I have spared you.)

So how would you redraft this?

The first rule is to work out what it is you wish to say. The 'White Book' (the *Supreme Court Practice*, containing the rules which you will be learning all about in litigation) has a commentary on each rule. On this one it says:

> '[The rule] enables a defendant to call upon a plaintiff firm ... to disclose the names and addresses of all the partners at the time when the cause of action accrued ... and [it] enables a plaintiff suing a defendant firm to call upon the defendant firm to disclose the names and addresses of all the partners at the time when the cause of action accrued.'

This is actually easier to understand than a reading of the rule itself. Can the rule be made to say this more accessibly? How about:

> If you are being sued by a partnership or you are suing a partnership, and you need to know who the partners are, you can serve a written notice on the partnership or its solicitors requiring the partnership to give you the full names and addresses of all the people who were partners in the partnership at the time the cause of action arose.

This is informal but effective. (I have not removed technical terms such as 'cause of action' and 'service of a notice', because these are terms of art which have defined meanings.)

You might think that in my drive for informality I have missed out something obvious, for example how long the partnership has to reply to the notice, or where the notice should be served if not on the partnership's solicitor. I did. It is also missing from the original rule, but because of the complexity of that rule's drafting, it was harder to spot the omission of these sensible points. Now – assuming it is in my power to declare that a reply is required within seven days, and where a notice should be served – here is a more formal version.

> If a partnership is a party to an action, any other party may serve a notice on the partnership requiring it to supply within seven days of service the full name and address of every person who was a partner in that partnership at the date when the cause of action arose. The notice must:
>
> > specify the date of the cause of action;
> >
> > be in writing; and
> >
> > be served either on the solicitor acting for the partnership, or at any address at which the partnership trades at the time of the notice.

Note that breaking this down into shorter paragraphs and subparagraphs helps to clarify the meaning.

Here is another example of drafting which can be improved. It is an extract from a contract guaranteeing damp-proof work. The client came for advice because he wanted the firm not only to remedy the damp, but to redecorate the damaged wall afterwards. It is an example of mediocre, rather than bad, drafting: it uses long sentences without punctuation, puts capital letters in wrong places, and hides rather than highlights its meaning. It fails to answer the important question about redecoration – a problem which you would have predicted if you had your research sorted out before starting to draft it (see Chapter 4).

> X Ltd Guarantees for 30 years from the end of the Month of Completion that upon being notified as soon as reasonably possible of damp continuing to rise from the foundations through the X Ltd damp-proof course inserted under the Contract we will, provided the Client has kept the property well repaired and maintained, upon production of the guarantee and the Survey Report (including any drawings) inspect the wall or wall structure in which such damp-proof course was inserted and carry out further treatment to that wall or wall structure to prevent such continuation without further charge.
>
> 3 This Guarantee shall not apply, however, if damp continues to rise from the foundations through the X Ltd damp-proof course because of any settlement or movement of the wall or wall structure or the foundations or any interference with such damp-proof course.
>
> 4 The benefit of this Guarantee shall be deemed to be automatically assigned upon the transfer of ownership of the property.

As always, when drafting or revising, work out what you intend to say. Here is what I assume the drafter's original instructions from X Ltd were:

■ We guarantee our work for 30 years.

■ The guarantee covers our client and future owners of the property.

■ If we receive a complaint we will inspect and, if we think necessary, carry out remedial work.

■ We don't want to be liable for problems which have been caused by interference or settlement.

■ We will not pay for redecoration or cleaning after carrying out remedial work. (I have added this; they might have decided they would pay for it, of course, but whoever drafted the guarantee should have made it clear one way or the other.)

Actually, now we have a checklist, the guarantee is almost complete. For ease of understanding, I have chosen to use 'we' and 'you' for the parties to the agreement, and assume that it has already been explained that 'you' includes any owner of the property during the 30-year period.

1   We have completed the damp-proof specified in contract number [ ].

2   We guarantee this work until [date]. You must keep this Guarantee, and the survey and drawings which form a part of it.

3   You must keep the property in good condition. We are entitled to refuse to honour this guarantee if you do not do so. (*Is this too widely drawn to be enforceable? We would have to alter it after consulting the client company to add:* if this affects the damp-proof work.)

4   While the Guarantee is in force, if you notice any damp rising from the foundations of any wall we have treated, you must notify us as soon as possible.

5   Once you notify us, we will inspect the wall. If we find that the rising damp is a result of a failure of our damp-proof course, we will do any necessary work to stop damp rising in that wall. We will (*or, if instructed to exclude this*, we will not) arrange for the wall to be redecorated at our expense.

6   If the rising damp was caused by movement or settlement of the wall or foundations, or by any interference with the damp-proof course, we will not be responsible for carrying out any further work.

3   Preparing oral communications

Students on vocational courses are facing assessments in interviewing and advocacy, which involve oral communication skills. You may have oral presentations assessed on your degree programme. In research, drafting, and possibly negotiation it is possible to communicate in writing only. Are there any key differences between oral and written communications?

Yes there are. But the similarities between the tasks are more important, and the principles set out in this chapter apply to most communication tasks: above all is the need to decide what it is that you intend to achieve before you start speaking and writing.

For an oral performance, here are a few special points.

You will be nervous. This is not a bad thing. Without adrenalin, there would be no excitement or motivation. Your assessors will be aware of the strain you are under, and your colleagues will be equally stressed. You can reduce, but not eliminate, the nervous stress in three ways:

■   First, allow yourself to accept that people are generally nice: clients, witnesses, even judges. They are not usually out to get you. On your assessed course they know that you are a learner; even if the lecturer who is to assess you lacks all characteristics of 'niceness', he or she knows what level of achievement it is realistic to expect from you. You only have to show that you are ready to learn from experience and further training; that you are on your way, not that you have arrived.

■   Secondly, practise: the first time you make a speech, or interview a client, speak in class, or even speak into a dictaphone, you may feel an utter fraud whose inadequacy is transparent. But over time, with practice, you ease yourself into playing the role more naturally, it begins to fit you. Use audio-visual facilities if they are available. It may be painful to watch your performance, but it helps you to learn. Refer back to the techniques of critical and constructive feedback in the previous chapter.

■   Thirdly, there are well-known techniques to assist relaxation. You may have gone to yoga classes, or been in a choir or drama group; preparation for childbirth or advocacy or exams involves some of the same techniques, which can be applied before times of stress. At the simplest, you can try to sit or lie down for a few seconds or minutes, concentrating on breathing regularly and slowly. You can try to calm your mind by, for example, focusing on each part of your body in turn, or counting slowly. If it comes naturally to you, you can pray. These kinds of techniques are used in high-powered management training, and may assist you too.

But, relaxed or not, you are going to be judged. Not just by the assessors, but by the person you are communicating with. You are going to be judged not just on the words you use. According to Adair (*The Effective Communicator*), words contribute a mere 7% of people's impressions, tone of voice 38% and body language/appearance a staggering 55%. This is not to say that slick body language is all you need. But you must pay attention to it. President Reagan was a popular and persuasive leader – not because of his (doubtful) political and intellectual acumen, but because he knew how to sound and look homely and sincere. Many politicians take professional advice on how to dress, how to intone their voices, how to stand and where to look – because they know they cannot afford to ignore the impression they, as opposed to their policies, create.

You should try to see yourself on a video tape, frequently, and see how your body speaks. Do you dress appropriately? Are your mannerisms annoying? Do you pace backwards and forwards? Do you make eye contact or look around shiftily? Because you are going to be assessed by human beings, who are not able or required to ignore these factors, you must try to come over in a way that is immediately pleasing. Aim to be polite, cheerful, smart and confident. Try to come over as enthusiastic: you may have to feign this for a while, although if it comes only with huge difficulty, is the law for you at all? Some people get over-enthusiastic and have to discipline this tendency: seeing yourself on video is the best way of judging this.

All three of these factors – words, tone and body language – are influenced by the confidence with which you approach the task. Confidence is itself largely a function of your preparation and understanding of the task.

You are not going to be good at any oral performance first time. You must practise. And you need to find out basic information: where is the assessed exercise going to take place? To what extent will it require you to project your voice? Is there any need to get used to the layout of the room? Are you free to alter it? Where are you expected to sit, or stand? If in doubt, ask.

Another key rule about speaking is getting the speed right. A fast delivery is almost always more difficult to understand and enjoy than a measured pace. Think about which lecturers you find the most effective; which lawyers you have found more convincing in court. You will probably agree that speaking fast does not aid communication.

Concentrating on speaking slowly, and remembering to take a breath before you run out of air, can help you to measure your pace. Experienced counsel and politicians share an ability to speak slowly, knowing that this helps to get the point across. You can practise with poetry, bedtime stories for children, or conversations with your mother-in-law, as well as with legal arguments.

However, there is often a mismatch between what the audience perceives, and what the speaker thinks he or she is doing. Generally, careful use of pauses, and an unhurried delivery, will sound acceptable to the audience; but to the inexperienced speaker it feels like drying up, or not getting through the material fast enough. A measured pace, especially to a speaker who is nervous or enthusiastic, feels just too slow.

Both as a lecturer and a solicitor I admit I need reminding of this, and the best lessons I can find are to watch other people speaking. When I am on the outside looking in, I can see when they are talking too fast and losing my attention. When I am doing this myself I cannot judge: I feel driven to finishing the material in time, and who knows, maybe slipping in some brilliant extras that have just occurred to me. You will be helped by watching yourself on tape, and asking colleagues to assess your speed – and learning from watching them. To slow the pace, try to pause after your main points (which is like providing an uncluttered layout in written text). By pause, I mean, as you practise, pausing for what seems a dreadfully long and uncomfortable time. (To a nervous speaker, five seconds feels an eternity, but a listener may not even have noticed that you have stopped.) Speak slowly, trying to deliver each word separately. Choose certain words or sentences to stress – by surrounding them with a short pause before and after. As you pause you have a chance to look at your audience and gauge their reaction before continuing.

Remember to make eye contact. Who is your audience? An interviewee? A bench of magistrates? Contact each one, regularly, and in particular when a point you wish to make is important. Look up, not down, for as much of the time as possible.

And a final point: should you read from a prepared text? This is not a possibility in an interview – at most you may have a set starting patter which you could prepare word for word. But in an advocacy task like a mitigation plea – rather than a contested hearing – you may have the opportunity to prepare text.

My advice is to avoid reading word for word. I normally find that if it is read out, the speech becomes harder to follow, less immediate, and intrinsically more boring. Exceptions to this seem to be so rare as for the advice to be categorical: do not read out your speech. Remind yourself: communicating is about getting a particular response from the receiver. It will often mean persuading them of the merits of your point of view. Reading from a prepared statement is unlikely to sound convincing.

What you therefore need to do is to prepare the key points, to be totally familiar with the subject, to have enough detail written in front of you to turn to as a guide, but then to choose the exact words as you go, responding to the subtle cues you are picking up from your audience. The key point is in-depth knowledge of your case, preparation of the major issues you will cover, and in the right order, and a belief in what you are doing.

We will return to look at what is going on in oral communications in interviewing (see Chapter 3) and advocacy (see Chapter 7), and in particular will ask you to pay attention to how subliminal messages are communicated and the cues you need to pay attention to.

Conclusion

I hope this chapter has set the tone for all of your assessed speaking or writing. I hope you did not expect to finish the chapter actually being a better communicator. I have given you some ideas, some principles and some tools. It's a bit like having been told how to swim, or ride a bike: you won't make any progress, however much you know, till you do it. The more you practise, revise, video, share, criticise, revise again, the better you will be. You do not have to be good yet: you have to show that you know what you are trying to do.

And do not be afraid of mistakes. As an American management guru Tony Parker has said: 'You get things right because you have good judgment; you have good judgment because of your experience; you have experience because you learn from mistakes; you make mistakes because you are prepared to try'.

Chapter 3

INTERVIEWING

'Too many beginning lawyers believe that interviewing is just something one does naturally, and that one's interviewing success is determined by one's personality.'

(Binder and Bergman *Fact Investigation, from Hypothesis to Proof.*)

'Do I have to talk to the client?' (title of training video tape for Bar students, Samwell-Smith and Keane, Blackstone Press 1994)

1 An introduction to interviewing and conferencing skills

Interviewing is both a generic skill used in many contexts, such as medicine or business, and a legal skill with its own specific dimensions, which will be different for different types of lawyers. Barristers even choose to call it by a different name, conferencing.

For the client, or indeed the witness, the name of the skill does not matter. Clients will judge your qualities as a lawyer more from meeting you than from any other part of your work for them. How do you want to be judged? You probably want to be thought to be good at it.

Although solicitors spend more time with their clients than barristers do, all practitioners will have spent hundreds, and, quite soon after starting, thousands of hours doing it. They like to believe they are doing it well.

But you do not have their years of experience, and yet if you are on a vocational course you have to show you understand the basic techniques and philosophy in a few months' or weeks' time. Most of the practitioners who are teaching you learned from trial and error. This was not a good start for them, and certainly will not do for you. There are techniques to bring you quickly to the point where you can start interviewing and then learning from live experience with less errors. For the assessment you have to show that you have reached that point of readiness, not that you are already as good as an experienced lawyer.

Is this chapter relevant to barristers?

Barristers receive a set of written instructions before first meeting a client. These may be of excellent or poor quality, but they will help them to formulate an agenda. Solicitors will have little more than a diary note. Barristers will also have a 'professional client' (the solicitor or her representative) present, which changes the dynamic of relationship and gives the barrister a source of support. Solicitors will have a closer personal relationship with the client – normally – than the barrister, who sees the client after some of the work, particularly problem identification, has been carried out. But both professions, in their different contexts, are dealing with the same task. I want to examine the task at a level which enables you to understand some of the dynamics. I will shortly recite the Bar and the Law Society standards for this skill, and you are going to encounter words like empathy, rapport, emotion, and questioning styles. I want you to understand these, and on the way I will provide a little psychology to help. You are not getting technique and etiquette: much of that is common sense, and in the case of the barrister, I commend the Inns of Court School of Law manual 'Conference Skills' (Blackstone, 1997). There the authors say 'There is, we are pleased to say, next to no theory about conference skills within the following pages'. Here, I am pleased to say, there is some theory, and it will help, whether you are aiming for the bar, to be a solicitor, or simply to understand one of the crucial parts of the legal process.

Is this chapter relevant to the student on a degree programme? Without a doubt. Interpersonal skills are crucial to employability. The government's agenda, in the light of the Dearing Report, is unambiguous about the need for transferable skills. But will learning about interviewing clients be relevant to your degree performance? Again, I have no doubt, even though in most universities interviewing skills are not assessed as such. What happens, as a student, when you meet a client? You are practising:

■ analysis of fact,

■ development of a legal theory to accommodate those facts,

■ integration of fact and law to develop advice, and

■ testing the validity of that advice against the reactions of the client and the feedback of any observer.

You are practising academic legal skills, in the same way, but under more pressure and with more focus and more individualised feedback, as you would as a member of a tutorial group. This chapter will enhance your understanding of the process, as well as giving you some concepts to help with the freestanding interpersonal skill which can give you vocational advantage. It is vital that the degree student reads the following chapter on research skills as well, so that the interpersonal skills can be fitted into a law context. Vocational students should also read that chapter, though you will get some benefit from this chapter alone if you are facing a discrete skill assessment in interviewing or conferencing.

The chapter tends to look at the skill from the solicitor's perspective, but the underlying skill is relevant to all lawyers and indeed others who work with client problems.

Since writing this chapter in the first edition I have looked in some detail at the skill of legal interviewing from the perspective of the counsellor. One thing I have learned from training in this new discipline is that the 'right' method of legal interviewing, the consensus that is building up in the literature, is based only on experience and supposition. It is not, in contrast to the work that psychologists have carried out in the context of therapeutic interviewing, backed by systematic research into what works and what doesn't. The result is that a lot of the guidance given is only common sense. Students can themselves produce checklists for a good interview – such as the stereotypical 'meet seat and greet' formulae – before they have any knowledge and experience. Is the professional relationship really that easy? For me the obvious deficiency with this kind of checklist approach is that it is based around the behaviour of the interviewer. Perhaps what matters is not what the interviewer does, but what the client experiences and what outcomes are achieved. You may have to put aside 'common sense' and your own experience as a guide, if objective evidence suggests there are better ways. I cannot tell you in this chapter the right and wrong ways – though I will give some guidance on the artificial tasks posed in a course assessment. What I will tell you is that there are ways you might evaluate what is going on, how you are performing; I will give a little insight into the psychological processes involved for interviewer and client. I will try to equip you to become a person who can reflect and improve. I will try to make you realise that getting the coveted label 'competent' on your course does not mean that you are competent in any real sense. You have passed a test, which was the goal, and that is all.

If you are on a vocational course the context is highly artificial. For a start assessed interviews are more difficult than real ones. You are likely to be assessed in a short role play. You will play the role of the solicitor, and you will not have the comfort of an established office, a coat stand for the client's coat, a cup of coffee to offer, or the reality of building a real relationship dealing with real needs and emotions. The 'client' is normally seeing the solicitor or barrister for the first time. This is not the typical client-solicitor interview, as most solicitor time is actually spent with existing clients. But that interview, where there is an existing relationship between solicitor and client, is hard to create in a role play. Role play alters the task further, because an actor – usually not a trained actor but another student – has to focus on the information given in a written brief. A role playing amateur 'client' who has been briefed to be difficult is far more difficult to handle than a real client with some difficulties.

The first interview with a client is also the hardest one. It involves you in building a relationship, formulating a theory of the case, giving initial advice, working out a strategy for the future conduct of the matter, as well as dealing with a 'client' who may have been briefed to raise difficult dilemmas of professional practice or to show distress.

On top of this, in an assessed exercise you may have to demonstrate your competence in 20 minutes or less, because of the demands of assessing large numbers of students.

Such a short initial interview with a non-real client, recorded on video, is enough to cause palpitations in an experienced solicitor. It will be like appearing on 'Mastermind' (but without choosing your subject). It will be hard for anyone to do well in these circumstances. As a student please remind yourself that the standard you need to demonstrate is that you have an idea of what you should be trying to do, and that you are able to enter into a training contract or pupillage and continue to learn there. You do not have to be a brilliant interviewer.

Will the assessor be looking for your generic interviewing skills, or judging you on the quality of the legal analysis? During joint interviewing training at Newcastle Medical School I recently role played a doctor. My patient was a middle-aged man complaining of chest pains. Imagining what I thought to be a good bedside manner, I took a history, showed interest in the whole person, not just the symptoms, nodded in the right places, asked open not closed questions, and made good eye contact. Good generic interviewing skills, I congratulated myself, until the patient wanted to know if he was going to have a heart attack just like his father had. Generic skills had been just the building blocks: I now needed medical knowledge in order to provide help.

From the moment my confidence left me, through lack of knowledge, I was unable to continue in any meaningful way. There was no longer a way to show interviewing skills. It may be like this for you if you are seeing a client in an area of law you do not know well. Is it fair to judge students for their failure to get the law right? What I came to realise through playing the role of doctor is that if we intend to assess your skills as an interviewer, we must set up the exercise so that you will be able to succeed; you cannot succeed if you are overwhelmed with the complexity or strangeness of the law and facts.

There are, therefore, two ways of approaching the task of assessing a student:

■   to assess your interviewing skills *and* your relevant legal knowledge, or

■   to provide sufficient information or time to prepare so that your legal knowledge is assured, and you can succeed (or not) on the skills you show as an interviewer.

It will be important for you to know how your institution has decided this issue so you can prepare adequately. Is it a test of your memory of legal and procedural knowledge as well as a test of communication skills? What is certain is that you cannot demonstrate your communication skills as a legal practitioner without knowing how to begin to solve legal problems in that area of law.

What is the appropriate level of competence for a vocational student? You have to demonstrate that you are ready to go into practice and continue to learn from experience. I believe there are some underlying principles which will enable you to demonstrate this competence:

1   You must take control of the process.

2   The client must be enabled to make the decisions.

3   You need to demonstrate some understanding of psychology.

4   Emotion matters.

5   You should know how to build a working relationship.

6   You should be prepared to anticipate common problems.

7   Show that you have a structured approach.

8   Show that you are ethical and professional.

A couple of anecdotes on point 8 to give you a short break from concentrating:

■ A judge calls the parties into court. 'I have in my left pocket £2,000 in cash from the plaintiff. I have in my right pocket a cheque from the defendant for the sum of £2,500. I do not intend to be influenced by such attempts to bribe me. I will return £500 to the defendant and try the case on its merits.'

■ A solicitor finds that the client, who has settled the bill in cash, has inadvertently handed over twice the correct sum. The solicitor is troubled by the ethical dilemma and eventually rings the confidential help line to explain what has happened, ending with the agonising question ' I just can't decide whether to tell my partners or keep the money myself'.

2 The LPC and BVC context for interviewing

The LPC Board's interviewing and advising standards are set out on the left, with the corresponding BVC conference skills standards (necessarily not in order) on the right :

'The student should be able to

identify the client's goals, gather information to identify means of realising those goals, and assist the client to reach decisions as to the appropriate means of implementing those goals.'

The student should be able to

(a) prepare for the interview;

(b) allow client to explain concerns;

The student should be able to

• conduct the conference in a structured and efficient way, follow an agenda as far as possible and cover all relevant issues in a logical sequence

• communicate effectively with the client and respond appropriately to the client's concerns and questions by putting the client at ease and using appropriate language

• listen to the client in a non-judgmental manner, empathising and reassuring the client when appropriate

• permit the client to raise concerns

• listen to what the client says

		• elicit the information required to advise the client
(c)	identify client goals;	• obtain the client's full instructions
		• demonstrate an understanding of the objectives of the conference
(d)	help the client reach priorities among those goals;	• set out the strengths and weaknesses of the case
(e)	elicit relevant information and distinguish between relevant and irrelevant information;	• demonstrate an understanding of the factual, legal, procedural and evidential issues which should be raised in a conference
(f)	use appropriate questioning techniques;	• select and use appropriate questioning techniques
		• ensure the client understands what has been discussed
		• demonstrate a clear understanding of the client's account of the case/facts
(g)	determine what further information is required;	• clarify the relevant gaps and any ambiguities
(h)	identify possible courses of action and the legal and non-legal consequences of selecting that *course of action*;	• explain fully and frankly when required
(i)	assist the client to make a decision regarding the best course of action;	• advise the client appropriately by explaining the legal, procedural and evidential issues in clear and unambiguous language
		• advise on the consequences of any course of action taken
(j)	agree action to be taken by both parties subsequent to the interview;	• adhere to the instructions
		• advise on what further action should be taken
(k)	accurately record the interview, confirm instructions and confirm action that needs to be undertaken;	

(1)   establish a professional relationship with the client and deal with any ethical problems that may arise when advising the client.

- Demonstrate an understanding of the need to observe professional ethics when conducting and concluding a conference

- Observe the rules of professional conduct

- Not invent facts

- Not mislead the client as to facts and law

The LPC standards finish with material which makes explicit the fact that skills are to be assessed, and that they are a foundation for further learning. This additional material is equally relevant to a bar student:

> The student should be able to demonstrate an understanding of the principles and criteria of good interviewing and should be able to:
>
> (i) conduct an interview in which those criteria are met;
>
> (ii) modify their own interviewing errors to meet those criteria;
>
> (iii) transfer skills learned in one context to other contexts
>
> (iv) develop techniques for appraising and developing their own interviewing style.
>
> Students should be aware of the need to deal with a range of personnel including other lawyers, professionals, witnesses and parties.
>
> Students should be aware of the need to take instructions from their principal and other supervising solicitors.

Documenting the interview is omitted from the Bar standards, because that skill is assessed on the BVC in opinion writing. This is not covered here, but is touched on in Chapter 2 on Communications (where we urged you to write with precision – see in particular p 71) and Chapter 5 on Drafting, which includes opinion writing.

What are the standards for the degree student? If you are being assessed your law school will provide the standards which it is using. You will probably find that in any involvement in interviewing there will be more emphasis on the identification of the problem and the analysis of law. But beware the tendency to see the problem as all important and the client as merely the vehicle through which your legal analysis is tested. The degree student cannot ignore the standards of interpersonal skill which the vocational standards set, for to do so removes the point of presenting you with a legal problem in this way. Additionally if you can relate to the client you will get to the problem.

So those are the standards. Great – but what do they mean and how do you achieve them. What is empathy? How do you allow clients to explain their concerns? Which questions are appropriate and which are not? Let's move on …

3   What is the point of interviewing clients?

Close your eyes and think of the answer to this question before you read on.

Was it a stupid question? To get the relevant information to solve the client's problem, of course, and to give the client advice. Did you end up with something like that? OK, you didn't do it, you want answers not questions, but that's probably what you would have come up with.

Turn the question round, and ask instead: I am the client, why am I going to a solicitor? You may not have consulted a lawyer yourself, which makes answering this question from the client's viewpoint hard, so think of yourself visiting a doctor; you have a worrying pain. What is the goal of the consultation? Again, close your eyes and try to identify what you, the patient, want.

Words crop up like reassurance; understanding; sympathy; explanation; cure.

Is there a difference between these two sets of expectations? Those of the doctor and those of the patient?

I used to conduct an exercise with law students preparing them for advice work at a Law Centre. To get them into an appropriate frame of mind for client interviewing, I ask them to picture a bad professional they have had dealings with. I never had a student who could not picture one. In fact, as the students go quiet, I see their eyes focus on remembered experiences; there will be perhaps a snort of laughter or a sigh of re-experienced indignation as the person comes to mind.

Typically we got estate agents, bank managers, lecturers and teachers, doctors, accountants, personnel managers ... and lawyers. I ask the students to write down in no more than a minute at least ten adjectives describing the person they have in mind; year after year the same sort of adjectives appeared:

>   aloof; bored; arrogant; pompous; uninterested; hurried; distracted; uncaring; disdainful; rude; overconfident; dismissive; smug.

If you close your eyes – last time, I promise – and imagine a bad professional who has blighted your life on one occasion, you can probably double this list within a couple of minutes.

OK, you haven't stopped to reflect. Never mind. Ask yourself: what is *not* there in the list?

>   lacked knowledge; gave wrong advice; useless diagnosis.

If I suggest this dimension to my students, they may well then say 'ah yes, that too'. But what initially defined the bad professional was the dreadful lack of interpersonal skills, and poor communications. And this seems to be how the Solicitors' Complaints Bureau sees it: from their 'Facts at a glance' in the 1992 Report: 'Over 80% of matters received concerned poor quality service including poor communications and delay.' (The Office for the Supervision of Solicitors has not broken down the figures in this way in its first annual report of 1997 unfortunately.)

I suspect most complaints can be distilled to the general concept of uncaring. In interviewing you must show (but really show, not just pretend) that you have a professional care for your client.

Hang on, you might be thinking: the lawyer is not a priest taking confession; caring is only a means to an end. This I accept. But if these adjectives indicate how clients judge bad lawyers, caring is what you too will be judged by. The 'right' result comes second, at least in terms of client satisfaction. In fact, of course, the two goals of getting the right result and caring for the client are entirely compatible; but the right result is immeasurably harder to achieve if the lawyer is lacking care and consideration. Client and lawyer may not even have a shared view of what is 'right'.

You get the best possible outcome for your client – an award at trial of thousands of pounds in damages; a tricky conveyancing chain that you struggled to manipulate into position – and not a word of thanks. Perhaps what it meant to the client was months or years of trauma as the case dragged on. The whole legal system, you as well, is judged as a nightmare, a horror story to be told to the stranger on the train who admits to being a lawyer.

On the other hand you get a result you find disappointing: completion is delayed by yet another week; the settlement your client accepts is half what you thought you would get at trial. The client cannot praise you highly enough: you are recommended to friends and swamped with work.

The client interview – indeed the whole of the client retainer – is about a relationship. Relationships thrive on confidence, trust, openness, and a caring professional approach.

Sometimes of course you have a problem client with whom confidence and trust are impossible. The client who fails to come to appointments, who systematically withholds information from you, who is rude, who makes you feel irritated. You no longer can be expected to be open and caring then.

100% wrong. To adopt the concept of the problem client is the easy way out, and it will not serve you well. Of course there are problem relationships, but it takes two to establish them. Of the two, whose job is it to make it work? Who has the training and experience? You. The client is paying you for this skill. You cannot just blame the client.

You doubt this? I challenge you to see your family doctor after reading this chapter, or your bank manager, or whoever, and try to redefine the terms that have been set for you. Will you say: 'Please move out from behind that big imposing desk so that we can relate on an equal basis'? 'Please do not ask me to strip until you have established that I can trust you'?

We doubt it. You will allow yourself to have the terms of the consultation dictated by the professional, according to their rituals. You may be upset or seething at the way you were treated; you will probably not have felt the power to alter the way the doctor or the bank manager treated you. You did not overstep the carefully erected barriers that prevent you taking charge of the situation – how could you, when you lacked any control of the information, the agenda, the decision-making, even the physical layout of the meeting space? All you can do is vote with your feet. If that is not open to you you too can become a problem client.

So it is up to you, the professional, to tackle problems of building a relationship. If things are not working out, you – no-one else – have to establish why, and how to learn from this, rather than say – as every one of you will at times inevitably say – 'that Mr Z is a real pain in the ...'. You will get a bit of popular psychology shortly, as a result of which you will, I hope, be better equipped to understand these situations.

Before we move on, what was the answer: what *is* the point of interviewing clients?

My answer is: to explore with the client why she is seeking legal advice and assistance; to ascertain what are the problems which have led her to seek this assistance; to offer an analysis of the range of ways of addressing the problems; to explore with the client which of those ways is preferred; to allow the client to make an informed decision at the appropriate stage; to ensure that the lawyer and the client both agree on the consequences of any decision made, in terms of costs, action, timescale and further decisions; and to achieve all of this in a manner which gives the client the maximum power to make the decision and in which the solicitor behaves in a professionally ethical manner.

(If you were hoping for a pithy quote, how about 'to empower the client'?)

Now we come onto our key principles. You will realise on reading these, and later from experience, that you cannot interview according to a schedule, or even by going through a list of points that must be covered. Checklists are useful (and start on p 161); but interviewing by numbers is impossible. We do not even attempt it in this chapter, although we do mention structure as a vital part of the skill.

4   The principles of interviewing

Principle 1: You are in control, and Principle 2: The client makes the decisions

Two conflicting principles? In a sense, yes, but they can easily be reconciled. A simple analogy. You want to go on a journey, but you have not yourself learned to drive. You can hire a car and a driver. The driver will go to your stated destination, and will take the route you prefer; but the driver will decide which gear to use, and do the map reading. You will rely on the driver to follow the rules of the road and not to get you into an accident. So long as you are prepared to pay, you can decide half way through to go a different way, even to a different destination. The driver can advise you that this is not a good route to take; the driver can refuse to take you on the particular route if the road is not open to traffic. (The driver, of course, obeys the law whatever your instructions.)

So which one of you is in charge? You both are.

Let us start with you, the lawyer. Principle 1 puts you in control.

When I went into practice nobody had advised me of this simple fact. I felt to start with intimidated by a fear of being exposed: 'they' would sooner or later find out I lacked knowledge and experience, and could not possibly help with their problems. These were men and women of the world, paying for a service I felt inadequate to provide. So I could not presume to suggest that I was in control.

But not taking control because of feelings of inadequacy is the worst way to tackle the problem of lack of experience. Anything is better; you could even start the interview: 'Ha! You think I'm a lawyer, but really, I'm just playing a role and I don't know much about this game.' But you would have to add: 'But let's get one thing straight. You came to see me, not the other way round, and this interview proceeds on the basis that only one of us is in control of how it is conducted, and that's me.'

Perhaps not? But there are two errors you may make:

1   fear of inadequacy prevents you from taking control; or

2   in order to take control you pretend you are more confident than you are – which is the advice I received.

Is there perhaps a middle way?

The middle way, in my opinion, is not to assume that because you are inexperienced you have nothing to offer. You have an ability to listen, to seek advice, and to research where your own knowledge is inadequate; you already have a lot of experience of legal problem-solving practice behind you, even if it all suddenly seems irrelevant or unusable. You have something to offer. You are going to start a process of tackling a problem that a client has decided to entrust to you. That can only work if you give the client the confidence that you are the right person for the job. (In real life, for a trainee solicitor at least, the job may consist of knowing who can handle the problem better than you can.) Use what you do know, admit what you do not know, but remain in control.

Why is this so important? Because out of the two participants in the interview, only one – you – will have worked out a structure for it. Only you will have an ability to sift the relevant from the irrelevant material. Only you can produce legally viable solutions to problems. Only you can stop the time being wasted in chasing down blind alleys. None of these things can your client do better than you.

In fact your client wants you to take charge. First, that is what he or she is paying for.

Secondly, put yourself in the client position. If necessary think back to being a patient with the doctor, pupil with teacher, or client with accountant. While you want to be listened to, you need structure and guidance as to what should be listened to.

Thirdly, in an assessed interview, time is short. Your 'client' has probably been overbriefed: the role instructions may contain masses of material, perhaps with both a presenting problem and a disguised sub-plot. (Perhaps you know the sort too well, beloved of academics: the client presents with an employment problem, but what she is reluctant to admit is her affair with the boss. The academic mind has a never-ending supply of such fictions.) There is simply no time for losing control.

How are you going to put yourself into the controlling position straight away? We suggest, always, show in your opening that this is how things are. For example, after a few pleasantries when you greet and seat the client (you take the lead in this process too), but before the client has started to pour out the problem (difficult to time this right, but the client must start to talk at your invitation if you can manage it, not into a vacuum) you impose your structure to the interview.

For example:

> My name is (*full name of solicitor E*). I'm a trainee solicitor with Collins Bradbury and Co. That means I am working under the supervision of a partner, Mrs Bradbury.
>
> May I check that I've got your name correctly? Mrs Emily Shearsby? Good.
>
> I'd like to start this interview by explaining how I usually go about things with a new client. What I usually find useful is to ask you to to give me an idea of the reason you have come to see me, in your own words, so that I can get an idea of the problem. I don't want to spend too much time on that, but I'd like to start just by listening and not interrupting; then what I'd like to do is to ask a few very quick questions to clarify any things that I may have misunderstood. After that I'll need to start to take down some notes, and to ask you specific questions in more detail. Towards the end of the interview I hope that I'll be able to offer some advice and suggest some course of action, and I often find that after an initial interview we have to agree on what further information I need, who is going to do what, and when we need to meet again.
>
> Well, Mrs Shearsby, I've spoken long enough. Is there anything at all about what I've said that confuses you. ...? (*Pause.*) Well, can we start? The first thing is, briefly, would you like to tell me why you have come here today to see me?

As you get more experienced, you can leave out half of that, or even all of it, and start with: 'OK, so what's the problem?' Or just a raised eyebrow, meaning: 'OK, shoot'. But if you are in doubt about being in control, a short spiel along the lines set out may help establish to the client and the assessor that you have decided it is your interview. On the other hand if you doggedly pursue a patter of this sort, and fail to notice the signals of incomprehension or anger coming from your client's body language, you are demonstrating incompetence right from the start.

How are you going to balance your controlling role against the other principle? **The client – not you – makes the decisions**.

It is not hard to think in terms of what to avoid. Some of you may remember John Cleese as Basil Fawlty, the overbearing bully, on television. Here is a solicitor in the Fawlty mode of legal interviewing seeing a nervous woman facing a criminal charge.

> *Solicitor A:* Hello, Mrs Evans. In a bit of trouble, are we? Don't worry, you've come to the right man here. Trouble with the police, I believe. Is that right? Nothing naughty, I hope. We haven't been in trouble before, have we?
>
> *Mrs Evans:* Well ... they arrested me for taking money from where I work. You see, I put these coins in my pocket that should have gone in the till. ...
>
> *A:* I see. Have you got the charge sheet? (*She hands it over.*) Oh dear, oh dear, this looks serious. That's a lot of money. And the magistrates around here – you really have to see them to believe them. This is what they call breach of trust, you know, theft from an employer. Did you do it? That's what I need to know, of course, so I can decide how to get the best deal for you.
>
> *Mrs Evans:* Well, yes, I suppose I must have taken those coins, they found them in my apron, but I have no. ...

A: Good, good, that's a whole lot simpler. And did you make a confession to the police when you were there. Of course, we'll get a transcript of your confession in due course ... did you confess?

Mrs Evans: Yes, if you mean, did I tell them I did it, I felt I had to, you see. ...

A: That's excellent. Co-operation with the police is always a plus. Had a case only last week where I managed to persuade the bench to keep a young lad out of prison, and you know, with the magistrates here, that's quite something nowadays. And it was his co-operation with the police that made all the difference, and of course the guilty plea. With him, though, the amount of money he'd stolen was a lot less, and that does present us with problems. Still, leave it with me, if anyone can get you out of this mess, I can. Now, let's have a look at legal aid and then I'll take down some details of what the police call your antecedents. (*To the intercom*) Jane, poppet, I need a criminal legal aid form 1 and form 5 – though it's probably a waste of time in this case, but we can try – and an antecedents form. Thanks. Oh, and I could murder a cup of coffee, can you fix that please? (*To Mrs Evans*) I didn't offer you a cup. Still, we're nearly finished, I just need to get a few facts I can use in mitigation, and we're away. Do you have any questions? I like to check that my clients understand what is going on. That's really part of the job, isn't it, you know, relating to customers and so on. Is there anything?

A guilty plea may be what the client, properly advised, would have chosen. The client may well get the best mitigation in town and a cheap, efficient disposal of the case. On the other hand she may feel so overwhelmed by the pace at which this has started, so lacking in choices or understanding, that her way of coping is to do nothing: not return for further appointments, not sign any forms that are sent, and not face up to the situation that brought her to the solicitor in the first place. She has been denied ownership of her problem and its solution.

This could be labelled the 'Don't worry your pretty little head; just leave it all to me' model. Many solicitors, doctors and other so-called caring professionals see it as their role to take the responsibility for the client/patient's problem.

My preferred model is one in which the client comes away feeling empowered. Why? I have already stated that the client is the one who gives instructions and makes decisions. If you enhance the client's power, you enable the client to make genuine choices. And anyway, solicitors are at the service of clients, not vice versa.

There is nothing wrong, where appropriate, with saying 'You don't need to worry about that' and 'leave it to me'. But it triggers alarm bells in assessors. For a start, a client who is worried is worried. A solicitor saying 'you don't need to worry' is saying, in effect, 'your concerns are nothing'. The client who felt worried about the problem now has to worry about the fact that she is still worried when she has been told she shouldn't be.

Secondly, you will notice on our checklist on p 162 that 'giving premature advice' is bad news. The LPC and BVC checklists don't explicitly say this, but it is implicit: bad advice is worse than no advice. So you only say 'leave it to me' if you know exactly what is being left to you; you only say 'don't worry' if you *and* your client understand why there is nothing to worry about.

From the receiving end, being told that there is nothing to worry about is usually a trigger for alarm. ('The level of radiation released poses no danger to the public'. 'The National Health Service is safe in our hands', etc etc! At the age of 25 I fell off my bike and had abdominal surgery which weakened my stomach muscles. I was told by the surgeon when

I went for a check up a few months later 'Don't worry about that little bulge old chap. Everyone gets a little middle age spread'. Up to that point I had not been worried.)

The BVC standards ask you to reassure the client. I take issue with this if it leads you to feel that the client must be given good news to go away with. Reassurance comes from within the client, as a process of understanding rather than as a process of being told everything will be fine. Reassurance is an outcome for the client and not a process that belongs to the lawyer, and certainly not something you should see as part of a checklist of behaviours to be got through. The giving of reassurance belongs, if anywhere, at the end of an interview or conference, where you summarise what is going to happen, what the client has agreed to. If there really is nothing to worry about, and you have agreed with the client who will do what, or you have explained what is going to be left to you, then the client already knows the score. The client could better be saying to you: 'Good, I see I shan't have to worry about that then'.

When giving reassurance are you actually trying to convince yourself that you are in control? Are you being lawyer centred rather than client centred? This is not the same as actually being in control; and the assurance is unlikely to be real. Watch yourself and your colleagues with this in mind. (The point is touched on again below under the heading 'Not knowing the answer to the client's problem'.)

If the solicitor takes charge of the whole process, this leaves the client as little more than the supplier of raw materials: fees, signatures and raw facts. The client has to suppress many other inputs: the emotions connected to the situation; the doubts; the opinions; the choices.

Here are some interview excerpts based on the 'don't worry about that' model.

Mr McAuley's cycle accident

> **Client:** I'm worried about how much this is going to cost. My Mum is on the dole, and I haven't got anything. Will I have to pay for you doing my case? I mean, I haven't got any money.
>
> **B:** Don't worry about that, old man, you've got green form legal aid, and we can do the whole thing on a conditional fee basis after that.

Mrs Evans's criminal charges

> **Client:** What happens if, in spite of what you're saying, they find me guilty? I don't want to go to prison, I mean, what would happen about my little girl if I went to prison.
>
> **A:** Oh, you won't have to worry about that. It's very rare that someone who hasn't got a criminal record is sent to prison, even in a case like this one where it's a theft from an employer, which they do tend to regard as more serious.

Mr Kader's business plans

> **Client:** ... and I'll be renting the office to the company, so I want you to ensure that I get the best possible return for it.

D: I'll get a valuer instructed to sort that out for you; I usually use Johnson & Co, they seem pretty reliable. I'll give them a ring later on today.

Mrs Shearsby's loan to Mr Kader

Client: ... but if I pulled out now I could pass the money to my children much sooner ...

E: Yes, but we've already discussed why buying into this venture would be far more profitable in the long run, and in fact the draft agreement is ready to send out to Mr Kader's solicitors. We should have the whole thing sorted in the next couple of months and you'll see the advantages when the profits start to come in.

Mr Green's and Ms Kennedy's conveyance

Ms Kennedy: ... so they said at the end of the phone call either we pay the full asking price or the deal is off; and there's no way we can pay more than the property is worth, is there darling?

C: Well, that should be fairly easy to sort out; we know they are wanting to move by the end of next month because they are moving to his new job in London, so I think they will have to agree if you say 'no way José'. Just leave this one to me, it's generally easier for solicitors to sort this kind of thing out between themselves.

In each of these situations, the advice given or steps proposed by the solicitor may be fine. But the client may leave the interview feeling that he or she has not been listened to before the advice is given. And perhaps there is another problem too. Things may not be what they seem to be. Often there are items that need exploring before assurance is given.

If you avoid jumping in with your professional decisions too quickly, the conversation might instead go a bit like this:

The business loan

The client has just said she's thinking of pulling out of this transaction:

E: You are concerned that it might be better for your children if you sell the property now.

Client: Well, it's to do with my husband's death and what he would have wanted, what with the children not being mine and the rows we had just before he died, and my step daughter rang up last night to say they had decided to send Nathan to a private school, and then I got a letter this morning to say that my husband's shares were only worth about half what I had assumed. (*More of the same follows while the solicitor does not interrupt.*) So it's no wonder I've been feeling ill. ...

E: You've been feeling ill?

Client: It's nothing really, you know, well, I mean, I don't know yet, but then I don't suppose I ever will; these doctors are just like your lot, they never tell you anything of what's going on. ...

D (*While making a mental note to come back to the illness in case it is relevant, but recognising that the client has something about lawyers that she may wish to get off her chest before she can start a useful relationship with E*): You've had a bad experience with lawyers.

Client: (*Describes a messy divorce, how her share of the sale of the matrimonial home got almost wiped out by the Legal Aid statutory charge ...*

The solicitor has not delved. But she or he has gleaned some information which will help to carry out the present task. Mrs Shearsby is very wary of lawyers, and needs to have an opportunity to acquire confidence in D; the client has an embittered relationship with a previous husband and is being influenced in her decision by the desires of her step daughter; the client has health problems. D can now make choices as to which of these are important issues to deal with or follow up in building a rapport with the client, obtaining relevant information, and carrying out her instructions.

For example the discussion could continue:

E: You've been feeling unwell.

Client: Yes, ever since my husband died and the arguments we've been having over what to do with this money that Brian left. I mean it's nothing really. My doctor said it's nerves. I suppose he thinks I'm whinging. My daugther is behaving as if the money really belongs to her. Well perhaps it does, really, though he left it to me and she knows it, and I know Brian wanted to get involved with Mr Kader's business ...

E: Well, it sounds to me as if you have been under a great deal of pressure. What I'm wondering at the moment is whether in the light of what you have said we should maybe take a bit of time to think again about what you want to do, maybe even leave it for a few days to let you sleep on it ...

Alternatively the conversation might have continued:

Client: Yes, but I'm better now. I think I must have got run down, you know, the kind of 'flu that just goes on and on. Now, you say the agreement with Mr Kader is almost ready. I'd like to take a look at it if it is ready? How long do you think it'll take from now?

The cycle accident

The client has expressed worry about payment. The solicitor says he'll get legal aid: an overconfident assurance. It might have gone like this.

B: Yes, legal work is expensive, and I can't even predict at this stage how much work is going to be involved. But there is a good chance of getting legal aid to pay for this help. You may have heard about legal aid at school, or read about it in the paper.

Client (*apparently disinterested*): Nope.

B: Would you like me to tell you a little about it? If you are worried about the costs of me helping you with this case, legal aid may be very important to you.

Client: Yeah, go on, I suppose so.

This little snapshot was not for the purpose of showing how you explain legal aid (I will deal with explaining costs under client care below). It was about learning something about the client and his attitude. The client is concerned about the funding of the case. Although he is worried he finds it difficult to relate to the solicitor and comes across as lacking interest. The issue of legal aid was merely the opportunity to express some of his anxiety. The solicitor needs to find ways of gaining some kind of trust before the interview is likely to make much progress.

The criminal charges

The client is worrying what will happen if she is convicted.

> *A:* Yes, it is very important to discuss this and I'm glad you asked. Would you like me to explain how the courts are supposed to make decisions on what kind of sentence is appropriate?

> *Client:* Yes, that would be a good idea. (*But A notices that she looks preoccupied, waits before speaking again. After a few seconds client continues.*) But my name won't get in the paper will it?

The client here has been given the space to address what is really on her mind, at present, so the solicitor delays the explanation about sentencing, and advice on plea and addresses publicity. But A does not say: 'Don't worry, it won't get in the papers', because A does not know.

The business plans

The client has just explained how he wants to maximise his rent from the property he owns which he will rent to the company. In the situation above the solicitor decided to get a valuer onto this. Here is another approach.

> *D:* Right, how do you want to go about fixing the right rent for this?

> *Client:* I've decided I want at least £30,000 a year with an increase clause after no more than two years.

> *D:* Yes, I see ... have you talked about this with Mr Khan?

> *Client:* Well he knows I am going to have to charge rent on the property, and he is going to have to agree to pay what the place is worth.

> *D* (*Noting that the question has not been answered*)*:* Did you discuss actual figures with him?

> *Client:* No. I didn't think that was necessary.

> *D:* (*Does not speak, to see if client will amplify, which he does after a pause.*)

> *Client:* He has to agree to the rent I set, because he knows I'm a fair man. And he knows he is coming into my business, the business I have built up.

> *D:* I wonder if we should look at how we would get round this if he doesn't agree to the rent you want to charge. Do you think we should explore that or wait to see what happens?

Client: Well, he is going to have to agree it, so there's no point.

D (*aware that the client seems unwilling to open the issue up any further, but still aware that entering the formation of the partnership with a fixed, possibly excessive, valuation in mind may be a risk to the new venture*): Yes, I suppose that is the case. But I wonder too if we should explore how things might work out if he is unhappy with the rent. What do you think might happen?

Client (*maybe after the question has had to be put three or four times – but no advice given*): It would be the end of the deal ... I suppose one way we could resolve this would be to ask a valuer to come to an independent opinion of the best market rent, so long as we could be sure I wasn't being undersold.

D: Yes, that is a very good idea. ...

The conveyance

Ms Kennedy has announced that there is no way they can pay more than the property is worth 'is there darling?'

C: (Says nothing, waits for 'darling' to reply.)

Mr Bennett: We could just call their bluff ....

C (*Instead of just 'leave it all to me' response which C has apparently now been given permission to adopt*): That may well be the best way to resolve this. Yes, I could well do that, and it probably would result in a climb down quite quickly. (*Looking at Mr Green*) Is that what you would like to do?

Mr Bennett (*sheepishly*): I'm not sure, I suppose so ... well (*and goes round the houses a little, before finally saying*) well, the thing is, I know we can get a loan of £1,000 from my parents, and to be honest, if the worst came to the worst, I would be prepared to use that if the sellers came down in price a little.

Ms Kennedy: (Either agrees, or says no way.)

C: Well, what I suggest is that you spend a little time discussing this together before deciding how to respond. I think we can leave it till tomorrow, and it is a very big decision you are having to make. What do you think about leaving it, and you phone me at 9.30 tomorrow? If necessary, you could pop in as I'm free up to 10.30.

In all of these rather simplified situations the solicitor had two basic choices. To use his or her professional judgement and get to a quick solution to the perceived problem; or to hold back, leave the problem area open for a little longer and see what else might need to come out in discussion.

Mind you, it is not just lawyers who might rush in too quickly with decisions made before the client has joined in.

'In 50% of visits the patient and the doctor do not agree on the nature of the main presenting problem. In one study patients were interrupted by physicians so soon after they began describing their presenting problem (on average within 18 seconds) that they failed to disclose other significant concerns.'

(Simpson et al 'Doctor–patient Communication: the Toronto Consensus Statement' *British Medical Journal* (1991) 303, 1385–1387.) The article then goes on to confirm my own view about dissatisfaction with professionals:

> 'Most complaints by the public about physicians deal not with clinical competency problems, but with communication problems, and the majority of malpractice allegations arise from communication errors.'

Empowering the client to make the decisions does not mean the solicitor for ever holding back and saying, as Peter Cook and Dudley Moore used to: 'I dunno, what do you think we should do?' 'Well, I dunno, what do you think?' ad infinitum. (Peter Who? Dudley What? Sorry, my knowledge of TV personalities is outdated, but we are up to the minute on skills theory.) Being in control means ensuring that adequate discussion has taken place. Choices still have to be made, and the solicitor, not the client, is in the best position to identify at what point those choices should be put, and to identify the range of choices that will need to be made. But the client makes them.

A helpful way of understanding the process of who has what power comes from Roger Neighbour's *The Inner Consultation*. His model for doctors is that, as the consultation progresses, the initiative gradually shifts from the patient to the doctor. In the early stages, the patient has the virtual monopoly on what is relevant – the patient is the expert and the doctor knows nothing – but as the doctor takes in the important information the focus shifts. It is now the doctor who has most to offer in defining and resolving the problem.

But the power never goes entirely to the doctor, or the lawyer because only the client gives instructions. Lawyers and doctors do not instruct, they only advise.

Every year the Solicitors' Complaints Bureau until its abolition in 1996 reported that not letting clients know what is going on is the greatest complaint. Not, as you might imagine, fouling up the case, getting the law and procedure wrong, merely not ensuring that the client is respected as the most important person at the centre of the transaction. Similarly, solicitors dealing with cases of medical accidents often report that the client was not eager for compensation – at least not initially – but was enraged at the way no-one ever told him or her what was happening, and, if there had been a mistake, not explaining or apologising. As Ann Whelan (mother of Michael Whelan, subject of a long running and eventually successful campaign to have his conviction for murder overturned) says in *Legal Action*, July 1993, first about barristers:

> 'Yet they don't come and tell you what's going on, you have to keep on asking. And even then they talk down to you as if you are an idiot and don't understand the law. Of course we don't. That's why we want it explained to us.'

And secondly, about the possibility of compensation for the miscarriage of justice:

> 'It would help if somebody would just say, in any of these miscarriages of justice, "We got it wrong, we made an awful mistake, we cannot compensate, but we are sorry." '

This kind of complaint appears to be about not listening. It is not quite so simple. If you asked the lawyers concerned, they would say, perhaps correctly, that they did listen. What seems to be missing is the ability to hear things from the client's perspective: from what is important for her, from what, as far as a stranger can understand it, is her world view, and taking that as the starting point.

Clients get angry if their power is taken away by professionals. To empower the client does not mean an abdication of your professional responsibility or a denial of your expertise. You remain the expert, the enabler, the one who can give the client what they otherwise could not achieve but what you have enabled them to choose. But don't forget that in terms of expertise on the relevant facts, the client knows more than you and deserves respect for this expertise.

Principle 3: Understand some psychology

'Helpful attitudes include a belief in the importance of ... an unconditional positive regard for patients. A physician's personal growth and self awareness are essential bases of effective communication.... Medical education is a stressful and sometimes abrasive experience that can produce cynicism and callousness.'

(Simpson et al 'Doctor–patient Communication: the Toronto Consensus Statement' *British Medical Journal* (1991) 303, 1385–1387.)

This quote applies to lawyers too. We must ensure that we remain in touch with people, despite our expertise and training.

This is my pop psychology section. Why do clients behave so oddly? Why – much harder to take on board – do *we* react so oddly to our clients?

You do not have to be a psychologist to increase your understanding of human behaviour. What will be helpful is to grasp the fact that much of what goes on in human relationships goes on at a level which is not verbalised, not conscious, and not overtly part of the transactions taking place. Nevertheless it is a truism that you pick up cues from other people that are vital to the relationship: you like someone, are put off by another; feel you can trust one stranger, but not the next; feel attracted to one, repelled by another. Some people make you feel uncomfortable, others are the sort you not only enjoy as clients but would enjoy as friends.

All of this feeling will intrude on your relationship as solicitor to client. There is no way to exclude these extraneous factors: extraneous, that is, to what appears to be the particular task of identifying a legal/factual issue and advising accordingly. Some awareness will enable you to do two things:

■ to see what is happening and remain professionally detached;

■ to use deliberate techniques for improving rapport with your client based on this understanding.

Why do people come to see lawyers?

This may be obvious – they have a legal problem. On the face of it this is true. But some do decide they need a lawyer, some don't, in identical situations: one person trips on a paving stone and puts it down to bad luck, another is incensed at the attitude of the highway authority and eager to sue for revenge. One person wants a cut and dried partnership agreement, another works in business without any formalities and hates the idea of inviting the lawyers to wreck a good relationship.

I want to look at three different psychological models for what is going on. They are not in conflict; they just offer insights from different angles. I will use them as pegs to hang discussion of wider points on.

A little psychology 1: people have to satisfy different needs all the time

The heirarchy of needs is a theory of the American psychologist Abraham Maslow (see for example *Towards a Psychology of Being*). People need to satisfy needs at many levels simultaneously:

■ they have basic biological needs – eating, drinking, breathing, sleeping and sexual release;

■ at a higher level they have what he calls 'safety needs': security, freedom from fear, predictability, boundaries;

■ further up again people have 'belongingness needs': for love, intimacy, confidence, acceptance, friendship, company;

■ then come esteem needs: status, approval, recognition;

■ finally there are self-actualisation needs: self-esteem, self-respect, expression, fulfilment of potential, finding of meaning.

The actual hierarchical organisation is not important for our purpose. What is important is awareness of all these needs, and the fact that the client is inevitably expressing those needs in any relationship, and so are you. If you doubt the latter, why do you get such satisfaction when a client says to you: 'I am so grateful to you for everything you have done. I'll recommend you to all my friends'? Your needs for esteem, acceptance, fulfilment are being met in an obvious way; the client is punching all the right buttons. Similarly, if the client is ungrateful, obstinate in refusing your advice, becomes too personal for your liking etc, the relationship is becoming difficult partly because your needs are being denied or your personal boundaries transgressed.

Understanding the client's needs

Is it the lawyer's job to *satisfy* the client's needs? You are not in the business of therapy, but the answer I suggest is still yes, where appropriate. And *recognition* of needs helps in all situations. You will not be expected to address the biological needs – that would be professionally inappropriate, save maybe to give your client a cup of tea and a ventilated interview room. Nor is it your responsibility to ensure that the other needs are satisfied for their own sake: that, if it is to be addressed, is the long-term work of a counsellor, spouse, friend or spiritual adviser. But it is appropriate for you to address those that can assist the professional relationship. 'Nice' people do this anyway. Here are some very easy techniques. You only need reminding: you have used most of them since you were a baby.

Smiling   Gives the other person approval, friendship. Smile as you greet your client: 'How nice to see you again, Mrs Evans'.

Eye contact   Shows acceptance, recognition.

Praise   'That is a very good point, Daniel; I'm glad you asked that.' 'Thank you for letting me have your instructions so promptly, Mr Bennett. This makes my task much easier.' 'I do appreciate you coming in at such short notice to execute this document, Mrs Shearsby.' (Be aware that too much of this may be patronising the client, however. Appearing sincere is no substitute for being sincere.)

Understanding   'Yes, I imagine that was very upsetting for you'; 'Oh, of course, it's only right that you should obtain the full market rent for letting them use your property.' (Understanding too has to be genuine. Telling the client how he feels is pointless and a put down if actually he doesn't.)

Respect for boundaries   What was meant there? This can be a cultural matter. In South America it is common to stand very close to a person you are talking to, and to touch during conversations; in France people kiss frequently when they meet; in football matches men kiss each other when they are pleased. There is nothing right or wrong with such variations, but it can be quite threatening to get closer than normal. You must be aware of and respect these boundaries.

There are psychological as well as physical boundaries. Psychologists generally agree that the process of growing up from babyhood involves a recognition by the child that he or she is a separate being, that the mother and other parts of the world are 'out there'. When a person falls in love, or becomes a close friend, one of the reasons this is so satisfying is that some of the separation is reversed, the boundaries can be let down and more intimate behaviour is allowed (see, for example, Peck *The Road Less Travelled*). When things go wrong, the parties re-erect boundaries, and distance and resentment can grow. You have practised the art of setting appropriate boundaries all your life. All we ask you is to be aware, in the professional relationship, of what the appropriate boundary is.

It is inappropriate, for example, to delve immediately into a person's intimate affairs – even though, when it becomes appropriate, your task requires you to do that; it is inappropriate, probably, to offer an embrace to a very upset client (not least because of the risk of misinterpretation); it is, perhaps, appropriate to lean a little closer. It is, I suggest, inappropriate to put up a massive boundary at this point by saying 'there's no need to get upset', or 'There there, I'll get you a cup of tea'. The client came closer by sharing the upset. You backed away, meaning: 'I can't handle this intimacy' which in turn means 'it's not safe for you to do that again.' No response might be a good response. Or a small gesture, for example, you may not be transgressing a boundary when you show sympathy by a light touch on the client's upper arm (generally reckoned to be the least threatening part of the body to touch).

Recognition of physical boundaries is easy to conceptualise, but not necessarily to get right. Emotional/personal boundaries are more difficult: but if you look at the higher order needs, such as self-esteem, you are crossing a boundary inappropriately if you do all the thinking for the client, come up with the solution before the client has arrived at the point where it can be 'owned' by him or her.

Before moving on from the hierarchy of needs, we want to check that you understand what to do with the information. If you recognise these needs, you can be aware of how you are responding to them. You do not have to articulate them, of course, nor make file notes of how you dealt with them. But you will have a more satisfied client to the extent that the client comes away with such needs appropriately met.

Understanding that you too have needs

Me? But I'm a detached professional.

If I may say so: what rubbish. No-one is detached. Your brain and your hormones function much like everyone else's. You wish to be respected, admired, you get angry, etc. You need to eat sleep and have sex. Detachment is best achieved by owning those needs but meeting them elsewhere than in the client relationship. Where it does not involve transgressing boundaries inappropriately, it is legitmimate for you to try to meet the client's needs, in particular some of the higher order ones that came at the bottom of the list, in particular respect and approval.

But can you really transcend your own needs while role playing the lawyer? If you could, clearly the concept of favoured and problem clients would never arise: but it does, for every solicitor.

Let us examine a sample of these potential needs.

Friendship   There is nothing wrong with you getting satisfaction – the client who says you are doing a good job and smiles at you is likely to be helping him or herself to get the best out of you – but there is a lot wrong with seeking it in the solicitor–client relationship. Where you should be looking to satisfy these needs is outside – in friendships with colleagues, friends, home life, church, counsellors or whatever. Inside the interview your needs, your personal agenda, are irrelevant.

Recognition   An example: I have a video tape of myself starting to tell a client (real, not role play) about my own son. She interrupts to carry on telling me about hers. I cringe now to think about it, but no doubt there are many instances where I have done this without the camera to teach me. I did not benefit the client by asking her to give time to my agenda.

Lawyers don't need to show off their knowledge and experience to their clients.

Physical needs   If your need for food has not been satisfied, your hunger may intrude, it may dominate the interaction. 'When can I get rid of him, so I can go out to lunch?'

Sexual needs   Your need for sex can intrude: you may find the client attractive, or be daydreaming about someone else.

I appreciate this is a sensitive area. It could simply be left as an ethical matter. There are simple rules, and your professional code will tell you when it is permitted to sleep with a client. You do not start romantic relationships with clients, and if you have to, you normally first cease the client-solicitor relationship. Not sleeping with the client is the easy bit. Such injunctions do not deal with the fact that people fantasise, and daydreams (or stronger) intrude on the relationship of solicitor and client. There is nothing wrong with recognising that this is happening. What you must not do is cultivate the fantasy: see it as something that floats in and out of your consciousness, perhaps something externalised – 'there I go again'. 'Sorry' you admit to the client, 'my attention wandered for a moment; I wonder if you could just tell me again what happened to the kitchen when the septic tank flooded in April?'

With physiological needs it is relatively easy to say: don't let them intrude. What of higher order needs? Are you not entitled to esteem? Friendship? Appropriate boundaries? The answer is yes, and in a relationship that is working, both sides adjust their behaviour to supply at least some of what the other person is looking for. The more you consciously attend to the client's legitimate needs, the more the client is likely to respond subconsciously to yours.

But you cannot demand satisfaction. This is part of what being a professional is about, and part of the reason why you learn a degree of detachment from your clients. You will learn not to become thick-skinned, rather to take responsibility for keeping your own self-fulfilment and self-esteem at a high level outside the interview, rather than blame your clients for failing to do so for you. By becoming professionally detached, you are not becoming uninterested. You are committed to the case, you are undoubtedly on the client's side. You are, however, keeping your own problems out of the relationship.

Unmet needs If you start to feel uncomfortable with a client – angry, depressed, inadequate – it may be that you are wanting and not getting the recognition, friendship, intimacy or other need fulfilment that you want. OK, admit it – 'there I go again'. Try not to associate those feelings (which belong to you) with that client (who happens to trigger them). Blaming your client for how you feel is the process called 'projection'. 'I feel angry/depressed; it is someone else's fault. My client's anger is the problem. Her behaviour is intolerable. No wonder I am depressed when she is here.' Admit that the client does not meet all of your needs, indeed, in his presence you feel some of them are being thwarted – the wrong buttons are being punched – but let it go, because your needs are not the ones that matter here.

Are you surprised that your own emotional needs are considered relevant? Put yourself into the position of patient; how do you feel if you see signs that the doctor is distressed by your symptoms? ('Oh my God, what a horrible load of pus, I can't bear it!') How would you feel if you knew that the offhand treatment you were receiving was because you remind the doctor of a much disliked relative? You would expect the doctor to be able to distance her or his feelings towards the situation from the behaviour towards you.

Warning signals   Here are symptoms that your emotional reactions are getting in the way of an effective professional relationship:

■ personal dislike of the client;

■ discomfort when the client expresses anger or other emotion;

■ you feel angry at the client;

■ you feel distress at the facts described – it may consciously, or subconsciously, trigger bad memories of your own;

■   you feel worried that you will not cope, and focus on that anxiety rather than listening to the client;

■   you suffer from personal prejudices, eg racial, gender, apparent sexual orientation, disfigurement, speech defect and this prevents you from listening to the client;

■   you feel a need to impress the client.

How are you going to deal with these problems? Unattended they will distort your ability to listen, to analyse and to advise dispassionately.

Stage one must be awareness. It is more comfortable to deny than to accept, and to blame the client for any difficulties, particularly if you are being asked to admit prejudices and lack of ability to cope. But no-one is actually asking you to reveal to the client or anyone else that you are having an internal dialogue or battle with a side of your character that you prefer not to reveal. These are enormously sensitive issues which you should not burden your client with. We are not asking you to say: 'Sorry, for a moment I was not listening to you, because I was having difficulty getting out of my mind that you are gay/black/female/short (or whatever)'. No-one is asking you to say: 'I've just realised that the reason I hate interviewing you so much is that your mouth is shaped just like my old headmistress's.' You don't have to say this to anyone – except to yourself. Then either allow yourself to dismiss it with indulgence: 'there I go again'. Or recognise that you are going to have difficulty accepting instructions.

No-one will ever convince me that they are so well balanced that these problems do not occur in their professional and other relationships. Hard to admit? Yes. But dangerous to suppress? Very. The person who says: 'Prejudiced? Me? Never!' is possibly more at risk of being dictated to by those prejudices than the person who says 'Yes, I personally find it difficult to accept that women should be in positions of authority'; 'Yes, I for a moment assumed that because my black client is refusing to tell me what I need to know he is ill educated and surly'.

The above discussion arose from the consideration of Maslow's hierarchy of needs. We need to return briefly to the hierarchy. The client may present you with one need – often for money, or security – when in fact other hidden needs provide the real motivation. Awareness of the possibility of several needs all jumbled up together can help you to unravel the problem, and help the client to identify which is the most important underlying need. The client may apparently present a need for compensation for an accident: money to provide for biological and security needs. In fact the client is desperately angry and really wants an admission that she is right, 'they' are wrong. It is the anger caused by the refusal to acknowledge her distress – rejection, lack of approval – that principally motivates her in giving you her instructions.

I do not mean to ask that you reinterpret the client's instructions and say: 'There there; I see that what you really need is love and friendship, so let's forget this silly dispute with your former partner, and why don't you lie back and tell me all about it.' I mean, instead, that in the pursuit of your client's objectives you will be better equipped to explain options and offer advice because you begin to understand what is motivating him or her. You can reflect back in a way that recognises the legitimacy of those feelings: 'It seems that this experience has made you upset.'

In our business law case study, it seems that your client is going all out to get the maximum rent on the property let to the company. It seems to you bizarre – the client is risking wrecking the prospects of the new business as a result of making this negotiation difficult. What is the real need the client wishes to have satisfied? Perhaps you can explore, subtly: maybe the client has worked for years to pay for these premises and fears being 'robbed' by his partners if he gives it away too cheaply; maybe he is desperately financially insecure. You do not have to come up with a diagnosis. Your client would not thank you for this, probably. But the possibilities allow you to search for ways of giving your advice in the way that allows the situation to be resolved and those needs to be satisfied. Maybe all that is needed is recognition from you – not even from the other parties (the ex-spouse, the business partner etc) whose lack of recognition seems to have been upsetting the client. Often the client needs a good listening to.

> **Solicitor D:** Yes, this must be quite a difficult decision for you, how much to rent out the premises for. You told me earlier that you worked – what was it? seven? eight years? – to save up the money to put into that building. You feel you are entitled to a fair return on it.

(Although the solicitor here is doing the talking, it is evidence of active listening – more on that below.)

Alternatively (exploring another hypothesis, that 'giving away' the premises makes him angry at his new partners who appear to be getting something for nothing): 'How do you feel about the fact that your partner is benefiting from a situation that you took so long to build up? I imagine you want him to recognise in some way the contribution you have already made, and I imagine he will be pretty grateful to you for the head start you have provided.' (The recognition by you may take away some of the intransigence of this client's attitude, who now has at least some of the recognition that he wanted, and perhaps he can look at the negotiations with a more open mind as a result.)

Similarly, take Mrs Evans's predicament. This was based on a real case, and she was offered a caution if she would admit her guilt. Instead she chose to fight for acquittal. The solicitor can advise that the prospects of a conviction are so great that conviction is more than likely; this may indeed be the best advice, and it is right to give it forcefully. But the client refused to countenance a caution, because it meant admitting her guilt, which she would not do. To admit her guilt – even though she was guiltless – was on one level expedient, and would meet certain needs: no punishment (no loss of money to pay for food, shelter etc) and no threat to self-esteem resulting from cross-examination and possible publicity and conviction. But what motivated her at the point of decision was the need for self-respect and self-confidence. If her adviser understands that this need is at this moment so powerful as to override other considerations, it is possible to empower the client to make choices rather than confront her. It may be important to give the client space and time rather than to insist on having a decision.

Here are two possible dialogues:

> **Solicitor A:** Look, Mrs Evans, I am going to have to be blunt with you. Do you understand how bad it looks? You have come up with no alternative explanation that the court will believe about the coins getting into your pocket. Our investigations unfortunately have not produced any evidence that will help us to suggest that the coins were planted in your apron pocket. The police are offering you a caution. I know it means you will have to admit doing something that you are saying did not happen, but that way you end up without a criminal conviction, no punishment, no trial. ...

Client: But I didn't do it, I can't admit to something I didn't do.

Let us try an approach recognising that our advice about how bad the case looks goes in the face of a strongly felt high order need – self-respect. (And note a very important point: it is not important to the solicitor to win the argument. All that is necessary is to help the client come to an informed choice that she can live with, preferably without later regret.)

A: Yes, I imagine that would be a very difficult thing for you to do.

Client: I just couldn't face myself if I did that....

A: It would feel all wrong saying to the police 'I did it'.

Client: Like, you know, like I'm a criminal ... like a terrible person ... someone people would want to avoid on the streets....

A: You feel people would look at you differently because of that. (Pause). I wonder if we could nevertheless explore what will happen if we go to trial. You are aware, I think, that I am not optimistic about winning a trial. I wonder if it will help to look that far ahead, and how you will feel if you get convicted ...

Client (*after a pause*)*:* The same ... a criminal ... I won't be able to face my friends and family....

And so it continues. These suggestions do not give a magic solution, where the client suddenly accepted your advice and resolved her feelings. In fact you are not advising, not least because if your client denies the offence it is wrong to advise her to admit it. What matters is that you gave space for the recognition of her needs and fears: the difficult choice is still hers, there is still much to explore in terms of personal cost, financial cost, chances of an acquittal, likely punishment and so on. But some of the client's needs are implicitly stated and made accessible to her (and you) during the discussion. What the solicitor is doing is to use his or her skills of predicting outcomes. It is not only the accuracy of the prediction that is crucial, but making it useful to the client.

A little psychology 2: Games people play

Here is another way of looking at what makes you and the client tick as you relate to each other. The area of psychology is called 'transaction analysis', but 'game playing' will do. A very popular book thirty years ago explained this theory in popular terms: *I'm OK, You're OK* (by Thomas Harris). Greatly simplified, the idea is that you can categorise behaviour patterns into three types, which were learned in childhood. Everybody behaves at any given time more as a child, a parent, or an adult. In doing so, they are re-enacting old patterns in a new environment. They do not literally become different people. They play old tapes of different messages – for parent mode, the messages my parents kept giving me (and I'm now giving out to others); and for child mode the messages of how I felt as a child (and am feeling again).

Imagine an inner dialogue, which the person concerned is probably not aware of:

■   'I shouldn't admit my guilt, I'd look so stupid.' (The 'child' is in control, admonishing and cajoling. Mrs Evans is listening to a tape of what her parents might have said, such as 'Don't let me ever catch you ... '.)

■ 'I'm not going to let her get a penny out of my husband's estate.' (The 'child' is in control, expressing anger; 'I used to have everything taken away from me when I was a child …'.)

■ 'Now really Mrs Evans, there's no need to get quite so upset.' (The solicitor is in 'parent' mode, an easy role to play.)

■ 'I can see that an independent valuation of the property would be the best way of moving forward.' (The adult gets to grips and makes more rational, considered, decisions. No old tapes are controlling behaviour.)

All of us, according to this theory, oscillate between these modes. A solicitor giving advice too readily 'I don't think you should set too high a level of rent, Mr Kader … ' forces the client into rebellious 'child' mode of responding – a mode of irrational feelings about the problem that results, for example, in surliness and anger, rather than co-operation. 'I'll do what I bloody well want' is the internal message running through Mr Kader's tape.

Child mode of response recurs frequently. The client may react, for example, to the solicitor setting out the risks of starting court proceedings, or buying the house on an endowment policy, by feeling: 'Oh, I can't go along with that, what if I ended up paying thousands of pounds? I can't contemplate that.' 'What if the endowment policy doesn't accumulate enough to pay off the mortgage?' 'Don't go out, it might rain; don't speak till you are spoken to.' When 'child' mode takes over the client can feel a loss of confidence, which triggers 'good child' mode, and start to apologise for taking up so much of the solicitor's time (Solicitors are Very Important People and you Mustn't Waste Their Time).

This happens. Most people have had an experience of trying to get past the receptionist at the doctor's surgery. You too? Do you remain an 'adult'? Or do you go into good 'child' mode? 'I know I shouldn't be bothering doctor, but it's this cough that's been going on a bit too long.' Or angry 'child' mode? 'This is the 57th time this week I've tried to see the doctor and if you don't let me see him now I'll burn down your surgery.'

What you, and the doctor, and indeed everyone who deals with people, should aim to do is to empower the 'adult' within the client. To do that you avoid reminding the client of any ways in which their parents behaved badly towards them (watch parents in supermarket queues or, indeed, in solicitors' waiting rooms for guidance on this – you can tell where children are being put down inappropriately, though it is harder to tell when you do it yourself!) If you accidentally remind the client of how it felt to be a child – subconsciously, of course – you may get child responses. You will less probably get an adult response from your client.

The 'games people play' relate to the various responses people make to each others' modes. It is a 'game' (also known as a 'racket') when 'parent' and 'child' lock into each other. Solicitor gives out parental messages (To paraphrase in Mrs Evans' case 'Grown women don't get upset; accept the caution and get on with it') and client responds as 'child' (for example by running away and ignoring the need to make a decision; for example by accepting the advice of the parental figure; for example by getting angry and making a decision that she later regrets). Adult to adult mode is not a game, not a racket. The lawyer can deliberately try to remain in adult mode, but this requires an act of will not to descend into parent mode (which is too easily confused with adult if the client plays the game of 'child').

Again, no easy answers through this theory. Just a chance of insights when you find clients responding in ways that drive you beserk. Have you behaved in such a way as to trigger that reaction? You can blame the client – who, in child mode, probably feels blameworthy already – or you can look back over the 'transaction' that just took place and identify at what point something you did triggered this response. Be aware of this, especially when you watch your own video performances or help to evaluate a colleague's interview.

No-one is blaming you for doing this. All of us trigger unexpected feelings in other people all the time, and they do it to us. Knowing it is happening starts to give you choices. Be aware that you, the lawyer, will be receiving stimuli that trigger 'child' in you (eg 'you're no good as a lawyer'; 'you're handling this client very badly'; 'I can't see why I should listen to this client's drivel any longer'; 'I am angry …').

A little psychology 3: The psychoanalytic approach

The Freudians, and those who took psychoanalysis further, recognised that people in adult life live out patterns of behaviour established in very early life. Whether these were caused by Oedipus complexes and penis envy, and whether the true state is revealed in dreams or not, is not important. The insights which help us as lawyers is that people are driven by forces they do not consciously use or understand. Relationships which became distorted, such as overdependence on a parent, or dysfunction caused by abuse, cause lasting effects. A person who did not learn to establish an independent relationship with his or her parents – to grow up – finds continuing problems with dependence and attachment to others. A person who had problems with a father may have continuing problems with people in authority – manifested by rebellion or eagerness to please.

Because of this, a person who is causing you distress, for reasons you cannot quite put your finger on, may be reliving, compulsively, a pattern of behaviour that makes it very hard for you either to relate to them or obtain clear instructions.

For example, our Mrs Evans cannot decide what to do in relation to the offer of a caution. She wants to accept it, she wants to refuse it. Perhaps as a child her dominant parent never gave her the power to make real choices, and now she lacks that ability. It does not particularly matter why she is like she is. What matters instead is that you recognise that the behaviour pattern is coming from somewhere, and that your behaviour unavoidably becomes another part of the pattern. Mrs Evans, in her subconscious, may identify you with that parent, and the pattern will go round and round without resolution.

You could say 'we simply don't get on, she doesn't listen to a word I say'. You could say 'she is one of those problem clients'. But you could say, instead, 'I am having difficulty in this situation. Something is not working in my relationship with this client. What can I do to make it work, not for its own sake, but to ensure that I can carry out my task as a lawyer?' I offer this brief excursion on the Freudian approach not because it offers techniques you can adopt, but because we want you take on board the possibility that the person behaving in a difficult fashion towards you is not malicious, stupid or unco-operative; that they should be accepted as simply having a pattern of behaviour, triggered by the situation, that is not their fault, not your fault, not to be judged. In accepting the client as he or she is you have crossed the first threshold to establishing a good working relationship. At this point you might like to remember the BVC standards' requirement that you be non-judgmental.

Another thing the Freudians taught us is the concept of the id, ego and superego. The ego is the one that may help to improve our understanding, but for a context I will describe the other two concepts. The id represents the instinctive, impulsive more primitive drives: for the Freudians this got very tangled up in sexuality and fantasy, but you could just see it as representing that part of the psyche that represents the most basic needs of the human being. The superego is at the other end, representing the internalised values of the person, the conscience perhaps.

Then there is the ego, what the person has learned to call 'I'. At the time of writing this chapter for the first edition my five-year-old son had just had a tantrum because in his game of whist his high card was trumped. This is the ego at work: the 'I' is threatened. If he wins his game and is praised, if I get a good review for this book and earn lots of money, my ego is happy. 'I' have done well. People invest large amounts of time and energy in attempting to satisfy the demands of the ego for proof that the 'I' is doing alright. The ego demands proof in the form of power, wealth, praise, material well-being, friendship, career success and so on. Both you, and your client, will inevitably be adopting behaviours that make your ego feel better. The ego can be a real pain – it can drive you to work yourself into an early grave, it can drive you to bully your children, it can drive your client to spend a fortune on fruitless legal proceedings, it can actually stand in the way of happiness and quality of life.

So be it: you are not a counsellor. Be content to recognise it as a potential explanation for what is going on in your professional relationships, and do two things:

1   Find ways of bolstering the client, who underneath, like everyone else, has a vulnerable ego. A little praise can go a long way: 'I know how difficult it can be to recall things that happened so long ago, and you are doing extremely well ... now that is exactly the sort of information that will help me, well done ... it makes such a difference when a client understands what is required ...'.

Respect for the importance of the client can help: keeping someone waiting indicates that you have power, they do not. Make sure they know your name for the same reason. Decide whether you want to sit behind a desk – to demonstrate your control and power – or whether you can create a more equal situation. (There is not a right answer to this question of layout, and I will raise it again later. But remember that it plays a part in how the client feels, and an intimidated client has a threatened ego.)

2   If any effort is to be spent protecting vulnerable egos, make sure it is the client's ego, not the solicitor's, that gets the attention. The professional, detached behaviour of the solicitor means putting your own egotistical needs aside. So the client makes you feel mad: count to ten, change the subject, anything, but do not hit the ceiling. You find yourself feeling worthless, inadequate: the ego tells you to inflate yourself (*go on, show off my knowledge and power, quote section 76 of the Police and Criminal Evidence Act verbatim, that'll make me feel better*; or *show him who is boss: I cannot possibly fit in another appointment until Thursday at the earliest, why, I'm in the High Court for the next two days and I have that oh so important meeting with that very important person on Wednesday ...*). Resist. You already are a lawyer, a highly respectable person with a great deal of power, and if you ever pay off your student debts, access to vast amounts of money. Tell your ego to take a back seat while you are dealing with clients. Watch out for warning signals that your ego is getting agitated, such as: *Uh oh, I'm using pompous language; I'm wanting him to be*

impressed with my knowledge; I'm worried she'll think I'm no good; I'm trying to stop her talking about this topic because it upsets me; I hope he likes me; now what did that last remark about 'are you sure about this?' mean etc.

A little psychology 4: client-centred counselling

The late Carl Rogers had much to teach lawyers. I did not include him in the first edition, but in the meanwhile have trained in counselling and learned that of all the pyschologists, reading Carl Rogers is the one I recommend most strongly. For me his writings are nothing short of inspiring. He even coined the phrase we now all pay such slavish lip-service to: 'client-centred'. Reading and then trying to apply Rogers' ideas taught me, above all else, that to be client-centred I have to focus on what I, the interviewer, am doing as well as what the client is doing. I have to confront my own behaviour. Read on.

Rogers' work underpinned new approaches to therapy, to education, to interviewing, and more. Rogers believed that client-centred work actually starts with three conditions which the counsellor must achieve. He called them his 'Core Conditions': Congruence, Unconditional Positive Regard, and Empathic Understanding (Rogers, 1961, pp 61–62):

Congruence: It has been found that personal change is facilitated when the psychotherapist is what he is, when in the relationship with his client he is genuine and without 'front' or facade, openly being the feelings and attitudes which at that moment are flowing from him. By this we mean that the feelings the therapist is experiencing are available to him, available to his awareness, and he is able to live these feelings, be them, and be able to communicate them as appropriate. No one fully achieves this condition, yet the more the therapist is able to listen acceptantly to what is going on within himself, and the more he is able to be the complexity of his feelings, without fear, the higher the degree of his congruence.

Unconditional Positive Regard: When the therapist is experiencing a warm, positive and acceptant attitude towards what is in the client, this facilitates change. It involves the therapist's genuine willingness for the client to be whatever feeling is going on in him at that moment – fear, confusion, pain, pride, anger, hatred, love, courage, or awe. It means that the therapist cares for the client, in a non-possessive way. It means that he prizes the client in a total rather than a conditional way. By this I mean that he does not simply accept the client when he is behaving in certain ways, and disapprove of him when he behaves in other ways. It means an outgoing positive feeling without reservations, without evaluations. Again research studies show that the more this attitude is experienced by the therapist, the more likelihood there is that therapy will be successful.

Empathic Understanding: When the therapist is sensing the feelings and personal meanings which the client is experiencing in each moment, when he can perceive these from 'inside', as they seem to the client, and when he can successfully communicate something of that understanding to his client then this third condition is fulfilled.

Elsewhere (Rogers, 1961, pp 33–34) Rogers suggests that the demonstration by the therapist of these conditions makes the client feel safe and valued, free to take risks with what he or she explores, and free from diagnostic judgements or threatening evaluations. 'When these conditions are achieved I become a companion to my client ...'

Rogers also suggests that effective counselling results in self-actualisation – the client becoming whole. A relationship with a counsellor who demonstrates the three core conditions of genuinness, unconditional positive regard and empathy will cause the client to become a more integrated person, one who has an 'internal locus of evaluation', and therefore has no need to search for 'external conditions of worth'. (The client essentially values him or herself, rather than relies on a perception of how other people value him or her as an indication of personal worth.)

But why is this relevant? It is definitely not the goal of legal interviewing to change the client. The lawyer is hired to fix external problems. Why, then, should a lawyer pay attention to these three conditions? Let's see briefly why they might be relevant.

Empathy, or at least the word empathy, is superficially described in many writings on legal interviewing, and is explicit in the BVC standards.

Does a lawyer need to 'prize' the client, or be genuine and transparent? It is only necessary to suggest the opposite: a lack of prizing, and a falsity of behaviour, to recognise that at least some demonstration of these attributes is appropriate. Taking prizing, for example, the following quotes, the first from a solicitor and the second from a client, throws into relief the way the client can be treated if there is no positive regard:

> So many defendants are, well, just stupid. They never seem to remember what they've done, or to understand what's happening to them.... you lose patience with them sometimes. (Bankowski and Mungham (1976) at page 52.)

> I get the impression that I'm one of his many cases.: 'Well, what's the latest ... get the file ... what shall we do about this.' There's no sense of get up and go; no sense 'Right, let's get this sorted'. (Matrimonial client interviewed in Davis Cretney and Collins (1994) at page 111.)

I am not seeking to cast stones. I have, as a lawyer, felt this way and treated clients this way. What matters is that it is unlikely that a client would obtain a professional service from a lawyer feeling this way and doing nothing about it.

What of genuineness? This is perhaps the most challenging of Rogers' conditions. As a trainee lawyer I was led to believe that I had a *role* to play. Lacking explicit guidance I modelled my behaviour on how I *thought* solicitors behaved. Given a choice between genuineness and the role, I would tend to choose the role. I recently taped an interview I conducted with a client, and also taped a discussion afterwards with her and an observer from a counselling background. While the client needed to tell me about her marital problems, she stated after the interview: 'I had to be sure I could trust you as a person first'. It is easy to try to please other people by telling them what I think they want to hear (responding to what Rogers labelled the 'external locus of evaluation' – I think I will feel better as a person if I behave the way I imagine other people want me to). This is bad news for the clients of counsellors and lawyers alike. They are not paying to be lied to. They can get that elsewhere.

My summary of Rogers would be as follows:

- ■ be yourself, don't play the role of a different lawyer; if you are aware of your own feelings, this may be giving useful guidance to how you handle the client

- ■ look at the client's issues from the client's perspective; your agenda, your satisfaction, are not important (but in being yourself you are aware of them)

■ treat – don't pretend to treat, actually do it – the client as the most valued person; change career if this is not possible.

The limits of psychology

Without studying these, and other schools of thought and research into human behaviour, in greater depth you cannot be expected to use the actual techniques mentioned or implied in the last few pages. The introductions to four different schools of thought dealing with human relationships are intended at best to help you to do two things:

■ to avoid being judgmental, since you can accept that the clients are behaving in a particular way for a particular reason (and who cares whether in fact you understand that reason?)

■ to avoid casting all the blame for problems onto the client; you have your own psychological patterns.

Taking this use of psychology further would require supervision of your work by psychologists or lawyers with a wider training – a process which I would recommend to the professions. (You can read more about my ideas for this in the Law Teacher – [1998] Vol 32 (2) Brayne: *Counselling Skills for the Lawyer: Can Lawyers Learn Anything from Counsellors?*).

Principle 4: Emotion matters

'Don't get all emotional' or 'lawyers have to learn to cope with emotion'. These are unhelpful comments, for they imply that there are emotional states and there are non-emotional states. All human states are emotional. Children tend to display these emotions without inhibition. Adults have gone through a process of hiding them, more or less successfully. I want to take you through a short logical process. Please accept the first two premises:

1 Hiding emotions can cause dysfunctional behaviour (ask 'Relate', the relationship counselling service).

2 Your job is helping clients solve problems.

Can you solve problems if your client is behaving dysfunctionally? Too often the advice I have seen offered to students veers towards the 'getting the emotion out of the way' approach. My advice is to get it out into the open. Why?

1 Your client's emotional state is part of the factual situation and will help the client to give you appropriate instructions

2 Your client will formulate those instructions more clearly and usefully as a result of acknowledging the emotional background to the problem and his current state.

So a starting point is to aim not to be afraid of expressed emotion. A good way of coping with the client's emotion is to reflect it back, to allow it to be vented: 'Yes, I can see the refusal to lower the price is distressing you'; 'You seem very upset about what your former wife did to you'; 'Did that worry you?' 'Would you like to tell me how that felt'. Words and emotions sometimes do not mix. Sometimes you cannot and need not put it into words. Let us go to E and a tense interview with Mrs Shearsby, who has agreed to lend money to Mr Kader to expand his business.

> **Mrs Shearsby:** So when she phoned and said she wouldn't speak to me again if I lent the money to Mohammed I shouted at her 'well go to hell then'.

> **E:** long pause, then if and when client appears ready to move on, (for example) 'And you haven't spoken to her again since ...' (or whatever)

Note in these examples I am not suggesting you tell the client about her own emotions. You do not need to say: 'That must have made you very angry' or 'If that had been me, you know, I would have been devastated'. Such reactions to signs of emotion from the client can be valid, but sometimes too powerful, because they assume something the client has not revealed, and may indeed be projection of the solicitor's own feelings, not a reflection of those of the client. It is important to allow for the expression of the emotion, but less desirable to leap to conclusions about what those emotions are. If you feel that an emotional charge is coming into the situation, you can usually address it by giving the client herself the space and the implicit permission to take it further if she wishes. Taking the above example, after the pause, if the emotional energy was still apparent the solicitor could have taken the essence of what the client had said as the way of conveying 'it's OK to be emotional'.

> **Mrs Shearsby:** I shouted at her 'go to hell'.

> **E:** (*after pause*) (*for example*) At that moment you had had enough.

Alternatively you could ask your client: 'how did you feel about that?' But the danger of asking questions is that you get answers, in words. Why do you want to know how she felt, and how she now puts those feelings into words? My advice is to give space and safety in the relationship to vent emotions. There is not great need to talk *about* them.

Creating space and safety is hard, however, and has to be deliberate. The easier way is to simply change the subject.

> **Mr Bennett:** And then the building society phoned and said they couldn't lend more than 95% on £50,000 and I just felt like screaming.

> **Solicitor C:** But you could try another bank or building society you know. (*Message to client: your distress is too much for me.*) In fact I know that the British Wide is currently offering very good terms; should I ring the manager now? (*Message: and it's so uncomfortable I'll use any means I can not to have to face it right now, and I'd rather hear no more about it.*)

Another approach might have been:

> **Solicitor C:** Yes (*followed by silence*).

Allowing space, saying nothing. This does not mean nothing is happening. The client may benefit from the opportunity to follow up with something important: 'You know how much we want to move, and that seemed the last straw. I'm not at all sure what to do.'

Silence is not inactivity. It is filled with eye contact, smiles, nods of approval, non-verbal cues like leaning forward rather than away, and semi-verbal cues like: 'aha', 'mmm' or just 'yes'. Silence is not a bad thing in an interview (see p 133). A compulsion to fill the silence reveals your insecurity. I don't blame you for feeling insecure – I feel that way about silences too – I simply ask you to use them as a professional tool. What else can be going on in a silence? What else can it tell you? It can mean that the client is thinking, imagining. According to Roger Neighbour, who cites scientific research in support, you can tell what is going on in someone's mind when they are not speaking by what their eyes are doing. (This is not just fantasy, since visual perception is linked to particular parts of the brain, and different parts of the brain are linked to different emotional states.)

If a person looks up, they are picturing something in their mind. It may be a real event they are remembering, in which case they look to their left; it may be imagined, in which case they look to their right. Test this hypothesis by asking a friend: describe the view from your bedroom window (up and left); picture a hot air balloon floating past (up and right).

If they look ahead they are listening to something in their mind, again left if it is remembered (a conversation) and right if it is imagined. Try with your friend: please think of the sound of waves crashing on the beach (ahead, left); imagine phoning your mother/boy friend to say you have just passed the interview skills assessment (ahead, right).

If the person looks down they are having some kind of kinaesthetic experience (meaning feelings or physical experience). Left means remembered, right means imagined. You could ask: How did you feel when you were told you had a place on the course? (down, left) or: What would it be like to have a headache? (down, right).

You don't agree? You didn't try? It doesn't matter. (Although it may be helpful to know that the school of psychology related to this, neurolinguistic programming, has a basis in solid research. Did you know that the cerebral cortex is split into a left half and a right half? The left half controls the right side of the body, and the parts of our behaviour that are concerned with reasoning and thinking. The right brain connects to intuition and emotion. We function best when we use and integrate our entire apparatus. By putting emotions to one side we are reducing our brain capacity by 50%. Except, of course, we cannot do this – instead we set our emotions and our thinking in conflict with each other, thereby reducing our brain functioning even further.)

What is, in any event, beyond doubt is that people change the focus of their gaze when they are thinking or imagining something; some even close their eyes. This is not a time to interrupt; this is a time to allow the client to focus on something internal. When the client's focus returns to you or the present situation, you can break the silence (if the client has not already done so) with a question, such as 'I wonder if you can tell me a little more?' or even directly 'Was what you have just been thinking about relevant to what we are discussing?'

Another way of 'dealing' with client emotions is to provide comfort. I do not think it is a good way unless you are very skilled or very sure of your ground. 'There, there, it'll be alright' does not make it alright; 'You'll feel better after a nice cup of tea' may be over-optimistic. The client facing a criminal trial, a violent home situation, a very risky business decision, an upsurge in anger at a former spouse, may feel these emotions discounted by such a reaction. It is a coded way for the solicitor to say: 'not for me, your emotions'. The client may feel misunderstood or simply uncomfortable. Again, this is the tendency for student lawyers, who have set themselves unrealistic targets, and the fault of lecturers who write wholly impossible roles for the 'client' to play. It is not surprising that all they can come up with is: 'Don't worry, we'll sort that out', or 'I'm sure you won't get a prison sentence', or 'You won't have to worry about your step daughter making a claim on the estate'.

The student in that situation is confused about his or her role. A lawyer must give the client reassurance, but not at all costs. False reassurance is no reassurance – it is either not believed at the time (because the giver lacks conviction) or it turns out to be false (which leaves the client unprepared when the worst happens, and probably angry). It is not the solicitor's job to be fairy godmother: there is no magic wand, and if you cannot make the situation right – whatever 'right' is – that is not your fault. Whenever you feel words coming up like 'don't worry' please pass them through a mental censor: is there really nothing to worry about, or am I trying to change the subject and divert attention from something I cannot deal with? Every time you watch your own performance on a video, ask at each act of reassurance which got past your censor if it was given with confidence. If not, should it have been replaced with: 'Yes, that poses a real problem'; 'I can see you are worried'; 'We're going to have to discuss that a lot further before we can decide if we are going to be able to deal with that'.

Another temptation when a client expresses emotion is to try to bring the situation under control by capping the story, putting your own emotional experience into the discussion. 'Yes, that reminds me of the time we moved house, and would you believe the traumas we had; first ...'. Does this help the client, or divert attention from their problem to your need for attention?

The story may, on the other hand, help the client, if it is a safe way to explore the problem, in much the same way as a problem can be externalised temporarily by discussing it in terms of a perhaps fictitious person in a similar situation. Neighbour calls this the 'my friend John' approach.

For example:

> **Mr Bennett:** If they don't back down and drop their price I think I'll go round and give them a piece of my mind.

> **Solicitor C:** Yes, I had a client once who was in a similar situation, and you know what he ended up doing? He actually went round and had a blazing row, but unfortunately the vendor simply took the house off the market after that. Would you believe how petty people can be? (*Advice has been offered: have you thought about the risks, but not in a paternalistic sense which would be harder to accept.*)

Alternatively:

> **Solicitor C:** Many people feel the same way when things like this happen/something very similar happened to me when we moved house, so I have some idea how you feel. (*Back to the present.*) Do you think going round for a frank discussion might help to move the situation forward?

Let us recap on what we have looked at so far in relation to needs and emotions:

- recognise your own emotional reactions (more on this later) but do not look to satisfy your needs here;

- recognise, by contrast, your client's legitimate need to express emotion;

- offer reassurance only if it is backed by genuine confidence;

- as you cannot usually take away the worries, allow them to be expressed.

Principle 5: The relationship matters

On almost any criteria for interviewing, you are going to be judged on some factor called rapport, empathy or relationship building. How do you demonstrate that you can do this?

There are some simple techniques, in addition to the psychological issues you have begun to think about. Of course you must observe the simple formalities: your client needs to know your name, so give it clearly and slowly, not garbled; remember the client's name – the simple technique to avoid forgetting it (and to avoid having to write it down right at the start, which breaks into relationship building) is to use the name a few times in the first few minutes. 'Nice to meet you, Mr Kader' ... a few sentences later 'I wonder, Mr Kader, if you'd be good enough to tell me why you have come to see me today' ... 'Now, Mr Kader, it helps me at this stage to take down a few basic details on paper'.

Should you invite use of first names? The only rule I offer is to avoid encroaching into the client's space. Between students, one of whom is role playing the client, the temptation to become informal is increased, but your control of the interview may suffer. Use of surnames may increase detachment, which is very valuable until the relationship is established on a professional footing. Wearing formal clothes can achieve the same result.

You will need to ensure your client is comfortable: if she is wearing a coat, or carrying a heavy bag, offer to take it and put it somewhere (make sure there will be a coat hook so that this is not an empty gesture; I have even seen students take a coat carefully and then have nowhere to put it). The offer of a cup of coffee can show that you are concerned about more than the legal problem – but again, you cannot offer something which, in a role play, you cannot provide. (One of my students in this situation buzzed through on an imaginary intercom to an imaginary secretary and asked for a cup – full marks for initiative!)

Who will sit where? If you wish to create formality and distance, you can put a desk between yourself and the client. If you wish to avoid such a barrier, you can arrange the chairs beforehand so that they are directly facing. (If you need a desk to write on, you can sit at the side of a desk.) Most solicitors sit behind desks. Most advice on interviewing says 'don't'. Try both styles in front of the video cameras or colleagues and make the decision after careful reflection. Ask the 'client' after a role play whether the seating arrangement was appropriate.

Your client is going to tell you something very significant; and yet you may have heard it all a thousand times before. The client will need to convince herself and you that it is significant, otherwise what is the justification for seeing a solicitor? Recognise the significance to the client, even if you then put the issue into a less exciting context.

You must remain interested. That means looking at her, nodding, encouraging her to go on, interspersing what she says with 'aha', 'yes' and so on; agreeing occasionally 'I see', 'yes that was quite something' or 'no, no of course not' as appropriate. This comes relatively easily, but you must watch your own performance to check that you really are doing it adequately.

These techniques are very important. An exercise I sometimes use is to set up two groups of students to carry out interviews.

One group is briefed to exaggerate the art of attentive listening, by doing as much as possible to show real interest. They should lean forward, maintain vigorous eye contact, avoid distracting mannerisms, nod and encourage further talking.

The other group of interviewers is instructed to show every possible indication of not being interested: looking at their watches, leaning away, looking down, coughing, manicuring their nails and so on.

Interviewees are not told anything about these briefings. They are asked to talk for five minutes about some topic of interest, such as 'my career plan' or 'my favourite holiday activity'. They then report on the experience, and not surprisingly, half the students found it very easy, pleasant, and time passed quickly; the others found the time dragged, the task was unpleasant, and the topic they wanted to talk about did not feel as interesting as they had anticipated.

Talking without being listened to is unpleasant and hard to sustain. Talking while being listened to and not being judged is fun and easy.

There is another insight from this type of exercise. Listening is partly the art of knowing when to talk, and more importantly, when not to talk. It is hard to judge an interview as competent when the balance of talking – who talks most – is too skewed towards the interviewer not the client. The person who needs to talk is the client. While you are performing the interview it is very hard, particularly if you are nervous, to know when to shut up. You are being judged on your performance, and you naturally feel you must do something. But the client has come – at least initially – to be listened to, much less to listen. Of course, the client wants to hear what you have to say – and possibly to gain your approval, as well as your advice. But it is a very dissatisfying experience to go to see someone who has then dominated the available time.

If in doubt: shut up and listen. Remember this advice: don't just do something; sit there. (In fact active listening is very demanding, far more so than chattering on.)

If you are listening attentively, the client will feel able to talk. Awkward silences need not be filled: they feel a good deal more awkward when you are in them than they seem to a client or an outsider watching, and what seems like minutes can actually be seconds. Silence may be the time when the client prepares to tell you something important.

Listening and interrupting are, of course, contradictory behaviours. If you interrupt what your client is telling you, you are in effect saying: What I have to say is more important than what you have to say. You are taking power and confidence away from the client. It is almost never appropriate, and it is nevertheless a common fault. Interruptions, by the way, sound even worse on tape than they do live, because the listener lacks the cues of hearing the voices coming from different directions and therefore the ability to hear them separately. You may be assessed on your video tape.

To avoid interruptions you need structure, and the structure must be one clearly understood by the client. Each of you – guided by you at the appropriate stage – must know when it is your turn to dominate the conversation. At the start of the process, especially in the first interview, the client dominates the available time; later on you take up more of a share, both because you are beginning to have an idea what the matter is about, and because the client will be ready to listen, having been listened to satisfactorily.

What if your attention wanders? What if listening and concentrating 100% is too much. Accept that this will happen, and do not treat it as a failure. Nobody is a perfect listener. As a parent I fail to listen to much of what my children say, even though I appear to them to be listening (nodding, smiling, aha, the usual things that appear on an assessment checklist but can be done on autopilot and without listening). The same can happen when I am teaching; attention wanders, a student speaks, I nod and then realise I have not heard. It happens in my legal interviews, and it will happen in yours. Admit it – what else can you do? If you pretend you were paying attention to save embarrassment, you are prevented from obtaining that bit of information, which your client thinks you have received.

The trouble is that while you are trying hard to listen actively – saying to yourself: *I should nod now, I must smile and say 'go on'* – you may be distracted from the actual listening. Yes, this is unavoidable. You will also be listening to a dialogue in your head that is saying: *What are the crucial facts I am supposed to get out of this interview? What legal analysis is needed? Am I up to this? Why is the client looking at me in that funny way? He doesn't half annoy me with that habit of poking his spectacles up his face every 30 seconds ... I wonder where his anxiety about his completion date fits into his hierarchy of needs (whatever that meant, never did really understand that – was it something about childhood potty training)? ... What was that he said? Zut! I missed it. Now I'll never pass this assessment....*

This inner dialogue is a bit of a problem. We doubt if you'll ever shut it up altogether, and it can give you helpful information – see p 139. Of course you will miss things. But here is one vital technique for dealing with the problem (as well as asking the client to run over a particular point again as soon as your attention returns from a daydream).

It is called recapitulation – a key ingredient of active listening. You could even define the purpose of the interview as getting to a point where you can recount the client's concerns and the client will say: 'Yes, that's just it' and mean it.

To get to that point you should try to erect milestones at every ... well, mile, we suppose, the equivalent being whenever you want to mark out having got to a particular point.

Here are some milestones from our case study interviews:

> ***A:*** *(five minutes into the (alleged) bakery theft interview):* So let me see if I have got the basic facts straight. You worked for Mr O'Connor for three years, he says money has been missing from the till for a period of six months, and the police arrested you yesterday because they say you put some marked coins into your pocket instead of into the till. Have I got that right?

You have proved you have listened carefully. And your client can correct you, as you wrongly stated that she had worked for this employer for three years.

> **B:** (*to Daniel, our cycle accident client (pointing at map)*): If I've got this clear, you were cycling about 200 yards along High Street, and at this point (*shows on plan*) you looked behind you and moved to this point in the middle of the road.

> **E:** (*to Mrs Shearsby, towards the end of the interview*): I'll get in touch with our probate department, just to reassure myself that your step daughter won't be able to prevent you using your late husband's money for this investment. You have asked me to get in touch with Mr Kader's solicitors to see how quickly Mr Kader is planning to go ahead with the expansion of his business. And just to be absolutely clear that I have understood your instructions clearly, I'll write and confirm what you have told me today, and in particular how you intend to invest the money your husband left you in the business that Mr Kader is setting up. I'll also confirm in the letter the likely costs of the work this firm will be doing for you and the stages when payments will be expected. You are going to sleep on things for a couple of days and confirm to me, after you have got my letter, whether you wish to go ahead in the light of your step daughter's concerns. Now, have I covered everything we've each agreed to do?

You can recap on facts, and agreements on who does what, as our examples above show. You can also recap on emotions as a technique of active listening:

> **Ms Kennedy:** And they think I'll just wait until after completion to get all the mortgage money; they've got a nerve.

> **C:** The delay is upsetting you.

> **Mr Kader:** The thing is, if World Wide Building Society carry out the valuation, I think they will undervalue it, they simply have no good people there any more. I've had nothing but hassle from them over the house.

> **D:** You've lost confidence in the World Wide.

In reflecting back some of the feelings behind the statements made, you are helping the client to feel understood, as well as checking subtly that your understanding of the situation is accurate. Note that you are reflecting back, not judging, or telling the client how they feel. People find it calming to have someone recognise their emotions, and yet they can get angry or defensive if someone tells them what those emotions are – a subtle difference which we hope will become clearer with your increasing experience.

A word linked to the process of recapping is *empathy*. It is a word almost bound to crop up on assessment checklists. A dictionary (*Collins English Dictionary and Thesaurus 1992*) describes this as 'a power of understanding, imaginatively entering into another's feelings'. You will need to demonstrate empathy – it may well be on the assessment checklist on your course. Active listening is a component of empathy – see page 133.

Neighbour describes another technique of rapport building during the early stages of the interview: tuning in. People do need to tune in to each other. If you meet someone at a party, or in your new seminar group, or wherever, it takes time before you get down to talking about the meaning of life or the perpetuities rule. First, you adjust to each other's presence, and take stock with small talk. It is almost like tuning the radio dial as you adjust the way you speak, your posture, your eye contact, your animation, tuning in to the other person's wavelength. The process is usually unconscious, except at a party where perhaps you are having to make an effort and wondering what you can find to say to that interesting looking person in the far corner.

If you fail to tune in, the client may feel discomfort and want to end the relationship. I have seen myself on tape with a client who has a strong regional dialect. I have failed to tune in, which I realised only on reviewing the tape. I appear to be dealing with her questions, but much of the detail I have not grasped. Although the detail was not relevant to the advice I gave, this client never came back. She was entitled to be listened to and hadn't been.

There is probably an optimum wavelength not just for each person, but for each relationship at a particular time. The start of an interview – the greet, seat and small talk section – is actually about tuning in to your client. Your client will also be tuning in to you, but remember who is in control: you. You are the one who needs to make the deliberate effort to tune in to the way your client communicates, not the other way round. If you understand this basic concept, there is no need to explain in detail why use of jargon is usually undesirable, or why you should not dominate the talking, at the beginning of the interview.

So, you understand the concept. How do you now apply it?

Fortunately, you have a lifetime of experience. You simply make conscious and available the behaviours that you actually use all the time. When meeting a new person, you normally choose neutral topics, or topics where you are likely to find agreement rather than disagreement. The weather, the difficulties finding parking, are examples for people you have never met before; the person's health, their family, their holiday, may be suitable for people who you know a little about each other from previous meetings. The idea is that you say something that your client can surely agree with, and you can observe how they behave in 'agreement' mode. They may smile, look you in the face, nod, lean forward.

Be sure such topics are genuinely neutral. For example asking Mr Kader how long he has been in this country can be insensitive, as it betrays assumptions you are making about his background. If these matters turn out to be relevant – for example the client has an immigration problem, or it is clear that there is a problem of understanding each other because of language – you can deal with them as part of the problem-solving.

You are now tuned, partially at least, to recognising how your client expresses agreement. Why do you need to know this? Because many clients appear to agree but in fact they are clueless.

> *C:* So you'll contact the mortgagee to query the retention? I'll deal with getting the transfer drafted and the requisitions on title. Is that OK?

> **Mr Bennett** (*not looking at the solicitor, not nodding, not smiling, in fact withholding all signs of agreement from his body language*)*:* Yes (*meaning 'I don't want to look a fool, I hope this is all over soon'*).

This is bound to happen. There is nothing wrong with having to retune every few moments. The solicitor, noticing that the client is not behaving in 'yes' mode despite his language, can simply start again.

C: I'm not sure that I have explained clearly what we're each going to do next. You've agreed to contact the building society to query the amount they want to keep back until the timber work has been completed – the retention; when do you think you'll have a chance to do that?

Client: I'll see the manager straight away after I leave here.

C: Good, let me know if there's any problem as a result. What I will do is draft the document that I have to send to Mr and Mrs Rigby to sign, which transfers the ownership of the property to you; and I will need to send their solicitor a list of questions called the 'requisitions on title': just a few questions which have to be answered to check that they actually can sell you a proper title to the house, if you know what 'title' means.

Client (*nods, looks at the solicitor*): Yes (*meaning 'yes'*).

Notice in the example that in ensuring the client understood it became necessary to split the two questions, and deal with each separately. It is likely that you will cause confusion if you ask two questions at once, because 'yes' may only apply to the last question asked. In fact if you want to check that you are not straying from your client's wavelength, keep what you say simple and divided into short chunks, and look for/ask for feedback after each chunk.

Unless you are tuned in to your client, the fact that you have said something does not mean that it has been understood.

B: Well, Daniel, there is no chance of getting any settlement of this case until we have a much firmer medical prognosis.

Mr McAuley: (*sits glumly and does not respond*).

B: Well, if you have no further questions, I'll see you after we've got your medical report. Next please.

If the solicitor had tuned in to this client more deliberately, he or she would know that this particular client sometimes copes with any difficulties by becoming withdrawn. You may have concluded from our little exhortation to bring psychology into the interview room that this young man has a hostile attitude to authority figures. You may be wrong, and should always be wary of labelling clients. What you certainly have discovered is that it is hard to win his confidence. Use of words like prognosis may be proof to him of his worst fears: you overwhelm him, intimidate him, confuse him. Of course he will not admit it, but his sullenness gives you the information that you are not in tune.

You cannot achieve miracles. You are not a therapist. If your client has, or wants to overcome, problems with authority figures, that is his issue. But you can at least recognise where your words are wasted, because it is not what you say that counts, it is what is understood. Try again.

B: I know this is all quite confusing and complicated. I know it would help if we could get things sorted out quickly. I'm afraid the law is quite slow. Because we will be trying to get compensation for your injuries, we have to know everything we can about those injuries before we can even think about what the case is worth. That means getting a report from a specialist doctor, and that is going to take some time. Do you understand, Daniel?

Client: What's compensation?

Hooray, you have an intelligent response and a sensible question. So you explain what compensation means, and make a mental note to be careful when you use that word again with new clients.

I mentioned silence earlier, and asked you not to be compelled into filling each silence. It is a time for the client to think – and for you. You may like to tune in to how the client behaves while using a silence to think: early in the interview you can give the client permission (and yourself) not to have to speak, by saying something like: 'I know it will be dificult to think of how it happened immediately. I want to give you a few moments just to collect your thoughts. Just think about what she actually said to you that day for a few moments, and then tell me what you can remember. Take your time....'

While your client is occupied thinking, reflecting, you can observe how he behaves: look at his eyes, as they probably focus inwards (or on some distant, or non-existent point); observe how the signals change as he comes out of the reflection and shows that he is ready to speak to you. You have now tuned in to how the client is behaving when trying to reflect or recall. Treat those signals as a 'do not disturb' sign, and wait until that sign is removed. Bear with it as long as you can, then knock gently, for example by asking, 'Are you ready to tell me what you think/remember? Or do you need a little more time?'

Another aspect of the use of silence which may contribute to your discomfort is the perceived length of a silence. You can try a simple exercise during a video practice. Create an opportunity for a silence, along the lines indicated, by giving both yourself and the client a period for reflection, and recall how long it seemed to last (do not time it). When you watch it on the video, time it. If you have no video, ask a colleague to time you. What is the difference? You are likely to have overestimated the length of the silence, possibly by a huge margin. People who are feeling uncomfortable think the silence is dragging on; to the outside observer it may have been a few comfortable seconds. Be careful not to jump in if it is clear, or even possible, that your client needs the time.

Let us return to the task of listening actively. We have seen many of the obstacles to achieving this.

First, you may fail to see it as your task, and see it as the client's fault if she doesn't tell a clear story.

Secondly, hidden agendas: for example you are in a tearing hurry and do not have time to listen, or the client is telling you about one thing but actually anxious about another.

Thirdly, the client appears (to you) quite unlikeable.

Fourthly, the client is so obviously seeking your approval that your ability to listen (your regard for the client, to return to the Carl Rogers phrase) dries up (*if she asks me one more time whether it was the right thing to do to agree to a 5% deposit, I'll throw Emmett on Title at her and scatter her title deeds over her grave!*).

Fifthly, you may be quite formidable to the client. Just like doctors have rituals, like covering themselves in coats and stethoscopes while their patients are stripped in a public ward wearing someone else's pyjamas, lawyers have rituals: big desks, long words, and keeping clients waiting. We all know who is important, and we don't feel comfortable sharing our feelings with Such an Important Person.

You can try and dismantle some of these obstacles – although however approachable you are, centuries of self-important behaviour by your predecessors may linger in the folk memory of your overawed client. With experience your detachment grows, and these obstacles seem less significant to you as a result. The deliberate use of listening techniques helps you to achieve detachment.

The techniques are simple: smile, nod, encourage with words or gestures: 'yes, uh huh, of course, go on, I see, really?' Lean forwards more than backwards. Look at your client for as long as it feels comfortable. Reflect back your understanding of what he has said, or conveyed without saying. Basically, care for the well-being of your client and be interested in this problem.

Active listening is the beginning of an empathic relationship.

Empathy is sometimes confused with sympathy. The *Collins* dictionary defines empathy as:

> '1. Feeling for another in pain etc. 2. Compassion, pity. 3. Sharing of emotion, interest, desire, etc.'

Can you tell the difference? Sympathy implies involvement, a stepping over the boundaries that should separate the two parties to the professional relationship. Sympathy is a very common pitfall for the beginner, and it is hard to explain at first why it is inappropriate. To say 'I understand how you feel' is dangerous. Do you? Do you need to say you understand to prove how good you are at interviewing? If you actually understand, it shows. Often the person best suited to tell the student lawyer why it was inappropriate is the person who role played the client: ask the 'client' afterwards.

Likewise, you say to a client: 'that must have been terrible' before your client has said how terrible it was. There is a risk that you are no longer reflecting the client's emotions, but defining them. But no-one likes to be told how they feel, and this becomes a barrier to understanding, not an aid.

Distress needs to come out, and you have played your part if you allow this to happen. You can encourage the expression of the emotion or distress: you do not have to 'deal' with it, your job is not to make the distress go away. Nor is it your job to offer sympathy. Attempts to sweep distress under the psychological carpet will not help the client or the tackling of the problem: 'There's no need to worry ... I'm sure everything will work out ... I doubt if it's as bad as all that ... I know exactly how you feel' do not make the client feel better, and may make him feel misunderstood.

Principle 6: Anticipate common problems

Problem 1: The client who is not revealing everything

Academics who write role plays sometimes assume that the core of the skill of interviewing is to uncover hidden agendas. They set a task which is like a crossword puzzle – they know the right answer, but you have to discover it. Most situations that a client brings are in fact straightforward, and there is no subplot. But in almost every situation there are some aspects of the case that you might think relevant that the client does not reveal. For example Mr McAuley in the cycle accident may not wish you to know that he may have given no hand signals. He probably does not understand that if this eventually comes out his case is damaged more than if he had told you straight away.

Clients in criminal cases can be reluctant to admit – may even have forgotten – their past convictions. You need to know these to prepare the case, both in case they may be revealed during the trial, and also for bail, legal aid and sentencing. You have to probe deeper than the client appears to want. You will have to explain that you are prying for a legitimate reason.

> *A:* I am going to have to ask you something which I have to ask every client who has been charged with an offence. Have you ever been in trouble with the police before?

> *Mrs Evans:* Yes.

> *A:* It will help me if you give me all the information you can remember. (If persuasion is needed.) The police have usually got the information on their computer anyway and if it comes up in court I don't want to be taken by surprise.

Someone may be apparently withholding information because of the need to protect someone else: in a criminal case, someone who might also get into trouble. They may be withholding information simply because what they have done was, in their eyes, stupid, and they don't want to appear stupid in front of such an important person as a lawyer.

The key issue is to cultivate your awareness of hidden issues. There are no simple solutions to winkling out the information. For a start you only think it is being hidden; you do not know, and have to be sensitive. Also if the client, or witness, is reluctant, the reasons will be different, and even if there is a technique for every reason you have to make an accurate guess at the reason.

Here are some possible reasons for withholding, and possible approaches from the solicitor.

■ *I'll look a fool if I make a fuss about this*

Possible approaches:

- ☐ 'I've known people who this has happened to who took their case to court and won ...'

- ☐ 'This is clearly a very important issue for you, and I can see that you are very concerned ...'

- ☐ 'You have given me some extremely useful information so far, and I'm just wondering if there is anything else you think I ought to know ...'

- ☐ 'Some people find it embarrassing to talk about personal issues of this sort, but I can see from our conversation so far that you are doing your best to be open and frank with me ...'

☐ 'I think you handled the situation very sensibly ...'

■ *It's not important, I'm wasting your time*

Possible solution:

☐ 'This is a very important issue and I'm impressed that you have sought advice so soon ...'

■ *I'm only going to talk about what I think relevant*

Possible solution:

☐ 'It may seem strange to you, but one of the areas we need to discuss is your business partner's wife's attitude to having her house remortgaged, and this is relevant because ...' (or possibly you change the subject and come back to it later – make a note of the need to come back).

■ *Reason for reluctance unknown*

Possible approach:

☐ 'You seem to be reluctant to talk about your children, Mrs Shearsby. Am I right? Do you want to tell me why? It may help me to help you.'

Of course, it is legitimate to argue, tactfully, with the client. 'Painful as it may be, you are going to have to tell me about the arguments you have been having with Mr O'Connor about working Saturdays and getting more pay because otherwise I cannot advise you about how we can defend the case in court. I may need to cross-examine Mr O'Connor to try to bring out the fact that he has a grudge against you and to do this ...'

It may be that the client does not understand that what is said to you is confidential. You will not disclose the contents of such conversations to anyone else without permission. You should find an opportunity at some stage in the interview to raise this issue, and to make sure your client understands it correctly. Confidentiality does not in fact mean the same as: none of this will ever go any further. It need go no further, but you also have to explain that to do the job for the client – in court, or in negotiations, in drafting – you may need to reveal the information that the client wants to keep secret; or that other people may reveal it anyway. So do not give the client the expectation that what is discussed in a solicitor's office is sealed in some verbal tomb for ever.

When you explain the right to confidentiality, it is, incidentally, wrong to say or imply that all contents of all communications with the solicitor will be confidential. There are some exceptions, such as a client saying she wishes to invest money obtained from drug trafficking or saying something which indicates to you that a child may be at risk of abuse, or a serious criminal offence is about to be committed.

If you are interviewing a witness as opposed to a client, there is no promise of confidentiality: all information obtained must be put at the disposal of the client. If a witness says 'Can I speak to you off the record' the answer, before the witness even starts to speak, is 'No'.

Problem 2: Not knowing the answer to the client's problem

Great! You recognised it instead of kidding yourself that you know everything. This is a theme which I looked at early in the chapter, so there are only a few points to add now.

You are rarely going to be able to solve the client's problem on the spot. It is unlikely that you know enough law or procedure, and it is probable that you lack sufficient experience to predict how things will turn out even if your law is sound. This is true for all self-aware lawyers, and an expectation that you can deliver straight away what you think the client wants will lead you into trouble. Barristers of course have been instructed in advance on what the problem is about, so 'I don't know' is less appropriate (until a problem is raised which was outside the instructions).

Do you think you will look more authoritative if you give out unequivocal answers and definitive advice? That was what your undergraduate law has probably led you to believe would be your role: to every problem a clear solution. But remember the marks you score as a degree student? 50% gives you a respectable degree, 70% a brilliant award. Yet here you are handing out advice with 100% confidence. The confidence is misplaced. It is, undeniably, misplaced if you assert the answer with more confidence than you actually feel. It is dangerously misplaced if you feel a degree of confidence which your experience does not justify: you are bordering on arrogance then.

You do not yet know enough to make any confident predictions about any factors outside your own control. Within your own control may be things like: I will send this in the post tonight; I will contact the Jones' solicitor right now; I will issue proceedings tomorrow.

- *Have I got a strong case? (Doctor, am I going to live?)* 'It is too early to say at this stage; I need to look up a number of points of law, and talk to a more experienced colleague, but I hope to be able to do so within a few days and will phone you within the week.'

- *Will you need to interview my partner?* 'I don't know yet, there are a number of aspects of this problem that I need to think about and probably discuss with you again at a later date. But for now, it would be good to have his name and address, and a phone number where I can contact him? Do you have these to hand?'

- *Will the court need to know about my conviction in 1998?* 'I'm going to need to refresh my memory on the rules of whether courts can refer to a person's convictions; I'll certainly have given this some thought by the time we next meet.'

Problem 3: Having to break bad news

You are not only a fact-gatherer and problem-solver. You are an adviser for your client. Breaking good news is not taxing. Anyone can play Father Christmas. 'The opposition has just admitted liability and offered to pay you £20,000 plus costs....' 'I've just had the surveyor's report and there is only minimal work to be done on the property....' 'There is no way the police officer will be allowed to give that evidence of your confession in court.' (Are you sure from research or sound knowledge before you say this?)

Breaking bad news is more difficult. We saw that clients sometimes withhold information; maybe solicitors are equally often to blame. Countless clients complain that they had no idea how much the solicitor was going to charge; they did not realise that instructing a valuer, an engineer or a barrister, for example, would have to be paid for by them; that winning the case did not mean recovery of all costs; that the draft contract describes the vendors as trustees and not as beneficial owners. You decide that you should not tell the client of these little local difficulties, and you will sort the problem out in time – and then you fail to sort it out and find it even more difficult to tell the client. I recall in my articles advising a client to settle a matter by making a payment into court. The advice was probably sound, except that I failed to advise him as to the cost consequences if it was accepted (which at the time I had never been taught). When I realised that my client was going to face a shock, what did I do? I put off the bad news. So the shock was even worse when it finally occurred. Don't do this.

This sort of situation can lead the adviser to mumble, omit, or gloss over. The temptation is clear. But there is one rule which I wish I had learned the easy way (that is, from someone else's experience rather than from my own). Take it on board now. A solicitor does not have to achieve for the client what the client wants. Do not promise what you cannot deliver.

The client comes wanting you to win the case; smooth the path of the conveyance or partnership ... and so on. The client will naturally hope that you can achieve this. But you can only achieve what the factual background and legal framework make possible. Do not judge yourself a failure if you cannot achieve more. Do not let your client retain expectations, therefore, that you cannot fulfil. Bad news, for the client, is the difference between expectation and reality: keep the gap narrow by keeping expectations realistic from the start.

But when you have bad news to deliver, do so directly and sensitively:

> *To Mrs Evans you will have to say:* I'm afraid to say that, looking at all the evidence that we can produce, and assuming the court believes the police officers and Mr O'Connor, the case does not look good. I think it is going to be very difficult to get an acquittal.

> *To Ms Kennedy and Mr Bennett*: I've done my calculations, as I'm sure you have, and if the sellers do not lower the price, you are going to have to find another £2,000 to get the work carried out before the building society agrees to release the £1,500 retention. Not good news I'm afraid.

> *To Mr Kader:* I'm sorry, but it does look as if there is a possible conflict of interest and I cannot advise both you and Mr Khan. I've thought hard about this and, you see, if I advise Mr Khan to mortgage his home to raise money to put into this business, and he says: 'Do you advise me to go ahead?', I will have to advise him to think very carefully about the risks involved, to study the accounts carefully, to ask awkward questions and so on. I don't think that would be compatible with my role of doing my utmost to get him to agree to your terms as soon as possible.

Problem 4: Having difficulty concentrating

I have already referred to the difficulty everyone has in maintaining full concentration. Admit it if you have missed something the client has said.

Here is an insight from Roger Neighbour which may help you. He calls his book about medical consultations *The Inner Consultation*. Oversimplifying his thesis, he describes two processes at work. There are the outward observable events, some of which can be captured on video or by observation – the dialogue, the body language in particular. At the same time each person is having an inner dialogue. *I wonder if I am making a good impression? Is now the point to renew eye contact? I wonder if the employer actually planted the coins – should I suggest that yet? I have to finish this interview by 12.00 because I want to pop down to the bank before lunch.* Some of the inner dialogue is irrelevant. Try to recognise as soon as you start on such a train of thought and try to refocus.

But some of it is a source of useful information. Neighbour talks of the two hemispheres of the brain: the right, which is primarily concerned with feeling, with intuition, with impressions; and the left, which controls in particular the rational processes, such as language and reasoning. Both hemispheres are at work all the time. But there is only one conscious mind. Sometimes the right hemisphere takes charge and gets you to smile, scowl, jump to conclusions or feel angry; sometimes the left hemisphere's work is most available to you, as you conduct a careful analysis of the legal issues involved. Listen to both. There is a clear place for the intuitive information, although as it comes up you may be dealing with another task. Stop for long enough to make a mental or written note of ideas that are generated; pay attention to what is going on in your head and allow both observers of this interview – right and left – to take a turn.

This is not the solution to improved concentration. It helps to explain lapses. Is there a solution? Some obvious points: prepare yourself, so that you are not going to be hungry, so that you are reasonably calm, so that you have anticipated things that may be coming up in the interview; allow yourself to admit you were distracted when it happens; be aware of the different messages that your inner voice is throwing up, and take time to pause and respond to them rather than repressing them entirely. Finally, watch your performance on video as soon as possible: when you felt your concentration going – did it show? How long did it last? What effect did it appear to have on the client's behaviour? What could you do differently to avoid it happening again?

The inner dialogue can also be useful in itself. What your right (emotional) brain keeps sending up to your consciousness uninvited may help you deal with the situation. If you are getting messages such as discomfort or anger about being with this client, you can first choose not to react (that is, you remain professionally detached) and, secondly, using your left brain's analytical powers, you can recognise that if you are uncomfortable and angry, perhaps the client feels that way too. Also you can bring the feelings to the surface for the client: 'How did that make you feel?' or 'I get the impression that telling me about being in the police station is making you feel uncomfortable ...'.

Problem 5: Timekeeping and the waffler

What are you going to do with the waffler? In practice time is money. In an assessed interview time is short. How you deal with this depends on whether you are expected to complete the whole interview in the time available, or whether you are allowed to demonstrate competence during the first part of the interview only? My clear preference is that you should learn not to rush; that to be thorough takes time, and trainees need more, not less, time. If your assessors want you to solve problems before you are ready you are going to acquire some bad habits. Unlearn these as soon as the assessment is done.

You must be clear from the start if you are expected to finish the interview or not. If you are not, then you may only get as far as beginning to build the relationship, starting to identify the problem, and offering a few clues that you are grasping some of the legal issues. That ought to be satisfactory, but you should ask what is expected, and obtain feedback from those who will eventually assess you, as well as your peers.

If the whole thing – like Dr Who's Tardis – must be contained within a tiny space, you somehow have to appear less rushed than you are. I believe that no-one can achieve much more than a very preliminary diagnosis of the issues involved in 20 minutes, and that any advice and predictions are speculative before thorough investigation is carried out. Therefore my advice is to set realistic targets and share them with the client:

> 'Thank you very much for coming in, Ms Kennedy. I am afraid that we only have a very limited time available to discuss things today, in fact only 30 minutes, which I hope the receptionist made clear to you when you phoned. I think it is likely that, if you want me to do any work for you after today, we will have to meet again to go over things in more detail. For today what I want is an overall impression, and to identify as far as I can if anything needs to be done urgently, and perhaps to be able to give you some very preliminary advice about what we can do.'

Then during the interview you will have to be very careful with the timekeeping, and tell the client how you are going to use the available time:

> 'That has been extremely useful, Mr Kader, in giving me a clear picture of your business plans; we've unfortunately only got five minutes before I have to be away, and so I think what we need to concentrate on now is....'

And when you have only one or two minutes left, you must start final recapping:

> 'OK then, we are agreed that you will pop the completed legal aid application in to me tomorrow, and that we will have a further meeting next week; I will be writing to the police in the meanwhile to find out who the driver of the car was, and to see if we can get an accident report, and you will be working out what all of your travel costs to and from the hospital have been. I'll write and confirm this, and also the advice I have given you about legal aid and how our firm will handle this case. Is there anything left that you want to mention?'

This topic, of guiding you how to conduct the very short initial interview, caused some real difficulty in writing this book. Richard took the view that no-one should even think of planning an interview with a new client and not leave enough time to go over all the facts and the queries raised. So what is the point of telling students how to do what we don't advocate? And I agreed – but the LPC/BVC assessment is not the real world. Nor is your degree assessment. If you are given too short a time, you may have to conclude your interview bluntly rather than subtly as time pressures build up.

Now, back to our waffler? If you have only 15 minutes, almost anyone can seem like a waffler. I have stressed throughout that you are in control, and that the signs of this become more obvious as the interview progresses. The waffler, like anyone else, must have the chance to speak without too much interruption in the early stages. Your intuition will indicate to you during the early stages that you have someone who is finding it hard to focus on what are going to be (for your task) the relevant issues. When it comes to time to take control – and don't leave it too long – you will have to be clear, but tactful, about the direction you now want the interview to go in. Be direct about the shortage of time, and use focused questions earlier in the interview than you would have with the less loquacious client. Form some of the direct questions in your mind as you listen to the client in the early stages. You may have to be more assertive than feels comfortable in directing the client's attention to the issues you need to discuss. 'I'm sorry, Mrs Shearsby, we don't have the time to go into all of that today, as we are very short of time. What I do need to focus on for now is. ...'

Principle 6: Show that you have a structured approach

'You cannot control and plan it unless you know exactly what you are aiming for; nor can you be certain afterwards that you have achieved your objective if you were not certain what it was in the first place.'

(From Binder and Bergman *Fact Investigation, from Hypothesis to Proof.*)

If the discussion so far has been of any use, you will not find any difficulty with devising a structure for the interview. Remember that while the final decisions are for the client to control, the way issues are brought up, analysed and repackaged is for you to determine. You are in control of the structure. Let it show, both for assessment purposes and in practice. For example, after a few 'tuning in' exchanges about the weather or did you find my office OK? etc, perhaps after the client has given a brief outline of the problem and you have done some active listening, you suggest your own agenda:

'Well, Ms Kennedy and Mr Bennett. That has been very useful to me, and I have some idea of what I now need to do in the time available. What I often find useful is to get my client to go over the problem in their own words in a bit more detail; then I will need to take down a few basic facts and check these over with you to ensure that what I note down is accurate; then we'll have to have a go at working out what needs to be done, which will include a bit of time for me to explain any law that may be involved; then towards the end we will have to agree whether there is any work to be done, who is going to do it, what it will cost, and to check whether we have left anything out. ...'

Or:

'So, first of all, you've told me it is about your cycle accident. Why don't you tell me about how it happened? I'll be taking some notes in a minute, but first it would help me just to listen and get an overall picture. ...'

Some writers prepare long lists of stages the interview must go through. These are perhaps helpful, with the warning that you cannot interview by numbers. Interviewing is a matter of forming a relationship, and you have to judge for yourself what is appropriate at each point, not necessarily go onto the next point of a list. As Neighbour has said:

'If I were to give you a list of do's and don'ts at this stage (even if I knew what to put on the list) I think I know what would happen: you would start to criticise yourself for not doing everything you were told. You might criticise me or my list for being too complicated. Finally you might start to criticise the patients for not making things easy for you.'

He advises doctors to be satisfied that they can recognise good and bad consultations, and refuses to prescribe a checklist of what to do and when.

Neighbour nevertheless uses a five-point plan, which contains the essential ingredients of a consultation. Although my plan is different, because I am writing for lawyers, his five points contain a useful overview. The doctor (lawyer) should go through these stages:

1   Connecting – that is, establishing a relationship, and hearing what the patient has to say.

2   Summarising – putting what the patient has described into a format that the doctor can give back with the added value of the doctor's understanding.

3   Hand over – giving the patient back the power and responsibility to deal with whatever comes next in the plan for tackling the problem.

4   Safety netting – checking that the patient has understood, can deal with what has apparently been agreed, and that nothing that should have been discussed has been omitted.

5   Housekeeping – space and facilities for the doctor to recover and be ready to deal with full attention with the next patient.

You can choose your structure from many different writers. For example Avrom Sherr (*Client Interviewing for Lawyers*) has 13 stages for a first interview, set out under three major headings: Listening, Questioning and Advising. Mike Wolfe, in a workshop for the Legal Action Group, suggests five: Listen; Analyse; Investigate; Decide and Implement. Actually, we all end up covering the same ground in different ways. We suggest a model for the first interview (and in fact for the continuing relationship) with 11 points:

1   Preparation

2   Connecting

3   Establishing the legal framework – costs and client care

4   Listening

5   Identifying the issues

6   Questioning

7   Analysing

8   Summarising

9   Handing over

10   Closing the interview

11   Housekeeping

This is not an 11 point linear progression. You will have to revisit some points on the journey several times. But do not pass any by completely. Like a very complicated treasure hunt: you have to check in at all clues at some stage, and possibly in a set order, but when you begin to find you have not got some of the clues right, you have to go back.

Stage 1: Preparation

This will take three aspects: preparing your physical environment, to the extent that you have some control; preparing yourself; and preparing any materials you may need.

The physical environment can create the relationship, or at least influence it strongly. I do not offer right answers, and in any event in an assessed interview where you are on a conveyor belt in front of the video camera, you may have less control than you would wish. But you must decide whether you wish to create a formal impression, with you and the client on opposite sides of the desk; or an informal impression, with no barriers, perhaps with easy chairs (but consider where you will put all the papers that you may need to work with). Watch yourself in practice interviews and decide which sorts of layout bring out the best in you as interviewer. Once in practice you will have control over things like the tidiness of your desk; flowers; dead coffee cups – or fresh supplies for you and your client.

The way you dress is part of the physical environment. People expect lawyers to dress formally, perhaps conservatively. Break the mould if you wish, but do so knowing that the way you dress forms part of the way someone will judge you.

Prepare yourself: Solicitors may – and barristers will – have been given some advance indication of what the meeting is about. You may have been given enough information to look up the relevant law and procedure. But you may only know that the interview will concern a general area, such as 'wants to form a partnership'. Whatever advance indication you are given, you must use. For if your interviewing competence is to be assessed, your legal knowledge must be there to support you.

Prepare the types of questions you will ask. You could even have some jotted down (though beware a wooden performance, like a child reading out loud at school). There are checklists at the end of the chapter, and there is more on research preparation in Chapter 4.

Get yourself calm. A few moments of quiet, with your attention focused on steady breathing, can help. If you can find somewhere, a quiet lie down can calm you. Work out how you can best relax in the available facilities. (There was brief consideration of relaxation in Chapter 2.)

Finally, prepare anything you are going to need to have with you. In real practice, you will have an office full of relevant forms, checklists and reference materials; in the assessed exercise you may have only limited access to these facilities, and probably none during the interview itself. Do you need a legal aid form and green form key card for assessing means? Do you need a checklist as an aide memoire? (See end of chapter for basic points that we think you should obtain in an interview in each of the core subjects.) Is there any previous file material that you should have available or have read? Clients naturally think you do not care if you have not studied their file. Have you made sure no phone calls will come through? Have you got a working pen which will not run out of ink? Do you have a box of toys for the client with a young child? Richard brought in the toys after his pot plant was destroyed by a can of coke poured in by a bored child. You could save your plants and get the toys now.

Stage 2: Connecting

This point on the journey is most important at the beginning, but needs to be returned to frequently. This is where you tune in. This is where the client dominates the available time, almost to the exclusion of the solicitor. You are already aware of rapport-building techniques.

At the start of the interview there are some simple formalities which must not be ignored. Students in role plays tend to be very casual about introductions, perhaps because they and the client are not thoroughly in role. How is the client going to get from door to seat? Are you going to offer a hand to shake, or not? Decide how you will tackle these small issues before you start. When will you start talking? Is there a long pause as you both walk from the door to the seats, or have you found some way of starting a conversation as you walk? Where is the dog, the child, the friend going to sit? (Should a friend be present during a confidential interview?)

You must make sure about each other's names; do not mumble them, do not give your name at a point where the client is preoccupied with something else, like taking her seat, or starting to talk about the problem; spell your name to emphasise it, or offer to write it down. Who are you? A pupil? A trainee? A solicitor? Do not, as many students do in an attempt at informality, give only your first name – your client is entitled to know your full name for future use. Who is supervising your work? If it is an initial interview, give yourself a lead in such as 'Very pleased to see you Mrs Evans; I don't think we've met before; my name is.... That's spelt.... I've got a card with it written down here. (*Students – you probably haven't, but could spell out your name instead.*) I'm a trainee solicitor in this firm....'

But do not talk for too long to start with. That will set a tone of solicitor dominance. Your talking at the beginning should be aimed at making the client feel at ease, and encouraging her or him to talk. I strongly recommend some ice-breaking chit chat, for tuning in purposes. This can seem a little insincere in a role play – 'Have any trouble getting here today?', for example, when both parties know they have been pulled out of the same classroom, can seem hollow. It rings truer in real life. Nevertheless it is worth using even hollow-sounding techniques and watching yourself on video – perhaps they come across better than you thought. Another opening gambit can be: 'Is this the first time you've been to this firm?' If the answer is yes, you can follow with 'You may be a little apprehensive about what is going to happen', which can lead in to you explaining what is to follow.

Another neutral gambit is: 'Hope I haven't kept you waiting too long'. It doesn't matter if you are starting bang on time, the client may have arrived early, and knows that you care about their time as well as your own.

And the weather: what is it like today? Even if you wrongly state it, in a moment of confusion, nothing hangs on it. It is a traditional British way of starting a conversation, designed to be without emotional importance. Both sides know the lines that are written for them, and it gives you both a chance to hear each other talk about something that doesn't matter to your consultation.

Whatever else happens in this introductory period, make sure that your client knows where to sit, and that he or she has had the opportunity to take off any outdoor clothing that they wish to remove (check beforehand where you will then place it). Who sits down first? It is courteous to wait until the client is seated before sitting yourself down.

What is your body language at this point? You are both seated. The client will probably be looking to you for cues. Are you leaning back or forward? Looking towards the client or away? Showing interest or lack of interest?

Despite the best laid plans, things do not work out exactly. The client may not be interested in the weather, the local parking or the test match score. He or she may start talking about the problem even before you have introduced yourself. What does that tell you? It tells you that the client's most important need is to unload the problem. OK, listen for a while, then at what you judge an appropriate moment, try to assert your own agenda. For example, Mrs Shearsby is saying after your 'good morning':

'It's about my husband's will. You see he made a will a few years ago after we married, and then he died last month and I really want to do things the way he would have wanted; but of course there's Christine and she thinks the money is rightly hers and I suppose she's right; after all he would have given it to her if he hadn't married me and we married late in life and the trouble was we never got on, me and Christine. I don't know why; we were two grown adults, but somehow ... oh I don't know, maybe it was because Brian just refused to get involved and just went back to his newspaper if Christine ever started to try and talk to me about things. That was the trouble with Brian, though now he's died I shouldn't be disrespectful...'.

And so it may go on for a while yet. This is actually very useful information, and you should try to store up some of the key points to help you through the analysis that will follow. It is not the time to interrupt, not yet. There will come a time when the client's flow slows, or where you are given a space to indicate your response, and then it is time for you to claim your responsibility, which is to structure the interview. For example:

'That's a very helpful overview, Mrs Shearsby. Can we just stop there for a moment?

You have given me a lot of very useful information already, and I intend to go over all the points you have raised in some detail in a few moments. I wonder if we could just pause for a few moments, though? I want to make sure that I've got your name right – it's Emily Shearsby, isn't it? Good, I'll just jot that down ... and my name, I'm not sure if anyone has given that to you already, it's [D]. Now Mrs Shearsby, what I often find helpful when I'm seeing someone for the first time is ...'

and here you have a chance to describe how you intend to conduct the interview.

In the early stages you will need to obtain your client's address, phone number (day and evening, but always ask whether you can phone a person at work). Write these down, and check back with the client that you have got any awkward spellings correctly. This is especially important if you do not speak the same dialect as your client. You may choose to do this before or after the client has started to talk about the reason for coming. I say choose, but it is wrong to interrupt a client in full flow just to get these details; and it is often a reasonable ice-breaker, to give you and the client a chance to settle in together as you deal with these formalities. We have provided a checklist of questions at the end of this chapter, to be used as an aide memoire, not a rigid drill.

It may be tempting to comment on someone's name. 'Ah, Winifred, I had a great aunt of that name; it's not so common nowadays.' Are you treading across boundaries that should be respected? What right have you to make that observation? (Again there is no right answer, just be sensitive.) Be careful with an observation that might appear to be prying: 'Mr Kader, yes, pleased to meet you. That's an Indian name isn't it? Is that where you're from?' Where Mr Kader is from is irrelevant until the context of the interview indicates otherwise. Anyway, is an interview a place for satisfying the curiosity of the lawyer?

Stage 3: Establishing the professional framework – costs and client care

There are many aspects of costs and client care which you may need to build into your checklist. We do not expect that you will deal with all of them together. As a student you may be conducting a role play in which you are instructed not to discuss charging, or to assume it has already been agreed. As a barrister your fees will have been discussed between your solicitor and your clerk, and then explained by the solicitor to the client. It is therefore not a necessary stage in the conference, although an understanding of how the client is meeting his or her legal costs is a vital part of the framework in which you are operating.

1   If you are training to be, or role playing, a solicitor: Make sure the client understands the position on costs. The professional practice rules require you to explain this (see further chapter 6 – drafting and writing). You need to cover the present interview (for which those setting the exercise may have given you a figure) and future costs. For this the professional practice rules say either give a quote or state the basis on which your costs will be calculated. The rules also require you to deliver bills or details of accumulated costs at least every six months of a retainer. Your client is entitled to be told what the terms for payment will be, and the mechanisms for disputing any bill. It is common for solicitors to add on to an hourly charging rate a percentage for 'uplift' or 'care and conduct'. This means that the client pays, say, 50% on top of the basic charging rate (the profit element). The client is entitled to know in advance that costs mean costs plus X%, plus VAT at 17.5%, and that disbursements come on top (disbursements is a word which will need explaining – it means those costs which you have to pass on to your client, such as paying for a barrister or an expert witness).

If the costs are to be met by the client, we hope in a role play you will have been told a reasonable charging rate rather than being left to invent one. If you are not briefed about your charging rate or the total estimated costs of the work, you can select one as follows:

☐   a figure plucked out of the air – but we would mark you down for this unless convinced by the evidence that this was a carefully considered figure which the client was entitled to rely on and which could be quoted back at you on a taxation of your costs;

☐   an admission that you haven't got a clue (which leaves the question unanswered); or

☐   an admission that it may well be a lot of money, but you lack the experience to make even a rough estimate, but that you will talk the case over with your principal and let the client have your best estimate as soon as possible;

☐   an evasion of the issue, which is what some solicitors still do. ('In studies a few years ago more than half the profession were found not to be complying in full with practice rule 15 of the standard': John Aucott *Law Society's Gazette* 90/44, 1 December 1993, p 2. He goes on to urge: 'Take a deep breath. Forget your training, your inherent caution and embarrassment and talk about money. Do not give estimates which are hopelessly out but tell the truth as you see it.' And: 'If a client is going to argue about the costs of a matter, let him or her do so at the begining, before you have spent any of your money on his or her job.')

2   Solicitors: You have a professional obligation to advise the client about the availability of legal aid; therefore in an initial interview you must consider this point, unless you are instructed before the exercise that legal aid is not available – for example a member of staff has already carried out the financial assessment, or it is an area for which legal aid is not available. If such an instruction is not given, you must be prepared in your knowledge of legal aid forms and procedures – the *Legal Aid Handbook* (updated every year) is the best single source of information.

Take into the interview a green form and current key card. You may have been taught how to use it, but not necessarily how to explain it. Does your client actually understand what two hours' worth of advice and assistance means? The difference between initial advice and legal aid for representation?

If you find yourself having to explain the availability and scope of the legal aid system, you must be able to explain contributions from income and capital, the process of financial assessment, and the grounds for granting a certificate or order. In a civil case, you will have to understand the operation of the statutory charge, and promise to follow up this advice with written confirmation of how the scheme affects your client.

3   If you are submitting a civil legal aid application for the client, explain contributions out of income and capital, the statutory charge, the likely time period before a decision, the need for co-operating with the Legal Aid Board, and the costs consequences of winning or losing. Do not even think of going into an interview about a civil litigation matter unless you are confident about explaining these. There are also two leaflets: the *Statutory Charge*, and *What Happens Next* which you should not only understand, but give to your client.

If you are submitting a criminal legal aid application, advise your client about weekly contributions from income and the possibility of a capital payment too.

Advice on legal aid should be confirmed after the interview. Tell your client you will be writing, and if anything is unclear now, please ask, and if on receiving the letter anything is unclear, please ask again.

4   If you are going to advise the client to proceed under a contingency fee arrangement, that will require careful explanation and follow up. The details of such an arrangement are covered in chapter 4, as contingeny fees are a topic our solicitor decides to do some research into.

5   Explain to the client your status (dealt with under Connecting above) and the firm's client care procedure. This means the client has to be told who, if they are unhappy about anything, they should contact. Details of the requirements are given in rule 15 of the Solicitors' Practice Rules. The imaginary firm you are working for should have a complaints procedure, preferably in a brochure which you hand to the client. You

should also let the client know who can be contacted if you are ever unavailable – for example, your principal.

6   Promise to follow up your advice in writing, making clear what you have agreed to do, the costs advice you have given, and what the client has agreed to do. This is not a substitute for clear point-by-point explanations face to face, but a safety net for both of you. If it is in writing, and unambiguously drafted, and confirmed, the client cannot blame you later for misunderstanding his or her instructions. If the client thinks you have recalled it wrongly, he or she can correct your mistake in time.

All of these points are not our advice, they are requirements of practice. For more detail see Chapter 13 of the Law Society's *Guide to the Professional Conduct of Solicitors*, which is part of the course material for the LPC. Barristers cannot ignore costs, just because the main onus is on solicitors. The costs of legal assistance are one of the major factors influencing a client's decisions. You need to know what it is costing your client to be speaking to you and to be following any advice you may offer. Degree students may be told to take costs into account, or to ignore them – but in learning about how your advice relates to real clients you have to allow the client to make economically sensible decisions about his or her legal rights and remedies. You need to be aware of costs of the actions you recommend.

Stage 4: Listening

In the early stages the client wants a good listening to. That in itself will help discharge some of the discomfort at coming to see you and the emotion attached to the problem. Clients of solicitors, patients of doctors, clients of therapists, all report a positive feeling if they have been listened to and taken seriously; stage one of that is to allow the client to have their say in terms that they find significant, without any packaging from the professional. Note-taking is itself a form of packaging of the client's experience – hence you should consider carefully when to start.

Clients rehearse what they are going to say. You do the same when you go to the doctor or bank manager. Do them the courtesy of listening without interruption or other signs of discouragement.

There comes a stage when you have listened, encouraged, heard a description from the client of what brings her or him to your office. It may have lasted only a few seconds, or ten minutes: ideally it will not go on longer, because you will run out of time to do what is your big task, to rearrange ideas into a shape that your legal knowledge and experience suggests, to offer solutions to problems. But ideally it will be a stage lasting longer than a few seconds; it is the only chance you have to hear what the client has to say before you have stamped your own observations onto the account. Even by saying: 'tell me a little more about the financial arrangements for the partnership' you have indicated to the client what is and what is not worth going into, before you have heard what the client thinks significant.

In these early stages you are doing two things: first, allowing the client to feel listened to, what Mike Wolfe, of Stoke on Trent CAB in a Legal Action Group workshop on client interviewing called 'venting' – getting the charge and emotion out into the open. Secondly, just plain listening, attentively and encouragingly but without directing, allows you to store up issues that you can come back to in due course when you seek to impose your sense of order onto the material you have received. 'Right, you mentioned earlier that you have had some arguments about the money with your husband's daughter. Let me check if I may that I have got an accurate picture of what you told me? Christine is not your own daughter, she is aged 28, and her own mother died some years back. She has been telling you that the property your husband left to you is rightly hers, and she is very worried about you letting it to Mr Kader.' In this way you are telling your client very clearly that you have listened, that you have taken her seriously when she was talking to you.

You are going to have to take notes at some stage during the interview. Solicitors sometimes assume that the client does not mind you taking notes, and they are probably right. But you should explain why notes are needed and confirm your client's agreement when the point to do so has arrived. For note-taking is an impediment to an easy relationship if one party is writing as the other speaks. The writer clearly exercises a dominant position, and can even use the pauses which result to control the pace of the interview. I have no objection to this dynamic; I only wish to make you aware that starting to take notes affects the relationship, and to ask you to make this overt: first in your own mind, and then in your relationship to the client. When you initially ask the client for her name, you can say 'I'll just write that down'.

But do you then continue writing throughout? Normally I would advise against it. ('Normally', because with a well-established client there is an understanding that can enable you to get through the connection stage so quickly that you could miss it altogether if both sides indicate they are willing.) In the early stages the bulk of the speaking time belongs to the client. For the client to feel ownership of this available time, and the right to speak uninhibitedly, there must be no sense of having to go at the pace the solicitor can write at; and the client should not feel there is any compulsion to put her or his thoughts into a different order that suits writing them down. The initial 'this is why I have come to see you' offering should come as free and flowing as possible. Notes are signals from the solicitor saying: *I want your thoughts to fit my format, please.*

Stage 5: Identifying the issues

We cover the topic of problem-solving and theory building in Chapter 4. In the interview you are involved in face-to-face fact finding. To do this, in your mind you are building, rejecting, modifying and testing theories about what the case/problem is going to be about, and as you do so you identify questions that you will need to ask. What is going on in the interview at this stage is that you are building, and noting, a reservoir of relevant facts.

Of course your first theories about the issues will need much refinement. The next stage is very much tied in with this.

Stage 6: Questioning

You probably don't need to be reminded that in conversation not all questions end with a question mark. Any comment inviting an answer is a question, as many of the examples below will show.

Pay attention to different styles of questioning. In particular there are open and closed questions, and you have used these in appropriate combinations since you started talking.

There are loaded questions, to be used with caution and preferably not at all, since you are supposed to avoid being judgemental.

An example of an open question is: Have you read anything on skills? A closed question would be: Don't you think it is a very fine book? A loaded question would be: Surely you bought the Legal Skills Book?

If you ask a closed question you only get the answer to that question. Sometimes you need specific answers, because you have determined that a particular piece of information is now necessary: When did you start work? Which building society have you applied to for the mortgage? Can you remember if you put your arm out before moving out into the middle of the road? You want, at that moment, that information, and nothing else.

But sometimes you want to find out what is available, and not just get answers to your questions. You need an open question: Have you thought about where you might find the extra £5,000? Tell me about your relationship with your employer. As well as you can remember, tell me everything that happened from the moment you decided to turn right.

The trouble with questions is that all you get is answers. The questions have to be excellent – and closed questions can only be guaranteed to be excellent if you already know the type of answer you are expecting (as should be the case in your cross-examination). Open questions are for the stage of your enquiry when you are open minded, before your analysis tells you exactly which mould to force the information into. Many writers, for example Binder and Bergman, use the T-funnel metaphor for deciding on your use of open and closed questions. At the start of any particular line of enquiry, the questions are broad (the top of the funnel), but as you become familiar with what the person is telling you, you narrow down the focus. You can use T-funnels repeatedly – an interview will have many little Ts rather than being one big one. Let us take an example from the interview with Mrs Evans.

> *A:* Tell me please what was going on in the bakery at the time the officers first came in. (*Nice open question.*)

> *Mrs Evans:* Well, it was a man and a woman; they came in … it must have been about a quarter to one; it was a busy time, and they were part of a crowd of people waiting to be served. I didn't notice them in particular, I only remembered them after they came in and told me they were police officers. I think it was the woman who ordered, I think she bought bread and buns or something like that.

> *A (who has a wide range of issues to pour into the T-funnel, and decides to focus on one part of what was said):* How did they behave, these officers? (*Still an open question, but narrower than the original one.*)

> *Mrs Evans:* Well, just like customers do, nothing out of the ordinary that I can recall. They just came in, waited their turn, bought their things and left.

> *A (not getting much that is useful, tempted to start with closed questions, such as: Did they appear to recognise Mr O'Connor? Did they see him? Instead forbears and asks):* Anything else at all you can remember?

> *Mrs Evans:* Well, it were that crowded, let me think; well, one thing that happened, I think, which I didn't remember till now, is that at some point around then I got really annoyed because I saw Sharon and the boss talking about something and what with the shop so busy, I wanted to shout at them to

deal with whatever it was later and let Sharon carry on serving. But you know how it is, I didn't want to make a fuss, and in fact Sharon wasn't away from serving that long.

A (deciding it is now time to go down the funnel poses questions such as):

> Was Sharon talking to Mr O'Connor at the time the officers were in?

> And you were the only person serving throughout the time the officers were there (NB an example of a question that is not phrased as a question, but invites an answer).

> Did you hear what they were talking about?

> Where exactly was this conversation taking place?

> How long for?

> etc

Eventually the T-funnel runs dry – there are no answers, or no further useful questions. A goes off into another T-funnel:

- 'Tell me now if you would about how you get on with Sharon' (a broad question, at the top of the T).

- 'So you are absolutely sure that at no time did Sharon have a chance to put anything into your apron?' (the final focused question at the bottom of this particular T).

Do not go overboard about the T funnel. (If I had invented it, I would push it harder; but it is just one metaphor among many.) Just be aware that there is a time for openness and a time for closedness. If ever you are in doubt, lob in an open question before a closed one.

There are degrees of closedness to questions. A loaded question is about as closed as you can get, with the negative question not far behind. Loaded questions are inappropriate to any open-minded enquiry. Words like 'surely' and 'obviously' are clear indications that you are expecting an answer of a particular type. Phrasing a question as a negative has the same effect: 'Didn't you think of asking for a solicitor?' is a very loaded question, making the person feel a fool for saying 'No I didn't' and tempting her to invent a face-saving answer which may be partially true (eg 'They said it would not be necessary'). Loaded questions put the interviewee on the defensive. You are making a judgement.

- 'Obviously you found that very difficult to handle, didn't you?'

- 'Surely the coins were produced to you at some time while you were being interrogated?'

- 'Didn't they offer you anything to eat at all during that whole time?'

- 'Didn't Mr Khan give you any explanation for not wanting to view the premises with the surveyor?'

To avoid feeling judged, the client may reply with false or incomplete information.

■ Solicitor: Daniel, I can't believe you can't remember if your bike had lights on.

■ Daniel: (To avoid the criticism, rather than reveal the truth) Yes I did have lights on it.

Watch in your own interviews for indications that you are loading your questions, and stop it. How could these loaded questions be rephrased? 'How did you feel about that?' 'Were the coins produced to you at any time?' and 'Did they offer you anything to eat during that time?'

Another type of question is the persuasive question: don't you think that …? For example, B says to Mr McAuley: 'Don't you think it is more likely that you did stick your arm out before you turned? After all, that is what they taught you in your proficiency test.' Or E says to Mrs Shearsby: 'You are creating a lot of unnecessary anxiety for yourself this way; why don't you simply give her a sum of, say, £5,000, to keep her quiet? Surely after that she would not create trouble.'

There is never a good reason for trying to persuade your client to answer a question in a particular way. It is, in fact, entirely unethical (the BVC standards rightly tell you not to make up answers). You may get the answer you want, but if it does not accord with what the client actually recalls or wants, you will be left with either a confused, disgruntled client or a poorly prepared case. Trying to get the 'right' answer means you are treating your theory of the case as if it were the truth and only looking for information that fits. When the police do this, we get miscarriages of justice. Keep an open mind, look for information relevant to your theory, but try as much to disprove it as prove it.

Which of the following questions/responses (borrowed from Binder and Bergman) do you consider most appropriate when, for example, Mrs Evans has just told you about her arrest and charge, or Mrs Shearsby has told you about recent negotiations with Mr Kader?

■ What exactly happened?

■ Did this happen in such and such a way?

■ That must have been very upsetting/interesting.

■ Are you sure?

■ Surely not!

Only one response shows interest in the client. The others may be appropriate later on in the T-funnel, once you have established that you are a listener and empathic.

The good questioner listens to the answer – and is seen to be listening. It is difficult, particularly as you start your career as an interviewer, to concentrate both on phrasing brilliant open and closed questions that earn you stunning marks and also to listen to the answers. As the client is speaking, inside your head you are conducting the factual and legal analysis, identifying the client's state of mind and emotion from verbal and other cues, phrasing the next question, and quite probably also worrying about other things ranging from domestic problems through to what you had for breakfast and why you didn't have a bath this morning.

If you think I have an answer to this hitherto unsolved problem of human concentration – sorry. The only thing I can offer is recognition that it is going on, some solace in the fact that you do not suffer from this problem alone, and the possibility of actually trying to listen. Two things are going on while you listen: the outward signs, as you nod, smile, say 'yes' and 'no' and 'aha' and 'go on' at appropriate moments; your eyes will focus on the speaker, who will feel willing to speak to someone who displays these signs of being interested. Then there is the inner aspect of listening. Nodding like a dog on the parcel shelf of a Ford Cortina (as Neighbour points out) does not actually prove that you have heard. You may have heard and immediately judged what you have heard according to what you think the speaker ought to be saying, rather than what the speaker actually wants to say.

The client has, for example, said again and again that she did not admit to the police that she stole the coins. The solicitor is writing as she summarises: 'So let's get this quite clear: you said nothing to the police … you said nothing to indicate that you might have stolen the money?' Client: 'I did say something like "If that's what you're saying".' The solicitor, still concentrating on the previous comment, writes down in her notes: 'did not confess'. It can happen to anyone – this is an example from a role play carried out by an experienced solicitor. Until it was pointed out to her, she was clear in her mind that the client had maintained the denial throughout the interview.

It is just like the First World War message mentioned in Chapter 2: 'Send three and fourpence, we're going to a dance.' It simply isn't what was said. Psychologists and linguists have done vast amounts of studies on human perception, and it is common knowledge that what people hear is not any objective reality. (All they are receiving is auditory and visual signals – meaning is constructed from the experience of the listener.) If you think the client did not confess to the police, you may ignore an answer that contradicts this view because you are not focusing on what the client actually says, but listening for confirmation of your own views. Or you may 'hear' something said that was not said, or reinterpret an ambiguous answer as being a clearer statement than it is.

This is inevitable. However carefully you listen, you are bound to interpret the material you receive in the light of what you expect to hear. Therefore go back over what you understand the client to have told you with an open mind: do not show irritation such as 'you didn't say that, look, you said this, I've written it down'. Remain open-minded to the inevitability that what you have heard and understood is not always what the client intended you to have heard and understood. It needs checking. You check this not only at frequent moments during the interview, but again when you write up a statement for the client to check over. And in your request to the client to read and sign the statement, you convey to the client (and the same to witnesses) that you are quite likely to have misunderstood some parts of the story; you want the client to read through with a very critical eye, and correct every misunderstanding.

Here is how not to do it:

> I'm going to write up everything you have told me and send it to you to sign; please sign and send it back as soon as possible.

(So you cannot accuse me later of having got the facts wrong.) Instead try:

> We will need to have a written statement of the relevant facts in your case. One reason is that this helps us to remember the facts and to prepare the next stages of the case; and the other reason is that

this gives you an opportunity to check that I have correctly understood what you have told me. I will have a statement typed up and sent to you in the next few days. Treat this as a draft, and let me know if any aspect of it is incorrect, even small details; and let me know if there is anything that I have left out. Then we'll get it rewritten if necessary and if you are then satisfied that it is accurate, I'll ask you to sign it. It may take two or three rewrites, or we may be lucky first time: don't be afraid to insist on changes so that you are sure that what it contains is accurate.

Also, when you write statements of what the client (or witness) told you, you are very likely to realise that you do not, after all, have the complete set of facts; you terminated the interview thinking there was nothing further to discuss, then you find you do not have some essential details such as date, address, details of precontract discussions etc. This is particularly so in your early years, and there is no point pretending as a student or trainee that you will get everything you need in an initial interview. Our clinical students sometimes take weeks to get all the relevant information together to complete a statement. That is entirely acceptable and your initial interview will not be judged a failure on these grounds.

Hear what is said. Listen also for what is not being said. People who do not know the answer to a question may feel silly and inadequate; but they do not want to admit this. So they gloss over the answer to avoid encountering this embarrassment; they probably do not know they are doing it. You as a lawyer are prone to the same tendency: you may be able to see when you watch yourself on tape when you were fudging and when you are clearly addressing a point. If you see signs of embarrassment, or just think some part of a question is being sidestepped, are you going to leave it there, or is it important to have another go?

For example:

> **Solicitor B asks Daniel McAuley:** What about the street lights? Were they on at the time?

> **Client:** It was only quarter past three, he should have seen me, he had plenty of time.

It is tempting to treat that as the answer – but unless you realise that you do not need the information, you have to press ahead with your closed question – tactfully.

> 'You are right that it may not be very important about whether you had any lights on. But I would like to have as much information as I can about every detail of what happened, and you have been extremely helpful in giving me these details. Can you remember whether you had your bike lights on at the time? It doesn't matter if you can't remember, but if you can, I'd like to know. I imagine if you take a bit of time, you may be able to remember.'

Expecting your client to remember and conveying this confidence will encourage more recall than simply 'I know how hard it is to remember and you probably won't get every detail.' Rewards along the way can help – 'well done', 'aha', 'it's not many clients I see who can remember as well as you are doing' etc.

Stage 7: Legal analysis

This process has already started; once you have encouraged the client to explain the problem in his or her own words, you begin to form a theory of what area of law is involved, and to frame your questions in order to test and develop the legal theory. You have done this in your head in the early stages, as you listen and question. But there must come a stage in the interview when you externalise your legal analysis; you start to share it with your client, and having given a legal context to the facts you have been given, you seek your client's views on whether the analysis fits those facts and the client's aspirations.

'It seems to me, Mr Kader, that there are two types of business organisation which we should explore. You could form a company, a limited company, in which you and Mr Khan would be the shareholders and the directors; or you could enter a partnership....'

'Essentially, Daniel, the law will allow you to get compensation from Mr Slater, or his insurance company, if we can show that the way he drove that car was not up to the standard of a reasonable, sensible driver; and we may have to show that the way you were cycling was normal and sensible, the way sensible cyclists ride their bikes. The sort of things we need to concentrate on are therefore whether he was going too fast; whether he was not paying attention; whether his car was in good order ...' etc.

'There is, as you rightly feared, Mrs Shearsby, a law which allows people to claim against the estate of someone even if the person left a clear set of instructions excluding her from any inheritance. Your step daughter Christine could make a claim against the estate, but she will only succeed if she can show that ...' etc.

Chapter 4 will help to show the process of legal analysis in more detail.

Stage 8: Summarising

This is the stage where the solicitor has sifted all the relevant facts and run through as many lines of analysis as the facts lead to. The client has been involved in all of these analyses, been taken head first down all the T-funnels, and should understand the analysis of each point that you have carried out, because you have checked with the client as you have gone along.

In each case there are now several threads. Some choices have to be made. The solicitor has a series of notes, perhaps with key points highlighted, and can read over these and summarise these to the client. For example, the various threads in Mrs Evans's case picked out in the first interview could lead to this summary, towards the end:

'I'm going to summarise all the points we have discussed so far. The reason I am doing this is to check for myself that I've covered everything I reasonably can manage to deal with in this first meeting; and to make sure that you understand where we have got to. Please stop me if there is anything at all in what I say that you do not understand, or do not agree with. (*Pause to ensure that Mrs Evans has taken that request on board. If no nod, or 'yes', is given, check.*) Is that OK? Good.

The first question we have looked at is what we think the prosecution are going to be saying, if the charges go ahead in court. What they are going to say is ... (*and the story is the same as we put together in Chapter 4*) ... and this is the evidence they will probably use. Mr O'Connor will go in the witness box and say ... (*as in Chapter 4*) etc.

What we are going to need to do to prepare a defence is....

You have agreed to give the question of accepting a caution a little more thought. Do you need to run over that again before you leave? ...

We have got to look very closely at any evidence we can find that might suggest that Mr O'Connor tried to set you up. What I will do is....'

And so on, through the whole set of notes that A has made, checking each time by looking for verbal or other cues whether it is safe to move to the next point, or whether the client needs to ask any questions or go over any points again.

The client has been making decisions throughout – what information to give, which questions to ask, which suggestions by the solicitor to encourage and which to discourage.

Before the end of the interview the client has to make some firm and overt decisions. She or he must be asked for these. It is perfectly acceptable for some things to be left open, however; a decision not to decide is a decision, and should be agreed and recorded, together with a decision about when the decision will be made. Mr Kader will want to think about all the suggestions E has made about the future structure of his business; Mrs Evans will need to decide if she wishes to explore the caution, or instruct A to interview her colleague Sharon Smith.

You need to use clear language to identify each issue where a decision is needed; you not only listen to the instructions you receive, but also watch for body language to ensure real agreement. 'Yes' (without eye contact, and accompanied by delay and fidgeting) can mean 'no'. Just like people confess to the police in order to get out of the interrogation, people appear to agree to things with their solicitors that they have little real intention of carrying out. Unlike the police, who have a confession on tape, you gain nothing in such a situation. Nor does the client, who fears returning to you and looking a fool for not doing what he or she agreed. (Studies in medicine, we saw earlier, have shown a non-compliance rate of around 50% after a consultation with a GP. Anything to keep the doctor happy – but the doctor's happiness was not the goal. Any fool can obtain apparent agreement: it is what the client does that is a measure of success.)

Make clear who is going to do what – confirm when deciding, summarise again at the end of the interview, and yet again in your follow-up letter. (Follow-up letters are followed up in Chapter 6.)

Stage 9: Handing over

This is a return to matters of psychology. The client came to you hoping, in some way, to dump the problem onto your shoulders. During the course of the interview she or he will have gained some relief as you understood the problem, showed you cared and could listen, and offered advice about how it could be tackled. During that period, you were in control, even while calling on the client to make decisions.

You have got to hand the problem back to the client. You – the solicitor – can achieve a lot in between meetings, in terms of analysis, investigation, contacting people, negotiating, and shielding the client from aspects of the problem. But it is still the client's problem, not yours. Somehow you have to hand responsibility back to the client, and ensure he or she accepts it. Agreement to do certain things, take certain decisions, is essential for the psychology as well as the efficient management of the case. Once again, be warned against the 'leave it all to me' approach. Whatever is left to you, do it and make clear that you have accepted that responsibility; everything else remains with the client.

Stage 10: Closing the interview

If you have completed the agenda, and made sure that your client has had a genuine opportunity to ask anything he or she might wish (throughout the interview, and again at the end) you can signal a close to the interview. (Do not, however, give any signals which contradict what you appear to be saying. As you give the client her coat and open the door, it is a bit late to be asking: 'Is there anything at all you wish to ask?'!)

Once the agenda is finished, do not wait for your client to give the signal that he is ready to go. Remember who is in control. And remember who is paying. You can say firmly: 'I think we've covered all the ground we can manage today' and maybe stand up. Once the signal has been clearly understood, you can perhaps repeat any key points, such as that you will be writing in the next couple of days, or 'don't forget to make an appointment with the receptionist for next Friday'.

It may be time to close, and yet you have not got through the agenda. This can be a cause of anxiety in an assessed exercise, and it is quite likely to happen on your course, because you may be time restricted. Make the client aware of how much time is available at the start and that you therefore cannot expect to cover everything in this single interview. A few minutes before the end, you must start to summarise and hand over, even if there is masses of ground to cover. Otherwise you look out of control. Explain to the client the areas you still need to explore, the decisions that are still needed, the information that he or she must provide, and agree another meeting soon. Leave enough time, even if you are hurried, for the client to ask any questions about what you have discussed so far.

In an unfinished interview, you must show your control of the ending. 'I'm sorry, that is all I have time for today, and I realise that there's a lot still to discuss. But I shall have to end the interview now (stand up) but I'll look forward to seeing you again on Tuesday....'

Stage 11: Housekeeping

This term is borrowed from Roger Neighbour. It is relevant to practice more than the student interview. You have got to allow time for recovery, so that you are ready for your next client or task; time to stretch, relax, eat etc.

You need time to reflect and write up or dictate. You have taken notes during most of the interview. Read them through and fill in any gaps immediately after the interview. Then write up forthwith – attendance note and client statement. As you write, look carefully for points you feel like fudging: *How annoying, I didn't ask how many shares Mr Kader would wish to allot to his wife, well I'll just say there will be three shareholders in the statement.* This is tempting but avoid fudging your notes. Any feeling of uncertainty is a useful source of information, not to be wasted. Make a note that you will obtain clearer instructions.

In Chapter 5 (Drafting) we look at writing up the content of an interview by way of a client statement and attendance note.

Principle 7: Show that you are ethical and professional

In your interview you are demonstrating many things: your skills at interpersonal relationships; your ability to obtain information; your knowledge of the relevant subject area; and, never forget, your awareness of the professional duties of a practising lawyer. You are going to have to be particularly careful not to fall foul of professional practice rules.

For example, a client who suggests to you that you mislead another party, or even worse, the court, must be clearly told that that is not possible. If a client who you do not know asks you to act in a mortgage application, because of the prevalence of mortgage fraud, you must satisfy yourself that the person is who he or she purports to be. If asked to invest money, you need to know where it comes from – for you have to report any suspicion that it may be drug money.

You must not put misleading information into a legal aid application, nor turn a blind eye to disposal of capital in order to qualify. If a client wishes to be known by a different name in court proceedings, you cannot agree if this would mislead the court. Indeed you risk committing a criminal offence. If your client insists on withholding proper discovery of documents you must refuse to act; if he or she instructs you to lie on precontract conveyancing enquiries, you must refuse. However economy with the truth may be the right side of the line, such as 'the purchaser should make her own enquiries on this matter' rather than 'of course the supertram is going to blight the property; why do you think I'm moving out?'

What if your client admits (to you) guilt in a criminal offence but still asks if he or she can plead not guilty? You must not suggest to the court facts you know to be false, but you can still act in the case, because the prosecution must prove the case. But if the client wants to put forward assertions in evidence or cross-examination that you know to be false, you cannot act and must advise the client to go elsewhere for representation. The new solicitor may guess why you have refused to act, but does not actually know the client is asking him or her to lie and is able to accept instructions (unless the client makes the same blunder again).

If Daniel McAuley were to ask if he could pretend that his bike had cost more than it really did, or pretend that he had signalled right when he did not, again, you cannot comply. You would have to explain to him why you cannot do this.

Be alert to the possibility of a conflict of interest between your client and yourself or between two potential clients. If alerted to the possibility, as will arise with Mr Kader who wants Mr Khan to see E about the business plans, do not even start to take instructions from the second. You have to explain sensitively but firmly why you will not act for both. See Chapter 5 for detail on this point.

Client care issues were covered on p 146, and come again in the client care letter in the Drafting chapter.

5   Dealing with witnesses

Barristers were formerly forbidden from talking to witnesses, except experts. Now they may, normally in the presence of the their instructing solicitor, but must not give the impression of trying to coach the witness (Code of Conduct 6.2.4).

Regardless of your professional status, before deciding to interview a witness, ask yourself a few questions:

■ What is my theory to which the witness' information is relevant?

■ What is the objective in the case?

■ What are the alternative ways of getting this information?

■ What are the pros and cons of talking to this witness?

If you decide to go ahead, ask: Am I ready to talk to the witness? Do I know what questions I need answers to? Can I be sure that I will not have to come back to this witness later because I had not worked out exactly what issues I needed to explore? For this reason, identify all possible theories before starting the interview.

Most interpersonal skills relevant to clients are also relevant to witnesses. The crucial difference is the way you may decide to treat the witness. Whereas the client instructs you, the witness is a tool you are hoping to use for your client's interests. If you can get information out of the witness in ways you would reject with the client – for example, aggressive questioning – it is ethically acceptable to do so, if you are satisfied this is the best way to get it. (It probably is not, because a witness who is unwilling to co-operate answers questions very guardedly. A witness who finds you empathic and a good listener may say things that you can use, even things they regret saying. Silence with witnesses is at least as useful as it is with clients. It is like a hole, into which the first person to break it will fall: let the witness speak first, you never know what might be said.)

If the witness is reluctant:

■ You can recognise their concern as legitimate – 'Yes, Ms Smith, I understand this is very difficult for you as you still work for the bakery, and I do not want to cause you any difficulties. My client is very grateful that you were willing to be interviewed at all, and we appreciate very much your agreement to help. All I want to find out....'

■ You can move to another topic for the time being, a less difficult one. You may choose to confront or even bully – 'Surely you can remember that, is there any reason you would not wish to tell me? Why so reluctant to answer my question? (The witness may deny reluctance and then answer the question.)

■ You can appeal to the witness' sense of justice – 'Try not to see this as taking sides in this, it's a matter of helping the court to get at the truth ... this is very important for my client, who otherwise may be convicted of something she is not guilty of....'

The witness may be embarrassed by the facts that he or she is being asked to reveal. They do not want to testify for the 'wrong' side, or admit to lapses of their own, such as Ms Smith herself has pocketed money in the past. The alibi witness may be reluctant to help because he told his wife he was at work. The witness may be embarrassed because he fears that you will be angry at his poor recall, so he prefers not to co-operate. The witness may not want to remember a distressing experience; or he or she may just want to avoid hassle.

These are real difficulties, and you stand a better chance of getting co-operation to the extent that you recognise them as genuine – and not your own fault. Just like there are no problem clients (once you stand back and take ten deep breaths) there may be no problem witnesses. Can you engage their sympathy? Get them started on neutral questions, so that they are too involved by the time you get to the difficult material. Can you make things easy by going to them, or offering travel expenses? Praise them for their assistance and recall. Fawn over their co-operation (through gritted teeth, if necessary). If the worst comes to the worst, and you are sure this is necessary, threaten to compel them to attend court (but you cannot compel them to be interviewed in advance).

The separate issue of expert witnesses is touched on briefly in Chapter 4 on Research. The key there is to be absolutely clear what opinion you seek from them.

Conclusion

> *Client:* And what really worries me is that I'll go to prison, lose my job, my daughter will be taken into care …

> *Student interviewer:* Good, fine, right, OK, I'll just take a few notes. Obviously we're now going to need to fill in a legal aid application.

If you remember nothing else from these pages, remember this when you are interviewing: things are rarely 'great' 'fine' or 'OK' for your client, and nothing is 'obvious'. Avoid these words.

I have tried otherwise not to focus too much on mechanical 'dos and don'ts' and 'all you have to do is …'. Interviewing is about relationships. If you have gained some understanding of aspects of what is going on in the interrelationship between a lawyer and a client, you can devise and adapt your own techniques. Each interview and each problem will pose entirely different challenges for you. You will get to the destination, and you will pass the milestones, in each case, but you will do so in a unique way each time.

I hope that you have come out of this chapter believing that there is no such thing as a problem client, only problems in the relationship between the client and the adviser. Follow our advice, drop the assumption that the client is the problem and, if you achieve nothing else, you are one stage nearer to satisfying the skill assessment of interviewing and counselling. Are you a problem student? Of course not. The client does not think of him or herself as a problem client either.

Appendix   Interviewing checklists

We put these forward for guidance only. They are not a substitute for expertise in the subject area, or for careful analysis and theory building. The lists remind you of points that are likely to be relevant, and which you therefore should not omit accidentally. Many questions can be omitted by choice, however. Do not go through the lists mechanically – some questions are not relevant, some cover information that you will already have received from the client before you get to that point. Students are welcome to photocopy these pages for use in interviews.

1   A self-assessment checklist

ATTITUDE TO CLIENT

How well did you:

- Introduce yourself to the client?

- Make the client feel at ease?

- Listen attentively?

- Notice any problems of understanding?

- Give opportunities to ask questions?

- Explain clearly?

- Allow client to make decisions?

EVIDENCE OF PREPARATION

How well did you:

- Demonstrate that you had prepared a structure for the interview?

- Understand any documents produced?

- Show appropriate familiarity with law/procedure?

OBTAINING INFORMATION

How well did you:

- Allow client to explain problem in own way?

- Ask questions at the appropriate time which were:

  ☐ open?

  ☐ focused?

- Accurately obtain available details of:

  ☐ the factual situation?

  ☐ the client's main concerns and wishes?

- Obtain/ask for relevant documents?

- Identify where further information was needed and how to obtain it?

- Use time efficiently?

IMPARTING INFORMATION

How well did you:

- Explain legal terms and procedures (where necessary)?

- Avoid giving premature or wrong advice?

- Summarise main points?

- Explain next steps to be taken by solicitor and client?

DOCUMENTING THE INTERVIEW

How well did you:

- Summarise factual issues?

- Identify legal issues?

- Summarise accurately advice given and instructions received?

- Clearly identify next steps for adviser and client (including dates)?

2 Basic checklist for conducting all interviews

- Full name of client(s)

- If under disability who is giving instructions?

- If more than one client, can instructions be given by one alone?

- Any previous name used if relevant, eg before marriage

- Address including post code

- Any reason for not contacting at that address, and alternative?

- Telephone at home

- Telephone at work

- Fax number (check messages will remain confidential)

- E-mail address (check confidentiality – see Chapter 6)

- Tel number where messages can be left (can confidential information be left?)

- Employment/source of income

- Family situation: married or not

- Number and ages of dependants

- Employment/income of any partner

- List of documents supplied

- Documents to be obtained

- History of problem – if problem is one of those listed below, use detailed checklist

- Name and role of any previous adviser – address if relevant

  (If solicitor, is client transferring instructions? Do not advise otherwise.)

- Client's objectives

■ Advice given on objective:

☐ cost

☐ likelihood of success

☐ time scale

☐ difficulties

■ Key names and addresses, eg opponent, insurer, witness, employer

Client care

■ Name of fee earner clearly given

■ Who else can be contacted?

■ Who can complaints be addressed to?

Fees

■ Green form advice available?

☐ statutory charge explained?

☐ scope explained?

■ Criminal legal aid application to be prepared?

☐ 3 months' wage slips for client and partner requested?

☐ contributions explained?

■ Civil legal aid application to be prepared?

☐ emergency application required?

☐ employer's form required?

- ☐ contributions, statutory charge, costs, co-operation explained? leaflets given to client?

- ☐ supporting documents requested?

- ☐ follow-up letter promised?

■ Legal aid not available

- ☐ costs of this interview?

- ☐ cost estimate for whole transaction given/promised?

- ☐ charging rates explained?

- ☐ money on account agreed/received?

- ☐ billing frequency/cost update explained?

- ☐ cost recovery explained if case won/risk if lost?

- ☐ other sources of funding? Trade Union? Legal expenses insurance?

■ Conditional fee discussed? If so:

- ☐ Success fee stated?

- ☐ Termination arrangements discussed?

- ☐ Disbursements discussed?

- ☐ Arrangements for drafting conditional fee agreement discussed?

■ *Summary of who has agreed to do what:*

- ☐ people to contact

- ☐ documents to obtain

- ☐ facts/law to research

- ☐ letters/documents to draft

- ☐ advice to be confirmed by letter

- ☐ next meeting/contact

3 Checklists for specific types of cases

Criminal

- Obtain summons/charge

- If no charge, is one likely?

- Arrested? If so date, time and officer

- Attended police station? Where?

- How long in police station?

- What happened in police station?

  - ☐ complaints?

  - ☐ admissions made?

  - ☐ details of questioning – times, frequency, who present, breaks, style?

  - ☐ solicitor attended?

  - ☐ doctor attended?

  - ☐ appropriate adult?

  - ☐ other (eg interpreter)?

- Police bail granted? If refused, reasons?

- Has there been a court hearing? Where? When? Representation? Outcome including bail decision

- Next court hearing? Where, when, what stage? (mode of trial; committal; trial?)

- Evidence against client – what does client know about:

  - ☐ what police/others say client did?

  - ☐ any confession?

  - ☐ identification evidence?

  - ☐ involvement of others?

□   witnesses for prosecution?

□   forensic evidence, eg fingerprints?

■ Client's version of events, consider in particular:

□   any alibi

□   mistaken identity

□   confession unreliable

□   mens rea

■ Names and addresses of possible defence witnesses – which ones will be contacted at this stage? When? By whom?

■ Names and addresses of anyone else involved

■ Who is representing them?

■ Details of any previous offences:

□   date of offence

□   date and court of conviction

□   plea

□   details of offence

□   sentence

□   disqualification/endorsement – ask to see driving licence

■ Explain you will obtain details from prosecution

■ Is client under a court order at date of alleged offence?

□   community sentence

□   suspended sentence

□   conditional discharge

□   deferred sentence

■ Name and address of any probation officer/social worker involved with client or family

- ■ Is bail likely to be refused? If yes:

  - ☐ take details of community ties

  - ☐ previous bail record

  - ☐ acceptable conditions, eg

    residing at given address (who will contact?)

    sureties (name, address, suitability, who will contact?)

    reporting to police (how often?)

    curfew

    avoiding witnesses

    avoiding certain places; surrender passport; other

- ■ Advice on plea given?

- ■ Consider whether to discuss:

  - ☐ advice on sentencing powers?

  - ☐ likely maximum sentence?

  - ☐ effect of custody on client/family/employment?

  - ☐ attitude to community sentences?

  - ☐ previous responses to sentences?

  - ☐ seriousness indicators for offence (see Magistrates' Association guidelines for offence)?

  - ☐ references, eg employer, church, voluntary organisation; letter or attend court? who will contact?

  - ☐ financial information (client and partner where appropriate) including:

    income (including benefits)

    capital

    debts

outgoings including: tax, NI, housing costs including council tax, travel to work, debt repayments and HP, food, gas, electricity, water, TV licence, car (tax, insurance, maintenance, petrol), court orders, maintenance payments, other?

☐ evidence of above requested?

☐ willing to pay compensation?

☐ TICs offered? to be accepted?

☐ willingness to obtain treatment for dependency? (eg alcohol, gambling, drugs)

☐ willing to seek relationship counselling?

☐ employment prospects, evidence of job seeking?

■ Any other questions?

A personal injury claim

- Date of injury

- Limitation date advised

- Time

- Place

If road accident

- Details of other vehicles (make, colour, ownership, registration, age, unusual features)

- Details of client's vehicle (as above, MOT, insurance, condition)

- Names and addresses of other parties, approximate ages, relevant observations, eg glasses worn?

- Details of any passengers/pedestrians involved

- Weather

- Road conditions

- Insurance details of other drivers

- Police involved? station, officers, comments made

Work accident

- Role of equipment/other employees?

- Any previous similar accidents?

- What warnings/precautions known?

- Accident reported/recorded?

- Any prosecution?

- Client's training, experience, and expertise?

- Any subsequent changes in practice?

- Photographic evidence to be obtained? Site visit?

All cases

■ Client's account of what happened and cause (have client draw plan if necessary)

■ Were any admissions made?

■ Medical information

☐ injuries suffered

☐ where treated (hospital and dates, name of consultant)

☐ GP details

☐ follow-up treatment given/required

☐ consent form obtained

☐ effect of injuries on work, other activities

☐ prognosis

☐ previous medical history

■ Loss of earnings

☐ name address and contact person for employer, reference number

☐ wage slips requested for past six months

☐ benefits received since accident, and NI number

☐ employment prospects

■ Expenses incurred/estimated – clothing, travel, prescriptions, care etc

■ Advice on potential defendants and enforcement – MIB, insurance company, employer

■ Advice on prospects and time scale

■ Advice on relevant welfare benefits or other claim, eg CICB, own insurance

■ Other sources of help – trades union; motoring organisation; own insurance

■ Any other questions?

A consumer or debt claim

- **Name and address of other party, including head office**

- **Details of agreement**

  - ☐ date

  - ☐ if written, copy obtained/requested?

  - ☐ price/amount

  - ☐ other significant terms

  - ☐ oral or written representations (obtain details)

- **What breach is alleged?**

  - ☐ date of any significant event

  - ☐ what happened?

  - ☐ evidence available or to be sought – witnesses, inspection, expert

  - ☐ consequences of breach – injury, damage, financial losses

  - ☐ receipts available for any losses?

- **If goods sold or services supplied:**

  - ☐ was it in course of business?

  - ☐ were descriptions given?

  - ☐ was purpose made known?

  - ☐ was agreement made away from business premises/visit unsolicited?

- **What financial arrangements – deposit, instalment, cash, credit card, credit, HP, cheque, other?**

- **Is it a consumer credit transaction?**

- **Any evidence of rescission/cancellation?**

- **Client willing to sue/defend/compromise?**

- Other methods of resolving dispute? Complaint or arbitration through trade association; guarantee; contractual remedy; arbitration

- Obtain details of any communication between the parties since breach

- Advice on choice of defendant including supplier, wholesaler, manufacturer, importer into EU – ascertain identity of these

- Advice on prospects including enforcement difficulties and early judgment

- Any other questions?

Conveyancing: sale

- ■ Full name(s) of client(s)

    - ☐ address(es)

    - ☐ telephone numbers (home and work)

    - ☐ date(s) of birth

- ■ Property to be sold

    - ☐ address

    - ☐ deeds (where?)

    - ☐ mortgaged? (with who and account number(s)?)

    - ☐ amount(s) outstanding on mortgages

    - ☐ occupied? (if so by who?)

    - ☐ fixtures and fittings included

    - ☐ sale price

    - ☐ items offered for sale with price

- ■ Details of selling agent

    - ☐ particulars of sale obtained?

- ■ Related purchase? (if so details)

    - ☐ related occupation of other property?

- ■ Completion date sought

    - ☐ alternatives

    - ☐ removal arrangements

- ■ Status of sellers (joint, in common, other)

- ■ Transfer of services (gas, electricity, water, council tax, telephone, cable TV, mail)

■   Insurance (existing or required)

     ☐   life

     ☐   endowment

     ☐   buildings

     ☐   contents

■   Any known problems? (with property, area, neighbours, boundaries, disputes, future developments)

■   Proceeds of sale? (to who, when and where)

■   Fees and disbursements

     ☐   profit costs

     ☐   VAT

     ☐   searches

     ☐   others (eg apportionments)

■   Payment of accounts

     ☐   selling agents

     ☐   removal expenses

■   Any other questions?

Conveyancing: purchase

■ Full name(s) of client(s)

    □ address(es)

    □ telephone numbers (home and work)

    □ date(s) of birth

■ Property to be purchased

    □ address

    □ occupied/vacant?

    □ if occupied, by who?

    □ price offered

    □ fixtures and fittings included in purchase

    □ purchase price

    □ other items to be bought (with price)

    □ type of property (terrace, semi, detached)

■ Details of selling agent

    □ particulars of sale obtained?

    □ deposit paid?

■ Sellers

    □ capacity of sellers (beneficial owners, trustees, others)

    □ details of sellers' solicitors

■ Financing of purchase

    □ mortgage required, if so with who?

    □ amount required

    □ survey fee paid?

☐   date of application for mortgage

☐   balance purchase monies provided by?

☐   notice required for release

■   Completion date sought?

    ☐   alternatives?

    ☐   removal arrangements

■   Related sale?

    ☐   details

■   Rented property?

    ☐   details (including notice required)

■   Transfer of service accounts (gas, electricity, water, telephone, council tax, cable TV, mail)

■   Insurance (existing and required)

    ☐   life

    ☐   endowment

    ☐   buildings

    ☐   contents

■   Fees and disbursements

    ☐   profit costs

    ☐   VAT

    ☐   searches

    ☐   Land Registry fees

    ☐   stamp duty

    ☐   other (eg apportionments)

■   Has client(s) made a will?

■   Joint purchasers (instructions on co-ownership and shares)

Business client

■ Full name(s) of client(s)

☐ address(es)

☐ telephone number(s): (home and work)

■ Name of business

■ Legal structure of business (company, partnership, sole trader)

☐ trading address of business

☐ if company

registered office

company registration number

company secretary

directors

shareholders and shares

Memo and Articles obtained?

☐ if partnership

names of partners

partnership agreement obtained?

■ VAT registered? If so number

■ Details of business accountants

■ Details of business bankers

■ Assets of the business

■ Land and buildings

owned

rented

☐   plant and equipment

☐   trading debts owed

■   Liabilities of business

☐   trading debts

☐   mortgages

☐   floating charges

☐   tax

■   Nature of business

■   Any other questions?

Chapter 4

RESEARCH SKILLS

1 An introduction to research skills

Some people think being a lawyer is dull. Don't fall for that. Every case you deal with can be exciting and creative. You may not match the drama of 'LA Law' (or the stress); even so lawyers have a daily diet of fascinating problems brought to them.

Law only ceases to be interesting when the lawyer, as a matter of course, tackles each new problem in the same way as a previous one. We want you to avoid that at all costs. A creative approach to each new problem benefits you in two ways:

■ being a lawyer will not bore you after the first few years, and you will continue to welcome as a challenge each new client, each new problem;

■ you will pass any assessment that involves the skill of legal research with ease.

The chapter has six parts:

1 An introduction to research skills

2 Research in the context of your course

3 The tools of legal research

4 Research in practice: the contentious cases

5 Research in practice: the non-contentious cases

6 Documenting your legal research

The biggest part, by far, is where we look at how you apply methods to actual problems; problem-solving in the four case studies. This is Parts 4 and 5 of the chapter.

This is a chapter written by both of us: it was too important, we felt, to leave to him! You don't need to know who did which part (except that Hugh did the contentious cases and

Richard did the rest), but we admit now that we approach research somewhat differently, and have presented our methods in different styles. There is no conflict, however. All we are saying, in our respective ways, is define the problem carefully, check your law, and check your facts, before taking action. In our examples you will see different methods; we have no wish to paper over these differences, as they are complementary. But the key agreement is that there must be a method. You can and should develop your own method. If you are being assessed on any task you must show that you used a method and how that method worked out. Nowadays, even on undergraduate programmes, you are expected not just to produce the 'right' answers but to show how you got there. Perhaps our approach to planning, doing, documenting and applying research will inspire you to start.

Whatever method you settle for, it must be creative. Let us look at an example.

What does a poor person do if she is libelled? Go to a solicitor? What does the solicitor do? There is no legal aid for libel, so she cannot sue. A five-minute consultation; hardly worth charging. Any law student knows that libel is only for the rich.

And yet a chambermaid in the royal family, whose character was attacked in a newspaper, made legal history recently. Why?

This particular solicitor refused to tread the time-honoured path of advising her that as she was neither rich nor eligible for legal aid there was no remedy. He rediscovered malicious falsehood, obtained legal aid, and a remedy for his client. (The defendant's attempt to have the action struck out is reported in *Joyce v Sengupton* (1992) Times, 18 September.) The lawyer concerned, Mark Stephens, was interviewed about his approach in the *Law Society's Gazette* of 25 November 1992 at p 14. This is what he said:

> 'There are two kinds of lawyer: the "fixed paradigm" type and the creative sort. The former treats the law as a rigid set of "cans" and "cannots", while the latter treats it as an art form, skilfully manipulating its rich pattern to evolve a solution.'

Which kind do *you* choose to be? We hope to steer you towards creative lawyering. We believe that proper professional care for each client demands this.

Even if you are not aspiring to make legal history, your professional duty to your client requires you to predict accurately the outcomes and risks of different courses of action (or inaction). You need a detailed understanding of the law, the facts, and the likely behaviour of known and unknown people: you need, in a word, research.

2   Research in the context of your course

Whether you are on a degree course, a CPE programme , the LPC or BVC you will need to do research and demonstrate how and why the research was done. At degree level a great deal of emphasis has been placed on the need for research. The Bar and the Law Society specifically require legal research to be conducted as an essential underpinning to the foundation subjects on qualifying law degrees (Joint Statement of the Law Society and Bar, 1995, 6). The criteria for legal research are stated to be:

'The ability to analyse a problem involving a question or questions of law, and through research to provide a solution to it. This involves the ability:

   (i)   to identify and find relevant legal sources and materials;

   (ii) to extract the essential points from those legal sources and materials;

   (iii) to apply the law to the facts of the problem so as to produce satisfactory answers to the questions posed; and

   (iv) to communicate the reasons for those answers, making use of legal sources and materials.'

The Lord Chancellor's Advisory Committee on Legal Education and Conduct also emphasises the importance of research (ACLEC, 1996, 72).

Indeed it is hard to imagine any aspect of law and the legal process being effectively learnt without the research skills as a central and integral feature of the programme. In our experience, however, the importance of research does not always come across on law degree courses. It is often more of an implicit expectation rather than an explicit requirement. Look at the learning outcomes for your programme. Do they specify how the research requirement ties into each module? How do you know if that research element is being met? Students studying at degree level may find the process described in this chapter helpful in addressing the need for research skills and an effective research methodology.

On the vocational courses research is equally important. It is not just law students who have to look things up. Practising lawyers have to research too – both law and fact. Research is an essential part of the daily business of legal practice, even if the research itself may sometimes take a more sophisticated or specialised form.

On the LPC research is more pervasive in nature than the other D(R)AIN skills. Research is required as part of every LPC core subject and every other DRAIN skill. The BVC Course outcomes are equally specific although they concentrate on legal rather than factual research (to a certain extent the factual research is covered by the subsequent section on Fact Management). The LPC Board's Written Standards and the BVC Course Specifications state:

LPC	BVC
Students should understand the need for thorough investigation of factual and legal issues and should understand the need for preparation and the best way to undertake it.	The student should approach legal research in a practical rather than academic manner and be selective, precise and efficient in the identification and utilisation of resources.
Students should be able to:	The student should be able to:
(i) determine the objectives of the ... client;	
(ii) identify and analyse factual material; ...	(h) summarise or paraphrase relevant materials;

LPC

(iv) identify the sources for investigating relevant facts; ...

(vi) identify and analyse legal issues;

(vii) apply relevant legal provisions to facts; ...

(xi) present the results of research in a clear, useful and reliable form'.

'Students should be able to demonstrate an understanding of:

(i) the use of primary and secondary texts;

(ii) the methods of locating cases and statutes;

(iii) the use of treatises, periodicals, digests and standard practitioner texts;

(iv) the use of indexes and citators;

(v) the use of computerised research tools.'

BVC

(e) distinguish between relevant and irrelevant sources and materials;

(a) analyse the issues raised by the case and identify which questions of law have to be answered;

(f) cross-refer between materials to ensure the answer is complete;

(j) come to a satisfactory answer to each of the questions posed;

(k) give brief reasons for the answers arrived at, showing how those answers have been reached.'

(b) identify and locate sources of information such as text books, *Halsbury's Laws*, etc;

(d) identify and locate relevant sources and materials, such as reported cases, statutes, statutory instruments;

(g) check that the law found is current (eg that the statute is in force, that the case has not been overruled);

(i) extract the key points from, and correctly cite, those sources and materials;

(c) make a correct identification of key words to enable efficient and effective use of an index;

In addition to the LPC standards set out in the table above, the ability to investigate law and fact is repeated in the Board's standards for each of three compulsory areas. Before you get any reference to knowledge of, say, conveyancing procedures, how to draft a statement of claim, or advise a business person on the formation of a company, it is a requirement that a student must be able to:

    '(a)   identify the client's goals;

    (b)   investigate and identify the relevant facts;

    (c)   research and identify the relevant legal issues;

    (d)   identify alternative means of achieving the client's goals.'

This is repeated in identical words for Conveyancing, Litigation and Advocacy and Business Law and Practice.

Regardless of which course you are studying on what do such words as 'analyse', 'apply', 'identify', 'investigate' and 'research' tell you? You must demonstrate that you can recognise gaps in your knowledge, develop strategies for obtaining that knowledge, and then go and get it. By knowledge we do not mean only legal knowledge; you must also research what the client wants from you, and therefore what the factual context is for researching that legal knowledge.

Research is therefore a foundation for learning and applying law and procedure in the rest of the modules of the programme of study.

Equally research is the linking skill in each of the other legal skills:

■   In interviewing or in conference you are either engaged in factual research; or you are advising a client in the light of the factual and legal issues, which you will have researched.

■   Drafting and writing is only effective if you have first found out what you want to say, discovered what is relevant in the light of the facts and law, and identified the correct drafting procedures. Again research is essential.

■   Advocacy is the presentation to a court of the results of your factual research, in the context of law and procedures that you have had to discover.

■   Negotiation and dispute resolution – the process of maximising outcomes for your client by agreement – can only take place effectively if you know what outcomes are possible and realistic in the light of all the appropriate facts, law and procedures.

Research has two strands: factual and legal. On an undergraduate law course you probably have little need to deal with factual research. A research task conventionally means you are handed a short summary of undisputed facts and told to find out what law you should apply. On the vocational courses, and when you enter practice, you will be unable to separate factual and legal research in this way, since you cannot find out much about the facts until you know what the law (including procedures) makes relevant. But you cannot know what law to look up until you know the basic facts of the case. Even in degree courses sometimes you need to investigate, or at least consider, the facts before turning to the law.

Research might sound like a grand title for the simple process of fact-gathering. Ask a practising lawyer if they do factual research, and they are likely to say no, they just get the facts from the clients, witnesses, documents etc. But that is research, every bit as much as a dialogue with LEXIS. Facts can't be said to exist, at least for any practical purpose, without some investigation.

The relationship between factual and legal research is well summed up in the contentious field by Binder and Bergman in *Fact Investigation, from Hypothesis to Proof*:

> 'Substantive rules are not self-activated. They are triggered by evidence which proves, to the degree of certainty required, that certain facts exist to which the rules in turn can be applied. The triggering mechanism itself relies on lawyers to present evidence in such a way as to convince a factfinder that facts occurred which render a given substantive rule applicable or inapplicable. And it is through factfinding that lawyers amass and shape the evidence presented at trial. Thus the gathering and shaping of evidence is as central to the operation of the law as is the application of rules once the facts are determined. Indeed, this gathering and shaping forms the the basis from which a factfinder decides whether or not to invoke a given rule.'

In other words, rules come into play after you have discovered the facts. But how do you know which facts are relevant to any particular issue? Because, of course, the law defines them as relevant. Catch 22? We cannot look up the law until we know the facts, and we can only investigate the facts in the context of the relevant law.

Legal research is therefore an art, relying on judgment and intuition. The key, however, is not just to *use* intuition, but to test it. In this sense, you are pursuing a scientific approach: you have a hypothesis. This hypothesis has two dimensions: you have a hypothesis as to what the facts are, and you have a hypothesis as to what the best legal framework is. The legal framework is chosen in the light of the facts as the one most likely to lead to a desirable result. Then you test the legal and factual hypothesis until it is either found to be the best available, or replaced with one which better explains or controls the available facts in the context of the available law.

This approach is particularly suited to contentious case preparation, and in Part 4 of this chapter we look at a process called theory building. To a lawyer imitating scientific method a theory is of no value unless tested; the theory should then be thrown out if it does not fit the 'facts'. ('Facts' in inverted commas, because there is only a fact if, when tested, the factfinder agrees that it was a fact. This applies to non-contentious facts too, because they are only non-contentious until a dispute arises!)

We will not press the claim to scientific method any further. The analogy only applies in the sense that scientists test their theories by trying to disprove them. Lawyers should do the same. If our theory stands up to our test, it may stand up to the court (contentious) and future events (non-contentious). But scientists claim to be detached; they want to find what is, not what they want to be. Lawyers are goal orientated: all research work is conducted in the light of the client's legitimate goals and ability to pay. We are only objective and detached in that this enables us to test our theory better; we test the theory because we are single-minded, involved and subjective in pursuing the goal. We may find

Research checklist

To what extent have you:

■ Identified appropriate client goal(s)?

■ Clearly formulated the problem in terms of:

    ☐ factual issues?

    ☐ legal issues?

    ☐ procedural issues?

■ Identified a strategy for researching/clarifying:

    ☐ the relevant facts?

    ☐ the relevant law?

    ☐ the relevant procedure?

■ Documented the research carried out?

■ Reformulated the problem as necessary?

■ Produced a result in a form which can be applied to achieve the client goal?

■ Demonstrated ability to use any of the following legal research techniques?

    ☐ up-to-date text books

    ☐ encyclopedias

    ☐ practitioner texts such as 'White Book' etc

    ☐ *Halsbury/Digest* or similar

    ☐ original statutory sources

    ☐ original case reports

    ☐ statutory instruments, circulars etc

    ☐ LEXIS or other database

    ☐ case or statute citators

■ Demonstrated an ability to use factual research techniques, eg where appropriate any of the following techniques?

☐ contentious cases:

obtain information from the prosecution (criminal cases)

interrogatories/discovery (including originating discovery) – civil cases

interview witnesses, including prosecution witnesses

experts

examination of real evidence and site visits

archives, eg newspaper reports

☐ non-contentious areas, eg

interview clients

searches of registers: Local Land Charges, Land Charges and Land Registry

enquiries of local authority

deeds and documents of registration

valuations

surveyors' reports

site visits

public information services (for example Information Office for Supertram)

accountant's reports

enquiries of other side (sellers, partners, directors)

■ To what extent is the resulting research reliable?

that we promote our client's theory even while we believe the facts and the law point to the opponent having a convincing case.

We will not use the term theory building in non-contentious cases, because there are no past events about which to hypothesise or construct your theory. But identifying the problem, the facts and the relevant legal framework, then testing these to see if they are really the best available, are all equally necessary.

What lawyers have always done is to get a hunch about the case. Whenever we say theory, or legal framework, say hunch if that makes you happier. But test your hunches as hard as your theories.

On top of demonstrating integration of your research abilities in the skills and subjects, you must demonstrate your research abilities as one of the identified legal skills or, as we have called them (in the context of the LPC) the DRAIN skills. The standards expected of you on your vocational course are, in terms of the assessment of the skill of research, set out above. The specifics of assessment will vary from one provider to another. Look carefully at what is being asked of you. You will be required to show your competence not only as a technical legal researcher but you must be able to justify the results of your labours by documenting the research process and showing how what you discover is applied. This may, as we will see in our case studies, result in the need for further research and re-application.

Clearly this involves demonstrating competence in the use of specific tools for legal research. But unless you are given a freestanding test on these research tools, you will have to use them for a purpose and in a context. The use of a computer database, or a loose-leaf encyclopedia, for its own sake, whilst involving transferable skills, is of little applied value – a case of means and not ends; you must use it to find answers to the problems you have identified. At this point in your education and training the correct identification of the problem is more important than the provision of a solution to the wrong problem.

Put more succinctly, getting the wrong answer to the right question is better than getting the 'right' answer to the wrong question. If the right question was asked, you can test the answer to see if that is also right.

A research self-assessment checklist

The research checklist on pp 186–187 does not take the form of the checklists you will see in the other skill chapters, as the research requirement varies entirely with the task set. For example, you may arrive at a correct formulation of the legal point via several routes, each of which is satisfactory if the task is correctly identified and a useful answer obtained. Getting the 'right' answer is likely to be only one part of the task, and having a thorough strategy ought to be rewarded whatever the result.

It will make more sense once you have completed the chapter and read the way our five solicitors carry out research. Although there are just four case studies solicitors D and E are on opposing sides in our business law example.

The check-list is not intended to be a complete guide, just one more tool to help you check if what you are doing is on the right road.

3 The tools of legal research

Much has been written on the techniques of, and aids to, legal research. Tunkel (*Legal Research*) is good; Thomas and Cope (*How to use a Law Library*) is clear and Clinch (*Using a Law Library*) is very user friendly. Tunkel and Clinch are now a little dated (1992), a significant consideration in this age of rapidly changing technology.

We presume that you are conversant with the main research material and can find your way around a law library. You must, if you are in any doubt about your competence in this field, address the problem without delay. Read Thomas, Tunkel or Clinch. Seek guidance from the law librarian – in our experience they are a helpful bunch. Set yourself practical research tasks to test your ability to use the resources available.

What follows is a summary of the main sources of legal research material. We will show examples of how to use these sources to address particular problems in our case studies.

We begin with the most general indexes and then progress to the more specialised tomes.

A starting-point must be *Halsbury's Laws of England*. The way into this enormous mine of information is the consolidated index. This index should, if you have a broad idea of what it is that you wish to research, point you towards the relevant subject matter. The index covers a wide range of legal topics, including crime, tortious liability, conveyancing and company law. The index gives a specific reference to the volume and page number where the detail on that subject matter can be found. Changes in the law, both statutory and judicial, are recorded in an annual *Cumulative Supplement* and a monthly *Noter Up*. You cannot ignore these updates, as you must ensure that the law upon which you rely is in fact in force and has not been amended, relevant case law formulated, or the statute repealed.

A further useful general work is the *Current Law* service. This consists of citators for both legislation and case law, together with a monthly issue.

The *Legislation Citator* lists statutes passed between 1947 and the date of the most recent edition (presently 1995), statutes (of any date) that have been repealed or amended since 1947 and all cases in the law reports since 1947 which have considered the sections of the statutes. Also included in the same volume is a *Statutory Instruments Citator*.

The *Case Citator* gives the full name of cases reported between 1947 and the date of the most recent citator (1995), a list of references to the law reports and journals for each case, and the history of any case (whatever date) that has been judicially considered since 1947. Reference is made in both citators to further detail on cited cases in the *Current Law Year Book* for the relevant period.

The monthly parts of the service summarise reported cases under different subject headings, and list articles published in the different areas of practice or law. These are collected every year in the *Current Law Year Book*.

Halsbury's and *Current Law* are a good starting-point for getting a sense of direction and an overview of the area, especially if you do not know which text book to use.

The above sources – except the citators, which are essentially indexes – are secondary sources: they rely on someone to summarise and interpret what the law means. The primary sources of law for research purposes are the statutes (including secondary legislation and European material) and the case reports.

Legislation can be found in a variety of sources ranging from the *HMSO* publication to *Halsbury's Statutes* and *Halsbury's Statutory Instruments*. *Halsbury's* provides useful annotations of the statute, and is generally easier to use than HMSO individual statutes (unless you are needing to look up something in a statute recently passed, and not yet available in *Halsbury's* or the monthly *Noter Up*).

Annotated copies of the Acts and Regulations are also published by the major legal publishers (Butterworths, Sweet and Maxwell and Blackstone).

Of major and increasing importance are the Directives and Regulations from the European Union. So far as EU legislation is concerned the *Official Journal* is the most comprehensive and up-to-date source and includes all secondary legislation. Alternatives include Sweet and Maxwell's *Encyclopedia of EC Law, European Current Law* and Butterworths' *EC Brief* (a weekly newsletter).

Whatever the source, you need to check that the version of the statute you are looking at is up to date, in force and whether it contains any amendments. A useful publication in this respect is *Is It In Force?* This annual volume gives details of the commencement of all sections of statutes passed since 1963.

Case law can be obtained from a wide variety of law reports, headed by *The Law Reports* (as the preferred authority, at least by the courts) but including the *All England Reports* and the *Weekly Law Reports*. Reports also exist in specialist areas such as housing and employment law. *The Times* and, until the early '90s, the *Guardian*, also carry law reports which are now indexed in the *Daily Law Reports Index*. The index is organised by parties' names and subject matter and even ships' names where relevant! The digest is up to date to about two weeks and is therefore a valuable source of recent case law. A cases digest gives a summary of the facts and decisions.

An index of case law known as *The Digest* is also available, although somewhat complex to use. This was formerly known as the *English and Empire Digest*. You will see solicitor A putting this to use on behalf of Mrs Evans below.

For the practitioner, specialist books are available that focus on particular legal areas. Increasingly these are presented in loose-leaf form and cover such topics as company law, family law, wills and probate, employment law, conveyancing, personal injury work and immigration. These are updated regularly and are an indispensable aid to lawyers. These publications often contain not only explanations of law and procedure, but also may give a copy of the primary source, for example the section of the Act, as well as precedents. The role of these for precedents will be looked at in greater detail in Chapter 5 (Writing and Drafting in a Legal Context).

Journals and periodicals also supplement the library, and include the *New Law Journal, The Solicitors' Journal, The Law Society's Gazette*, and more specialist publications on, say, criminal law or welfare benefits. These contain regular updates on the law, with articles and commentaries. Since 1986 there has been a *Legal Journals Index* which lists articles by author, title and subject matter and is published monthly. From this you can find the article itself – solicitor A does this below.

Several dictionaries may also help in focusing research. These include *Jowitt's Dictionary of English Law* and *Stroud's Judicial Dictionary of Words and Phrases Legally Defined*. Use the most up-to-date dictionary available, and check in any supplement available in case a definition has been modified.

Last, but certainly not least, is information technology. With the ever-increasing bulk of statute and case law, important strides have been made in handling this through computer-based technology. You may be familiar with several of these programmes and systems, including Lexis, Justis and Lawtel. More recent developments using CD ROM have now begun to make their impact on legal research. The use of on-line research through Lexis is pursued in this chapter, and in more detail elsewhere (Tunkel *Legal Research* and Thomas and Cope *How to Use a Law Library*).

The internet or 'web' is now a significant growth area in terms of research potential for lawyers. Our recommendations will no doubt be rapidly overtaken. One website that will give you links to a large range of other resources, such as the Law Commission, legal publishers, the House of Lords and many more is: http://www.sosig.ac.uk/roads/subject-listing/UK/law.html. Perhaps this is one of the best beginners' websites for lawyers. Try it.

We will take you to some of these sources when we look at research tasks generated in the four case studies. But the sources are not in fact our primary concern. What we will try to help you realise is that finding the law is the (relatively) easy bit – formulating the precise question and knowing when you have answered it is your challenge.

In Parts 4 and 5 we will take you through the case planning, problem-solving and research strategies in each of our four case studies. We intend to illustrate possible approaches, not necessarily to solve the detailed problems of each of our clients. Usually our approach follows similar stages, although not always in the same order.

1   *Preparatory research*: before you have taken instructions, or in the early stages of the interview, formulate a series of questions which will enable you to obtain some of the relevant facts and start the process of theory building or identifying objectives and strategies. Obtain any checklists that we, you, or others have provided (see appendix to Chapter 3).

2   *Identify the goal*.

3   *Set a framework for detailed research*: once you have taken preliminary instructions, formulate one or more theories about the law and facts, or in a non-contentious case, the legal framework for pursuing the goal.

4   *Make sure you research the right legal points*: formulate legal questions which you will research. Make sure that each question is precise enough for you to know if you have found an answer.

5   *Make sure you research the right factual points*: predict the existence of relevant facts (contentious case) or of relevant obstacles to achieving goals (non-contentious case) and investigate these.

6   *Agree decisions* on case strategy (the means to the goal) with your client. If you cannot, go back four spaces. Do not pass Go.

7 *Review*, review, and review again. Unless you are certain that you are right, go back four or even six spaces. Do not pass Go yet.

8 *Go* – which means implement the decisions through your drafting, negotiation or advocacy, while always reviewing, reviewing and reviewing.

You will not find all stages covered in all of our case studies. Even the criminal case, where we go into the most depth, is only an extract from the life history of the case. (Would you have wanted to pay even more for this book?) In any event, if you get the picture, it's now your turn to try and do it. You do not have to copy our method. Lawyers have got by for centuries without it – but the best ones have always had some kind of method like this. Now you can be like them.

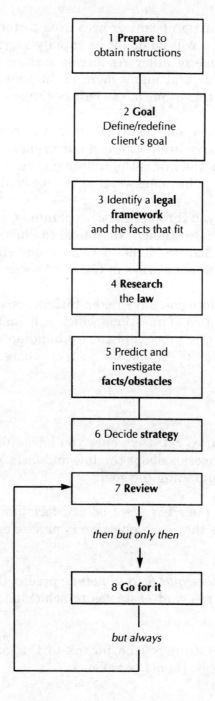

4 Research in practice: the contentious cases

Some definitions

In Parts 4 and 5 we will be taking you one by one through our four case studies. In the two contentious cases, we are going to use some words that we need to explain in advance: these words are *theory* and *story*. For the purpose of contentious and non-contentious cases alike, we also want to define *research*.

Theory   This is a bit like a holy grail. It is what every lawyer is looking for to guide his or her preparation of the case and the decisions that the client is advised to make. It is not quite as elusive as the holy grail, but can tend, once found, to slip away, or to change its form. You thought you had it but now you need to go out in quest again. (The process should not be that elusive, but your theory or theories will need constant reshaping.)

What is theory? The 'theory of the case' is an American concept. (If you are someone who has a prejudice against American terminology, please hang in there, take it easy and chill out. If we can explain this concept to you, it will serve you for life.)

Your client comes to you and tells you, more or less directly, the problems or opportunities in their affairs which they think need a lawyer's involvement; and they tell you the outcomes they desire. They tell you many things; you listen, and gradually decide that certain things are very relevant, some are marginal, and others of no relevance at all. The theory is the yardstick by which you make these decisions. The theory underpins your ordering of the facts into a coherent whole. Coherent means fitting into a legal framework that, in your best judgement at that time, matches the information available to you.

The facts may be uncertain; the legal framework you choose may turn out to be the wrong one, as and when further facts are introduced. The 'facts' you discarded as irrelevant may need to be revived. The facts may be past, present or future; they may be facts in the sense of being established beyond any doubt, or 'facts' only in the sense that they are an assessment of what happened in the past or may happen in the future. The facts may be welcome, or unwelcome. Taken together and in the legal framework you are currently invoking, they are the best model of reality available to you. The theory which organises them together enables you to make decisions on resolving your client's problems or exploiting their opportunities.

In summary you are saying: taking this legal framework, at least for now, the relevant facts fit like this – the way I make the facts and the law fit is my current theory of the case.

You will be lucky – or foolish? – if you immediately identify one best theory and stick with this one. Usually there will be a number of possible theories, and you have to evaluate one against the other until you decide which one(s) can be eliminated for the time being, and which one(s) merit exploration.

A theory about past events applies to contentious work. You want a factfinder (a court) or a negotiator to make decisions based on the version of events, or theory, that you are putting forward. The court can never go back to visit the event itself – it has to decide between competing theories of past reality, based on the evidence presented.

(On the other hand you may be concerned about anticipating future behaviour, and controlling it in your client's favour. This is non-contentious practice. You predict what relevant events might happen and plan your client's affairs in the light of such predictions. You cannot test any theory about the future, so we do not use the term theory in Part 5.)

Theories have to be tested. If they do not work they must be discarded or modified. This means forming predictions based on them. If theory A is true, then fact B (and perhaps facts C and D) should be found to exist. (Or at least evidence should point to their probable existence.)

For example, in our civil litigation case one theory of the case might be that the driver was speeding (presumed fact A). If the theory is a good one, we can predict and then investigate evidence of facts B, C and D, such as:

■   tyre marks would be found on the road;

■   a witness would have heard screeching;

■   the driver will have been prosecuted;

■   expert examination of the bicycle damage, or injuries, will be consistent with impact at speed.

We can now investigate these predictions. We look for witnesses; those we identify we ask particular questions, not just 'What do you know about the accident?' Do we find some or all of the expected evidence? If not, is the theory that he was speeding of any use to us? Should we scrap speeding and try for a new theory, such as 'not looking where he was going'. Every theory should lead to predictions; every prediction should be tested, as far as you are able, *before* it is tested by events over which you have incomplete control: the judge/jury.

Story   This term is again relevant in contentious cases. If the theory is to be useful (credible to the factfinder), the facts must fit together into a coherent story. The story is both a way of testing the theory and a way of conveying the content. Assume, for example, one of our current theories is that Mrs Evans did not steal the coins, and in fact Mr O'Connor planted them in her apron and conspired with the police. The legal framework for this theory is absence of actus reus. We have to put all the known and hypothesised facts into a narrative, or story, that, through our evidence and cross-examination, hangs together credibly for the factfinder. If it does not carry this conviction, what use is this theory? (Of course, in the absence of a better theory, it may still be the one we end up using, after advising the client of the likely outcome.)

Research   We imagine that most legal practitioners do not see themselves as researchers. But if research simply means asking questions to which you need an answer (which is the most difficult bit), and answering them with the best information available, then you should be a researcher throughout your professional life.

Research can be *factual*: you will need to find out about the client's problems or opportunities from the client directly; to investige the existence of further facts which you hypothesise may exist, by interviewing potential witnesses, talking to people, obtaining documents etc.

And it can also be *legal* research: finding out through a textbook, a colleague, a statute, a case report, a database etc what the legal framework is in order to formulate or modify your theory, and take decisions.

We will take you through over 30 research tasks as part of our four case studies. We call them legal research tasks, but they also involve elements of factual research.

Case study 1: The money that went missing from the bakery

Before we start, a word of caution: the title, which you have just read, to this case study is misleading. Why? It has not been proved that money has gone missing – we are using someone else's theory as if it were a fact. It is the theory probably held by the prosecution, and it has to be tested. That is solicitor A's job. As with the Second World War poster, careless talk costs convictions. That many solicitors are failing at this basic level of professional responsibility was claimed in a study at Warwick University by Professor Michael McConville. The headline and first paragraph from the report in the *Guardian* of 29 October 1993 gave the alarming flavour:

> **'Legal aid lawyers push for guilty pleas**
>
> Criminal defence solicitors routinely process legal aid clients into guilty pleas rather than explore the possibilities of a defence, according to a study of 50 law firms published today.'

The *Guardian* report later states:

> 'Defence advisers worked on the assumption that their clients were guilty. Prosecution evidence was accepted uncritically and defence advisers' activities "rather than designed to oppose the prosecution, are tailored to legitimate and support it", the study found.'

Hardly a proper standard of work!

Mrs Evans's case, on the face of it, does look hopeless, ready to process as a straightforward guilty plea. But we owe her a professional duty to advise her in relation to her actual instructions, not our superficial opinion of what really happened.

Stage 1: Preparing for interview

Solicitor A knows that Mrs Evans is coming to see her or him charged with theft. A list of initial questions would include:

- What is the exact charge?

- What does she know about the police allegations?

    - who is she alleged to have stolen from?

    - what if any is her connection with the alleged victim?

■   What has she told the police?

■   What is her version of events?

■   Who else can give relevant information?

■   What is the client's tentative decision on plea?

Further questions which can be used to prepare for an interview in relation to a criminal charge are set out in the appendix to Chapter 3 on pp 163 and 166.

Before even speaking to the client, solicitor A must check his or her knowledge of what constitutes theft. A finds that theft in its simplest form is found in section 1(1) of the Theft Act. This is a research task at its easiest: any up-to-date criminal text will reveal a definition. Just look in the index. Better, though, is to get used to looking in one of the practitioner texts that is updated at least annually: *Blackstone's Criminal Practice*, *Archbold: Pleadings Evidence and Practice in Criminal Cases*, or *Stone's Justices' Manual* in particular. The subject index under 'theft' takes A to the definition. Here is the definition found in *Blackstone's* (1998 edition) at section B4.1:

> 'A person is guilty of theft if he dishonestly appropriates property belonging to another with the intention of permanently depriving the other of it; and "thief" and "steal" shall be construed accordingly.'

A now adds to the list of questions to ask Mrs Evans a note to look in the interview for the following information:

■   What evidence does there appear to be indicating:

    ☐   an act of appropriation by my client?

    ☐   an intention to permanently deprive another?

    ☐   the property belonged to another?

    ☐   my client was behaving dishonestly?

Of course, when A has the charge sheet and more information about the case, it may turn out that A looked at the wrong offence, and will have to look again at definitions. Perhaps the client is wrong, when she tells your receptionist it is about a theft charge; maybe it is handling. (In this case, it turns out that section 1(1) of the Theft Act was the right one to look up.)

A interviews Mrs Evans and writes out her statement:

> I, Winifred Evans, of 6 Manor Close, Sheffield 5 will say as follows:

> I am 46 years old. I am a married woman with two dependent children, Alan (aged 15) and Tracey (aged 12). My husband Eric works as a car salesman.

> I work part-time as a shop assistant at Tasty's baker's shop on Granville Street, Sheffield. The business is owned by Mr Andrew O'Connor.

I first started working at the shop about six years ago. The owners then were a Mr and Mrs Smiley. The business was sold to Mr O'Connor some time last year and he kept me and the other assistant, Sharon Smith, on.

My duties at the shop include stocking the shelves (the bakery is in another part of town and deliveries are made three times a day), selling the bread and cakes and generally looking after the shop.

I share this job with Sharon. She works in the mornings and I work in the afternoons, Monday to Friday. We overlap by about an hour usually as dinnertime is our busiest time and it is useful to have more than one pair of hands then. I arrive at work at about 12 o'clock and Sharon leaves about 1 o'clock.

Although Sharon is a good bit younger than me we get on alright. She must be about 24. We have worked together for the last three years.

On 1 September I was at work as usual at about 12. We had been very busy all day and especially so that dinnertime. Sharon left just after 1.00. Mr O'Connor was doing some paperwork in the back of the shop during this time.

Two people came into the shop. It must have been at about 1.15. They asked me if I was Mrs Evans and told me that they were police officers. They were in plain clothes. I recognised one of them, the woman, because I had served her earlier that day with some sandwiches.

They asked me to go into the back of the shop and then asked me to turn out my pockets. I was very shocked and felt confused and upset. When I put my hands in my apron pocket I found three £1 coins. I was told to look at these and asked if they were marked in any way. I saw a small cross on each which had obviously been put on the coins by someone. I was then told that these coins were ones that had been used to buy the sandwiches earlier and they had been marked by the police. The male police officer asked me how these coins had ended up in my pocket. I said that I did not know how.

I was then told that I was under arrest and was taken to the police station.

At the station I was put in a cell where I was kept waiting for what seemed like ages. Eventually a sergeant brought me a cup of tea and asked me if I wanted to talk to a solicitor. I felt I had nothing to hide so I said 'No' and I was then interviewed. To be honest I can't really remember what was said, it was all so dreamlike. I do remember that the interview was tape recorded. I was asked lots of times how the coins came to be in my pocket. I told them that I did not know how or why but that I suppose that I must have put them there.

They also asked me questions about other sums of money that Mr O'Connor said were missing. I said that I knew nothing about any other money.

One of the officers went on about how I had been seen going into the bakery late one night, which may be true, as I once or twice have gone back if I have forgotten something. I have keys to the premises and can operate the alarm system.

After the interview I was taken before another policeman who read out two charges and gave me some papers, telling me that I had to go to court later.

I still do not know how the money ended up where it did. All I can say is that I do not remember taking it and if I did so I did not take it on purpose. I have certainly never taken any other money. I don't know who has been taking the money.

I am in good health, although I am now under the doctor with my nerves as a result of all this.

Of course I lost my job at the bakery.

A also obtains the charge sheet from Mrs Evans, which reads:

Theft contrary to s 1(1) Theft Act 1968

1   On the first day of September 1998 stole £3 belonging to Andrew O'Connor.

2   Between about March 1998 and September 1998 stole £545 belonging to Andrew O'Connor.

Stage 2: The goal

On our instructions Mrs Evans is not guilty, and the goal is to obtain an acquittal. This goal may change in the light of Mrs Evans's instructions, which may change in the light of A's advice, which will develop in the light of research.

Stage 3: Theory building

So now we know what the case is about?

> 'An initial interview provides all the information one needs to assure success for a client about as often as one is dealt a laydown hand in gin rummy.'
>
> (Binder and Bergman *Fact Investigation, from Hypothesis to Proof.*)

No, we do not know what the case is about, yet. We have a first version of events, which we call our instructions. We do not have a clear idea of what the prosecution story will be, nor what the defence version will be. If we carried out no further analysis, we would have a hard time advising our client to plead other than guilty – things look pretty bleak.

We have to build two theories: one is the theory we predict the prosecution will be offering as their explanation of how all the facts fit together; and the other the most credible defence version of the facts inconsistent with the section 1 definition of the offence. The goal is going to be to produce for the defence a theory of what actually happened; a theory or explanation of the 'facts' that, when tested, is more internally consistent, credible and convincing than the prosecution's version; a theory that will convince the factfinder (magistrates or jury), or at an earlier stage the negotiator (Crown Prosecution Service).

The defence theory must fit the legal framework. It is partially defined by the prosecution, in that the charge they must prove is that of section 1(1) of the Theft Act. But A has to explore other legal dimensions now A has an outline of the relevant facts. A returns to *Blackstone's, Archbold, Stone's* or a reliable textbook, to see if there are any obvious statutory or common law defences.

Definitions of 'property' and 'belonging to another' appear to offer no relevant assistance. We are not assisting A by suggesting a theory around the idea that the money was not property or did not belong to another person.

However, section 3 defines 'appropriation' and may assist:

'(1) Any assumption by a person of the right of an owner amounts to an appropriation, and this includes, where he has come by the property (innocently or not) without stealing it, any later assumption of a right to it by keeping or dealing with it as an owner.'

Mrs Evans has instructed A that she had no idea how the coins came to be there. This is a good theory. If a court accepts a defence based on this theory, she has not assumed the rights of an owner.

Section 2 may also assist:

'(1) A person's appropriation of property belonging to another is not to be regarded as dishonest—

(a) ...

(b) if he appropriates the property in the belief that he would have the other's consent if the other knew of the appropriation and the circumstances of it;'

This could be explored further with Mrs Evans or in cross-examination of the owner: would he have consented to her putting money into her pocket temporarily if someone else was using the till? (If he would have, there would also be no appropriation.)

'Dishonesty' is itself not defined in the statute. But A cannot understand the prosecution case or prepare the defence without obtaining a definition. Again, an up-to-date textbook or practitioner work gives the clue: the definition of dishonesty currently used, which we have taken from *Blackstone's Criminal Practice 1998* B.438, is from the case of *Ghosh* [1982] QB 1053. This provides a two stage test: 'whether according to the ordinary standards of reasonable and honest people what was done was dishonest' and if so 'whether the defendant himself must have realised that what he was doing was [by the standards of reasonable and honest people] dishonest'.

The facts and inferences needed by the prosecution to prove dishonesty will be tied in with proving appropriation. If she did not intend to put the money in her pocket or keep it for herself, there would be no dishonesty: this can found another theory of what happened.

We need to research if there is any guidance on intention permanently to deprive. Section 6 of the Act says that this is an 'intention ... to treat the thing as his own to dispose of regardless of the other's rights'.

This again ties in with the issue of dishonesty and appropriation, and leads to no new factual theory of events.

And finally: is there any law on what is sufficient to prove the mental elements of these offences? Research starting from the indexes of the textbooks brings solicitor A back to *Ghosh* and the general approach that 'In most cases, where the actions are obviously dishonest by ordinary standards, it will be obvious that the defendant himself knew that he was acting dishonestly'.

We have a legal framework now, which defines what facts are important.

But we are still not ready to generate useful defence theories. Before we carry out a brainstorm to generate defence theories, we need a prosecution theory, since the defence task consists of casting sufficient doubt on their story. We have to work out from the information we can obtain what their theory of the case will be and what story they will be telling.

As this case is triable either way, we do not have to carry out this process until after we receive the advance information from the prosecution setting out the facts on which they rely.

Under the Magistrates' Courts (Advance Information) Rules 1985 A requests a summary of the prosecution case. The following statements are provided:

I, Andrew O'Connor, of 16 Scott Street, Sheffield 4 will say as follows:

I am 32 years of age. I have been the proprietor of 'Tasty's' bakery and retail shop for the last 18 months. I bought the business as a going concern from a Mr and Mrs Smiley. At the time that I took over there were two staff in the shop, Sharon Smith and Winifred Evans.

About six months ago, in or around March, I began to notice that the till takings were down on what the till roll indicated they should be. I have a simple cash register in the shop which records sales on a paper roll as and when they are entered by the shop assistant. I also noticed that the shop stock sold did not equal the amount in the till at the end of most working days. I check the till each day at about 3 pm, just before I go to the bank to pay in the takings. What struck me as odd was that the till was always 'light' by an exact number of pounds, say 4 or 5. It was rarely out by an odd number of pence. I accept that in the retail trade, especially when dealing in small amounts, errors do occur, for example when change is given. I would have expected that this would show up as an irregular figure, not as a round number of pounds each time.

I don't serve in the shop myself so I thought the irregularity must be due to someone taking money from the till or not paying in money received from customers.

The amounts missing were never great but it was becoming so regular that I felt I had to do something about it. The only people who handled money were Sharon and Winnie, and I began to notice that Winnie behaved in a furtive manner sometimes, so I suspected her. I believe she has been in some financial difficulties in the past few months.

I decided to take advice from the police and they said that if money continued to go missing they would set up a test for me.

On 1 September they did so by coming into the shop to make some purchases with marked coins. I knew they were coming on this day so made myself scarce in the back of the shop. I heard the voices of two 'customers' who I knew were police officers.

After they had made their purchases I went into the front of the shop to check the till. This would have been about 12.50 pm. I discovered that the till was £3 short. The only other persons apart from me in the shop during the time from when the police officers had come in until the time I had checked the till were Mrs Evans and Miss Smith. Miss Smith left at about 1.00, before the police came back.

I then went into the back of the shop and made a call to the police who were waiting nearby in their patrol car.

The police came back into the shop and searched Mrs Evans. They found the three marked coins in her apron pocket. Mrs Evans was unable to give an explanation to the police and she was arrested and taken away.

I can confirm that no-one apart from me has authority to take money from the till or to keep money that should have gone into the till, unless it is to give change to customers.

From the records that I have kept since April I can also confirm that in addition to the £3 taken on 1 September, £545 has gone missing from the till or from stock.

I wrote to Mrs Evans on 2 September telling her that in view of the circumstances I had no choice but to dismiss her. Since then apart from small and irregular discrepancies (odd pence), the shop takings have been accurate. I have now extended Sharon's hours and she works virtually full time.

Since the incident on 1 September my son, Darren, who is 13, has told me that he has seen Mrs Evans pocket money from customers before. He thought that she was just collecting money in her apron pocket because she was busy and was going to pay it in later.

Darren O'Connor

I, Darren O'Connor, will say as follows:

I am 13 years old and live with my mum and dad at 16 Scott Street, Sheffield 4.

My dad runs the baker's shop on Granville Street. I often go to the shop after school to meet Dad who then takes me home. When I get to the shop Mrs Evans is usually there. I either sit in the back of the shop until Dad is ready to go or I hang around the shop and talk to Mrs Evans or the customers.

When I found out that Mrs Evans had been caught stealing I told my dad that I had seen her put money in her apron pocket several times before. The shop was often very busy and I thought that she was doing this to save time or something. As she has worked in the shop for a long time I guessed that she knew what she was doing. I can't remember exactly when I saw her do this but it was very often and quite recently.

DC Regan

I, David Regan, Detective Constable 417, based at North Bar Police Station, Sheffield will say as follows:

On 30 August I received a telephone call from a man I now know to be Mr O'Connor, proprietor of the bakery business known as 'Tasty's'. He told me of his suspicions regarding money unaccounted for in his retail outlet.

In the company of WPC Higgins, and in plain clothes, I visited the premises at Granville Street, Sheffield, on 1 September at approximately 12.45 hours. I went into the shop whereupon WPC Higgins purchased some sandwiches from the salesperson now known to me as Winifred Evans.

Prior to entering the shop I had marked three £1 coins with a small cross above and to the right of the letter 'd' in the word 'pound' on the coins.

WPC Higgins made the purchase tendering the coins in payment. The purchases came to exactly £3 (we had been advised by Mr O'Connor of the shop's prices beforehand). Mrs Evans handed over the goods and we left the shop. Mrs Evans still had the coins in her hand as we left the shop.

WPC Higgins and I then sat in our patrol vehicle and about twenty minutes later received a telephone call from Mr O'Connor who told me that the till was missing the marked coins.

In the company of WPC Higgins I went back into the shop and revealed my identity to Mrs Evans. This was at approximately 13.15 hours.

I asked Mrs Evans to come into the back room of the shop where I asked her whether she had any money on her person. She replied that she had not, all her money being in her handbag which was hanging up in the staff toilet.

I then asked her to reveal the contents of her pockets. She did so and produced three pound coins from her apron pocket. She said that she had no idea that they were there. I examined the coins and identified them as the coins that I had marked earlier that day.

I asked Mrs Evans if she could explain how the coins came into her possession and she could not. She admitted that she had no authority to take any coins that were the property of Mr O'Connor, other than to put them into the till on the sale of merchandise, or to give change following any purchase.

Mrs Evans was then told that she was under arrest and she was taken to North Bar Police Station where she was interviewed.

WPC Higgins

I, Mary Higgins, WPC 634, based at North Bar Police Station, Sheffield, will say as follows:

On 1 September at approximately 12.45 hours and in the company of DC Regan, I visited the premises known as 'Tasty's' on Granville Street, Sheffield. With three £1 coins provided to me by DC Regan, which were marked with a small cross above and to the right of the letter 'd' of the word 'pound', I made a purchase of various items the total value of which was £3.

I was served in the shop by a woman who I now know to be Winifred Evans. I was given the goods and left the shop. I did not see Mrs Evans place any of the coins in the shop till, nor did I see her ring in the sale.

I left the shop with DC Regan only to return at approximately 13.15 hours following a telephone call that DC Regan had received whilst in the patrol vehicle.

In the shop DC Regan identified himself and myself to Mrs Evans and asked her to go into the rear room of the shop. There Mrs Evans was asked whether she had any money on her. She replied that she had not. She was then asked to reveal the contents of her pockets and she produced from her apron pocket three £1 coins.

I examined these and identified them as the coins which I had tendered for my purchases earlier that afternoon.

After failing to give any satisfactory explanation of why the coins should be in her possession, Mrs Evans was arrested and taken to North Bar Police Station, where she was interviewed.

There is also a Recording of Taped Interview (ROTI). The prosecution provide a 'balanced summary' (meaning a summary – the balance is an aspiration towards neutrality) to the defence. (A copy of the tape is available on request and should normally be listened to; to avoid pages of transcript, assume nothing apart from the extract below is found to be of any significance.) The following exchanges between DC Regan and Mrs Evans took place:

> *Q:* We have evidence that you have been seen several times in the vicinity of the bakery after closing time. What do you say to that?
>
> *A:* I may have been back once or twice to collect things I have forgotten. That's all. I didn't go in to steal if that's what you mean. Why would I? I could take anything I wanted during the day. I mean, I didn't, but I could.
>
> *Q:* You admit then that you have had every opportunity to take money when you are working in the shop? And you admit that you were caught red handed with the three marked coins in your pocket? And you admit that you cannot explain how they came to be there. And you admit that you were seen on several occasions in the area of the shop after closing time? Don't you think all of this adds up? It's obvious that you are the one who took this money from the bakery, and have been doing so since March.
>
> *A:* Yes, well, I suppose I must have done it; it looks like it. I don't know.

A now has everything the defence will normally receive from the prosecution about the case.

In a criminal case, we cannot build a defence theory without first predicting what the prosecution theory is likely to be. This is because the definition of the defence task is to challenge, or create a reasonable doubt against, the prosecution's theory of what happened. The prosecution have a theory (they may not call it such, but in matching the 'facts' to the charge of theft, they have a theory of what happened and what legal framework fits). We do not yet have all the information. We will not have it until we hear, at trial, what their witnesses actually say on oath. So we have to make the best guess at their theory on the information we do have.

You know from studying criminal law that for Mrs Evans to be convicted, each element of the charge must be proved beyond reasonable doubt. (Some knowledge of criminal procedure is assumed, but if you did not know how the case has to be proved, it is a matter not for shame, but research: look in a basic procedural textbook, such as *Emmins on Criminal Procedure*. The index entry on *proof* takes you to p 291. If you need more detail, try researching in a practitioner text, such as *Archbold 1998*, where the index on standard of proof takes you to para 4–384.) Proof can be by direct or circumstantial evidence.

A takes each element of theft in turn. The prosecution theory A constructs takes first the facts which will be alleged for that element, then the evidence available to prove it. Because there are two charges, A has to do the same process for each.

Charge 1: The coins

The charge says on 1 September Mrs Evans stole three £1 coins belonging to Mr O'Connor. Under the section 1(1) definition of theft, we know this includes elements of appropriation, dishonesty and intention to permanently deprive.

Element 1: Mrs Evans The prosecution will be saying it was her, not someone else, who received the coins from the police and it was on her person that they were found. Evidence in support comes from the two police officers.

Element 2: Appropriated property There appears to be no direct evidence that she did this. No-one saw her put the coins in her pocket. The prosecution will have to ask the court to infer that this is what she did, since the coins ended up in her pocket. The court will also have to infer that this is an appropriation – an intention to treat as hers – from these facts. There is evidence in the police interview which can be construed as an admission by her of an appropriation ('I suppose I must have taken it').

Element 3: Dishonestly There is no direct evidence, and again the prosecution theory will rely on inferences based on the *Ghosh* definition: if the appropriation took place, right thinking people would agree it was dishonest, and Mrs Evans would have known such people would call it dishonest.

Element 4: Belonging to Mr O'Connor There is direct evidence from two officers that the coins found in Mrs Evans's apron had been paid into the business owned by Mr O'Connor.

Element 5: With the intention of permanently depriving the owner Evidence for this is entirely indirect (meaning circumstantial), in the absence of an admission by Mrs Evans. An inference from conduct can be made if the court is satisfied that there was an appropriation. Because Mrs Evans is also accused of a series of thefts, the prosecution may be intending to ask the court to infer that this course of past conduct shows dishonesty on the present occasion.

Charge 2: The £545

The charge says that Mrs Evans stole £545 belonging to Mr O'Connor between March and September. The Theft Act 1968, section 1(1) tells solicitor A that Mrs Evans will have to be found to have appropriated this money dishonestly with the intention of permanently depriving Mr O'Connor of it.

There is no set way to break down the elements, so long as no essential element is omitted. To prove the point we do so slightly differently for this charge.

Element 1: Mrs Evans There is some direct evidence: a young boy appears able to testify that he has seen her put money in her apron. Mrs Evans appears to make an admission in her interview with the police. Otherwise the evidence is indirect: Mr O'Connor states that he suspects her because of her attitude and her financial difficulties. She is one of only a small number of people who could have taken the money. She is said to have visited the shop after hours. Although we know this to be true, the prosecution have supplied no evidence, save that the police put this allegation to her.

Element 2: Dishonestly As with the coins, the prosecution will need to rely on inference.

Element 3: Appropriated There is evidence from till rolls and stock records (according to Mr O'Connor's interpretation of them) that money amounting to this total has been appropriated; there is evidence from Darren indicating that he has seen Mrs Evans on occasion put money in her pocket, from which an inference can be drawn that she has appropriated all of the missing money.

Element 4: Property belonging to another   Mr O'Connor can give evidence that the missing money comes from his business.

Element 5: With the intention of depriving Mr O'Connor of it permanently There is no direct evidence; the prosecution will again rely on an inference that, if the appropriation was proved, Mrs Evans must have had this mental element. The admission 'I suppose I must have done it' looks like evidence of intention.

The missing £545 – a prosecution story

Before constructing defence theories, let us see how the prosecution theory translates into a story. We use the word story, because each side of the case will be trying to tell the factfinder a coherent narrative story through the evidence available at trial. On the facts we have available we imagine the prosecution story could be structured as follows. Direct evidence is available to support part of the story, but the court will have to draw inferences (these *inferences* are shown in italics).

1   Mrs Evans was an employee of Tasty's bakery with unsupervised access to the till. She received customers' money. *Inference: She has the opportunity to take money from the till or to divert it.*

2   Mrs Evans was short of money. *Inference: She was open to temptation and has a motive to steal.*

3   Over a period of six months money went missing from the till. Mrs Evans was seen by the proprietor's son to take money from the till on occasion and put it in her apron. *Inference: Mrs Evans had the opportunity.* She was found with the three £1 coins. *Inference: It was she who took the rest.*

4   Mrs Evans visited the bakery after hours during the period the money went missing. *Inference: She went back to steal.*

5   On 1 September three £1 coins were marked and used by police officers to buy goods. Three identical marked coins were found in Mrs Evans's apron pocket. *Inference: Mrs Evans removed them from the till, or never put them in the till after receiving them. This is what she had done on other occasions.*

6   Mrs Evans admitted the coins were in her pocket and said she had no idea how they came to be there. *Inference: She must have put them there; it is a lie to say she has no idea.*

7   Mrs Evans admitted the allegations during police interview.

Research tasks

We now intend to demonstrate techniques available to carry out legal and factual research in order to build and test your theory of events. We have not got enough space to do this in relation to every aspect of these two charges. For the sake of brevity, we will shortly abandon one of the charges, leaving it to be picked up in Chapters 6 (Reaching Agreements and Resolving Disputes) and 7 (Advocacy). Before doing so, we will show how solicitor A begins to reach the conclusion that there may be a chance of negotiating the dropping of one charge – money missing over a long period.

Solicitor A notes that some parts of the story of the missing money are supported only by indirect evidence:

■ she worked there (*inference of opportunity*);

■ the till rolls show money missing (*inference that a theft did take place*).

There are parts where the case against Mrs Evans is not only inferential, but where A considers the evidence is potentially inadmissible:

■ she had the opportunity;

■ Mr O'Connor suspected her;

■ she visited the premises after hours;

■ if she stole the £3 then it must have been her who stole the rest.

And there are parts where the evidence, though direct, is less persuasive:

■ the owner's son saw her putting money in her apron on occasion (appropriation);

■ she made an admission.

Before entering into negotiation with the prosecution, A would research admissibility and weight of these points of evidence. To show the approach, we have picked on researching the evidence of the boy and the confession. These are the only points of direct evidence connecting Mrs Evans to the allegedly missing money.

Legal research task 1

What is the weight/admissibility of such evidence from a child?

■ *Objective*: to minimise or eliminate the damage caused by the evidence of the child witness

■ *Question*: can a child of 13 give evidence for the prosecution in a criminal trial, and if yes, can the damage be minimised?

This is our first research task. We will use a similar process each time, in contentious cases and, later in the chapter, the non-contentious cases. As we go on we will become briefer; our purpose is not to do all the research for you, but to show how you formulate the research question and devise a strategy. For each research task, therefore, we set a client objective – what we want to achieve as a result of the research – and a specific question which we wish to answer. As the research progresses, we may wish to modify the question.

We catalogued our research as we carried it out: blind alleys are included. All the tasks were identified before the research started. As a result, some questions are answered already by the time we get to them.

We use a variety of research techniques and legal sources. There is usually more than one way to the research outcome; do not presume the one we illustrate is the best.

(Please do not rely on the actual answers, since the research may be out of date by the time you read this. More recent cases may have been decided. New legislation may have been passed. It is the process, not the result, that matters.)

In task 1, we are faced with damaging evidence from the 13-year-old son of the main prosecution witness. The objective? To exclude the evidence at trial, failing which, to have it rendered less credible.

The research question is easy to formulate: can a child of 13 give evidence in a criminal trial? If yes, can the weight of this child's evidence be minimised?

The answer may be easy to find, if we can identify the area of law. What is it? Procedure? Evidence? A standard text on either area should lead to assistance. Using a library catalogue if necessary (A finds a range of potential sources). A decides to look at *Emmins on Criminal Procedure*. In the index A looks up 'child' and 'children' – but finds there is nothing relevant to whether they can give evidence. A tries under 'Evidence: children' and again fails. Under 'witnesses' nothing is listed.

Has A failed in the first research task? No. You may have to try several leads before finding an answer. The library catalogue also mentioned *Blackstone's Criminal Practice 1997*. 'Witnesses, children as' takes A to F4.16. Under section 33A of the Criminal Justice Act 1988 Darren is able to give evidence, which will be unsworn.

Does his evidence, as a child, carry reduced weight? The same section of *Blackstone's* suggests that there is no reason to treat a child's evidence as inherently less credible than that of an adult.

We have answered the questions, but not achieved the objective. The right answer to the wrong question is easy. The wrong answer to the right question is better. Best of all – but you know what is coming....

So can the question be reformulated? Is there any other approach, forgetting that he is a child, to limit the damage caused by Darren's evidence? How can he be challenged? He is the son of the owner. He did not report what he saw until much later. We need to formulate another question. The index words are likely to be 'weight', 'credibility', and 'bias'. The question could be: has a witness who is connected with the complainant less credibility? Can his lack of credibility be put to him in some way which impeaches his credibility?

For the sake of variety, this time A starts with a textbook, *Evidence: Law and Practice* by Cowsill and Clegg. 'Witness, credibility of' leads to 'Cross Examination' in the index, and to pp 131–135. A finds that he or she can cross-examine a witness for bias. But the information in this book is brief, and A is worried by the 1990 publication date. So A turns to a fuller, more recent text, *Cross and Tapper on Evidence* (8ᵗʰ edn 1995). The index gives 'character and credibility – bias and' at page 336, where we find only a general statement

'In the modern law it is quite clear that many witnesses, such as parties and their close relatives, are likely to be biased, and there is no special need to bring this out'.

So can A give Darren O'Connor a grilling in cross-examination on bias? We don't really know, but this statement is discouraging. A tries Archbold. The index under 'cross examination as to credit' leads to 'see credibility' under which A finds 'bias' at 8–148 to 8–150. A can put it to this witness that he is biased, but cannot cross-examine further once the answer is given (unless A has independent evidence on this question of bias).

The objective of legal research task 1 was to exclude or reduce the effectiveness of Darren's evidence. A concludes that Darren's evidence is admissible but may be attacked once only for bias.

The other damaging evidence in relation to that charge is the confession.

Legal research task 2

What is the evidential value of this confession? Is it admissible?

- *Objective:* To exclude the confession.

- *Question:* Are there any recent cases indicating that in similar circumstances a confession has been excluded?

Wait – that is a vague definition. It begs a further question – what do we mean by similar circumstances. Precision in your question is essential if you want precision in your answer. The circumstances are: no known impropriety by the police, fairly intense repetitive questioning, a fatigued client who says she was in a dreamlike state, and no solicitor present.

For illustrative purposes, we approach this task from more than one angle, and do not take the path we used in task 1 of using a textbook.

This time we assume you have some background knowledge, or can obtain it from the textbook, and that what you are unsure of is whether there is any very recent case law that could help you to exclude this confession. You know that any argument on admissibility will centre round sections 76 and 78 of the Police and Criminal Evidence Act 1984.

There are several ways into case law – summaries of recent cases in journals are very useful, for example, in this field, *Criminal Law Review*; you can also look through indexes to law reports. The *All England Reports* have subject indexes in each volume. You can use a database (which we will do for a later task).

For this example we started with the *Criminal Law Review*. Working back from the most recent (at the time of writing May 1998) A searches the index. For a year that is not completed each monthly part has a cumulative index; the bound annual volumes have an index for that year. The first result under 'Evidence – confessions' comes in 1995 with *R v Weeks* at page 52. The Defendant was told he would have to stay in custody if he did not tell all he knew. The court decided that in the overall circumstances the confession was still reliable. The police gave more of an inducement here, and the defendant was more robust, than in Mrs Evans's case. Looking further back the next hit is in 1993, a case note on *R v Glaves* [1993] Crim LR 685. Oppressive repetitive questioning of a juvenile in the absence of an appropriate adult led to admissions of arson after repeated denials. The admissions were excluded.

Does this answer A's question? Not really, although the repeated questioning was a part of the oppressive conduct.

Going back still further, the 1992 index (which is consolidated and covers the years back to 1988) produces under 'Evidence – confessions' reference to several cases. A reads the report on *R v Gline* in [1992] Crim LR 122 and finds that extensive questioning, in the absence of bad behaviour by the police, but when the accused is suffering stress, can lead to exclusion of a confession under section 78 of the Act. Interestingly, the Court of Appeal accepted expert psychological evidence supporting the defence theory that stress made the confession inadmissible under section 78.

We could go back over further years, and we could look in, say, Archbold, but as we are only on a guided tour, we skip across to *Current Law*. This is a monthly publication which lists cases and articles under subject headings such as Criminal Evidence. Each month has a cumulative index and each year is bound with a consolidated index. 1998 and 1997 reveal nothing likely to help the enquiry, with cases covering bugging of cells, police misconduct, informers and a mentally disabled defendant. There are several in 1996, including an unreported case of *R v Sullivan* at paragraph 96/1317. We have to go back to 1994 and further to find much else. (A carries out a LEXIS search by looking for all cases where Sullivan appears in the title. This case should be found, but surprisingly is not. Even LEXIS is fallible.)

1994, 1992 and 1991 indexes under the same headings show up some well publicised cases: *R v Miller, Paris and Abdullah* (1993) 97 Cr App Rep 99 and *R v Silcott* (1991) Times, 6 December. In both, on appeal, the court held the confessions should have been excluded because of the oppressive questioning (*Miller*) and the state of mind of the suspect (*Silcott*). A has found, so far, nothing directly comparable with the mild pressure which Mrs Evans endured.

Let us try another approach. Are there any relevant journal articles that can lead us to authority?

Another source of journal article references is the *Index to Legal Periodicals*. This also covers US cases. The February 1993 index – for example – takes A to an article in the *New Law Journal* vol. 142 p 1277 by Gudjonsson on the pyschological vulnerabilities of people under interrogation, and suggests to A the possibility of calling expert psychiatric evidence on the *voir dire* (the process also known as the trial within the trial where the admissibility of the confession is decided). A would need to reinterview Mrs Evans in more depth to discuss her state of mind before pursuing this possibility. If A decided to go ahead, that would lead to further questions – will legal aid pay, will such evidence be admissible? A does not undertake the research now, as A notes that the case of *Gline* (above) dealt with the admissibility point, and research task 11 will deal with legal aid costs.

So far A has nothing conclusive from recent case law. A would go through further journal index dates, but we move on to another source. We know that we are concerned with section 76 of the Police and Criminal Evidence Act. A is looking for cases where the confession may be unreliable despite the police not breaching the codes. What do the commentaries say about this in *Halsbury's Statutes*? Evidence is in volume 17. At p 226 we find commentary on section 76, and on 'things said and done' which might make the confession unreliable. We are referred to *R v Goldenberg* [1988] Crim LR 678, and *R v Crompton* [1991] Crim LR 277. Both involved drug addicts who confessed during a period of withdrawal. The resulting confessions were admissible. A looks in the cumulative supplement for 1997 of *Halsbury's Statutes* and the *Noter Up* (in case there is any new case law since 1993, when volume 17 was published). There is nothing similar to this case.

A tries one further source of case law (apart from a database), *The Digest*, which gives a potted summary of cases going back as far as you could wish on indexed topics. Volume 15(2) deals with this aspect of evidence, and in the index we can choose from a large range of headings. A finds nothing apart from *Goldenberg* (at para 18353).

A is satisfied that there is case law from which it can at least be argued that the confession be excluded. This can be used in any negotiation and at trial – if, after advice, Mrs Evans so instructs. But the confession is probably going to be admitted, in the absence of good authority to support exclusion. Further research by A, not demonstrated here, into whether the questioning breached the codes of practice will in fact confirm that a challenge is unlikely to succeed. A might look in an up-to-date text such as Blackstones under 'Confessions' and find this conclusion confirmed at F17.16 onwards.

A has now looked at the key evidence relating to the charge of the long-term theft, and decides to explore a negotiation. This takes place in Chapter 6, but in terms of chronology, it would happen now. Depending on the outcome, A will prepare both charges for trial, one only, or none.

To illustrate the method of preparing the case for trial, we have solicitor A prepare just one of the charges for trial, the theft of the three coins – but that is not necessarily what happened. Did the prosecution drop the other charge? Find out in Chapter 6.

A now starts to build defence theories. As onlookers, we can allow ourselves a frisson of excitement, as we may be able to start pointing the finger of blame at someone else. Hercule Poirot would have loved it!

We do not have to end up with a theory that is different in every aspect from the prosecution story. One element on which the court has a reasonable doubt is, in theory, sufficient for an acquittal. In practice, we want a story that hangs together credibly, more so than the prosecution's, but at the same time our story aims to be most coherent at precisely the point where the prosecution story is vulnerable.

In our theory creation we should not worry about aspects of the prosecution theory that are not disputed. Nor should we invent theories that are inconsistent with anything our client has told us, for we are not in the business of inventing stories, only fashioning them from the material which we find. Inventing facts is professional misconduct; predicting facts and then looking to see if evidence supports them is creative and professional lawyering.

First we brainstorm the possibilities. This means casting our net widely to try to create theories around the prosecution facts, theories that may contain plausible stories consistent with a not guilty verdict. A lists some possible theories around each part of the prosecution story.

Element 1: Mrs Evans had the opportunity to steal

■ *Theories*:

  ☐ the prosecution won't be allowed to use that evidence;

  ☐ so what? (ie it is not damaging to the defence);

  ☐ so did others: employee, family, friends, burglars.

These theories, once generated, need both legal and factual research so that A can test if they are useful. The factual tasks are all taken together below, but we get A to tackle the legal research tasks for each of the brainstormed theories as we go along.

Legal research task 3

Is opportunity by the defendant or others admissible evidence?

■ *Objective:* A wants to exclude evidence of opportunity.

■ *Question:* The word 'opportunity' does not show up in any textbook index, so how can A formulate the exact question? A must find a generic word to describe the type of evidence he or she is going to research. To help arrive at this, try thumbing through the contents pages of a textbook. Words like 'relevance' (*Cross and Tapper*, for example, at p 56) lead to discovery of the concept 'circumstantial' evidence.

The research question could now be: Is circumstantial evidence admissible? *Cross and Tapper* (p 23) states that it is. Blackstones (F1.10–F1.15) gives as examples of circumstantial evidence motives and lies. Is this a satisfactory answer?

It is too brief, it does not cover the possibility that there may be kinds of circumstantial evidence that may be excluded. So knowing what the relevant term is (circumstantial evidence) A turns to something more weighty, in this case *Cross and Tapper on Evidence*. A finds there that such evidence, including opportunity, is admissible (p 28).

The objective has not been achieved, in that the answer is not what A wanted on behalf of Mrs Evans, but this is better than preparing the case without this knowledge.

Element 2: Mrs Evans is short of money   Again, A brainstorms to generate theories. A will try to show that this is not the truth, or that this type of evidence cannot help the prosecution. Here are some theories that A generates.

■ *Theories*:

  ☐ Mrs Evans is not short of money;

  ☐ so what if she is? (not damaging);

  ☐ others with access are short of money: the owner, Sharon, Darren?

  ☐ such evidence is not legally admissible.

Legal research task 4

Is shortage of money admissible in evidence?

Happy are we: we have already researched opportunity. We know that shortage of money will be categorised under circumstantial evidence and is intrinsically admissible. Is there any way to stop it? It doesn't seem very fair.

FAIR? This triggers another avenue of legal research: is evidence supposed to be fair? In Blackstone we look up 'fair' unsuccessfully – but do not give up, trying its opposite 'unfair' which leads eventually to F2.14, where we discover section 78 of the Police and Criminal Evidence Act and the power of the court to exclude evidence which it would be unfair to adduce. To get an idea of how section 78 works is now easy, because A can use the table of statutes in any book, or for example in *Halsbury's Statutes*, or can look up any cases on LEXIS where section 78 has been cited. (A does not use LEXIS here, but we will show you LEXIS in action shortly.)

What does A find? A finds no cases supporting a theory that the evidence of motive can be excluded. (*Cross and Tapper* p 538 onwards found by looking for section 78 in the statutory index at the beginning.)

Oh well, we tried ....

Element 3: Over a period of six months money went missing from the till. Mrs Evans stole while serving in the shop and when visiting after hours

■   *Theories*: After a brief brainstorm, A has generated the following possible theories:

☐   money did not go missing at all;

☐   Mr O'Connor is lying, conspiring, or mistaken;

☐   the till or the records are inaccurate;

☐   someone else took the money;

☐   others visited after hours;

☐   stealing after hours is inconsistent with the type of theft reported by Mr O'Connor;

☐   this kind of evidence is not admissible.

These theories all require factual research, but they generate legal research tasks too. A will need to find out to what extent he or she can be allowed access to the factual information (see research tasks 8, 9 and 10); and A needs to find out:

Legal research task 5

Is evidence of visiting after hours admissible in evidence against Mrs Evans on the charge of stealing the three coins?

■ *Objective*: To exclude evidence which identifies Mrs Evans with this other offence.

■ *Question:* A first has to work out what kind of evidence is this that he or she is trying to exclude? How do we categorise evidence relating to a different charge? Is it possible to use evidence of one offence to prove commission of another?

It is hard to identify the key words if you have not obtained some knowledge of principles of evidence. Assuming you know a little, you could look, rather than at an index, at the contents page of a textbook. Early on in most evidence texts comes 'relevance' and at some point there are chapters dedicated to 'character'.

Relevance does not answer the question immediately, but under character we find that evidence suggesting Mrs Evans has offended on another occasion is not relevant (eg *Cross and Tapper*), unless her behaviour on that occasion is proved to be strikingly similar to how she is alleged to have behaved this time. (Found by looking for 'Relevance, character and' at pp 58 and 353.)

This evidence is, then, inadmissible to prove theft of the three coins. But if both matters are tried together ... can they be separated? Another research task for A to do later, if a trial on both charges takes place. (But not for us, we skip happily forwards into the theory building.)

Element 4: Darren O'Connor saw Mrs Evans put money in her pocket on other occasions   A brainstorms the following theories:

■ *Theories:*

  ☐ he is mistaken;

  ☐ he is lying or conspiring;

  ☐ he is correct but there was no appropriation;

  ☐ what happened on another occasion is not admissible.

Factual investigation is undertaken later, but A needs to check out the legal theory.

Legal research task 6

■ *Objective*: to exclude evidence of previous incidents.

■ *Question:* Is what happened on a previous occasion admissible evidence?

A remembers task 5. If this amounts to character evidence, we have answered the question: no further research needed. But if A concludes this is not character evidence, he or she has to go back to first principles. Where do we look in the index? Nothing comes to mind except ... yes, is the evidence relevant? A already knows where to find relevance in the texts. *Cross*, for example, has under 'Relevance' 'conduct on other occasions', p 58. A finds the evidence is probably not legally relevant if its sole purpose is to show that a person has a tendency to behave that way.

Element 5: On 1 September police officers marked three one pound coins and used them to purchase goods from Mrs Evans   What factual and legal theories can A generate to combat this element?

■ *Theories:*

☐ the police are lying, mistaken, conspiring with others to implicate Mrs Evans;

☐ it is true but not damaging.

These theories generate factual investigation – see below.

Element 6: Mrs Evans put the coins in her apron pocket as an appropriation

■ *Theories*:

☐ they were not the same coins;

☐ someone else put them there;

☐ they were planted by the police;

☐ she put them there absent-mindedly.

(Note A does not try a theory that the coins were not there at all – we have our client's instructions on this point already.)

Again, A has not generated, at this stage, a legal question (having earlier researched the meaning of appropriation – p 195).

Element 7: Mrs Evans admitted the coins were in her pocket and said she had no idea how they came to be there

■ *Theories*:

☐ this is true, since she has told A the same – A's theory is simply that she is telling the truth;

☐ it is not admissible as evidence against her.

Only the legal theory needs research.

Legal research task 7

■ *Objective:* Some of the evidence helps us – a denial of knowledge right from the start. Some is damaging – that the coins were in her pocket. A already knows that the damaging part is admissible as a confession – and anyway, it is not disputed. The objective, therefore, is to admit the helpful denial.

■ *Question:* Is an early denial of some part of the offence admissible to assist the defence?

A, a great lover of variety and knowing how librarians love re-shelving law books, takes another textbook: Carter *Cases and Statutes on Evidence*. In the index A finds under 'Confessions': 'Excupatory [sic] statements'. At p 390 Carter cites two authorities, one Canadian which held such statements inadmissible and one English that rules (*obiter*) that they are admissible: *R v Sat-Bhambra* [1989] Cr App Rep 55 (at 61–62). A does not want to rely on persuasive authority only.

In Keane *The Modern Law of Evidence* under 'confessions' A finds 'mixed statements' at p 109. The case of *R v Sharp* [1988] 1 All ER 65 is cited. A checks in this case and finds that in a mixed statement (both damaging and helpful to the defence) both parts are admissible at trial as evidence of the truth of their contents. A checks for further citations of this case in the *All England Books on Screen* index (where all cases are listed alphabetically; any further case in which a particular case is discussed within the All ER is also indicated, and linked by hypertext: just double click the mouse to find that further case). A similar manual check could be made in the most up to date All England Reports index, or the case citator (which would give citations of all reports, not just those contained in the All ER). The case of *R v Bey* [1993] 3 All ER 253, a House of Lords case, is shown as having considered *Sharp*. However *Sharp* was only considered in the context of whether a lie – the damaging part of the statement – by a suspect is admissible in evidence, not the question of whether a statement supporting the defence is also admissible. No other citation of *Sharp* occurs within the All England series.

A can now run the case of *Sat-Bhambra* through LEXIS, to ask LEXIS to cite cases where it was considered. If there is a more recent case which confirms or overrules the principle of admitting the favourable parts of a mixed statement A will have a definitive answer. Because Sat-Bhambra is an unusual name, the search request within ENGGEN cases is simply Sat-Bhambra. Nine citations are found, the most recent being *Western v DPP* [1997] 1 Cr App Rep 474. This confirms that Mrs Evans's denial of knowledge should be accepted as evidence by the magistrates.

Stage 4: Factual investigation

A has carried out legal research, but needs to look now at the factual elements of the various theories. The defence theories seem to be falling into two clusters: *she was framed* or *she did not mean to take the coins for herself*.

Only two overall theories? Why not try more?

A speculated during the brainstorm that the police are lying when they say it was Mrs Evans who found the money in her pocket, and that they planted it when they searched her. But A has Mrs Evans's clear instructions to the contrary. If the instructions were unclear, A could work further with that theory. As it is, A abandons it as not worth further pursuit.

There is of course a very plausible theory that she did take the money deliberately. It is a theory that coherently explains all of the known facts; after A's investigations if it seems the most convincing what should A do? The opponent has the best theory – help! But it is not for the solicitor to judge, merely to advise. A would be right to tell her that, given the weaknesses of her defence, and the strength of the apparent prosecution evidence, a not guilty plea looks unlikely to succeed. But A's task is to promote theories consistent with Mrs Evans's instructions.

We are not at the stage yet of counselling despair – not yet anyway. A needs to test the two theories with thorough factual investigation. Contentious lawyers are not in the business of trying to force facts to fit; nor of influencing witnesses to tell anything other than the truth as they perceive it. The theory tells A where to look and what are the relevant questions to ask. A does so with an open mind.

A has already obtained through theory generation a number of 'facts' which need investigation. But a good theory also helps to predict the existence of further evidence, and to guide A as to where to look. If Mrs Evans was framed A would expect to find evidence of some of the following:

■   someone having a motive to frame her, eg a grudge, covering up own misdeeds, financial problems, incompetence;

■   someone showing changed behaviour towards her, before or after;

■   someone having done things like this before;

■   inconsistencies in the story, eg the till, the till rolls, the books, the timings;

■   implausibilities, eg why these three coins in the apron and no others?

■   opportunities to frame her, eg getting at the apron;

■   pressure put on witnesses such as the boy to lie;

■   some of the above may be revealed by witnesses, eg the other employee; suppliers.

If she put the coins in her pocket innocently, this also generates factual predictions. Some of these may be true:

■   she has acted in a similar way in the past;

■   others have acted in this way in the past;

■   putting coins in the pocket is normal practice in retail work at busy times;

■   missing money is an error of bookkeeping;

■   there is evidence of Mrs Evans's general honesty;

■   her confession is untrue, because she was put under pressure.

We need to investigate to see if the predictions in either theory may be valid. If a theory is true we expect to find facts consistent with it. Not all of our predictions could be true simultaneously; after investigating, we can reject or refine theories.

The primary source of relevant facts is our client; but the predictions also suggest other sources. A wide-ranging approach could include:

■ interviewing all other people concerned in the bakery;

■ finding out about the criminal records and backgrounds of people who might have been involved in framing her;

■ looking at the till rolls, the till itself;

■ visiting the shop to look at the layout and who might have seen what from where;

■ seeing the apron and other aprons;

■ looking at the coins themselves and submitting them to analysis;

■ fingerprinting the coins (if they have been kept sealed); and

■ finding out about Mrs Evans's personal circumstances.

These factual investigations cannot be carried out before more legal research questions are answered.

Legal research task 8

■ *Objective:* To interview whoever we choose.

■ *Question:* Is there any restriction preventing a solicitor approaching anyone he or she chooses?

The key task is to identify what type of problem this is. A asks: if a solicitor were to talk to someone and this was not allowed, what might happen? It might be a criminal offence. It might be a breach of professional conduct.

Now it is easy. To learn about criminal offences, A tries a practitioner text, *Blackstone's Criminal Practice*. Under 'witnesses' A finds 'interference with' at B14.31. It is an offence, A finds, to threaten, attempt to bribe, harass or frighten a witness. A of course intends to do no such thing (though what about offering expenses?). It looks as if there is no criminal penalty.

Is it professionally acceptable?

A looks in the Law Society's *Guide to the Professional Conduct of Solicitors* under 'witnesses' and finds 'interviewing'. On p 338 A finds the answer: the principle that there is no property in a witness, and the guidance that there should be no possible suggestion that a solicitor has tampered with a witness. If the witness has been interviewed already by the prosecution, A is advised to let them know of the intention to interview and provide the prosecution with the chance to be present.

Legal research task 9

■   *Objective:* To obtain access to this evidence.

■   *Question*: Is the defence allowed access to the till, the rolls, and the premises? No: A needs to formulate this into a question that can be researched. What kind of evidence is this that A wants to see? Assuming some basic knowledge, A knows it is 'real' (things). So is A allowed to inspect real prosecution evidence in preparing a criminal defence?

It is a practical question so A turns to a practitioner text, in this case *Blackstone's*. Surprisingly, A draws a blank in the index under 'real evidence': there is only mention of categorisation and admissibility.

The question needs reformulating. It is not the fact that the evidence is real that is relevant to A's objective: it is the fact that it is in the control of prosecution witnesses. Fortunately A is aware of recent miscarriage of justice cases relating to non-disclosure of prosecution evidence. Will this formulation help? The question becomes: is the defence entitled to disclosure of available prosecution evidence?

A looks in *Current Law* for disclosure of prosecution evidence. Working back from the present date, A finds two cases in 1993 at paras 805 and 808. A looks up the first, a Privy Council case from Jamaica, *Vincent v the Queen* [1993] 1 WLR 862, and finds the principle stated that the full prosecution case should normally be supplied to the defence on the basis of fairness. A also finds *R v Davis* [1993] 1 WLR 613 where the Court of Appeal decided the court has a power to allow evidence to be withheld from the defence if it is sensitive or otherwise in the public interest to do so. Otherwise evidence should be disclosed, and various authorities are cited, which A looks up: a Practice Note called *Criminal Evidence: Unused Material* [1982] 1 All ER 734 and a number of cases, including *R v Ward* [1993] 1 WLR 619. To check if IT may reveal anything more recent A conducts two further searches. Using the All England Books on Screen, with a search request: prosecution disclosure evidence, 162 'hits' are obtained. The most recent are the ones A is interested in, for example *R v Mills* [1997] 3 All ER 780 which confirms the general principle that a fair trial requires disclosure of prosecution evidence reflecting on their witness's credibility. A LEXIS search (Prosecution W/15 disclosure and witness) produces over 100 hits. The most recent confirm this finding, so there is no need to narrow the search.

Another way to track down material relating to a new topic is to look for journal articles. Lawtel provides quick access to abstracts, though as it does not search the articles in full text, it will only discover material if your search matches the editor's judgement as to what the article is about. Using keywords: Evidence and disclosure, A finds three highly relevant articles in the New Law Journal by David Corker at (1997) 147(1) p 885, and (1997) 147(2) pp 961 and 1063. These articles, entitled Maximising Disclosure, reveal to A that the common law obligation to disclose prosecution evidence is now complemented by a statutory regime under the Criminal Procedure and Investigation Act 1996, and codes of practice. The prosecution have a duty to make a schedule of all relevant evidence and, A discovers, reveal any evidence which 'might undermine' the prosecution case (section 3(1)). There is a right to apply to the court of trial if material is not disclosed.

A asks for fingerprint test results, of which no mention has been made (and is told that no tests were carried out). A knows that if access to the coins, tills and rolls and the premises is refused there will be grounds for an application to the court or an appeal against conviction. A therefore is able to insist on inspecting these items of real potential evidence.

Legal research task 10

■   *Objective*: To obtain access to information held by police on witnesses (with the aim of using it to discredit them).

■   *Question*: Can A obtain access to criminal records and other information about any other people involved – employer, Sharon Smith, Darren O'Connor, police officers involved?

It is tempting to assume that task 9 answered this. Assumptions are not the same as research. This would be to extrapolate too widely – *Ward* is not authority for allowing the defence everything they want, only a fair trial and information actually held by the prosecution. A has a wider objective – to uncover dirt. The research question is whether A can obtain details of convictions of people connected with the case or the bakery.

An obvious trigger word for the search is 'privacy'. A also guesses that any information about convictions is likely to be held in a computer, if anywhere.

Is a person entitled to have details of their convictions withheld from enquiry by others? Is the situation different if they are to be a witness for the prosecution?

Where to start? *Halsbury's Laws*? Volume 8(2) para 110, according to the index, deals with 'privacy'. But this deals only with the constitutional lack of a right to privacy, and the possibility of actions for trespass. Well, A does not intend to use Watergate methods, so this is not relevant.

If there is nothing instantly available under *Halsbury's Laws* (and A finds nothing under data protection either), how about *Halsbury's Statutes*? Volume 6 contains the Data Protection Act 1984 at p 899 onwards. Section 2 of the Act says that general principles of data protection are set out in Schedule 1. There A finds no general principle against disclosure of data, but does find that any person holding data can only divulge it in accordance with the purpose for which the data was held in the first place. Under section 9 of the Act A finds that it is possible to inspect the Data Protection Register to find out for what purpose the police are registered to hold data. But A decides that enough has been learned – it is most unlikely that there is a general right to find out from the police about people's convictions.

What about disclosure of convictions of witnesses? Where would an answer be found? A realises that this is a matter of criminal procedure. A basic text (*Emmins* is used) shows (at p 269) that A is entitled to details of convictions of witnesses. The authority cited is *R v Paraskeve* (1983) 76 Cr App R 162, which A can look up. A asks the CPS for this disclosure.

Legal research task 11

■   *Objective*: To be paid.

■   *Question:* What expenses can be incurred in investigating all of this?

This is straightforward – under a criminal legal aid order what limits exist as to the work which a solicitor can be paid for in preparing the defence?

Where to look? A library catalogue shows that among other things there is a *Legal Aid Handbook* published every year. What is the index word? A thumbs through the index under 'Criminal Legal Aid' and finds 'scope' at p 205. This is a Note for Guidance and says that A can use legal aid to prepare the client's defence. That is not an answer – it begs the same question. A goes back to first principles. Legal Aid is a statutory scheme: A can be paid according to the statute or the regulations. These are available in the handbook. Section 19 of the Legal Aid Act says that the scheme allows representation and section 25 says costs can be recovered according to the regulations. So A turns to the 1989 Legal Aid in Criminal and Care Proceedings (General) Regulations at para 54. A may apply to the Area Committee for authorisation before 'performing an act which is either unusual in its nature or involves unusually large expenditure'.

A does not, from experience, know what this means. How long is a piece of string? What should A do? A leaves the library and uses a research strategy that is one of the most important of all: A asks someone with more experience. We asked each other and agreed almost all of the investigations apart from witness interviews we would like to undertake should be authorised if we want to be sure of payment. In accordance with the regulations A looked up, A applies to the Area Director for authorisation, setting out the steps he or she wishes to take, the reasons, and the likely cost.

A now has some more interviews to carry out and investigations to make. In this factual research A must look for both consistent/helpful evidence that supports the theory, and also damaging evidence. The latter is perhaps the most important, because 'the lawyer who consciously avoids discovery of harmful evidence learns for the first time at trial what the adversary has known all along' (Binder and Bergman *Fact Investigation, From Hypothesis to Proof*). Indeed, if we are in any way emulating a scientific process, we must have A do his or her best to disprove the theory, testing it harder than the court will. In court we may permit A to be partisan, and try to prove our version. We can expect the prosecution to explore any weaknesses. In preparing for court, A must look for the weaknesses.

The results of these factual investigations turn out to be as follows:

The shop A visited the shop and observed the layout. It is a cramped shop which, at busy times, is very crowded. There is a big counter in front of the till, but this does not obscure sight of the till. A customer could watch money being put – or not put – in the till.

Mrs Evans In a follow-up interview Mrs Evans tells A that Mr O'Connor's management has been laxer than the previous owner's; that on occasion he will take money from the till without apparently noting this in any books, for example to pay for supplies or to give to Darren.

Mrs Evans has noticed changes in his behaviour over the previous months, a general sharpness towards her where he was previously more relaxed; during the summer he started to put pressure on her to work on Saturdays, which she resisted. There had also been some tension in the early summer when she asked for a pay increase, which Mr O'Connor not only refused but became very angry about. Also he used to allow her and Sharon to take unsold goods home at the end of the day; around that time he stopped this practice, although he takes stock home himself. Unsold food is now thrown away.

Mr O'Connor's approach to bookkeeping was casual. The old owners used to cash up (reconcile the till with the cash in the register) twice a day. Mr O'Connor can go for more than two days without cashing up.

Pressed by A, Mrs Evans cannot recall Sharon's or Mr O'Connor's movements during the time between the visit of the plain clothes officers and their return. They were both in the premises much of the time, and both she and Sharon would have been serving. She cannot recall taking off her apron at all during that period, though if she had gone to the toilet she normally would hang it outside the toilet. It is unlikely she would have used the toilet during such a busy period – as far as she can remember she did not stop serving the whole time.

Asked if anyone could have removed the three coins from the till, Mrs Evans says that while Mr O'Connor was mainly working at the back of the shop at the time, he was not seated all the time and would have come into the customer area several times to check stock, or talk to her or Sharon. As far as she can remember she would have put the money in the till, not her pocket, and has no conscious recollection of putting the coins in her apron. She has no doubt at all that if she, not the police, had discovered the coins, she would have put them back in the till and thought nothing further about it.

A had asked her to bring to the interview an apron similar to the one used in the shop. Mrs Evans tries it on, and A observes that the pocket opening is quite tight against Mrs Evans, who is a well built person. A, with Mrs Evans's permission, tries to put a hand into the pocket and finds it difficult to do so without Mrs Evans's co-operation. A concludes that slipping coins into the pocket of the apron while Mrs Evans was wearing it was unlikely to happen. The coins would have had to be put in while Mrs Evans was not wearing the apron, which is unconvincing on two fronts: firstly, Mrs Evans's instructions that she does not think she took it off; and secondly, Mr O'Connor would have had to be certain of her taking it off at the right time in order to be sure to frame her.

During the interview A forms another prediction and tests it. If Mr O'Connor would have needed to be sure that Mrs Evans was going to take off her apron, something unusual must have happened, such as him offering to take over at the counter so she can take a break. A puts this to Mrs Evans: Did something like that happen? Would you have remembered if it had? She answers that she is fairly sure it did not.

Mrs Evans is asked again how certain she is that she herself found the coins when the police asked her if she had any money on her; or whether a police officer searched the pocket and produced the coins. Mrs Evans confirms her original instructions that she is certain that she herself found the coins in the pocket.

A now is forced to drop that part of the theory that would have Mr O'Connor or anyone else putting the coins in the pocket. In consequence A decides not to examine the coins. There is no prediction from any theory that we would find any relevant evidence, since we know she handled the coins, and even if sealed since produced from the apron, they would show only what we know – her fingerprints.

Finally she tells A that she has never liked having Darren on the premises, finds him a badly behaved young man. On occasion she has had to be quite firm with him as he has been rude to her in front of customers. She denies that she is in the habit of taking money from the till into her apron, as alleged by Darren, but states that once at a busy time she did find money in the pocket and returned it to the till immediately, and presumes she had done so out of absent-mindedness.

Pushed hard about Sharon Smith, Mrs Evans is utterly convinced that she would have had nothing to do with any conspiracy; indeed Sharon phoned her up the night after her arrest to commiserate. The idea of running a story based on such a theory would clearly not please Mrs Evans; A decides that even if it had a strong theoretical basis, it would be a non-runner for this reason.

(In fact an alternative prediction could be formulated and tested in interview or cross-examination with Sharon: she telephoned to cover her tracks. But A does not pursue this as Mrs Evans is clear in her instructions on this point.)

Mrs Evans is also unwilling to believe that the police could have misbehaved in any way, and confirms that the account of what she told the police in interview is accurate. Though she felt very anxious, she thinks they treated her fairly. A asks why she said the words 'I suppose I must have done it'. She says that she must have meant: 'I suppose I must have put the coins into my pocket' not 'I must have stolen them and the other money'. She also says that she felt that she had to say something 'helpful' because the interview had been going on for quite a while and she was becoming very anxious to get out of the police station.

We have flagged up confession evidence as a research task (number 7).

A asks Mrs Evans if she has any previous convictions, which she says she does not; and about Mr O'Connor's allegation that she is short of money. She confirms that until this incident both she and her husband have been working, that while not well off they can manage. She also states that she has had responsibility for handling money in the past, including as treasurer of her son's football club, which involves collecting subscriptions, running the account and making out cheques for purchases. She gives the names of committee members, and A obtains letters from the chair and secretary who confirm what she says and personally vouch for her honesty.

Sharon Smith A then interviews Sharon, who willingly co-operates and appears to A to be a truthful person; she too has occasionally gone to the premises after hours (neutralising any inference from the fact that Mrs Evans admits such visits). She had no knowledge of missing money or any plan to plant the marked coins and catch the thief. She can remember nothing of the incident of the plainclothes police officer buying items for £3. She says that she was aware that Mrs Evans once found money in her apron pocket, and that Mrs Evans remarked on finding the coins before putting them in the till. Sharon Smith has never done this herself.

She states that the staff take their aprons off to go to the toilet at the back of the shop, and there is a peg outside the toilet which she and Mrs Evans use. On the day in question she and Mrs Evans were both serving customers and had access to the till.

She hints that Darren is a mischievous child, and hints at not trusting Mr O'Connor – she cannot be pushed further on this and is still working at the bakery, indeed is working full time since Mrs Evans left.

She has seen Mr O'Connor occasionally take money from the till to pay suppliers without ringing it through the till. She is unwilling to say that Mr O'Connor's bookkeeping is different from the previous owner's, but gives A the impression that she is reluctant to say anything against her employer rather than that this is what she has observed.

She is very anxious about attending court and did not reply when A sent her a copy of the statement asking her to sign it.

Legal research task 12

■   *Objective*: To compel Sharon Smith to give evidence and to ensure that it is not then damaging to Mrs Evans's case.

■   *Question*: Can she be made to go to court? What will happen if she comes to court but refuses to give the evidence we are expecting?

This is a straightforward procedural question followed by a reasonably easy evidence question. Compellability is dealt with in any procedural text.

For the second question A looks up 'witnesses' in a standard text – in this case *Cross and Tapper* – and on flicking through the index finds 'witnesses – party's own – previous inconsistent statements' at pp 313–318.

The police   A did not in the end interview the police because there were no outstanding predictions to investigate; Mr O'Connor, as expected, declined an interview, and refused an interview with his son.

The real evidence   The till rolls and the till were inspected. The figures entered in the books matched those shown on the till roll. The roll for 1 September shows no entry of £3 in the till. The theory that someone removed the coins after Mrs Evans placed them there is abandoned. (But A makes a note that the other thefts were supposed to have been from the till – a point on which cross-examination of Mr O'Connor may damage his credibility.)

Convictions of witnesses   The CPS, after some chasing, supply details of a criminal conviction of Mr O'Connor three years previously for furnishing false information under the Value Added Tax Act 1983, section 39. He was fined £500 at Leeds Crown Court. Legal aid has been refused to pay for an enquiry agent to investigate the circumstances, but solicitor A researches sentencing guidelines for such offences (for example in *Blackstone's Criminal Practice 1998* at B4.9) and concludes that the offence although a breach of trust was relatively minor; the usual sentence is a community sentence.

There are no convictions of any other prosecution witnesses.

Theory evaluation time

We have two contenders. We turn them into narratives and hold a beauty contest between them.

Facts over which we can still only speculate but which are likely to exist if the theory is true are italicised. If we were using this theory at trial, these matters would have to be put in cross-examination.

Theory 1: Mrs Evans was framed   Because of the information received from our further investigations we have eliminated Sharon as a potential conspirator; we have found no evidence suggesting conspiracy with the police (which was one reason we decided not to interview them – see research outcomes on pp 219–222 for other reasons).

We are left with Mr O'Connor and possibly Darren as the villains if this theory is to run. Here is the story (with the predictions in italics):

Mrs Evans is employed by Mr O'Connor. *Mr O'Connor's business is in trouble/*his accounting is poor and he is removing money from the business without putting it through the books. *In order to avoid any suspicion falling on him* he accuses an employee of theft *of the amounts that are missing from his books. He chooses Mrs Evans because* she refuses to work on Saturdays and asked for a pay rise; *he prefers Sharon* and increased her working hours after Mrs Evans left.

His son Darren has seen her put money in her pocket *and this gives him an idea for a 'sting'.* He *wrongly* tells the police of his suspicions; there is no objective evidence of any money going missing before this day; as arranged with him, the police buy the goods for £3 *and place the coins in the till. Mr O'Connor then takes the money from the till and somehow gets the marked coins into Mrs Evans's apron, perhaps when she takes it off to go the toilet.* The coins are found in the pocket by the police, as planned.

There are some strengths to the theory. It accounts for some known weaknesses in the prosecution case:

■   of all the coins received by Mrs Evans that day, those three, and only those three were found in the apron;

■   money missing on previous occasions went through the till;

■   Mr O'Connor has a highly relevant conviction.

But there is a lot in italics, a lot of speculation. We will need to ask a lot of questions in cross-examination, to which we do not know the firm answer. A key point, on which we ought to be in a position to give evidence, turns out to be italicised: Mrs Evans cannot confirm taking off the apron and believes she did not. (And we must not ask her to make up such evidence.)

The theory has a further weakness: A's discovery that it would be extremely difficult to place the coins in her apron pocket without her noticing. A could choose not to refer to this point – there is nothing ethically wrong in choosing which information to withhold. But if A is not in the position to put a coherent story together, which explains how the coins got there, the theory will be rejected. The court will be impressed by Mrs Evans's truthfulness in admitting that it would have been hard to plant the coins, but the planting story now has no evidential basis.

Two legal research tasks arise from the theory, and should be investigated before making a final decision:

Legal research task 13

To what extent, if at all, is the evidence of Mr O'Connor's conviction admissible?

■ *Objective:* To get the evidence admitted and for the court to decide it dents his credibility.

■ *Question:* Can we?

We have not yet tried *Stone's Justices' Manual*, an important procedural text published annually. The index under 'witness, convictions of' leads to 2–193. But this only deals with how to prove the conviction, not the principle of whether it is admissible. A reformulates the question: can A bring in evidence of the witness' character? This leads to para 2–492, where the consequences of attacking the character of a prosecution witness are set out (for Mrs Evans the loss of the shield against being cross-examined on her own convictions – if any).

A feels fairly safe in the inference that if there is a procedure for proving Mr O'Connor's character and a consequence of doing so, it must be admissible. A finds no other leads under 'character' via the index however. A tries a new tack: 'cross-examination – character as to'. A is entitled to cross-examine a witness on previous misconduct (para 2–476) – and indeed adduce evidence of the witness' character if it is relevant to an issue in the case.

Legal research task 14

What if any is the danger of casting such an aspersion on Mr O'Connor?

This was answered on the way to the answer to 13. There is no danger as Mrs Evans has no convictions.

Theory 2: Mrs Evans did not appropriate and was not dishonest   This story runs as follows (again, the points on which there is no direct evidence are in italics):

Mrs Evans is a hard-working employee on behalf of her employer Mr O'Connor. She has served him well for 18 months and before that the previous owners. She is honest and of good character and these allegations are the first of their kind.

On 1 September she was serving in the shop at a particularly busy time. The shop was full; two people were serving, *and both of them could not get at the till simultaneously*. She served the plainclothes police officer as alleged, and *put the money in her pocket in the rush*. Past behaviour *indicates that she would have put it in the till when she had the opportunity. No such opportunity had arisen, but she would have noticed the coins at the latest when she took the apron off at the end of the day.* She is an inherently honest person *and this is therefore likely*. There was no appropriation.

This leads to a further research task:

Legal research task 15

Can evidence of her honesty and good character be used in this way?

■ *Objective:* To use her good character as part of the defence.

■   *Question:* Is evidence of an accused's good character admissible?

The index in *Cross and Tapper* shows 'character – accused good character' at pp 347–350. Good character is admissible and probative.

This story has fewer italics; does that make it the most convincing theory? It accords closest to our client's actual instructions, and to the prosecution evidence. The only fact in issue, given that no evidence of previous losses from the shop is admissible (see p 213 where this turned out to be the research outcome) is the inference that her putting the coins in her pocket was an act of appropriation, and, if that is accepted, the further inference that it was dishonest, and done with the intention to deprive Mr O'Connor permanently.

Which theory we choose to run with is now a matter for the client, on our advice.

Assuming our client opts for one of these theories, is that it until trial? No more hard work on theory building and testing? Maybe, but please keep an open mind, modify them if better predictions can be made in the light of further thought or new information.

For example, we have assumed the Legal Aid Board has refused authority to use an enquiry agent to investigate Mr O'Connor's conviction. What if it had authorised this enquiry, and we find that Mr O'Connor's business is again under investigation by the Revenue?

Legal research task 16

What rights would we have to obtain information from the Revenue about the current or the past investigations?

■   *Objective:* To find a bit more dirt about Mr O'Connor which we can cross-examine him about and discredit his evidence.

■   *Question:* Is information held by the Revenue confidential?

Books on tax law – *Butterworths Yellow Tax Handbook*, or *Revenue Law* by Mayson and Blake – yield no answer. Feeling bold A decides to try a database strategy.

This is our first demonstration. The database we used is the most widely available at present, LEXIS. Getting access to the system is a matter for you. Our concern is getting at the information once you have switched on.

LEXIS is a literal, unintelligent system – it will find exactly what you asked it, and nothing else. It will not read your mind. It operates according to the RIRO principle: Rubbish In, Rubbish Out. You should work out what you want, and what instructions to give, before you log on, as it is an expensive system to use. You ask it to search its memory banks for key words; if you ask for all cases where 'Inland Revenue' is mentioned, you will get thousands. If you ask for all cases where 'obtaining confidential information from the Inland Revenue' occurs you will probably get none, because LEXIS can only give you cases where those exact words were used.

A decides 'Inland Revenue' is one of the key phrases to search against; A asks for any English (ENGGEN) cases where 'Inland Revenue' occurs within 25 words of 'confiden!'. (The exclamation mark shows the search word has been truncated; it will allow for 'confiden(tiality)' and 'confiden(ces)'. The actual instruction to LEXIS is phrased: 'Inland Revenue w/25 confiden!' (W/25 means please give cases where the key words or phrases occur within 25 words of each other somewhere in the case transcript.)

But this throws up 42 cases. To read even the headnotes (or KWIC, which highlights the key words A has chosen in their context) would take hours and a lot of expensive LEXIS time. LEXIS allows an existing search to be modified: A modifies the search by typing 'm', pressing 'transmit', and typing in a modifier: 'and confidential'. Lexis now finds those cases among the 100 where the word 'confidential' occurs somewhere – a safe assumption that somewhere in the judgment (if it is to be relevant to our task) the word confidential will be used?

This produces 23 cases, still a little unwieldy and expensive if A has to trawl through each; so A tries a new search with even narrower parameters: 'Inland Revenue w/20 confidentiality'. This is narrower, because the words chosen have to be within only 20 words of each other, and the second word must be confidentiality, not confidential or confidence. If this is too narrow, A can always open up the search again.

In fact, nine cases are revealed, and A looks through the headnote to each. In many of them the headnote alone confirms the general principle that information obtained by coercion by the Inland Revenue from taxpayers is to be kept confidential. (For example *H v H* (1980) 52 Tax Cas 454, which cites the case of *R v Inland Revenue Commissioners, ex p Rossmouth* [1980] AC 952 – which A looks up in the usual way.)

Conclusion of case study 1 research

This has been a long process. And we are not yet at 'Go' (see p 192 and Chapters 5–7 where the preparation is turned into action). A has not, for example, prepared questions to put to each witness in examination and cross-examination to bring out the key points of evidence which will support the chosen theory of what happened.

To go through this analysis and research as we have done would take up more time than can be profitable on criminal legal aid rates. This does not matter. When you learned to write, you had to form each letter slowly and deliberately. Now you write at speed and accurately. Invest in learning. Eventually everything that we have analysed here could have been achieved by an experienced practitioner by intuition – but you cannot rely on intuition until you have acquired years of experience of thorough investigation of the facts and theories. As you gain experience you can turn theories into hunches.

Case study 2: The bicycle and the car

This is our second contentious case. We use a similar approach, but avoid the level of detail used in the criminal case. If this were your case, you would continue where this analysis leaves off.

Stage 1: Before and in the early stages of taking instructions

We know early on that Daniel McAuley has been involved in a cycle accident involving a motor vehicle. Early questions will be based around our need to know what happened.

- When (exactly) did the accident happen? Where (exactly)? Have a local map available; get client to draw a map.

- Who was involved?

- What was the sequence of events?

- Why does our client think it happened?

- What were the conditions at the time?

- What injuries and losses occurred?

- What continuing consequences, if any, does our client suffer from?

- What is the client's relevant history (experience with cycling, previous accidents, medical)?

- Does the client have good sight and hearing?

- Were there any witnesses?

- Were the police involved?

Solicitor B asks these questions, and others that come to mind as the issues begin to come clear during the interview. B uses, of course, the checklist on pp 163–166 and 170–171 in helping to formulate the questions.

In Blue Peter fashion, here is a statement that was prepared earlier.

I, Daniel McAuley, of 12 Fenton Place, Newcastle 12 will say as follows:

I am 14 years of age and was born on 16th October 1984. I live at home with my parents and attend North Lees Comprehensive School.

On 1st December 1997 I went for a ride on my bike. I was going to see my aunty who lives nearby. I left home at about 3.00 in the afternoon. It was not raining but it was very cold. I went from our street into the High Street. The road was quiet.

As I rode westward along the High Street I needed to turn right into Hanley Street so I looked behind, saw there was no traffic coming, I think I indicated right with my arm and went into the centre of the road. I waited there for a car coming in the opposite direction to pass. As I did so I heard a screech of brakes and the next thing I remember is that I was thrown up in the air.

I must have passed out because I don't remember anything else until I was in the back of the ambulance. I knew I must have been hit by a car or something, but that is all I can remember.

In hospital they gave me X-rays on my head, arm and leg and I had to have an operation on my left leg, which was broken. I was in hospital for a week and have kept having to go back for treatment. I can walk OK now but limp a bit as my left leg is a bit shorter than my right. The doctors say this should improve over time. I am very afraid of going out again on a bike. I missed four weeks off school, and still can't play games like I used to.

My bike was a Ridgeback mountain bike and cost about £350. I had only had it for Christmas. Before I could have it my Mum and Dad made me do a proficiency course, which I am sure I would have passed but unfortunately I was ill on the day. My jeans and shoes were also quite new and were worth about £100. My jacket was an old one, which I got from my older brother who had bought it two years ago for £40. These were all damaged beyond repair.

I don't know if anyone saw the accident. The police took a statement from me in hospital.

I do not know the name of the driver. The police told me he had been drinking. I am sure he was driving too fast and that's probably why he hit me without seeing me.

I am an experienced cyclist, and I have good sight and hearing.

Solicitor B finds the name of the driver by phoning the police, and details of his insurance. The police accident report is not yet available, because a prosecution is likely.

Stage 2: Theory building

To keep it simple, we illustrate the process in relation to theories on liability. B would do the same for quantum. See Chapters 5 and 6 for the research into the amount of damages Daniel might be able to obtain.

The first question is to establish a useful legal framework for the theory or theories. In the criminal case, the legal framework was provided by way of the charge. In a civil case the plaintiff has to define it for him or herself.

The framework is based around the cause of action. This case study is relatively simple; there is only one, and you can probably identify it without help. The cause of action is inevitably in tort, and within tort it is breach of the duty of care – negligence. (It is not always this easy: if the injuries arose at work, for example, the legal framework could not be identified until we had researched, for example, the statutory duties of the employer, perhaps issues of vicarious liability and case law on negligence and breach of safety regulations in the workplace.)

Negligence here is breach of one road user's duty to another road user, causing loss: what is the standard of the duty of care? Before formulating any theories you may need a little legal research simply to brush up on and define the appropriate standard.

What is the standard of care of a road user to another? This is basic textbook research, and we have to have an answer to continue the analysis. For once we give you the answer without the process.

B finds the standard is that of the reasonably competent driver. To formulate our theories, we have to think of all possible ways that Mr Slater failed to live up to this standard. Please consider all possibilities at this stage and do not reject any until they have all been given a chance.

After a brainstorm B lists as possible plaintiff theories within negligence:

1   Slater was driving too fast.

2   Slater was drunk.

3 Slater was not paying attention to other road users.

4 Slater's car was not in good order.

5 The windscreen was obscured.

6 Slater has poor eyesight.

7 Slater does not have any experience of driving.

8 Slater had no lights on.

9 Slater was preoccupied with other matters.

10 Slater intended to run down McAuley.

As this is a contentious case, we must assume also that those advising the potential defendant will have their own theories; we must consider those too. He is likely to be looking at both a denial of liability and contributory negligence. Their theories may suggest:

1 McAuley does not know how to ride a bike.

2 McAuley had no lights/reflective clothing.

3 McAuley did not look behind him before going into the centre of the road.

4 McAuley was drunk.

5 McAuley did not indicate.

6 McAuley swerved at the last minute.

7 McAuley was obscured by other traffic.

8 It was foggy or otherwise visibility was bad.

9 McAuley was hit, if at all, by another vehicle altogether.

The defendant will be carrying out investigations into the best of these theories. So must we, in order to produce from the start the more convincing of the two sides' theories.

We are going to concentrate on an exploration of plaintiff theories. However, there is one critical research task before we can do this. The issue of contributory negligence is likely to be raised, if our predictions are correct. We must know what standard of care Daniel owed to look after his own safety, particularly in light of his age.

Legal research task 17

■   *Objective:* To show that even if Daniel did not behave according to the standards of a reasonable adult cyclist, he was careful according to the standards expected of a 14 year old cyclist.

■   *Question:* What is the standard of care children must exercise to avoid being harmed?

B looks first at a general tort book: *Atiyah's Accidents, Compensation and the Law* by Cane. Under 'standard of care' B finds at page 53 that the standard for the defendant is objective – that is, it does not take into account that in a road case the driver is a learner or old or infirm. The same is expected of everyone. Looking up 'contributory negligence' B finds at p 120 that the standard is more subjective. The authors propose that children can only be expected to behave like children – but the only authority given is actually in favour of an objective standard. That is *Stavely Iron & Chemicals v Jones* [1956] AC 627. A notices that Atiyah is a 1993 text, and looks elsewhere.

A decides to use that case as the start of a more detailed search in a tort textbook. A turns to *Clerk and Lindsell on Torts*. The case index shows this case cited several times, and A finds the relevant section at 3–22. There it is made clear that the standard expected of a child 'of tender age' is subjective – not that of the adult. However, B looks up the cases cited and notes that the ages of the children in most of them was under ten, so the point is not conclusively made. However, *Gough v Thorne* concerned a child of thirteen and a half who made a road crossing which would have been foolish for an adult, and it was held there was no contributory negligence.

B conducts a LEXIS search to find cases where *Gough v Thorne* is cited (Gough w/3 Thorne does the trick). He or she finds the case of *Morales v Eccleston* [1991] RTR 151 where an eleven year old was held 75% to blame – but he was playing football in the middle of the road between traffic passing on both sides.

This research task is used as the example for documenting your research: see p 271 for more detail.

To illustrate the many approaches to a single research task, here is a completely different way to the same information. A loads the CD containing the All England Reports 1936–1998. Telling the computer to search for any case containing (in any order) the words contributory negligence child, A finds 51 'hits' (though fewer cases – for some reason many are duplications). The most recent is 1969, *Jones v Lawrence* [1969] 3 All ER 267. This, along with many of the cases referred to above which we also found, confirms that the principle that a child's standard of care is that of a child of that age. Usefully, the All England Reports always cross refer to where to find more cases: in this case cases on contributory negligence and children can be found in Vol 28 *Halsburys Laws* and at 36 *The Digest*.

Evaluation of plaintiff theories

Each theory leads to lines of enquiry, which can be pursued with witnesses (including the police accident report), by visiting the site of the accident, and talking again to our main witness – Mr McAuley. We are condensing the process, compared with the bakery case, to show that if you wish you can generate predictions and lines of factual/legal enquiry all at once.

1   *Slater was driving too fast*

Predictions:

☐   someone saw Slater driving fast – seek witnesses, knock on doors, ask police if there were any;

☐ there will be skid marks on the road – obtain expert opinion on speed based on any marks found;

☐ the street will have a maximum permitted speed limit – ascertain speed limit; there will be hazards making slow driving necessary – do test drive, note any hazards in the street;

☐ there will have been screeching – client confirms this in his instructions, seek witnesses;

☐ impact at different speeds damages cycles/injures riders in different ways – have cycle seen by expert, have expert consider report on injuries;

☐ Slater will be prosecuted for speeding – check with police;

☐ Slater was trying to get somewhere in a hurry and was late – ask Slater; ask people who knew his movements on that day.

2 *Slater was drunk*

Predictions:

☐ this will have been noticed if the police interviewed him;

☐ witnesses may have noticed signs of alcohol or erratic driving;

☐ his car may contain empty bottles;

☐ Slater will be prosecuted – check with police.

3 *Slater was not paying attention to other road users*

Predictions:

☐ he was talking to someone else in the car – seek information from police; from witnesses; from Slater himself;

☐ he was reading a map, adjusting the radio – same lines of enquiry;

☐ he was looking in the mirror – same lines of enquiry, suggests possibility of another vehicle behind – possible witness?

☐ he was about to change direction or carry out some other manouevre – same lines of enquiry;

☐ there is room between where Mr McAuley was waiting to turn right and the side of the road where Mr Slater could have driven past – check scene with client, take measurements;

☐ Slater will be prosecuted – check with police.

4   *Slater's car was not in good order*

Predictions

☐   the car will have defects that the police will have discovered;

☐   we can discover the defects by having an expert inspect it and service records – or the absence of service records;

☐   Slater will be prosecuted – check with police.

N.B. Possibility of another theory – the garage that maintained the vehicle was negligent. Prediction from this new theory: Slater will blame the garage himself if this is the case.

5   *The windscreen was obscured*

Prediction:

☐   Slater will himself say this by way of excuse;

☐   if there was an obstruction that he deliberately ignored, someone else may have noticed it – members of his family, people in his street, police;

☐   it was frosty, Slater had travelled only a short distance before the accident and the windscreen was still obscured – find out where Slater lives, investigate the weather that day, ask police for observations.

6   *Slater has poor eyesight*

Prediction:

☐   he will fail to see things clearly in court – ask questions at trial to expose this;

☐   he will have a history of consultations with the optician – ask Slater;

☐   he will have glasses and contact lenses but was not wearing them – check with witnesses, especially police;

☐   he will have been advised/required to give up driving – check with licence authorities;

☐   Slater will be prosecuted – check with police;

☐   he will be old – find out through police; cross-examine him; check with people who know him.

7   *Slater does not have any experience of driving*

Prediction:

☐   he has no licence – ask to see it, check with police;

☐   he rarely drives – ask him; ask family and friends.

8 *Slater had no lights on*

Prediction:

- ☐ it was dark enough to need them – check with client, eye-witnesses, lighting up time for that day, meteorological office for weather conditions;

- ☐ his lights were not on when the police came – ask police; ask witnesses.

9 *Slater was preoccupied with other matters*

Prediction:

- ☐ he was on his way to an important appointment; he had just split up with his wife; lost his job – ask questions of those who know Slater.

10 *Slater intended to run down McAuley*

Prediction:

- ☐ Slater has a grudge against McAuley, boys of McAuley's age or background, cyclists in general – ask those who know Slater;

- ☐ the car moved from the edge to the middle of the road and was found well towards the centre – ask witnesses of the scene, police in particular.

We can imagine that Mr Slater's solicitors, who have also had the advantage of reading this book, are doing the same to the theories of liability and contributory negligence. Knowing this we would scrutinise defence theories too, so that we can compare the two and predict which of ours, in the light of the facts investigated, are the best explanation to rebut the best of theirs, so that the factfinder agrees there was negligence by Mr Slater leading to the accident, and no/minimal contributory negligence. But we do not do that here for lack of space. It is sufficient if you can see the way the process can work.

A number of lines of enquiry are thrown up. Some cannot be investigated without disproportionate expense – for example, an enquiry agent to obtain details of where Mr Slater goes – if at all – for eye tests. Some cannot be investigated without investigation of associated legal issues – for example, what is our right to talk to Mr Slater and people who know him, for example his family? Some can be investigated with ease – by talking again to our client, by observing the scene of the accident, and by asking the police for their report. Beyond that it is harder to say which lines of factual investigation can be pursued without some legal research and some initial investigation and further theory evaluation.

Assume that the answers thrown up by the easy lines of enquiry show the following:

- ■ it was not dark, it was not foggy, but it was freezing;

- ■ Slater lives very close to the scene of the accident;

- ■ Mr McAuley has no personal knowledge of Mr Slater, and Mr McAuley's father, who is giving B instructions, does not know or know of him either;

- there is no information in the police accident report to indicate a frozen obscured windscreen;

- there are no immediate hazards making slow driving in that street necessary;

- the speed limit is 30 mph, skid marks have been found (but are not necessarily associated with that vehicle and the police carried out no tests);

- Mr Slater is 34 and there is as yet no evidence relating to his eyesight or personal circumstances;

- the police reported no defects on the vehicle;

- the police report no other vehicles involved;

- the police are aware of no witnesses to the accident;

- Slater is to be prosecuted for excess alcohol as his breath test showed an alcohol reading of 35 microgrammes alcohol per 100 millilitres of breath;

- he admitted the collision to the police, but blames Mr McAuley for pulling out suddenly.

Solicitor B knocked on a few doors in the street, but was unable to find any witnesses.

B also investigated the defence theories listed above: many of the factual aspects overlap, for example to do with the weather. Where they concern Mr McAuley's experience and how he rode the cycle on that day, we have found no witnesses other than Mr McAuley himself and his parents. His instructions in relation to Mr Slater's presumed theories are as follows:

1   *McAuley does not know how to ride a bike*

Denied, he has taken a proficiency course.

2   *McAuley had no lights / reflective clothing*

Not relevant, visibility was good. He had lights but there was no need to switch them on.

3   *McAuley did not look behind him before going into the centre of the road*

Denied – but B concludes memory unclear and client may not perform well on cross-examination.

4   *McAuley was drunk*

Denied.

5   *McAuley did not indicate*

Denied – but client's memory appears to B to be based on what he would like to be the case; may not do so well in cross-examination. He was also traumatised by the accident and admits his recall of the incident is hazy.

6 *McAuley swerved at the last minute*

Denied – he moved out into the road some time before he was hit, and waited for oncoming traffic.

7 *McAuley was obscured by other traffic*

Client aware of no other traffic.

8 *It was foggy or otherwise visibility was bad*

Not the case.

9 *McAuley was hit, if at all, by another vehicle altogether*

McAuley has no knowledge – but Slater admits collision to police.

Which plaintiff theories do we now wish to pursue, modify or discard? Those that remain potentially useful – bearing in mind the expense of pursuing those that are merely fanciful – might be the following. We have noted beside each the legal issues that would then require research.

1 *Slater was driving too fast*

Worth retaining.

Legal research task 18

Of what evidential value would skidmarks be, if interpreted by an expert to support a theory of speed?

■ *Objective:* To use an expert to show that these skidmarks belong to Slater's car and that it was driven fast/braked late.

■ *Question*: Is an expert allowed to give this evidence to the court?

B looks up in the 'White Book' (the *Supreme Court Practice*) the word 'expert'. (The first thing A sees is 'authority to incur costs under legal aid'. A makes a note to do that research too.)

Nothing shows up under 'admissibility'. But there is a note on 'restrictions on expert evidence' at 38/36. B finds that to use expert evidence, a direction from the court is required. B concludes that admissibility is impliedly stated. But to be certain B checks in a text on civil procedure, say Sime *A Practical Approach to Civil Procedure*. At p 267 authority is cited to confirm that B may call expert evidence.

Legal research task 19

■ *Objective:* To prevent Slater from using the lack of a conviction as evidence of his careful driving.

■   *Question*: Of what evidential harm is the lack of a conviction for speeding?

Is this to do with the admissibility of convictions? At first sight this seems to be the question, and B looks up in the 'Green Book' (the *County Court Practice*) under 'convictions'. Page 299 makes clear the procedure for admitting a conviction where it is relevant. It says nothing, however, about the absence of a conviction. How can the question be reformulated? What is conviction evidence? B looks up conviction in *Cross and Tapper*. Under 'conviction' there is, predictably, nothing helpful, such as 'lack of'. B thinks more laterally: what is similar to a lack of conviction? An acquittal. This is found on p 116, and the acquittal is inadmissible – so, presumably, would be the lack of a prosecution in order to prove his good driving.

2   *Slater was drunk*

Very useful, on the evidence probably available.

Legal research task 20

■   *Objective:* To use the conviction for excess alcohol as evidence of negligence.

■   *Question:* Is there case law showing that the presence of alcohol can lead in itself to a finding of negligence.

In our 1994 edition B decided on a LEXIS search. B then searched the ENGGEN cases using 'excess alcohol w/15 negligence'. (This instruction, in case you have forgotten, means that LEXIS will throw up references to any cases where these chosen words occur within no more than 15 words of each other.) Three cases were revealed. Two were relevant, neither a reported case: *Gould v Official Solicitor* (14 June 1982, unreported), CA and *Skilton v Blackmore* (12 October 1990, unreported), QBD. *Gould* makes clear that capacity to drive is affected by drink and is a factor in concluding negligence – but if there is another explanation for the collision the alcohol is not conclusive. *Skilton* is authority for the prima facie presumption of negligence where a driver has drunk excessively.

In 1998 B tries to update this, but for purposes of illustration uses a different database: Lawtel. This database searches against case summaries, not full text, so it has its limitations. But it is far cheaper to use for each enquiry. B, having loaded Lawtel's internet home page, clicks onto 'search tips' to identify the search conventions. For example, on Lawtel negligen* will throw up cases where the summaries use the words 'negligent, neglience, or negligently'. Putting the search text into inverted commas means the programme searches only for those exact words. For example 'drink driving' will not look for anything containing the separate words drink and driving, only the exact combination of those words.

How about:

   alcohol conviction negligen*

or

   drink or drunk driv*

Each of these produces over 400 hits: too many for any easy look at each. B narrows down the strategy as follows:

> aolcohol conviction evidence negligen*

Surprisingly there are no cases containing all of these words. Has B narrowed the search too far? No. Like all search engines, Lawtel will only look for what you give it. B misspelled alcohol. With it correctly spelt B hits 350 cases. How to get it down further. What word will eliminate all the criminal cases which are cluttering up the search? A word that is bound to occur in any damages claim will be plaintiff. B searches for:

> plaintiff alcohol negligen* driv*

and scores two direct hits. *Johnson v Kohler* 1998 QBD, a case not reported as yet, is summarised as follows: 'Despite being convicted for driving with excess alcohol the defendant had not breached his duty of care to three children with whom his car collided because the careful driver would not have expected children to run into the road at eight o'clock in the evening, let alone travel at speed on a single skateboard.' B can look this case up on LEXIS to find what cases are cited, what detail is given in the judgment. A search strategy? How about

> Johnson w/3 Kohler

As we have shown LEXIS at work elsewhere we will move on rather than run through that exercise here.

Legal research task 21

■ *Objective*: to admit the drink/drive conviction as evidence.

■ *Question*: can the conviction be used or must the level of alcohol be proved afresh?

B has found an answer to this in the 'Green Book' search above – task 19 – and notes the necessary procedure.

3 *Slater was not paying attention to other road users*

> We have no firm evidence, and are not aware of any witnesses who could help us. But Slater did hit our client's cycle from behind. This theory is compatible with the other retained theories and can be at least put to Slater in cross-examination. Can it be presumed from the facts that he was not paying attention? B decides to find out if the vaguely remembered doctrine of *res ipsa loquitur* and things happening without explanation is relevant.

Legal research task 22

■ *Objective*: to use the fact of the collision as evidence of negligence.

■ *Question*: does res ipsa loquitur assist here?

B decides on a LEXIS search. Because this is the last of the contentious research tasks, apart from the question of funding the case, B takes a short cut and does not formulate an objective and a question because B thinks he or she is now very experienced. The task is relatively easy: B types in 'res ipsa loquitur w/10 road' to see if there are any cases where the doctrine is linked to road (presumably the word road will occur in reasonable proximity in the judgment if it is a road accident case – but if not the search can be widened.)

B finds four cases. This is a small number, and suggests that *res ipsa loquitur* is not often used. In *James v Parsons* [1975] 1 Lloyd's Rep 178 the court held that if a car ran off the road with no other explanation, prima facie, negligence is established.

Similarly if Mr Slater runs into the rear of Daniel? Suddenly, belatedly, B realises that Slater will offer an explanation, which is what the case will turn on. B has predicted that Slater will claim Daniel changed course without warning or looking. *Res ipsa loquitur* is not going to apply. Which all goes to show that LEXIS is not an intelligent system – it produced the cases, but not the analysis. B should after all have formulated a precise and intelligent question before asking LEXIS – a waste of time and money.

4   *Slater's car was not in good order*

Discard for now for lack of any evidence. If there were evidence worth pursuing, Chapter 7 shows as an advocacy task how B might go to court to seek discovery of relevant documents.

5   *The windscreen was obscured*

The frost theory is worth pursuing; interview the police officer and ask if he or she can recall this one way or the other. Consider putting it to Slater in cross-examination, starting with innocent questions about how far he had travelled before the accident.

6   *Slater has poor eyesight*

No basis at present to pursue investigation – could be put carefully in cross-examination as not incompatible with any other theories.

7   *Slater does not have any experience of driving*

No basis at present to pursue.

8   *Slater had no lights on*

No evidence at present that this was the case, or that it is relevant to the accident. Abandon.

9   *Slater was preoccupied with other matters*

No evidence so far, but cross-examine Slater on events before the accident and where he was going to.

10   *Slater intended to run down McAuley*

No basis to pursue.

(If new information comes to light in relation to any of the abandoned theories, they can be revived. What if, for example, we learned that our client's father had made allegations to the police about Mr Slater being a child molester? We may decide to revive our fanciful notion that the running down was deliberate – and of course then bring in another legal framework of trespass to the person to run in the alternative to negligence.)

The plaintiff's story

'A complete theory of the case combines legal theories and descriptive and explanatory hypotheses in a story which has both rational and psychological appeal.'

(Binder and Bergman *Fact Investigation, from Hypothesis to Proof*, p 184.)

We do not know how the evidence will develop; we have not seen the defence and not yet had an exchange of witness statements. But before we are entitled to any of that, we have to draft our own claim in order to start proceedings; we have to set out a narrative story of the material facts that, if believed, will demonstrate that Slater was negligent in the manner that he drove. This is, essentially, a short story. Ignoring the technicalities of drafting style (see Chapter 5) our story can be constructed from our retained theories.

On a cold winter day at about 3.15 pm on 1 February the Plaintiff, Daniel McAuley, a 14-year-old boy, was riding his cycle southwards along High Street; intending to turn right into Hanley Street he looked behind him, saw that the road behind him was clear, indicated right by putting out his right arm, and moved into the centre of the road.

While waiting there for the oncoming traffic to pass, Mr McAuley was struck from behind by a car driven by the defendant, Mr Slater. The defendant was responsible for the accident because:

- he was not paying attention to the presence of the plaintiff in the middle of the road; had drunk more than the permitted maximum of alcohol;

- his windscreen was obscured by frost;

- he was driving too fast for the frosty conditions and speed limit, evidenced by expert opinion on the skid marks found on the road.

The consequential injuries to the plaintiff are ...

B checks this story with the plaintiff, obtains legal aid to commence proceedings, and the case continues – in fact, into Chapter 6 on Negotiation.

Legal Research task 23 – funding the case

- *Objective*: to carry out the work for Daniel in a way which enables B to be paid and Daniel to minimise the risk of costs.

- *Question*: Can this be achieved through conditional fees?

At the time of writing this edition proposals, but not regulations, are underway for the abolition of legal aid in personal injury litigation. The government expects cases to be funded either through insurance or through conditional fees. B wants to find out a bit more about conditional fees.

Let's introduce B to the internet, which has become a more and more useful tool. For example, current bills, legislation since late 1996, parliamentary debates and government information can all be accessed quite easily. House of Lords cases, and some Court of Appeal cases, are there, and all the press releases of government departments. Large numbers of solicitors' firms have websites. If you are at a university or college you will have on your Faculty homepage a list of resources under various headings, one of which should be Law (ask your technical adviser if you cannot find this). From here you will expect to find links to various web based sources of law, accessible just by pointing the cursor and clicking the mouse. All we seek to illustrate in this little part of the conditional fees research task is that the internet is one more tool for conducting legal research.

B loads up his or her internet access programme and selects a 'search engine': a tool on the web, accessible through whichever company or organisation provides you with net access, used for trawling through all websites looking for the words you are asking for. A good search engine – B used Excite – finds the data in seconds. B types in, quite simply, 'conditional fees'. B finds a large number of sites – large meaning 49,220 at the time of writing – where the words occur. In the list of 'hits' he or she finds beside each a short summary of whose site it is and what the contents are. Beside each entry is the offer to produce 'more like this'. The second entry on the list mentions the word 'personal injury', and when B clicks onto 'more like this' it leads to a number of useful results. Several firms of solicitors are listed, some of which have displayed on their website information for clients explaining how they operate conditional fees.

For example James N Doran of Derwentside (this firm is now incorporated within Stanton Croft), to whom we are grateful for permission to quote this extract, tells prospective clients:

Personal Injury Conditional Fees Explained

1. What are conditional fees?

Conditional fees are a new way to pay for the services of a solicitor in certain types of cases.

If you choose a Conditional Fee Agreement the money you will have to pay your solicitor depends on whether you win or lose your case.

If You Win:

You can receive from your opponent

    damages;

    money to pay for all or some of your solicitor's basic costs, VAT and expenses (expenses are also known as 'disbursements').

You Pay:

    your solicitor's basic costs and expenses;

    a success fee to your solicitor.

If You Lose:

You pay:

    your solicitor's expenses;

    your opponent's legal costs.

(but see section 4 – insurance costs – Accident Line Protect)

2. Some terms explained:

    'basic costs' – refer to the normal charges of a solicitor worked out on an hourly rate basis;

    'success fee' – is a percentage (up to a maximum of 100%) of your solicitor's basic costs added to your bill;

    'disbursements' – are your solicitor's expenses which may include court fees; expert's fees; accident report fees; official search fees; travelling expenses; and in some cases barrister's fees.

3. Other ways to pay:

You should discuss with your solicitor other ways to pay for legal help. Ask your solicitor how likely you are to win. That helps you to decide which way to pay for your case.

Legal Aid

You should ask your solicitor:

    whether you are entitled to legal aid;

    if you are, what contributions you will have to pay (if any);

    what difference having legal aid would make if you win or lose your case.

Paying your solicitor privately

You should ask your solicitor how much you would have to pay if you did not have a Conditional Fee Arrangement. And ask what would happen about payments if you won or lost your case.

4. Insurance cover – Accident Line Protect

Solicitors who are members of the Law Society's Accident Line Scheme can arrange this insurance for you. It can provide cover up to £100,000 for a premium of £85. The policy covers you for your opponent's legal costs and for the expenses for reports etc obtained for you by your solicitor (but not barrister's fees), in the event of you losing your case.

You should discuss the scope of this insurance cover and other insurance policies which may be available with your solicitor.

ask for the leaflet on 'Accident Line Protect';

make sure you understand what the policy provides;

discuss what you may have to pay out if you are not covered.

5. The conditional fee agreement:

If you decide to go ahead, you will be required to sign a written agreement. This sets out all the terms of the contract between yourself and your solicitor. For example, it will say what happens if you or your solicitor want to end the agreement.

The Law Society has published a model Conditional Fee Agreement. Your solicitor does not have to use this. But any other agreement must cover the same issues. You should discuss the agreement with your solicitor to make sure you know what is expected of you and your solicitor.

All agreements must say whether there is a limit on the success fee, (see section 2 above – 'Some Terms Explained'). For example, the Law Society agreement says that the success fee cannot be more than 25% of the damages you receive. Your solicitor must discuss this with you.

Now returning to conventional sources, while still at the computer, B asks Lawtel to do a periodical search against the words conditional fees. This will enable the database to list those journal articles where the words have been included in the summary prepared by Lawtel's editors, so it is dependent on how the editors choose to repackage the contents (it is not a whole text search, only a search of summaries). There are 28 hits, a large number of which, however, are newspaper articles. Conditional fees have been in the news a lot, because of the government's decision to remove personal injury work from legal aid. But newspaper articles are not what B is looking for. An article in the New Law Journal looks interesting, however: Improving Access to Legal Justice, at 148 pages 245–246. B looks up this article and, amongst other things, finds a reference to the Courts and Legal Services Act 1990 and the 1995 Conditional Fee Agreements Regulations (SI 1995/1675, in force 5 July 1995).

B is beginning to find how these fee arrangements work. The regulations state that a conditional fee arrangement may be made which states, in writing:

■   the particular proceedings or parts to which it relates

■   the circumstances in which the fee is payable by the client

■   how the fee may vary in different circumstances

■   what happens if the agreement is terminated

■   liability for the other side's costs or of the party's own solicitor

■   how costs are taxed

B is not yet an expert, but realises there is a framework. If he or she wants to offer Daniel's parent the opportunity to conduct the case in this way he or she may next turn to the Law Society to see if there is any guidance on how the scheme operates. He or she looks through the Legal Journals Index to see if there has been anything further written which may be useful. Given that the regulations came into force in 1995 he or she starts in that year and 1996, and finds, under the heading conditional fees, reference to two articles each of which contain model agreements, one by Jenny Levin in [1996] Personal Injury 3(1) 35–46 and one by Michael Cook in [1996] Legal Executive Feb 16–17.

B is still not an expert, and indeed has probably reached a point where some training is called for, or guidance form an experienced colleague. But at least B now knows the basics.

Some issues in contentious research and problem-solving

We have finished looking at the two contentious case studies.

We will dwell for a little while longer on research and problem-solving as they relate to contentious cases. Some of these issues are not so relevant in non-contentious cases, which we discuss next.

Perhaps you have been able to see from the criminal and civil analyses that theory development precedes all but the initial stages of the factual investigation. Once you have obtained an idea of what the client's principal concern is, you are guided in what questions to ask, and what lines of factual research to follow up, by the theory that is telling you what is relevant. With limited resources for investigation, your choice of what theories are likely to succeed then guides you further. If you start to pursue your investigations without first articulating a theory, you risk wasting time (and money). For example, interviewing a witness and asking them to tell you all they recall about an accident will not help you ask perhaps the most crucial question: for example, did you notice that the windscreen was frosty? Only when you have the theory do you know that that is a crucial question to ask. To the witness, it may not be something they recall or believe to be significant until you ask the question.

There are certain techniques that you can use once you have a theory. They help you to predict what facts to look for. For example, if a person claims he has been attacked, and that is the theory you are currently probing, would you predict bruises? If you have, for example, a theory that the driver was speeding, you can generate predictions using the 'especially when' technique. Drivers speed *especially when* … they are in a hurry to meet a person … to make an appointment … late for work. This approach gives you a line of enquiry, and even if you can unearth no evidence before trial, you can use the probability of such a fact being true to strengthen your negotiations or to cross-examine the driver at trial.

Legal knowledge/research is integral to theory building. The wrong legal framework gives a theory that, while factually coherent, is ineffective. If the charge is one of drunk driving, 'I did not realise I was drinking alcohol, my drink must have been spiked' is not of any use on a not guilty plea. Your research will reveal that this only affords evidence to use in mitigation after conviction. Similarly, in a civil case (a real example this one) the plaintiff was claiming damages for disrepair of a lavatory pan. The landlord's defence was that the tenants had failed to repair it once they noticed it was faulty. This indeed was factually correct, but as a theory on which to base the defence it was no more use than the lavatory pan itself. Legal research would have revealed that the landlord had a duty to repair it as soon as he was notified. The facts, even if accepted by the court, were worthless because they were irrelevant to advancing the landlord's case within the correct legal framework.

5   Research in practice: the non-contentious cases

Introduction to the non-contentious context

The need for thorough and accurate research is as important in non-contentious cases as it is in the contentious ones. You cannot serve the client's best interests if you have not identified the relevant questions and researched the answers to them. But to suggest that the process of problem-solving can be explained in the same way for each type of case is to understate the differences between contentious and non-contentious cases.

Our contentious cases (indeed most contentious cases) involve a dispute primarily about what has already occurred. We are talking here of past events. We have demonstrated that a contentious matter can be analysed in terms of the theory of the case. Presumptions are made, questions asked, instructions taken, investigations carried out and theories formed. These theories are then systematically tested by the application of the results of legal and factual research to see whether the theory holds up. In this way the lawyer can prepare for trial in the knowledge that on the available information – the client's evidence, the evidence of witnesses, the likely cross-examination and the legal framework that has been researched – the theory of the case should stand the test. Of course during preparation theories may have to be remoulded or abandoned. At trial the magistrates, judge or jury may prefer the other side's evidence. What defines contentious cases is that the theory of the case is tested, or is capable of being tested, at some point.

The non-contentious case is different. The subject matter is seldom concerned with past events (although the history behind a transaction, for example the chain of ownership of property, may be relevant). We are dealing instead primarily with the present and future. The client may want a house conveying or a will drafting. The client may wish to set up a partnership or limited company. There is, at least at the outset, no dispute. The past may colour the transaction, in the sense that it provides detail and meaning, but is not the subject of disagreement. The case will focus on the completion of an objective, the house purchase, will, or company formation. There is no hearing to prepare for and nothing needs to be proved; it is not appropriate (although we did try) to look for a theory of the case.

Of course a simple transaction may become contentious. The buyer of a house might complain after completion that the property is infested with dry rot, which the seller lied about. Probate of the will may be contested by a relative who argues that the will does not make reasonable financial provision for him or her. The partners in a business may disagree over the time spent by one of them in a rival concern. The case becomes contested – the parties disagree over who did what. A theory of the case will be needed. Allegations and assertions are being made over events that have taken place. The court may have to decide between versions of events.

In non-contentious cases the use of theory cannot be pursued in the way seen in our first two case studies. There is, as yet, nothing to test, or at least no final arbiter to convince. This does not mean that research and investigation are unnecessary. Far from it. You need to be able to identify your research tasks and execute those tasks with the same degree of skill and professionalism as for any other case.

In order to illustrate and explain how research in non-contentious cases can effectively be carried out we use the following approach:

1   define what it is you wish to achieve (the objective);

2   identify what might prevent you from achieving the objective (the prediction of obstacles);

3   discover what must be done to secure the objective and avoid the obstacles (the means).

By objective, we mean the client's wishes as guided by the solicitor's advice.

The obstacles may be technical difficulties, for example the wording of a document to satisfy the seller's solicitors or the Registrar of Companies. They may also be problems that could arise in the future and which you wish to guard against, for example, the possibility of a tenant subletting to someone who proposes to carry on a business the landlord does not approve of – perhaps a competitor.

The means are the devices and procedure that you intend to adopt to achieve the objective. These may range, for example, from the general use of reference material such as a conveyancing precedent to a particular clause in a lease appointing an arbitrator to settle the amount of rent payable.

The starting-point in non-contentious cases is the generation of questions to identify the objectives, obstacles and means. In the appendix to Chapter 3 (Interviewing) we set out some standard questions that might be asked in particular types of cases. These can be used, say, in the first interview to initiate the questioning process. With answers to these standard questions you can then proceed to draw out of the client the full detail of the proposed transaction, and identify the objectives and some of the obstacles and means. Further questions will be generated by what the client tells you, and by your research.

A research strategy is needed. The experienced solicitor may already have a good idea of the issues that are likely to arise during the transaction. His or her questioning will no doubt be shaped by that knowledge and experience. You, however, lack the benefit of years of practice. (We are not calling you ignorant – just experientially challenged!) Put another way, you have an opportunity to research the case fully and will not take short cuts that might miss out on important issues.

Asking the right questions is an integral part of the research brief. After the first interview you may have to brainstorm the possibilities – obstacles and means – in the case so as to throw up the points for investigation.

The generation of questions does not finish until the transaction is completed. We have seen the concept of the application and reapplication of legal skills at various stages in this book. Research is no exception. Indeed it is the very essence of good research that you continue to search for questions and then answers until you are satisfied that what you have dealt with obstacles and met your client's objectives.

The next stage in the process is to identify your research tasks. The questions that you ask will point you in the direction of these tasks. Some may lead to dead ends in that the answers are irrelevant or inapplicable to the objectives. Others will give you answers in the form of relevant legal or factual material that you must apply as part of the means. The results of your research may lead you to reformulate your questions and conduct further investigations. After advising your client and taking instructions following that advice you may have to reformulate your client's objectives in your research plan.

The research process involves you in the identification of the research source. This, as will be seen shortly in the research exercises created by our non-contentious case studies, may be in the use of an expert, looking at plans or documents, or referring to a textbook, statute or case law. One source may not provide the answer that you need and another must then be consulted.

Each research task must follow a plan. This is necessary to ensure that the purpose of the research is both understood and achieved. The formulation of such a plan is relatively straightforward. What is the aim of the research? What is it that you wish to discover? Where do you intend to conduct this research and what are the means by which you will pursue it? How will you know when you have discovered what is needed?

The last question is perhaps the most difficult to apply. One simple answer is that the result of your investigations suits your objective. This in itself is glib – but not very helpful.

A better approach is to ensure that each research task produces a result. This may be a positive result in that it provides you with an answer, say in the form of a case or statutory provision supporting your client's goals. In our conveyancing case, for example, C needs to know whether the person occupying the house that Ms Kennedy and Mr Bennett want to buy has any rights over the property and if so how those rights can be extinguished so that they do not affect the purchasers. C's research shows that the occupier may have an overriding interest but the occupier can be asked to sign away these rights. Case law is found that provides authority for this and C's research then uncovers a form of words that would do the job (see page 254).

The result of research may be positive in that it clearly answers the question by showing that you cannot meet that particular client objective in that particular way. For example Mr Kader's solicitor, D, has been asked by his or her client whether being a majority shareholder in the company will mean that he can run the company as he used to run his business – that is, however he likes. Can Mr Khan object? D's research reveals that minority shareholders do have rights in the event of the company being run in a way that is unfair or prejudicial. As Mr Kader cannot guarantee having his own way at all times D may have to consider whether to redefine objectives, or advise the client that this is as good as it gets.

The research may, however, result in no definitive answer, or indeed, no answer at all. Although an outcome has been obtained it is not necessarily the conclusion of the research. The point is that all research undertaken must produce some result that can be applied to the objective. If a negative response results, then further questions need to be asked, or objectives changed. For example what if Ms Kennedy and Mr Bennett inspect the property they intend to buy? They notice a gate at the end of the garden which leads onto some land that appears to be uncultivated. On the opposite side of the land is a public road. A rough path leads from the gate to the road across the land. This path provides a convenient short cut to the road. Does the seller have a right of way over the land and if so can this right be passed on to the buyers? The clients ask solicitor C, who carries out the initial research by looking at the copy title documents that came with the draft contract. To the research question 'is there a right of way over the land?' the answer C gets from looking at the copy title deeds is 'no'; although the land at the rear of the house and the road beyond it are clearly identified on the deed plan. There is no right of way referred to.

If this answer were taken as definitive C would advise Ms Kennedy and Mr Bennett that there was no right of way. But C knows (from his or her general knowledge of land law or from further research on how rights of way can be created) that it is possible to have a right of way other than by grant in a deed. Further enquiries of the sellers (who have lived in the house for 30 years) show that they have used this path as a short cut for the entire time that they have lived in the house. More research then follows into what has to be done to safeguard the buyers' interests in the use of the short-cut. (See p 343 for a solution on similar facts.)

The tasks end when the solicitor has raised all of the questions that he or she thinks are relevant and when all the resulting questions have been researched, to the extent that answers have been generated or it is clear there will be no answer. This point may sometimes be reached only after the solicitor has had to start all over again, with redefined objectives, obstacles and means, and a fresh batch of research tasks; perhaps more than once.

Once the solicitor is armed with this mass of legal and factual information, the client's objectives can then be tackled. You can now 'go for it' – apply the means.

Two questions must always be asked:

1   When evaluating your research, can the transaction be completed so that it is legally effective and satisfies the client's purposes?

2   Does the resultant position safeguard the client, so far as is possible, against the intervention of any of the predicted obstacles?

If the answers to these two questions are both 'yes', the solicitor has reached the point where the transaction can be finalised. No solicitor can of course prevent another person from later taking hostile legal action in respect of that transaction. Neither can the solicitor guarantee that the documentation in the case will stand up to judicial examination.

What the competent solicitor can do is to say that in the light of all of the legal and factual research carried out, the likelihood of future problems is remote (or at least predictable). If anyone does complain, they should find the transaction will stand up to another lawyer's scrutiny. In other words, you cannot prevent someone suing you, but if a matter has been properly prepared and executed any such action should be unsuccessful. If all goes to plan your client or their successors will, of course, avoid the test of litigation.

For each research task appearing below, the appropriate question(s) are posed.

Case study 3: The conveyance

Ms Kennedy and Mr Bennett wish to buy 1, Paradise Road, Sheffield. They make an appointment to see solicitor C, who agrees to act for them. Although this case study is intended to show a relatively straightforward non-contentious transaction, you must not assume that the research element is insignificant. An experienced conveyancer may appear to spend little time actively engaged in research. You, as a learner, cannot take anything for granted.

What factual investigations are necessary may be indicated, initially at least, by the use of standard forms of search and enquiry. The Law Society's National Conveyancing Protocol for domestic freehold and leasehold land (Law Society 1994) uses a number of standard questions that provide much factual information for the buyer's solicitor. To presume, however, that this obviates the need for your own focused research is inaccurate and dangerous.

An example will make this point clear. Let us say that C conducts his or her searches and receives replies from the local council. These indicate that the property is affected by planning proposals, say the widening of a road, or the installation of a tramway. C must be able to identify what this means for his or her clients, and to investigate the extent of this proposal. The local authority search itself is not the answer; all the implications must be researched. Even the most experienced of solicitors must be able to recognise when a research task has arisen and how it must be followed up. The standardisation of conveyancing and other procedures may make the initial information-gathering more efficient, but it does not do away with the need for a thorough analysis of all aspects of the case.

Let us look at the research implications in the conveyancing case study by starting with the three points made earlier. We must be able to define the clients' objectives, we must be able to predict the possible obstacles and we must define the means by which the objectives will be reached and the obstacles avoided.

Objectives

What are the objectives in this case? C is being asked by the clients to complete the purchase of a particular property for them, whilst safeguarding their interests. This means that the purchase should result in the property being unencumbered by any unwanted or avoidable restrictions. The house must be at a price that the clients are willing to pay, and should be completed within the time scale that the clients want. The means by which they own the property should reflect their wishes. These are the objectives that C is likely to have in mind even before receiving specific instructions.

Obstacles

What might prevent this from being achieved? C must be able to identify the possible obstacles to progress in order to ask the right questions. These questions will direct C to the requisite research. C makes a list of potential problems:

1   The house may be defective.

2   The property may be affected by disputes between the sellers and their neighbours.

3   People, other than the sellers, may have rights over the property.

4   The property may be the subject of plans or restrictions imposed by central or local government.

5   The sellers may not be able to show good title to the property.

6 The contract for sale may not reflect the agreement that the buyers and sellers have made, for example on price, contents or completion date.

7 The property may be subject to a mortgage or other charge.

8 There may be onerous restrictions revealed by the title deeds.

9 The property may be adversely affected by its location, for example it is in an area where mining has taken place.

10 The buyers may not be able to finance the purchase.

11 The buyers may not agree on the basis of their co-ownership.

The list could go on. All of these matters could prevent the objective being achieved in total or in part. C must now investigate the facts and any relevant law.

The research starts at the initial interview between solicitor and clients. C will take instructions on a range of issues that will enable him or her to begin to define objectives, obstacles and means. The interview begins with C asking a number of questions that can be found in the appendix to Chapter 3 (Interviewing). These are designed to elicit the fundamental information relevant to the conveyance, and will include the identity of the buyers, the address of the property, the price, the type of property, the arrangements for financing the purchase and the desired completion date.

C should supplement these answers by asking further questions triggered by them. C may well explain to the buyers that the solicitors for the seller will either provide, or can be asked to provide, answers to a wide range of questions concerning the sellers and the property. C should ask the buyers if there is anything in particular that they wish to find out. After all it is the buyers who have presumably seen the property and their own inspection of it might give them reason for raising queries.

C has not met either Ms Kennedy or Mr Bennett before. At first interview C (who has already read, enjoyed and digested the Interviewing chapter of this book) greets the clients and adopts an impressive interviewing manner in which the clients are made to feel at ease. They are encouraged to talk broadly about the proposed transaction. After some dialogue and questioning it transpires that they intend to buy the property as soon as is possible and plan to live in the house together. They are unmarried and have no intention to marry in the foreseeable future. Both work full time, Ms Kennedy as a social worker and Mr Bennett as a welfare rights adviser for the same local authority. They are willing to pay £55,000 for 1, Paradise Road, which is a large terraced property in inner city Sheffield. They intend to borrow £50,000 by way of mortgage, and have £6,000 in savings. £5,000 of this will be provided by Ms Kennedy. This was left to her by her grandmother who has recently died. The balance of £1,000 is money that they have saved jointly.

At this early stage, C conducts some simple factual research by asking the clients for information on what is to be included in the sale price (for example, curtains and carpets?). This question may be prompted by the questions contained in the checklist from Chapter 3 used by C at the interview.

C then receives a draft contract from the sellers' solicitors. It is proposed to conduct the conveyancing under the terms of the Law Society's protocol. The sellers' solicitors also send office copies of the entries on the Register (the property being registered land) together with a set of answers to standard pre-contract enquiries and a list of fixtures and fittings to be included in the sale.

C is therefore armed with a mass of information in the form of instructions from the clients and the documentation forwarded by the sellers' solicitors. What does C need to do to formulate his or her research tasks and to activate the necessary research?

Some question generation is required to focus on the research tasks. Let us concentrate on C's instructions. The clients noticed willow trees in the garden and, knowing a little about gardening and trees, they ask whether there is any water course running under or near to the property. Willow trees apparently thrive close to a water supply. Water could mean dampness and structural defects. This is a new possible obstacle that has come to light.

The clients also tell C that they wish the house to be bought in their joint names.

Two research task are thrown up here:

First, as a matter of fact, C must enquire as to the existence of a water course affecting the property. He or she can do this by asking a specific enquiry of the sellers, through their solicitors. With the clients' consent (for additional costs may be involved) C might contact the local water authority or consult maps or plans of the area. C may advise the clients in the light of this information to obtain a further surveyor's opinion before committing themselves to the purchase.

Secondly, C needs to consider the co-ownership issue. The clients wish to buy the property jointly. You may be aware from studying land law that there are different options available to would-be co-owners. C needs to know the clients' objectives and then identify possible obstacles. Since the clients may find it easiest to state their objectives if they know some of the problems that might occur in joint ownership, C identifies three potential obstacles:

■ What might happen, in terms of the property, if the clients were to separate after buying the house?

■ What if one of the clients were to die after the purchase was completed?

■ What if one of them wanted to alter or end the co-ownership arrangement?

If C is to ensure that the house purchase is completed, and that the clients are satisfied and mutually safeguarded, he or she must be able to answer these questions, clarify the clients' objectives and apply the results to the conveyancing process. We will presume that C knows there are alternative means of co-ownership, but needs to check the detail.

Where does the research start here? Even without the benefit of this knowledge C could conduct the relevant research as follows:

Legal research task 24

■ *Objective:* To advise the clients as to the forms of co-ownership and the advantages of one form over another.

■   *Questions*: What types of co-ownership are there? What are the implications of each?

C could consult one of a number of texts and reference materials. We wish to show a range of possibilities in the various research tasks dealt with in this section. A starting-point for researching co-ownership could be *Halsbury's Laws of England*. The consolidated index (1996) volume 55, 590, reveals: 'Ownership in common' vol. 5, 1245 and 'Co-ownership classes of,' vol. 39, 525.

On looking up this reference C finds 'tenancies in common' and 'joint tenancies'. These are defined in terms of their nature and effect. The information, however, is limited to a brief description of each and has little on termination of co-ownership.

An alternative source for this legal research might be *Emmett on Title*, a well-known practitioner's text. The index reveals nothing under 'co-ownership'. 'Joint tenancies' and 'tenancies in common' are, however, listed at Index 12 and Index 28 respectively. More particularly 'survivorship' (what happens when a co-owner dies) and 'severance' (the ending of co-ownership by one or both co-owners) are examined in the main body of the work at 11.131 and 11.143–145. C may not have been aware of the relevance of such terms as 'survivorship' or 'severance', but their mention in the research source would focus C's mind on these issues, and C could explore how they relate to the clients' objectives. The process is becoming an exercise in redefining the issues that are important to the client and the case.

In the text C discovers case law on the meaning and consequences of co-ownership (*Martin v Martin* (1987) 54 P & CR 238). This is of interest and relevance to C, for the case deals with ownership in equal and unequal shares.

Through this very simple, but extremely important research, C has located the basic information that he or she requires to advise the clients of the choices before them. C can tell Ms Kennedy and Mr Bennett that they can either hold the property as joint tenants or as tenants in common. In the former, the survivor of them would stand to inherit all of the property were one to die. If a joint tenancy is declared this can be terminated by either party on notice. If however a tenancy in common is created each retains an interest in their own share, which the survivor does not automatically inherit. The tenancy in common can be held in whatever shares the parties wish, that is, the shares need not be equal. C might add advice that if a tenancy in common is formed there would be nothing to stop either or both of the clients from making wills, giving the other rights over the property, in terms of inheritance or rights of occupation.

Aware of the possible obstacles identified already, C could research in a similar way the rights of married and unmarried couples in respect of the right to occupy the 'matrimonial home'.

C can now seek instructions from the clients as to their wishes in terms of the ownership.

Before doing so, C points out to Ms Kennedy that she is proposing to contribute the lion's share of the deposit. C identifies another potential obstacle to achieving client objectives: that of a conflict of interest between the clients. Alternatively, a potential obstacle is the possibility of a failure by the buyers to agree on the terms of joint ownership. The research task would be 'is there a conflict here?'. The factual research (the clients' wishes) and the legal research (the meaning of conflict of interest) must be carried out, and answers obtained. A similar problem arises in the business law case study, and is dealt with fully there. In this case C's factual enquiries indicate no potential conflict. Unless C feels that Ms Kennedy is being pressured in some way, so that a conflict of interest has arisen, or is about to arise, then there is no reason why the purchase cannot proceed. In the event, the clients wish to hold the property as tenants in common in equal shares, notwithstanding the unequal contributions.

The research tasks identified above arose out of questions stemming immediately from C's instructions from the clients. Other tasks may arise elsewhere. Let us say that C receives from the sellers' solicitors a draft contract and supporting documentation. The answers to standard pre-contract enquiries reveal that the sellers live in the property with a Mrs Shaw. Mrs Shaw is the mother of Mrs Rigsby, one of the sellers. The question which revealed this information asked whether any person aged 17 or over occupied the property other than the sellers? It is a standard question raised by buyers' solicitors for reasons that will become apparent below – but C does not yet know.

Why does it matter if a person other than the seller occupies the property so long as the sellers are contractually bound to vacate? Is this another potential obstacle?

Legal research task 25

■   *Objective:* To protect the buyers against a claim by an occupier of the property to an interest in it.

■   *Questions*: What are the rights of a non-owning occupier? What effect do such rights have on the purchaser of property occupied by the non-owner?

In *Emmett on Title* under 'occupation of land', the index refers to 'overriding interests' (5.126–5.143). Paragraph 5.127 refers to paragraph (g) in section 70 of the Land Registration Act 1925: 'This paragraph constitutes by far the most important class of overriding interests ...'.

What are 'overriding interests'? We need to know this because Mrs Shaw's occupation may just be one. We have to send you on a paper chase.

Try a law dictionary. Jowitt's *Dictionary of English Law*, vol. 2, p 1299, refers us back to section 70 of the same Act. That is not an answer to our question. Look up the section in the Act to see if there is a definition.

Section 3 defines them as 'all encumbrances, interests, rights, and powers not entered on the register but subject to which registered dispositions are by this Act to take effect'. Do you understand it? Does it help? It still begs the basic question – is Mrs Shaw's occupation one of these things or not?

Further research is still needed. An explanation from *Emmett* might help.

Emmett describes the classification of overriding interests (5.123–5.127). This shows that a person in actual occupation of registered land has rights to remain on that land despite the fact that some third party may, for example, have purchased it, unless enquiries are made of the seller and the rights of occupation are not disclosed. C checks the exact wording of section 70(g) and finds that it says exactly the same as *Emmett*. (Does C know what registered land is? If not, by now C has got the message....)

Factual and legal enquiries have led C to a problem: Mrs Shaw would seem to have rights of occupation which continue after the clients' purchase. More research is now needed. Two further research questions arise: first, *when is a person in occupation for the purposes of the Act* (refining the answers obtained), and secondly, *can anything be done to safeguard against the person exercising this right* (seeking the means to achieve the objective)? Unless both questions can be answered, C cannot protect his or her clients' interests and must advise them accordingly.

C finds another useful reference work: *Conveyancing Practice* (Kenny). C looks up the relevant section of the Act at 8.074. Cases are cited that focus on the meaning of occupation including the decision in *Abbey National Building Society v Cann* (1990) . The occupier in our case would indeed appear to come within the protection of the statute – bad news, the obstacle remains.

So what can C do to progress matters and overcome this obstacle? The answer may lie in a number of sources, but to illustrate the range of possibilities let us look at a student text on conveyancing. *Storey on Conveyancing* deals with the difficulties at length (pp 86–88, 102–103 and 479–480). The Law Society's *Conveyancing Handbook* (Silverman) also addresses this problem (B.3.5.10, D.2.3.3, G.3.14.3, G.3.15.1–2). Silverman asks whether the agreement of all non-owning occupiers has been obtained and says that: 'it may be thought desirable for the occupier to sign a release of his or her rights ... The validity seems to have been met with the court's approval. ...' (B.7.3.3)

Silverman then refers to *Appleton v Aspin* [1988] 1 All ER 904. C checks the law report. This case supports the view that an occupier can agree contractually to vacate property by, for example, signing a declaration in the contract of sale or by a separate contract. C now knows the meaning and effect of the term non-owning occupier of land. The way of solving the problem has also been discovered. Mrs Shaw should be asked to formally agree to forgo her rights over the property, in a separate contract or by endorsing the contract between the sellers and buyers. (If you doubt the contractual significance of this why not conduct your own research. As a starter, has there been consideration for Mrs Shaw's promise to leave before completion?) If she refuses to do so, the clients should be advised to abandon the purchase.

A suggested form of words for a release of rights is suggested by Silverman in *Conveyancing* (p 107). C takes this and adapts it for use in our conveyancing case (with relevant details inserted and some minor alterations made to the text to fit in with our keep it (effective but) simple campaign. The clause is typed onto the draft contract and sent to the sellers' solicitors. It now reads:

'In consideration of you today entering into a contract with Paul Rigsby and Janet Rigsby for the purchase of 1, Paradise Road, Sheffield (the Property), I, Mavis Shaw, of 1, Paradise Road, Sheffield agree to release any equitable interest which I may have in the Property (such interest, if any, being transferred to the proceeds of sale of the Property) effective from the date of completion of the sale of the Property. I agree to effect the cancellation of any registration of such interest and to vacate the Property, on or before completion.'

We can leave the obstacle of the occupier behind. C has found positive answers to this problem and the means to move forward. Mrs Shaw is legally obliged to leave the house by the time of completion.

More research is still required in the transaction. C knows, from having struggled through conveyancing on the LPC, or checking in a basic procedural text, that he or she must make a search of the local Land Charges Registry and enquiries of the local authority. These enquiries will reveal whether there are any planning or related matters that affect the land or buildings on it. To conduct such a search is standard practice for conveyancers. What is not standard or routine is the nature of the follow-up research element. C must be able to identify first whether any additional questions need to be asked of the local authority and then be able to analyse the answers received and the entries on the Register that may be revealed. C might discover from the clients' instructions that the property was once probably occupied by tenants. Let us say that the house has sinks in all the bedrooms, a good indication that the rooms may have been used as bedsits. C may now decide that the house could be affected by notices issued by the local authority in connection with multiple occupation of the house. C would need to raise a specific enquiry of the council dealing with this.

C's search and enquiries are returned. As a mundane but vitally important piece of factual research, C must read through the responses. In this case there are two entries that strike C as warranting further investigation. First the register entry indicates that the property is affected by an order made under the Clean Air Act 1956 (as amended). What does this mean? An experienced conveyancer would almost certainly know that this order compels people to use smoke-free fuels. But actually this is not what the Act says. To be more accurate, the Act in fact bans the emission of dark smoke, rather than smoke *per se*. A student, a trainee solicitor or even a recently qualified solicitor, may well not know this.

Legal research task 26

■ *Objective*: To discover the meaning of a smoke control entry so as to advise the clients of its effect and to see if the clients are prepared to proceed with the purchase despite the restrictions imposed.

■ *Questions*: What is the meaning of a smoke control entry in the Land Charges Register? What is the effect of such an order?

Where does research take you to check this detail? Again, several sources could be used. What about the statute itself? The Clean Air Act (referred to in the register entry) specifies (section 34) that smoke emissions darker than shade 2 on the Ringlemann Chart are prohibited. What is the Ringlemann Chart? You either decide that you don't need to know – but how could you decide you don't need to know until you do know enough to know that that you don't need to know? – or you check it out. So, find out about the chart. Look up the Act, consult the local fuel board. Ask the local council. If needs be, some factual research must be carried out, by asking the clients whether they intend to burn fuel that will emit smoke. If they do, the local fuel supplier may advise on the compliance or otherwise of the various fuels. In fact the restriction prohibits dark smoke and dark smoke is normally produced by non-smokeless fuels, for example wood or household coal. In this case Ms Kennedy and Mr Bennett tell C that they only intend to use gas-fired central heating with perhaps a gas coal-effect fire in the lounge. C's factual research tells him or her that neither will emit dark smoke (unless things go seriously wrong!). There is therefore no problem caused for the clients by the smoke control order.

This example is perhaps unlikely to call for the detailed research described as most conveyancers should know the effect of such an order but the process of asking the question: 'what does this mean and how might it affect the client?' and the discovery of the answer is important. If you think you do not need to check this kind of information (at least once in your career), do you really think you want (or ought) to be a conveyancing lawyer? What is the point in carrying out enquiries if you cannot advise the clients what the answer means?

A second matter is revealed by the search. In answer to the enquiry whether there are any plans that adversely affect the property, the answer given by the council is that the house lies within 200 metres of a proposed supertram line (a development that ravaged Sheffield at the time of writing the first edition of this book and will do so again if the proposals to extend the scheme are actually carried out). Is this another obstacle? If the transaction is completed and the clients then discover that a supertram depot is to be built next door they are likely to be unimpressed with C's work. C must tell them of the possibility before they buy the property. C might otherwise be reaching for the firm's indemnity insurance policy.

C must, in order to advise the clients properly, carry out some factual and, if necessary, legal, research. C must look at any relevant plans and see what the proposals amount to. These reveal that there is to be a station built about 150 metres away on an adjacent main road. C informs the clients. As it turns out on hearing this news they are delighted as this will give them improved transport facilities and the conveyancing can proceed.

Research may seem a sophisticated description for sending the client off to visit the tramway's PR department, but it is research nonetheless, both in the meticulous identification of the problem and the seeking out of relevant information. If the clients did not like the idea of a station being so close to the house at least they would have had the chance to withdraw from the purchase.

Although the permutations are potentially endless, the last two conveyancing research tasks that we will examine relate to the content of the title deeds themselves. The property is registered land and the copy of the entry in the Property Register shows that the title is registered under title number SYK 12345. The land is held under the terms of a long lease dating from the end of the nineteenth century, for a period of 800 years at an annual rent of £5. The lease, a copy of which is provided by the sellers' solicitors, shows that there are various covenants imposed on the lessee and successors in title, including an obligation to maintain (with others) a right of way to the property, and a restriction against using the property for business purposes.

Legal research task 27

■   *Objective*: To advise the clients about their potential liability under the lease.

■   *Questions*: Will the covenants in the lease bind C's clients as the new owners?

What research is needed here? What are the relevant questions that define the research needs? At a basic level C could ask whether a lease can make such impositions on a lessee, who after all is the 'owner' of the property? We will presume that C knows enough about land law to be able to answer this for him or herself on the basis of privity of contract and estate. If you do not know, perhaps you should look carefully at the notes accompanying your contract, land or conveyancing course.

C must also ask: what are the implications for his client of such specific restrictions? Are the conditions imposed in the lease obstacles to achieving the client's objectives? If such covenants are legally enforceable what possible liability would this impose on the clients? That is, what obstacles can be predicted to occur in the future, and what are the means if any to prevent significant problems from arising?

We are trying to show as many research sources and techniques as possible. Having raised the right questions, why not look around the office and ask? You should make the most of the resources available to you, especially if you are a trainee solicitor, with a principal supervising you. Ask whether such restrictions are commonplace in the locality. Are they to be considered onerous? If in any doubt about the answers given, conduct your own primary research. Some excellent book s on conveyancing are listed in the bibliography at pages 469–471.

Legal research task 28

■   *Objective*: To advise the clients on potential liability for maintenance of a right of way.

■   Questions: Who is responsible for maintenance of a right of way? Who bears the cost?

One way of tackling these questions would be to seek information from the sellers, through their solicitors. The extent of liability to maintain the road, for example, might be gauged by writing to ask if the sellers have ever been called upon to make a financial contribution to the road's upkeep. Similarly, the sellers may be aware of disputes that have arisen in respect of covenants or conditions in the lease. Why not ask them about these matters? C will look at their responses and analyse the situation in the light of them. If the sellers have never been asked to contribute to the maintenance of the right of way does this mean that liability has lapsed? If they have been asked to pay, when was this and for how much? Was the demand for payment legally enforceable?

C clearly needs to conduct more research. He or she should look carefully at the plans (if any) on the title deeds or office copies. What do the title deeds and office copy entries have to say on maintenance of the right of way? Why consult these? You may find that they give you more information. The office copy entries are likely to contain a plan that indicates the exact route of the right of way. The lease may also have a plan showing a coloured area that is stated to be the right of way. What further questions can be raised? One might well be, has anyone else now assumed responsibility for the maintenance of the roadway since the property was built (in the late nineteenth century)? A long time has elapsed since then and legal liabilities can change. Has the local highway authority adopted the road? Has a management company taken on responsibility for it? Where do you check these details? C will of course have conducted a search of the local Land Charges Register and made enquiries, at least in standard form, of the council. Replies to these enquiries reveal that the roadway is maintained at public expense. If C compares the answer to enquiries with the plan he or she will discover that the adopted roadway and the area covered by the right of way are one and the same. The research is over for this task, for C can now advise the clients that they would not be liable to maintain the right of way. The council has taken over responsibility for the road.

Legal research task 29

■   *Objective*: To advise the clients about restrictions on use and take their instructions on whether they wish to proceed despite those restrictions.

■   *Question*: Are the clients concerned about restrictions on use?

Finally, in this case study, C has discovered a restriction in the lease concerning use. The lease states that the lessees cannot carry on any trade or profession from the property. It is for residential use only. Without repeating the research methodology in full again, C must raise the relevant questions, starting with whether such a restriction is likely to be an obstacle to achieving the clients' objectives, and if so, whether the condition is legally enforceable? The clients' instructions must be taken – simple factual research. In the event, Ms Kennedy and Mr Bennett tell C, having been advised of the restriction, that this is not a problem for them, as they do not intend to run a business from home. The house will be used for residential purposes only.

An apparently straightforward and seemingly routine conveyancing matter therefore provides numerous requirements for research. You must, in order to properly discharge your professional duties and satisfy your clients, be able to ask the right questions, define your objectives, carry out the requisite enquiries of both fact and law and eventually apply the results until the objectives are met.

Case study 4: Expanding the business

The final set of research tasks come from the instructions of Mr Kader and his business expansion plans.

Again, we can analyse the research needs by asking the three broad questions used previously: what are the client's objectives, what obstacles might prevent the attaining of these goals and what means are to be adopted to achieve the objectives?

The overall objective is relatively straightforward. D took Mr Kader's phone call when he rang to arrange an appointment, and has noted the following key facts: Mr Kader wishes to bring Mr Khan into the business and to raise funds for the building of a new factory and production line. D's objective therefore is to facilitate the achievement of the client's plans for the expansion of the client's business whilst safeguarding the client and his interests.

D must start to make plans at this early stage in preparation for the interview that is about to take place. Raising the right questions now – the initial research task – will focus on the issues that may have to be researched later.

D brainstorms and makes this list:

1   Who is the client? D is presently dealing with both Mr Kader and Mr Khan. A conflict of interest may arise and this may affect D's ability to represent either.

2   The client may be, or may become, insolvent.

3   Personal liability for business debts may be incurred. The client needs protecting as far as possible against such a contingency.

4   Mr Kader and Mr Khan may not agree as to the form or content of the new business structure.

5   The creditors may require collateral security that is in a form that is unacceptable to Mr Kader or Mr Khan.

6   Employees in Mr Kader's present business may object to the restructuring, especially if it means job losses.

7   The re-organisation may have tax implications that are disadvantageous to the parties.

8   Mr Kader and Mr Khan may disagree in the future about the business.

9   The business may be adversely affected by the economic climate and may not be viable.

You may think of other, actual or potential, problems.

For the first interview, D should prepare a list of questions that will allow instructions to be taken and that will enable D to focus upon the wishes of the clients and the research that will be needed. The appendix to Chapter 3 (Interviewing) sets out some of these basic questions. They are a starting-point for the research process.

Following the interview D has a better idea of what it is that Mr Kader and Mr Khan want, and is also clear about some of the possible difficulties that will have to be addressed.

We have given many examples of research strategies and techniques in the other case studies and we do not intend to dwell in this case on all the possibilities that may arise. Rather, in the business case study we will presume that the clients discuss with D the options facing them and decide that the formation of a limited company would best represent their interests. Whether a company or a partnership was more suitable would in itself have been a research exercise for D. Rather than look up this very wide-ranging topic, we will presume that, for the present, D has enough knowledge and experience to know the relative benefits or otherwise of the two basic business structures. On the basis of the client's instructions, D now identifies the following questions as needing investigation:

1   *Is there a conflict or potential conflict between the two clients? If so can the solicitor properly represent both or either?*

2   *What are the tax implications if a company is formed?*

3   *What do the business changes mean for Mr Kader in respect of the present workforce?*

4   *How might the internal organisation of a company be drafted to reflect the clients' own interests? The answer to this may depend on the answer to 1.*

It is not suggested that this is an exhaustive list of all of the relevant questions that arise in this case. We suggest that it is, instead, a useful selection from the likely obstacles that were itemised above. They have been triggered by the instructions that D receives and the questions that D asks the client in response.

From D's instructions the following emerges:

Mr Kader insists that D act for both him and Mr Khan. It becomes very clear to D from what the clients say (remember that at this stage D is being consulted by both Mr Kader and Mr Khan) that a conflict of interest could arise. Both clients have vested interests which may not be the same. Mr Kader already owns the business and has strong views, expressed in the interview, over what is now to happen. Mr Khan wishes to become involved but does not have this existing proprietorial interest. The interview also reveals that the business' bankers will require collateral security for a proposed loan. This will impact on both clients. D must solve the problem of whether there is a conflict of interest and if so what is to be done about it.

The tax question may have been raised directly by the clients. 'What does all this mean in terms of tax liability?', they may have asked D. Similarly, the clients could have raised the question of what a change in business structure might mean in terms of the employment rights of the business' workforce. Alternatively, D might have asked who the business' accountants were, with a view to carrying out some factual research on present tax liability. D would have been prompted to ask this question by virtue of the standard interviewing questions (see the appendix to Chapter 3 (Interviewing)). D may also have asked the clients for information on the number of employees at the factory and this will have triggered questions about the effect of a change in business structure on them and on the clients.

Mr Kader has strong views as to how he wishes the business to be structured. His instructions clearly indicate that he wants to retain control over the business in whatever form it ultimately takes. The question now arises: how should the business be structured? In Chapter 5 (Writing and drafting in a legal context) we see that the parties decide on the formation of a limited company. We presume that D has some expertise in this area, at least to the extent of understanding the basic characteristics of each. We concentrate on the company formation to illustrate the research point.

D's objectives are to protect the client and to ensure that the company documentation reflects the proprietorial interests of Mr Kader. D might ask: *How do I safeguard the client's position? Can the wording of a company's rules give a controlling interest to one person? Can the rules limit the involvement of others, for example, Mr Khan?*

Each of the above questions need to be answered by research. Other issues may arise, which require a reassessment of the research need, depending upon the answers that result. Let us look at the research tasks generated by D's questioning.

Legal research task 30

■ *Objective*: To decide whether D can act for Mr Khan and Mr Kader or either of them.

■ *Questions*: Is there a conflict of interest between Mr Kader and Mr Khan? When does a conflict arise and what must a solicitor do if there is such a conflict?

As a matter of priority, D must resolve the question of whether there is a conflict of interest or not. The question here is: *Do the interests of Mr Kader and Mr Khan compete in any way?* Put another way, the question is: *Are Mr Kader and Mr Khan's interests in the business expansion entirely complementary?* As seen in Chapter 5, the answer to this will determine who, if anyone, D can act for.

What is the source for this research? First, D's research is of a factual nature: to explore the extent to which he or she can protect the interests of both clients. This is very much a matter for judgment in this case. The two clients intend to co-operate as co-directors and owners of a business. If they are in apparent conflict at this stage, the business is doomed. But is there potential conflict of interest in the negotiations leading to the formation of the business? D has formed the impression that Mr Kader wants his own way, in terms of how the business is run and financed. D should assist him, as a client, to achieve those objectives. But acting for Mr Khan, D would have to advise caution: Do you really want to settle for Mr Kader having majority control of the voting shares? You seem unhappy with Mr Kader's idea of mortgaging your home to secure the bank loan. Why don't we suggest he part secure the loan on his own property? D has no choice but to conclude that the advice given to protect each client would be adverse to the interests of the other.

D may well know, or may find in the library, the leading work on the law and practice affecting solicitors: *Cordery on Solicitors*. D will see that this loose-leaf reference work deals with many aspects of the rules that regulate solicitors, especially those laid down in the form of professional duties and responsibilities. In the index D finds;

'conflict of interests'

which seem to be mainly located in section F, but also in A,E,J and M. D looks up section F and discovers:

'F – carrying out instructions'

Subsection I,C is headed 'conflict of interests' and I,C,3 refers to conflicts arising during the retainer. D knows that this means after taking initial instructions from a client. Had he or she not known that there would have been more research to do.

The text (which we quote in a slightly shortened form – the meaning is unaltered) states:

> 'A solicitor ... must not continue to act for two or more clients where a conflict of interests arises between those clients ... unless he (sic) can continue to act for one client with the consent of the other. Irrespective of the consent of one client, the solicitor will not be able to continue to act for either if he (sic) has acquired relevant knowledge about one client which would affect the way in which he (sic) advised the other.' (128)

As for '(sic)', if you don't know what this means or why we have put it in, think about why you might object to the drafting of this paragraph given the principles set out in Chapter 2 (Communication for lawyers) and 5 (Writing and drafting in a legal context).

D checks when the work was last updated and finds that it was on 8th January 1998.

D concludes from this research that a solicitor is obliged to ensure that he or she does not allow a conflict of interest to arise between clients, between the solicitor and the client and between the client or the solicitor and the court. Where a conflict between two or more clients arises, or may arise, the solicitor should not generally act for either. The solicitor may continue to act for one of the parties if the other consents and is not prejudiced in terms of what the solicitor knows about the former client and how he advises the actual client in consequence. Would Mr Khan be disadvantaged by D continuing to act for Mr Kader? D does not consider that he or she does have information that would prejudice Mr Khan. D feels therefore that he or she can quite properly act for Mr Kader but cannot act for both.

Just to demonstrate that there are alternative means for conducting this research D could have consulted the Guide to the Professional Conduct of Solicitors (Law Society, 1996). Perhaps this, rather than the more costly tome of Cordery, was on D's bookshelf.

In the index under 'Conflicts of interest' are various headings, for example borrower and lender; buyer and seller; and lessor and lessee. Using the Guide, D tries a different tack. Under 'Clients – conflicts of interest' D finds reference to pages 194, 274–81 and 276–78. On looking up the page references D discovers a whole chapter devoted to conflicts of interest – Chapter 15. It would have been quicker to look at the table of contents rather than the index; but speed is not the issue here – it is accuracy. Paragraph 15.01 of the Guide specifies when instructions must, in principle be refused. Paragraph 15.03 deals specifically with conflicts arising between two or more existing clients. We are getting closer. The Guide states:

'15.03....

1. If a solicitor has already accepted intructions from two clients in a matter or related matters and a conflict subsequently arises between the interests of those clients, the firm must usually cease to act for both clients. A solicitor may only continue to represent one client if not in possession of relevant confidential information concerning the other obtained whislt acting for the other. Even in such a case it would be prudent to confirm that the other party does not object.'

Spot the difference between Cordery and the Guide. One says that the consent of the former client is needed the other that it is wise to obtain the consent. So is consent actually rquired?

D now knows what the Guide recommends (but he might go on to ask him or herself what is the status of the Guide and what would happen if he or she continued to act – not that we recommend it!).

It is perhaps worth pointing that it is not clear from section of the Guide quoted above, or indeed from Cordery, what a conflict of interests actually amounts to. D, however, feels confident that he or she could recognise a conflict if he or she saw one. Look at D's letter to the clients (page 299) for further clues.

D reaches the conclusion that he or she must make a decision as to whether a conflict of interest exists, or is likely to exist in the foreseeable future. He or she must use the available facts and for once ask no further questions – no more factual research! This is because D must not act – which will include obtaining further instructions – for either if there is a potential conflict, except, as provided for above, with the permission of the one whom D has to show politely to the door.

The facts known to D are that both Mr Kader and Mr Khan do or may have differing interests in this case. As you will see in Chapter 5, D composes a letter to both of the clients raising the problem. You will see that Mr Khan eventually decides that it would be better for him to be independently represented. As D considers that there would be no unfair advantage over Mr Khan in doing so, he or she is able and willing to act for Mr Kader in this matter.

D can now turn to the outstanding matters. What are the tax implications that need to be addressed before D can give the client full and proper advice? What is the precise research question here? If the business is restructured as a company or a partnership, what will Mr Kader's tax liability be? Will he pay more or less tax depending on the form of business adopted?

Legal research task 31

■   *Objective*: To advise the client about the tax implications of restructuring his business.

■   *Questions*: What would the tax position be for Mr Kader and the company, if Mr Kader's converts his business enterprise from that of a sole trader to a limited company? What relief, if any, can the company claim?

A good starting-point might be a text on revenue law. *Revenue Law – Principles and Practice* (Whitehouse) dedicates a chapter to incorporations, acquisitions and mergers (Chapter 35). This deals with the tax implications on the transfer of an unincorporated business into a company. Consulting the index would also have revealed specific tax issues on such a restructuring, for example: 'VAT, taxable persons, going concern, transfer of a business'.

In fact D finds that Chapter 36 deals with a comprehensive list of tax and other related implications, including: income tax; VAT; capital gains tax; inheritance tax; stamp duty; and the position of employees. Out of (good) habit D looks at the date of this otherwise seemingly pertinent text – 1995. D knows (as all good lawyers – qualified or not – do) that the law can change frequently and significantly, especially in the tax field. D needs to be sure that the information he or she has found is up to date. Perhaps it is. Maybe the rates of tax payable have changed. There may be entirely new schemes for claiming relief from tax. Clearly more research is needed. *Butterworths Tax Handbook* (1998) may help, particularly with D having a good idea of what he or she is now looking for (either the rules described in Whitehouse or specific changes to them). D could of course always turn to the primary sources for research – the legislation enacting the tax law. D might fnd the whole of a Finance Act rather heavy going although he may need to check on the wording of a particular section at a later stage. He could use computer based technology. A search on a CD-ROM database such as Butterworths Tax Law might answer specific queries.

It may be, in this case, that D has been fortunate to hit so quickly upon very useful and pertinent texts. This may have occurred by chance or design. D may know very little about tax law and picked out the first book that came to hand (or perhaps the only book on revenue law in the firm's library) hoping it would contain what it is that he or she required. Alternatively, D may remember that these particular research sources are an accurate and reliable reference point having used them before.

So what has D discovered by way of this research? D will now know that tax is levied on individuals, partnerships and companies in different ways. The rules governing the tax allowances and reliefs, as well as the rates of tax, differ as between income tax and corporation tax. If the business is converted from the position of a sole trader to that of a company the tax implications are considerable. D now knows that for tax purposes the original business will be discontinued and Mr Kader will be liable to pay income tax to the point of discontinuance. Corporation tax will be payable once the company is formed. The rates of tax and the reliefs and allowances that can be claimed also differ. The transfer of the business from Mr Kader to the company may also attract capital gains tax in that there will be a disposal of the assets being transferred to the company, for example plant and machinery. 'Roll over' relief is allowed which is linked to share disposal, effectively postponing liability. Stamp duty may be payable if any assets pass by document. VAT may also be chargeable.

The subject area is so wide that we have not itemised each point of this research task. On this occasion we have presumed that D has found a definitive answer to all of the general issues relating to the tax implications of the proposed changes to the business. Armed with this overview D must go back to Mr Kader and clarify the client's instructions. D needs to carry out some factual research (asking Mr Kader questions) and assist Mr Kader to set objectives for a company structure that is tax efficient.

Once D has, for example, described the capital gains tax and stamp duty implications to Mr Kader, the client may ask whether it would be advantageous for him to retain personal ownership of, say, the factory building, and perhaps lease these to the company? D may also have raised this as a possibility. The wide-reaching tax research initially embarked on would now be redirected towards the very specific question of what the tax implications would be if Mr Kader rented the factory to the company. On this point, D, thinking back to days on the LPC and conscious of using all available resources (and perhaps not wanting a walk to the local Law Society library unless he has to) consults *Business Law and Practice* (Harvey, Harvey, Longshaw and Sewell). Paragraph 27.3.1 describes the disadvantages of transferring assets to a company from an unincorporated business. These include the rule that all assets of a business need to be transferred to the company if certain tax advantages (known as 'roll over' relief) are to be secured.

On balance Mr Kader decides to keep the business premises in his own name and to lease these to the company. In this way, should the company become insolvent, the creditors would not be able to lay claim to the premises.

D must look at each of the tax implications in turn and, against the general advice given to the client, must re-direct the research to answer the specific questions raised. These questions will come from what Mr Kader may ask, from what D discovers from his or her initial research and from subsequently questioning the client.

Legal research task 32

■ *Objective*: To advise the client about the liability for employees currently working for the client if the business is restructured.

■ *Questions*: What rights do employees have on the transfer of a business? Is Mr Kader personally liable? Would the company take over liability?

The third research task set out above concerns the employees that Mr Kader has and what effect, if any, the change in business plans would have for them and for Mr Kader. D may well be familiar with employment law and know that although a company is a separate legal entity, this does not mean that the employees will necessarily lose their employment protection rights on transfer. Mr Kader may also want to use the restructuring of the business as a means of slimming down the workforce. D must research into the question of employees' rights.

D knows that employment protection is both significant and complex and Mr Kader must be aware of the consequences of his plans in this respect before he makes any decisions. There are many texts that deal with employment law, including the loose-leaf reference work, *Harvey on Industrial Relations and Employment Law* (Butterworths). The index mentions:

'Employer – change of

transfer of undertaking, where C473, F74'

C473 says:

'where the Regulations apply the contracts of employment of the employees in the undertaking are automatically transferred to the new owner of the undertaking along with all rights, liabilities etc.'

What regulations? In the same paragraph reference is made to the Transfer of Undertakings (Protection of Employment) Regulations 1981 and cros-referenced to Division F in the same reference work.

If D looks up these provisions he or she will discover that employees have considerable rights in respect of a change in business structure, especially where the business is taken over as a going concern. These rights include the option for the employee to elect for redundancy, or to carry forward the continuity of employment to the new company. Contractual rights are in fact preserved in such cases. Armed with this, D looks up the statutory provisions on employment rights, in particular those relating to unfair dismissal and redundancy. Back to *Harvey*.

Section 94 and Schedule 13, para 17 of the Employment Protection (Consolidation) Act 1978 provide that an employee who is offered work on the same terms as before with a new employer is not entitled to claim redundancy. Furthermore, if the employer changes and the employee is kept on, the employee preserves his or her employment record in terms of continuity of employment. The Transfer of Undertakings (Protection of Employment) Regulations 1981 automatically ensure that, on a transfer of a business, the contract of employment is transferred to the new employer. If the employee is not offered work then either a redundancy situation or unfair dismissal may arise. If the employee is offered work on dissimilar and disadvantageous terms then the employee can claim redundancy.

Hold on a minute you say, and D says – the EP(C)A 1978 – hasn't that changed? It is time for a check on how up to date this version of *Harvey* is. The record indicates that the volumes were last up-dated on 1st April 1995. How appropriate! This came out of the actual research done in a law library where the law school concerned has a 5-star research rating!! Perhaps this was a deliberate mistake to keep researchers on their toes.

The useful point we can make here is that research must be done in context. Be aware that the law is ever changing. Always check if what you have is up to date. D needs to do some more work. This time he or she goes for an up to date text book: Tolley's Employment Law Service – Employment Handbook (1997). Here there is a useful history of the transfer of undertakings provisions – they came from a EC Council Directive in 1977 on acquired rights. The 1981 Regulations are, according to the book, still in force (amended in 1987, 1993 and 1995) and the EP(C)A 1978 has been replaced by the Employment Rights Act 1996 (section 141 deals with the unreasonable refusal of suitable alternative employment with a new employer and the loss of redundancy payment rights). D is concerned to ensure that there have been no further changes that affect the law here and so checks in *Halsbury's Statutes* and *Statutory Instruments* and the *Noter Up*. We now have the up to date position.

A further consideration occurs to D. Are these findings affected by laws emanating from the European Union since the directive in 1977? This is another research task but we leave this to you and D, whose time and energy are inexhaustible.

D can now advise Mr Kader that the employees will either have redundancy entitlements or will be able to preserve their contractual and statutory rights in the new company. Any employee who has statutory protection against redundancy or unfair dismissal may claim compensation if not taken on by the new company.

The advice that D gives is that each employee retains continuity of employment with the company on its incorporation and takeover of the existing business. Mr Kader will have to decide whether he wishes to revise his objectives of slimming down the workforce in the light of these findings. D may need to research, if requested by Mr Kader, exactly how much the entitlement of named employees would be if not taken on. In the event Mr Kader is hoping to expand the business after a short period and prefers, in the light of D's advice, not to lose any workers. He modifies his objectives and employment protection ceases to be an obstacle.

Legal research task 33

■   *Objective*: To secure Mr Kader's control over the company.

■   *Questions*: What must the company documentation state to ensure that Mr Kader's stays in effective control?

The next item of research arises from the broad question of how Mr Kader's interests can be preserved in the new company format. What are these interests? Mr Kader until now has been a sole trader. He has run the business on his own terms. He has invested heavily in the business for many years and has given the last ten years of his working life to it. All of these facts are confirmed in the interview. The protection of his proprietorial stake in the business is of crucial importance. D now acts for Mr Kader and so can properly direct the necessary research to protecting these interests, not necessarily Mr Khan's. (Of course any deal that does not suit Mr Khan may be against Mr Kader's objective of working with Mr Khan and raisng capital through him.)

In order to advise the client properly D must ensure that Mr Kader is aware of the role of and responsibilities incumbent on company directors. We will presume that it has been proposed (by lawyers for Mr Khan) that both Mr Kader and Mr Khan be made directors of the company (see Chapter 5). This would give both a say in company affairs and is part of the attraction, for Mr Khan, of investing in the business. The ultimate control over the company vests in the shareholders, who are, of course, the owners of the company. The day-to-day management is left to the directors who are accountable to the company and to the shareholders. It is likely, in such a relatively small business concern as the one in the case study, that the directors and the shareholders will be one and the same.

Mr Khan's lawyers are prepared to see Mr Kader retain the majority shareholding and the division of shares is set at 75/25 in Mr Kader's favour. D explains that this gives Mr Kader a controlling interest in the company. This matches Mr Kader's wishes. What research issues therefore remain to be addressed?

Mr Kader asks D whether he can outvote Mr Khan in the event of their not agreeing on company policy and if necessary whether Mr Khan could be removed from his position as director. D should have been aware of questions of this nature, for the company structure, as well as company law, will dictate the relevant duties and responsibilities.

Before D answers the initial research question – what the company paperwork would have to state to give Mr Kader control – D identifies more questions that require researching: *Can a majority shareholder simply outvote the minority on any issue? Can a director who is no longer approved of by the majority shareholder be removed from office?*

Where might D look for answers to these questions? Several reference texts might help: D decides to consult a specialist text. First, E consults *Butterworths Company Law Handbook*. Nothing is revealed under 'minority shareholder' and 'shareholder' only gives 'notice to'. On close inspection it turns out that this volume is a compilation of statutory rules and does not provide the commentary that D is looking for.

D then consults *Mayson, French and Ryan on Company Law* (Blackstone Press, 1997). The index refers D to 'minority shareholders and in particular to 'dissentient minority questioning decisions' (388–90) and the 'dismissal of directors – by' (451). Reference is also made to actions under the Companies Act 1985, s 303. D goes to a copy of the Act itself for the full wording (a well thumbed copy, bought from HMSO, is sitting on the library shelf). But 1985 was a long time ago, even if the particular section is still good law. D decides, as you might predict, to check that it is up to date.

Having done that D is now confident that he has answered the subsidiary questions about minority actions – a shareholder who feels that he or she is being unfairly treated can complain to the courts. Such treatment could be where the majority shareholding outvoted the minority and that the result was an outcome unfavourable to the company as a whole.

D's advice therefore to Mr Kader should be that the majority shareholder(s) can legitimately overrule the minority providing the process that is used is fair and that the company's interests are being followed. If Mr Khan felt that the Mr Kader was using his controlling interest to prejudice the company Mr Khan could complain to the courts by way of a minority shareholder's action. D could look up in more detail what is meant by 'fair', or 'prejudice' and what are the 'company's interests', by following up any statutory definitions or case law on the point. In fact you know by now the kind of person D is, and D is already on the way to the firm's library. Mr Kader should be made aware of the possibility (if unlikely event) of a minority action if he is to understand fully the implications of using his majority shareholding to control the company.

We, meanwhile, move back to D's principal research question – what must the company documentation state to secure Mr Kader's control (subject to what has already been said about minority actions)?

D knows, from his company law course at university, that the rights and responsibilities of directors (amongst other things) are set out in the articles of association of a company and that these rules will determine when meetings of directors will be held and how they will be conducted. D knows or soon finds out that directors owe a responsibility to the company, as they are in a position of trust and must act in the company's best interests at all times (unless sanctioned by the company to do otherwise). More specifically, the articles will lay down voting rights, the conduct of meetings and the circumstances under which the directors may be removed from office.

The question, for example 'Can Mr Kader remove Mr Khan from his position of director?' can now be answered. Depending upon exactly what the articles of association say, directors can be removed from office by a simple majority vote of the shareholders at a duly convened meeting of the company. All directors, not just Mr Khan, will be subject to the same rules. The rules would therefore apply to Mr Kader as well as Mr Khan, but as Mr Kader would have the controlling interest in the company, this would give him a very strong position from which to operate. D therefore tells Mr Kader that directors can be removed by ordinary resolution but as Mr Kader will have 75% of the voting rights his position should be secure.

From his or her research D can advise Mr Kader that, subject to the rules laid down in the articles, Mr Kader could effectively run the company mostly according to his own wishes providing what he does is in the general interest of the company. Despite this apparent imbalance of power, Mr Kader must be made aware that the rules which impose duties on directors and companies are applicable equally to him and Mr Khan. There would undoubtedly have to be some negotiation between the client and Mr Khan on how the articles are worded. The content of the articles would be researched and then probably negotiated and drafted. Chapters 5 and 6 deal with aspects of this.

For the present, suppose that D wants to find a precedent for articles of association from which he or she can work. To demonstrate a further research tool let us say that D's firm have recently invested in Butterworth's Books on Screen, a reference work available on CD-ROM. The software has been installed and the password successfully entered.

D hits the start menu or Books on Screen icon. The Books on Screen Desktop appears on the screen. D follows this sequence:

1   clicks on card index

2   clicks on Company Law icon (others include the All Englands and Civil Litigation)

The screen now shows icons for a variety of books and materials on company law including Halsbury's Laws of England (vol. 7 (1), (2) and (3)), Tolley's Company Law, Company Law cases and Company Forms and Precedents.

D:

1   selects Company Forms and Precedents

2 clicks on 'search' and then 'find'

3 enters 'articles of association precedent'

4 enters in 'search – how' - 'all words appearing in any order in the same paragraph'

5 enters in 'search – through' – 'everything'

6 enters in 'search – where' – 'current book'

(The entries under 'search' are selected from prompts)

7 and hits enter

The screen displays that there are four matches. On selecting the first – Companies vol. 9, Part I, Formation and Registration, a precedent comes on screen (initially hidden by the list of matches – click on the left hand box at the top right corner of the window to send it to the tool bar and reveal the precedent underneath). This is all about pre-emption rights over shares (precedent 26) although it does mention the words identified in the search.

D tries the second match – Companies Vol 9, Part 4, Off the Shelf Companies. This time D gets a resolution creating weighted voting rights (precedent 332)!

Clearly the search needs to be more carefully targeted. D tries again and searches simply for 'articles of association' and in 'forms/precedent' rather than' everything' – this was an experiment for us too!

This time there are 18 'hits'. The second is Companies Vol 9 Articles of Association of private company adopting table A – short form (precedent 259). Table A? Where might D find that? (he or she does know table A can be used to incorporate standard clauses in articles). Scrolling down the page D finds table A (precedent 260). Clauses 42 and 91 refer to the appointment of a chairperson for general meetings of the company and meetings of the board. Have a go and look these up for yourself.

D decides that adopting these clauses would not in fact guarantee Mr Kader the chairperson's role (as under clause 91 the chair is elected by the directors) and so drafts a new clause making the appointment of the chair a matter for the general meeting (where Mr Kader would have the majority of votes) and using Table A for other less contentious matters.

We have looked at a large number of research questions in this chapter and we presume that you are getting the message on how to go about your research. Let us look at just one more in our business case study.

Legal research task 34

■ *Objective*: to ensure that the company can sublet part of the factory premises without undue restriction.

■ *Questions*: Can a lessor prohibit subletting? Can subletting be subject to restrictions?

Our final research task concerns the lease for the factory. Elsewhere in this book you will pick up that Mr Kader and Mr Khan want to have the freedom to sublet part of the factory. Mrs Shearsby is not keen to allow this as she wants the minimum of complications in the transaction. The draft lease prepared by Mrs Shearsby's solicitor, E, prohibits the lessee from subletting. Before entering into negotiation with her solicitor E, D wants to check the position. Can a lease outlaw subletting? Alternatively if D can persuade E and his or her client to allow subletting what restrictions, if any, can a lessor impose? Can the lessor effectively veto a proposed subletting?

Having found help before in *Drafting and Negotiating Commercial Leases* (Murray Ross, Buterworths 1994) (see Chapter 5) D finds his suspicions confirmed – the lease can prohibit subletting (see Chapter 13). Another book in the library (the firm order the annual editions of the books produced for the LPC course to keep abreast of changes and to give their trainee solicitors some familiar material to consult) is Kenny and Hewitson's Conveyancing. This (page 213) deals with covenants against subletting and confirms the position that subletting can be ruled out in a lease. The section (18.3.6) then refers to subletting with the landlord's consent and the provisions of the Landlord and Tenant Act 1988. D looks this up in *Halsbury's Statutes* (Vol 23, 474) where the Act is set out in full with annotations. It transpires that where subletting is permitted the landlord's consent cannot be withheld unreasonably and a decision must be given within a reasonable time. The annotations include reference to subsequent (post 1988) case law.

The position is therefore clear. Mrs Shearsby can stick to her guns and refuse to allow subletting but if D can negotiate the inclusion of such a cluase then consent can only be refused on reasonable grounds. Armed with this D takes Mr Kader's instructions and begins talking to E about amending the lease. Surely Mrs Shearsby would not want to prejudice the whole letting over one clause? See how the negotiations develop more generally in Chapter 6.

6   Documenting legal research

Carrying out research is only one part of the challenge. Demonstrating and recording the results is at least as important, and may be part of the way your research work is assessed.

Factual research is omitted from this writing-up. The reason is that factual research on a client matter will always show up in an attendance note, as well as documents, reports and witness statements that are part of the client file. How to set these out is considered in Chapter 5. But you risk overlooking the recording of the legal research unless you create a system. Like school maths problems, where working out is shown as well as the actual answers, you must show how you carried out the research as well as what your answer is. In that way you, or anyone else, can go back over it and develop it further. Document your blind alleys too – see the LEXIS search below as an example.

We suggest below a couple of ways of recording research. The first was used by Hugh in the Student Law Office at Northumbria University, and the second by Richard in the Law Clinic at Sheffield Hallam University. We think both offer useful guidance whether your research is in practice, on the LPC or BVC course, or simply, but importantly, as a way of helping you become more accomplished at research at degree level. Details of the research actually carried out under the Newcastle method come from research task number 17 (p 230). We have included a blank copy of the pro-forma used in the Sheffield scheme for you to copy and adapt for your own use in one of the research exercises left for you to do in this chapter (for example the European law dimension in research task 32).

Documenting legal research – an example (research task 17)

Research record – Daniel McAuley

The nature of the problem

Identify the issue/s you are researching and their purpose

Daniel McAuley is aged 14. There may be evidence that he failed to look behind him, or to indicate, before he started to turn right. I need to find out whether his age is going to assist us in defeating an allegation of contributory negligence.

Identify any limitations, such as time limits or lack of legal aid

We must have an answer before seeing Mr Smith from the defendant's insurers next Monday, 9 June 1998.

The relevant law

First list *all* sources looked at, including discussions with lecturers or colleagues, and including those that did not provide you with the results you were looking for.

Summarise the relevant law, citing all relevant sources correctly and fully

1 *Atiyah's Accidents, Compensation and the Law 1993*. See p 53 – the standard of care for the defendant towards the plaintiff is an objective one.

2 See p 120 – the standard of care for the plaintiff towards himself is subjective. *Stavely Iron and Chemicals v Jones* [1956] AC 627.

3 *Stavely*: One employee injured by another, a crane driver. One question the House of Lords had to deal with was whether the standard owed by the one who drove the crane was any higher than the duty of the injured man for his own safety. Held by House of Lords that the duty owed by the company (ie vicariously through the crane driver) could be higher than that owed by the employee to himself. See Lord Tucker at 647–648.

4 *Clerk and Lindsell* 3–24: Conduct on the part of a child contributing to an accident may not preclude it from recovering in full in circumstances in which similar conduct would preclude a grown person from doing so. What is negligence in a grown person

272 · **Research skills**

is not necessarily negligence in a child. Negligence means want of ordinary care, and 'ordinary care must mean that degree of care which may reasonably be expected of a person in the plaintiff's situation' [footnote: per Lord Denman in *Lynch v Nurdin* (1841) 1 QB 29 and several further cases cited], which in the case of a very young child would be nil [footnote: The Occupiers' Liability Act 1957, section 2(3)(a) warns expressly that 'an occupier must be prepared for children to be less careful than adults']. Note to self: argue by analogy?

A number of further cases cited there, where children's contributory negligence up to age nine considered, and even a boy playing with petrol and lighting it aged nine held not contributorily negligent (*Yachuk v Oliver Blais Co Ltd* [1949] AC 386).

5 From *Clerk and Lindsell* again: 'Where a child aged five ran across a main road and was hit by a car, the court held the driver and the child equally to blame.' (*McKinnell v White* [1971] SLT 61)

6 At 3–32: burden of proving contributory negligence is on the defendant (cases cited in footnote all old).

7 3–32 and footnote 17 lead to case of *Gough v Thorne* [1966] 3 All ER 398, CA – 13½ year old girl injured not on a crossing. Per Lord Denning: 'A very young child cannot be guilty of contributory negligence. An older child may be; but it depends on the circumstances. A judge should only find a child guilty of contributory negligence if he or she is of such an age as reasonably to be expected to take precautions for his or her own safety: and then he or she is only to be found guilty if blame should be attached to him or her. A child has not the road sense or the experience of his or her elders.' Of the defence suggestion that the child should have looked around the lorry that had stopped to let her cross: 'That indeed might be reasonably expected of a grown up person with a fully developed road sense, but not of a child of 13½.'

8 Per Salmon LJ in the same case, the standard to be expected is that of the ordinary girl of that age.

9 *Clerk and Lindsell* 3–24 leads to *Morales v Eccleston* [1991] RTR 151: CA increased the contributory negligence from 20% to 75% where plaintiff, age 11, was playing football in the middle of the road with traffic passing in both directions.

10 Is there any case law on breach of highway code as pointing to contributory negligence? Contributory negligence not in title to All ER on disk. Under 'negligence' found 'breach of highway code', *Powell v Phillips* [1972] 3 All ER 864 CA - 19 year old woman stepped on and off gutter at night to avoid slush on pavement. Not facing oncoming traffic, hit by speeding car. Held no contributory negligence despite not acting in accordance with highway code.

Review and assess your findings, bearing in mind the following considerations

What is your answer? If no answer, why not? What will you do, if anything?

Damages can be reduced for contributory negligence even where the plaintiff is a child. The older the child the more this is possible, but the standard expected is what you would expect of a reasonable child of Daniel's age. Given *Gough v Thorne* we can argue convincingly that he is not yet to be expected to cycle according to the standard of an adult.

Breach of highway code by Daniel (if alleged) not on its own proof of contributory negligence.

Is the law you found authoritative and reliable?

Yes, the general principles are repeated in several cases, backed up with the analogy of the Occupiers' Liability Act 1957. But need to check any citations of cases of *Gough v Thorne* and *Powell v Phillips* – case citator? LEXIS?

Can you identify the relevant statutory provisions?

Occupiers' Liability Act 1957 section 1 by way of analogy with the common law standard, and argue that Mr Slater should have taken particular care because of the known risk that child cyclists may not be careful for their own safety. (It seems to increase the duty on the defendant rather than deal specifically with contributory negligence.)

Can you identify the leading cases?

Lynch v Nurdin, Gough v Thorne, Morales v Eccleston, Powell v Phillips.

Are you aware of the different weight given to any conflicting cases?

The authority is consistent, if we take into account that *Morales* was concerned with a very stupid game of football which any 11 year old would have known was dangerous. The way Daniel rode his bike is not comparable, even if he did not signal as he should have.

Is your research as up to date as possible?

LEXIS search on citations of cases discovered still to be completed [this is an accurate search report, in that it identifies where it is incomplete].

Legal research put into practice

Specify how your research has been or is to be used

(Eg letter to client explaining situation, follow-up interview with client, letter to opposing lawyer, draft defence, submission at court.)

Have to hand when talking to insurance company representative; if necessary, prepare opinion for use at trial; use as basis for commissioning expert road safety opinion on standard expected for 14-year-old cyclist (check legal aid situation before doing so).

Sheffield Hallam University

School of Financial Studies and Law

LAW CLINIC

RESEARCH PRO-FORMA

Case number .... Name(s) of client(s) ....

Firm .... Student Adviser(s) ....

Law Clinic Supervisor ....

Date ....

Research Objective ....

....

Research Location (Library/Law Clinic, etc) ....

....

Research Material (Statute, Regulation, Case, Book, Article, LEXIS, etc) ....

....

....

Research Finding ....

....

....

....

Further Research Required ....

....

....

Time spent on research ....

Please use a continuation sheet if necessary

Conclusion

Research is never finished.

Chapter 5

WRITING AND DRAFTING IN A LEGAL CONTEXT

1   An introduction to drafting

The authors (hereinafter referred to as we) hereby assert and maintain that by diverse means and in a manner hereinafter contained we will address forthwith and without undue procrastination the aforementioned matter known as writing and drafting in a legal context and that the relevant part (or parts) of the learned volume known as *The Legal Skills Book: A Student's Guide to Professional Legal Skills* entitled 'Writing and Drafting in a Legal Context' shall pertain wholly and exclusively to the said writing and drafting unless and until the reader (hereinafter referred to as you) is advised by us to the contrary.

What?

This chapter is devoted to the legal skill of writing and drafting. Let us use 'drafting' to cover both concepts for now.

The skill of drafting is rightly seen as central to the lawyer's function. The need for an ability to use words and language for a particular and specified purpose arises regularly during legal practice.

In contentious work accurate and effective drafting is needed as a prelude to, and during the conduct of, litigation. Prior to the issue of proceedings, in either civil or criminal cases, lawyers will be called upon to communicate in written form, particularly by letter. The audience for the letter or other document may be the lawyer's own client, an opponent, his or her solicitor, a witness, the court, or a third party such as an insurance company.

Once proceedings are under way even greater emphasis will be placed on the written word, particularly in a civil case. Your theory of the case (see Chapter 4 – Research) is outlined in witness statements and in pleadings. You may be drafting instructions to counsel, giving formal legal opinions or composing letters of advice. Frequently you will need to take notes, send memos, draft applications or prepare affidavits.

Non-contentious work also depends heavily upon drafting skills. Not only are informal letters important, but also transactions are progressed and completed by the use of formal documentation. A conveyance, a will or a business agreement may be the end result of that transaction. These need to be carefully worded, first, to achieve the desired result (that is, to finalise the house sale, execute the will, or form a company), but secondly, to avoid potential conflict at some later stage.

A carelessly worded lease may store up difficulties in the future if, say, the lessor wants to restrict subletting only to find that the lease actually permits this. A conveyance that fails to reserve a right of way, or does not give an indemnity against breaches of a lease by a subsequent purchaser, invites trouble.

Drafting is therefore a skill aimed at constructing a document that achieves a purpose required of it by the client, the lawyer, and the law. In its popular sense drafting is the initial preparation of that document. This might be a first attempt at producing the letter or deed. By drafting, however, we mean something much more comprehensive. Drafting in this chapter is taken to mean the whole process by which the necessary paperwork, be it a letter, a deed or a court pleading, is created. It will start with a first attempt and should end with a document that achieves the desired result. It may take many goes to reach this point. Indeed, particularly with a student or trainee lawyer, it should take time to produce a product that meets a professionally acceptable standard. It is the process of planning, research, drafting and redrafting that must be worked through. With experience of course the process will take less time. Not all drafting is subject to the ultimate scrutiny of being tested by another lawyer or a court. Relatively little drafting may be. The aim, however, must be to cater for such a possibility. The drafted document must be able to stand up to any test of its potential weakness. Case law may provide the test that shows the mettle of the final draft. But you hope it is not your case, or your document, that is taken through the courts.

Research is inextricably linked with drafting skills. You will need to discover what the law and procedure is on any particular point before starting or completing your draft. You must ascertain the relevant facts.

This chapter will see further progress being made in our case studies. The drafting of the conveyancing documentation will be examined. Court pleadings and witness statements in the personal injury case will also be dealt with as is counsel's opinion. The form and content of documentation to create a company will be mentioned as will the drafting of particular clauses in a lease.

Less obvious, perhaps, are the drafting implications in the crime case study. Drafting here includes letters to the client, and to the CPS, together with a brief to counsel.

As a lawyer or law student is often judged by what he or she produces in written form, an understanding of the skill of legal drafting is imperative.

2 Learning outcomes and assessment in legal writing and drafting

The standards expected of students, whether on degree or vocational courses, should be clearly stated, as should the means by which the performance of students is assessed. For undergraduates drafting is unlikely to form a compulsory part of the curriculum in the sense of modules dedicated to this specific skill. From recent surveys of law school practice it does appear that drafting is being given increasing prominence as part of other units or as an elective to be taken as a specialist area of study. In either case you should look carefully at the specified learning outcomes and assessment regimes for the modules concerned. It is hard to imagine that drafting cannot be seen as anything other than central to law study, if for no other reason than it is tangible evidence of students' ability to communicate their comprehension of a particular subject in written form. This skill is as relevant to the undergraduate as it is to the law practitioner.

On the vocational courses expectations are clearly stated. They are:

LPC

Students should have developed a basic skill in the preparation of a range of documents and should be able to formulate and present a coherent piece of writing based upon facts, general principles and legal authority in a structured, concise and, when appropriate, persuasive manner.

BVC drafting

The student should be able to demonstrate a sound understanding of the nature, function and value of pleadings and learn to draft a full range of pleadings and other documents from simple to complex in civil and criminal proceedings using precedents appropriately.

The student should be able to draft a variety of documents, for example:

(a) Indorsement on a writ;

(b) Any pleading;

(c) Order;

(d) Affidavit;

(e) Indictment;

(f) Grounds of Appeal and Advice on Appeal in a criminal case;

(g) Originating Summons;

(h) Contracted or negotiated settlement.

BVC opinion writing

The student should be able to write concise well-structured Opinions in a variety of cases and should be aware of the need to adopt a practical approach to the needs and objectives of the client.

They should be able to draft documents that:

The student should be able to draft documents that:

A student should be able to write an Opinion which:

(i) meet the client's goals, carry out the instructions or address the client's concerns;

(j) accurately state the client's case, and identify the relief sought"

(c) identifies and addresses the needs and objectives of the client and seeks to solve the client's problems;

(j) adopts a practical approach, avoiding an academic discussion of the law;

(ii) accurately address all relevant legal and factual issues;

(i) set out the material facts and tell a clear story, identifying the material issues and omitting all immaterial matters;

(d) accurately indentifies and shows a thorough grasp of all the material facts, the relevant law, the real issues, the relevant procedure and evidence;

(h) is complete in that it covers everything that needs to be covered, is fully reasoned and follows a clear line of reasoning;

(l) identifies and asks for relevant further information/evidence explaining where appropriate, why the further information is needed;

(m) gives clear, identifiable, appropriate, sound practical advice on the matters identified in the instructions and implicit in the instructions and advises on any practical steps to be taken.

(iii) where appropriate, identify relevant opinions;

(k) answers all the questions expressly or implicitly raised by the instructions by expressing clear conclusions where appropriate, alternatively explaining why there can be no clear conclusions, gives a whole answer to every question, explains any legal and factual alternatives, sets the conclusions out clearly and prominently and gives full advice;

(iv) where appropriate, demonstrate a critical use of precedents;	(g) make a critical use of the appropriate precedents;	
(v) are logically organised;	(c) are properly headed and laid out, neat on the page, contain all necessary formalities and are appropriately structured;	(e) distinguishes one issue from another; (g) has a clear and appropriate structure in that it deals with each issue in a logical order and separates issues into paragraphs in a sensible way, dealing with one isue at a time and giving each its due weight and significance;
(vi) form a consistent and coherent whole;	(e) are in compliance with the requirements of practice, sound in law, settled in the appropriate court and drafted to achieve all the client's objectives; (h) relate structurally to other documents and are consistent with any accompanying advice;	
(vii) follow the rules of grammar;	(a) are written in clear grammatical English, correctly spelt and appropriately punctuated;	(a) is written in clear grammatical English, correctly spelt and appropriately punctuated;
(viii) demonstrate appropriate use of language;	(b) are written fluently and concisely in language and style appropriate to the document;	(b) is written fluently and concisely in language appropriate to an Opinion;

(ix) are succinct and precise;

(d) are accurate and contain correct figures and sums;

(i) is concise, contains no irrelevancies, and is no longer than is reasonably necessary;

(f) are drafted precisely and unambiguously in terms that are appropriate;

(x) meet any formal requirements.

(f) is properly headed, laid out, makes sensible use of sub-headings where appropriate, is signed and written in a style appropriate to an Opinion;

Students should be able to explain the principles of good drafting practice and should be able to:

(i) identify pieces of drafting where those criteria and not met;

(ii) modify their own drafting errors to meet these criteria;

(iii) transfer drafting principles or criteria learned in one context to other contexts;

(iv) use techniques for appraising and developing their own writing and drafting styles.

Students should have developed a basic skill in the use of precedents, in setting out documents, in drafting clauses and should be able to write letters to other lawyers, clients and ... non-lawyers.

The assessment regime followed in the vocational courses will vary from provider to provider but is likely to focus on practical writing and drafting exercises. The exact assessment standards should be made available to you in each case.

Drafting checklist

RESEARCH AND PREPARATION

To what extent does your preparation display evidence of research of:

- Relevant facts?

- Relevant law?

- Relevant procedure?

STYLE, APPROACH AND STRUCTURE

To what extent do you:

- Use correct punctuation?

- Use correct grammar?

- Use clear, precise language avoiding ambiguity?

- Avoid wordiness and repetition?

- Use straightforward sentence structures?

- Convey information in an organised, coherent way?

- Use appropriate format/layout for the task and audience?

- Use appropriate vocabulary and style for the task and audience?

- Distinguish between relevant and irrelevant information?

INFORMATION CONTENT

To what extent does the draft:

- Cover all relevant points?

- Display clear understanding of the factual situation?

- Show understanding of legal issues raised?

- Provide appropriate citations/references?

Subject to these particulars how can you gauge your own progress when studying and applying drafting skills?

A self-assessment checklist may be of use here (see p 282). You can use it to assess any particular drafting exercise that you undertake.

Achieving your purpose

From both the professional standards and our checklist you will realise that drafting is about your ability to communicate. Be accurate and target the objective at hand. Chapter 2 (Communication for lawyers) and Chapter 4 (Research skills) contain material that will give you a sound foundation for good drafting.

Before you hand in any work to be assessed (or commit any document in practice to the post, the court or the client) can you answer the following questions?

1   What is it that you want to say?

2   Why do you want to say it?

3   Who is your audience?

4   What is the result you hope to achieve?

5   What is the likely effect of the draft?

6   Are you satisfied with the first, second or subsequent drafts?

7   If appropriate does your client understand and approve the draft?

The general principles of drafting may now be examined, followed by a look at drafting in the context of our case studies.

3   The principles of drafting

First, some ground rules need to be established.

Preparing the task

Drafting is a skill that involves the construction of documents, both formal and informal. It necessarily involves the selection and application of words and expressions. You must be aware of what it is you want to convey; that is the aim of the document. Who is your audience and how do you intend to convey the information?

Let us use an example. Solicitor D has just interviewed Mr Kader. The objectives of the client have begun to take shape. D wishes to write to Mr Kader. D identifies that the main purposes of writing a letter are, at this point, threefold.

First, the letter should verify D's understanding of the facts. The letter should record the salient points of what Mr Kader has told D.

Second, the letter will set out the options available to Mr Kader at this stage, based on the information that D has received so far. The advice given in interview will be confirmed by the letter.

Third, the letter is aimed at the immediate future, that is, what is to happen next. If Mr Kader has opted to form a company limited by shares, D will now draft the appropriate documentation.

The letter also fulfils certain ancillary functions. It will be a record of what has been discussed and agreed by the parties. If there is ever any dispute about what the client's instructions were, D can point to the letter which, in the absence of any objection, can be presumed to have met with Mr Kader's approval. The letter may not be conclusive proof of any binding agreement, in a contractual sense, but is indicative of the nature of the transaction, and would support D's evidence of what he or she said those instructions were. Mr Kader should be encouraged in the letter to contact D if he feels there is anything wrong or unclear.

You should also remember that the letter is a building block in the relationship between solicitor and client. Well structured, promptly sent and accurately detailed correspondence reaffirms the client's view of the efficiency and reliability of his or her legal adviser.

The letter is therefore designed to:

1   verify D's understanding of the facts;

2   set out the options and confirm the advice given;

3   confirm the action to be taken.

(We will see that this formula arises in each of the letters written by our solicitors to their clients. We will look in detail at these letters shortly.)

D therefore has a set of specific aims and objectives when sending the letter.

Before looking at the 'how' it is also necessary to think of the effect on the recipient of the letter. Who is the audience in this case?

The letter is going to a client. It needs therefore to be targeted at that person. This particular client is quite sophisticated in terms of his knowledge of business matters but is not familiar with the law. The tone of the letter should reflect this.

A different sounding letter might be appropriate if the recipient is a possible opponent or another solicitor or a court. These issues will be expanded upon later.

Now that D knows the purpose of and audience for the drafting task, he or she is in a better position to assess how that task should be carried out. We will draft D's letter to his or her client and a set of other letters a little later.

One final point can be made on preparation. We stressed in Chapter 2 some principles of effective communication. These call above all for brevity and clarity. The use of correct spelling, appropriate punctuation and 'good' grammar all aid the communication process. When preparing your drafting task be aware of the use of language. Words are your stock-in-trade.

It is well beyond the scope of this book (and perhaps either of us), to provide definitive guidelines as to the use of the English language in general and grammatical rules in particular. We do think, however, that Chapter 2 made a good start. We suggest that you reread this chapter if necessary and think about the use of language in the context of drafting, as well as in communication generally. We want you to think about how you best achieve the aims and objectives of drafting and expressing yourself effectively as part of this process.

Conventions and interpretation

Drafting often relies on conventions and rules of interpretation. By conventions we mean procedures which you are expected to follow. Slavish adherence to conventions can be as much of a hindrance as a help, but an ignorance of those expectations can bring dangers.

Certain words and expressions carry, in legal drafting, very particular meanings. Their interpretation is important. You may use words intending them to cover one particular set of circumstances, whereas, when they are tested (by another lawyer if your draft has to be approved, or by a court if the document is tested in litigation) they may be attributed with a different meaning. You may wish to impose a particular interpretation in your document.

Conventions

Convention dictates who is expected to produce certain drafts. In our conveyancing case study, C will expect the sellers' solicitors to draft the contract of sale and to provide C with this. C will be expected to approve (with or without amendments) that draft contract and, eventually, a version that is acceptable to both buyer and seller will be agreed. Later on, in the same transaction, convention dictates that C will draft the purchase deed for approval by the seller. The roles are therefore reversed.

How do you know which convention applies to your case?

So entrenched are many of these conventions that experience will soon show which paths will be followed. A better answer, however, starts with research. In the conveyancing example the lawyer, who is uncertain as to the largely informal rules of the game, might consult a basic text in that subject. (For example, see *Storey on Conveyancing*, pp 20–24).

Conventions that are less rigid can be found in the formatting of certain documentation. Conveyances are a good example. When solicitor C's drafting a conveyance for Ms Kennedy and Mr Bennett he or she will probably follow a precedent adapted to fit the objectives of that case. The precedent may give a layout that is, by convention, followed in legal practice. For example, convention dictates that a deed begins with 'THIS CONVEYANCE' in capital letters. Legal convention also favours the absence of punctuation. We suggest that these two conventions are of little, if any, worth and can be properly and safely avoided.

As we are concerned with convention and not formal legal requirements, it is important to realise that conventions need not be rigidly followed. They should not, however, be lightly ignored. Working models and precedents tend the follow conventions and have often been devised either as a result of litigation (where perhaps a document has been judicially scrutinised and found lacking), or through years of use and adaptation to suit changing circumstances. In other words they have stood the test of time and practical application. Many of these precedents are commercially produced and published, for example *Parker's Modern Conveyancing Precedents* (Taylor). The precedents can however be adapted and used by practitioners themselves. Word processing has greatly added to this development with many precedents now available in software packages or created by law firms for use in their own practices. Be sure therefore if and why you want to depart from precedents and established convention – there may be good reason for doing so, but know what it is.

A solicitor's office may have on disc model precedents for a wide range of transactions. These may include company formation documents, leases, partnership agreements and wills.

The point we are making here is that the basic form of precedents, be they the commercial publication, or the home grown variety, set out a form and style which you may find useful to follow. But this must suit the objectives you have for your client. The use and abuse of precedents is examined in the case studies appearing later.

Formal documentation may by law take a particular form. Court pleadings are perhaps the best example. The Rules of the Supreme Court and the County Court Rules prescribe many written forms for the various stages of litigation. These will set out the nature and layout of the contents or even the exact form which must be used. An originating application, or a writ, or a defence, or a request for further and better particulars must be in the prescribed form and contain prescribed information – or it will not achieve its purpose. As well as being set out in the court rules many such precedents are available commercially in hard copy or on disk (for example, Oyez, the legal stationers, supply many law offices with conveyancing precedents).

Interpretation

Someone somewhere will have to interpret what you have drafted. That interpretation may arise in the course of litigation when another lawyer makes submissions on the meaning of words used in, say, a will or a conveyance. The judge will have to apply the law in deciding what these words mean. Perhaps the matter never reaches the court, but instead, a few years on, another solicitor acting for a subsequent buyer who wishes to buy Ms Kennedy and Mr Bennett's house will look at the purchase deed drafted by C, and simply advise: 'Don't buy – defective title'.

How therefore will your words be interpreted and what meaning will they carry?

We are concerned with legal drafting; legal words will usually be given their legal meaning. If, therefore, you use words or expressions that carry very particular meanings you will be burdened with the meaning the law gives them, not the lay meaning you intended (unless it is the same).

The legal meaning may be defined by statute. This can arise in two instances. First, the Interpretation Acts 1889 and 1978 lay down the rules for the interpretation of certain words and phrases. Let us say that, in the conveyancing case, the contract says that completion shall take place on a particular day. Failure to complete on the agreed date would give the aggrieved party the right to make 'time of the essence'. Doing this makes the date for completion a condition of the contract (breach of which would allow rescission). This is carried out by serving a notice to complete. What if this notice specified a month as the requisite period? The Interpretation Act 1889, section 3, dictates that 'month' shall be a calendar month as opposed to a lunar month (28 days). In the absence of agreement to the contrary a month in the contract would carry this meaning.

A second aspect of interpretation comes from statute. Many Acts of Parliament and statutory instruments contain their own definitions of words and expressions. Thus, the Law of Property Act 1925 section 205 defines 'conveyance', 'land' and 'purchaser'. The Companies Act 1985 section 741 defines 'directors' and section 744 'articles' and 'memorandum'. Even these definitions are not always the full answer. For example, section 62(1) and (2) of the Law of Property Act says what a conveyance of land includes (buildings, drains, fixtures and fittings, and dozens of other things). So when you call something a conveyance of land you should know that you mean the kitchen sink too!

Part of the research task you must perform will be to ensure that the words of your draft use terminology in the sense that is intended and not in conflict with provisions laid down in statute. If in doubt look up the word or expression in a very up to date legal dictionary.

The definition or interpretation of the word or clause may also come from case law or practice directions.

Let us use an example from the case studies. B is drafting the particulars of claim in Daniel's case. B wishes to claim the cost of Daniel's attendance at a private physiotherapy clinic. 'Where, if at all, should I claim this expenditure?' is the question that B asks. B knows from experience, from research on the case or from his or her recall of the detail of a civil litigation course, that it is usual to claim costs against an opponent. Order 38 of the County Court Rules covers costs generally. Order 38 rule 1(2) states that: 'costs of and incidental to all proceedings ... shall be in the discretion of the court'.

The Order goes on to list those items that can be claimed under the heading of costs, and these include: solicitors' charges, VAT, counsel's fees, attendance allowances for witnesses, interpreter's charges, expert witnesses' fees and court fees. If this is the working definition of 'costs' it does not include the expense of medical treatment. Can such an item be included as damages? B looks up 'damages' in an academic text and is referred to general and special damages (*O'Hare and Hill* Chapter 4).

This in turn refers to a Practice Direction ([1984] 1 WLR 1127) and to the Law Reform (Personal Injuries) Act 1988 (section 2(4)) which deal with the items that can be included under the head of special damages and the right of the plaintiff to claim for private medical care.

If therefore it is B's intention to claim for Daniel's medical costs he or she must ensure that they are pleaded under the heading of special damages in the particulars of claim. The drafting of this pleading is examined later.

The final point to be made on interpretation concerns the inclusion of your own definitions and interpretations. Remember that your drafting skill is based on research. This involves you in predicting or assessing certain risks and outcomes. Good drafting includes you deciding in advance how a word or expression is to be interpreted and building into any agreement the actual interpretation that you want applied in the context of an agreement. If you want a word or phrase to have a certain meaning, or if you want the agreement to be interpreted in a particular way, write it into the document.

Take for instance our conveyancing case. The draft contract or draft purchase deed may contain a definitions clause. This can be taken from established precedents or created as need dictates in the particular transaction. *Kelly's Draftsman* (Ramage) contains many such examples (pp 61–63).

What if the sellers of Paradise Road live abroad? A clause might be inserted into the draft contract that reads as follows:

> This contract shall be governed by English law and the parties consent to the exclusive jurisdiction of the English courts in all matters regarding it. ... (Based on *Kelly's Draftsman* p 61, precedent 145.)

We can also use our business law case studies to illustrate the point. Let us say that D is instructed by Mr Kader to draw up an interim agreement between Mr Kader and Mr Khan to enable them to start their joint business venture. They wish to do so before the company documentation has been finalised. D may draft a contract between them which acknowledges that Mr Khan is to lend Mr Kader money and that in return Mr Kader will allow Mr Khan access to the business accounts pending the formation of the company. But the parties do not want to create any legally binding relationship yet. How can this be prevented? The agreement between them might contain a clause that interprets the overall meaning of the agreement and defines the parties' intent. The clause reads:

> Nothing in this agreement shall be construed or have effect as constituting any relationship of employer or employee or partnership between the parties. ... (Based on *Kelly's Draftsman* p 61, precedent 144.)

You do not always have to rely on the precedent books for such aids to interpretation. So long as you understand what it is that you are including and why, and you are sure that they would be interpreted in a way that supports your case, you can design your terms with confidence.

For example, let us suppose in our civil litigation case that Daniel's solicitor reaches agreement with the lawyers for Mr Slater for the payment of compensation to Daniel staged over a number of years, from now until he reaches majority – a structured settlement. A clause could be inserted in the agreement defining a particular word or expression or provide for a particular consequence. This may define the basis on which payment is to be made including the rate of interest applicable and the calculation of the periodic payments to Daniel.

Interpretation, whether imposed on you or created by you, is part of the drafting process and must be both understood and applied. The message must be: be creative but do not use words without understanding their legal meaning – EVER!

Reference material and precedents

Before looking in detail at both informal and formal drafting, we must now consider drafting aids. We have already introduced the concept of models, or precedents. A walk around any practitioner's library will reveal how important such materials are in the work of drafting. Of course they may be there just to impress, but that is an aside.

As we shall see in the drafting examples that follow, we prefer not to start at this end of the solution to the drafting problem. Before you consult a precedent you should work out what it is that you wish to achieve. The precedent should be used in the light of your own first draft. Before we put this into practice, however, it is useful to know what these aids to drafting are so that they can be intelligently consulted at the relevant stage of the drafting process.

Aids to drafting fall into two main categories. The first are general encyclopaedias that cover a broad range of legal matters. At one end of this category are the expansive publications that provide material on almost all conceivable (and some inconceivable) matters. There are two main collections of works that fit this description. The *Encyclopaedia of Forms and Precedents* covers such diverse areas as agricultural holdings, matrimonial settlements, rights of way and wills. A vast amount of material including both precedents and explanatory notes can be found. *Atkin's Court Forms* concentrates on precedents used in civil litigation and includes useful commentary .

Let us say that you are looking for a precedent for a transfer of registered leasehold property into the name of Ms Kennedy and Mr Bennett, as tenants in common in unequal shares. (Where did the tenants in common come from? – see Chapter 4 (Research skills).) Where might you find help in the *Encyclopaedia of Forms and Precedents*?

Volume 36 (1990) entitled *Sale of Land*, contains a precedent (form 229, para 1397) which sets out a transfer of the whole of the land to joint proprietors as tenants in common.

What about a precedent for the approval by the court of a settlement in Daniel McAuley's personal injury claim? *Atkin's Court Forms* can assist.

Volume 21(3), pp 427–429 give the forms for a summons that is required for the settlement of an action involving a minor.

You might benefit from looking up these reference books for yourself – study the relevant entries and work out whether they fit the required purpose. Do they need adaptation? It is all good practice in terms of developing both research and drafting skills.

At the other extreme there are a number of very useful general reference works that deal with a wide range of legal forms that commonly arise in legal practice. Possibly the best known is *Kelly's Draftsman*. This comprehensive volume (and it is only one compared with 42 for the *Encyclopaedia of Forms and Precedents* and 41 for *Atkin's Court Forms*) includes many of the areas of law regularly arising in private practice. The range of topics covered is still wide, running from arbitration through commercial documents to family, partnership, trusts and wills. Many of the requirements for precedents in our case studies could be satisfied here, at least in terms of finding a starting-point.

Kelly's also includes some useful models that can be adapted in a wide variety of situations such as the correct form of attestation for a statutory declaration or affidavit (p 73, standard clauses 218 and 219). This could be useful in the context of our civil case. If proceedings were issued against Mr Slater, who failed to enter a defence within the time limit, judgment could be entered. Mr Slater on discovering this may take legal advice and his solicitors could apply to have judgment set aside. Look at the provisions of the County Court Rules, Order 37, rule 4. You will discover that the application to set aside must be supported by affidavit evidence. The rules will tell you the grounds on which a judgment in default can be set aside. Your affidavit must address these grounds only but completely. The form of attestation for such a document can be found in *Kelly's Draftsman*. (So often is this form of words used, that it should soon be a formula that you are able to recite at will. Indeed, if you become a solicitor, you can earn a modest sum for the administration of oaths and the taking of statutory declarations (Solicitors Act 1974, section 81).)

The general precedent books are therefore a basic tool in the lawyer's library.

The second category of drafting aids is of a specific nature. Either these contain sets of precedents relating to one particular practice need, for example conveyancing, or they are part of a slightly wider look at an overall subject area, for example company law.

Examples of such sets of precedents include *Parker's Modern Conveyancing Precedents* and *Parker's Modern Wills Precedents* (both Taylor). These volumes contain a large number of models that provide comprehensive coverage of conveyancing and will making needs. *Parker's Modern Conveyancing* gives a very useful set of precedents that provide the practitioner with adaptable forms of assignment, conveyance, lease, mortgage and transfer. Should solicitor C require such documentation in our conveyancing case study, he or she would find that this slim volume covers the relatively straightforward transactions and gives a base for the drafting of more complex deeds. Standard clauses (for example, for indemnity in the case of breaches of covenant, or the acknowledgment of the right to the production of deeds), can be found alongside complete precedents for particular transactions. Examples of using such precedents can be found later in the chapter.

Such books deal with specialist areas and are available in areas other than conveyancing and wills, including matrimonial law and commercial and company law.

There are also an increasing number of specialist texts and journals that include, as part of their content (as opposed to their reason for being), sets of useful forms and precedents. *Butterworths Company Law* is one comprehensive loose leaf service. The *Law Society's Gazette* also publishes, from time to time, precedents relevant to practice. The Legal Action Group journal *Legal Action* often provides precedents in the field of employment, immigration, social security and housing law. Litigation based publications offering both law, commentary and precedents include *Butterworths County Court Practice* and *Butterworths Personal Injury Litigation Service*. Both are looseleaf publications, to which updating services are available. Forms for use in court proceedings can also be found in the 'White Book' (Rules of the Supreme Court), the 'Green Book' (the County Court Rules) and *Stone's Justices' Manual*. These are based on the procedural requirements and usually set out in the actual court rules. They are therefore to be followed (with the blanks completed in relation to the particular case) rather than adapted for use as more general precedents might be.

Finally, there are several publications which provide precedents for letter writing and record-keeping. Some useful models are available, for example, *Specimen Letters For Solicitors* (Blackford, 1989).

Faced with all these possible sources for guidance, you may feel somewhat daunted and at a loss to know where to begin your drafting. It might assist if we put the use of legal precedents in context. Some might say that you should look up a suitable precedent and then adapt it to suit your needs or case theory. Others (including us) prefer an alternative approach that requires you to attempt to draft, at least in outline, what it is that you wish to achieve. You can then consult a precedent to see how far it supports you. The reason why we prefer this system is that it complements the research component and makes you work out what you really need rather than assuming that you can find what you need, as a package, elsewhere.

Precedents are not, in the technical sense, intelligent. Like research data-bases, eg LEXIS they only give you what you ask for. You have to ask intelligent questions to use these devices to their full advantage.

Perhaps the issue is not so much whether you consult the precedent first, but whether you thoroughly assess your aims and objectives, and identify the factual and legal issues that must be covered, before drafting the document in question. Using precedents as a yardstick or checking device, rather than as inspiration, should at least put your drafting on the right footing. At your stage of education and development, you are wise to check your draft against a precedent.

Not all drafting tasks allow for the same degree of creativity. A transfer of registered land into the joint names of two purchasers is unlikely to overtax the average conveyancing solicitor.

A more complex commercial transaction, such as drafting a partnership agreement or the forming a company, may require considerable use of precedents and careful adaptation of what you find.

Where do you start? We suggest a few simple guidelines:

1   Be sure of your client's instructions. Develop the theory of your case or define your overall objectives and the legal framework for achieving them (see Chapter 4).

2   Outline what it is you intend to achieve in the draft. Check this with another lawyer (your tutor, your principal, your pupil master, one of your colleagues). List all key legal and factual matters that must be covered and arrange them into a logical order. This may be chronological order for parts of a pleading or affidavit, or subject-based for a conveyance, lease or will. Take into account any constraints or requirements; for example, the Rules of the Supreme Court (RSC) or County Court Rules (CCR) lay down what must be included in pleadings and for particular applications.

    RSC Order 18, for example, sets out a complete code for pleadings. Order 18, rule 6 dictates that the pleading must state the title of the action, description of the pleading and date of service (all of which must appear on the face of the pleading). Order 18, rule 7 stipulates that facts and not evidence must be pleaded. If you look at this rule and commentary in detail you will see that pleadings should be statements that summarise all material facts that are relied on but not the evidence that would go to prove those facts. Order 18, rule 8 covers matters that must be specifically pleaded including the expiry of any limitation period, a claim for exemplary damages and any claim for interest. This latter point will be noted in the Daniel McAuley case shortly. The Rules go on to cover the particulars of the pleadings including the amount of damages claimed and medical reports relied upon. Importantly, Order 18, rule 15 specifies that the statement of claim must specifically plead the remedy or remedies sought but tells you that costs need not be expressly claimed.

Your first draft must take into account all these requirements. Substantial research and preparation will therefore be necessary before you are in a position to begin drafting.

3   Attempt an outline of the draft, indicating at least the issues that you see as pertinent.

4   If you are unable to make progress towards a completed first draft, or if otherwise in need of guidance, or perhaps if urgency dictates, consult the appropriate forms and precedents.

5   Trace these either from a general reference work or a text that deals with that particular subject. The indexes to most volumes are quite comprehensive.

6   Take a copy of the precedent or precedents that you think may be of help. You can then make comments and notes on the copy, or even cut and paste certain sections.

7   With whatever peace and quiet you can muster, take time to work carefully through your draft, comparing this with the precedents you have found. Extract from the precedent any suitable wording and amend any inapplicable material. Merge your words with those provided to ensure that your draft reads as if it makes sense. (Perhaps it even will make sense!)

Ensure that the style of the draft is consistent.

8   This is the important bit – once you have a draft to hand that has emerged from the sequence above (with greater or lesser reliance upon precedents), test your best theory or your client's objectives. Does the draft stand up to scrutiny? If your theory is that Mrs Evans had no *mens rea*, ensure that the proof of evidence that counsel may have to rely on (yes, this is part of drafting too!) supports this theory. If your objective is to allow Mr Kader and Mr Khan to sublet part of the factory site ensure that the amended draft lease (by convention the lessor's solicitors produce the first draft so your drafting role is to check this and suggest drafted amendments) secures this right. This point will be developed later in the chapter.

Unless you are very able, very lucky, or prepared to be slip shod, it is unlikely that your first draft will pass the test. This is particularly the case if you have little or no experience as a drafter. So what should you do? The answer must be to thoroughly test your draft against your objectives – your theory of the case or the aim in the transaction. You may find it does not meet the objective or you may be uncertain as to whether it does or not. What then? The answer must be to conduct further research into the substantive law and/or procedure until you are sure that the draft you have produced will meet your requirements.

If the particulars of claim in Daniel's case do not make out the allegation of negligence, or list all of the heads of general damage and contain a schedule of special damages, or otherwise fails to comply with the court rules (for example omits the case number and is sent back by the court registry), they will fail their purpose. This failure may be fatal to the action (for example not revealing a cause of action) or may incur the displeasure of the judge resulting in an order of costs against you or your client and/or cause unwarranted delay. You must check and recheck to ensure that the end result supports the theory of the case or the case objectives.

We hope that by now that you realise that legal skills are all about a continuing process of analysis. It is only when the will has been drafted or the conveyance drawn up, and that it appears that all angles have been covered, that your job is done. In non-contentious work, you may never know whether your drafting has passed the ultimate test of satisfying a judge. Also you cannot guarantee that someone in the future will not complain about your draft. You can, however, predict whether or not your draft would satisfy these tests were they to arise. You should spot its inadequacies before someone else does.

Drafting and legal writing is therefore a skilled art form applicable to both contentious and non-contentious cases. Before we look at formal drafting in these individual areas, let us deal with informal drafting common to both.

4   Drafting informal documents

What do we mean by informal in this context? Formal documentation is taken to mean court pleadings, deeds and other written material which is produced as an official record of a particular transaction or is prepared for a particular stage in litigation. Informal documentation is really everything else. There are no specific legal requirements in drafting informal documents and there are perhaps fewer precedents to follow. Professional obligations are, however, incumbent on practising lawyers. Good sense and good practice demand competence and skill in this area. The Law Society, for example, dictates that clients must be given information about how long a case is likely to take and how much it will cost. These rules will affect the content and form of informal documents, especially letters.

We intend to concentrate on five aspects of informal drafting:

1   letter writing;

2   drawing up witness statements;

3   recording file notes;

4   instructing counsel;

5   writing an opinion.

This list may not be exhaustive but these five areas are of central importance in legal practice, in the solicitors' office and barristers' chambers. They may well form part of the assessment tasks you have to perform on your course.

Letter writing

This section looks at perhaps the least understood and potentially the most important aspect of drafting, both informal and otherwise. Although of most practical concern to solicitors the principles which underlie letter writing are highly relevant to all lawyers, students, solicitors, counsel and judges alike.

What does a letter do? It sets the scene for the relationship between lawyer and client. It is the channel through which advice and instructions are confirmed. It is the record through which the history of the case can, or ought to be able to, be traced. It is a means of focusing attention and of setting agendas. It is also a tool through which others may be persuaded, cajoled, threatened or compelled to take certain action. It is the means by which constructive discourse can take place between opponents, third parties and other lawyers. In a word, drafting letters is pivotal – pivotal to much else that then happens. You must get it right.

You might also consider this. Your own self-preservation may depend on good letter writing. If you don't get it right, you may let your client down. If you let your client down you may face proceedings in negligence or investigations by, for example, the Office for the Supervision of Solicitors.

We have some key suggestions to offer you on letter writing:

The first is that there is no right or wrong way of drafting a letter but there are certainly better ways. Practice rules affecting what the letter should contain do exist and obligations fall on the solicitor to ensure the proper discharge of these professional duties. Examples are given below in Letters 1 and 2.

As with any drafting task, the base must be in the planning. Work out in advance what it is that you wish to say, who your audience is and what you wish the letter to achieve.

Convention may lay down certain forms and styles which are not in themselves binding. Rather like good grammar, letter writing conventions can help to convey clarity through good structure. A well worded letter that follows conventions may also create the desired effect through meeting the recipient's expectations. There is virtue in conventions that are effective. A letter should clearly identify such important details as:

■ the name and address of the person to whom it is to be sent;

■ the date on which it was sent;

■ the identity of the sender;

■ the matter the letter addresses.

Solicitors in private practice must use note paper which will conform to additional requirements. The Solicitors Publicity Code 1990 dictates that all professional stationery must include a practising address and the names of the partners of the firm.

We will presume for the present that the stationery upon which your final draft appears complies with these various needs.

Some conventions relate to style. If you use a form of address that includes a name, for example 'Daniel' or 'Mr Kader', the letter should end with 'Yours sincerely'. If the form of address is impersonal, such as 'Dear Sir/Madam', then the preferred ending is 'Yours faithfully'. Other forms for ending a letter may also be acceptable such as 'Yours truly'. Much depends on the house style of the firm or on your personal preference, but impressions do count and it is as well to remember some of the more entrenched letter writing conventions.

It is usual to address a letter to a client or potential witness in the personal form, using their family name or even, if you have been encouraged to do so by the client, their first name. In some cases, for example where the client is a child, such as in our personal injury case, it may be appropriate to use the more familiar form of address in any event.

By contrast, when writing to members of the public who are neither clients nor potential witnesses, a less personal approach may be preferable. A letter before action (of which more presently) to, say, Mr Slater (who is as yet unrepresented) should begin 'Dear Sir'. A letter to the Chief Clerk of the County Court, who is known to be female should be to 'Dear Madam'. In writing to solicitors or other commercial concerns in connection with your professional work the convention is to use 'Dear Sirs'. In these possibly more enlightened times, especially where the gender of the recipient is unknown, 'Dear Sir/Madam' or even 'Sirs/Mesdames', might be appropriate (although as the letter will surely be read by a man or a woman why address it in the plural?). We have seen letters where 'Dear Partners' has been used in addressing a firm of solicitors or even 'Dear Insurance Company'. These are moving some way from conventional approaches. The letter can be addressed to an unnamed individual in an organisation, such as 'The Managing Director' or 'The Secretary', in which case, 'Dear Sir/Madam' is a suitable opening.

In any event, use a reference if it is provided, by which the person or organisation with whom you are corresponding will be able to trace the matter. This not only enables the recipient to find the relevant file more speedily, but also looks, and is, efficient.

Addressing a letter appropriately sets both a scene and a standard. Inappropriately addressed letters create the wrong impression of your professionalism.

Once the letter has been appropriately opened what rules should then be followed? We suggest that the following are essential guidelines:

1   Tie the letter in with any history; for example, if you are writing in response to the recipient's letter, say so.

2   Identify the issue about which you are writing.

3   Identify what your purpose in writing the letter is.

4   Communicate your planned message.

5 Ensure that the letter clearly states what outcome is sought.

6 Unless necessary, do not repeat the same message (emphasis may be required).

Having achieved this you should ensure that you:

7 Comply with any technical, procedural or professional requirements.

8 Use plain English wherever possible and follow the recommendations concerning precision and clarity set out in Chapter 2 (Communication for lawyers).

9 Send the letter off as soon as you are satisfied with its contents and that it matches your objectives and client's instructions. Send it by the most appropriate form – post, document exchange or local mailing service. If necessary despatch it by hand or messenger service. Letters sent by facsimile should be backed up by the original being sent by one of the other forms of delivery. A copy of any letter sent should be kept on the file. The recent development of electronic mail (e-mail) adds another dimension here. Whilst there may be good reason to communicate in this way (by sending typed messages from one computer terminal to another) there are important issues of confidentiality at stake and the sender must ensure that confidentiality is preserved where practically or professionally necessary. Remember it is not just access to the message at the computer terminal that has to be considered but also access to the servers through which the message has been routed.

As many of these guidelines are somewhat abstract, let us look at working examples from our case studies to emphasise the important points here. We will look at several letters to illustrate differences in style and content. We will also look at letters sent that serve a technical as well as communicative purpose.

In each example the type, purpose, requirements and content of the letter are summarised.

Letter 1

- *Type*: Letter to client following an initial interview.

- *Purpose*: To confirm instructions, advice and action to be taken.

- *Requirements:* To comply with the Solicitors' Practice Rules and guidelines concerning client care.

- *Contents outline*

  ☐ refer to interview;

  ☐ tell client about the decision to prosecute;

  ☐ ask client to contact you as and when charges are made;

  ☐ confirm you will contact CPS to stress client's innocence;

  ☐ clarify legal aid position;

☐   enclose details of firm;

☐   invite client to contact you if she has any queries.

Presume that the following letter is drafted:

A & Co
Solicitors
1 Main Street
Sheffield
S1 1XB

Tel: 0114 212345
Fax: 0114 223456

Our Ref: A123

Your Ref:

3 September 1998

Mrs W Evans
1 Manor Close
Sheffield
S5 1TL

Dear Mrs Evans,

Thank you for visiting my office yesterday. I was sorry to hear of your present difficulties. As you will remember, I promised to write to confirm our discussions.

From what you have told me I understand that you were released from the police station on 1 September 1998 without being charged. The police have told you that you are suspected of having stolen from your employer. The police are sending a report to the Crown Prosecution Service who will decide whether you should be prosecuted.

Until I have had the opportunity to see the details of the case against you and the exact charges you face I am unable to advise you fully. What I can say for the present is that if you are charged with theft the prosecution would have to prove that not only did you take the money in question, but also you intended to do so.

I suggest that you contact me if you receive any further contact from the police or you receive a summons from the court – this will specify the charges against you and tell you to go to court on a particular date.

In the meantime, I will contact the prosecution stressing that you believe you are innocent and asking them not to prosecute. The decision to prosecute is normally taken within two weeks.

I confirm that you are eligible for help at this stage under the Legal Aid scheme. This initially consists of up to two hours of my time. Should the case go to court I can make an application for legal aid on your behalf to cover the cost of representing you in those proceedings. For a case of this sort the Sheffield courts will generally grant legal aid but as the decision is their's I cannot guarantee this. I will advise you of this at our next meeting if necessary.

I enclose a pamphlet explaining more about my firm and in particular about the procedure which applies should you ever have any cause for complaint.

Please do not hesitate to 'phone, make an appointment or write if there is anything you need to discuss. A good time to 'phone me is generally between 4.30 and 5.30.

Yours sincerely

Solicitor A

Enc: Firm's pamphlet

Partners:
Solicitor A, LLB MA; Solicitor B, BA; Solicitor C, Commissioner for Oaths.

Letter 1 sets out the basic ingredients for an effective letter to the client. It addresses the professional practice requirements (see the commentary to Letter 3 for details). The letter is supportive and friendly. It summarises the facts as known. It indicates the action to be taken by the client and/or solicitor and it deals with the issue of costs. We hope that Mrs Evans will feel reassured by the tone and content of the letter and by the advice contained in it. The letter should confirm what she was told at the interview. She will no doubt still be very worried but the letter should show that all that can be done at present is being done.

A more complex letter serving a similar purpose follows (presume that the letter head and layout is as before, but this time it is solicitor D writing to his or her clients).

Letter 2

■   *Type:* Letter to client following interview.

■   *Purpose:* To confirm instructions, advice and action to be taken.

■   *Requirements:* To comply with the Solicitors' Practice Rules and guidelines concerning client care.

■   *Contents outline* (A full example is given in Letter 1. We will now use key words to indicate the process of planning the following letters):

☐   tie to interview;

☐   proposed expansion plan;

☐   reason for possible conflict;

☐ explanation of problem;

☐ proposed action;

☐ costs.

The letter is drafted as follows:

Mr M Kader & Mr B Khan
c/o Kiddies Clothing Co
1 Upminster Road
Sheffield
S4 6BJ

Dear Mr Kader & Mr Khan

Re: Your Proposed Business Venture

Thank you for calling at my office yesterday. As promised, I am writing to you to confirm your instructions and my advice.

You told me that you both wish me to act for you in your plans to expand Mr Kader's present business. These plans include building a new factory. The expansion will be funded in part by a loan from Mr Khan (£30,000) and in part by a mortgage from Mr Kader's bankers (£70,000). You have both asked me to look into the restructuring of Mr Kader's present business arrangements. At present Mr Kader operates as a sole trader.

We discussed Mr Khan's concerns. He is worried that that the business expansion plan will almost certainly result in the business' bankers asking for additional security for the loan. This is likely to take the form of a mortgage on both of your homes. As I understand it, Mr and Mrs Khan are reluctant to allow their home to be mortgaged in this way.

Whilst I am very pleased to help you both in this matter, I do have a professional duty to act in the best interests of both of you. I am concerned that the present situation could give rise to a position where your interests are in competition, or in other words, a conflict of interest could occur.

You both have a joint objective in seeing this business plan through, but equally you each have your own agendas so far as the risks and benefits are concerned. I wonder at this stage, in view of such a potential conflict, whether each of you should be separately advised.

As you will both be aware I have acted for Mr Kader for many years. My professional responsibilities allow me to continue to do so, but if a conflict arises, I must then initially decline to act for both of you. Were you, Mr Khan, to decide to take independent legal advice, at this stage, I feel that I would be able to continue to act in this matter for Mr Kader. Were I to continue to act for both of you and a conflict were to arise in the future I would have to decline to act for both of you. This is because I could, by that point, have discovered information about both of you that would give me an unfair advantage in acting for just one of you.

I am confident that there is no such conflict at present. However there is a strong possibility of one arising in the future and I prefer to confront the issue at this stage. The type of conflict that could occur, for example, would be if the two of you were to disagree on how to divide the shares in any company formed to run the business. We did discuss this at some length at our meeting and you both said that you would think about what I have raised.

Before I continue to act further I would like to discuss with you both the content of this letter. Would you please contact me as soon as possible either by telephoning me or making an appointment to see me. I will not take any further action until I have spoken to you both.

Can I assure you that once this issue is resolved we can then make progress as agreed and as soon as is practically possible?

At that point, I will confirm my further advice including the terms upon which my services will be provided. As discussed, there is no charge for our initial consultation and for writing this letter.

As instructed, I have addressed this letter to you at Mr Kader's place of business. In view of the content, I have also sent a copy of it to Mr Khan's home address.

Best wishes
Yours sincerely

Solicitor D

cc Mr B Khan
7 Stern Road
Sheffield
S7 7FY

Is this a good letter?

The letter complies with the standards expected of solicitor D, both in terms of professional obligation and good practice. It is in language that should be readily understood. It is a cautious letter which is intended to cover both the clients' interests and D's, in terms of his or her professional position. It is a clear letter, in that it sets out what action should be taken and why. It is an honest letter that highlights what the client needs to know. In the real world, the commercial reality is that a solicitor will not readily turn work away but, sometimes, must do so. This may attract the client's disapproval. Nonetheless D must take such action if he or she feels this is required professionally.

Two small points of style can be noted here. The letter is headed by the words 'Re: Your proposed business venture'. First, it is good practice to identify what you are writing about. It focuses attention. Mr Kader and Mr Khan probably know why D has written to them but they are told anyway to avoid any ambiguity. In a letter to another solicitor, court or other organisation, this may be even more directive as it identifies the issue. The court may have several parties called McAuley or Slater and the heading can direct the court to your particular case. The court would also have a case number which should always be quoted.

The second point concerns the use of 'Re'. This is a rather old fashioned, Latin, way of indicating what something is about in the sense of 'concerning' or 'to do with'. We accept this as it is well used and understood. We don't normally become tempted by Latin terminology. Here however, its use and meaning is very clear. 'About' could be just as effective but no-one else uses it! Omitting it altogether is arguably worthwhile, leaving only the subject matter in place in the heading. We do that in Letter 3.

Let us now move on to the next stage in this case. We have already seen in Chapter 4 that Mr Kader eventually accepts the point of a possible conflict of interest, and Mr Khan sees the wisdom of getting independent advice. A letter can now be written to Mr Kader as D's client. The heading of the note paper, address, and date can be presumed to be as set out before.

Letter 3

- *Type:* To the client confirming instructions.

- *Purpose:* To clarify action to be taken.

- *Requirements:* To satisfy 'client care'.

- *Contents outline*:

  ☐ willingness to act for Kader;

  ☐ Khan separately represented;

  ☐ summarise benefits of company/partnership;

  ☐ company option – action plan;

  ☐ costs;

  ☐ firm's details.

This is what D writes:

Dear Mr Kader

Your Proposed Business Venture

Thank you for phoning yesterday. I am writing to confirm the position as I understand it.

After talking with you, I met Mr Khan. He has decided to consult another solicitor. At his request I have recommended a solicitor to him who I know, from previous dealings, is efficient and reliable in these matters. As agreed, I will continue to act for you.

In view of the circumstances I do not propose to make any charge for my services to date to either you or Mr Khan. I set out the basis for my charges in the future later in this letter.

From what you tell me it is my advice that your business needs to be restructured.The business venture with Mr Khan should be put on a footing that protects your interests. Mr Khan now wishes to become formally involved in the business, and, as I understand it, you want to involve him. There are two ways of achieving this:

- entering into a partnership; or

- setting up a company in which you both hold shares.

Let me explain this more fully:

A partnership would give you a set of rules regulating your business but making you both liable (together and individually) for all the partnership's liabilities. A company would offer you protection against liability as well as giving you a set of rules that set out how the business is to be run. By this I mean that you cannot be held personally liable for any of the company's debts (unless you have given a personal guarantee for them). The rules of the company would set out the extent of your ownership (through shares) and your position in the company (you would presumably wish to be managing director). Although slightly more formality and expense would be involved in setting up a company, it is my view that this alternative would better suit your purpose. As I understand it, you also prefer this option and I am waiting to hear from Mr Khan's solicitors as to whether it suits him.

We need to agree with Mr Khan and his solicitor which structure best suits you both and the ground rules that would apply. These include the details of the company to be formed, the role that you and Mr Khan as its directors and shareholders will occupy and the financial arrangments involved. We did discuss some of this in detail at our last meeting but I will go over the important matters, including the responsibilities of directors, when we next meet. I have agreed to work out for you a draft proposal covering all of these points and to send this to you as soon as possible and in any event by 30th September. We can then discuss the arrangements further before sending our proposals to Mr Khan's solicitors.

I have contacted Mr Khan's solicitors to suggest that we proceed on this basis and also I have suggested that the cost of forming the company should be shared between you. Both you and Mr Khan will of course be responsible for your own legal fees.

So far as my charges are concerned this is not a matter for which you are entitled to legal aid. My firm's fees are calculated on time spent and responsibility involved. As I do not yet know how long this transaction will take to complete (because I have not yet heard what Mr Khan's solicitors have to say and I have not yet discussed with you all of the implications) I cannot give you a precise assessment of the final cost. As and when I am in a position to do so, I will. What I can say is that my firm has an hourly charging rate of £100.00 (plus VAT at 17.5%) which in this case covers both the time and responsibility involved in a case such as yours.

All time spent on your case will be closely monitored to keep costs to a minimum, and you are entitled to see how this has been computed at any stage. I will in any event account to you at the end of each month so that you will be aware of the extent of these costs. In addition to the hourly charging rate my charges will also include any expenses incurred on your behalf, such as your share of the fees payable on the registration of a company. As and when these costs arise I will advise you.

I will conduct your case personally with assistance from other members of this firm. Should you at any time have any queries or feel cause to complain, please contact me immediately. If you are dissatisfied with my response my firm operates an internal complaints procedure. Any client in such circumstances can write to the senior partner 'F' who will investigate the matter as soon as possible and convene a meeting of the partners to discuss what action, if any, is to be taken.

It is difficult to estimate exactly how long this transaction is likely to take but if we can agree on the basics with Mr Khan relatively quickly and finalise the financial aspects, the restructuring of the business could be completed within 6 to 8 weeks.

I enclose a leaflet which provides you with what I hope is useful information about the firm. You have no doubt received a similar leaflet when I have acted for you previously but this is the most recent version.

If you have any queries at all please do not hesitate to contact me. I will write to you again as soon as I have heard from Mr Khan's solicitors and when I have prepared our draft proposals.

Yours sincerely

Solicitor D

Is this another good letter? At first sight, it may appear very long-winded. One of our guidelines for letter drafting was the need to be precise. Let us think about this for a moment. Can a long letter be precise? We think that the answer is yes.

Being succinct is being to the point. If there are lots of points at issue then the letter may well be long. This one could have been much longer. All of the implications of partnership and company law could have been recounted. We do not think that this was necessary. It was discussed at length during the interview. The overall position was reviewed in the letter. The detail should have been recorded in attendance notes (of which more later) and subsequent correspondence. The letter also had to address issues other than the summary of instructions and advice given. Rule 15 of the Solicitors' Practice Rules requires that the client be given certain information relating to complaints procedures, the identity of the person handling the matter, the length of time the case is likely to take and developments that may occur.

The Law Society's written professional standards offer guidance on costs, legal aid and related matters. The client is entitled to know how much a case is likely to cost as well as how long it will take.

D's letter would appear to satisfy these requirements and our own objectives at every stage – what we are doing and why.

Having seen a couple of 'good letters' what about one that is lacking in some of the basic ingredients?

Consider this:

Letter 4

- *Type*: To the client confirming instructions.

- *Purpose:* To confirm action to be taken.

■   *Requirements:* Satisfy 'client care'.

■   *Contents outline:* Didn't bother!

The letter reads as follows:

> Dear Sir,
>
> **Re: Kiddies Klothes – Proposed Company Formation**
>
> Further to our interview on 20th inst. we confirm we are willing to accept your instructions.
>
> Our Commercial Law Department will attend to the drafting of the Memorandum and Articles of Association of the aforementioned company and submit these for approval to your proposed co-director and legal representative and your good self.
>
> Please contact the writer in the event of difficulty.
>
> Yours faithfully

This letter stands in stark (and deliberate) contrast to the previous two examples. It is perhaps an extreme, but realistic, case of a poor letter. It raises a possible breach of rule 15 by failing to refer to any complaints procedure. The actual requirement of the rule is that such a procedure should be maintained and this procedure must ensure that 'clients know who to contact in the event of their being dissatisfied with the services provided by the solicitor' (Silverman *Handbook of Professional Conduct for Solicitors*, p 25). The letter also fails to refer to the appropriate information and the issues raised by the case as required by the rule.

There is in fact no specific requirement that such information be in writing, although Law Society recommendations are that it should be. It is conceivable that Mr Kader could have been advised at the interview or over the telephone. Where better (for the record), however, than in a letter? (If you follow our view (expanded on later, p 316) a telephone call would have to be written up in an attendance note anyway.)

Professional obligations apart, what else is wrong with this letter? We have said that a letter drafter should try to follow several important guidelines. The letter should be clear and precise. It should use plain English and avoid unnecessary legalese. It should clearly state outcomes and communicate the message so the recipient understands what has been said and why. This letter falls down on many of these objectives. What would you feel if you received such a letter? At best you may feel that someone is looking after your affairs (but who is the Commercial Law Department?) and if there is a problem, you could contact 'the writer' whoever that might be. At worst you may feel that the letter is wholly inadequate. It sounds as if the solicitors are doing you a favour. You are just a number to them; they don't even give you a name.

What were your instructions? Did you decide a company was what you wanted? As you understood it, it was a possibility but this had not been decided on.

What about the language? What are Memorandum and Articles of Association? Who is the proposed co-director? When was the 20th inst? It may not be too difficult for Mr Kader to make the correct assumptions, but should a client have to play such a game?

How long will it all take? What will it cost? And who will pay? When will I hear something else? Will they discuss it with me? All these unanswered questions must have the possible effect of making Mr Kader uncomfortable and in need of reassurance.

It must be said that rule 15 does have a caveat or an exempting provision which states that some or all of its provisions need not be complied with if the solicitor considers it inappropriate in the circumstances. One example given is where the transaction is a repetitive one and the client is a regular client of the solicitor or is a commercial client who is sufficiently familiar with the business in hand. It is doubtful that these conditions apply in Mr Kader's case, at least on the facts brought out so far.

So it is back to the letter drafting board for 'the writer'.

Before leaving letter drafting, several other types of letter need to be examined. Particular drafting issues need to be addressed for particular types of letter.

Let us have a look at a letter before action. For this example we can turn to the personal injury case.

Solicitor B has taken instructions from Daniel and now intends to write to Mr Slater. The form and content of this letter is important. The letter before action is a chance for you to set out your case clearly and lead the opponent towards the resolution of the case. The letter may prompt Mr Slater to refer the matter to his insurers, in which case a negotiated settlement may be more likely, or it may clear the way for the issue of proceedings. It is also courteous to tell an opponent what you are intending to do. Your claim may even be struck out if there was no letter before action or at least your costs may be disallowed. Take care to make the letter accurate, for errors may be quoted back at you. For example, you may claim a breach of the Health and Safety at Work etc Act without having looked up the provisions to see if there was a requirement to act in a specific way. Making claims that you cannot substantiate cannot help your cause.

The key requirements of the letter before action are:

- Who you act for.

- What happened (be brief but accurate, there is no need to provide or even refer to evidence at this stage).

- Why the recipient of the letter is said to be responsible (the cause of action).

- What you are claiming.

- What you want the recipient to do, for example, pay, report the matter to the insurers etc.

- When they must do it, and what will happen if they do not. (On the last point do not make idle threats; if you threaten proceedings in 14 days, you had better be sure that your client means it and that you have everything you need by then to do it. 'Proceedings may be issued against you' could be another line, but why make threats if you are not willing to proceed?)

How might such a letter be written? Again the letter heading will be taken as before.

Letter 5

■   *Type:* Letter before action.

■   *Purpose:* To elicit a response from opponent and to set out exactly what the case is.

■   *Requirement:* To safeguard position on costs.

■   *Contents outline:*

☐   identify client;

☐   specify incident;

☐   outline allegations and loss;

☐   define objective;

☐   state action to be taken.

This letter goes like this:

Dear Sir,

Re: Road Traffic Accident, 1st December 1998

We act on behalf of Daniel McAuley.

We understand that you were the driver of a motor vehicle registration no. ABC 123 on the above date, when your vehicle was in collision with our client. The accident happened at approximately 3pm at High Street, Jesmond. Our client was cycling westwards along High Street when you collided with him from behind.

From our instructions it would appear that the accident was caused by your negligence. We believe that you drove in a manner that was below that expected of a reasonable driver. We have advised our client that he has a strong case against you for compensation for the injuries he suffered and damage to his property caused by the accident. It is our client's intention to claim such compensation from you.

Our client is still undergoing medical treatment and we are not yet in a position to quantify his claim but we anticipate that we will shortly be able to do so.

We suggest that you refer this matter, if you have not already done so, to your insurers with whom we will correspond.

We must point out that if we fail to hear from you or your insurers within 14 days of the date of this letter, proceedings may be issued against you without further notice. We trust that this will not be necessary.

In view of the contents of this letter you may wish to take independent legal advice in which case we suggest that you contact a solicitor.

Yours faithfully

What is the purpose of this letter?

First, the letter makes out a cause of action. It alleges that Mr Slater was negligent or careless. As you know, if a duty of care is owed, and that duty is broken, and damage results, then compensation can be claimed.

This is a basic principle of tortious liability.

There is little point in going through all of the detail of the accident in a letter to Mr Slater, but you must identify the basis upon which compensation is being claimed. No detailed facts are given and none of our evidence is revealed, but enough information is set out to give the basis for Daniel's claim. There is little point (and indeed some danger of saying something that you may later regret) in making detailed allegations at this stage. It is enough to pinpoint the incident, the cause of action and the remedy sought.

Secondly, the letter is aimed at getting a response. It contains a suggestion – see your insurance company or your lawyer; and it backs this up with a lawful threat – if you don't respond constructively we will sue you.

The third purpose is to give Mr Slater the chance to meet his liability without the expense of full blown litigation. Remember that the court has a discretion in matters of costs and unless you or your client have behaved reasonably, costs may be at risk.

Fourthly, if you can quantify a claim so much the better. In Daniel's case, however, it is too early to ascertain what the case is worth (quantum). As you will discover from a study of civil litigation, proceedings cannot normally be issued without serving a medical report and a list of special damages (for example, loss of earnings, damage to a vehicle or damage to clothing). The letter before action therefore rightly leaves open the figure claimed by way of compensation.

Three other points should be raised:

Technically the letter confirms that you act for Daniel and that all future correspondence should be sent and pleadings served on you as his legal representative.

The letter opens with an impersonal form of address – 'Dear Sir'. This is, we believe, preferable as it indicates a professional distance, through formality. You are not acting for Mr Slater.

The letter closes with a reference to the possibility of taking legal advice. Solicitors have a general professional responsibility to act fairly and properly. Making threats to sue should be tempered with a non-oppressive stance. There is, however, another compelling reason to use this tactic. What you want is progress in the case. If Mr Slater feels compelled to take legal advice, this will open up channels of communication that will at least bring about a response, if not lead to a settlement. If you already know who Mr Slater's insurers are, say, from the police, you might omit the reference to seeing a solicitor and end the letter 'I have sent a copy of this letter to your insurers AB & Co'.

The next type of letter which we need to mention is a letter endorsed with either 'subject to contract' or 'without prejudice'. The general purpose of these letters is intended to convey proposals or suggestions without the risk of the maker being held to them in the event of no agreement being reached.

An example should illustrate the point. In the personal injury case, the solicitors for Mr Slater (or the insurance company) may enter into negotiations with solicitor B. Firm proposals are about to be put. B receives the following letter from the solicitors for Mr Slater's insurers:

Letter 6

■ *Type:* 'Without prejudice' letter to solicitor.

■ *Purpose:* To propose a settlement.

■ *Requirement:* To avoid admission of liability and legal implications in the event that the offer is not accepted.

■ *Contents outline:* What would the other side include here? This is a letter to B. Work out for yourself the content plan of Mr Slater's insurers' solicitor. There are plenty of examples of content plans in this chapter if you need guidance.

This is what B receives:

Dear Sirs,

Our Client, AB & Co Insurance, Your Client, Daniel McAuley

Further to our previous correspondence, we have now received our client's instructions. Entirely without prejudice and without admission of liability, we are instructed to offer the sum of £10,000 in full and final settlement of this matter. Our clients are also willing to meet your reasonable fees and expenses incurred on behalf of your client.

This offer is to remain open for a period of 14 days after which it may be withdrawn without further notice.

We await hearing from you once you have had the opportunity of taking your client's instructions.

Yours faithfully

The general purpose of the endorsement 'without prejudice' is that the content of correspondence or discussions cannot be used in court at some later stage to bind the party who made the relevant proposals. The solicitors for Mr Slater's insurers indicate this by the use of the magic words 'without prejudice'. Remember, however, that if proposals are accepted, then according to the principles of the law of contract, a binding agreement arises, even if the correspondence was entered into on a 'without prejudice' basis.

B's reply should also be 'without prejudice', especially if attempting to negotiate a variation in the original offer.

As a matter of drafting technique, it is perhaps preferable to mark the whole letter with the words 'without prejudice' at, say, the head of the letter, perhaps in block capitals, repeating this on every page if the letter goes beyond one. This avoids the danger of parts of the letter being taken as without prejudice and other parts not. If a letter, or part of a letter, is not endorsed in this way it will be assumed that you intend it to be an 'open letter' and it may be referred to in the course of court proceedings.

In matrimonial cases (and in any other case where no payment into court can be made – see RSC Order 62) there is a particular type of letter known as a 'Calderbank' letter which is written 'without prejudice', but reserves the right to refer to it, after the main issues have been decided by the court, on the issue of costs. As it does not fit into our case studies we will note it only in passing.

Similar provisions (although with different effect) can apply to correspondence conducted in the course of contractual negotiations. 'Subject to Contract' can be used to demonstrate that the parties do not intend to be bound by the content of, say, a letter or memorandum. This matter was of particular relevance in conveyancing until the enactment of the Law Reform (Miscellaneous Provisions) Act 1989. This now provides that all contracts for the sale of land must be in writing, rather than simply evidenced by writing, so you need not be quite so cautious as previously when writing letters about buying and selling land.

A 'subject to contract' letter might be used in Mr Kader's case to show that any statememt made in negotiations in the run up to the formation of the partnership or company are not to be taken as contractually binding.

The next letter relates to routine standard correspondence passing between solicitors. What is the purpose and plan here?

The conveyancing case study well illustrates the point. Solicitor C has conducted factual and legal research leading to the despatch of enquiries before contract. He or she needs certain information before being able to approve the contract on behalf of the client. As seen in Chapter 4 (Research skills) much of this is now in standard form. However, looking at the contract C notes that the sellers (who are co-owners of the property) are described as selling as trustees for sale. C knows (or finds out) that covenants for title are more extensive if the seller sells as beneficial owner rather than as trustee for sale (Law of Property Act 1925, section 76(1)). C therefore wants to ensure that the contract is amended, to refer to the sellers as beneficial owners.

Letter 7

- *Type:* Letter between solicitors.

- *Purpose:* To raise enquiries and propose amendment to contract.

- *Requirements:* Not to commit clients to contract.

- *Contents outline:*

    ☐ identify clients and property;

    ☐ enclose enquiries;

    ☐ approve contract (subject to proposed amendments);

    ☐ indicate progress.

C's letter appears like this:

Dear Sir/ Madam,

Re: 1 Paradise Road, Sheffield, Kennedy & Bennett from Rigsby

Thank you for your letter of 20 January.

We enclose our enquiries before contract together with a copy for your file. Please note the additional enquiries raised. In particular we would prefer your clients to sell as beneficial owner. We have taken the liberty of amending the draft contract in this respect.

We enclose the draft contract otherwise approved subject to your satisfactory replies to our enquiries.

We expect to be in a position to exchange contracts shortly and await only your replies to our enquiries and the result of our local authority search. We have received our mortgage instructions.

Yours faithfully

enc: Enquiries before contract and copy draft contract.

This letter is somewhat different from the others in that it assumes a certain formality and legalese. Think of what it tries to do and who it is being sent to. Lawyers have their own conventions, coded words, and technical language. If this assists then it may be followed providing clarity and precision are not lost.

The letter indicates that the transaction is progressing along a predictable and routine course, even though particular matters remain to be answered. C has carried out the necessary initial research and simply awaits the result of the local authority search and the replies to pre-contract enquiries.

The letter informs the seller's solicitors of what C is waiting for before progress can be made. It attempts to move matters along by returning the contract with conditional approval. This means that, subject to satisfactory answers to the enquiries being given, the contract can be taken as agreed in principle, even though it is not yet in force. Technically, C could continue to raise queries in respect of it. In fact the letter allows the sellers' solicitors to take their clients' instructions and to obtain their clients' signatures in anticipation of exchange.

Seemingly, the letter conveys the right message – what we want to know from you, what you need to do, and where we go from here. The letter is written in a formal but efficient manner and extends the sort of courtesies (for example, sending a copy of documents for the other solicitor's file) that oil the machinery ensuring smoother progress. At the same time it does not yet commit or compromise either the buyers or C.

What about a letter to the court? Mrs Evans's case can be used to provide this example. The example can be a simple one to illustrate the point.

Presume that A has completed a legal aid application form for Mrs Evans. The first hearing before the magistrates is scheduled to take place in a week's time. A needs to have the issue of legal aid resolved before that hearing, so that he or she can be sure of payment. If legal aid were refused, solicitor A could discuss this with the client before the hearing to settle whether she will pay A's costs herself and if so how payment of the fees would be made.

Letter 8

■ *Type:* Letter to court.

■ *Purpose:* To enclose legal aid application.

■ *Requirement:* To elicit decision before court hearing.

■ *Contents outline:*

☐ identify client and hearing date;

☐ enclose legal aid application;

☐ stress deadline.

B writes the following letter:

Clerk to the Justices
Sheffield Magistrates' Court
North Square
Sheffield
S1 6PJ

Dear Sir/Madam

Re: Winifred Evans Date of Hearing 24.11.98

We act on behalf of Mrs Evans and enclose an application for criminal legal aid.

As the hearing date is only a week away, we would be grateful if you would advise us as soon as possible if legal aid has been granted. If necessary would you please telephone the result of the application?

Yours faithfully

Enc: Legal aid form, statement of means.

The letter is formally addressed. It identifies the client, the hearing date (this is important to enable the court to trace the case and deal with it expeditiously) and it informs the court what A needs to know and by what deadline. The enclosures are noted at the end of the letter. This is a useful checking device.

Letter writing is therefore an important skill that underpins much of the work that you will do in legal practice and is central to building and maintaining relationships with clients and third parties. Because it is so important we have taken the time to illustrate a number of different examples. For most of us writing a 'good letter' comes neither naturally or easily. It takes many drafts and many letters to get it right. However, if you are aware of the general guidelines to letter writing, set out above, you should be able to reach the desired objects with greater speed and efficiency.

Remember also that you will be judged by the letters you send. The client will form a view of you and so will others including assessors on your course! Importantly, the Office for the Supervision of Solicitors may take a view of your letter writing and so may a court.

It pays, therefore, to get this very basic skill right.

Before turning to the drafting of formal documents something needs to be said of four other informal drafting matters: statements, file records, instructing counsel and opinion writing.

Statements

By statements in this context, we mean a statement by your client of their instructions. This is not to be confused with witness statements (which may or may not be by your client and which are for use in litigation). These are examined later in the section on formal drafting and also in Chapter 7 (Advocacy).

The drafting skill here centres on the accurate recording of a client's instructions in a form that the client can read and approve and the lawyer understand. There is no legal requirement for such a statement to be produced, and for the experienced lawyer, a statement may sometimes be seen as an excessive requirement. If there is any element of complexity, and certainly if there is any possibility of the matter becoming contentious, a statement is a necessity. We believe it is good practice for lawyers to reduce their clients' instructions into a statement in any event, as this adds to clarity in the case. The statement is no more than an attempt to record what the client has told the lawyer. It also means that everything you know about the facts of the case can be found on file.

For you, both as a student and in your early years in a law office, we recommend that you regard the statement as a starting-point in the preparation of all cases. Whether you are experienced or not, there is always the need to record your instructions fully. You should do this to ensure that you understand what it is your client is saying and so that you can check with your client that he or she agrees. Using the form of a statement is one way, we say the best way, of directing your mind to this recording task. You also have a double check in place, for not only have you produced what you think your instructions are, but also you have the chance to ask your client to confirm these details. If properly done, two stand less chance of getting it wrong than one.

We suggest, therefore, that you draft a statement for your client and then send it to the client for his or her comments. Ask the client to correct, amend or add to the statement. Don't be worried about asking the client to do this more than once. Careful preparation is a strength and not a weakness. Inadequate preparation is a potential disaster maker.

You should end up with an accurate record of what your client has said and what it is that your client wants to achieve. You may need to amend this statement in the light of fresh instructions.

In contentious matters it may be worth producing a statement in a form that can be later adapted for use in litigation. Examples of this can be found in Chapter 4 (Research skills). The starting formula reads:

I (name) of (address) will say as follows. ...

Write down in chronological order the history of the case, noting, in particular, dates, people present, addresses, locations and any relevant documents, for example letters, deeds and contracts, and where they are to be found. Read back through the statement to see if it makes sense as a story and to check for any obvious omissions, errors or ambiguities. When you are happy with the content, send it to your client. We use the word 'send' deliberately, for it is preferable in our view to let the client have the statement with an explanatory letter and time to reflect on the content. Make the explanation clear that the statement is a draft and it is to be used as such, that is, it is amendable. Tell the client that it has been prepared to help you and him or her, and it will not be shown to anyone else without the client's consent.

Go through your draft extremely critically, looking for ambiguities or points that are not made clear. For example:

'I looked behind, saw that there was no traffic, and went into the middle of the road, before turning right.'

When and where did he look? For how long? Did he then signal? Did he wait in the middle of the road before turning; if so for how long?

The end result should enable you and the client to understand better the tasks ahead and to highlight those areas requiring further legal or factual research. For example, if Mrs Evans states that she saw Mr O'Connor taking money from the till on numerous occasions to pay bills or buy goods, you will need to find out how many times, when and under what circumstances. In this case, the statement acted as a prompt to asking further important questions.

In a non-contentious case there is no less a need for a statement. It is not necessary to use the same form of words as in a contentious case ('I will say as follows....'), but it is essential to record, and have the client check, the instructions.

In our view a statement is as good a way of doing this as any we know and probably better than most. As non-contentious matters mostly relate to present and future facts rather than past (contested) ones, the format of the statement is likely to be somewhat different. For a routine transaction parts might even be standardised like a questionnaire. A record is needed in any event.

In your draft, outline what the client has identified as the problem or task, specify what it is that the client wishes to achieve and list all of the pertinent facts as you see them. In the accident case, for example, Daniel (perhaps with help from his parents and prompting from B) will have told B about himself and his family (names, ages, addresses and other personal details). He should have related the details of the what happened on the day of the accident so far as he is able to remember them (what time he went out, what he was wearing, what the weather conditions were like, where he went, what time it was, the details of the collision, what happened afterwards and what injuries and damage was caused). Compose a description of these details and seek the client's confirmation of them. This is factual research. Clarifying and recording fact is as important a feature of research as the discovery of new material.

Regardless of whether the statement is in a contentious case or not, be prepared to take on board new facts and to amend the statement, or add to it, as the case progresses. In the conveyancing case study, the initial position may be recorded on the strength of the client's instructions, following the first interview. Later, however, this record will have to be amended to take into account the client's wishes on co-ownership, the reduction in price for the property, and the alteration in their financial arrangements. Factual changes should either be recorded in an amended statement, or by adding to the statement in the form of a memorandum.

Many of the points raised in this chapter also apply to file records. Drafting skills do not end with the letter, the contract, the lease, the client's statement or the pleadings.

File records

Unless you have the good fortune, as a barrister, to be able to get rid of all your paperwork, perhaps by tying it up in red tape and sitting on it, you will have files to maintain. For solicitors file maintenance is of great importance. Undergraduates too should know how to keep records for this is useful as a tool to organising your study and may be a requirement in terms of assessment (for example presenting coursework in the form of a case file).

You must ensure, both as a matter of good practice and professional duty, that your file management is accurate and efficient. You should make a record of all developments. There is a dual reason for doing so. First, if you are a practising lawyer, there are professional standards to meet. If you are charging for your time, or otherwise having to justify your claim for payment, the file is your record of what has been done. You can calculate charges appropriately and justify them if called to do so later, by reference to the information on your file.

What are file records? Excluding clients' statements, which have been dealt with above, the file records include a range of matters. The most important are attendance notes, records of telephone calls, memoranda of meetings, research notes, copy correspondence and draft documentation. This list is not exhaustive.

What are you setting out to achieve? Quite simply, your file should reflect everything that has happened in the case, from your initial instructions, through correspondence, court pleadings and other documentation. The file records are those that you keep on your file to record what has taken place. The file will contain other material that has been sent to you. You should hold the originals of letters from other parties such as the opposing solicitor. You may also hold deeds, experts' reports and other related documents. These should be kept along with the other records in good condition and in a logical order. It should be possible at any time for you or any other person (for example, your principal or the solicitor who takes over if the client sacks you) to consult the file and to be able to read easily the content of it, so as to know exactly where the case has reached.

When drafting the records (as opposed to filing documents received) think about the purpose. You need to know what has taken place. You may be called upon to justify your actions. You may need to refer back to your records. Ensure therefore that any record placed on file is both comprehensive and accurate. In some cases pro-formas may assist in this respect. These are standardised forms used for particular purposes, for example to record a telephone conversation. A well drafted pro-forma will be user-friendly and ensure that the detail is completed in such a way that it is readily understood by you or anyone else who has to use the file. Pro-formas also encourage standardised practice within a law office.

An example will make this clear. A great deal of a solicitor's work is conducted over the telephone. Short of tape recording all that transpires (there are professional practice guidelines in this respect, see Silverman *Handbook of Professional Conduct for Solicitors*, p 40), you need to record manually what has been said. Not only is this a general requirement but it can have specific legal consequences.

Take the conveyancing case. C is ready to exchange contracts in Ms Kennedy and Mr Bennett's purchase. Both C and the sellers' solicitor are ready to proceed. C telephones the sellers' solicitor. Both wish to exchange contracts over the telephone. This is an important moment in the transaction for, if the matter is handled correctly, both sets of clients will become contractually bound. Both solicitors should record the telephone conversation noting the date and time of exchange, the date for completion and the parties concerned.

According to Law Society guidelines (*Law Society's Gazette* 9 July 1986, 2139), contracts can be exchanged in this way either under formula A, B or C (depending on whether one solicitor holds both copies of the contract, whether each holds their own client's copy or whether the exchange forms part of a chain to be synchronised).

An effective memorandum with the details completed could read as follows:

Memorandum

Exchange of Contracts by telephone

DATE: 1 February 1998

TIME: 11:30 am

SELLER'S SOLICITORS: A B & Co.

PURCHASER'S SOLICITORS: C & Co.

PROPERTY: 1 Paradise Road, Sheffield

SELLER: Mr & Mrs Rigsby

PURCHASER: Ms Kennedy and Mr Bennett

COMPLETION DATE: 1st March 1998

LAW SOCIETY FORMULA: A/B/C (delete two leaving one)

Signed:

(C – solicitor completing memo).

This memorandum should then be filed immediately (no later than 11.31 am).

Other file notes must record:

■ who talked to who;

■ time (exact start and finish) and date;

■ name of client;

■ detail of conversation or action;

■ follow up action required.

The file record must be legible.

Compare the following file notes:

1 Mrs Evans telephoned this afternoon. She said she had received a summons from the court. She made an appointment for Thursday at 2pm.

2 *Note of telephone call*

Name of caller: Mrs Evans – crime

File number: A123

Person taking call: A

Date: 21/10/98

Time start: 2.30 pm

3 Time finish: 2.40 pm

Instructions: Client has received summons
Two charges of theft (£3 and £545)
Court hearing – 24/11/98

Advice: I will request advance disclosure and antecedents. Client to see me as soon as possible and bring summons.

Action: Appointment made for 2pm 23/10/98 to see me.

Which is the better file record? Why?

The standardisation of file records makes sense, especially when you consider that Mrs Evans's criminal case or Ms Kennedy and Mr Bennett's conveyance may be one of many that you have in your cabinet at work and one of many more current in your practice. We are making a case for organisation, for accuracy and for efficiency. This is as much part of the drafting process, however mundane, as the more obvious drafting tasks.

The last of the informal drafting tasks dealt with here concern the use of counsel – instructing counsel and opinion writing.

Instructions to counsel

Whilst this quite properly fits into the section on informal drafting, instructing counsel is governed by conventions in practice that give a certain formality to this process. We will look at these conventions shortly.

Counsel should not be used as a short cut to problem solving. The solicitor must address the problem concerned directly. A barrister should be consulted at a point when the solicitor has already researched the facts and law and is in a position to determine the theory of the case or the case objectives. Until this point is reached the solicitor cannot know what it is he or she wants the barrister to do. In the absence of the results of the legal and factual research, it is not possible for the solicitor to instruct counsel adequately. The barrister is therefore a resource to which the solicitor can refer from time to time as need dictates. Some examples may make this clear.

A barrister could be asked to give his or her opinion as to liability and/or quantum in Daniel's case. As seen in Chapter 4 (Research skills), B has already investigated the facts of the case and has carried out extensive research on the applicable law. Nonetheless, B feels the need to take a second opinion to ensure that his or her view of the law on, say, contributory negligence, is right. This may be particularly relevant if the case may eventually be heard in court and counsel is to be used at that hearing. This is explored in more detail in the following section – opinion writing.

In Mrs Evans's case the matter may go before judge and jury in the Crown Court. At the time of writing few solicitors have full rights of audience in the Crown Court and counsel would probably have to be instructed. Given this requirement it makes sense to involve counsel sooner rather than later to take advantage of counsel's views which may assist in the preparation of the case.

Other constraints may call for a barrister's services. Daniel may be receiving legal aid and the certificate may be limited in the following terms: 'for all steps, up to and including taking counsel's opinion, but not including the issue of proceedings'. Counsel's opinion would therefore be required if legal aid were to be extended. From research, B knows that Daniel has a strong case and is willing to move forward with confidence, if necessary to a hearing. Counsel's opinion will have to be taken. If this supports B's view that proceedings should be issued, the Legal Aid Board is almost certain to lift the limitation on the certificate and to authorise B to proceed with the case. With the lifting of the limitation, B may decide to ask counsel to draft the particulars of claim. This is likely especially if counsel is to be used at any subsequent hearing.

Counsel can therefore be used for a variety of purposes, from giving opinions to appearing on a client's behalf. The function of counsel is not limited to contentious cases. You can ask counsel to draft documents in a legal transaction, for example a contract, or provide an opinion on the wording of a complex provision in a will that seeks to create a trust. It is in contentious cases, however, that barristers are more commonly used.

If counsel is used to give an opinion, or to draft court pleadings, the document drafted by the solicitor is known as 'instructions to counsel'. If counsel is being asked to represent a client before a court or tribunal the term 'brief to counsel' is used. Both instructions and briefs are governed by the same considerations in terms of defining the purpose and plan.

We suggest that the following guidelines should be applied when instructing counsel:

1   Conduct all necessary research, both factual and legal. Reach the point in the case where you have defined your case theory or objectives. These may have to be remoulded following counsel's advice, especially where further investigations are needed.

2   Formulate the question or questions that you want counsel to answer and/or the task that you want counsel to perform. This should be generated by the theory of the case or case objectives. Is liability at issue? Is contributory negligence relevant and if so to what extent? What is the appropriate level of quantum of damage? Do you need a conference with counsel (jargon for a meeting between you, the barrister and the client)?

3   Set out the issues that you wish counsel to deal with in an ordered way. Number the paragraphs if this helps. Plan this before starting the draft instructions or brief. Write out all of the matters that you wish to cover and use this as a checklist.

4   Enclose copies of all relevant documents that counsel might need and list these in the draft. Ensure that all copy documents are legible and in order. (Do not send the originals unless there is a compelling reason, in which case tell counsel.) The enclosures should include all witness statements, records, deeds, photographs, experts' reports etc. If the matter has previously been before counsel, enclose those previous instructions, enclosures and opinions. Any legal aid order or certificate must be copied.

5   Begin the draft by telling counsel who you act for and in connection with what. Go on to summarise the pertinent facts so that counsel knows at the start what the case is about, its history so far, and what is required of him or her. Pertinent issues include any knowledge of how other parties to the proceedings are planning to conduct the case – for example co-defendant's plea or third party allegations.

6   Set out the questions that you want counsel to answer and the tasks that you want counsel to perform.

7   Explain what you think the relevant legal and factual issues are. Highlight the matters that are in dispute and those that are not. Give counsel your opinion on fact and law and on difficulties that may arise.

8   Ensure that you give counsel all relevant information concerning your client. If the client is very nervous or apprehensive mention this in a tactful but clear way. The

barrister may have to meet your client and needs to know if there are any issues that should be handled with care or delicacy. Remember that you (we hope) already have a good working relationship with the client, but the barrister is a stranger.

9   Invite counsel to hold a conference if you think this is needed or if counsel wishes to have one. Ask counsel to contact you if there is anything that he or she needs in connection with the case.

10 Conclude by summarising what you want counsel to do and with any deadline that must be met, for example, a court hearing date or limitation period.

11 Advise counsel if the client is legally aided and quote the certificate number. This will assist counsel in considering liability for costs if the case proceeds to court. It might help counsel in planning tactics in the case and it will affect what counsel can charge. Also, if the instructions are not marked 'legal aid' the solicitor, not the Legal Aid Board, is personally liable to pay counsel's fees.

12 Comply with the conventions applicable to instructing counsel. We are, in part, reluctant to press this point, for, as we have said before, good communication should not hinge on slavish adherence to custom and habit. It may well be that some of the conventions set out below are unnecessary and anachronistic. A failure to observe them however may result in poor relations between you and counsel and possible delay if, say, a brief is returned by a haughty counsel's clerk. It may also mean that you score badly on a course assessment. Some of the conventions can be circumvented but only if you know counsel well and know that he or she is happy to proceed in their absence. For the time being stick to the rules.

What are these conventions?

- The document instructing counsel should have a backsheet (a sheet giving the court and title to the action, the name of the parties, the name of counsel and the instructing solicitor's details. Mark it 'legal aid' if appropriate).

- The document should be typed or word processed on brief paper (heavy quality, traditionally foolscap).

- The solicitors instructing counsel are normally referred to as 'your Instructing Solicitors' not 'we'.

- The barrister is called 'counsel', not 'you' or Mr Jones.

- After the title to the action, the document is headed 'Brief to Counsel' or 'Instructions to Counsel'.

- The whole is folded lengthways, with enclosures, and bound in pink ribbon! Your course assessment may not insist on this.

Let us put these principles into action and draft a brief to counsel to appear in the Crown Court on behalf of Mrs Evans.

The backsheet would read:

IN THE SHEFFIELD CROWN COURT   Case number CC001

IN THE MATTER OF:

R

v

WINIFRED EVANS

BRIEF TO COUNSEL TO APPEAR IN THE CROWN COURT ON 15 APRIL 1999 AT 10.30 AM

LEGAL AID

A & Co.
Solicitors
1 High Street
Sheffield
0114 2123456

After repeating the title, the content may read as follows:

1   Your Instructing Solicitors act on behalf of Winifred Evans, the defendant in this case. Mrs Evans has been indicted on two counts of theft. She is due to appear before the Crown Court at Sheffield on 15 April 1999 at 10.30 am where she intends to plead not guilty. Counsel is requested to represent Mrs Evans at this hearing and any subsequent trial.

2   Enclosed for counsel's information are:

(a)   Witness statement of Mrs Evans

(b)   Draft indictment [*note to student reader: the copy served on the defence solicitors by the CPS is invariably referred to as the draft because it has not yet been approved by counsel for the prosecution*]

(c)   List of Mrs Evans's antecedents (note to student reader: antecedents are details of previous convictions)

(d)   Copy correspondence between your Instructing Solicitors and the CPS dated 1/9/98 and 28/10/98

(e)   Copy grant of conditional bail order

(f)   Committal papers as detailed in the attached schedule

(g)   Record of taped interview of Mrs Evans by the police

(h)   Copy of custody record

(i)   Copy unsigned statement of Sharon Smith

3   Mrs Evans is 46 years old and is a married woman who lives in Sheffield with her husband and two children. She worked for approximately 6 years as a sales assistant in Tasty's bakery, Sheffield, owned presently by one Andrew O'Connor.

4   On 1/9/98 Mrs Evans was arrested on suspicion of theft. The circumstances of her arrest and subsequent charge are detailed in her statement. 3 marked £1 coins were found in her apron pocket and it is alleged that these coins were given to her by a plain clothed police officer buying food at Tasty's. It is also said by the prosecution that Mrs Evans took the coins and placed them in her apron pocket. When asked during the interview at the police station if she had put the coins in her pocket, Mrs Evans replied, 'I suppose I must have done it'. Mrs Evans was summarily dismissed from her employment by Mr O'Connor following her release from police custody on 1/9/98.

5   Counsel will see from the draft indictment that Mrs Evans faces two counts of theft. The first relates to the 3 £1 coins and the second to the sum of £545. It is alleged that Mrs Evans stole money totalling £545 on dates between 1/6/98 and 1/9/98. Mrs Evans denies committing either offence.

6   Mrs Evans elected Crown Court trial and was committed by the Sheffield Magistrates' Court on 1/2/98 under s 6(2) Magistrates' Courts Act 1980 on conditional bail, the condition being that she reside at her home address. All prosecution witnesses were fully bound.

7   The interview with Mrs Evans at the police station on 1/9/98 (counsel has a record of this in the form of the ROTI) took place in the absence of legal representation. The custody record shows that Mrs Evans was offered the services of a solicitor (which she does not dispute) but she declined this. Her explanation for this is that she wanted the matter dealt with as quickly as possible and that as she had not done anything wrong she had no reason to seek legal help. Mrs Evans is inexperienced in these matters. It was only after her release that she was persuaded (by her husband) to take legal advice. On consulting your Instructing Solicitors she was advised of the need for the prosecution to prove criminal intent in such cases. She now says that when she told the police in the interview that she must have taken the coins, she did not mean that she intended to permanently deprive Mr O'Connor of them, or act dishonestly. Rather, she must have put the coins in her apron pocket, intending to place them in the shop till at some later stage when she was less busy. Mrs Evans cannot in fact remember putting the coins in her pocket at all but she says that she may well have done so without thinking. Mrs Evans has never admitted taking any other money or stock from Mr O'Connor. She denied all knowledge of this in the interview and still does.

8   Your Instructing Solicitors consider evidence of this confession is admissible under s 76 of the Police and Criminal Evidence Act 1984 but counsel might consider if a voir dire is merited.

9   As Counsel knows [*more traditional briefs might say 'In your Instructing Solicitors' respectful opinion'. Is this necessary? We think not*] the prosecution must establish two elements if a conviction is to be upheld. First, there must be an appropriation of property belonging to another. If Mrs Evans did take the coins, but in her capacity as Mr O'Connor's employee, was the placing of the coins in her pocket an appropriation for the purposes of theft? She had permission from Mr O'Connor to handle money in the shop. Secondly, the defendant must act dishonestly and must intend to permanently deprive Mr O'Connor of the property. Mrs Evans will say that she had no such intent. Your Instructing solicitors draw counsel's attention to s 3(1) Theft Act 1968 (appropriation – assuming rights of an owner) and to the case of *R v Ghosh* [1982] QB 1059 (definition of dishonesty).

10   Counsel will note from the statement of Mr O'Connor contained in the committal papers that Mr O'Connor will say that he noticed money missing from the shop till for a period of over 6 months. According to Mrs Evans, Mr O'Connor regularly used money from the till to pay for shop supplies and for his own use. Your Instructing Solicitors suggest that the accounting system in the shop is suspect and that Mr O'Connor could properly be challenged with this evidence. Mr O'Connor also has a criminal conviction for dishonesty (VAT fraud 1993) which counsel will wish to consider putting to him notwithstanding loss of Mrs Evans's shield against character cross-examination. The only person who would appear to be able to substantiate Mrs Evans's assertions about the shop accounting system is Sharon Smith. Ms Smith works on a part-time basis at the bakery. Despite agreeing to be interviewed Ms Smith has so far declined to sign her statement and has indicated since making the statement that she does not wish to give evidence in the case. She says that she fears for her own job security if she is seen to support Mrs Evans. The statement given by her is, however, included with this brief. Your Instructing Solicitors will obtain a witness order if counsel so advises. Although reluctant, Ms Smith would be likely to be a truthful witness.

11   The evidence in respect of the second count of the indictment (the theft of £545) would appear to be very weak. The only direct evidence comes from Daniel O'Connor aged 13 who claims that he saw Mrs Evans taking money on previous occasions. Counsel will no doubt want to cross-examine him on why he did not mention this earlier. Your Instructing Solicitors have corresponded with the CPS on this matter and copies of the relevant correspondence are enclosed for counsel's information. Counsel may consider whether it is appropriate to raise with counsel for the prosecution the possibility of no evidence being offered in respect of the second count. On present instructions your Instructing Solicitors understand that Mrs Evans will continue to deny liability on both counts.

12   Counsel will no doubt require a conference in this case and your Instructing Solicitors await confirmation. If counsel needs any further information or clarification he (she) will no doubt advise.

13   If Mrs Evans is found guilty counsel is asked to address the court in mitigation. Counsel will be aware of the seriousness of a theft from an employer, but will note the particular effect a custodial sentence would have not only on Mrs Evans but also on her family. Up-to-date details of Mrs Evans's finacial circumstances will be prepared for the hearing.

14   Counsel is therefore requested to represent Mrs Evans at the Sheffield Crown Court on 15th April 1998 at 10.30 am. Counsel will note that Mrs Evans is legally aided.

We suggest that this brief summarises all relevant points in the case and leaves the barrister with clear instructions as to what is required of him or her. The solicitor should send the brief to the barrister of his or her choice. This might be on the basis of the solicitor's personal knowledge and preference. It may be by way of recommendation. It may be on the suggestion of the clerk to the barristers' chambers. Either way, it is for you to decide who you want to represent your client and you have a professional duty to ensure that a suitable person is instructed.

The 'cab-rank' rule (a professional rule applying to members of the Bar) says that unless there is good reason (such as lack of experience or expertise, or prior commitments) the barrister nominated should take on the case (Code of Conduct of the Bar, General Council of the Bar 1990 (amended 1991) para 501). Practicalities dictate that the barrister of your choice may not be able to take on the case, especially at short notice. In such cases you are, of course, free to instruct another. Counsel's clerk will normally advise of any such difficulty and may well recommend a barrister to you who can take on the case. Because of the chance of a last minute substitution of counsel, the brief must say it all. The new barrister relies on your preparation and has no time to supplement it. Counsel's clerk will also discuss fees (unless the case is legally aided).

So much for drafting instructions to counsel. What about counsel's advice or opinion?

Opinion writing

Opinion writing is, in a legal practice sense, the exclusive preserve of barristers. It arises when a solicitor's office instructs counsel to provide his or her views and assistance on a particular aspect or aspects of a case. You will be required to draft an opinion as part of the BVC. You may be required to perform this task at undergraduate level as part of the coursework and/or assessment for particular modules. Whether you are asking for an opinion as a solicitor, providing one as counsel or carrying out opinion writing as part of your course it is important, to achieve the most from the exercise, that you understand the drafting considerations involved.

We do not intend here to supplant the material available from the BVC providers. We simply make the point that opinion writing is an important drafting function and a drafting task that calls for the use of specific considerations and conventions as well as the general principles of good drafting practice discussed in this chapter.

First, let us be clear about terminology. A barrister's opinion or advice is a written document that answers specific questions asked by the solicitors on behalf of the client. The solicitors are normally referred to as 'Instructing Solicitors'. By convention counsel's 'opinion' is restricted to matters of law and liability. 'Advice' refers to evidence and procedure. Many instructions will cover both and we suggest that the distinction between 'opinion' and 'advice' is unimportant. For simplicity's sake we will use the word 'opinion' to cover both.

The general principles of good drafting apply equally to opinion writing as to any other legal drafting task. These can be summarised as follows:

1   be sure of the client's instructions – for barristers there are two clients, the professional one (the Instructing Solicitors) and the lay client (the Instructing Solicitors' client). The opinion is a response to the professional client but must take into account the objectives of the lay client;

2   be thorough in your preparation and research – analyse the facts as presented, identify the research issues, conduct the research methodically, plan your response;

3   compose your draft in plain English with a clear, consistent and logical structure – avoid legalese wherever possible, use numbers and headings to set out your advice, deal with each issue arising separately, reach a conclusion in respect of each point of advice sought;

4   comply with any legal, procedural or appropriate conventional requirements – ensure that your draft meets any or all of these;

5   test the draft against your instructions – does the draft fit the theory of the case or client's objectives?

If these are the general principles applicable to opinion writing, as one form of legal drafting, what are the specific considerations for the opinion writer?

The starting point must be to understand the purpose of the opinion. The provision of advice by a barrister is not an academic exercise. The advice that the barrister provides will be used to assist the client in resolution of their problems. It needs therefore to focus on possible practical outcomes – how the opinion can help the client achieve his or her goals.

In the useful manual *Opinion Writing*, produced by the Inns of Court School of Law (ICSL) (Blackstone Press, 1997), the drafting process is helpfully described in two stages – the thinking and the writing. In the thinking stage the barrister should ensure that he or she:

- reads the instructions carefully;

- understands what the client's principle objectives are;

- manages the facts (identifying what is relevant, what is not and what else may be needed);

- constructs a legal framework;

- sees the issues arisng in the context of the case as a whole;

- identifies all of the questions which require an 'answer';

- forms an objective view based on the facts, the law and the practical considerations applicable.

The seven stages of this thinking process are essential elements of preparation. They are consistent with our approach to contentious case research as shown in Chapter 4. We will see how these apply in the setting of our personal injury case study shortly.

The writing process is the transfer of the thinking process onto paper, in the form of the opinion. It should take into account:

- who is to read it (Instructing Solicitors and their client);

- the clients goals (a practical resolution of the relevant problem(s)); and

- the physical lay-out and form (to ensure any relevant conventions are met, procedural rules followed and, most importantly, that the client understands, in the clearest possible terms, the relevant issues and options available).

A well worded and structured opinion is rather like a preliminary judgment – assessing how matters are likely to turn out based on the facts and law as presented.

Although there are no absolute rights or wrongs the ICSL manual suggests (and we agree) that an opinion should include the following:

- a backsheet with the name of the case and details as set out in any pleadings. This will come from the instructions. Underneath should be the word 'OPINION' or 'ADVICE'. In Daniel McAuley's case this might read:

Daniel McAuley v Roy Slater

OPINION

As proceedings have not yet been issued details of the formal title of the court and parties are not required;

- by convention the opinion begins on a following page with the heading detailed above repeated;

- the opinion be set out in logical, paragraphed, manner. For ease of reference paragraphs should be numbered and/or headed. Numbering helps organise the opinion and headings sign-post content. In the case study the headings might include:

1. Introduction

2. Liability of Mr Slater

3. Contributory negligence of Daniel McAuley

4. Quantum of damage

5. Conclusion

- the opening paragraph(s) start with the material facts, or, if the facts are not thought to be at issue (for example if liability is not being contested), a summary of them, for example:

1.1   Daniel McAuley, who is 14 years old, was injured in a road traffic accident on 1st December 1997 when he was knocked off his bicycle by a car driven by Roy Slater. As a result of the accident Daniel suffered from a compound fracture to his left leg, concussion and abrasions to his arms, face and torso. I am asked to provide an opinion as to liability and quantum in this case.

- the main body of the opinion separate out each issue (general principle of law applicable, evidential matters, parties, liability, quantum) with the issues clearly identified, what your views are in relation to that issues, your reasons for forming those views and your conclusions in respect of each, for example:

(under *4. Quantum of damage*)

4.3   In my view quantum, for general damages, on a full liability basis, can be realistically assessed at between £10,000 and £16,000 presuming that Mr Healy's prognosis eventuates. In reaching these figures I have taken into account the cases of *Howe v Moore* (1992), unreported, cited in *Kemp and Kemp on Damages*, 12–317 and *Breese v Darnton* (1996), unreported, cited in *Kemp and Kemp on Damages*, 12–312/1. The latter was somewhat more serious than the present in terms of the number of operations undergone by the plaintiff and the extent of the long-term affects suffered by him. The former involved a full recovery but with a slight risk of stiffness developing in later life.

- restrict the citation of legal authority. Remember that this is not an academic exercise. Although a barrister might properly refer to case and statute law to justify his or her reasons this should only be done where such justification is necessary. It is not constructive, given the purpose of the opinion, (or perhaps ever) to cite authorities simply to show how well versed you are in the law;

■ if additional information or evidence is required this be included as specific advice either in the main body of the opinion, at the appropriate point, or in a separate advice on the evidence. This might for example include:

(under *4. Quantum of damage*)

4.1 My Instructing Solicitors have kindly provided me with a medical report by Mr Healy of 1st March 1998. As helpful as this report is I am conscious that it is now over 3 months old. In view of the somewhat speculative nature of some of the consultant surgeon's comments, those instructing me might wish to consider a further report before concluding negotiations or setting this matter down for trial. I am in particular concerned about the possibility of the limp that Daniel apparently suffers from becoming a long term disability.

■ a conclusion which summarises the main points of your opinion and addresses the overall concerns of the client, for example:

5. *Conclusion*

In conclusion I am of the opinion that Daniel has a strong case for damages based on the negligence of Mr Slater. There is a possibility of some contributory negligence on Daniel's part but this should not exceed 25%. The range of general damages applicable in this case, on the basis of full liability is between £10,000 and £16,000. If the element of contributory neglignce is taken into account this reduces the range of general damage to between £7,500 and £12,000. If those instructing me were to obtain further medical evidence that could substantiate the probability of longer term detrimental effects of the accident these figures would have to be revised. I would be pleased to assist in the provision of further advice and the drafting of any relevant papers in this matter. I wish Daniel a full recovery.

■ counsel's signature, name, date and address of chambers. In our case study this might read:

Barrister F

2 Morgan Court
Temple
London EC4

Before turning to a worked example of the opinion one further point can be made. It is an essential part of good drafting practice and central to ethical conduct that people communicating with each other should do so in a civil and constructive way. There is little to be gained and much to be lost through doing otherwise. Would-be barristers might take careful note of this general principle as and when they come to dealing with solicitors. When drafting your opinion ensure that it is a polite response to what is being asked of you. As the expert being asked for advice it is all too easy to be patronising in reply. If the solicitor has missed out what you consider to be vital information, or if the solicitor's view of the law is not necessarily your own, do say so in your opinion (or in a phone call made before you complete the final draft). But make sure that it is said in a tactful way. You and perhaps your chambers' clerk will not be getting briefs and instructions in future otherwise!

So how might counsel's opinion read in the *McAuley v Slater* case? Presume for the purposes of this example that solicitor B has asked for counsel's views on liability and quantum, enclosing Daniel's statement, the police report on the accident, a medical report on Daniel's injuries and a set of photographs showing the site of the accident, the damaged cycle and scarring to Daniel's body. Proceedings have not yet been issued. (An example of a brief to Counsel was set out earlier at page 320.) We have seen above some examples of what might be included in counsel's opinion in this case. The whole now reads as follows:

Daniel McAuley v Roy Slater

OPINION

1. Introduction

1.1 Daniel McAuley, who is 14 years old, was injured in a road traffic accident on 1st December 1997 when he was knocked off his bicycle by a car driven by Roy Slater. As a result of the accident Daniel suffered from a compound fracture to his left leg, concussion and abrasions to his arms, face and torso. I am asked to provide an opinion as to liability and quantum in this case.

1.2 From my instructions it would appear that the facts, in so far as the details of the accident and the injuries to Daniel are concerned, are unlikely to be disputed. I note that my Instructing Solicitors, having discussed the matter with solicitors for the prospective defendant, do not anticipate a denial of liability but do expect an allegation of contributory negligence on Daniel's part to be raised.

1.3 In consequence I deal first and briefly with the liability of Mr Slater, secondly with the possibility of the contributory negligence of Daniel and thirdly with the appropriate quantum of general damages. I note that I have not been asked to settle the Particulars of Claim in this case but in view of the conclusions that I reach, I should be pleased to do so if my Instructing Solicitors wish me to. As and when pleadings are drafted it should be remembered that Daniel is under the age of majority and any litigation should be commenced by his next friend, presumably one of his parents.

2. Liability of Mr Slater

2.1 It is a well established legal principle that road users owe a duty of care to all those who are likely to be affected by their acts or omissions. Mr Slater owed a duty of care to Daniel and this duty can be regarded as having been broken if it can be shown that Mr Slater's driving was below the standard to be expected of a reasonable driver in such circumstances. I note from my instructions and, in particular from the police report, that it is probable that Mr Slater was driving at an excessive speed. In any event he failed to avoid the accident and according to his statement, Daniel was an easy to be seen road user. The responsibility on any driver approaching another person or vehicle from behind is considerable. My Instructing Solicitors have suggested that a reasonable driver should have avoided a collision and it is hard to imagine a court reaching a different conclusion unless some other intervening factor (such as the way in which Daniel manouvered his bicycle) made the accident unavoidable. I will turn to the possibility of contributory negligence shortly. Mr Slater's subsequent and related drink-driving conviction, although not conclusive of negligence in itself, is useful and admissible evidence to support the allegation that he was driving in a condition and in a manner that resulted in a breach of the duty owed.

2.2 I conclude, therefore, from the evidence available that Mr Slater would be likely to be held liable in negligence. Should my Instructing Solicitors require a more detailed explanation in this respect or supporting authorities, would they please advise me? In addressing the rest of this opinion I am presuming therefore that liability in negligence on the part of Mr Slater can be established. As I will show the extent of this liability and its effect on quantum of damage requires more detailed consideration.

3. Contributory negligence of Daniel McAuley

3.1 The law is relatively clear on the principles upon which tortious liability can be apportioned. Blame can be allocated as between two or more persons causing loss, including plaintiff and defendant. In this case the onus would be on Mr Slater to show that Daniel committed some act or omission that contributed to the accident. I am unaware from my instructions whether or not it is alleged that Daniel caused damage to Mr Slater's car or whether Mr Slater was injured as a result of the accident. Given that I have not been instructed in this respect I presume that any question of negligence on Daniel's part is restricted to contributing towards his own injuries and loss. I should be grateful if those instructing me would advise me if this is not the case.

3.2 The liability of Daniel in any event (that is for damage suffered by Mr Slater or for Daniel's own losses) would be determined on the same basis as described in paragraph 2.1 above, that is, was Daniel behaving as a reasonable road user would? However, whereas Mr Slater would be judged by the standard of a reasonable and competent driver Daniel's conduct would be measured against that of a person of his age. There is a long line of authority for this proposition and I note in particular the case of *Gough v Thorne* (1966) 2 All ER 298. In this case the plaintiff was a boy of $13\frac{1}{2}$ who was injured while crossing a road. The court held that even though it may have been unwise for an adult to cross in the applicable circumstances it was understandable that a child of this age might. No contributory negligence was found. I note from Daniel's statement that he has passed a cycling proficiency test and is well acquainted with the rules of the road. He distinctly remembers looking behind before moving to the centre of the road although he cannot recall indicating with his arm. A failure to indicate could be held to amount to contributory negligence and much would depend on what the judge determined on the evidence. I note that there is no corroborative evidence in the form of independent witnesses to support either side as to whether Daniel did in fact look behind and/or indicate. What is clear is that the law generally expects less of a child than of an adult. Any contributory negligence on Daniel's part would, in my view, be likely to be low, perhaps less than 25%. As can be seen below this would affect quantum.

4. Quantum of damage

4.1 My Instructing solicitors have kindly provided me with a medical report by Mr Healy of 1st March 1998. As helpful as this report is I am conscious that it is now over 3 months old. In view of the somewhat speculative nature of some of the consultant surgeon's comments, those instructing me might wish to consider a further report before concluding negotiations or setting this matter down for trial. I am in particular concerned about the possibility of the limp that Daniel apparently suffers from becoming a long term disability.

4.2 For the present purpose, I can give an indication of the range within which quantum for general damages might fall, on the basis of a full recovery. A more up to date report will allow my Instructing Solicitors to satisfy themselves as to the likelihood of any long term complications, which would, if they materialised, affect the assessment of damages. Daniel's injuries are fully documented in Mr Healy's report. He underwent a lengthy and complex operation and was hospitalised for a week. He was in plaster for 8 weeks and although he has made a good recovery he still has (8 months after the accident) a noticeable limp, which in Mr Healy's view may well improve in time. There is some risk (unspecified) of arthritis. Daniel is still anxious about cycling and his injury prevented him from playing sport for 6 months. His scarring is fading but he will be left with visible marks on his left leg where the operation was carried out. On the present evidence there is no suggestion that Daniel's injuries will affect him in terms of his future studies or job prospects.

4.3 In my view quantum, for general damages, on a full liability basis, can be realistically assessed at between £10,000 and £16,000 presuming Mr Healy's prognosis eventuates. In reaching these figures I have taken into account the cases of *Howe v Moore* (1992), unreported, cited in *Kemp and Kemp on Damages*, 12–317 and *Breese v Darnton* (1996), unreported, cited in *Kemp and Kemp on Damages*, 12–312. The latter was somewhat more serious than the present in terms of the number of operations undergone by the plaintiff and the extent of the long terms effects suffered by him. The former involved a full recovery but with a slight risk of stiffness developing in later life.

4.4 In reaching my view on quantum for general damages in this case I have also taken into account the Guidelines for the Assessment of General Damages produced by the Judicial Studies Board (Blackstone Press, 1994). A range of £11,500–£16,000 is given for complicated or multiple fractures of the leg with the possibility of degenerative changes, limitations of movement and unsightly scarring. A lower range of £7,500–£11,500 is suggested where there is incomplete recovery (for example a slight limp) but without the other aggravating features mentioned above. For a simple fracture and complete recovery a figure of up to £6,000 is stated as appropriate. In Daniel's case, based on the medical evidence currently available, the court would, in my view, be likely to award general damages, on a full liability basis, at least at the top end of the range of £7,500 to £11,500. The court may well venture into the higher band of £11,500–£16,000 taking into account the scarring and risk of arthritis. The guidelines were of course drawn up over 4 years ago and inflation must be considered appropriate.

4.5 If one takes into account a possible finding of contributory negligence on Daniel's part of 25% the range of damages I suggest is reduced to between £7,500 and £12,000. My Instructing Solicitors have not instructed me to advise on special damages and I presume that they have full details of these as identified in Daniel's statement.

4.6 My Instructing Solicitors will of course be aware of the need to obtain the court's consent in such a case as this to any settlement that may be negotiated.

5. Conclusion

5.1 In conclusion I am of the opinion that Daniel has a strong case for damages based on the negligence of Mr Slater. There is a possibility of some contributory negligence on Daniel's part but this should not exceed 25%. The range of general damages applicable in this case, on the basis of full liability, is between £10,000 and £16,000. If the element of contributory negligence is taken into account this reduces the range of general damage to between £7,500 and £12,000. If those instructing me were to obtain further medical evidence that could substantiate the probability of longer term detrimental affects of the accident these figures would have to be revised. I would be pleased to assist in the provision of further advice and in the drafting of any relevant papers in this matter. I wish Daniel a full recovery.

Barrister F

2 Morgan Court
Temple
London EC4

Does this meet the standard we set ourselves in the introductory comments to Opinion Writing? The advice is clear. The questions set by Instructing Solicitors have been answered. The style is logical and the language straightforward. Perhaps more could have been added to explain the basis for the conclusions on contributory negligence. Why 25%? Remember we are not trying to show you how to draft the perfect opinion but what you should take into account in the preparation and drafting. If you think you could do better be our guest.

Let us now turn to drafting formal documents.

5   Drafting formal documents

In this section we are concerned with the drafting of documents that serve a formal purpose. This may be to record and complete a transaction (for example a conveyance), or to present aspects of a claim before a court (for example, alleging negligence in the particulars of claim in a road traffic accident case). Drafting in contentious and non-contentious cases will be considered in turn.

Drafting in contentious cases

Witness statements

We have already looked in the informal drafting section of this chapter at statements taken from the client. These are a record of the client's instructions. Witness statements, which may be made by the client or by any other person, are different, in that they are statements that are designed to be used in court or tribunal proceedings. As such they must be drafted to fulfil your objectives and at the same time comply with any legal requirements.

By objectives what do we mean? Why is the statement being prepared? Who for? In this context it is prepared for use in court. It may have to be disclosed to the other side and it may be used instead of the witness giving evidence-in-chief (though normally the witness can expect to be cross-examined). If the statement does not have to be disclosed it will be used as the basis for examination-in-chief – for the advocate to utilise as a benchmark for questioning. Therefore your purpose must be to set out what that witness can say that is relevant to the case, including in particular those parts of the evidence that are crucial to your theory of what happened, and excluding parts of the evidence that either do not assist or are inadmissible.

We suggest that if a case is likely to end up before a judge or other arbitrator, early drafts of witness statements should be prepared as soon as possible. Not only will this enable you to focus on the facts of the case (and to conduct the necessary research) but the nearer the taking of the statement is to the actual event, the more likely the record is to be an accurate account of what happened.

So what is a witness statement? It is an account of events that relate to the case in question, made by a person who is able to give the details from his or her personal knowledge or experience. It is a device to record the witness's account of what has taken place.

It can be used for a variety of purposes, the most important of which are:

■   as a proof of evidence for the lawyer to use for examination-in-chief in court (or a tribunal);

■   as a statement that will be disclosed to the other side in advance of the trial in a civil case (RSC Order 38, rule 2A and CCR Order 20, rule 12A);

■   as a statement that may be used in criminal proceedings (usually by the prosecution), in committal proceedings (Magistrates' Courts Act 1980, sections 6 and

102) or as a statement that is not disputed and will be read to the court without the witness being produced (Criminal Justice Act 1967, section 9);

■ as a statement that will be given in evidence under the permitted exceptions to the hearsay rule (Civil Evidence Act 1995 and RSC Order 38).

The witness statement must comply with its objectives, the theory of the case and the requirements of any procedural rules in that particular type of case. As well as satisfying yourself of the objectives the statement has to serve, and what legal rules, if any, are relevant, you need also to ensure that the statement supports the story that you are attempting to establish.

In a civil case RSC Order 38, rule 1 and CCR Order 20, rule 4 dictate that witnesses must attend court and give evidence on oath. However, as seen above, the orders go on to require that the statements of witnesses must be disclosed to the other side in advance of any trial.

As the exchange of witness statements in civil proceedings is now a very important part of the litigation process (and as you may well be asked to draft such a statement on a vocational course) we summarise the main points below. (These are based on the commentary to RSC Order 38, rule 2A with our own additions.)

The statement should:

1 be in numbered paragraphs with each paragraph dealing with only one matter;

2 be typed and double spaced, using one side of the paper only;

3 be paginated;

4 give the witness's full name and address (work address if that is relevant);

5 state whether the witness is a party to the proceedings and if not what the status of the witness is;

6 be as far as possible in the witness' own words;

7 relate events in chronological order;

8 contain only admissible and relevant evidence;

9 be signed by the witness;

10 the signature should preferably be witnessed.

We would add:

11 be complete (leave will be required to amend a disclosed statement or to introduce material at trial that is not contained in the original statement, so you must know what your theory and this witness' part of your story will be);

12   be consistent with your theory of the case;

13   preferably not be revealed until the other side has revealed – or agreed to post – theirs;

14   the contents must be sustainable in court. The witness will not be examined in chief, except to confirm his or her name and address and that this is their statement. Then the witness is subjected to cross-examination, and every part of the evidence that the other side disagrees with will be challenged. You must have tested what the witness can say during the interview, and again when sending the statement for signature.

When taking a statement from a witness, especially your client, you will almost certainly take down details of the case that later prove to be inadmissible in proceedings or which you would not want to disclose to the other side (for example, reference to an adverse medical opinion that you do not intend to rely on). You must ensure that the statement that is eventually produced to satisfy the requirements of Order 38 excludes this additional material.

Let us see how this might work in our civil litigation case study. Look at Daniel's statement in Chapter 4 (Research skills, at p 227). Would you disclose this to solicitors for Mr Slater? Does it comply with Order 38? Not yet?

The paragraphs need to be numbered, and the statement must be signed and witnessed.

Does the statement contain information that is either irrelevant or inadmissible? What about Daniel's views on Mr Slater's speed? What about Daniel having heard that Mr Slater has been convicted for drink driving?

These matters are legally irrelevant and inadmissible.

What about what the doctor told Daniel?

This is clearly hearsay.

Does B want to reveal whether Daniel has passed a cycling proficiency test or not?

If he has not, we think not.

Daniel's statement must therefore be amended and reformatted before it is disclosed.

Before we leave witness statements let us consider a further drafting exercise. We will say that B wishes to call Dr Healy, the hospital consultant, to give evidence of the extent of Daniel's injuries. Dr Healy treated Daniel on his initial admission to hospital after the accident. Dr Healy has since died. Can his evidence be admitted in the form of a statement given out of court?

Automatic directions will have already required B to disclose the report. If Dr Healy is not to testify his report is hearsay and in this case the Civil Evidence Act 1995 would apply. What is the drafting exercise involved here?

Look up the provisions of the Act. You will find that the 1995 Act can be used for any category of hearsay evidence. Hearsay notices must be served within 28 days of setting down in the High Court (RSC Order 38, rule 21(4)) or within 28 days of trial in the county court (CCR Order 20, rule 15(4)). For it to be effective the notice must state that it is a hearsay notice and must identify the hearsay evidence at issue. It must name the person making the statement and specify why he or she is not to be called. If the evidence in question is part of a witness statement the notice should specify the relevant part. Such a notice in this case might read:

> TAKE NOTICE that at the trial of this action the plaintiff desires to give in evidence the statement made in the following document, namely a report dated 1 March 1998 from Mr John Healy MD FRCS to the Plaintiff's solicitors.
>
> A copy of this document is annexed to this notice. And further take notice that Mr John Healey cannot be called as a witness at the trial because he died on 12th July 1998.

How do you like the language? 'Take notice that' goes against our general advice on drafting. Why not make it less pompous? It turns out that this form is one of the county court standard forms from the 'Green Book'. This is not a precedent, it is a requirement, so we backed down just for once.

It may well be that the evidence is not in dispute, in which case it can be admitted by consent.

Affidavits

An affidavit is a statement which is either made under oath or affirmed. Unlike pleadings (see below), the affidavit is intended to provide evidence of the matter contained in it. The person giving this type of statement is known as the deponent. This person may be the client, a witness in the case or his or her legal representative. The affidavit is either sworn under oath or affirmed to be true. Either way, to give a false statement in such a form is perjury.

It is rare for affidavit evidence to be given in court during a trial (leave is required) but such evidence is used in interlocutory applications.

From a drafting perspective, the composition of an affidavit must take into account the following:

- formal requirements are dictated by the court rules. These are set down by RSC Order 41 and CCR Order 20, rule 10. The affidavit must: state the title of the action; the name, address and occupation of the deponent; be expressed in the first person (that is 'I'); be divided into numbered paragraphs; be paginated and bound; give dates and numbers in figures and not words; and be endorsed to show on whose behalf it is filed.

- the affidavit must be sworn or affirmed by the deponent before a solicitor (other than the one who drafted it or the firm which is acting), a commissioner for oaths, or a duly authorised court clerk. The Oaths Act 1978 governs the execution of oaths and affirmations and the jurat (the wording indicating how the affidavit has been executed) must be worded appropriately. Any alterations to the affidavit must be initialled by the person administering the oath or affirmation. You should learn the form of words by heart because you will often use affidavits (and statutory declarations, of which more later) in practice.

The affidavit should begin by indicating whether the deponent is swearing or affirming and the jurat should read either:

Sworn before me at

this   day of   199

or

Affirmed before me at

this   day of   199

■ The requirements of the action. The affidavit must contain the details required for the particular task for which the affidavit has been drafted. For example, RSC Order 13, rule 9 states that if an application is made to set judgment aside an affidavit must be filed by the solicitor acting for the defendant which shows some defence on the merits, that is an arguable defence or triable issue. Clearly research will be necessary here. The rule does not tell what, other than that, the affidavit should contain. Similarly, if you were applying for an interim payment, you would look up RSC Order 29 to find the grounds you need to prove through your affidavit. However good you are at drafting affidavits, they will be of little or no use if they do not comply with the procedural requirements.

Let us take an example from the case studies to illustrate the point. What if judgment has been entered by B in the absence of any defence having been filed by Mr Slater's solicitors? They may wish to apply for judgment to be set aside on the ground that service of the summons was defective in that it was delivered to the wrong address and that it was only when the order giving judgment was received that Mr Slater knew of the existence of proceedings. What should the affidavit do and what should it say? Mr Slater's solicitors would have to give reasons by way of affidavit to support the application.

Some research is again needed. What do the rules of the court dictate? CCR Order 13, rule 7 deals with what the affidavit must contain and includes the possible ground of non-service.

The affidavit could therefore state that the summons was never received, or if it was, having been sent to the wrong address, the time limit for filing a defence had passed. It must go on to outline the nature of the defence that would have been filed (and indeed will be if the application succeeds).

The affidavit must consist of information that the deponent knows or believes to be true. We have already seen that to give false information amounts to perjury. You must give careful thought as to who is best placed to provide affidavit evidence given this constraint. Although hearsay evidence is permitted the deponent must reveal the source of the information. Any documents referred to in the affidavit should be exhibited, that is mentioned in the affidavit with the copy document endorsed accordingly. Let us say that in Daniel's case Mr Slater's solicitors file an affidavit to support the application to set aside judgment. The affidavit refers to the police report. The content of the affidavit should include reference to the report saying that the report is 'now produced to me and marked HD1' (the exhibit usually carries the initials of the deponent and the number of the exhibit). The exhibit itself should be endorsed with the words 'This is the exhibit marked HD1 and referred to in the affidavit of (name of solicitor B or other deponent) sworn before me this   day of   199X'.

The affidavit should follow the guidelines set out above for witness statements. The information contained in it should be set out in chronological order, make sense in the reading and be in short numbered paragraphs. Once drafted it should be carefully scrutinised by the drafter and deponent.

Have a go yourself at drafting the affidavit for setting aside judgment for Mr Slater. If you want an example to follow see page 342 where we use a similar document – a statutory declaration. This should provide you with the layout and style used in such formal documents.

Pleadings

In criminal cases the pleadings are few and far between and will consist of a charge sheet or summons, and if the case proceeds to the crown court, the indictment.

Although simple in principle, the drafting of an indictment is often a highly technical matter. A defectively pleaded indictment may result in the acquittal of the defendant. The indictment must recite a statement of the offence, with the relevant statutory authority (unless the offence is a common law one). Examples of indictment drafting can be found in the ICSL manual *Opinion Writing*. As this book is about the principles of good and effective drafting and not the technicalities of specific tasks we suggest that if you are interested in drafting indictments your read carefully this BVC material.

In civil cases the formal documentation, in particular court pleadings, is of far greater prominance. The legal, and factual, elements of the case are made out in advance by documents submitted to the court and served on the various parties. Other than in exceptional circumstances the parties to proceedings will be bound by the content of their pleadings. No evidence on any other point is allowed. You must get it right at the moment of serving the pleading. Your case theory must be ready then. If amendments become necessary, do them straight away. (Look up the rules, you may need leave although amendment is normally possible, without leave, if pleadings have not closed).

What are the pleadings in a civil case? The pleadings are a formalised record of the claims and denials of the parties and they consist of:

1   the particulars of claim or statement of claim;

2   the defence; and sometimes:

3   a counterclaim;

4   a defence to the counterclaim; and only rarely:

5   a reply to the defence/defence to counterclaim; and even less common:

6   a rejoinder and surejoinder.

In tribunal cases, for example, a claim for unfair dismissal before an employment (formerly industrial) tribunal, pleadings may be relevant but do not have the same technical requirements; nor do they appear as formal. Nonetheless what is said in them is highly relevant and care must be taken in their preparation. They set out the key facts of your claim/ defence.

The purpose of pleadings is to ensure that each side and the court is as fully aware of the other's assertions as is possible. What drafting skills are relevant to pleadings? *O'Hare and Hill* (p 163) state that:

> 'The art of pleading lies in deciding which facts are material and in deciding which details are necessary.'

Be aware of two considerations when drafting pleadings. First, the pleading must comply with the detailed procedural rules laid down in RSC Order 18 and the CCR where expressly provided (the CCR are less comprehensive and the RSC are otherwise normally followed). These requirements cover both form and content. Secondly, pleadings must support your theory of the case, for you will be bound by their content.

Let us look at our civil litigation case to see how these considerations apply and how pleadings should be drafted. We will presume that a letter before action has been sent and there has been no response to it, or if there has been a response it has not resolved the case. B discusses the case with the client and it is decided that proceedings should be issued. B must now draft the necessary documentation to initiate the claim. B must initiate the process by issuing a writ (High Court) or summons (county court) or by asking the court to issue a summons. The choice between High Court and county court will be determined normally by the amount of the claim. Let us say that the action is brought in the local county court. B must draft the particulars of claim. He or she could of course instruct counsel to do this but B is keen to tackle this drafting task alone, confident in the light of having read this book and having fully researched the case.

As a research exercise, B might look up the County Court Rules to check on the requirements for such documentation. Alternatively, B may consult one of the practitioners' loose-leaf reference works, such as *Longmans Litigation Practice*. B would discover that not only do the particulars of claim have to conform to certain standards but that a medical report and schedule of special damages must be filed (CCR Order 3, rule 1 and Order 6, rule 1).

In his somewhat lighthearted but readable account of legal drafting (*Pleadings Without Tears*), William Rose refers to the four Cs as a philosophy for drafting pleadings. Pleadings must be:

1   Concise.

2   Comprehensive.

3   Comprehensible.

4   Accurate (his joke not ours!).

It is beyond the scope of this book to look at all of the rules affecting the form and content of pleadings but it is necessary to consider, for drafting purposes, the basic principles. These can be found in RSC Order 18. We illustrate the application of these principles in drafting the particulars of claim in Daniel's case but the principles are equally applicable to all pleadings in any civil action.

Order 18 specifies that three general rules apply to drafting pleadings. First, the pleadings must state facts and not law. The pleadings must not go into the evidence that will be adduced to prove the facts. Secondly, the facts that are pleaded must be material to the case. Facts are material if they are necessary to substantiate the claim or defence. They must establish the cause of action and support the remedies sought. Thirdly, the facts pleaded must contain sufficient but not excessive detail. 'Concise' and 'precise' is one judicial description of a good pleading (*Re Parton* (1882) 45 LT 756).

In a negligence action such as Daniel's, the particulars of claim should contain sufficient detail to show the cause of action. Mr Slater owed a duty of care to other road users, including Daniel; this duty was breached by the standard of his driving and damage resulted. Basic principles of tortious liability are applicable here.

The particulars of negligence need to be pleaded to support the general allegation. When, where and how was Mr Slater negligent? Specific issues also need to be pleaded, for example that Daniel intends to rely on Mr Slater's conviction for drink-driving in support of the allegation of negligence (Civil Evidence Act 1968, section 11 and Order 18, rule 7A). The extent of the loss and damage Daniel has suffered must also be included.

The particulars of claim will include the remedies sought, in this case, damages for personal injury and other losses, for example the damage to the bike and clothing and medical expenses. In our case, the claim is for an unliquidated sum for general damages (for Daniel's pain and suffering) and a liquidated sum for special damages (for the value of the bike, clothing and medical expenses). Interest must also be specifically pleaded. In this case section 69 of the County Courts Act 1984 would apply (the court has a discretion to allow interest on a claim for such period and at such a rate as it shall think fit). It is usual to ask for an order for costs although strictly speaking this need not be included in the pleading (see the 'White Book' 18/15/1). The part of the pleading that deals with the orders or remedies sought is known as the prayer for relief.

B must therefore plan the drafting task by clearly identifying the material facts, by detailing the remedies claimed and by observing the procedural requirements of the RSC and CCR. In doing so B might follow a schedule such as this:

1   specify the court;

2   identify the parties;

3   describe the title of the pleading;

4   set out the cause of action (negligence);

5   outline details of the negligence;

6   describe the nature and extent of the injuries;

7   list the other losses;

8   claim all orders and remedies;

9   comply with any particular rules relating to the case, for example, if wishing to rely at trial on a relevant conviction of the defendant.

B is now in a position to draft the pleading. The particulars of claim might be drafted to read as follows:

IN THE NEWCASTLE COUNTY COURT   CASE NO. 98 ....

BETWEEN

DANIEL McAULEY (A MINOR)   PLAINTIFF

by NORMAN McAULEY (HIS FATHER AND NEXT FRIEND)

and

ROY SLATER   DEFENDANT

PARTICULARS OF CLAIM

1   The Plaintiff was born on 16th October 1984 and is a minor appearing through his father and next friend, Norman McAuley.

2   At approximately 3pm on 1 December 1997, the Plaintiff was cycling along High Street, Jesmond, Newcastle upon Tyne, on his Marin bicycle, when a collision occurred between his bicycle and a Vauxhall Astra motor car, registration no. ABC 123, driven by the Defendant. The Defendant was travelling in a westerly direction from Newcastle towards Jesmond at the time of the collision. The Plaintiff who was also travelling in the same direction was positioned to turn north from High Street into Hanley Street at the time of the collision.

3   The collision was caused by the negligence of the Defendant.

PARTICULARS OF NEGLIGENCE

The Defendant was negligent in that he drove his vehicle along High Street:

a)   at an excessive speed;
b)   whilst under the influence of alcohol and/or whilst his blood/alcohol level exceeded the permitted legal limit;
c)   failing to brake, steer or otherwise manoeuvre his vehicle so as to avoid the collision, and without reasonable care for the safety of other road users, including the Plaintiff.

4   The Plaintiff will seek to rely on the fact that on 8 January 1998, at Newcastle Magistrates' Court the Defendant was convicted of the offence of driving a motor vehicle with a blood/alcohol level in excess of the permitted legal limit. This conviction is relevant to the alleged negligence.

5   By reason of the Defendant's negligence the Plaintiff suffered personal injury, loss and damage.

PARTICULARS OF INJURY

The Defendant was 14 years old at the date of the collision. He was taken by ambulance to the Accident and Emergency Department of Newcastle General Hospital, where it was diagnosed that he had incurred a compound fracture of the tibia of his left leg, which was set under general anaesthetic. He also suffered abrasions to his arms, face and torso, and concussion as a result of the collision. He was detained in hospital for 7 days for observation and treatment. His leg remained in a plaster cast for 8 weeks. During this period he was unable to attend school. The Plaintiff underwent physiotherapy for a period of 12 weeks following his discharge from hospital. Full details of his injuries and the prognosis are disclosed in the medical report of Mr Healy FRCS, dated 1 March 1998 and served with these particulars.

PARTICULARS OF SPECIAL DAMAGE

These are disclosed in a schedule served with these particulars.

6   The Plaintiff claims interest at such a rate and for such a period on both general and special damages as the court may consider just pursuant to Section 69 County Courts Act 1984.

The Plaintiff claims:

    1   Damages

    2   Interest

Served this   day of   1998

B & Co Solicitors
1 River View
Newcastle upon Tyne
NE1 3RT

To: The Court
       The Defendant.

B would need to compile a schedule of special damages to include all of the losses over and above Daniel's personal injuries. The list should include the cost of the bicycle, clothing, shoes, medical expenses and travel costs. Mr Healy's medical report would also be filed. The request for the default summons or the summons itself needs to be completed (form N201 or N1) and a cheque made payable to Her Majesty's Paymaster General for the correct amount to cover the plaint fee.

The request for the summons or the summons itself, the particulars of claim, the fee, the medical report and the schedule of special damages are then sent to the court for service on the defendant.

So how do you, as an inexperienced drafter, begin to compose these complex and highly significant documents? Three principles can assist:

1   Plan what it is you wish to achieve. List all of the factual matters that you must include in the pleading to make out your case. This may be the detail of the plaintiff's claim or the content of a defence to such a claim.

2   Discover what formalities you need to comply with. Look up the RSC and, if relevant, the CCR. See what is required. By now you are aware of the principles applicable to drafting pleadings. Check that there are no additional requirements in your case. For example, if you are drafting a defence the pleading must give a comprehensive account of the defendant's position. If the defence fails to deny any allegation, the defendant will be taken to have admitted that fact (RSC Order 18, rule 8).

3   Consult precedents to check your plan and compliance with it.

Some would argue (but not us) that you could go straight to 3. Why not just find a similar precedent to your case and copy it? We believe that there are several dangers in this approach. First, you may use a precedent that is not in whole or part appropriate. If you rely on one set format, you may be persuaded that this, and only this, is the correct form and you may lose track of your own requirements. Secondly, if you do not plan your requirements and check the formalities you will not begin to appreciate or learn the art of drafting. It is the same principle that we have seen before. Do not simply imitate. At best, you will not learn the process and at worst you might imitate bad habits and poor practice.

Having said that, precedents are extremely useful. They fulfil a very important role in drafting. We will encounter them in the following section on non-contentious document drafting. One further point can be made. There is a halfway house that falls somewhere between using model precedents and creating your own. If you have successfully drafted, say, pleadings on a previous occasion, there is nothing wrong, and indeed much to gain, by referring to those pleadings in future cases. You (or perhaps someone in your office) will have drafted the original having conducted the necessary research and investigation. If this document satisfies all the needs of the case (you will only know this if you have fully researched the law and facts), why not follow this in the drafting exercise? Of course, it must be modified and adapted to suit, but you should do this in any event, as part of the drafting process. The key difference between other people's precedents and your own is that *you* know why you did things in a particular way last time. Your use of precedents is based on research. Adaptation is likely to be informed and intelligent.

In the context of pleadings, the use of precedents is therefore a yardstick to drafting the correct document in any particular case. We have only looked at a relatively simple example of pleadings for an action in negligence in the county court. The drafting of pleadings in other proceedings, for example a breach of statutory duty, may be more complex. The general guidelines, however, we would argue, are equally applicable.

Drafting in non-contentious cases

Let us return to our non-contentious cases.

What general principles apply? Some of these have been seen before but are worth repeating for their importance and significance:

1   The document(s) must satisfy any relevant legal requirement.

2   The words used should be simple, clear and relevant. Tautology makes lawyers appear ridiculous. As seen in Chapter 2 (Communication for lawyers) the use of anything other than plain English is normally unnecessary and does nothing to serve either the client or the lawyer.

3   The structure of the document should be logical and comprehensive. Use a system of consistent and obvious numbering and paragraphs. Ensure that the same term is used in the same context throughout, for example, call one party in the conveyance 'the buyer', and the other 'the seller'.

4   If using legal terminology (sometimes this is both necessary and unavoidable) ensure that it is used accurately, for example 'covenants', 'real property' or 'the Articles of Association'.

5   When looking through a draft document (your's or someone else's) be able and willing to make amendments and be able to justify why such amendments are made.

6   Plan your document with your goal (that is your client's needs), the relevant information (for example the details of the parties) and the legal requirements in mind.

7   Produce a plan and then make a first draft of the document.

8   If relevant (and it usually will be, especially in the early stages of your career), check the initial draft against a suitable precedent.

9   Be critical as to the form and content of your draft. Test it against your case objectives and only be satisfied with it when it meets all the relevant standards.

Statutory declarations

Our first formal drafting in the non-contentious cases involves statutory declarations. These are the equivalent in non-contentious cases to affidavits in litigation. A statutory declaration is a written statement of fact which is declared before a solicitor or court officer. The maker, or declarant, commits perjury if false information is given. The same rules applying to affidavits in terms of form and content are applicable here. Statutory declarations must contain facts that are within the maker's own knowledge or belief. A slightly different form of words from those appearing in affidavits is used. The declarant must 'solemnly, sincerely and truly declare and affirm that the contents of this declaration are true'.

Exhibits are dealt with in the same way as for affidavits.

When are these statements used? They are relevant in cases where a person wishes to make a statement that is intended to be used as a formal record, or where legal rules require it. Some examples may make this clear.

Mr Bennett has recently changed his name. He used to be known as St. John-Bennett. This was the name that he was given at birth. He produces his birth certificate during the mortgage application procedure. The Hallam Building Society – who used to know him under his old name – request evidence of the change of name. Mr Bennett asks C for advice on the point. Having researched the relevant law C tells Mr Bennett that legally he does not need to follow any formal process to change his name, but that it might be useful to be able to produce a document that evidences the change of name (to avoid delay and questioning in the future). This can be done by statutory declaration. The declaration simply records the fact that Mr Bennett has since a specified date been known as Bennett and not St. John-Bennett. Mr Bennett thinks that a declaration might be useful to him in other situations so he instructs C to prepare one. C prepares a statutory declaration setting out the history of events and concluding with the statement that the client now intends to be known as Bennett. The document must be set out to comply with the terms of the Statutory Declarations Act 1835 and be declared before a solicitor or other authorised person. As a matter of good drafting practice it should bet set out in a logical order and in numbered paragraphs, as in the case of witness statements and affidavits.

How would C go about the drafting tasks here? As seen many times throughout this book, the starting-point is the formulation of a plan. What is the purpose or object of the exercise? C knows that there is no legal requirement for a change of name but that evidence of change can be useful. A declaration would be good evidence. Research shows that the Stautory Declarations Act 1835 has certain formal requirements. But what should the detail of the declaration be? In order to show what Mr Bennet was originally called and what he is now known as C needs to specify what Mr Bennett's full name was and what he now says it is. It would be useful to know the date when this change occurred. Having worked out what is likely to be needed C could look up a precedent and compare what he is planning with what is recommended.

C may have a precedent he has used before (based on research done then). It is a good idea to build a stock of your own precedents that have worked for you in the past. The firm may have a precedent on the word processor that it uses in such cases. Let us suppose that C has to start from scratch. He or she looks at the index to the Encyclopaedia of Forms and Precedents. 'Name, change of' is contained in Volume 29. The research that C conducted before advising Mr Bennett confirmed that a name could be changed by deed poll but that this was not a legal requirement. Knowing from this research that Mr Bennett does not need to undergo any formal legal process to effect his name change, C is drawn to the section entitled 'Informal change of name' at 112 where a form of statutory declaration is set out for the use of an assumed name where there is no intention to execute a deed poll.

Look up the precedent for yourself. Trying to keep things simple but effective, we find it rather over wordy and so what appears below is our amended version:

I, Simon Mark Bennett of 46 Weston Road, Sheffield, S5 6AL do solemnly and sincerely declare as follows:

1. I am the person named Simon Mark St. John-Bennett in the birth certificate now produced and shown to me and marked 'SMB1' (the Birth Certificate).

2. I have since 1st December 1997 used the name Simon Mark Bennett and I have been known by that name in all matters and on all occasions.

3. It is my intention to continue to use the name of Simon Mark Bennett and I renounce the name of Simon Mark St. John-Bennett appearing in the Birth Certificate.

4. I consequently request all persons to address me by my assumed name of Simon Mark Bennett for all future purposes.

And I make this declaration conscientiously believing the same to be true and by virtue of the Statutory Declarations Act 1835.

Declared at (place) this   day

of   199X   (signature of declarant)

before me

(signature of commissioner/solicitor)

A commissioner for oaths/solicitor empowered to administer oaths

Another example of the need for a statutory declaration can be taken from the conveyancing case. Let us suppose that when raising the pre-contract enquiries with the sellers' solicitors C is told that the sellers have used a piece of land at the rear of Paradise Road as part of their garden, without interruption or objection, throughout the time that they have lived in the property (six years). They have assumed rights over it. The ownership of the land is unknown. C may consider that it is prudent to ask the sellers, through their solicitors, to provide a statutory declaration confirming their use of the land. This can be used as evidence at some later stage of the assumption of possessory rights over the land. As you may recall from studying land law, this does not as such give title to the land but provides some reassurance for the buyers, who may also wish to use the land, and may eventually give rise to possessory title.

The drafting of all these sworn or declared statements is within the regular remit of solicitors. The drafting plan must be as described before: assess your purpose, set out the detail in chronological order and comply with any legal requirements. The draft should then be checked against the case objective to ensure that it fulfils this end.

Drafting formal documents in non-contentious cases can now be taken into the case studies. Let us look at each case study in turn and draft some of the relevant documents.

The conveyancing case

Solicitor C has the task of conducting Ms Kennedy's and Mr Bennett's conveyance. The principal task in conveyancing is either drafting the contract for sale, or drafting the deed that transfers ownership. We have already seen that convention dictates that the buyers' solicitors draft the purchase deed. In the case of freehold property, this would be a conveyance and in the case of leasehold property an assignment. If the property involves registered land this deed is known as a transfer. You will become familiar with these terms if you are on the LPC conveyancing course. If we concentrate on the drafting of the purchase deed in this case, what should C take into account; what are the objectives?

1   to transfer ownership of the exact property;

2   to ensure that the buyers are not liable for any acts or omissions of the previous owners;

3   to preserve for the buyers any benefits that go with the property;

4   to reflect in the purchase deed the extent of the buyers' co-ownership;

5   to comply with any legal requirements, for example the payment of stamp duty or land registration fees;

6   to produce a deed that will be accepted by another buyer's solicitors if C's clients decide to sell the property.

Solicitor C may well be an experienced conveyancer and the formulation of this plan would be less of a deliberate or articulated exercise. If, however, you are to acquire the relevant drafting skills, you must, in the absence of such experience, rehearse the process quite deliberately.

Although you have developed your drafting plan it is unlikely that you will yet be familiar enough with conveyancing to enable you to produce a draft without recourse to conveyancing precedents.

Be warned, yet again, of the shortcomings of such precedents and of their use. As a guideline, especially in conveyancing, they are invaluable. An inflexible adherence to them, however, will restrict your own skills development. You can become stale, and stagnant (accepting old and inappropriate expressions without question). You may be tempted to use a precedent that is less than perfect, rather than take on the drafting task afresh. Unless properly adapted, a precedent can be of little use and may indeed fail your client.

A starting-point is to work out what you need and then consult a precedent to see if that can help you. An example should make the point clear.

1, Paradise Road is a leasehold terraced house. Ms Kennedy and Mr Bennett wish to own the property jointly as tenants in common (remember this was researched in Chapter 4). They want to hold the property in equal shares. What precedent should you look for?

What is the task? – to transfer ownership of leasehold property to joint purchasers. Is there a precedent entitled something like this? *Kelly's Draftsman* contains a large number of conveyancing precedents. The contents page reveals: 'assignment of leasehold house to joint purchasers subject to covenants'.

In Part 2, pp 882–887, a precedent for the assignment of a terraced house can be found (precedent 3586). On looking up this precedent it cross refers you to other precedents. Footnotes raise issues such as the applicability of stamp duty.

Are these precedents suitable? The book does not give us the exact heading that we are looking for. The cross-references, however, reveal further details. The index points us to Part 6, pp 911–923 and in particular to precedent 3362. This refers to a conveyance of property to joint purchasers. The tenure of the property is in fact immaterial for C can adapt this by extracting the joint purchaser clause from the precedent and inserting the reference to leasehold property to suit his or her drafting purposes.

What about preserving rights of way that the property may have the benefit of? If the rights were created by the lease under which the property is held precedent 3583 paragraph 4 covers the matter. What if the land is registered? Precedent 3351 (p 845) gives the heading and explains that precedents on the sale of land can be utilised for both registered and unregistered titles. We could go on.

OK, stop for breath. The first point can now be made. Using precedents is complex. In some ways you need to know what it is you are looking for before you can possibly know when you have found it. *Kelly's Draftsman* has been used deliberately at this point. It is not that this publication is in any way deficient (although we all have our preferences in terms of content, style and layout); rather, it is a difficult book for the novice drafter to use with any confidence.

Let us compare other precedent books to see if they better suit your purposes. Another text well thumbed in practice is *Parker's Modern Conveyancing Precedents* (Taylor). This books warrants a mention for two particular reasons. First, it is a comprehensive but concise text that specialises in conveyancing. It is less bulky than many of its rivals and it is somewhat easier to use in consequence. Secondly, *Parker's* heralded the start of a campaign for the use of plain English in legal drafting. The precedents contained in it use simple but effective wording – an aim to be commended. The book sets out precedents, in full, for commonly occurring transactions (for example a conveyance by joint sellers to joint buyers) as well as including a range of clauses to deal with particular issues (for example a clause for the production and safe keeping of title deeds to be retained by the seller).

A look at the table of contents will reveal:

'Part 2

Precedent 67   Assignment of the whole of the property comprised in a lease: p 164

Precedent 68   Assignment of part of leasehold property by reference to an attached plan, the rent being apportioned: p 166.'

The section goes on to cover other possibilities. Section B sets out a list of precedents that deal with joint ownership, including (precedent 18) a conveyance to two persons as beneficial tenants in common. The book also contains a number of precedents termed 'Standard Clauses', which can be incorporated as required in the particular deed.

What does C need to include in the draft deed in order for it to achieve its purpose? If the content of this can be planned, C can then check with some of the precedents referred to above, to ensure that the deed achieves its objectives.

The draft deed should address the following:

1   identify the parties, that is the sellers and buyers;

2   identify the property and the price;

3   identify the tenure of the property, that is whether it is leasehold or freehold;

4   transfer the legal title;

5   include in the transfer the conditions to which the property is subject and the benefits it enjoys;

6   give protection to the sellers against breaches in the lease (this would be required by the sellers' solicitors);

7   comply with legal requirements, for example the rules relating to land registration or stamp duty.

Try to draft a deed that appears to meet these objectives. Let us take two clauses of the draft deed to illustrate this process. These clauses deal with the identity and tenure of the property. We have already seen that 1, Paradise Road is leasehold and dates from, say, 1890. A first draft at this point may read:

> The property to be transferred is known as 1 Paradise Road, Sheffield, and is a leasehold terraced house which was created by a lease made in 1890.

Now compare this with precedent 67 (*Parker's*):

> 1   The vendor acknowledges the receipt from the purchaser of £   the purchase price of the land and house known as   ('The Property'), which is fully described in a lease dated   ('The Lease').
>
> 2   The property is leasehold for a term of   years from   created by The Lease.

What is the difference between the two? The first draft covers the required issues but uses imprecise language and omits certain important details, for example the date of the lease. The precedent contains additional information, for example the price.

Importantly, it also uses qualified expressions ('The Lease'and 'The Property') that can be used to save lengthy repetition in the deed. Each separate item is numbered and this adds to clarity.

A further example may be useful. It was an objective of C's to include the conditions to which the property is subject, and from which the property benefits. A first draft in respect of this could read:

> 1 Paradise Road is transferred subject to the obligation on the part of the buyers to maintain the right of way shown on the plan in the lease dated 1 March 1890, but the buyers also get the benefit of that right of way.

By comparison, the precedent uses an all encompassing clause:

> The Property is subject ... to such covenants and restrictions contained in The Lease as are still effective.

Shorthand ('The Property' and 'The Lease') is again used and the contents of the lease are expressed as being transferred, so far as they are relevant.

After checking the drafting objectives, and after consulting a suitable set of precedents, C may finally settle on the following:

> This assignment dated   is made between Paul Ian Rigsby and Katherine Rigsby of 1 Paradise Road Sheffield (The Sellers) (1) and Victoria Kennedy and Simon Mark Bennett of 46 Weston Road Sheffield (The Buyers) (2).
>
> 1   The Sellers acknowledge receipt from the Buyers of £50,000, the purchase price of the land and house known as 1 Paradise Road, Sheffield (The Property), which is contained in a lease dated 1 March 1890, and made between John Smith (1) and Albert Jones (2) (The Lease).
>
> 2   The Property is leasehold for a term of 800 years from 1 March 1890 created by The Lease.
>
> 3   The Sellers, as beneficial owners, assign to the Buyers their leasehold estate in The Property.
>
> 4   The Property is subject to a yearly ground rent of £5.00, made payable by the Lease and is assigned subject to, but with the benefit of, the covenants and conditions contained or referred to in The Lease as are still effective.
>
> 5   The Buyers declare that they hold The Property as tenants in common in equal shares.
>
> 6   The Buyers covenant with The Sellers, by way of indemnity only, to perform and observe the covenants and conditions contained or referred to in The Lease, and to indemnify The Sellers against liability arising from any future breach or non observance.
>
> 7   It is certified that this transaction does not form part of a larger transaction or series of transactions, in respect of which the amount or value or the aggregate amount or value exceeds £60,000.
>
> Signed as a deed by the sellers
> in the presence of:
>
> Signed as a deed by the buyers
> in the presence of:

This draft is an amalgam of C's own words and precedents 18, 67 and the standard clauses contained in *Parker's*. How would C have known to include clauses 6 and 7? The title deeds may have contained previous assignments in which such clauses appear. Blind repetition, however, is dangerous. You must satisfy yourself why such clauses are used and if they achieve the objectives sought.

Parker's refers to the need for them. If you are studying on a conveyancing course this may guide you. The sellers' solicitors would also no doubt make comments on any omissions, especially where these would affect their client. Again, do not rely on these comments without having first checked the validity and relevance of them. The answer is, of course, to do your own research. Other solicitors' comments may reactivate this research requirement.

So what is the answer? We have done most of the hard work so far. Why don't you find out why an indemnity clause and a certificate of value are needed?

The drafting has been completed by the use of a plan of action, by C carefully considering each stage of the process and, where necessary, by reference to suitable precedents.

Wait a minute, we hear you say, isn't this drafting exercise wrong? Surely the land was registered? Well spotted! The description above has been included to show how a deed, transferring interests in land, can be drafted from scratch. In the case of registered land, the process, although the same in principle, is normally more straightforward. This is for two reasons.

First, once registered, property is referred to by title number and is transferred subject to current entries on the Register (so far as they are not removed, or a solicitor's undertaking given to remove them on completion, for example a mortgage). The drafting exercise is therefore simplified by reference to the title number and registered matters.

Secondly, pro-formas are now in common use that not only set out the form of the transfer, but also deal with joint purchasers. For example, Land Registry approved form 19 (JP) covers the transfer of the whole of a registered title to joint purchasers, sets out the content of the deed and requires the completion of the detail of that particular transaction. Such a form is commercially produced (Fourmat Publishing, 1988).

Many firms produce their own in-house models. Not only may these set out the form as required under the Land Registration Acts, but they may also contain standard clauses which can be deleted and amended accordingly.

The conveyancing case study is almost complete, save for the financial arrangements on the day of completion itself and the post-completion formalities including the stamping of the purchase deed and the registering of the transfer. The draft deed is, by convention, sent to the sellers' solicitors for approval. Once approved (amended or not) the engrossment (the final version, for the signature of the sellers and buyers) is prepared. C must ensure that he or she is happy with the draft and that the engrossment (the final document) accurately repeats the content of the draft and contains no typographical or other errors. The deed must then be executed and completion can take place. As for all records, copies of the draft and any amendments should remain on C's file.

Can the same principles be applied to the other non-contentious case study and do other issues arise in this cases?

Mr Kader and the expansion of his business

Here we look at two drafting tasks:

■ the company formation documentation; and

■ the lease.

Forming the company

From the research chapter you may remember that the task here is for solicitor D to draw up the Memorandum and Articles of Association of a company, or perhaps draft a partnership deed.

Again the general principles of drafting apply. Work out a plan, and keep the draft simple and concise.

Both sides here are legally represented. D has been given the job of producing a first draft for the restructuring of Mr Kader's business. D should draft this with the client's interests uppermost in his or her mind whilst being aware that Mr Khan's solicitors will read it.

Mr Kader has strong views on his own proprietorial position and may want these reflected in the drafts. Mr Khan's solicitor will no doubt be endeavouring to protect his or her client and ensure that the documents serve Mr Khan's needs. Whilst the formation of a company or partnership deed can be planned and checked against a variety of precedents (or even be purchased 'off-the-shelf' in the case of a limited company), D must bear in mind the fact that the content of any draft document is likely to be scrutinised and that amendments, alterations, and negotiation are likely. D's drafting therefore must be pitched to achieve the desired ends, but also must be targeted, to persuade the other side of its value. It is almost as if it is a contentious drafting exercise.

What plan will D follow?

In the research chapter, Mr Kader and Mr Khan decided to form a limited company. The plan might now include the following:

1   the need to comply with the requirements of formation as dictated by the Companies Act 1985 and related legislation, including European law;

2   the allocation of shares;

3   the allocation of responsibilities within the company (secretary and directors);

4   the drafting of the Memorandum of Association to reflect the trading interests of the parties and the objectives and structure of the company;

5   the drafting of the Articles of Association to dictate the day-to-day running of the company;

6   the drafting of any contract of employment under which the directors are to be employed.

Where should D start in drafting the appropriate paperwork? Two options are available. D could start from scratch and draw up the Memorandum and Articles of Association using precedents and taking advantage of the Tables contained in the Companies Act.

In the alternative, D could arrange the purchase of a ready-made company which Mr Kader and Mr Khan could take over. Resolutions could be passed altering the content of the company documentation, to reflect fully the interests of the parties.

Regardless of which approach is taken similar considerations will apply. D must be aware of what it is he or she wishes to achieve and how that objective will be reached.

In particular the company must have sufficiently wide trading powers within the Memorandum of Association to enable it to operate effectively. The company must also have a structure, through its Articles, that suits its needs and complies with legal requirements.

The Memorandum is perhaps the simpler of the two documents from a drafting point of view. The drafting challenge lies more in the construction of the Articles of Association.

These regulate the internal operation of the company and hence the activities of both Mr Kader and Mr Khan. These rules must ensure that both parties have a clearly defined role in the company's affairs with proper accountability as between each other and the corporation. Who is to do what? What proportions of their time are to be given to the company's affairs? How are dividends to be divided? When are meetings to be held and how are they to be conducted?

Having worked out the objectives, D may consult a suitable precedent, for example, from *Butterworths Company Law Service.*

Model Memorandum and Articles of Association are set out at A211 and A213 respectively. We suggest that there would be little point in D drafting each and every clause of these documents from the beginning (as we would normally recommend), as the precedents lay down comprehensive rules governing the workings of the company. In this case D could locate the precedents and read through them, checking their suitability against the drafting objectives.

How would D know where to look? Research in any good academic text (such as *Pennington's Company Law*) or one of the practitioner's guides (for example *Butterworths Company Law Service*) will lead D to the possibility of using a model for the company documentation.

Let us look at how this might work. Clause 3 of the specimen Memorandum of Association in *Butterworths Company Law Service* deals with the object or purposes of the company. In the precedent, these are expressed as:

'(1)   to purchase as a going concern the business of a   now carried on by

at

(2)   (main objects)

(3)   to carry on business as a general commercial company.'

The clause goes on to detail specific trading powers.

Does this fit D's purposes? D needs to check the wording of the precedent and insert the main objects of the company in paragraph (2). The objects of the company are drafted widely in the precedent and D may consider that it is appropriate to retain these objects so as to give Mr Kader maximum flexibility. D may therefore draft as the main objects clause the following:

(2)   to trade as a manufacturer of clothing for wholesale or retail sale.

and retain clause (3).

The Memorandum would also contain the name of the company, its registered office, a statement as to the share capital of the company and the names of the subscribers together with their shareholding.

The Articles of Association give far more scope for the exercise of drafting skills. The precedent contained in *Butterworths Company Law Service* runs to some 30 clauses.

Bearing in mind the client's instructions, D needs to look closely at each of the clauses to see whether they are suitable for the client's purpose. In particular, D will need to ensure that the powers and obligations of the directors are clearly stated. These should be regulated by the Articles.

Clauses 8–15 of the specimen Articles set out various matters relating to directors. Clause 15 in particular deals with proceedings of directors. D can find no mention of appointing a chairperson of directors. D must ensure that the rules regulating the conduct of these meetings is in a form acceptable to the client. D may prefer to include in the Articles a provision dictating that the chair is to be elected by a general meeting of the shareholders, thus enabling Mr Kader to have a controlling interest in the appointment.

Ever vigilant, D of course checks when this loose-leaf reference service was last up-dated – 13th May 1998.

D will probably discover, having checked the precedents, that apart from the need to draft a clause governing the appointment of the chairperson of directors and subject to the filling in of the necessary detail, the specimen Articles do in fact provide adequately for the business and client's needs.

The process, however, is to plan and check. The extent to which the precedent consulted is relied upon will, of course, vary depending on the circumstances arising. In this case study Mr Kader is to have 75% of the shareholding. This, subject to any minority action by Mr Khan, would be sufficient to give him the control he seeks over company affairs both in terms of general policy and day-to-day management.

The point here is that so long as D is aware of the client's needs and the essential framework of company law, the source of the drafting materials used is of limited relevance. In practice much time may be saved by using a practitioner's text on company formation. Providing D knows what the client's specific needs are, the precedent can be followed and adapted accordingly. It is in this case a sensible and reliable course to take. In the alternative, D's firm may have its own in-house company precedents.

Once reduced into written form, convention and practice dictate that D should submit this documentation to Mr Khan's lawyers for their approval. D will retain a copy of the draft. No doubt Mr Khan's lawyers will return the draft either approved as drawn, rejected out of hand or, as is more likely, amended with various suggestions.

The process of drafting and redrafting may take some time especially if sustainable amendments are raised by either side.

Ultimately a version may be agreed and by convention D would be expected to arrange for the engrossment of that draft. This would be the final and formal record of the agreement.

The drafting skill does not end with the approved draft. Care must be taken to check the engrossment to be sure that it accurately reflects the agreement and that the parties' objectives have been met. Completion is reached by the signing of the documents and the submission to Companies House for registration along with the relevant supporting documentation.

The lease

By convention the lessor's solicitor submits a draft lease for the approval of the lessee. We will follow that here. We have already seen in Chapter 3 (Interviewing) and will see again in Chapter 6 (Reaching Agreements and Resolving Disputes) that Mrs Shearsby, for a variety of reasons, wants to maximise the income potential of letting the factory. When she explains this to her solicitor, E, he or she advises her that there are several ways of doing this. One way would be to grant a lease for a relatively short term. When it expires, a further lease could be agreed at a higher rent level. Without going into the detail here (particularly the possible implications for the tenant under the provisions of Landlord and Tenant Act 1954) this may be an unattractive option as Mr Kader and Mr Khan, or more accurately, the company they are set to create, may not take up the lease if it for too short a period. Perhaps a better way forward would be to consider a clause in the lease that allows for the rent payable to be varied.

We will presume that solicitors D and E have done their homework (yes, it is research again) and have advised their respective clients fully on the options open to them. The fundamental terms of the lease have been agreed in principle – they are based on the late Mr Shearsby's discusions with Mr Kader (a five-year lease at a rental of £25,000 per annum) but the detail has not yet been committed to paper. As we will see, in this brief scenario, both sides have something to say on the question of the inclusion of a rent review clause. For the purposes of this exercise you could use any one of a number of potential terms in the lease – the right to sub-let or the parties' repairing obligations for example.

With the client's instructions clear (rent to be increased at the end of the third year of a five-year term) E sits down to draft the lease and in particular the clause dealing with the rent.

Suppose E's firm has a model lease in the form of an in-house precedent. On checking it E discovers that the rent payable according to the precedent is fixed (that is there is a blank in the rent clause for a fixed rent to be inserted) for the duration of the lease. If the rest of the precedent suits E's purpose he or she will have to adapt it to include a variable rent clause.

Before hunting for further guidance (that word research crops up again) E pencils out a plan – what must the rent review do?

E writes:

'1. Rent to be varied after 3 years of 5 year term.

 2. Amount of future rent? Mrs S wants a minimum of 10% increase.

 3. Procedure eg notices.'

E, who has drafted one commercial lease before, with a fixed rental payment in it, has a go at a first draft in this case:

'5. *Rent*

The Lessee covenants with the Lessor to pay by equal quarterly payments in advance, on the usual quarter days, the rent of:

- £25,000 per annum for the first 3 years of the Lease; and,

- £30,000 per annum for the remaining 2 years of the Lease.'

The clause goes on to cover other issues such as what will happen if the rent is late being paid or remains unpaid.

E submits the draft lease with this clause in it.

Mr Kader's solicitor, D, takes instructions. Mr Khan's solicitor no doubt will do the same. We will limit our example to D's response. Mr Kader objects to any increase on the grounds that the rent agreed with Mr Shearsby was supposed to be for the whole period and in any event is a fair price. He is, however, keen not to lose the property and begrudgingly accepts that a fixed rent for 5 years is, in commercial terms, unusual. Mr Kader instructs D to write back initially resisting the rent increase. If Mrs Shearsby insists on a rent increase Mr Kader is prepared to consider a rent review which would be preferable to a 20% increase on the rent as envisaged by E's draft variation clause. Mr Kader thinks £30,000, even in 3 years' time, is too high and a review would be unlikely to fix future rent as such a level.

What does D do? Does he simply write back saying no increase or a rent review please? He might do the former but could seize the initiative by drafting a rent review clause him or herself – to move matters along and to present a concrete alternative to E.

If so, where does D start? Once you start to think about a review rather than set variation other issues crop up. D's plan has these headings:

■ timing of review – stick to end of third year

■ assessment of rent – ignore Lessee's improvements

■ use of arbitrator if agreement cannot be reached

Knowing what the client wants, D is able to look at the intelligent use of precedents. First, he or she goes to the, by now well thumbed, Encyclopaedia of Forms and Precedents, this time volume 22(3), Landlord and Tenant (Business Tenancies). Paragraphs 6711–7035 set out a variety of rent review clauses. Having taken on board the call for plain English made in this book, however, D is less than impressed with some of the seemingly complex wording in the precedents he or she finds so turns instead to another drafting tool in the library – Drafting and Negotiating Commercial Leases, Murray Ross. Here D finds extensive narrative on rent review clauses (Chapter 6). Things look more complicated than D initially thought. The book highlights a number of considerations (for example, factors such as the effect of goodwill or subletting on rent reviews) that need to be taken into account in drafting the right clause. The book contains a seemingly useful precedent at pages 330–333. Helpfully the review clause follows on from the clause containing the covenant to pay rent. The clauses are contained in a model lease.

The rent review clause includes:

■ a definitions section – with review dates, review periods, assumptions and disregards all specified;

■   a review section – setting out how the review will be carried out and by who; and

■   arrangements pending the rent review.

Although the clause runs to 38 sections and sub-sections, it is comprehensive, clear and appears to meet D's client's needs and concerns. A sample from the precedent reads as follows (we have inserted in square brackets the words that put the clause in context. They do not appear in the original but are needed here to make the extract make sense):

'4.1.4   "Disregards" are the following matters at the relevant Review Date [defined earlier in the section] that must be disregarded [in the review of the rent]:

4.1.4.1   any effect on rent of the fact that the Tenant or anyone deriving title under the Tenant or their predecessors in title have been in occupation of the Property

4.1.4.2   any goodwill attached to the Property by the carrying on at the Property of the business of the Tenant....

4.1.4.3   any increase in rental value of the Property attributable ... any improvement to the Property carried out:

•   during the term ...

•   by the Tenant ... with the consent of the Landlord ... or at the expense of the Tenant

•   not in pursuance of an obligation to the Landlord.'

D is rightly impressed with the simple but effective form of this precedent and adapts only by altering the terminology to match that used in the draft lease (for example calling 'the Tenant' 'the Lessee' and 'the Landlord' 'the Lessor'.

Having checked the rest of the draft lease D makes other minor amendments (perhaps Mr Kader's, or the company's name is incorrectly spelt) and additions (the first quarter's rent is to be waived by the Lessor (as agreed with Mr Shearsby) in return for Mr Kader and Mr Khan carying out some structural repairs). The draft is then returned to E.

There is no need to follow this process through any further. There may be several letters or phone calls between the solicitors for Mrs Shearsby, Mr Kader and Mr Khan. Eventually a form of lease may be agreed. If it is, the drafting process will have borne fruit, in this case, as a joint enterprise between the respective lawyers.

Conclusion

Parker's Modern Conveyancing Precedents contains a fitting postscript to this chapter. (It talks of the objectives of that book but it could read as the objectives of good drafting.)

We can do no better than to set out the following (p xiv):

'1.   To produce the legal effect intended.

2.   To make the document more comprehensible to the client and thus to assist in relations between solicitors and the public.

3.   To avoid the abuse of the English language found in the traditional precedents.

4.   To avoid the confusion of thought and expression found in some of the traditional precedents.

5.   To make documents shorter and so save time and money.'

---- Chapter 6 ----

REACHING AGREEMENTS AND RESOLVING DISPUTES

1   An introduction to dispute resolution

There is no definitive stage when the means by which disputes are resolved appear on the agenda. Negotiation, arbitration and mediation may arise at particular points of a case and, utilising alternative dispute resolution (ADR) methods, require specific lawyering skills. Importantly these skills may be relevant in both litigation and transaction contexts and we will shortly revisit our case studies to see how the techniques for reaching agreement and resolving disputes negotiation can assist our clients.

In this chapter we focus on negotiation as this is central to the work of solicitors (even if it is no longer included as a discrete skill on the LPC). It is also an assessed part of the BVC and it may well form an optional module on your degree programme. As a negotiator you are engaged, on behalf of the client, in a process that is aimed at achieving the maximum possible benefit, in the circumstances, for your side. There are other skills which a lawyer may develop and even earn a living from. You may become an arbitrator or a mediator. These are very important skills for lawyers to develop but are fundamentally different from those of a partisan negotiator. We will look, in this chapter, primarily at the skill of negotiation but, to place dispute resolution in a realistic context, we conclude with some brief thoughts on other means of reaching agreement. Dispute resolution is very much the business of lawyers.

Before looking at how agreements can be reached in practice let us examine the concept of agreement and the processes that enable agreement to be reached for they are both complex in their nature and application.

In his book *The Selfish Gene* Richard Dawkin discusses the issue of natural selection. He talks of organisms that gain evolutionary advantage from co-operation, even though 'selfishness' by one particular individual would appear to be more valuable in the short term. Lawyers receive a mention as a temporary group of parasites whose evolution may be thwarted by maladaptive behaviour! Two concepts are introduced. In a zero sum game, any advantage gained by one player is an equal loss to another. A non-zero sum game, however, is very different, for if played correctly, the game can allow all the 'players' to benefit. Dawkin notes in particular:

'In what are called civil "disputes" there is often great scope for cooperation. What looks like a zero sum confrontation can, with a little good will, be transformed into a mutually beneficial non-zero sum game.'

He then proceeds to look at a divorce case, identifying a good marriage as a non-zero sum game, and stating that even in breakdown the parties have much to gain by continuing the co-operation. He identifies the interests of the children, and the cost of going to law, as two compelling reasons for this. He continues:

'So obviously a sensible and civilised couple begin by going together to see one lawyer don't they? Well actually no, at least in England and, until recently, in all fifty states of the USA the law, or more strictly – and significantly – the lawyers' own professional code, doesn't allow them to.'

We see that:

'the hapless couple have been dragged into a zero sum game',

and ironically the lawyers are perhaps in:

'a nice fat non-zero sum game with the [parties] providing the payoffs and the two professionals milking their clients' joint account in elaborately coded cooperation'.

This view of the legal practitioners is vividly portrayed in an oil painting that hangs in the old magistrates' court in Beaumaris, North Wales (I was last there in the mid 1980s – the court house is well worth a visit). The picture depicts two people pulling at opposite ends of a cow. One is labeled 'plaintiff' and the other 'defendant'. A bewigged and robed character is busy at work on the cow's udders!

As cynical as some of this might sound, the adversarial nature of legal advice and consequential legal proceedings compounds the problem.

As will be seen later, this course of action – the zero sum game – is not inevitable. Steps have been taken in both Britain and America to encourage movement towards a non-zero sum game. Conciliation and mediation both attempt to move along these lines. ADR is a fast growing alternative to the traditional polarised forms of litigation.

In this chapter we look at the skills implicit in reaching agreements and resolving disputes and concentrate specifically on negotiation as this features regularly in the work of barristers and solicitors and underpins much of the ADR process. As a rapidly expanding facet of lawyers' work and involving somewhat different, if related, skills, work we also look at mediation.

Negotiation is a core skill for trainee barristers. It is an important skill too for would-be solicitors even if it is no longer assessed as part of the LPC. For undergarduate law students negotiation is also an important topic. It provides a vehicle through which law can be studied in its operational context – how real people are affected by legal 'solutions' to problems.

If the aim of the lawyer is to help solve problems to the client's satisfaction, it is as important to be able to negotiate skilfully as it is to perform well as an advocate or researcher. It will be seen that negotiation is often the key skill underpinning the means by which to achieve the client's objectives. It may range from all the parties having open and frank round the table discussions to simply making contact to discuss agendas. The skills integral in successful negotiation are therefore all pervasive.

Game theory is a useful tool for aiding understanding. On a similar tack to the zero sum game is something called the 'prisoner's dilemma' (Axelrod *The Evolution of Co-operation*). This can in fact be applied to many areas of law and practice as elsewhere, but the fate of people awaiting trial on a criminal case is as good as any to illustrate the point. This example is not designed to describe the actual legal system, but rather the potential for co-operation in certain cases. Suppose that two people are charged with the same offence and have similar histories. Each knows the rules of the game. He or she could co-operate with the other prisoner, or give evidence against the other. The outcome will depend on what the other prisoner does. There are four possibilities:

1 Both co-operate with each other. If convicted both would receive a similar and relatively lenient sentence. For example, both plead guilty and act remorsefully. Both may be sentenced to, say, two years' imprisonment.

2 Both could defect to the prosecution and give evidence against each other. Both will be convicted, and receive a harsher sentence, as they would not be in a position to mitigate meaningfully. Let us say both receive a five-year prison sentence.

3 Prisoner A could co-operate and prisoner B could defect. B receives a one-year sentence as a reward for going over to the prosecution, and A receives a seven-year sentence.

4 In the converse, prisoner B could co-operate and prisoner A could defect, A gets one year, B gets seven.

Each might think: 'If the other co-operates, I get one year by defecting, but two years by co-operating, but if the other defects I get seven years by co-operating and five years by defecting. Therefore, I do best every time by defecting.'

However, if both co-operated they would receive two years each, a total overall of four years. If only one defects, it goes up to eight, and if both defect it goes up to ten. Defection serves the individual, co-operation serves both. In a one-off situation, not knowing the sentencing outcomes and given the lack of opportunity for communication between the parties, coupled with a probable lack of trust, it is likely that the prisoners will choose to defect. However, what would be the position if the game were played numerous times? Computer programmes have simulated such a possibility, playing the games with a particular set of instructions on when to co-operate or defect. Results suggest that those strategies that do not defect every time, but co-operate with those who are co-operative, and defect only after the opponent defects, score highest against all other strategies. Co-operation is therefore the long-term name of the game – at least if you are a computer!

The co-operative strategy in the prisoner's dilemma is therefore a non-zero sum game. Both sides gain more on balance and on average from co-operating than from defecting, so long as they are willing to defect rather than being walked over by someone who takes advantage of co-operation. Retaliation, or a threat of it, is required to prevent the defector always coming out best. Detailed discussions of games theory in general and the prisoner's dilemma in particular can be found elsewhere (Axelrod).

Further compelling arguments against the confrontational model of problem-solving or the win/lose approach can be found in *Getting to Yes* (Fisher and Ury).

In this influential volume, the authors coin the term 'principled negotiation'. This may involve negotiating the price of goods or services, or the resolution of disputes. The book suggests a theoretical base from which negotiations take place, contrasting hard and soft negotiating strategies and highlighting the weaknesses in both. A negotiator taking a 'hard' stance may be inflexible, unresponsive and destructive, and runs the risk of being in an all or nothing situation. Solutions may be arrived at that are unworkable, in that they have been coerced, with attendant resentment. The end result may be an unsuitable solution for all. The 'soft' negotiator, by contrast, is driven by the need for agreement, frequently yielding to pressure and accepting one-sided loss. The consequences are frustration, regret and possibly unworkable or inappropriate 'agreements'.

The alternative is described as neither hard nor soft. Indeed it can, at different stages, be both, and is based on the twin concepts of mutual gain and merit. The negotiator aims to establish objective criteria for measuring the fairness of any proposed agreement. The objective is a wise, efficient and amicable settlement to a problem.

The book advises four principles for the negotiator, as follows.

Separation of people from problems

Concentrate on the subject of the negotiation and not the personalities involved. Of course the target or audience of the negotiation may affect your style and content. This is the same for drafting or advocacy, but the real point of negotiation is addressing the matter in hand and not the personalities of the people involved. The parties are clearly highly relevant, and the negotiator is aware of their personal attributes, but attention must be focused on what it is that you are discussing and why. Separating the two allows both to be taken into account. What you are trying to achieve in the negotiation is highlighted. Personalities are background.

A simple example should make this clear. Let us presume that the person you are negotiating with has strong or controversial views. He or she makes these known during the course of the negotiation. You must avoid being distracted by these views if they are not material to the substance of your negotiation. Similarly a person may have a jovial manner or offensive habits. Whatever these personal traits, they should not be allowed to dominate the negotiation. It is the problem that you are concerned with, and not the person articulating it.

If, in our case study, the insurance company's representative, Mr Jones, tries to patronise you – perhaps a young and relatively inexperienced, if qualified, lawyer. He tells you that it is not the case law that matters but the amount of the settlement normally offered by his company in such circumstances. He adds that once you have been around a bit longer you will learn this. Should you take exception to his attitude and ask him to leave your office? Should you get defensive? Should you get stuck into an argument? We think not, at least not unless things get much worse! Rather you should concentrate on what you know you can rely on by way of authority and ask him to explain why he thinks his company would not be bound by such principles were the case to reach court.

Focusing on interests and not positions

Centring attention on rigid and immovable positions creates obstacles. You cannot have negotiation if neither side expects to move or concede. The better approach is to target your interests whilst avoiding entrenched views of the only acceptable outcomes. A range of possibilities should result that give flexibility and a potential for responsiveness on both sides. Ask the question: 'What is it that I want to achieve?' Use this as your starting-point rather than 'What am I prepared to accept?' As we will see, bottom lines (that is, minimum acceptable negotiated outcomes) are an important part of the negotiation process. These are fall back positions and are not positions from which you commence the negotiation. Look at the possibilities in a case before defining a bottom line.

Again an example might be useful. Going back to the road traffic accident case study, if Daniel's lawyer maintains, based on his instructions or his advice to the client, that Daniel is not contributorily negligent and will not conceed this at any stage as a possibility, the lack of flexibility on his or her part may act as a hindrance in the negotiation process. It may exclude the possibility of a more substantial offer for general damages or make the other side more resistant to quantum in other aspects of the claim.

Generation of options for mutual gain, not just selfish advantage

What are the possibilities? What is it that both sides can achieve? If we agree this, what does it mean for both parties? This approach stresses the expectations of the parties. Be aware both of your own case and that of your opponents. In legal terms this is very important for it enables you to plan your negotiation properly. It requires an awareness of strengths and weaknesses and likely attitudes of both sides.

The head on push to establish full liability, whilst admirable in terms of trying to maximise any payment that Daniel may receive, might ignore the realistic possibility of the court upholding an element of contributory negligence. There is no point fighting battles and losing wars. A careful appraisal of the pros and cons of each side's case and the theories they underpin is necessary if an acceptable and realistic settlement is to be reached.

Use of objective criteria to measure fairness, not subjective whims

Whatever the response, do not be diverted from what can be independently sustained. If there is a case that supports your assertions, quote it. Avoid conflict by redirecting your attention to the authorities or to accepted or indisputable facts.

The civil litigation case study illustrates these points. Look in particular at the dialogue between B and the insurance company representative (pp 380–384).

As well as describing the theoretical base of principled negotiation, *Getting to Yes* also takes into account the practical realities that the negotiator may encounter. Strategies are examined where the other participant is reluctant ('negotiation jujitsu'), or where the other person plays dirty tricks ('taming the hard bargainer'). In addition, the problem of imbalances in bargaining position is examined. We recommend reading this book.

Most importantly, the concept of the 'best alternative to a negotiated agreement' (BATNA) is described. This will recur at several points in this chapter and it is worth describing the principle here. In the negotiation process you may well have a strong idea as to what would be an ideal outcome in terms of an agreement. By contrast you are likely to establish a bottom line below which you are not prepared to negotiate. In the course of the negotiation the best outcome and the bottom line may be modified, but they are yard sticks against which possible agreements can be measured. A BATNA is somewhat different in that it is a course of action that one side proposes to take in the event of no agreement being reached. It too should be flexible, in that you are prepared to modify it during negotiations, but it also should be realistic in the sense that it will be implemented in the absence of an agreement. It is essential to calculate your best outcome, your bottom line and your BATNA prior to the commencement of negotiations. We will use these concepts in the case studies below. It is valuable to impress upon your negotiating opponent that your BATNA is realistic and not just a bluff – that you will sell the house elsewhere, issue proceedings, or (not to be recommended) resort to the Queensbury Rules. Of course, if you can bluff your opponent into believing you have a better BATNA than you have, well done. But if you get a reputation for bluffing you will have little clout.

The flip side of this coin is the WATNA (worst alternative to a negotiated settlement). What is the real price of not agreeing?

Both the BATNAs and WATNAs are examined in more detail in the context of our case studies a little later.

When preparing to negotiate, principled negotiation is a good starting-point from which to explore the possibilities of a settlement. The long-term effects of principled negotiation may be those illustrated by the prisoner's dilemma, in that everyone begins to benefit when each co-operates. One point, however, must be stressed. Principled negotiation is one model of negotiation, albeit, we think, a very useful one. It is not the only approach to negotiation and it indeed may be an inappropriate tool in some instances. The use or avoidance of principled negotiation, or for that matter, any one negotiation model, may raise important ethical issues and some of these are explored later.

Whether you are by now convinced or not of the need for co-operation in negotiation or of the value of win/win negotiating, the cost of legal action, the uncertainty of litigation, the trauma of adversarial proceedings, the failure of your client's transaction and the requirements of the assessment criteria of your course, may all persuade you to at least take this dispute resolving stance seriously. The skilful lawyer will use principled negotiation as part of the resolution strategy. There may well be times when other approaches are called for. Victoria Kennedy and Simon Bennett may not decide to buy that house after all. Daniel may well end up in the witness box in a full-blown trial.

What are the expectations in relation to ADR so far as your course is concerned?

2 Learning outcomes and assessment on dispute resolution modules

As noted in the Advocacy chapter (Chapter 7) the aims, objectives and assessment criteria for a module on ADR, or one of the specialisms within this generic heading (negotiation, mediation etc), is likely to vary from course to course within undergraduate programmes. Recent research has shown that, of all the legal skills included at first degree level, negotiation is included the least. That is not to say that it is of no importance or relevance to a law student. To understand the hows and whys of dispute resolution tells us a great deal about the workings of law and the legal system. As a learning tool negotiation, for example, can be used to develop and demonstrate knowledge in a wide variety of subject areas. Basic principles of negligence could be studied in this way with a role-play based on similar facts to our road traffic case.

In this chapter we have not tabulated the LPC and BVC standards and set them side by side. This is because negotiation is no longer a discrete and assessed part of the LPC and there are therefore no standards for negotiation as such. Instead we have listed the LPC standards for the compulsory areas in so far as they relate to dispute resolution. We have followed this with the BVC standards for negotiation. Negotiation is a distinct and assessed part of the BVC.

Leaving the arguments on the merits or otherwise of the removal of negotiation from the LPC it would be wrong to think that the resolution of disputes through negotiated settlement is, however, irrelevant in the LPC context. ADR is mentioned specifically in the core and compulsory areas. Under 'Conveyancing' a specified learning outcome is to:

> '... xi) recognise the need to resolve problems through negotiation and be able to advise the client on disputes arising out of the transaction and possible remedies'

This, as will be seen, is given a practical setting in our conveyancing case study later in the Chapter.

In the unit concerning Litigation and Advocacy a stated objective is to:

> '... appreciate the range of methods available to resolve disputes, and in particular, [students] should appreciate that it may be in the client's interests to resolve a dispute by settlement'

The elective areas on the LPC could specifically include ADR.

The specified skills areas of the LPC include aspects of ADR largely by implication, for example, under Interviewing and Advising students should be able to:

> '... viii) identify possible courses of action and the legal and non-legal consequences of selecting that course of action:
>
> ix) assist the client to make a decision regarding the best course of action'

The inclusion of ADR in the written standards for the LPC clearly indicates the need to be aware of alternative methods of resolving difficulties and requires in our view preparation and practice if ADR is to have any meaning at all within the context of the LPC (and most importantly afterwards in the law office).

The Outcome Specifications for the BVC are more clear cut. Here negotiation is specifically included in the syllabus. The overall aims are stated as:

> 'The student should be able to:

Negotiation checklist

EVIDENCE OF PREPARATION

1   To what extent did you show understanding of the essential strengths and weaknesses of the case?

2   To what extent did you identify for your own client:

☐   the best possible negotiated outcome (target)?

☐   best alternative if negotiations fail (BATNA)?

☐   the worst acceptable outcome (bottom line)?

3   To what extent did you realistically identify the opponent's likely strengths, weaknesses and strategy?

4   Did you identify a strategy for dealing with the opponent's strategy?

DURING AND IMMEDIATELY FOLLOWING A COURSE OF NEGOTIATION

5   To what extent did you carry out your planned strategy?

6   How well did you deal with unexpected material?

7   How did you deal with ethical issues?

8   How well did you represent your client's instructions?

9   How well did you deal with legal and factual issues?

10   Where is the result in the range of possible results?

(a) demonstrate an understanding of the importance of negotiation as a means of settling a case;

(b) demonstrate an understanding of the importance of planning a negotiation;

(c) select strategies and methods for conducting a negotiation that further the client's best interests;

(d) demonstrate an understanding of the need to observe professional ethics when conducting and concluding a negotiation'

The Specifications go on to refer to the detailed expectations on planning and conducting negotiation.

To give these various standards some practical meaning, look at our self-assessment checklist (see p 363). Photocopy this list if you wish and try to make use of it when you practise.

After a practice dispute resolution session, get together with your negotiating partner to compare notes on what was achieved. Did you accurately predict their strengths, weaknesses and range of outcomes? Could you have got a better result now you see their bottom line? Did you accurately spot their BATNA? Did you fall for their bluffs?

What sort of assessment tasks are likely on your course? For the LPC student there is, for better or worse, no formal assessment of negotiation other than it forms a component part of one of the core or compulsory areas. The undergraduate student will have to refer to the specific assessment requirements for the module in question. On the BVC, negotiation is assessed. What follows here may be of assistance to anyone undergoing assessment on ADR but obviously the exact assessment criteria will be specified in relation to the individual programme and module.

Whereas in real life a negotiated outcome is often the result of a series of communications between the parties, you may, depending on the assessment regime, be given just 15 minutes to complete the whole process. You may be required to reach an agreement on the spot, and be penalised if you do not. We hope you do not have to perform in such unreal conditions, and will be rewarded for making progress towards a settlement (or not – you may be a good negotiator if you have to resort to your BATNA as long as you can justify doing so).

If you have to get a result, as part of the assessment rules, then make sure you do so. Be prepared to make concessions towards your bottom line earlier than you would choose. If your opponent is refusing to make concessions, remind them that an agreement has to be reached. Make plain to the examiner that if the process breaks down, you do not bear the responsibility.

3 Negotiating: a practical example

Before turning to the case studies let us look at negotiation in a non-legal setting to illustrate the dynamics. The facts of this example are both simple and, we hope, realistic (as anyone with parental responsibilities might agree). The principles enshrined within it, however, are applicable to more complex situations and certainly to negotiation in a legal context. Take this as a scenario:

It is bedtime in a family household. Child has had a wonderful afternoon playing with toys and entertaining him or herself and perhaps other children. Child's bedroom is awash with pens, paper, toys, books and bedclothes. The most liberal and tolerant of parents (like us) might want the bedroom cleared of at least enough of the debris to allow Child to get to bed. Others amongst us might prefer some semblance of order so that toys are not lost or damaged, so that Parent can eventually hoover the carpet, or so that Child learns of the value of looking after possessions. We do not necessarily advocate (or mutually agree upon) any or all of these objectives.

For the purposes of the example let us make some factual presumptions. The bedroom is by any standards disorganised. Child is happy to go on playing (although it is late and there is school tomorrow). Parent wants Child to tidy the room and then go to bed. Parent is an understanding and caring person who does not like confrontation, oppression or violence. Child is seemingly unconcerned by the state of the room, the lateness of the hour, or the fact that it is a school day tomorrow. A negotiation takes place.

Parent plans a negotiation strategy. The key points are:

1   Best possible outcome – Child tidies room immediately, well and without protest.

2   Bottom line – Child tidies room for a bribe by tomorrow.

3   BATNA – Parent tidies room but Child loses some privileges (for example, later bedtime, pocket money or going out).

4   WATNA – Parent and Child row, unhappy consequences (Child late for school, Parent late for work).

As part of the negotiation planning, Parent tries to assess the objectives and intentions of Child. The key points, for Child (according to Parent) are:

1   Best possible outcome – Child does not tidy room and carries on playing without losing privileges.

2   Bottom line – Child tidies room and gets something in return.

3   BATNA – Child screams and shouts.

4   WATNA – Child and Parent upset and others unhappy (for example at school).

This scene can be represented diagrammatically as follows:

	PARENT LOSES	WIN/WIN AREA	CHILD LOSES	LOSE/LOSE AREA
PARENT	BATNA Parent tidies room and withdraws privileges	BOTTOM LINE Child tidies room for bribe	BEST POSSIBLE OUTCOME Child tidies room immediately	WATNA Row makes both upset and late
CHILD	BEST POSSIBLE OUTCOME room not tidied – Child carries on playing	BOTTOM LINE Child tidies room but gets reward	BATNA Child screams and shouts	WATNA Child and parent upset and school teacher unhappy at child being late

This simple example ignores one factor (presuming Parent's assessment of Child's position is accurate). Parent has considerably more power than Child. Ultimately Parent can impose penalties, argue more coherently perhaps or simply shout louder. However, Parent no doubt likes Child and does not wish to push Child towards the perceived BATNA. Parent recognises that he or she may suffer in the long term as a consequence of any breakdown and resort to BATNA. The win/win area therefore offers a possible outcome which focuses on the overlap of interests and the acceptability of agreement. Aiming for win/win, Parent recognises that the area of negotiation is the shape or size of the bribe. Parent will no doubt realise that the WATNA will assist no-one and that the lose/lose possibility is to be avoided at all costs.

Let us say Child agrees to tidy the room in return for an extra half hour in front of the television. Parent ends up sitting with Child and both enjoy the television programme and each other's company. Child goes to bed a little later than usual, but with a tidy room and on good terms with Parent. The battle resumes tomorrow – but this never was a book on parenting!

Let us now look at the case studies.

4   Negotiation in the case studies

We said in Chapter 1 (Introduction) that not all of the case studies fit the same mould. In some you will be able to utilise negotiation more effectively than in others. All, however, are susceptible to dispute resolution to some degree. Look at the standards set for your course (pages 361–364 refer to the Law Society and Bar Council's expectations). How far do the case studies that follow demonstrate the principles of how to prepare for negotiation and reach agreements? Let us begin by looking at the civil litigation case.

Daniel McAuley and the road traffic accident

Some general issues

The client is claiming damages for personal injuries suffered as a result of a road traffic accident. B, the solicitor for Daniel McAuley, the plaintiff, will be mindful of several issues in shaping the claim. These were analysed in Chapter 4 and are summarised here:

■ As a base line, is there a cause of action? It is not enough that Daniel has been injured. We do not have 'no fault' compensation. Trespass or negligence would have to be proven in such a case. It is necessary to show that Mr Slater owed Daniel a duty of care, that the duty was broken by the standard of Mr Slater's driving and that damage resulted.

■ If a cause of action can be established B would have to ask whether Daniel contributed in any blameworthy sense to his own misfortune.

■ B must then go on to consider the amount, or quantum, of damage.

■ How is Daniel's case to be funded – is he legally aided, is there a conditional fee agreement, are his parents or an insurance company paying?

■ Does Mr Slater contest liability?

■ Presuming Mr Slater to be insured, are his insurers willing to accept that Mr Slater is liable and move to a discussion of the appropriate level of compensation?

Questions of legal liability are crucial, not only to the negotiation process, but also to any other consequential court proceedings. Other factors, for example whether or not Daniel is legally aided or on a no win/no fee agreement with B, are equally important and may considerably strengthen B's negotiating position (by making his BATNA more attractive).

B's attempt to establish answers to the questions posed above and the predictions he makes are neither certain nor clear cut. Most of them can be answered by careful research and thorough investigation, but the answers cannot be tested until trial. B will, however, if the job has been done correctly, have reached a position where the relative strengths and weaknesses of Daniel's case have been assessed. B will not even think of negotiation before he or she has done this. Chapter 4 (Research skills) revealed the extent of the questions B has to answer in determining the merits of Daniel's case. Armed with this information, negotiation may well be considered by B as an appropriate means by which the case may ultimately be resolved. A failure to consider negotiation would, in our view, be a significant short-coming on the part of B.

The practice of legal skills necessitates an understanding of not just how to do it, but when to do it. So when might negotiation occur, who will initiate it and how might the process develop?

B must be able to assess accurately the strengths and weaknesses not only of Daniel's position, but also those of Mr Slater. A theory of the case based on factual and legal research has to be developed (for the workings of this refer back to Chapter 4). We have a theory that Mr Slater drove negligently. Mr Slater's theory may be that Daniel was contributorily negligent. The answer to the question, 'When should negotiation be commenced?' is therefore, 'Only when you are prepared for it'. Who initiates the process is to a certain extent irrelevant, although the initial approach may suggest to the other side that the person making that move wishes to settle because they are not confident of success.

In order for B to be sure that he or she is at the point where negotiation is relevant (regardless of who later initiates it) B must be certain that all that can be investigated has been, and that the information and evidence gathered supports the theory of the case (or *vice versa*). For this reason B is not planning to use all of the theories (for example, the frosted windscreen, on which no evidence was obtainable), although they may not yet have been abandoned.

B should have obtained a medical report or reports detailing Daniel's injuries, the pain and suffering associated with them, the extent of his recovery and the prognosis. Having carried out his or her own analysis and research, B may wish to obtain counsel's opinion on liability, or quantum, or both. Not only would this be a prudent course of action in the client's best interests, but also it would act as a qualified second opinion for B and a marker for possible negotiations. Counsel's opinion can also act as a tool for the solicitor. For example, in the course of negotiation B may be able to gain time and increase pressure on the insurance company, by saying that he or she wishes to go back to counsel to take counsel's further advice. This is explored further in the Chapter 4 – Drafting (see the section entitled Opinion Writing on page 327).

The theory building approached the case from both sides – B's and Mr Slater's. B's theory of the case is that Mr Slater drove with excess alcohol, and failed to pay attention, and that liability should rest fully with him. If so, he is responsible for putting Daniel in a position (so far as money ever can) that he would have been in had the accident never occurred.

Case law gives guidance as to the value of pain and suffering and loss of future mobility. One research task that B should carry out is to ascertain the appropriate level of compensation, in the light of Daniel's losses and injuries. This was one research task that we did not follow through in Chapter 4. Why don't you try this as an exercise for yourself? Where might you go to discover such information? There is a well-established reference text known as *Kemp and Kemp on Damages*. This work deals specifically with the assessment of damages in personal injury cases and catalogues awards for a wide range of injuries and conditions. A specific section deals with injuries to the lower limbs. *Kemp and Kemp* is regularly updated and through research you will discover recent cases and cases of longer standing. In older cases an element for inflation must be added to give the more dated cases contemporary values. If using this source B would carefully compare the diagnosis and prognosis in Daniel's case with the relevant decisions in the text.

Where should you look presuming that you know about *Kemp and Kemp* (if you do not, how might you have tracked this information down – from a text book or by asking someone more experienced than you?)? What about the Table of Contents? Here you will find 'I Lower Limbs' and under I2 iv) 'severe leg injuries I2–301' and 'vi) other leg injuries I2–501'. In both sections cases are named giving details of the extent of injuries suffered, treatment undergone and any future disabilities described. The amount of damages awarded is given in each case.

In 1992, for example, in the case of *Howe v Moore* general damages of £10,000 were awarded in respect of compound fractures of the right leg. The person concerned underwent one operation, was left with surgical scarring of the leg and was thought likely to suffer stiffness and aching within the next 10 years.

In *Breese v Darnton* (1996) a young plaintiff (16) suffered from compound fractures of the femur and tibia and underwent two operations. He had 7 months of physiotherapy and was unable to resume his normal physical activity for 9 months. The medical evidence suggested that he would have a permanent but minimal limp. He was left with surgical scarring and a mild toe deformity. General damages of £20,000 were awarded.

An award of £30,000 was made for general damages in *Hamilton v Bender* (1988) but the plaintiff underwent 6 operations and was still in pain at the date of the trial.

Does this research take into account the most recent authorities? Don't forget to check when *Kemp and Kemp*, a loose-leaf practitioners' reference manual, was last up-dated (as well as using all other the resources available to you). If you look in the front of the first volume the person who inserted the new material from the publishers should have filled in the details of what was inserted and when on the filing record card. In our case it was done by MM on 17th March 1998. Knowing her as I do I can safely rely on this! Reliable research material depends on management systems as well as the printed word.

We may be dealing with negotiation here but the need for research is ever present! Look up *Kemp and Kemp*. See if there are other cases that you could use that match our case study and that could be used to assess accurately the proper level of general damage in Daniel's case. See counsel's opinion on pages 328–329 for barrister F's view on quantum.

B needs to be armed with an accurate and sustainable analysis of the value of the claim, before he or she can begin to draw up the negotiation plan.

B's theory of full liability with maximum damages becomes the best conceivable negotiated outcome, but the target is reduced once weaknesses of the theory are incorporated.

Another theory, only this one we anticipate from Mr Slater's lawyers, is that Daniel's own conduct caused or contributed to the accident. Was he looking where he was going? Should he have seen Mr Slater? Did he indicate while attempting to turn right? Did he have lights on? The extent of any contributory negligence may range from 1% to 100%. This research task was explored in Chapter 4. There it was discovered that the duty of care incumbent upon a road user to look after his or her own safety is not the same for a child as it is for an adult. Age is clearly a material factor when determining the extent of the duty of care in contributory negligence.

Before the negotiation process can commence, other constraints must be fully researched. If Daniel is legally aided, B owes a duty to the Legal Aid Board to incur only those fees and expenses that are reasonable in the conduct of the case. If therefore an offer of compensation is eventually made, this will have to be reported to the Board as continued litigation at public expense may be deemed unreasonable. These problems for B are strengths for Slater's legal team in any negotiation. They know that B's BATNA – 'We'll see you in court' – is not guaranteed to bring B success as legal aid may disappear if an offer of settlement is reached. The possibility of legal aid in cases such as Daniel's will soon be history. His ability to proceed will probably depend on the conditional fee terms agreed with B.

To complicate matters further, as Daniel is under the age of majority, the consent of the court will be required before any settlement can be finalised (unless proceedings have not yet been commenced).

There is then the issue of costs. Great care must be exercised here. A legally aided client is normally immune from an order for costs against him or her if unsuccessful in the action. The rationale of this is that if a person cannot afford to pay their own costs, they should not be ordered to pay those of the other side. This will clearly weigh heavily in the mind of the defendant or insurance company. The insurers could perhaps successfully defend a case, only to find that despite 'winning', they have to bear their own, often considerable, costs. B notes that this reduces the attractiveness of Slater's probable BATNA which is also likely to be, 'Drag me through the courts', or a payment into court of a low figure. At the time of writing changes are pending in the legal aid scheme which will impact on the funding of such legal actions. The removal of legal aid from most personal injury claims and increased dependence on contingency fees will no doubt add a further dimension to dispute resolution, one where the actual cost of litigation impacts more dramatically than is presently the case.

Under the present rules (as of August 1998) a solicitor representing a legally aided client must be aware of the effect of the statutory charge. Any money preserved or recovered, as a result of legally aided proceedings, will be held by the solicitor to the order of the Legal Aid Board until the exact extent of the solicitor's charges against the legal aid fund is known. Those charges will then be effectively taken from the damages to defray the legal expenses. In other words, a successful client who is legally aided will pay for the cost of his or her own legal fees out of the winnings. The corollary of this is that if a legally aided client (or for that matter any client) is successful, they would normally expect an order for costs against the other side.

In Daniel's case were he legally aided, any money recovered by way of costs would mitigate against the statutory charge in the sense that the charge on the legal aid fund would be effectively reduced by the amount of costs recovered from the defendant. Any negotiation must take recovery of costs into account.

This question of costs raises a serious ethical issue. B must not allow the issue of his or her own costs to determine the outcome of the case, where the settlement is not in Daniel's interest. It must not be a consideration for settlement that B is able to recover his or her costs with relative ease, or improve the firm's cash flow. It is a proper matter, however, for B to insist on the payment of costs as part of a negotiated settlement, given that costs in general, and the statutory charge in particular, would directly affect the amount of money that Daniel might receive.

With increased use of conditional fee agreements another ethical issue in a negotiation context may arise – how much it is in the lawyer's own interest to secure a settlement when his or her fees are contingent upon the outcome? If our case study was conducted under a conditional fee agreement should B recommend that Daniel settle for £5,000 plus B's costs or should Daniel be advised that a larger sum is due (with B getting his costs and the opportunity to increase the amount of his 'share' but at the same time exposing Daniel and B to the risks that full-blown litigation might bring)?

B now has sufficient information to consider negotiation as a viable option. B may, or may not, have issued proceedings. To have done so will have convinced the opponent that

Daniel's BATNA is powerful, but it is quite legitimate to respond to signals made by the insurance company before proceedings are issued – indeed B intended to achieve this result with the letter before action (see Chapter 5 – Writing and drafting in a legal context).

There are two essential and significant issues that must be addressed now:

First, B must carefully plan for the negotiation.

Secondly, B must be aware of the ethical issues inherent in the negotiation process and how these affect Daniel's interest.

Let us look at each in turn.

Planning the negotiation

The first thing that B must do is to take instructions from the client. B's views on liability and quantum need to be discussed. B needs to ensure that Daniel and his father (the next friend) are fully conversant with the facts of the case, the arguments in favour of both sides, and the likely chances of success at trial. This requires B to advise Daniel not only of the positive aspects of the case, but also of the dangers contained in the action. The possibility of contributory negligence, for example, would have to be raised.

It will assist B and Daniel to draw up at this stage a list of strengths and weaknesses for both parties. B aims to predict, with some certainty, factors for and against his or her client's case succeeding on liability and quantum. So far as trying to see the case from the perspective of Mr Slater is concerned, B's attempt to assess the merits of his case are, to a certain extent, speculative, but the thorough preparation that has already been carried out should, at worst, involve B in educated guess work, and at best should allow B to arrive at a reasonably accurate assessment of the wishes and intentions of the other negotiating party.

B feels confident of being able to prove, if necessary before a court, that Daniel was injured by Mr Slater, that Mr Slater was driving negligently, and that a proper figure of compensation would be in the region of £10,000–£16,000 based on full liability. B is aware that Daniel may have been contributorily negligent, but that the extent of any contributory negligence would be relatively minor. What are the strengths of Daniel's case?

1 Slater had been drinking alcohol and was convicted of it. The court will take account of this conviction.

2 Drink-driving, although not conclusive of negligence, is indicative of it. Driving under the influence of alcohol is likely to affect driving standards.

3 Slater hit Daniel from behind. Slater should have been able to see Daniel at all material times.

4 The medical evidence in Daniel's favour is consistent with the sort of accident Daniel has described.

5 The content of the medical report has not been disputed.

6 For the present, Daniel may be legally aided, at least up to close of pleadings.

7 Subject to legal aid being extended (of which B is confident) B is prepared to go to trial and is confident of success (in whole or part).

If legal aid were not available, this could be a weakness as Daniel could be at risk on costs were he to lose or not receive at least the amount of any payment into court. Reliance on a conditional fee agreement with insurance cover in respect of the costs of the other side might be applicable and if so would be a strength, as might a more general policy of legal insurance.

Some of the above facts have not been introduced previously, but are quite usual in this kind of case.

Other strengths may occur to you. See Chapter 4 (Research skills).

What about weaknesses in Daniel's case as B imagines the insurers will view them? These may include:

1 Possible contributory negligence. Daniel cannot remember whether or not he indicated or looked behind him when manoeuvring into the middle of the road, although this admission is not yet known to the defence.

2 Damages will not be aggravated by any permanent disability. It would appear that Daniel will make a full recovery apart from a slight risk of arthritis in older age.

3 If legal aid had been granted Daniel's certificate is likely to be limited, requiring counsel's opinion before the issue of proceedings, or counsel's opinion on continuing beyond the close of pleadings. If this is a case where a conditional fee agreement applies – B's willingness to carry the risk of going to trial and perhaps not being paid.

4 There are no independent witnesses who can say whether or not Daniel did cycle negligently and no witnesses to say that Mr Slater was, say, speeding or otherwise driving carelessly.

Again, you may think of other weaknesses of the case.

This is only one part of the preparation. B must now look at the strengths and weaknesses thought to be on Mr Slater's side. What are the strengths?

1 The onus of proof is on Daniel to establish negligence as the plaintiff in the case, yet he did not see Mr Slater's driving and has no eye witnesses.

2 Daniel must make all the running as the insurance company is the one who is being asked to pay out. This gives it the tactical advantage of having to do nothing unless pushed. Insurers may practise substantial delaying tactics.

3 The insurance company is a large commercial concern with substantial financial backing behind it. It is unlikely to be upset if threatened by legal action.

B believes, however, that Slater's case has very particular weaknesses. These might include:

1   Slater had been drinking and was convicted of a drink/drive offence.

2   There appear to be no independent witnesses to corroborate Slater's account that Daniel failed to indicate or look behind him when turning right in the road.

3   Skid marks on the road, as itemised by the police report, indicate that Slater was either travelling at speed and/or had to manoeuvre suddenly. This might be indicative of negligence. (But it might support Slater if he says Daniel pulled out without warning.)

B must also be aware that the insurance company or Mr Slater's lawyers will no doubt engage in a similar exercise. The insurance company is likely to want to keep any payment to a minimum by stressing Daniel's culpability, Mr Slater's limited liability and by downplaying the nature of Daniel's injuries. All of these matters are as yet unsustainable, to the extent that the evidence that would prove one point or another is disputed. Only the conviction is likely to be beyond dispute – but that does not prove negligence on its own.

With a careful assessment of the relative strengths and weaknesses of the two sides, B must attempt to draw up a negotiation plan, in much the same form as seen in the Child and Parent example earlier in this chapter. B must be able to set out the best possible outcome for Daniel, the bottom line that Daniel is prepared to accept and the BATNA that will be adopted in the event of no agreement being reached. A similar exercise must be carried out for Mr Slater so that B assesses, on all the available information, what the insurer's negotiating position is likely to be.

Let us look at these items individually.

For Daniel, the best possible outcome would presumably be an amount of compensation that represents at least as much as a court would be likely to award, with payment being made as soon as possible. B's opinion, backed up by counsel, is that the case could attract an award of up to £16,000. If B was able to negotiate a settlement of at least £16,000 with payment in the very near future, this must come close to the best possible outcome. Of course more than £16,000 could be sought, but the best possible outcome has to be a realistic one, or there is no point in entering a negotiation.

The bottom line by contrast is the amount that Daniel would accept as a minimum figure. B's research suggests that a minimum of £12,000 would be likely to be awarded by the court. If contributory negligence of, say, 20% were upheld, this would reduce the minimum to £9,600. The risks of litigation are such that an award of any particular amount cannot be guaranteed and the avoidance of uncertainty may make a lesser sum attractive. Let us say that the bottom line agreed with Daniel and his father is £8,000.

Assuming that the case can be funded what is the BATNA in Daniel's case? This must be to issue proceedings immediately upon the failure to negotiate a settlement, or to continue proceedings if already issued. We will presume for the purposes of our case study that proceedings have not yet been issued although there is an important tactical question to be answered: Are you in a better negotiating position having issued proceedings? This will be examined shortly.

	McCAULEY LOSES	WIN/WIN AREA	SLATER LOSES	LOSE/LOSE AREA
McCAULEY	BATNA proceedings issued or continued	BOTTOM LINE £8,000	BEST POSSIBLE OUTCOME £16,000+	WATNA Fails to secure sufficient costs to make amount of damages adequate compensation
SLATER	BEST POSSIBLE OUTCOME no liability	BOTTOM LINE £11,000	BATNA defends proceedings and/or makes payment into court	WATNA Cost of case outweighs any savings on damages

Can B assess the same elements in Mr Slater's case?

The best possible outcome for Mr Slater would presumably be to pay nothing, on the basis of no liability. A realistic bottom line may be that some negligence is likely to be upheld. If B feels confident as to the quantum of damages (as evidenced by the researched cases) then Slater's bottom line is likely to be the upper figure of compensation (approximately £12,000) less an element for contributory negligence on Daniel's behalf. If that element were said to be around 10%, it would give a bottom line figure of, say, £11,000. Let us suppose that B presumes this to be Slater's bottom line. Of course B can only make an educated guess at this figure. B will have to listen for signals that indicate what this actual figure may be.

What about the BATNA for the defendant? This might be to continue to defend the action, or perhaps, and more realistically, to make a payment into court. You will learn more about this in civil litigation. Simply put, a payment into court increases pressure on the plaintiff, for if the court eventually makes an award of no more than the payment in, costs from the moment of the payment in are usually awarded against the plaintiff. The rationale behind this is that the defendant will have done all that is possible to settle the case and should recover costs incurred after Daniel unreasonably refuses that payment.

The BATNA should be regarded as a strategy rather than an outcome. The BATNA could of course lead to the WATNA. The WATNA, or lose/lose situation, would be protracted litigation which results in neither side securing any real gain either in terms of adequate compensation or order for costs.

If the BATNA for both sides is to meet in court they could both end up losing. The intention of sticking to the BATNA is an intergral part of the lawyer's plan. It gives a point of reference – what is to be done if the bottom line cannot be secured. Seeing the BATNA through, however, can result in a losing position for either side or a WATNA for both. Find that confusing? Let us try to represent B's plan, and the options for the parties as he or she sees it, in diagramatic form, similar to that given in the parent/child negotiation scenario earlier.

B has now prepared the substance of the case, analysed the strengths and weaknesses of both sides and prepared a plan for the negotiation. An overlap is revealed between the respective interests of B's client and Mr Slater (through his insurers). This must suggest negotiation potential.

What must B now do?

If B is seriously considering negotiation (and we suggest that this will be appropriate on the facts revealed so far) then B must check with the client whether the content of the negotiation plan is acceptable. This involves two matters.

First, Daniel must be made aware of all factors in his favour and of any inherent difficulties in the case. The client can only make an informed choice if he or she has the relevant information. One of the jobs of the lawyer is to advise what steps should be taken, but ultimately it is the client who must dictate, in the light of the advice given, what he or she wants to do. B therefore advises Daniel on liability and quantum. The chances of success are clearly described and the proposal to commence negotiation is discussed. The elements of the negotiation plan are explained and the client's comments and agreement (or not) on the best possible outcome, the bottom line and the BATNA/WATNA are sought (without of course using technical terms – see Chapter 2, page 73).

Subject to what is now to be said on ethics and negotiation and the client's agreement, B is in a position to proceed to negotiate.

Negotiation and ethics

Let us be clear why negotiation is taking place. B has, as his or her objective, the best possible outcome for Daniel. A failure to act in the best interest of a client is a breach of professional duty. B must not only know what Daniel wants (on the basis of informed choice), but also must ensure, so far as is possible, that Daniel achieves this objective. B must also give Daniel the benefit of his or her advice as to what is deemed best.

It means therefore that, when negotiating a possible settlement, B must have a clear idea of what it is that Daniel wants and is entitled to. The two may not be compatible. Daniel may have wholly unrealistic expectations of the value of his claim, having perhaps talked to friends, or heard that people have received far more than £16,000 for personal accident claims.

Here is our first ethical issue. If Daniel (or his next friend) insists on pursuing an unrealistic claim, B is duty bound to advise Daniel of such. Should Daniel carry through with his wishes, he may well lose. B would serve nobody's interest by allowing this position to develop. If the client is unwilling to accept the solicitor's advice, the solicitor must continue to act in accordance with instructions. (In limited circumstances, a solicitor is entitled to decline to act further for a client, for example, if the relationship between them has deteriorated to such an extent so as to destroy the confidence between solicitor and client.) The solicitor must act on instructions and must not, for example, settle a claim even if the level of compensation negotiated is thought by the solicitor to be reasonable.

This ethical issue becomes more complex, for if Daniel is legally aided, and an offer is made, B may be under a duty to report this to the Legal Aid Board who in turn may discharge the legal aid certificate, on the grounds that further legal action is no longer justifiable as a drain on the public purse. B, therefore, must be sure of the client's objectives and of his or her duty to the Legal Aid Board.

A second ethical issue would arise if a conditional fee agreement applied. To what extent would and should B be driven by the need to maximise the level of damages that Daniel might receive when B's fees are tied to the amount of any award or settlement? In short there may be a conflict of interest here. This is further explored in Chapter 4 (Research skills).

A further concern then arises. Let us say that B adopts a principled negotiating stance. Perhaps B has had regular dealings with this particular insurance company before and they now have a good working relationship. It may be that B is an inexperienced solicitor in this field, but has read this book carefully, and is both well prepared and committed to co-operative negotiating. Should the long-term gains of co-operation as illustrated by the prisoner's dilemma have any bearing of the settlement of Daniel's case?

The simple answer to this must be no. If principled negotiation does not result in a settlement that is in the client's interest, another approach must be taken. Of course, early settlement of the case at a reasonable figure, which research indicates is within the range a court might award, may well be in the client's interest. But the principle of co-operation of itself must not dictate an outcome. It is a means and not an end. B may well try a principled approach using objective criteria and focusing on issues and not personalities. If this does not either accord with the client's instructions or produce a result that B's research indicates that Daniel should receive, then the principled approach for the time being must be abandoned. This is why it is so important to have a well worked out plan, containing a bottom line and a BATNA. At least these can be used as warning bells against settlements that are not in the client's interests. If B is confident that the case is well prepared and that both law and facts support the claim there may be little role for negotiation beyond stating the issues in a letter before action and responding to any offers of settlement. Negotiation for negotiation's sake does not serve the client's best interest.

B must also be sure what his or her own interests in Daniel's case are. There might be two overlapping concerns that directly affect B in terms of the outcome of the case. Both form part of the ethical dilemma in negotiation.

The first concerns B's continuing relationship with the insurance company's representative (or perhaps other representatives from that firm or other insurance companies). Whether or not B develops a good working relationship with Mr Slater's insurers should not be allowed to blur the boundaries of Daniel's own interest. The pressure on B to settle the case and to show willingness to negotiate, which may then have long-term effects on a relationship between the negotiating parties, could well give rise to a conflict of interest. Principled negotiation may well give a better context for long-term discussions, but this should only be allowed to lead to a settlement if the settlement in itself is appropriate for the client.

Using the analogy of the prisoner's dilemma, B and the insurance company are repeat players to the extent that the negotiation is a long-term process. There is a meeting and correspondence after the meeting. It will probably pay Daniel as well as B to use a principled approach at each stage. The final measure, however, must be: is the negotiated settlement in Daniel's best interest?

On a related point, B may also feel some pressure to settle, to conclude the case so he or she may be paid. Solicitors have to earn a living. They earn this by charging fees. It is quite proper, professionally, for B to ascertain whether or not any settlement includes the payment of costs and, if so, what those costs might be. A failure to recover full costs will clearly affect B's client, for Daniel's compensation, that has been negotiated, would be reduced accordingly. If the client is legally aided the situation becomes even more pressing. The question of costs in the global sense, that is when taken alongside amounts of compensation, must be carefully analysed, for it is the effect of the package to the client that will determine whether the settlement is in the client's best interests. Costs alone must not pressurise B into settlement. Again the dilemma posed by conditional fees and a potential conflict of interest arises. It may be less risky for B to settle now and get costs plus the percentage 'success' fee on top, than to go on to seek a higher figure through further negotiation or trial. But B is not entitled to take the bird in the hand if two in the bush are better for Daniel!

The negotiation process

Let us follow through a negotiation in Daniel's case. We will suppose that the medical report indicates that Daniel should make a full recovery. He has experienced pain and suffering over a period of six months on a gradually decreasing basis. There is a slight risk of arthritis in the knee joint in later years. Our opinion, confirmed by counsel, is that the defendant is likely to be held liable, but that Daniel's own conduct (in possibly not looking behind or indicating) could be a minor contributory factor. With the use of authority, B believes that such blameworthiness should not exceed 20%. (As a research exercise, you could check this; see Chapter 4.)

Based on full liability, B estimates quantum at between £10,000 and £16,000 to include pain and suffering, minor physical deformity and the increased risk of arthritis. His employment prospects do not appear to be harmed and there is no element for loss of earnings, present or future.

Let us say that the insurance company which represents Mr Slater has denied liability on behalf of the insured (by blaming Daniel for the accident), but the tone of its most recent correspondence is conciliatory to the extent that it reads:

> According to our insured's instructions, Daniel McAuley failed to give any indication of his intention to turn right. On making his manoeuvre he failed to notice our insured's vehicle approaching from behind. Our insured maintains that the resultant collision was unavoidable.
>
> We note, however, the contents of the police report and the fact that our insured has subsequently been convicted of drink-driving.
>
> Without prejudice to the above, and without any admission of liability, we would suggest that our Mr Smith and your B meet to discuss liability generally. Our Mr Smith would be pleased to call at your office at any reasonable time convenient to you.
>
> Kindly contact us with dates of availability.

The letter indicates a willingness to meet, and implicitly to settle. The evidence in the case is strongly persuasive that liability, at least in part, rests with Mr Slater. Presuming B is willing to meet Mr Smith (and it is difficult to know of a reason to make this unwise, unless B has instructions to the contrary) what steps should be now taken prior to the scheduled meeting?

The preparation has already been completed. B was aware that negotiations in such cases often take place, and in anticipation has prepared the plan referred to earlier. The fact that the insurers wish to meet B should be reported to the client and the client's final approval to the negotiation plan and the meeting itself should be obtained.

There is of course no need for this negotiation to be conducted through a face to face encounter. Such meetings are, however, both likely and useful in practice. There may of course be more than one meeting, or there may be an initial discussion between the parties followed by further negotiation in correspondence.

Armed with the negotiation plan B must now decide upon relevant tactics.

We have suggested that B start by using the concept of principled negotiation – remember:

■ separating people from problems;

■ focusing on interests not positions;

■ generating options for mutual gain;

■ using objective criteria.

Negotiation theory suggests that this base for negotiation offers the most in terms of potential settlement, although there are inherent dangers in it for both solicitor and client. B therefore decides to follow a principled approach, but will be conscious throughout the process of the need to re-evaluate the position and to change this strategy if necessary.

B will also have to decide whether, prior to negotiation, proceedings should be issued. There are certain tactical advantages to be argued both for and against the early issue of proceedings. Issuing a writ or summons at a very early stage indicates a clear intent on the part of the plaintiff to take the matter seriously. Once embarked upon, certain information (for example, the content of medical reports) is brought out into the open. A timetable is established which can then be used to force the hand of any party who is dilatory or tries to use delaying tactics. On the other hand the early issue of proceedings may polarise matters. It may act to block the negotiation and it removes the ability to threaten proceedings if negotiations do not proceed promptly and constructively. There are arguments for both. We suspect there is much to gain from the issue of proceedings prior to negotiation for this lays down a clear intent and purpose, but this should not delay B's meeting with Mr Smith – it can be reserved as B's BATNA. However, issuing proceedings when a defendant has indicated a desire to settle could mean that you will fail to recover costs.

The style and conduct of the negotiation is not limited or predetermined other than by the professional practice rules (for example, the solicitor must not lie, but may withhold information from the negotiation, especially if it is damaging to the client's case, such as an unfavourable medical report, or the fact that B has a limited legal aid certificate). Convention may dictate procedure. Meetings in conveyancing cases, for example, tend to take place in the office of the seller's solicitors. Negotiation in personal injury cases frequently takes place at the office of the plaintiff's solicitors. There are, however, few hard and fast rules.

The time for the meeting is approaching.

B reads through the file one final time to ensure that the negotiation plan is clearly in his or her mind and that he or she is fully familiar with all of the detail of the case. B decides to formulate a personal agenda. The agenda will help focus the parties' minds and enable B to stick with the issues and avoid other distractions. The agenda might run as follows:

1   Discover whether the insurance company accepts, formally or otherwise, that its insured is fully liable.

2   What degree of contributory negligence (if any) is alleged?

3   What does the insurance company believe is the appropriate quantum of damage – that is: what level of compensation will the insurance company accept as being appropriate in this case, and does this match the results of B's research?

4   If liability and quantum can be agreed, when would payment be made?

5   What costs – or mechanism for determining the costs – would be agreed on settlement?

6   If no settlement is likely in the immediate future, would an interim payment be made?

B also intends in setting this agenda to find out where the parties stand, not to win arguments on each of the points. This agenda is based on the best possible outcome, the bottom line and the BATNA as agreed by the client (see p 374). This of course is not going to be revealed to the other side, or at least not yet.

It must also be stressed that the purpose of the meeting is simply to sound out the possibility of a settlement. B, especially at this early stage in negotiation, is unlikely to be able or willing to accept a sum offered unless this equals or exceeds the best realistic outcome. If by any chance such a result occurred in the meeting, B might reflect on why the insurers were willing to make such an offer at the outset and might wish to look again at the results of his or her research. The need to take instructions would buy time in such an event.

How might such a negotiation progress? Set out below is a suggested likely dialogue between Mr Smith from the insurance company and solicitor B. Remember that much will depend on the attitude and personality of the participants concerned, even though B will try to ensure that the negotiation concentrates on issues and not people.

We will presume for our purposes that Mr Smith and B have not met previously, but they quickly demonstrate a constructive view to negotiation, that is, a willingness to settle, if at all possible. Both have vested interests. Both have no doubt worked out their best possible outcomes, their bottom lines and their BATNAs. As we know, B has tried to assess the insurance company's position from his or her perception of their strengths and weaknesses. Their conversation is subdivided for our purposes into the following stages:

Stage 1: Setting the agenda

B's telephone rings. The receptionist informs B that Mr Smith has arrived. B in accordance with his or her usual practice goes into reception, greets Mr Smith and invites him into the interviewing room. The meeting then progresses as follows.

> *B:* Do come in. Nice to meet you at last, Mr Smith, are you well?
>
> *Smith:* Yes thanks, are you?
>
> *B:* Yes, but life in the office gets no easier. There are big changes afoot in legal aid and court work that'll make things increasingly difficult for both us and the clients.
>
> *Smith:* I know. It's not much different in industry either. Some huge insurance claims have certainly hit our business and there is always pressure on us to hit targets and show greater efficiency.
>
> *B:* Sit yourself down. Can I get you a tea or coffee?
>
> *Smith:* No thanks, I've only just had a cup.
>
> *B:* Well thank you for coming to see me, I hope we can explore some of the possibilities in the McAuley case. I thought we might begin by setting out the common ground on which we agree and then perhaps establish our differences, whatever they may be.
>
> *Smith:* That's fine by me. Why don't you tell me what you think about this case? In my view it's not as clear cut as it looks.

Several important points have arisen in terms of the negotiating process, even at this early stage. B has clearly demonstrated to Mr Smith that he or she is receptive to discussing the case in a constructive and effective manner. Politeness, consideration, ease and planning all come across. B intends the meeting to be conducted on a basis which allows for an exchange of views whilst following a structured agenda. The small talk is important as a prelude to the substantive discussion. It sets the tone of co-operation. Mr Smith has agreed to follow the structure suggested by B. As the negotiation progresses, not only will areas of agreement and disagreement arise, but also information may be discovered which both sides will be able to use to adjust their expectations and tactics.

Stage 2: Making a case

In some ways this is the most difficult stage in the negotiating process in that someone has to start somewhere in putting forward a view which inevitably involves the perceived case merits. B has taken the initiative in that he or she has suggested what plan should be followed and Mr Smith has agreed, although Mr Smith has indicated that, in his view, the case is not an open and shut one. The conversation continues:

> *B:* As I see it, there are five facts that we can, I hope, agree on at this stage. First, Mr Slater was driving along High Street and was at all times up to the collision at the rear of our client (that is behind him). Secondly, there was nothing to obstruct or hinder your insured's view along High Street. Thirdly, your client had been drinking as evidenced by his drink-driving conviction. I understand he pleaded guilty?
>
> *Smith:* Yes, but that's not in itself any evidence of negligence.
>
> *B:* I agree it's not conclusive, but you may be interested in some of the case law I've discovered on this point. Understandably the courts take a critical view of drink-driving and if a person has an accident, the fact that they have been drinking alcohol may well suggest that the person was driving negligently. I think you will find that it puts Mr Slater in some difficulty.

Smith: Okay, what are your other points?

B: Fourthly, our client was injured when your insured's vehicle collided with his cycle and the extent of his injuries are detailed in the medical report.

Smith: We don't disagree with the content of the report unless you intend to make mileage out of the fact that he is now unable to ride a bike or go out on his own.

B: Perhaps we can come to that when discussing quantum. It is unlikely to form a major part of the claim, but it has affected his lifestyle and is part of the overall result of the injuries. The fifth and final point is that our client is young and in the law's eyes his age is a consideration, when taking into account his own conduct.

Smith: Yes, I agree with all that, but let me put our point of view.

B: Very well, I was going to outline the possible differences, but perhaps you can do that for us.

Smith: We see it like this. Your client is only fourteen; I don't know if he's passed his cycling proficiency test at school, but even at his age he should be aware of road traffic rules and safety standards. He went to make a right hand turn out of High Street into a side road. He didn't look behind him and didn't give any hand signals. Our insured saw him in front, went to overtake him and your lad pulled out in front of our man who had no chance to avoid the smash.

B: Go on.

Smith: It is very difficult for us to get round the fact that our insured had been drinking and that this would have affected his driving ability to some degree. In the magistrates' court hearing, where you rightly say our insured pleaded guilty, the court found that he was only just over the legal limit. He was ten points over the thirty-five limit in breath, and they imposed a pretty standard fine and the minimum period of disqualification. And as you will know even a drunk driver is not responsible for an accident that he could not have avoided if sober. What I am saying is that although we are prepared to make you an offer, it cannot be on a full liability basis. Your client must accept some responsibility for his own conduct.

What has now taken place? Certainly the parties have different negotiating strategies and approaches (whether intended or not). B sticks to his or her plan and does not become drawn into allegation and counter-allegation. B makes no assumption about Mr Smith's case and keeps to the indisputable facts. B also makes an important and noticeable concession by letting Mr Smith outline the differences, recognising that Mr Smith is becoming defensive and anxious to have his say. Mr Smith then takes a contrasting approach by alleging that Daniel was contributorily negligent. Mr Smith does make assumptions and creates a setting where polarised views could easily come into play. Defensiveness is sometimes used to hide weakness. If there is now to be a useful discussion, B must try to move matters away from confrontation and towards common ground, so long as this is within the terms of his or her overall plan. Winning arguments about what happened is not going to be productive, and is probably not possible anyway.

B has, of course, carefully researched the issues raised by Mr Smith, for example, whether drink-driving is evidence of negligence or whether age is material to the standard of care in relation to contributory negligence.

Stage 3: Bargaining

The conversation proceeds as follows:

> *B:* I accept that Daniel has a duty to be careful on his bike, and that your insured is not liable for injuries that occur come what may. The important point, however, must be that Mr Slater owes a duty of care to all other road users. The fact that he had been drinking must have impaired his ability to react, even if he wasn't otherwise driving badly. Also, from what you say, he had our client in his view at all relevant times. Counsel advises us that the case could run on a full liability basis. There may be a possibility of a small degree of contributory negligence on Daniel's part if indeed he failed to look behind him and indicate. My instructions are that Daniel did look behind him, didn't see anything behind, didn't see anyone coming, and pulled out to the centre of the road and waited there while oncoming traffic passed by. He thinks he indicated, but cannot remember. The accident must have really shaken him up.

> *Smith:* I think we are not too far apart on this point. We seem to be in agreement that there may have been some contributory negligence. Would you take a seventy-five/twenty-five split in favour of your client?

> *B:* I'm glad to see that we are making some progress. I would need to take instructions on that. The split you suggest attributes far more blame to Daniel than either I or counsel feels is reasonable, but I'm sure we can discuss that further.

The first piece of hard bargaining has arisen. By now both B and Mr Smith have acknowledged various possibilities; a settlement based on Mr Slater's negligence; recognition that drinking alcohol will have affected the standard of his driving detail; and, the relevance (however slight) of contributory negligence, based on the admission that Daniel cannot remember if he indicated his intention to turn right. B and Mr Smith are testing the water. B could have confronted Mr Smith at this stage by rigorously defending Daniel's position and rejecting the suggested 25% contributory neglience outright. This indeed may be necessary at some later stage. The important point, however, is that some progress is being made and B would not wish to prejudice this unless there was a good reason for doing so. B therefore indicates to Mr Smith that the split suggested is probably not acceptable, but that further negotiations on the point can be held. Whilst B would need to take the client's instructions, this device also enables B to take some time to consider the matter and to increase pressure on the insurance company, who will be waiting for B's response.

Further bargaining now takes place:

> *Smith:* Okay, what about quantum?

> *B:* I must be mindful not only of what we feel is reasonable, but what the client and his parents are willing to accept. If proceedings are issued, I will have to seek the court's consent as Daniel is under age. Any possible contributory negligence on Daniel's part and the correct figure for quantum will have to be balanced, so that a reasonable overall outcome is achieved.

> *Smith:* Yes, I understand that. Whilst we accept your medical expert's report as to the extent of Daniel's injuries, it is clear that he didn't suffer very much for very long. If you are saying that damages should be aggravated by the fact that he does not now go out or ride a bike, I would have to insist on a further specialist's report looking at that particular aspect. Taken as they are, his injuries,

from which it looks like he will make a full recovery, are relatively light. A young man of his age should bounce back pretty quickly. Is he in general good health?

B: I think so; I know of nothing to suggest otherwise. I accept what you say, but he was hospitalised for a week and wore a plaster for over eight weeks. He had a number of minor injuries, he missed school, he couldn't play sports and was badly traumatised by the accident. He could also suffer from arthritis in later life and although that is a risk we all have to bear, the accident has slightly increased the possibility in his case.

I feel that on a full liability basis general damages of at least £17,000 would be appropriate. When assessing quantum, I had in mind the case of *Breece v Darnton* in 1993. This involved similar circumstances and injuries. The *Breece* case was perhaps slightly more serious than our's in that the plaintiff underwent two operations rather than just the one. The extent of the injuries, the scarring left by the operation and the slight residual limp are almost identical to what has happened in my client's case even though Daniel McAuley does not have the mild toe deformity that the plaintiff was left with in *Breece*. The court has awarded considerably more in other cases, for example *Hamilton v Bender* for similar consequences, aggravated by more medical intervention. Even in a relatively straightforward case of a broken leg with a full and uncomplicated recovery the courts have awarded around £10,000 in general damages. In this case we have a young man with a limp and a significant risk of arthritis in later life. I think £17,000 can be justified here. I am optimistic about being able to persuade both my client and, if necessary, the court, of the wisdom of accepting such an offer were it made.

Smith: I can see you have done your homework. I would have to look at those cases in more detail. From my experience, damages for the sorts of injuries which your client suffered might more properly be around £8,000–£10,000. Then of course there is the question of contributory negligence. Even at twenty percent it would reduce an award to the region of £6,800 to £8,000.

B: Mr Smith, would your company be willing to make an offer of, say, £14,000 for general damages, inclusive of any possible contributory negligence? (*This is a figure that B had discussed with Daniel and had in his mind as his first bargaining position.*)

Smith: I will ask, but I feel it's on the high side. Would your client be prepared to accept such a sum?

B: I would obviously have to take his instructions, but this figure would be within the range supported by the cases I have mentioned and it would reflect some degree of blameworthiness on Daniel's part. I cannot guarantee that he will accept it, but in my view it would be a minimum he would be likely to get if the case went to trial.

Bargaining has taken place and figures have been mentioned. B is not keen to press Mr Smith. B needs to take instructions and Mr Smith needs to be given time to consider the position. What B has done is not to dwell on the factual dispute (whether Daniel indicated or not or how drunk Slater was). Instead B has concentrated on the agreed facts and on reasoned and sustainable argument. B has demonstrated in a non-threatening manner that he or she knows the case and the law very thoroughly. Mr Smith is unlikely to be tempted – as some insurers are – to bamboozle. At some point figures have to be mentioned and each side has reserved the right to alter their position should that be necessary.

Stage 4: The end game

B: I have given you my reasons justifying our claim. Will you think about it and see if there is any further room for discussion?

Smith: Certainly.

B: As you are aware we are legally aided. Our client has no wish to go to court, but he is prepared to do so if a proper settlement cannot be reached. His parents are rightly concerned that he receives the correct level of compensation due to him. They feel they owe him that. There is also the court's view to be taken into account, as Daniel is under age. When I discussed this matter with my client before our meeting, we decided that we would try to reach a settlement if at all possible. If that settlement cannot be reached, then of course we will have to issue proceedings.

Smith: Yes, I see that. Leave it with me and I'll get back to you as soon as possible.

B: We obviously don't want to take proceedings unless necessary and add further to the costs of the case, so I would appreciate your answer as soon as possible.

Smith: I should be able to get back to you within fourteen days.

B: I will take no further action until I hear from you, or until I write to you telling you otherwise. I presume that if we can settle the matter, your company will meet our reasonable fees and disbursements and any special damages relevant to the case.

Smith: We will of course meet your costs. Presumably the special damages consist of Daniel's clothing, the damage to his bike and any medical expenses.

B: Yes, I will let you have details of these as soon as possible. Well, unless there is anything else, let me see you out and I'll look forward to hearing from you soon.

Smith: Goodbye. I will write to you shortly.

The end game is important for several reasons. It avoids continued and unstructured discussion. It provides a conclusion to this stage, so each party to the negotiation knows what is to be done next and who will do it. B has not yet had to fall back on his or her BATNA – although Mr Smith knows that proceedings are likely. Nothing that was said or done made this necessary. There is still some room to manoeuvre and importantly B can report back to his or her client on progress that has been made. An offer is certainly likely, although whether it will be sufficient remains to be seen.

Mr Smith has also made progress. He can report back to his employers that an element of contributory negligence is likely to be accepted. Damages will therefore be reduced proportionately and costs saved by negotiating a settlement without further dispute or court proceedings. The legal aid and costs position has been introduced by B. There is a strong practical incentive for the insurers to settle. Even if they were to defend the case successfully, it would be unlikely that costs would be awarded in their favour.

The negotiation process may well proceed further. After taking further instructions B may be prepared to accept £12,500 on Daniel's behalf as a settlement figure. Mr Smith may respond by making an offer of less than this amount. Negotiations may continue through correspondence, but it is likely that a deal will be struck. Remember that B's bottom line was compensation of £8,000. Unless there is good reason for altering this bottom line, the BATNA will come into play (that is, proceedings will be issued or continued). Let us say that Mr Smith offers £8,500 as an initial response and, through correspondence, this figure is eventually increased to £10,000. Both parties have made gains, both have made some degree of concession, compensation is paid promptly and without the uncertainty inherent in litigation. The negotiation was principled to the extent that it followed the model described earlier. A payment into court has been avoided. The end result is a level of compensation that can be said to be in the client's interest and fits the theory of the case researched by B.

What would have happened if B had taken a different approach? Let us say that B decided to take a hard negotiating stance, insisting upon £16,000, otherwise the BATNA would be activated. On the one hand, this would result in difficulties for Daniel in that polarised views emerge and the parties resort to their respective BATNAs. Of course, if the court decides in Daniel's favour and makes an award of, say, £16,000 the hard negotiating approach will have been successful. There are, however, considerable risks attached to this strategy. Both B and Mr Smith will be aware that if the negotiated settlement cannot be reached, the insurance company is likely to make a payment into court; let us say it pays in £10,000. The figure is, we suggest, a likely figure for a case of this nature taking into account the possibility of contributory negligence. Refusal of the payment has considerable implications as far as costs are concerned, and much of the advantage that B may have had in the negotiating process will have been lost. B may have to advise Daniel to accept. Did the hard negotiating stance serve Daniel after all?

What we are saying, therefore, is that, based on careful research and preparation, principled negotiation can be used as a constructive basis from which to resolve a dispute. Providing the objectives of the negotiation are clearly understood and any settlement measured against the bottom line in that case, there is no reason why an agreement that is in the client's best interest cannot be pursued. But all this presupposes that, if a suitable settlement cannot be reached that meets the relevant objectives, the parties are ready and willing to embark upon the BATNA. In this case this would be issue or continuation of proceedings. But this is not the end of the negotiation. It is not untypical for cases to go as far as the court door or even into the hearing before a settlement is reached. The negotiating process can therefore be relevant at any stage.

The process must be continually reviewed for, as more information is revealed, the strengths and weaknesses of each side may alter. B may have to modify the negotiating plan. Daniel's case is, we suggest, a realistic example of what is likely to happen in practice, especially in a relatively small scale and, in this case, legally aided personal injury dispute.

Before leaving the personal injury case study, several concluding points can be made.

First, before B reaches the negotiation stage, the case must be prepared as if each and every relevant fact and argument has to be proved. You cannot fully understand the case without fulfilling the research need. How can you assess the weight of your case, or that of your opponents, unless this is done?

Secondly, part of the lawyer's skill is the ability to predict outcomes. The client's best interests are served, not only by technical skill and substantive knowledge, but also by an ability, through using all available tools and resources, to see what outcome is most likely. In negotiation this is of crucial importance. B must be able to advise Daniel as to whether an offer to settle is reasonable or not in all the circumstances. B must also be able to say what might happen if the case did go to court.

Finally, the BATNA must be one which in itself is a realistic option. The issue or continuation of court proceedings should not be feared. Of course, clients may not relish the prospect of litigation – few do. However, there is no need for lawyers to feel the same. If a case is well prepared and researched, litigation is one route down which a case may proceed. It may be the only viable alternative to other forms of dispute resolution. We suggest that such processes as negotiation, if properly conducted, may render litigation to trial a last resort, but a resort nonetheless. You must aim to establish a reputation as someone who pursues their BATNA where necessary and wins cases.

What of the other cases? Negotiation as a means to resolving disputes can occur in all areas of practice, although some are perhaps more amenable to the application of this skill than others. All of our case studies realistically encompass some possibility of negotiation.

Mrs Evans and the allegations of theft

Negotiations in the criminal case could take place at various stages. The release of Mrs Evans on police bail (as opposed to being produced at court from custody) might be the subject of negotiation. If Mrs Evans was legally represented at this stage, discussions with the police might arise over bail. Theft from an employer is regarded as a serious breach of trust and although the amounts involved are relatively small, it might be sufficient for the police not to grant bail. Representations in favour of bail could therefore be made.

In order to prepare for this possibility similar principles to those outlined in Daniel McAuley's case would have to be adopted.

First, solicitor A would have to carry out the necessary factual and legal research. When can bail be legitimately refused? A looks up the rules and discovers the grounds for refusal in the Police and Criminal Evidence Act 1984 and the Bail Act 1976. If the police do not grant bail to whom can A apply and what procedures must be followed?

Secondly, what plan would A adopt? What are the respective best outcomes, bottom lines and BATNAs?

The negotiation potential in this instance is relatively limited. Can you spot why? It is because A effectively has no BATNA. A discovers that Mrs Evans will come before the court next morning whatever he or she does.

What, however, of the decision to prosecute the two charges to trial? Here there is considerable potential for negotiation. This could involve A in discussion with the police or, once proceedings have been commenced, the Crown Prosecution Service. Arguments in favour of, say, administering a caution might be made out if Mrs Evans were prepared to admit guilt. If a caution is not offered, there are possibilities for negotiation in terms of pleas and sentencing. Whilst it is not yet officially sanctioned (unlike, say, in the United States) it is well known that plea bargaining does take place within the British criminal justice system.

Whatever the circumstances, negotiation can only be considered once the relevant research has been carried out and the results analysed. As seen in the Daniel McAuley case, the cornerstone of effective negotiation lies in preparation. Solicitor A must be able to assess the strengths and weaknesses in the case against Mrs Evans and must be able to identify the likely intentions of the prosecution. A can only properly advise Mrs Evans on the likelihood of success of a not guilty plea – her BATNA – if the investigations into law and fact have been completed. Mrs Evans must be advised whether such a plea is supported not only by her instructions, but by the evidence. Ultimately Mrs Evans's plea to the two charges will be a matter for her, but good legal advice must incorporate a prediction as to the likely outcome, on the known evidence.

Negotiations in this case may follow one of two options. If Mrs Evans maintains that she is not guilty after having been advised in the light of all known evidence, then A can approach the CPS and try to persuade them that the facts do not support the charges at all. The negotiation process here is a little different from that described in the Daniel McAuley case. It is different because there is perhaps no identifiable bottom line or at least the bottom line is no different than the BATNA. The best possible outcome would be the dropping of all charges against Mrs Evans. However A knows that the CPS is generally over-stretched and drops many cases. A may take this into account in assessing the weakness in the prosecution case.

The BATNA and bottom line would be following the not guilty plea through to trial. By contrast the prosecution's best outcome would be a conviction on both of the charges and their bottom line and BATNA in the case would be to continue with the case against Mrs Evans. You should remember in this context, that while we are using the structural framework for dispute resolution outlines at the beginning of this chapter, there is a duty on the prosecution in any criminal trial to act in the interests of justice and not pursue a conviction for its own sake.

There is no shared WATNA, or lose/lose situation here. The WATNA for CPS (bringing the prosecution and failing to secure a conviction) is the best outcome for Mrs Evans, and vice versa.

Negotiations could take place by exchange of correspondence or dialogue or on the phone or at court, in an attempt to persuade the prosecution to drop the charges by using reasoned argument and identifying the weaknesses of the prosecution case. It is difficult to see, however, where there is an opportunity for mutual gain through exploring the win/win territory. The negotiation here is more of an all or nothing exercise.

Compare this with the possibility for negotiation if Mrs Evans is willing to plead guilty to one or both of the charges. Let us look at the relative strengths and weaknesses of both cases. Mrs Evans may argue the following in support of her assertions that she did not steal any money:

1   She had no need for extra money.

2   She had been in a position of trust in the shop for some considerable time and there had never been any previous complaints.

3   She co-operated with the police.

4   She admits that she may have physically taken the coins, but that she had no intention of keeping them.

5   She has no previous conviction for dishonesty.

6   Mr O'Connor does have a relevant previous conviction.

7   Mr O'Connor's system of accounting is suspect.

8   There is no direct prosecution evidence linking Mrs Evans to the theft of any monies other than the three £1 coins found on her.

The main weaknesses in Mrs Evans's case can be described as follows:

1   That she made a confession to the police that she took the coins.

2   That the coins were found on her.

3   That money was missing from the till.

4   That there is no evidence that anyone else took any money.

5   That Mrs Evans had the opportunity to take money.

A may well come to the conclusion, based on the the relevant research, that the circumstantial evidence against Mrs Evans, coupled with her confession to the police, makes for a strong case against her. However, there is little evidence, if any, that Mrs Evans is implicated in taking money in any context other than the three £1 coins. If Mrs Evans were prepared to accept that she is guilty of theft in respect of the coins, there is a distinct opportunity for negotiation.

The best possible outcome in a negotiation would be for both charges against Mrs Evans to be dropped. The bottom line might be, she would plead guilty to the theft of the three coins, if the other charge against her were withdrawn. The BATNA would be a not guilty plea and a trial on both counts.

What are the prosecution's interests? They are under pressure to achieve results, even within the ethical constraints placed on them (acting fairly). A concludes that the best possible outcome for the CPS would be a conviction on both counts, the bottom line might be to accept a guilty plea on a lesser charge. Their BATNA would be to proceed to trial in the event of there being no negotiated settlement.

The overlap here is obvious. If A can pursuade the CPS that there is insufficient prosecution evidence on the more serious of the two charges, the opportunity for a successful negotiation from both sides is apparent.

Again ethical considerations come into play. The fact that a negotiation is possible does not mean that A should proceed down this line. If the negotiation is to proceed, it will almost certainly require Mrs Evans to accept guilt on the lesser of the two charges. A solicitor must not allow him or herself to be drawn into a settlement unless this accords with the client's instructions, and pressure must not be brought to bear on the client to agree to the substance of the proposed settlement, just to bring the case to a conclusion. The outcome must be in the client's best interest as measured by the strengths and weaknesses of the case and the client's wishes.

If Mrs Evans is prepared to plead guilty to the theft of the three one pound coins, she not only benefits from the dropping of the other charge, but could also use her admission as material for effective mitigation against sentence.

It is in our view entirely appropriate and ethical for A to provide for Mrs Evans advice that gives her an informed choice about her plea. Mrs Evans must be made aware that the court is bound to apply a subjective test so far as criminal intent is concerned, but in assessing this, it may infer from all relevant circumstances what that intent was. A can properly advise Mrs Evans that it will be a difficult task to convince a court of her innocence, on the coins charge, in view of the evidence against her. Acting in a client's best interest is not simply giving them the advice they want to hear, but rather is identifying the possibilities in the case. A can quite properly raise with Mrs Evans the question of her guilt and the opportunity that a plea of guilty might give for bargaining with the prosecution. If Mrs Evans does indicate a willingness to accept guilt A can then prepare for negotiations; otherwise the matter proceeds to trial.

The strengths and weaknesses in a case like this can be rapidly reappraised. If the prosecution turn up at court without their key witness, for example, Mrs Evans's BATNA is suddenly very attractive, and therefore the bottom line might be to drop both charges. If negotiations fail and, in the absence of their witness, the prosecution get an adjournment, the BATNA of defending the case becomes unattractive again.

Before leaving the criminal case study, let us go back to the beginning. What if Mrs Evans had been offered a caution at the time of the first police interview with her, following her arrest? The police may well have said: 'Look, if you accept that you stole the money, we will probably only caution you. You've not been in trouble before and we don't want to have to take you to court.'

Mrs Evans is adamant that she did not steal the money, and turns down the chance of a caution, even though this would mean that she had no criminal record in respect of this offence. By sticking to what will turn out to be her BATNA ('if they are not willing to drop the proceedings, I will plead not guilty'), she loses the chance of the caution. Later, following legal advice, negotiations are entered into and she eventually decides to plead guilty. The BATNA has now become her WATNA (worst alternative). Looking for a caution at the door of the court is not realistic. The time and place for that was earlier.

Ms Kennedy and Mr Bennett and the purchase of 1, Paradise Road

The conveyancing transaction too may well involve negotiation. Two parties have to agree to one transaction. We will look at some snapshots within the overall negotiation that leads to a completed purchase.

Let us say that Ms Kennedy and Mr Bennett receive the result of the building society's survey. This reveals that the house is basically sound, although there are a number of items of disrepair and improvement that require attention. Building regulations now insist on a certain structure for timbered roofing supports, and older properties such as 1 Paradise Road do not comply with this. The building society requires the roof timbers to be reinforced as a condition of the mortgage. Damp is also said to be penetrating the property in several places. The wiring to the property needs to be updated.

The building society is willing to make a mortgage advance, but says that it will retain £2,000 until the various works itemised in the mortgage offer are completed. It values the house at £50,000, some £5,000 less than the asking price. As the mortgage is calculated on a percentage of the building society valuation, this is of some significance, for although the buyers are obtaining a 90% mortgage the calculation is based on the survey value and not the price that the buyers have offered. This means that not only would the buyers have to meet the cost of the repairs before the release of the £2,000, but also that the amount of the mortgage is some £4,500 less than they anticipated.

The buyers have several options. They can try to negotiate with the building society over the retention and the valuation. Solicitor C advises them that this is not likely to succeed. The building society is in a very strong position over the terms and conditions on which it is willing to lend money. The buyers could withdraw from the purchase. This may be a very unattractive option for them as they like the property and have already incurred considerable expense in terms of survey fees, legal costs and related expenses. As a BATNA it is unattractive. They could resign themselves to having to raise additional finance, perhaps from parents or friends or through other loans. The latter option may affect their borrowing potential from the building society. This could be explored as a better BATNA. They could, as an alternative approach a different lender although this would no doubt incur more expense (application and survey fees) and delay.

The most attractive option is to pay less for the property. They must try to renegotiate the purchase price with the sellers. They could approach the sellers or selling agents directly, or ask the solicitor to intervene on their behalf.

The negotiating process should, to be effective, involve the parties in predicting each other's strengths and weaknesses. What are these likely to be?

So far as the buyers are concerned the strengths in their case are as follows:

1   They are able and willing to proceed with the purchase with a mortgage offer ready.

2   Subject to the negotiation they are in a position to complete the purchase in the very near future.

3   The conveyancing process has reached an advanced stage for both the buyers and sellers and if the sale falls through the sellers will have to look for another buyer and go through the process again. This might mean the sellers losing their own related purchase.

4   The house is presumably not worth as much now defects have been exposed.

What weaknesses face the buyers? These might include:

1   The sellers' need to sell for a certain price in order to finance their own purchase.

2   A chain of buyers and sellers may be involved and the agreement of each of them may have to be negotiated if any alteration of the price of one property is made. This could present difficulties.

3   The sellers may refuse to sell to the buyers.

4   The buyers are known to want the property very much.

5   The defects are typical of older properties.

The strengths and weaknesses are similar, on both sides, as they each have much to lose from the transaction falling through, but also have much to gain from proceeding with it. The win/win area is likely to be large and both sides' BATNAs – a withdrawal – seems more like a WATNA.

What about the negotiating plan? The best possible outcome for the buyers would be a reduction in the price of, say, £6,500. A bottom line may be a reduction in price of £2,000 which would at least help finance the transaction. The BATNA the clients agree to would be to look for another property if a negotiated agreement in this range could not be reached.

So far as the sellers are concerned the best possible outcome would be to receive the full asking price for the property and their bottom line may be to accept a reduction of £2,500 only. Their BATNA might be to readvertise the property for sale elsewhere; or C predicts their BATNA might just be to go ahead for the price demanded by the buyers. This is hard to predict and there may be bluff about BATNAs and bottom lines on both sides.

C should advise Ms Kennedy and Mr Bennett as to the sellers' position so far as it is known. The sellers hope to buy another property. They say they are ready to exchange contracts. They too have invested much time and effort in the sale and purchase. There must be room for manoeuvre here. Not only is there pressure on the sellers to sell, in order to facilitate their own purchase, but there is also a promise of a speedy conclusion based on a price reduction.

Remember that C, if using the technique of principled negotiation, can cite the results of his or her research to legitimise reasons for a price reduction. The building society's valuation might be a starting-point. The defects in the property give additional ammunition to C.

After discussing the matter thoroughly with the clients and getting their instruction on the negotiating plan, C decides to write to the sellers' solicitors. A letter is sent in the following terms:

Kennedy and Bennett from Ford: purchase of 1 Paradise Road, Sheffield

We are pleased to confirm that our clients have now received their mortgage offer. However, our clients' building society has imposed certain mortgage conditions as a result of its survey of the property. Before it will release the mortgage advance, it requires our clients to undertake to carry out a number of repairs and improvements to the property. In particular, the Building Society require the roofing timbers to be strengthened, the damp that is penetrating the property to be cured and the wiring to be replaced. The total cost of these repairs and improvements is estimated at £2,000.

According to the survey the property is said to be overvalued by some £5,000.

As you may appreciate, our client's mortgage is calculated as a percentage of the building society valuation and, therefore, the mortgage offer to our clients is less than they anticipated when making their offer to buy the property.

For your information we enclose a copy of the building society survey detailing the defects in the property and giving the society's valuation.

We are instructed that our clients wish to proceed with this purchase as soon as possible, but owing to the building society's stipulations our clients are not able to finance the transaction on the basis that they first calculated. Although our clients do not wish to withdraw from the purchase, they may be compelled to, unless the selling price can be reduced. We might add that the reduction would have to be substantial to allow our clients to proceed.

We would be grateful if you would take your clients' instructions on whether they are prepared to reduce the purchase price and, if so, by how much.

Can we emphasise that subject to a satisfactory renegotiation of the purchase price our clients are able and willing to proceed and indeed wish to move to completion at the earliest possible date?

We should be grateful to hear from you as soon as possible.

Yours faithfully

Such a letter is, we suggest, a constructive attempt to start the negotiation process. It sets out in a clear and positive manner the objectives involved. The buyers do wish to complete the purchase of the house, but have a practical problem arising from the building society's survey. With the client's instructions, C has justified the reasons for the reduction, by providing evidence of the defects in the property and of the overvaluation. The incentive held out to the sellers is that the buyers will proceed very quickly with the purchase, if the price can be renegotiated. The most difficult part of the negotiation, that is setting a new price, is left open. C does not want to commit his or her client to a particular figure, without first testing the water.

There is much to lose for both sides if the transaction falls through and a mutual benefit to be had from seriously considering a reduction in the selling price.

In the event we can tell you that the sellers agree to reduce the property by £3,000 in view of the repairs needed and of the overvaluation. The buyers borrow the necessary funds from parents and repay some of this when the retention is released. The transaction could, however, have easily fallen through, that is, the BATNA would have been realised.

Mr Kader, Mr Khan, Mrs Shearsby and the lease

Reaching an agreement in our business law case study is central to the progress of the case. The number of isues that could call for protracted discussion and negotiation are considerable. Our objective here is to illustrate the approach, not the detail.

What might arise here?

We have already seen in Chapter 3 (Interviewing) that there is tension between the Lessor (Mrs Shearsby) and her step-daughter. There may be hidden agendas which Mr Kader's solicitor, D, could not have anticipated, but which Mrs Shearsby's own solicitor should have explored in interview. Mrs Shearsby may be negotiating in the shadow of her dispute with her step-daughter and, in any event, of the grief at her husband's death. The result might, for example, be that Mrs Shearsby would be almost relieved if the deal fell through, since that would satisfy her step-daughter. On the other hand, she may be willing to let the factory on any terms, because that is what the late Mr Shearsby would have wanted –

he was a man of his word. Mrs Shearsby might even want to let it in order to show her step-daughter who is in charge. We simply don't know.

Mrs Shearsby's solicitors should not enter into negotiations without clear instructions. What follows assumes that they have successfully brought out into the open what Mrs Shearsby wants to achieve in the negotiations and, that they have her (preferably written) instructions to negotiate some tough terms.

In our case study take it that Solicitor E has been instructed to prepare a draft lease that imposes a range of restrictions, for example on use of the property and on subletting, as well as onerous repairing obligations on the tenant and a rent review clause that ensures that the rent is increased at a rate and frequency that suits the interests of the Lessor.

There may also be some agreeing to be done as between Mr Kader and Mr Khan. What are the terms of their business venture? Some of these matters are explored in Chapter 3 (Interviewing), Chapter 4 (Research skills) and Chapter 5 (Writing and drafting in a legal context).

Let us take just one of these potential issues and explore briefly the room for, and principles applicable, in negotiating a deal. Let us say that the Mr Kader's present business needs are not such as to occupy the factory fully he and Mr Khan are interested in leasing. There is ample room for future expansion (which is the plan) but in the short-term the prospective tenants want to be able to sublet part of the factory to maximise income generation from its use. As chance would have it the factory site is ideally laid out to allow for a section of it to be used by another enterprise without causing difficulties for Mr Kader and Mr Khan. When the draft lease arrives from Mrs Shearsby's solicitor, E, it contains a blanket ban on subletting.

You may remember that Mrs Shearsby is relatively inexperienced in business matters and relies heavily on the advice of her lawyer in such matters. If E suggests that there should be no sub-letting then she is happy to go along with this. In any event Mrs Shearsby does not want to make matters more complicated by having several tenants using the factory.

To move this example along we can presuppose some of the client's instructions and summarise the position, from the solicitors' perspective, for the respective sides as follows:

Mrs Shearsby:

■ if she is to let the factory she wants a steady income from it;

■ she is happy in principle to go with the plan her late husband had to let to Mr Kader and Mr Khan;

■ it is important to her that she has a simple and workable arrangement with as little complication as possible;

■ for sentimental reasons she does not want to sell the factory, at least not yet;

■ she wants to achieve the above objectives without causing difficulties with her step-daughter.

Mr Kader and Mr Khan:

■ based on terms discussed with the late Mr Shearsby and an inspection of the site the factory ideally suits their needs in terms of facilities, location and rent;

■ the factory is large enough to allow for future expansion;

■ in the short-term it would enable them to sublet – they have a sub-tenant in mind who is in a similar, but non-competing, business and with whom they could achieve some economies of scale in terms of ordering and processing;

■ they are keen to make speedy progress and the site is ready for occupation; no planning consents (change of use) are required and minimal alterations are necessary to make the factory productive.

How do these factors fit into the negotiation theory described earlier? Of course precise terms, such as rental figures, would be need to be included in the final plan.

Again the results can be tabulated:

	SHEARSBY LOSES	WIN/WIN AREA	KHADER AND KHAN LOSE	LOSE/LOSE
SHEARSBY	BATNA Withdraw and let or sell elsewhere	BOTTOM LINE Sublet but high rent or longer lease secured	BEST POSSIBLE OUTCOME Lease with no subletting	WATNA Unable to let or sell; step-daughter proved right!
KHADER AND KHAN	BEST POSSIBLE OUTCOME Subletting allowed	BOTTOM LINE Subletting but other conditions eg higher rent or lessor's approval	BATNA Lease other property	WATNA Unable to find property as good

The possibilities here are many. Presuming agreement is reached it may well be on the basis that Mr Khader and Mr Khan agree to pay a slightly increased rent in return for the right to sublet for the first year of the agreement. Mrs Shearsby may be persuaded to allow sub-letting providing she has the right to vet and approve prospective sub-tenants.

The principles described in this chapter can be followed through in any of the case studies, contentious or not. Getting to yes on workable and mutually acceptable terms is the objective. The game plan must include what is to be done in the event that the agreement is not reached, minimising the risk that the WATNA might bring.

Other forms of dispute resolution

It is unrealistic to call on you at this stage to develop the skills of arbitration and mediation. However, as a negotiator you should be aware of other ADR possibilities in your work generally and in the negotiation process in particular. They may even form part of your negotiation strategy.

Arbitration is the use of a neutral party to determine the outcome of a dispute. It is like using a judge but out of court. Often the arbitrator will have the subject knowledge and professional skills relevant to the issues at stake. Arbitration may be an option open to the parties (requiring their joint agreement before it can be activated) or it may be the forum for dispute resolution agreed in advance of any dispute actually arising.

Mediation is somewhat different in that it is not a form of decision-making but rather is a process through which agreement can be reached. It differs from negotiation in that the mediator has no vested interest in the outcome of the case (other than to help the parties resolve their differences) and strives to avoid making a judgment or favouring one side against the other.

The mediator does not offer legal or other advice – this would inevitably be seen to result in apparent partiality. Mediation is voluntary, in that no agreement is made without the agreement of the parties (who should normally take advice from you, their lawyer, before concluding a binding agreement). Because it is voluntary the parties can back out at any time and fall back to their BATNA.

So what do mediators do? They create a structure in which issues are aired and the parties can hear what each other has to say. Facts and agendas are elicited by the mediator and options for settlement proposed by the parties. The mediator tries to help the parties to hear each other, including their concerns, allegations and wants. Everything that is aired is by way of trying to find a solution and is confidential to the parties and their advisers.

Mediators may see the parties alone or with their lawyers. Either way they enable negotiators to focus on a win/win approach.

Why do you, as a lawyer, need to know about ADR? The answer is that it may be in your client's interests – and therefore be your professional duty – to advise your client of the possibility of reaching workable agreements and to consider suggesting to the other side that they enter into the ADR process. This may involve negotiation, arbitration or mediation.

Organisations which promote mediation and other forms of dispute resolution now exist across the UK. One source for information is the Centre for Dispute Resolution.

Conclusion

Several points must be made in conclusion.

First, negotiation, especially in contentious matters, is always a possibility. In non-contentious cases it can be used at particular junctures, where interests coincide or conflict. You must therefore be aware of the need to consider negotiation in all case work, contentious or otherwise: in non-contentious cases agreement may be of the essence. In contentious disputes, the BATNA may have to be resorted to: that is often the court.

Secondly, you can only negotiate effectively if you are well prepared. This means working from a position of intimate case knowledge and thorough research – factual and legal. Negotiation cannot be fully effective unless the negotiator is able to assess the strengths and weaknesses of both his or her own case and, so far as is possible, that of the other side.

Thirdly, negotiation must be based on a plan and strategy. This requires the lawyer to be sure of what it is that is being negotiated. What are the objectives of a meeting or a letter in the negotiation process? What is the best outcome for the client? What is the least that the client is prepared to accept? Ensure that not only are the client's instructions taken, but that those instructions are based on an informed choice. What BATNA is to be followed in the event of a failure to agree? A well prepared lawyer should be in a position to predict chances of success in the event of, say, court proceedings resulting. Not only will the BATNA preserve a client's position, but it will also be a yardstick against which any prospective settlement can be measured.

Fourthly, we recommend that you follow the guidelines for principled negotiation. Use facts and law that support your arguments and that can be proven or examined. Concentrate on these to justify your case and focus on areas of agreement rather than dispute.

Fifthly, do not allow the concept of principled negotiation to compromise your client's best interests. Check your bottom line and your BATNA. Check your client's instructions at every relevant opportunity. Where necessary, stick to your BATNA and do not shirk from taking steps that render further negotiation unlikely, at least in the short term. The threat of the issue of proceedings or the continuation of them may well refocus the opponents' attention and lead them back to the negotiation table. If not, your plan confirms that you are serving your client's best interests.

Sixthly, avoid the WATNA! If you can't do this at least ensure that your client is aware of the real price of failure to agree.

Finally, be aware of the relevance of timing in the dispute resolution and settlement process. This should of course form part of your preparation and planning. For Mrs Evans the possibility of a caution as an alternative to prosecution will only exist for a relatively short period of time. For our house buyers timing may be all important, especially if the sellers are being held up in the purchase of their own property as a result of Ms Kennedy and Mr Green's attempt to negotiate a reduction in the purchase price of 1, Paradise Road.

Dispute resolution can only be said to work if two consequences result. First, the settlement must be acceptable to your client (as it will have to be to the other side too). In our case studies Daniel must see the settlement as reasonable, and the court may need to sanction it. Mrs Evans must be genuinely prepared to admit guilt; Ms Kennedy and Mr Bennett must be prepared to proceed on the basis of the price reduction obtained. A negotiated settlement for its own sake is likely to please no one. Secondly, any agreement must work. It is no good extracting an agreement that fosters resentment and bitterness between parties whose relationship must continue, or results in a deal that cannot be financed. Winning on principle can be very hollow and often costly.

On a more pragmatic level, dispute resolution may be seen as a game of bluff and counter-bluff. In following your negotiation strategy and plan, you may make assertions that are intended to increase pressure on the other side. 'If you do not settle, we will issue proceedings.' 'If you do not reduce the price, we will withdraw from the purchase.' 'If you do not drop the charges, we will defend.' These may be justified as an articulation of your BATNA. Principled negotiation suggests that you should follow this line in the absence of an agreement. We suggest that there is nothing unethical in this exercise, providing you are acting under instructions and you are not telling untruths. Your credibility in negotiation may suffer, however, if you make veiled threats, but do not see them through as necessary. Giving the other side, say, a deadline, may well focus their attention on the possibility of settlement. Subsequently ignoring that deadline makes your position weak. Your BATNA, however, must be carefully worked out as you may need to act on this if all else fails.

Using a co-operative approach to dispute resolution enables both sides to pursue their own ends and interests without necessarily resulting in a win/lose situation. The client's interests can be fully served when a settlement is fair in the context of the problem and is likely to be workable. The process by which the agreement is reached should follow a plan in which each point claimed is backed up with provable fact or established legal authority. If this approach also aids future developments, this is a valuable by-product.

For the lawyer, however, all of these processes are at the outset and the finish determined by the client and his or her wishes. The skill of the lawyer is to clarify these objectives and to realise them within the constraints of law and fact. Negotiating and other methods of alternative dispute resolution are just one part of this process and an integral step in reaching workable agreements.

Chapter 7
ADVOCACY
---

1   An introduction to advocacy

Of all the so-called 'legal skills' none is more readily associated with lawyers than advocacy. It is perhaps the most exciting part of the contentious lawyer's work. This chapter will explore the skill of the advocate and the importance of advocacy in legal practice.

This chapter is dedicated to how to do advocacy. After looking at the general principles, we move on to identify the goal of specified advocacy tasks, the legal framework within which that task is found and how the task can be carried out to achieve the desired objective. Again our case studies are used to illustrate the theory and application of advocacy in practice.

In an adversarial system such as that found in Britain, where one side is seemingly pitched against another, the role of advocacy is vital. Even those with little or no legal training can quickly conjure up visions of bewigged and robed lawyers arguing the merits of their clients' cases. Advocacy, however, does not begin nor end before a judge and jury, or even in a courtroom.

For our purposes, advocacy is the function of representation and the articulation of a client's case before the appropriate body or authority.

Taken in its broadest sense, advocates may use their skills to progress the client's case. This may include communications and discussions between the 'rival' lawyers themselves. Advocacy skills, therefore, arise in, say, drafting or negotiation. But in its narrowest meaning, advocacy is limited to the presentation of a case before a court or tribunal. Either way, two common features emerge. First, the lawyer, in exercising skills as an advocate, must be able to marshall the relevant law and facts and present them in a disciplined and relevant way. Secondly, the advocate must be able to persuade the judge or jury, magistrates or tribunal members, or opposition, that this account of the law and facts is the correct one.

Lawyers in an adversarial system operate from a partisan standpoint. They take sides. They owe a duty to the client to act in his or her best interests. You will remember, however, that a lawyer also owes a duty to the court and the profession.

Balancing these potentially conflicting obligations – to the client, the court, and the profession (not to mention the truth) – is yet another aspect of the lawyer's skill. As will be seen, standing by your client, whilst conducting a case with scrupulous fairness, is as essential as it is sometimes difficult. The challenges thrown out by these competing demands are not impossible to achieve. As a student you have to show your awareness of these obligations as they arise.

So, if advocacy is about representing the client is it also about discovering and presenting the truth?

Moulton and Bellow in *The Lawyering Process* suggest that it is not the zealous quest for truth that advocacy seeks to uphold but, rather, a devotion to the *process* through which it is hoped the truth will emerge.

Is there such a thing as truth anyway? There are many accounts of 'the truth'. These will be based on alleged facts, personal interpretations, perceived concepts and sustainable evidence. In cases of conflict those in authority, for example a judge, may have to decide whose account of 'the truth' is acceptable. In other instances the facts may not be in dispute, but it is the law and its interpretation and application that must be judged. We have already seen that the lawyer may not lie to or mislead the court or an opponent; the task is to do his or her best to persuade the audience of the merits of the client's version of 'the truth'.

If the advocate's role can be summarised in three words they must be: preparation, presentation and persuasion. We look at the first two in the context of the case studies. Persuasion we pick up at the end. Suprisingly it is perhaps the least important. Every advocacy task will, to a greater or lesser extent, rely on the ability of the lawyer to handle the three Ps.

2   The assessment context for advocacy

Before examining the components of advocacy skills, let us identify the standards to be expected of students and the methods of assessment likely to be used.

On undergraduate law programmes advocacy rarely forms a compulsory or discrete part of the course. It may be offered as an option on some law degrees. Where it does there will undoubtedly be a set of learning outcomes and assessment criteria. Given the likely variations from one institution to another it is impossible to list these. It is, however, important to recognise the significance of the skill of advocacy as a component part of degree level study, particularly in the student's capacity to communicate clearly and effectively. Advocacy is highly relevant in tutorial contributions and seminar presentations. It requires students to prepare thoroughly and express relevantly, succinctly and persuasively, the issues at stake. Much of what is said in this chapter focuses on advocacy in the context of the court room but the general principles on which work in this setting are based can apply equally to the undergraduate as to students on vocational courses.

What are the aims and assessment requirements on the LPC and BVC?

Given the differences in rationale and emphasis between the two vocational courses the standards set for the LPC and the BVC do not correspond in all respects. We have listed them making appropriate comparisons and noting the necessary differences. *Words in italics are not quotations from the standards. The rest is direct quotation.*

LPC

The student should be able to formulate a coherent submission based upon facts, general principles and legal authority in a structured, concise and persuasive manner. The student should understand the crucial importance of preparation and the best way to undertake it. The student should be able to demonstrate an understanding of the basic skills in the presentation of cases before various courts and tribunals and should be able to

  (i) identify the client's goals;

 (ii) identify and analyse factual material;

(iii) identify the legal context in which the factual issues arise;

(iv) relate the central factual and legal issues to each other;

 (v) state in summary the strengths and weaknesses of the case from each party's perspective;

BVC

A. The student should be able to prepare and deliver each of the following

(a)   an opening speech

(b)   a closing speech

(c)   an unopposed submission

(d)   an opposed submission

The student should be able to examine, cross-examine and re-examine witnesses.

In relation to any of these tasks, the student should be able to prepare the case effectively, understanding the relevant law, facts and principles, observing the rules of professional conduct and planning the advocacy task in question.

B (Preparation), C (Presentation), D (Examination-in-Chief), E (Cross Examination), F (Re-examination) – the Student should be able to:

B(a) formulate and use a theory of the case
B(I) adhere to instructions from the client

C(d) explain the strong points in the client's case
C(e) explain, excuse or justify the weak points in the client's case

(vi) develop a case presentation strategy;	B(h) structure the speech or submission in a clear, logical and coherent manner
(vii) outline the facts in simple narrative form;	B(b) outline the facts in clear narrative form
(viii) prepare in simple form a legal framework for the case;	B(e) relate legal authorities to propositions of law
(ix) prepare the submission as a series of propositions based on the evidence;	B(c) indicate the relevant legal principles to the court as concisely as possible B(d) cite cases and statutes as appropriate, giving full citations to the court when necessary B(f) relate evidence to legal principles B(g) make suitable use of affidavit evidence
(x) identify, analyse and assess the specific communication skills and techniques employed by the presenting advocate;	*The BVC Course Specifications set out in detail the expectations in relation to Presentation (C) including pace of delivery, stance in court, confidence in performance, anticipation of opponent's points, appropriate responses to the court, use only of arguments with merit and concession of points in argument. BVC students should refer to their course materials for the specific requirements.*
(xi) demonstrate an understanding of the purpose, techniques and tactics of examination, cross-examination and re-examination to adduce, rebut and clarify evidence;	*The BVC Course Specifications set out in detail the expectations in relation to Examination in Chief (D), Cross Examination (E), and Re-examination (F). BVC students should refer to their course materials for the specific requirements.*
(xii) demonstrate an understanding of the ethics, etiquette and conventions of advocacy.	

The assessment for both the LPC and BVC is therefore geared towards knowing how to make submissions and examine witnesses. It always involves preparation, and inevitably requires some presentation and persuasion.

Your starting-point in demonstrating competence must be clearly understood in advance of any court appearance. Before standing up and speaking, planning should be complete. Not all contingencies can be catered for, but the plan should be fully mapped out, even if it is later amended, once proceedings are under way. We are, at this point, reminded of the need for a theory of the case. This theory, identified in Chapter 4 (Research skills) matches the then available facts and law and is targeted towards the client's objectives. For Mrs Evans the best theory chosen is that she has no *mens rea*. For Daniel McAuley it is that Mr Slater drove negligently and that Daniel was not contributorily negligence.

There is also the distinct possibility that new theories will be required as the preparation progresses. These are not necessarily alternatives to the theory of the case, but rather, are sub-theories that relate to particular advocacy tasks, such as an interlocutory hearing in the civil case, or a bail application in the criminal one. For example, a bail application may be built around the theory that bail should be granted as none of the reasons for refusing bail exist (eg likelihood of the commission of further offences, or the failure of the defendant to surrender to custody).

The advocate's plan must:

■ set out objectives;

■ contain a full appraisal of law and facts applicable to the task;

■ identify the relevant strengths and weaknesses; and,

■ include the likely sequence of events that will take place when the hearing is under way.

The plan is therefore a strategy for achieving objectives. The case studies will shortly be used to illustrate the construction of a suitable plan and the consequential skills of the advocate.

The actual performance of advocacy is not a required part of the Law Society standards. It is a requirement for the BVC.

Establishing competence in advocacy on the LPC will require (dependent upon the assessing institution) a demonstration or performance of some advocacy. It certainly requires an understanding of the relevant skills. These are likely to be based on identified stages in litigation, for example, a plea in mitigation, a bail application, an interlocutory hearing, a legal submission or a closing speech.

The staging of mock trials to be heard in full are perhaps less likely, given available resources and the emphasis of the standards themselves. Paper exercises may cover other aspects. It is likely that demonstration of the preparation for trial may be part of the assessment. Emphasis may be laid on preparing to examine or cross-examine in particular.

In order to ensure that all possibilities for assessment are covered this chapter will look at all the relevant advocacy skills. The whole should be sufficient for you not only to pass the advocacy element of the LPC skills course, but also provide the aspirant advocate with grounding in the theory and practice of such skills.

The Bar Council's BVC Outcome Specifications specifically refer to presentation and examination of witnesses with repeated reference being made for the need to make, through assessed performances, appropriate and competent submissions and the necessity to deal effectively with the examination of witnesses. The form of assessment may vary from one BVC provider to another but the emphasis is on oral presentations.

Sample advocacy assessment criteria

A self-assessment checklist may assist you to focus on the applicable criteria for your own and each other's practice (see pp 404–405).

3   The principles of advocacy

There are two ways to learn to be an advocate:

- you can emulate others; or

- you can work from a theory of advocacy. The theory can be supported by experience, including observation.

Learning advocacy solely by emulating others is not in our view a good idea. It is how many learn their craft. We were exposed, as articled clerks (trainee solicitors as they are now known) to sitting behind counsel, or tagging along with our principals; after qualifying we watched for endless hours while waiting for our own short appearance before the magistrates. We learned that was how it was done – there was nothing else to teach us.

There are two flaws with this process: first, you see what other advocates are doing, not how and why they are doing it that way. Learning by imitation is of limited value, until you know how and why it is being done that way. Paradoxically, we are convinced the best thing that ever happened to our own advocacy skills was to stop doing it, when we became lecturers, and learn some law and procedure. Having forgotten how other people are doing the job around us, when we return to court nowadays, we have to ask ourselves the most fundamental questions. Who has the burden of proof here? What law is raised? What facts will have to be accepted to achieve the desired result?

The first problem therefore is that you may be copying a good performance in the wrong way and at the wrong time. You risk being, at best, an actor speaking the right lines in the wrong play. At worst, you risk being an incompetent lawyer.

The second problem is that, in copying, you become stuck with the process of advocacy rather than seeing advocacy as a problem-solving activity.

Personal recent and frustrating experience illustrates the point; a magistrates' court in which one of us was appearing wished to allow a summary of 'the facts' to be given by a solicitor, despite the fact that the solicitor had no witnesses or other admissible evidence of those facts (you perhaps already know this – lawyers making opening speeches cannot refer to matters they are not in a position to prove by evidence). I objected. The court clerk insisted: 'We always do things that way in this court'. That statement may well have been true but was not legally correct and could not be accepted as a benchmark of good standards. Remember, that using a mentor as a model presupposes that the person emulated has got it right in the first place. Bad habits, poor tactics and wrong procedures can be learned just as easily as the right or good ones.

This raises a further issue: your ego. Like an actor, you are probably going to feel great after a good performance, and lousy after a poor one. This is natural. Good advocates enjoy the limelight. However, do not go into court with two goals – being seen to be great and getting the right result. It is your argument, your law, your facts and, above all, your convincing control of these, that deserve the limelight. Making self-aggrandisement subservient to this is a measure of real ability.

There are some key words that can be emphasised in this section on the general principles of advocacy. We have already encountered three: preparation, presentation and

Advocacy checklist

EVIDENCE OF PREPARATION

(evidenced both in written outline and oral performance)

To what extent did you show that you:

- Identified the goal for the hearing?

- Identified appropriate factual material?

- Identified appropriate legal material?

- (If appropriate) anticipated opponent's likely goal/tactics?

- Anticipated contrary legal argument?

- Anticipated contrary factual material?

THE ORAL PERFORMANCE

To what extent have you:

- Kept to time?

- Spoken clearly and avoided reading the submission?

- Shown courtesy to court and opponent?

- Used English which was

  ☐ correct?

  ☐ free of unnecessary jargon?

  ☐ easy to understand?

- Revealed a structured approach?

■ Kept to correct procedure?

■ Argued the law appropriately?

■ Identified appropriate facts?

■ Established facts through evidence as necessary?

USE OF WITNESSES

(if appropriate)

If witnesses were involved, to what extent have you shown in each instance:

■ An understanding of role of examination and re-examination?

■ Use of appropriate questions for own witness?

■ Understanding of use of witnesses to establish relevant facts?

■ Understanding of role of cross-examination?

■ Use of appropriate questions for other side's witness?

■ Use of evidential rules?

MAKING THE POINT

To what extent have you asserted the argument:

■ Clearly?

■ Relevantly?

■ Persuasively?

■ Taking account of law established in hearing?

■ Taking account of facts established in hearing?

persuasion. Two others are organisation and control. In some of the conventional guides to advocacy, the authors, often skilled and experienced advocates in their own right, seem fixated with the concept of 'greatness'. Brilliantly inspired questioning, cutting cross-examination, rapier-like probing and silky eloquence, all single out the consequently famous advocates. Examples can be taken from performances of leading counsel of the day such as Sir Edward Carson and Sir Richard Muir (*Munkman*, pp 67 and 80).

We are rightly impressed with such expertise. Most of us can perhaps never realistically aspire to such heights of acknowledged fame. For many of us (we include ourselves), our advocacy training consisted of little else than observing more experienced solicitors and barristers on their feet in court. (This wasn't difficult as one of the advocacy skills not yet developed was securing the usher or clerk's attention and favour, to ensure an early place in the court list. Others tended to get on before us!)

On such occasions we waited and watched and practised and hoped for greatness to descend. We must not be too self-effacing, but neither of us has any claim to greatness. More importantly, in the absence of any guide (written or otherwise) to judge one's own progress was difficult, other than in terms of 'winning' and 'losing'.

This learning by experience is of course an important part of any job. Law is no different. But learning by copying is fraught with danger.

The situation is further compounded by a common weakness, especially on the part of inexperienced advocates. You properly take your client's side. You believe what your client says. You find evidence to support the client's assertions. You start a case with a view that you are in the right. Once the case begins you listen to the opponent's witnesses. A parade of convincing characters give evidence. They gush credibility. In the face of this unexpected strength, you have no line of attack.

Why had you not anticipated that your opponent would also have strengths to display? You may not have had the benefit of a book such as this! Certainly we had not, as novice advocates. The reason for the difficulty that you are now in is that there is no case theory. None of your evidence has been tested prior to the start of the case.

This is, if you like, something akin to a secret weapon here. Test the theories of the case before the hearing. You may not be able to examine all of the evidence, particularly that which can only be revealed in skilful cross-examination, but there is nothing to prevent an advocate from scientifically examining the available evidence (from both your own client's case and from the opposition's, for example, advance information in criminal trials and witness statements in civil matters) and testing this as fully as possible. As we will see, in our criminal case this means looking at all of the available evidence and formulating questions for both Mrs Evans and the other witnesses. The actual or anticipated answers will test whether the theories stand up to scrutiny. What was the accounting system in the baker's shop? Who had access to the till? Did Mr O'Connor use money from the till and if so did he keep records of it? Did Mrs Evans (or others), when busy, wait until things were quieter before putting money in the till? You may not be able to test the theory exhaustively, for you do not as yet know what will actually be said by the witnesses in court, but you should be able to test your theory on the available (and likely) evidence.

Expose the weaknesses in your own client's case to the likely critique that may come from the other advocate or the judge.

Advocacy here relies on meticulous and well focused preparation. You must anticipate what may happen and stay in control. No greatness in that? Sorry!

4   The ethics of advocacy

As a background to the general principles, and the specific advocacy tasks that follow, you must understand a set of ethical standards. A lawyer must, in order to meet these ethical expectations, maintain due respect and courtesy towards the court and other members of the profession whilst also acting in the interests of the client and to the client's best advantage within the limits of the law. Useful guidance can be found in principle 43 of the Code of Conduct of the Bar of England and Wales (1990). The rule sets out helpful guidelines for solicitors too. The explanatory memorandum to this rule states that it reflects the necessary balance between respect for the court on the one hand and the interests of the client on the other. Solicitors should take heed.

The Solicitors Act 1974 does not specifically mention advocacy. Since December 1993, however, the Solicitors' Practice Rules (rule 16A) require that the solicitor advocate shall comply with the Law Society's Code for Advocacy. Further principles are set out in the Law Society's *Guide to the Professional Conduct of Solicitors*. The Solicitors' Practice Rules, the Code and the *Guide* together form a framework within which that practice must take place. All solicitor advocates should be aware of and follow the rules and guiding principles.

To understand the nature of ethics in the context of advocacy you must focus on the tripartite duty owed by the lawyer to the client, the court and the profession. To succeed as an advocate and to survive and impress on a vocational course you must demonstrate your understanding of the standards that are expected of you.

So what are these ethical issues?

Don't mislead the court

Certain principles are sacrosanct. Let us illustrate these with reference to the rules and codes of practice for solicitors. Equivalent provisions apply to barristers. For instance, a solicitor who acts in litigation must never deceive or mislead the court (Advocacy Code 2.2). Knowingly allowing a client to proceed in a case before the court with, say, a false name would be a breach of this duty.

The Law Society's *Guide to the Professional Conduct of Solicitors* makes clear that you can argue each point on behalf of your client but anything known to be wrong cannot be used. For example, A could not put to the police officer that he or she planted the coins in Mrs Evans's pocket, even if this would help the case. A knows that it is not true from his or her instructions. Legal authorities that go against as well as those that support what you are arguing ought to be revealed. For example, B discovers, as part of his or her research, that there is authority to support the view that 14 year olds are expected to look after their own safety and can be found contributorily negligent to a high degree (see p 230). The court should be told of the case in the legal submissions. As part of proper preparation and planning, a good advocate would instead be ready to deal with arguments that reveal a weakness in his or her case; or would have advised the client of ways of avoiding ending up in court with a fundamental weakness in the case. In this way an advocate not only assists the court, but can counter in advance damaging allegations by the opposition. This can be done by explaining the weakness or at least conceding the point, if it is unavoidable.

The duty not to deceive or mislead is, however, a qualified one. There is no requirement to reveal factual omissions that the opponent has failed to raise in support of his or her case. For example, say Mrs Evans has previous convictions. These are highly relevant to the issue of 'seriousness' in sentencing. If the prosecution omit to mention them, A may in mitigation also properly omit reference to them, but cannot say that the client is of previous good character. That claim would be an act positively misleading the court. Similarly, the advocate for Daniel cannot suggest that he looked behind and signalled before moving to the centre of the road if in fact Daniel cannot remember whether he did so or not.

Respect the parties and witnesses

The Solicitors' Advocacy Code stipulates that a solicitor must not make an allegation intended to vilify, insult or annoy an opponent, witness or other person (7.1(e)).

For example, solicitor A might properly raise as an issue in the criminal case evidence or cross-examination on Mr O'Connor's business integrity (or lack of it), in an attempt to explain why the till was 'light'. Accusing Mr O'Connor of being a habitual liar, or of holding offensive views on race or gender, may well be held by the court to be both irrelevant and insulting, even if true.

Observe expectations of fairness

The Code for Advocacy (7.1(b)) states that a solicitor must not give personal opinions to the court (unless invited to do so). A's personal opinion as to the integrity of his or her client is not permitted. The evidence presented in the case may, of course, suggest such integrity and A should stress this in the closing speech.

According to the Code, the advocate must provide the court with all relevant case law and legislation applicable in the case, and is obliged to notify the court of any procedural irregularities even if these hinder the advocate or the client's position (7.1(c)).

It is permissible for a solicitor to interview and take a statement from any prospective witness whether or not that person has been interviewed or called as a witness by the other side (the Law Society's *Guide to the Professional Conduct of Solicitors* 21.10). The guidelines suggest that if a witness is interviewed and this person has already been interviewed by the opposing lawyer, the subsequent interview might take place in the presence of a representative of the other lawyer (to avoid the possible allegation of tampering with evidence). We would add that it is courteous to notify the other lawyer of the intention to interview 'their' witness, even though there is no property in that witness.

It should be remembered that barristers too can interview witnesses but must not rehearse, practise or coach them (Code of Conduct of the Bar, para 607 and Annexe H, 6.1) although it is normally the solicitor's job to discover and prepare evidence.

The advocate must not put any pressure on the witness to give anything other than a truthful account of their evidence. If the witness has been interviewed by another lawyer the content of that interview is confidential and there should be no attempt to discover what has already been said in any subsequent interview. According to the Code (6.5(a) and (b)) a witness should not be rehearsed or coached as to the content or form of their evidence. We suggest that this is not the same as checking with the witness that the evidence that he or she is to give is relevant, cogent and admissible. The witness can also quite properly be advised on the conduct of the ensuing trial, the likely cross-examination that may follow and the manner in which the witness is expected to behave in court. This may inevitably involve a detailed examination of the witness' evidence.

Any form of tampering with evidence is strictly forbidden (the Code 6.5 and 6.6). Payments to a witness contingent upon their giving evidence is also outlawed. This does not, however, prohibit the payment of proper expenses, including loss of earnings (Law Society's *Guide* 21.11).

A solicitor must therefore resist the temptation to tell the witness what evidence he or she should give. It is perfectly acceptable, however, for the advocate to shape questions on the content of possible evidence in terms of whether it supports the present theory of the case. Not only might the advocate's intervention in the shaping of evidence amount to a breach of the Code (a disciplinary matter) but such action could also be highly damaging to the conduct of the case. A witness may fail to come up to proof, or worse, may inform the court that the answers had been suggested by the lawyer in the case preparation. The temptation here can be enormous. Let us say that A is instructed by Mrs Evans that Mr O'Connor took money from the till to pay his personal expenses. A can legitimately ask the witness, Ms Smith, in interview if anyone took money from the till and if she had ever seen Mr O'Connor do so. The witness should not be persuaded to say so at trial just because it otherwise fits the theory of the case. (Asking such matters in cross-examination is somewhat different as will be seen.)

For the purposes of this section we used the word 'witness' to include the client and any other witness in the case.

Clients and truthfulness

The next important ethical principle concerns the possibility of the client misleading the court. Where a client, prior to, or in the course of, any proceedings, admits to the solicitor that he or she has committed perjury or has misled the court in any material matter, in relation to those proceedings, it is the duty of the solicitor to decline to act further, unless the client agrees to disclose his or her conduct to the court (the Code 2.2 and 5.2). (Remember that this point may arise at the interview and will need to be discussed there.)

This raises a question that a lawyer is often asked to explain at parties: how can you act for someone when you know that they are guilty? Of course, you rarely know that your client is lying to you or the court, and it is not your job to judge the truth. Remember the point about the lawyer's task being to get at the process of truth-finding, and not necessarily the truth itself. This rule deals with the exceptional case of the client who admits having lied and the case is still continuing. To act for the client further in the case, without rectifying the perjury, is to take part in the deception. Be watchful therefore for situations where you know – not just suspect – that the client wants to mislead the court. But so long as your client does not require you to mislead the court, you can still test the other side's case in court – even if you have been told by your client that the opponent's case is true.

If you are suspicious of the truth of what the client is telling you, you are obliged to probe your client's instructions but, unless you unearth anything that clearly shows that your client will be lying to the court, you cannot decline to act merely on the ground that if you were the court, you would disbelieve him or her.

Standards of dress

A solicitor appearing in court as an advocate must always wear suitable clothing and should appear duly robed where this is customary (Law Society's *Guide* 21.17). The Code of Conduct of the Bar dictates that 'a barrister's personal appearance should be decorous, and his (sic) dress, when robes are worn, should be compatible with them' (Annexe H, para. 5.12). The ICSL *Professional Conduct* manual (Blackstone Press, 1997) suggests that this means dressing conservatively and gives detailed guidance on the appropriate garments (pp 93–94). You may dislike formal clothes. You may think lawyers in fancy dress are an anachronism. However, you must follow the rules, including in your practice in front of the tutor or video camera. See how well you perform in the actual context in which you will be assessed. Whatever the merits or otherwise of formal dress, it is the client who may suffer if the court is antagonised by your appearance. Solicitors wear robes and 'tabs' in the county court when it is sitting as an open court, rather than in chambers. In chambers and in the magistrates court and tribunals, sober suits, or other conservative clothing will do. Loud colours and high fashion could antagonise the court. The same will apply when you are being assessed.

Other ethical issues affecting the advocate

The Law Society's *Guide* (21.19) deals with the solicitor as prosecutor, which is an area in which the trainee will receive specialist instruction. The prosecutor is not supposed to have a partisan client and does not 'want' a conviction as such. The prosecutor is supposed to represent the interests of society and the operation of a fair system. You are entitled to expect the prosecutor not to mislead the court, but also to be fair to the defence and to reveal information that may be helpful.

A solicitor who appears in court for the defence in a criminal case is under a duty to say, on behalf of the client, what the client should properly say for him or herself if they had the requisite skill and knowledge (21.20). There is a similar provision for advocates in civil proceedings (21.21). Under this rule you are acting for the client first and foremost. It does not mean you have to do exactly what the client says. You are the professional advocate. If you cannot do a good job for the client by following his or her instructions you can decline to act further (but you cannot then disclose why, to the court or the other parties, because your client's instructions are given to you in confidence). The insistence of the client in pleading not guilty in the face of compelling evidence to the contrary would not be a reason for declining to act unless it adversely affected confidence in the solicitor/client relationship.

In criminal proceedings, the defence solicitor has a concurrent duty to ensure that the prosecution discharges the onus placed on it, to prove the guilt of the accused. In civil cases, there is no equivalent to the presumed neutrality of the prosecutor and each side is responsible for the conduct of its own case with the judge as final arbiter.

On a more general level, the Code dictates that the advocate 'must promote and project fearlessly and by all proper and lawful means the client's best interests' (2.3(a)).

This is more than just representing your client to the best of your ability. It may require you to stand up in the face of judicial comment that verges on the intimidatory. Let us say that the court has made it clear that it wishes to proceed with a trial. You, however, have discovered some evidence that you have not yet had the opportunity to research fully. You want an adjournment. The court is not minded to give it. You must stand by the best interest of the client and put forward your arguments in favour of your proposed course of action. Do not be railroaded by the judge's immediate preferences. Ultimately you must respect the judge's decision (even if you later decide to appeal against it) but this is only after you have exhausted the arguments relevant to your case.

The Code also spells out the circumstances in which an advocate may accept instructions and as importantly when instructions can be declined, a retainer ended or a brief returned. These include anti-discrimination provisions on grounds of race, ethnic origin, gender, religion, sexual orientation and political persuasion (2.4). The advocate may have reasonable grounds for declining to act. These may include the circumstances of the case, the nature of the advocate's practice and the advocate's own competence or experience (2.5). Strict rules apply to the advocate who wishes to withdraw from a case (5.1).

As advocates, barristers must 'promote and protect fearlessly and by all proper and lawful means (the) lay client's interests', preserve client confidentaility and recognise, and if neccesary avoid, conflicts of interest. The way in which barristers conduct proceedings, their obligation to the court and the relationship between barristers and witnesses are all addressed. Annexe H of the Code of Conduct (Written Standards for the Conduct of Professional Work) lists the general expectations in this regard (paras 1–8) and lays down specific requirements of counsel engaged in advocacy in criminal proceedings (paras 10–17). These rules cover the roles and responsibilities of prosecuting and defence counsel as well as specific requirements in relation to particular aspects of a case (eg confessions, video recordings and appeals). The rules can be found in the ICSL *Professional Conduct* manual (pp 209–224) along with useful commentary (pp 83–91). A substantial section of the manual is devoted to equality issues and anti-discrimination provisions (pp 51–82) and these now rightfully form part of the standard of conduct expected of the barrister advocate.

5 Advocacy in action

Against this background of ethical issues let us now turn to the doing of advocacy. It helps to divide this into separate but interrelated headings:

1   Identify the tasks.

2   Construct the plan.

3   Prove the facts.

4   Establish the law.

Identify the tasks

In this section we look at the need for advocacy in a case and how that can be recognised and prepared for.

The first question to ask in preparing any advocacy task is: 'Why is the case being heard?' The second and related question then follows: 'What outcome do I (as advocate) want to achieve?'

In our criminal case study, Mrs Evans is to appear in court on several occasions. Each appearance has a specific purpose or purposes and the desired outcome will vary accordingly. Similarly, the civil case will involve hearing dates when certain issues are before a court and specific aims and objectives are pursued. You must be able to accurately identify the nature and purpose of the advocacy task. There is, for example, no point in trying to persuade a court of Mrs Evans's innocence if the hearing is to determine mode of trial. Similarly, there is no value in addressing the District Judge on the level of general damages if the court is hearing an application to set aside judgment. The aims and objectives of the particular advocacy task must be clearly understood and prepared for.

The two questions posed above are not restricted simply to court proceedings. The same might be said of appearances before tribunals (although none of the case studies will in fact be resolved in this way). Less obviously perhaps, the questions also arise in the context of advocating your client's case for, say, a price reduction in conveyancing, following an adverse house survey, or during negotiations leading to the settlement of our personal injury case.

A useful device to help identify issues is the closing argument. This is an address to the court at the end of a case or a particular hearing. Usually all sides have a chance to make this speech. The main exception is at the end of a criminal trial in the magistrates' court where the prosecutor is denied a closing speech (unless given leave or in response to legal submissions). It outlines issues of both law and fact that bolster your theory of the case. To formulate the main points of a closing argument, when preparing the advocacy task, will focus the advocate's mind on the matters at stake.

Is this not a topsy turvy way of going about preparing for advocacy? How can this approach be used before all of the evidence has been heard and the opponent's case fully argued? The answer is that you have prepared your own evidence and argument, anticipated that of any other party, and controlled the proceedings in such a way that the points you wish to bring out in your closing argument will be made in the evidence.

Clearly, not all eventualities can be anticipated at this stage but it is feasible to prepare, at least in outline, a closing argument. The fine tuning will occur as the case progresses. We have seen this point on several occasions – the need to review progress at every stage of the case as it develops.

In this way, the advocate should know what conclusion he or she wants the court or the other side to come to. From that point, you can work back in your preparation. If this proves unsustainable it perhaps begins to beg the question of whether the case should indeed continue to a hearing, or if there is no choice (for example, for the defence in a criminal prosecution or an advocacy assessment on your course), whether the correct strategy is being used.

Identifying the advocacy tasks in the criminal case study

The first opportunity for the advocate to display his or her skills will come in the preparation for and appearance at the initial court hearing. In order to prepare A must be able to identify the reasons for the hearing and the objectives of it.

Mrs Evans faces two allegations, both contrary to section 1 of the Theft Act 1968. The first is the theft of three £1 coins, the second the theft of £545. In both instances the property is said to be that of her ex-employer Mr O'Connor.

She could appear from police custody or on police bail, that is, bailed to attend court at a given place, date and time. In the alternative she could have been reported on summons, information having been laid by the police before the magistrates and a summons having been issued.

For present purposes it makes little difference. We will presume that Mrs Evans has been charged at the police station and bailed to attend court. She has instructed A to appear.

What is the purpose of the first hearing? This will clearly define the advocate's objectives.

A first hearing in the magistrates' court on an either way offence is concerned with several separate, but related, matters:

1   Identifying the defendant.

2   Ensuring that the defendant understands the charges.

3   Deciding if the matter can proceed on that day, and if so, how.

4   If in a position to do so, determining the mode (or venue) of trial.

5   Once determined (if summary trial is accepted by the court and chosen by the defendant), ascertaining the defendant's plea.

6 If a plea of guilty, deciding sentence.

7 If a plea of not guilty, arranging the trial (normally at some later date).

8 If summary trial is not accepted by the court or chosen by the defendant, arranging the committal (also normally at a later date).

9 If adjourned, setting a new date.

10 Adjudicating on any ancillary issues (for example bail and legal aid).

Mrs Evans's solicitor, A, has certain aims and objectives when attending the hearing. As seen in Chapter 4 (Research skills) Mrs Evans does not accept that she is guilty of either offence. She accepts that she must have taken the coins as they were found in her apron pocket. She cannot recall taking them and in any event did not intend to permanently deprive Mr O'Connor of them.

The purpose and objective of this hearing may well include:

Requesting and securing an adjournment to allow time for the prosecution to provide information by way of advance disclosure This stems from A's need to obtain further details of the prosecution case in order to advise the client fully. Is A entitled to information about the prosecution case?

Clearly some research is necessary. *Emmins on Criminal Procedure* (Sprack) reveals rights under the Magistrates' Court (Advance Information) Rules 1985 (SI 1985/601) to the disclosure of the evidence that the prosecution would rely on at trial. This may consist of copies of written statements of prosecution witnesses, or a summary of the facts on which evidence will be adduced. This entitlement extends to all offences that are triable either way. Theft is one such offence.

A therefore has the right to make an application to the prosecution for the disclosure of advance information which should be made direct to the CPS. If A is to have this before mode of trial is decided, an adjournment of the case against Mrs Evans is necessary. In planning this advocacy task, A must be able to explain to the court the reason for the application, with legal authority if called upon to do so (Magistrates' Courts (Advance Information) Rules 1985 and Magistrates' Courts Act 1980).

It may well be the case that, at court, the solicitor for the CPS produces the statements, having had the request from A prior to the hearing, or having anticipated that the request might be made. Here A must modify the application to be made to the court. He or she can no longer say that time is needed to obtain advance disclosure but, instead, A needs time to take Mrs Evans's instructions on the content. Is A entitled to an adjournment for this reason? The inherent jurisdiction of the court allows it to conduct proceedings as it thinks fit, subject to the content of the Magistrates' Courts Act 1980 and related legislation. The court may adjourn for good reason. It is suggested that good reason would include the need to ensure that a defendant has had the opportunity to give his or her representative full instructions on mode of trial.

To secure unconditional bail until the adjourned hearing What are Mrs Evans's rights so far as the grant or refusal of bail is concerned?

Again some research is needed. The legal framework for bail is governed by the Bail Act 1976 as amended. *Emmins* gives detailed guidance on the applicable law. A knows from his or her research that there is a statutory presumption in favour of bail, which means that Mrs Evans should be granted bail unless the statutory criteria for refusing bail or imposing conditions upon the grant are satisfied.

In order to identify the nature of the advocacy task in this instance A must therefore be sure of the circumstances when bail can be refused (Schedule 1) and when conditions can be imposed on the grant of bail. A must also be aware of the procedure applicable to bail applications. Case law and statutes dictate that after the first two refusals successive bail applications cannot be made unless fresh considerations are now relevant and have not been previously heard (see the Bail Act 1976 Schedule 1, Part 11A and *R v Blyth Juvenile Court, ex p G* [1991] Crim LR 693).

A must be armed with full details of Mrs Evans's background and personal circumstances so as to be able to counter any objections to bail that the prosecution may put to the court. A prepares these according to the Bail Act framework (grounds for refusing and relevant factors in Schedule 1).

We look at a bail application later in this chapter.

To secure the grant of legal aid   A needs to know for both the client and him or herself whether Mrs Evans is eligible for legal aid. What is the procedure for applying for legal aid in criminal cases? When can legal aid be refused? If granted, can it be subject to conditions?

A will know, or can discover from research, that legal aid in criminal cases is governed by the Legal Aid Act 1988, sections 19–26 and the Legal Aid in Criminal and Care Proceedings (General) Regulations 1989 (SI 1989/344). The magistrates' court may grant an application if the statutory criteria are met. These are twofold: first, there is a merits test, that is, is it in the interests of justice that legal aid be granted? Factors such as the likelihood of a custodial sentence should be considered by the court (section 22). Secondly, there is a means test. The applicant must give the court details of his or her income and capital. If beyond certain limits, either legal aid will be subject to a contribution, or it will be refused altogether. A must be aware of the detail of these provisions in order to be able to make the application effectively.

If convicted, Mrs Evans could face a custodial sentence. Theft from an employer involves a serious breach of trust. As part of the preparation needed for the bail application A might anticipate the prosecution's possible objections to bail. One might be the chance of Mrs Evans absconding in view of her likely sentence if convicted. This preparation can be used for purposes of the legal aid application, in that A could argue that legal aid should be granted given the possible sentencing outcome. (Case law supports the view that imprisonment can be properly considered in such cases: *R v Barrick* (1985) 7 Cr App R (5) 142.)

In the event of the court not agreeing to an adjournment (unlikely), to make representations on venue   What factors should influence a magistrates' court when determining whether to hear a case? When does a defendant have the right to demand Crown Court trial? What are the consequences of agreeing to be tried in the magistrates' court? If Mrs Evans will choose Crown Court, is it worth making representations about whether the magistrates should accept or decline summary jurisdiction? (Yes, A should, so that if the Crown Court judge says 'Why on earth was such a simple case sent here?' A's barrister might blame the magistrates and prevent a costs penalty.)

In order to plan for and prepare the advocacy task, A must have researched these issues. He or she needs to have answers to these questions in order to advise the client and make the necessary representations.

Mode of trial or the determination of venue is provided for in the Magistrates' Courts Act 1980, sections 18–21 and 23. Guidance to magistrates can be found in Practice Note (*Mode of trial: Guidelines*) [1990] 1 WLR 1439 (as amended by Criminal Justice Consultative Council, 1995). *Emmins* deals with the matter at pp 109–121. In cases of theft, the offence being one that is triable either way, the court may accept or decline to take a case in accordance with the statutory provisions and Practice Note but in any event the defendant has the right to elect to go to the Crown Court. Under certain circumstances, the magistrates can commit to the Crown Court for sentence even if guilt has been determined by them.

We have looked in some detail at the planning for this first hearing. We will return to this on p 429 when we see how it is actually conducted.

A will therefore prepare for this stage of the case by fully researching the applicable procedure. It is very unlikely that the client would be advised on mode of trial until the advance information requested from the prosecution was to hand.

We will presume that the application for an adjournment is granted and that Mrs Evans has been released on bail (see p 432 for details of the bail applications). Legal aid has also been granted. The adjournment was for three weeks to enable A to obtain advance information and to take instructions.

A second hearing therefore takes place. What is the purpose now?

1   to confirm the identify of the defendant and her understanding of the charges;

2   to decide on mode of trial;

3   to hear any applications, for example further adjournments or extensions of bail.

The advocate's objectives are now:

1   To make representations on venue that will secure trial at the Crown Court. We have already seen that where offences are triable either way, the defendant has the right to elect trial at the Crown Court. Unless experienced in such cases, A will need to check the procedure applicable. In the event of the magistrates being willing to hear the case, the court clerk will ask the defendant whether she wishes to be tried by the magistrates or by the Crown Court. A must ensure that this option is put to her and that the client knows what it means and what she must answer.

2   To extend bail to the next hearing (which will presumably be the committal hearing). If bail was granted previously, A will ask the court to extend bail on the same terms to the next hearing. Applications for a variation to the terms of the grant of bail can be made by either the defence or prosecution at subsequent hearings (Bail Act 1976,

section 3(8)). A should ask the prosecution if they do intend to object to the renewal of bail and be prepared to counter any objections by reference to the law or facts.

The agenda therefore shifts as the case progresses. One final example will illustrate this progression.

Let us say that Mrs Evans elects Crown Court trial and the case is committed to the Crown Court, where a not guilty plea is entered. A date is set for the trial. What are the purposes and objectives now?

The purpose of the hearing is to:

1   ascertain, through trial by jury, Mrs Evans's guilt or innocence;

2   if found guilty, to sentence Mrs Evans.

The advocate's objectives are:

1   To cast sufficient doubt on one or more elements of the prosecution case that an aquittal must follow; in effect, to convince the judge and jury of Mrs Evans's innocence, by proving that she lacked *mens rea*. Within this objective are more detailed agendas. A may want to show that some prosecution evidence is inadmissible (for example, Mrs Evans's confession) or may wish to prove certain facts (for example, that Mr O'Connor often took money from the till).

2   In the event of a conviction, to minimise the sentence to be imposed by addressing the judge on Mrs Evans's circumstances and on the appropriate sentence. This is normally known as a plea in mitigation, save that the fact of her plea will not allow certain mitigation factors to be raised. The court has not accepted her professed innocence and will not therefore hear of, say, the defendant's regret at having committed the offence. Mrs Evans could not now get any credit for a guilty plea.

Construct the plan

The key to preparation is organisation and detailed knowledge. Able lawyers are those who understand what it is that is expected of them and who know the client's case in every relevant detail.

The would-be advocate must be aware of the procedural requirements applicable in the case. This, as will be seen, is as important as the facts of the case and knowledge of the law. The extent of procedural requirements may vary, but you cannot avoid them. At its simplest, advocates must be conscious of who it is that they are to appear before. Personalities count. If you watch the same judge or magistrate over a period of time, you realise their own preferences, prejudices and attitudes. Skilful advocacy plays to these factors. (Read the *Rumpole* stories for further insights.)

The court, tribunal or meeting may have its own procedural rules. Some may be formal and prescribed, others expected or preferred. At one extreme are the important issues of rights of audience. Your client's case will not be advanced in his or her favour if you arrive at court expecting to appear only to discover that you have no right to speak on the client's behalf, which can be caused by merely not wearing the right clothes!

Rights of audience

The relevant rules are now contained in part in the Courts and Legal Services Act 1990. They are also based on convention, custom and practice.

Presently, solicitors can appear in the magistrates' courts without restriction. This covers the adult crime court, the youth court, the family proceedings court and the court that deals with licensing and miscellaneous matters. Trainee solicitors are not allowed to appear as advocates in the magistrates' court. Limited rights of audience are available to solicitors in the Crown Court in relation to appeals against conviction or sentence and in certain civil matters on appeal. Solicitors have rights of audience before certain Crown Courts for historical reasons (for example Caernarfon and Lincoln).

Solicitors can also appear in all county court hearings and in certain matters in the High Court (for example formal unopposed applications). All tribunal hearings are open to solicitors and trainee solicitors.

In chambers applications (that is not in open court) a solicitor has the right to be heard. Barristers have rights of audience before all courts and tribunals including the appellate courts. Solicitors have no such rights before the appellate courts.

The 1990 Act permits full High Court and Crown Court rights of audience for solicitors upon authorisation by the Law Society. This possibility will not affect a solicitor until several years after admission and requires considerable advocacy experience and the passing of an examination.

Barristers have unrestricted rights of audience before all courts and tribunals.

Proposals are currently under debate to equalise rights of audience.

Addressing the court or tribunal

In constructing the plan for action, the advocate must also be aware of the way in which proceedings are conducted. The 'batting order' is of supreme importance for it determines who says what and when. This is often determined only by convention but your compliance is required. An inability to understand and apply these rules may result in difficulty, embarrassment, delay and, at the very least, an unimpressed client.

How do you know when to jump up and make your submissions? When is the other side allowed to make representations or question your client? Some basic rules of procedure must be researched. You will know that the burden lies with the prosecution, plaintiff or applicant, in most proceedings, to prove their case. Occasionally, this is reversed (for example the defence must prove diminished responsibility on a murder charge). It is usual therefore for the person who has to prove the case to speak first and for the other party to respond. Consequently, the defence or defendant normally has the last word. Where an application is made, for example for an adjournment, the person making the request will usually make the initial move and the other party will be allowed to respond.

Emmins on Criminal Procedure (Sprack) and *Civil Litigation* (O'Hare and Hill) deal with the order of proceedings in criminal and civil matters respectively. Court and tribunal procedures do vary within these general parameters. If in an unfamiliar court or tribunal, ask the clerk what procedure the court or tribunal follows and then check this against the general legal rules. Try to avoid appearing in a totally alien environment. Go and watch before it is your turn to perform. Take a careful note of how the court (or tribunal) works. Check this against the rules if necessary. Even the courts can get it wrong!

Not only must the advocate understand the way in which the proceedings will be conducted but he or she must also comply with the expected form of address.

Magistrates are collectively referred to as 'Your Worships', but when addressing a stipendiary magistrate or chairperson of the lay magistrates the correct form of address is 'Sir' or 'Madam'. District judges are also addressed as 'Sir' or 'Madam', as are chairpersons of tribunals.

A circuit judge in either civil or criminal proceedings is referred to as 'Your Honour' and a High Court or Appeal Court Judge is referred to as 'Your Lordship' or 'Your Ladyship'. 'Master' is used for a Master of the High Court.

Other lawyers in court are normally referred to as 'My friend' (for a solicitor) or 'My learned friend' (for a barrister) and the clerk to the court is normally referred to as 'The learned clerk'.

Clients and witnesses should be referred to by their proper titles such as 'Mr, Mrs, Ms, Dr or Reverend'. Do not use first name terms except with young children. (If you want an example of overfamiliarity with a witness see John Cleese as the barrister in the film 'A Fish Called Wanda'.)

Using the accepted form of address is essential to avoid criticism and disapproval, both of which are likely to affect the client's case.

In criminal trials the onus is of course on the prosecution to prove beyond all reasonable doubt each element of the charge. The advocate for the prosecution therefore normally opens the case by introducing him or herself and his or her opponent, outlining the charges and what the prosecution must prove to establish guilt and providing a summary of the evidence that will be given by the prosecution witnesses. If any evidence may not be admissible, it must not be mentioned as part of the case at this stage.

The content of opening speeches will be examined shortly.

Prosecution witnesses are then called. The order of witnesses is not prescribed but presentation of evidence in chronological order makes sense in terms of the logic and flow of evidence.

After the examination-in-chief of each witness (that is, questioning by the advocate for the prosecution) the defence have the opportunity to cross-examine that prosecution witness. The prosecution may then re-examine the witness on issues raised by the cross-examination.

The defence case may then be put. An opening speech can be made but this is in practice rare. It is usual to call the defendant before any other witness, although it is not necessary to call the defendant at all. Inferences can now be drawn from a failure to testify

(Criminal Justice and Public Order Act 1994). The same procedure for examination-in-chief, cross-examination and re-examination then follows.

In criminal cases, no witnesses, except the defendant, may be in court prior to the giving of their evidence. They may remain in court (and indeed should remain, in case further clarification is needed) afterwards.

At the conclusion of the defence evidence the defence advocate will make a closing speech, summarising the evidence and drawing from it the issues favourable to the defendant. The advocate will also address the court on issues of law. If the defence did make an opening speech, the prosecution would be allowed to respond with a closing speech.

The prosecution may also reserve the right to be heard on law (as opposed to fact), if a legal submission is raised by the defence in the closing speech. Procedures also differ depending on whether the case is tried before the magistrates' or Crown Court. In the magistrates' court, for example, if the defence makes an opening speech it may not usually make a closing speech. In the Crown Court an opening speech by the defence can only be made if witnesses to fact are to be called. The rule about allowing a reply on a point of law applies at any time during proceedings.

In civil cases some significant differences can be seen. Witnesses are not excluded from court as in criminal trials. There are also specific rules of evidence and procedure that relate exclusively to civil proceedings. The plaintiff will normally open the case (for it is the plaintiff who must prove the case on the balance of probability). The advocate for the plaintiff will make an opening speech outlining the issues, the evidence to be called and the applicable law. Evidence is then called, examined, cross-examined and re-examined for the plaintiff and then the defendant. The defendant normally makes the closing speech. With the court's consent the plaintiff may also be heard in closing.

Procedure before tribunals is technically in the hands of the chairperson of the particular tribunal (for example an employment tribunal or social security appeal tribunal) but again by convention tends to follow (with possibly less formality) the same pattern sketched out for civil trials above.

Once a case has been conducted to its conclusion further considerations may arise, in particular the implementation of orders, the enforcement of judgments and the issue of costs. The procedures relating to these points must be understood.

In constructing the plan therefore the advocate must be mindful of the way in which the proceedings will be conducted and the various stages that need to be completed.

Within these broad rules and guidelines, how do you construct a plan that fulfils the objectives of the individual advocacy task?

Planning the objectives of the task

Let us look at the civil litigation case study. We will presume for the present example that a writ or summons has been issued and that a trial has taken place. On the evidence the judge finds that Mr Slater was driving his car negligently and consequently is responsible for the injuries suffered by Daniel. The judge is not persuaded that Daniel is, in part, to blame for his own misfortune and no element of contributory negligence is upheld. An award of damages is assessed at £14,000. The advocate for Daniel would appear to have 'won'. The strategy of conducting the case to trial would appear to have proven successful.

There are, however, several further tasks that the advocate must complete, that should have been planned in advance. First, what about costs? The outcome of the case clearly indicates that Daniel was justified in bringing the action. Surely Mr Slater should bear Daniel's costs in consequence?

What are the advocacy implications here and how might B go about preparing for this task? We suggest that there are four elements to the advocacy plan which can be followed in each individual task, be it civil or criminal.

The elements are:

1   purpose;

2   framework;

3   theory; and

4   outcome.

By *purpose* we mean what the advocacy is meant to achieve. In our example B intends to make an application for costs to be paid by Mr Slater. The purpose is to obtain a court order compelling Mr Slater to pay an amount equivalent to what it has cost Daniel to bring the claim.

The *framework* in which the claim can be brought will determine how and to who the application will be made and what the claim can consist of. B therefore must discover what rules govern costs and orders for their payment.

What of the *theory*? We have seen the development of the theories of this case (Chapter 4, Research). We are now talking about the theory relating to the outcome of research for this particular advocacy task.

We will look up the relevant rules. If they say that a successful party to proceedings can seek costs against an opponent then our theory will be that Daniel is entitled to the payment of his costs (or such part of them as the court may allow – the theory will be shaped by the actual research findings). Remember that there are two aspects to theory. Each side will have its own version (whether articulated or not). Work out what the other side is likely to say in response and the theory that it is attempting to follow. Because B's theory relating to Mr Slater's negligence was well researched, the need for the further advocacy task (applying for costs) should have been predicted. B might have said to him or herself: 'If the court accepts that Mr Slater was driving negligently judgment will be given for Daniel in which case I must make an application for costs.' This preparation should therefore have been done in advance of the hearing.

The *outcome* is what is anticipated as a result of the testing of the theory and what B therefore expects to achieve. It is the realisation of the purpose.

The purpose of the advocacy task here is to get an order for costs against Mr Slater. What do the rules say? Look at the RSC and the CCR. RSC Order 62 and CCR Order 38 both state that the court has discretionary powers on the issue of costs. This is qualified by the expectation that 'costs follow the event', that is, they are awarded in favour of the 'winner' against the 'loser'. The rules specify situations when a party or their legal representatives can be ordered to pay costs, for example, where undue delay has been caused or where orders for costs have already been made against a party in an interlocutory hearing. B's theory might be, for example, that Mr Slater's solicitors have behaved in such a way that they should be personally liable. This could happen for example if adjournments were caused by their failure to get witnesses to court.

In legal aid cases, costs cannot be recovered against a legally aided party until the court has determined how much, if anything, the legally aided party should pay (Legal Aid Act 1988, section 17). In practice it is unusual for a legally aided party to be ordered to pay another party's costs. If B had lost the case, B's theory would be that it is unreasonable to make any cost order against Daniel's next friend. (Legal Aid will not be a consideration in most personal injury cases shortly – see Chapter 4).

Detailed rules apply to the definition of costs and to the calculation of allowable costs. Unless the court specifies the exact amount or the parties agree, the person in whose favour the order for costs is made is only entitled to costs that have been taxed. In the county court Order 38, rule 19 provides for costs to be awarded on either a standard or indemnity basis. The standard basis covers those costs reasonably incurred, with any element of doubt exercised in the payer's favour. The indemnity basis applies to all costs other than those unreasonably incurred with doubt being resolved in favour of the party who is receiving them. Authority shows that the standard basis should be used in all but exceptional cases (see *Billson v Residential Apartments* [1992] 2 WLR 15).

B's research also showed that costs in the county court are, according to Order 38, rule 3, assessed on the basis of scales. For cases such as Daniel's, where damages exceed £3,000, the appropriate scale is scale 2. This determines the amount allowable for each item claimed on taxation.

Armed with the results of the research B is in a position to prepare for the advocacy task. The purpose of this part of the hearing is clear – to apply for costs. The framework suggests that costs normally follow the event and as judgment will have been given in Daniel's favour costs should also be granted. The theory is that as 'loser' Mr Slater should be ordered to pay Daniel's costs. The outcome should therefore be an order for costs on the standard basis against Mr Slater.

Although it is unlikely that B would be asked by the court for authority for the proposition that Mr Slater should pay the costs (as the principle of costs following the event is well established) B must be prepared to produce this if needs be and the plan should encompass this possibility. B also needs to prepare this in advance of the trial itself, for an application for costs will usually follow the giving of the judgment.

If Daniel is legally aided this has further implications for the advocacy plan. If Daniel loses, Mr Slater's lawyers could make an application for costs. B must be prepared for this possibility and be ready with appropriate representations. B will know from his or her research that a legally aided person cannot be ordered to pay costs unless it is reasonable in the circumstances for him or her to do so. In practice this seldom occurs. What representations might B put forward? Daniel's inability to pay as evidenced by the fact that he is unable to afford to pay for his own legal expenses (he is after all in receipt of legal aid) should be persuasive. At least this would have been the case if Daniel had been over the age of 18. He is not though. His next friend is technically the one against whom the costs order could be made. Yet another research task has arisen. When can the next friend be ordered to pay costs? Why not look this up? CCR Order 10 will provide a starting-point.

Let us turn to Mrs Evans's case to see how to plan for advocacy. It is the process of planning that we are concerned with here rather than the range of tasks that might arise. The section entitled 'The stages in advocacy' on pp 426–465 looks in more detail at the different advocacy tasks.

Suppose that Mrs Evans eventually pleads guilty. She accepts that the £1 coins were found on her and she also accepts that she must have intended to take them. She is prepared to plead guilty on this basis and states the value of the money that she took was only £3. For the sake of argument let us say that the prosecution claim they also found 20 £5 notes in her pocket, and allege that she stole those too. Mrs Evans is prepared to accept that she stole some property but not everything the prosecution say she did. If the court is satisfied that some property was stolen, the actual value of the property would be immaterial to guilt. It may, however, make a difference in terms of sentencing. The court may take a much more serious view of say, £103 than £3, because of the amount and the repetitive, dishonest behaviour that must have been involved. The value itself may therefore be material. The theft of a few pounds is different from the theft of tens or hundreds.

If the prosecution and defence cannot agree on the value, then the court will accept a guilty plea, but may feel unable to proceed to sentence without hearing evidence as to the value stolen (if the value would affect sentence). The advocate for both prosecution and defence must be in a position to produce evidence to the court of the value of the theft. On the facts, the court would probably adjourn to another date to enable such evidence to be presented. In any event the advocates must be prepared to proceed down this route.

How would A prepare for such an advocacy task? First the preparation should be completed well in advance of the hearing. If Mrs Evans's intentions were known in advance of the hearing (which they should be unless she changes her plea during the course of the hearing) A can anticipate the complication described above. A knows from his or her factual research that the only evidence that the prosecution have relates to the theft of the coins found on Mrs Evans. The case theory has now been remoulded to show that Mrs Evans took the three £1 coins but nothing else. B has already seen copies of the prosecution evidence by way of advance disclosure and feels confident that the prosecution cannot prove the theft of any other property.

What is the purpose of the hearing? It is for the court to decide, before sentencing, the value of the property taken.

What is the legal framework within which that decision will be taken? Research is again called for. Case law states that where there is a substantial conflict on the facts of the offence the court must either accept the defence version or hear evidence of those facts (*R v Newton* (1982) 77 Cr App R 13). The prosecution bears the burden and standard of proof on the same basis as if the case involved the dispute of guilt. The rules of evidence apply. The court will then decide after hearing the evidence, whose version it prefers, but given the standard any doubt must be exercised in the defendant's favour.

A therefore will include in the advocacy plan the theory that the prosecution have no evidence of the theft of anything except the three coins. If necessary, A must examine Mrs Evans and any witnesses of fact on the point and cross-examine the prosecution witnesses. This will be explored under the heading 'Stages of advocacy; trial' (p 440).

Having identified the purpose and the framework, and having tested the theory, A would expect, if the evidence given comes up to proof, that the court would find that the value of the property was £3. A can then proceed to deliver a plea in mitigation on Mrs Evans's behalf. This is carried out later in the chapter.

Before turning to the individual advocacy tasks in litigation, what other considerations must the would-be advocate take into account?

Prove the facts

We have said throughout this book that careful planning is essential and involves theory supported by relevant facts and an accurate interpretation of the law.

Let us take the matter one stage further. Whilst your theory will be shaped by the available facts, in order for it to carry sufficient weight with the court – that is, for it to be accepted as the preferred and credible version of what allegedly happened – the facts must be proven, or the prosecution facts discredited.

An advocate must give careful thought to what can be proved and how that is to be established. The rules of evidence are both detailed and complex. In the litigation courses of the LPC and BVC you will encounter these rules. It is not the purpose to recount them here. Rather we are concerned to create a framework for advocacy tasks within which these rules operate.

Evidence can take several forms. The most important is oral evidence from a witness. This is usually referred to as 'witness testimony'. The evidence obtained by oral examination in court will be considered shortly. A witness needs to relate to the court, in a clear and concise manner, all relevant and admissible evidence consistent with the case theory. It is the advocate's task to elicit this evidence. The court will be asked in cases of conflicting evidence effectively to choose between one version and the other. The court may hold as a matter of fact that a certain event has occurred, thus 'proving' the fact at issue.

What the advocate has to do is to construct an account or story in which all the testimony is consistent with the facts alleged, as between all of the witnesses and in terms of overall credibility. Corroboration, for example, would be one way of supporting an asserted set of facts.

Evidence may also come in documentary form.

The production of a tangible item of evidence is normally referred to as real evidence and includes both written material and other property used as an exhibit in the case. This would include the marked coins to be produced at Mrs Evans's trial.

All of the evidence, whether in the form of testimony or real evidence, must be presented and delivered in a manner that lends credibility and consistency to the case. The theory is therefore acted out in court.

It may be, of course, that the theory is shown to have flaws in it. Unexpected evidence could emerge from the other side. (Although in many cases the existence of rules aimed at the disclosure of evidence may make this unlikely, for example the use of written statements for committal. If Mrs Evans's case reaches the Crown Court the committal papers will reveal the prosecution evidence.) A witness may simply not come up to proof or may be discredited in cross-examination. Unexpected evidence may, at best, require a readjustment of the theory, or at worst defeat the client's case. Better though to expect the unexpected and have a theory to meet it.

Bear in mind that your theory is unlikely to be perfect. It will be more like the best fit available. It will include potentially damaging parts, such as the finding of the coins in Mrs Evans's apron pocket; it will not deny the undeniable.

In attempting to prove fact, the advocate must be aware of the strength of evidence available and be able to monitor the progress of it during the trial.

Let us look at the facts to be proven in Mrs Evans's trial for theft. For the prosecution, the facts to be established are that:

1   Mrs Evans took or 'appropriated' property.

2   That property belonged to another (Mr O'Connor).

3   Mrs Evans intended to take the property.

4   Mrs Evans intended to deprive Mr O'Connor of the property permanently.

The *actus reus* of the offence of theft involves the taking of the property belonging to another, the *mens rea*, the dual intent of taking and depriving permanently.

The evidence called to establish these 'facts' consists of the testimony of Mr O'Connor, the two police officers and Mr O'Connor's son, Daniel.

For the defence, Mrs Evans will try to establish, through her own testimony, and perhaps that of her ex co-worker Ms Smith that:

1   The system of book-keeping in the shop was unreliable. (That is, the prosecution cannot show how much was taken, by whom and when.)

2   That in relation to the £1 coins Mrs Evans had no criminal intent.

Although all facts need to be proved, not all facts are in dispute. A witness may give evidence that is largely uncontested by the opposition. Thus Mr O'Connor may describe the working arrangements in the shop, the involvement of the police, the discovery of the coins and the subsequent dismissal of Mrs Evans. Little, if any of this, may be disputed. The facts here therefore set a scene, in which other facts can be judged. The evidence over missing money or book-keeping systems may be disputed in cross-examination and by the defence witnesses.

A good account of the general techniques in proving facts can be found in Thomas Mauet *Fundamentals of Trial Techniques*, which, while produced for the US market, gives a valuable insight into the successful conduct of court proceedings.

Establish the law

Law students learn at an early stage of the need for legal authority to be used to support submissions. Thus, if the test of *mens rea* concerns the concept of dishonesty, statute or case law specifying the rule or interpreting it must be used (see *R v Ghosh* [1982] QB 1053).

In terms of proof, the authoritative text should be produced in court. This means that either the Act or the law report should be available. So far as the latter is concerned, there is a preference for *The Law Reports* (produced by the Incorporated Council of Law Reporting), but others, for example the *All England Law Reports*, can be used where necessary.

There may of course be a dispute between the advocates on the interpretation of that law and its consequential application. The opening and/or closing speech can be used to develop arguments on legal submissions. Skeletal arguments are increasingly used to give both the advocates and the court advance warning of the legal arguments likely to be raised. Part of case preparation will be ensuring that skeletal arguments are prepared and distributed and the authorities available for the court to consult. The strength of your case is enhanced by the proper presentation of the law.

When citing authority the advocates should direct the court towards not only the case in question, but to the paragraph of the judgment on which the advocate relies. Each authority should be ready to hand with the appropriate section flagged. Legal authority, however persuasive, is of little consequence if it cannot be produced when needed.

6   The stages of advocacy

In this section we focus on the actual advocacy tasks that are likely to arise. In each instance we look at how you would plan that particular task and how it should be executed. We give examples of the presentation of particular tasks; ones that may well arise in your advocacy skills assessment.

Pre-trial

Although the advocate is most often associated with the conduct of trials, a considerable amount of time and skill is expended in pre-trial hearings. This is true of both civil and criminal cases. The pre-trial process involves specific advocacy tasks.

The criminal case

We saw on pp 413–417 the sort of issues that A must prepare for at the first hearing for Mrs Evans. Let us now return to the case.

Mrs Evans arrives at court with solicitor A. It is an important part of the prosecution case that Mrs Evans has confessed to the crime in her statement to the police. She remembers saying in her interview, 'I suppose I must have done it'. A needs to see a copy of what Mrs Evans is alleged to have said. This may be in the form of a statement written contemporaneously by the police as it was related by Mrs Evans or, as is more likely, in the form of a tape recorded interview (ROTI).

A therefore wishes to make an application for an adjournment to allow time for the prosecution to provide the information to which the defence is entitled and that A has requested (under the Magistrates' Court (Advance Information) Rules 1985).

How should the advocate prepare for this hearing? In such cases the defence solicitor makes a request of the CPS for the production of the information. The court must then be asked to adjourn to enable the information to be disclosed and for the solicitor to take the client's instructions on the contents.

Let us look at the four principles that guide preparation:

1   *What is the purpose of the hearing and what outcome is sought by the defence?* The court will expect to progress the case by finding out; can it hear the case (mode of trial)? If not, can it commit to the Crown court? If it can hear the matter, is the plea guilty? (An indication of plea is now taken before a mode of trial decision on offences triable either way – Criminal Procedure and Investigations Act 1996, section 49. This is not the plea itself but an indication in the event of the matter proceeding to trial. Unless the accused requests otherwise the indication of a guilty plea will be taken as a guilty plea and the court can proceed to sentencing). If yes, can it proceed to sentence? If no, can the trial be held? If the case is to be adjourned should bail be granted? Is there a legal aid application to be made? Any of these stages may occur subject to the readiness of the prosecution and defence and of the court itself. These are the various purposes of the first hearing. A expects to secure the adjournment.

2   *What is the legal framework at this stage?* There are a multitude of legal rules that lay down the framework for the various issues that might arise at this hearing. Given the different possibilities set out above A would have to be aware of:

   ☐   The operational rules of the court, found principally in the Magistrates' Courts Act 1980. When, for example, can a court adjourn a case?

   ☐   The rules on mode of trial found in the 1980 Act and the Practice Note [1990] 1 WLR 1439.

   ☐   The entitlement to advance disclosure of the prosecution case. A may have to advise the court of his or her right to this information in order to secure the adjournment. As we have seen, the law is to be found in the Magistrates' Court (Advance Information) Rules 1985.

☐ The provisions affecting offences that are triable either way, particularly when a defendant can elect Crown Court trial and the procedures governing committal. These are found in the Magistrates' Courts Act 1980.

☐ The rules that govern sentencing. These are found in a variety of statutes and cases, principally the Criminal Justice Act 1991.

☐ The law on bail. This is contained in the Bail Act 1976 and subsequent case law.

☐ Legal aid. The Legal Aid Act 1988 sets out the relevant provisions.

The list is long. It is highly unlikely that all will apply at the first hearing. Because A does not yet know what will happen at that hearing the advocacy planning exercise must take into account the various possibilities.

We will look in greater detail at the legal framework as the need arises in each advocacy task.

3   *What is A's theory at this stage?* On present instructions A knows that Mrs Evans intends to plead not guilty to the charges. A also knows that the defence have a right to advance disclosure and the court must recognise this. It follows, therefore, that if A has been diligent in the conduct of the case, in that an application for advance disclosure has been made at the earliest opportunity, the court will be bound to adjourn the case so that the papers can be delivered by the prosecution and the client's instructions taken. The theory therefore supports the view that the adjournment should be granted. A must, however, be prepared to deal with questions from the court on why an adjournment should be granted and to know what to do were the adjournment to be denied.

In the unlikely event of the request being refused A should be prepared to deal with mode of trial. A's research has shown that the client has the right to trial at the Crown Court and the client could simply make this election.

A might also be mindful of an application for judicial review if the court rode roughshod over Mrs Evans's rights and the process was thereby defective.

A's plan has been formulated. Perhaps it sounds extravagant to prepare such a detailed plan for such a relatively straightforward task. We believe that the plan is an essential part of advocacy, even if it is not articulated as such by the more experienced advocate. The more experienced you become the easier the preparation for advocacy should be although the preparatory process is the same. You just get better at it.

We can now move on to the performance of this pre-trial advocacy task. In the final section of this chapter we look at the technnique of persuasion. For now we will simply recite the performance based on the preparatory work.

At the hearing the clerk to the court would ask Mrs Evans for her name and address (or ask her whether she is Mrs Evans of such and such an address), and then read out the charge or charges that she faces. This is to open the proceedings. Thus, the case may begin like this:

Clerk: Call case number 46, Winifred Evans.

(*Mrs Evans is ushered into the dock.*)

Clerk: Are you Winifred Evans of 6 Manor Close, Sheffield?

Mrs Evans: Yes.

Clerk (*who is unaware of the virtues and principles of plain English*)*:* Mrs Evans, you are charged first that on the 1st day of September 1998 you dishonestly appropriated property namely three £1 coins belonging to one Andrew O'Connor, intending to permanently deprive him of the same, contrary to section 1 of the Theft Act 1968 and secondly that between 1st March and 1st September 1994 you dishonestly appropriated property namely £545 belonging to the said Andrew O'Connor, intending to permanently deprive him of the same, also contrary to section 1 of The Theft Act 1968. Do you understand?

Mrs Evans: Er, Yes.

Clerk: Are we in a position to proceed?

Prosecution advocate: I understand that there is an application from A (the defence solicitor).

A should have forewarned the prosecutor and the court clerk of his or her intention to make an application for an adjournment. It oils the machinery of justice.

In this instance A may make the following submission. We presume that the court consists of a bench of three magistrates, the chairperson being a woman:

A: Madam, my name is A. I appear on behalf of Mrs Evans. May she be seated?

Magistrate: Sit down, Mrs Evans.

A: This is a case where the defence needs advance disclosure of the prosecution evidence against my client. An application has been made for such disclosure to the Crown Prosecution Service and I am told by my friend for the prosecution that the information will be disclosed within the next seven days. In order for this to be effected and so that I will have the opportunity of taking my client's instructions, I ask for this matter to be adjourned for, say, 21 days, by which time the defence should be in a position to proceed to mode of trial.

This is a clear and reasoned argument which the court will undoubtedly accept. Contained in the submission are several pieces of information, including the reason for the adjournment, an assurance that matters have already been set in motion, an estimate of the time that will be necessary for matters to proceed and a prediction that once this has occurred progress will then be able to be made.

At this juncture A may have other matters which he or she needs to raise with the court. A might continue:

A: Mrs Evans presently appears on police bail. I would respectfully submit that unconditional bail is suitable in this case. Whilst the offences charged are serious, there is nothing to suggest that Mrs Evans will commit further offences, interfere with witnesses or fail to surrender to bail. She has attended court today and has a settled address in Sheffield where she lives with her family and has done so for the past five years.

A flags up the fact that objections to the grant of bail would be contested. A's actual bail application would come after prosecution objections. On the other hand A may know (from discussions with the advocate for the prosecution) that bail will not be opposed, in which case A simply says: 'Mrs Evans appears on police bail and I ask for unconditional bail to be granted to her today'. There is more:

> **A** (*continues*)**:** Finally, Madam, there is the question of legal aid. An application has been submitted to your learned clerk, who will no doubt advise me before the end of today's hearing of the outcome of that application.
>
> Those are my applications, Madam.
>
> **Clerk** (*turning to the bench*)**:** I can advise you, Madam, that I am in a position to confirm the grant of legal aid. (*Addressing the prosecution*) Does the prosecution have any observations on the issue of bail?
>
> **Prosecution advocate:** I have already indicated to my friend for the defence that the prosecution has no objection in principle to the grant of bail. However, theft from an employer is a serious matter and to ensure that the defendant attends at court on any adjourned date the prosecution would ask for bail to be made conditional upon the defendant continuing to live at her present address.
>
> **A** (*who has already taken instructions from the client on bail and possible conditions*)**:** I have no objection to conditional bail in those terms, Madam, if the court feels that such a condition is in fact necessary in view of the provisions of the Bail Act.

(Although no satisfactory ground has been made out for refusing bail under the Act, A makes no objection to this condition as it is not onerous. We will look at the issue of bail generally and the imposition of conditions in particular, later, in the bail advocacy task.)

> **Chairperson of magistrates** (*having consulted her colleagues on the bench*)**:** Very well, please stand up Mrs Evans. Your case will be adjourned until the 5th of November 1998 to enable your solicitor to obtain details from the prosecution of the case against you. You must contact your solicitor as soon as this information is available so he (or she) can discuss the case further with you. You are granted conditional bail, the condition being that you must continue to live at 6 Manor Close, Sheffield unless the court otherwise agrees that you may live elsewhere. This condition is imposed to ensure that you can be contacted and that you attend court on the adjourned date. I must remind you that it is a criminal offence to fail to answer to your bail. Do you understand?
>
> **Mrs Evans:** Yes, thank you.
>
> **Magistrate:** You may leave.
>
> (*The parties then leave court.*)

There was no real contest in this scenario. The court and the two advocates were following a routine coloured only by Mrs Evans's name and brief details of the case. The application could, however, have been very different. Let us suppose that Mrs Evans had appeared from custody having been charged with the two alleged thefts and having been refused police bail (despite representations having been made by A at the police station). The police have produced Mrs Evans in court from custody. Once the application for the adjournment has been made, on the same grounds as before, the prosecution will normally make submissions if they object to the grant of bail.

We are now concerned with a bail application that is opposed. This is a new advocacy task. How does A go about preparing this? Again we use the four-point plan.

1   *Purpose of hearing*: to determine whether Mrs Evans should be remanded in custody or released on bail (conditional or unconditional).

2   *Legal framework:* Bail Act 1976 and case law. Court must grant unconditional bail unless it is satisfied that there are substantial grounds for believing that the defendant would fail to surrender to custody, commit an offence whilst on bail or interfere with witnesses. Bail can be refused or be made conditional only if the terms of the Act are satisfied. A list of factors relevant to the three grounds for refusing unconditional bail is set out in Schedule 1. Two full bail applications can be made but no more, unless there is a new circumstance that was not brought to the court's attention at the time of the previous application.

3   *The theory:* can be viewed from two aspects. First, A believes from the legal and factual research that bail should be granted as Mrs Evans has no history of failing to surrender to custody or of committing other offences whilst on bail. On the evidence available to A she is unlikely to interfere with witnesses or contravene any provision of the Act. However, the prosecution theory could be that she might abscond given the possibility of a custodial sentence. A must be able to counter this; for example, Mrs Evans is settled with her family in the local area and is very unlikely to fail to surrender to custody if granted bail. Although the offence is serious, it is not so serious that prison is the only possible outcome if she is convicted.

4   *The outcome:* A will seek to persuade the court that none of the reasons for refusing bail can be upheld or if the court does have concerns about the possibility of Mrs Evans absconding they could impose conditions to make this less likely.

A's plan for this advocacy task is therefore based on a sound understanding of the law and procedure relating to bail coupled with sufficient factual research to back up the submissions to be made. For example, if there is a real danger of the court concluding that Mrs Evans may abscond A should be prepared to produce evidence of the client's links with the locality (for example, in different circumstances, a letter from an employer) or details of a person willing to act as surety (who could be asked to come to court to give evidence of suitability).

For the purposes of our example we presume that Mrs Evans does have previous convictions. These include an offence of dishonesty when she was a juvenile (shop-lifting) and a recent offence of criminal damage which was the result of a matrimonial disagreement, for which she was fined.

The prosecution have outlined their objections to bail by raising the seriousness of the offence (a breach of trust) and the fact that a custodial sentence is possible especially as she has a recent history of offending. This in their view increases the chances of Mrs Evans absconding.

A might properly say:

> My friend has outlined prosecution objections to bail in this case. There is of course a statutory presumption in favour of bail and this should only be rebutted if there are substantial grounds, and I emphasise the word substantial, for believing that Mrs Evans would fail to surrender to bail or might commit other offences or interfere with other witnesses.
>
> It is conceded that theft from an employer is a very serious matter and one that could ultimately attract a custodial sentence. It is my submission that such an outcome in this case is in fact unlikely. Mrs Evans is 46 years old and is a married woman who lives a settled family life in Sheffield. She is a well respected member of her community. Her children attend the local school and her husband works in local industry. Whatever the eventual outcome of this case, in my respectful submission, the court would be looking for a non-custodial sentence. My client has appeared in court today and whilst this matter causes her grave discomfort and embarrassment, she maintains her innocence and is determined to resist these charges to the end.
>
> Although she does have one previous conviction for dishonesty, that was many years ago when she was a juvenile, and should not in my view be used against her in this instance. The only other conviction, whilst relatively recent, was the result of an isolated incident, following a domestic disagreement when a window was broken. This too in my submission should not affect a decision on bail today as it does not – being an unrelated offence – increase the risk of custody.
>
> My application is for unconditional bail. Your Worships, do I need to address you on the question of conditions?
>
> [*If the answer is yes, as it is likely to be, then A continues as follows:*]
>
> If Your Worships are concerned with the likelihood of Mrs Evans absconding it would be possible to limit this risk by the imposition of conditions, such as residence, or if necessary, reporting to a police station. Mrs Evans's aunt, who is in court this morning, would be prepared to act as surety in this case. She has investments totalling over £10,000 and is in full-time employment. If Your Worships consider the imposition of conditions necessary I would respectfully submit that a condition of residence or reporting or the imposition of a surety would minimise any risk. It must be said that the risk is, in my submission, low. In any event, I would respectfully remind the court that the statutory right is to unconditional bail unless the provisions of the Bail Act apply; that is, you have substantial grounds for thinking, for example, that Mrs Evans will abscond.
>
> Finally, Madam, I should point out that Mrs Evans has never failed to attend court in the past and has never committed offences whilst on bail. Neither has she ever been implicated in the interference with witnesses. These were not raised by way of objection by the prosecution.
>
> I would invite you, Madam, therefore to grant bail in this case. Unless the court has any questions of me, that is my application.

Similar considerations to those raised on the application for the adjournment and in the bail application can arise at other stages in criminal cases, for example, when determining venue, or at any committal hearing. For instance, A will have to decide, if the case is to be heard by the Crown Court, whether to require a committal hearing with consideration of the evidence, or whether the case can be dealt with without, under the Magistrates' Courts Act 1980, section 6(2). These matters will be examined in your criminal litigation course. In each instance the lawyer should prepare for the advocacy task in the way that we have indicated.

What of pre-trial matters in civil proceedings?

The civil case

Proceedings differ in detail as between county court and High Court but are to a large extent similar and complementary.

Once proceedings have been issued a timetable of events becomes activated. Procedural deadlines have long existed in civil litigation to give each party to litigation a base line from which to work, for example, time to file a claim, a defence or a counter claim.

Greater impetus has recently been added to this procedure by the introduction of a specific timetable and automatic directions in county court actions. The idea behind these changes was to speed up the judicial process and cut backlogs.

Two points can be made at the outset. First, in civil litigation generally pre-trial procedures centre on applications to, and hearings before, the District Judge or Master. Some administrative matters can be made in written form without the need to attend (for example issuing a writ or entering judgment in default of a defence). Applications to the court (for example an application to set aside judgment) are heard in chambers and are referred to as interlocutory applications in the county court, and interlocutory summonses in the High Court. The purpose of these pre-trial procedures is to facilitate progress towards trial (or settlement) by concentrating attention on the issues in conflict and by ensuring that each party is aware of all relevant material. If a trial does follow the parties should be in a position to proceed without adjournments and the court should possess all of the case details. It is therefore an enabling and vetting procedure.

Secondly, in many cases, including personal injuries, directions are now automatic and do not need a specific court order to advance the case (for example the service of medical reports, the discovery of documents, exchange of witness statements or the setting down for hearing). Any additional directions required can be sought at a directions hearing if necessary.

What advocacy skills are therefore called for at this stage? We return to the key words – the 3 P's – used earlier: preparation, presentation and persuasion, along with control.

Let us look at our personal injury case study to see how the advocate might conduct the case and what skills may be utilised. We will say that the action is started in the local county court. The summons has been issued (CCR Order 3, rule 1). In accordance with Order 6, rule 1, B has also filed the medical report and statement of special damage.

If B is to prepare, present and persuade, and exercise the necessary control what must be done? First B must be aware of the timetable of events. This will provide the general framework for the conduct of the case and can be simply put as follows:

■ Plaintiff issues proceedings (summons, particulars of claim, medical report, special damages calculation).

■ Plaintiff or court serves summons (within four months).

■ Defendant files defence and/or counter-claim (within 14 days).

■ If appropriate: plaintiff files reply or defence to counter claim (within 14 days).

■ Pleadings close (14 days after service of defence or reply or defence to counter-claim).

■ Discovery of documents (within 28 days of close of pleadings).

■ Exchange of experts' reports and written statements (within ten weeks of close of pleadings).

■ Plaintiff sets action down for trial (within 6 months of close of pleadings; automatically struck out if not set down within 15 months).

■ Trial.

■ Judgment.

According to this timetable if Mr Slater or his solicitors do not file a defence within 14 days, B is at liberty to enter judgment on Daniel's behalf. Whilst this may appear to be a short-term victory – Daniel has won – it is likely to be followed by an application to set judgment aside. This results in more work for everyone and possibly a worsening of relationships prejudicing negotiation prospects. (In the alternative it might show that B is a formidable opponent with a strong BATNA – see Chapter 6, Negotiation). Before taking such steps B may prefer to contact Mr Slater's solicitor (if known) to advise him or her that judgment will be entered if a defence is not filed by a certain deadline. Nonetheless B may properly enter judgment if progress cannot otherwise be made. If a defence is filed then the timetable of events proceeds.

Where no defence is entered Daniel can succeed by default. There is no advocacy to be performed at this stage, for the entering of judgment in default of a defence is an administrative step only and does not require a hearing. This is, instead, a drafting task. Research will be needed to check on the legal and procedural requirements. B finds out that CCR Order 9, rule 6 covers the entering of judgment in default.

Some discrete advocacy tasks do, however, emerge from the pre-trial preparations. If the procedure is not governed by automatic directions B must formally apply to the court for the order that he or she wishes. What if Mr Slater does enter a defence but B considers that the defence does not contain legally relevant grounds or contains insufficent detail for B to be certain what the exact justification is for defending the action? Having researched the matter B may decide to apply to the court to have the defence struck out or at the very least apply for further and better particulars of the defence.

How does B prepare for this advocacy task? We can use the formula demonstrated in the criminal case – purpose, framework, theory and outcome.

Purpose   The court is being asked to rule that the defence filed is no defence at all (legally) and should be disgarded or that further details of the defence should be provided.

Framework   B's research will show that striking out a pleading is governed in the county court by Order 13, rule 5. This rule details the circumstances under which this may occur and includes the failure of the pleading to disclose a defence that is known to the law. This is a question of law and not fact. The application must be made to the district judge on notice, that is, allowing the other side to attend and make representations. The procedure was discussed in *Williams and Humbert v W & H Trade Marks (Jersey)* [1986] AC 368.

If in the alternative B considers that there is a defence but insufficient details are revealed, he or she can apply for further and better particulars of it with a court order specifying that the defendant be debarred from defending if the particulars requested are not provided. CCR Order 6, rule 7 and Order 9, rule 11 cover this application. The request is in fact made in writing to the other side and, if it is not complied with, the application is made to the court for an order compelling the defendant to provide the details sought.

B should consider in either of the examples given asking the court to impose a strict time limit within which certain matters must be filed (the amended defence or the further and better particulars) and to seek costs from the defendant for the hearing itself (which was necessitated by the defendant's actions or inactions) (CCR Order 38).

Which course of action should B follow and why? We need to add some facts to the civil case to illustrate the point. We can then go on to look at the performance of the advocacy task. Presume for the present that Mr Slater is unrepresented and files a defence that states that Mr Slater did not mean to collide with Daniel and what happened was not Mr Slater's fault. Although it refers to the accident it does not contain any denial of negligence. B may consider, on the basis of Order 13, rule 5, that there is no defence as negligence is not disputed. Intent is not a pre-requisite to liability. The test of negligence is an objective one. B needs to prepare for an application (that may well be contested) to strike out the pleading.

In the alternative, the defence may contain a blanket denial of negligence but does not give any specific detail as to what Mr Slater says happened on the day of the accident. There may well be a defence at law, but B requires further and better particulars of it. For example, if Mr Slater has said he was travelling at a reasonable speed along High Street, B may ask for details of the exact speed that Mr Slater says he was travelling.

It is likely in practice that the request for futher and better particulars will have been made in advance of any application to the court. B might expect to justify the application (that is, being able to say why the details are required), but also should expect to have allowed the defendant a reasonable time in which to provide the details. Let us assume that B has asked for this detail in writing and Mr Slater has not replied.

In either instance, B must apply to the court and prepare for the advocacy task that follows.

Theory   What is B's theory underpinning the advocacy? The legal framework says that a defence that reveals no substance can be struck out. The defence appears to B to fail to contain a denial of liability. An application to strike out can therefore be justified.

In the alternative, the defence is imprecise or provides insufficient detail. The theory is that B is entitled to know the factual case being mounted by the defendant and is entitled to further and better particulars.

What about the defence theory? On the question of whether there is a defence at all B might predict that Mr Slater will take legal advice and that his representatives may resist the application on the ground that the defence should be amended. It would be a hard judge that allowed an unrepresented party to suffer the consequences of his or her ignorance. B must be alert to this possibility.

The outcome   B is confident as a result of his or her research that the application for the defence to be struck out is well founded, subject to the likelihood that Mr Slater may be allowed to amend the defence, particularly if he is now legally represented. The application for further and better particulars is supported by B's legal and factual research. To illustrate the process, we have B deciding to pursue only the striking out application.

We presume that B has drafted the notice of application correctly. Chapter 5 deals with drafting. B can now plan the content of his or her submissions. The outline of the plan might read as follows:

1   *Introduction*: As it is B's application, B is the first to address the court. As a matter of courtesy B should be prepared to introduce the parties or representatives to the district judge.

2   *Case outline:* B must tell the judge what the case is about (that is the overall case, not just today's application). This should be briefly put, but with enough detail to set the scene.

3   *Specify the order:* The judge should be told what order the plaintiff seeks.

4   *Specify the material facts:* The facts surrounding the application must be related, for example a defence was filed on a particular date, or a request for further and better particulars was made, and when.

5   *Give the legal authority:* B should explain the legal justification for the order(s) sought citing the appropriate order, statute or case.

6   *Request the order:* B should conclude with a request for the order(s).

7   *Listen and note the defendant's submissions:* As the defendant will be given the opportunity to respond B should take a careful note of what is said and be prepared to reply accordingly. Although hearings in chambers are relatively informal each side must be given a fair hearing under the principles of natural justice.

8   *Respond if necessary:* B should be prepared to answer any questions the court may ask. This involves complete familiarity with the facts of the case and a clear understanding of the applicable law.

9   *Other matters:* Ancillary issues such as costs should be covered. If the application is successful other requests might be made, for example, that judgment be entered and that damages be assessed at a later hearing.

10   *Record the decision*: B should write down what the court decides including the exact wording of any order.

One final preparatory point can be made. These hearings do not operate in a vacuum. It is likely that both sides will meet before the hearing either whilst waiting to be called in before the district judge or as a result of a pre-arranged meeting to discuss the matter. Use this as an opportunity to discuss common ground. An order may be agreed by consent obviating the need for a contest but not the need for the preparation. Prepare a negotiating strategy if you expect this to occur (see Chapter 6).

How might such an application be presented?

The following dialogue could take place:

Usher (*showing the parties into the district judge's chambers*)*:* McAuley and Slater, Mr (Ms) B for the plaintiff and the defendant in person.

District judge: Good morning, please take a seat.

B: Good morning, Sir, I appear for the plaintiff Daniel McAuley, Mr Slater appears today unrepresented.

District judge: Yes. (*To Mr Slater*) Have you consulted a solicitor in this matter?

Mr Slater: No, I cannot afford one.

District judge: That is clearly a matter for you but you are aware that Legal Aid could be available to you [or perhaps a conditional fee arrangement once Legal Aid is largely removed from personal injury cases]?

Mr Slater: I don't know much about that.

District judge: I must say that it may well be in your interests to see a solicitor who can advise you about these matters. First we will hear from Mr (Ms) B and then I will hear what you have to say. You might consider then whether you need to take legal advice. Yes, Mr (Ms) B?

B: Thank you, Sir. This is an action alleging negligence against the defendant following a road traffic accident in which the plaintiff was injured. Particulars of claim were filed on 23rd January of this year detailing the claim. A defence was filed by the defendant on 14th February. It is my respectful submission, Sir, that the defence reveals no defence known to the law.

The order I seek, Sir, is that the defence be struck out and judgment be entered for the plaintiff as claimed with damages to be assessed.

I rely, Sir, on Order 13 rule 5 of the County Court Rules which allows for a pleading to be struck out if it discloses no reasonable defence. This is, Sir, a legal and not factual matter. If I may draw your attention to the defence, you will note, Sir, that the defendant pleads in the first paragraph that he did not intend to collide with the plaintiff. He neither denies his involvement in the accident nor gives any account of the accident that would suggest that he contests the allegation of negligence. Sir, it is a well-known principle of tortious liability that negligence does not depend on motive or intent, but rather on behaviour objectively viewed.

In my respectful submission I would say that the defence clearly reveals no substance. The defendant has not countered the allegation of negligence. I ask therefore for an order that the defence be struck out and that judgment be entered for the plaintiff, with damages to be assessed.

District judge: Mr Slater, you have heard the application, what do you have to say?

There then follows an explanation by Mr Slater that demonstrates that he does not fully understand the implications of his pleaded defence but that he believes that the accident was not his fault.

> *District judge:* I have the power today to strike out the defence as requested if it fails to disclose a defence at law. I am of the opinion that the defence is lacking in this respect but I am also mindful that the defendant is not represented. I have to say that I find it difficult to understand why someone in your position did not take legal advice and I am considering offering you the opportunity to take advice. Do you have any observations, Mr (Ms) B?

> *B:* Sir, you have heard my submissions. In my view the defence is wholly inadequate and could be properly struck out. I recognise, Sir, that this is a matter for you but I would endorse the fact that the defendant has had the chance to seek legal advice and would appear not to have done so. Indeed this was made quite clear in my letter before action which you may wish to see. If on balance you do decide to allow the defendant to take legal advice I would ask, Sir, that you impose a strict time limit for the filing of any amended defence failing which judgment be entered for the plaintiff. I also ask for an order for costs against the defendant in respect of this hearing in any event.

> *District judge:* Very well, Mr Slater, I am prepared to dismiss this application, but I order that an amended defence must be filed within 21 days of today, failing which you will be debarred from defending this action. The costs of today's hearing will be the plaintiff's in any event. I would urge you to see a solicitor without delay. Are you insured, Mr Slater? If so you should ask your insurance company to deal with it. Do you understand?

> *Mr Slater:* Yes.

The parties leave the district judge's chambers.

What were the important points in this performance? First, B presented the application in a structured and clear way, giving the material facts and relevant law. Once the issue of Mr Slater's lack of representation was made, B made the point that the judge had the power to make the order as sought, but then covered the other possible contingencies by asking for time limits and costs.

The fact that Mr Slater was unrepresented might be thought to give B an advantage. But if B is well prepared the existence of a legal opponent should make no difference. It could be said that the court was more lenient in this case than it would otherwise have been.

The advocacy task here was relatively straightforward. The principles of good preparation and the use of a plan are, we suggest, the same even in more complex cases.

A further example of civil pre-trial advocacy can now be given. We do not intend to work through the example with the dialogue before the court but the process to be followed in terms of systematic preparation can be seen.

In the county court the scope for applications, or directions appointments, has since 1990 been limited due to the introduction of automatic directions. A timetable setting out the stages in the litigation process applies to nearly all county court actions. As already seen this covers discovery, expert evidence, exchange of witness statements and trial details (CCR Order 17, rule 11). These provisions cover routine matters likely to arise in a case such as Daniel's. There is, however, nothing to prevent an application being made for an order for directions if the automatic directions are considered inappropriate or inadequate. In the High Court directions appointments are more common, although automatic directions apply in personal injury cases such as ours (RSC Order 25, rule 8).

When might B decide to make an application for directions and what considerations in terms of advocacy must be taken into account?

Discovery is an important stage in the litigation process. This is where each side reveals to the other the existence of documents which have been in their possession or control. According to the automatic directions this should be carried out within 28 days of the close of pleadings.

In personal injury cases there is no automatic discovery on the defendant's part. Therefore if B does want to see certain documents an application must be made for discovery. Let us say that one of B's theories is that Mr Slater's car was in poor condition at the time of the accident and B wants to see if there was a valid MOT certificate in existence. The request is made to Mr Slater's solicitors for this and a copy of the service record of the car. Although willing in principle to reveal this information (perhaps knowing that it would be likely to be ordered by the court on application in any event) Mr Slater's solicitors tell B that their client canot find the documents that B has requested. B decides therefore to try to obtain copies from the garage where Mr Slater has his car serviced. (The name is volunteered by Mr Slater's lawyers.) The garage does not respond to B's request.

The preparation of this task can follow the previous pattern:

■ *Purpose:* To obtain a court order for discovery compelling the garage to disclose the documents.

■ *Framework:* Section 53 of the County Courts Act 1984 allows for disclosure of documents by non-parties in cases involving death or personal injuries. Any document must be relevant to the proceedings. The procedure is set out in RSC Order 24, rule 7A(2) by virtue of CCR Order 13, rule 7. The application is made on notice and must be supported by an affidavit. Costs are normally awarded against the applicant in respect of the hearing and of the production of the document. B makes a point of obtaining legal aid authorisation (while legal aid still exists in such cases!) for this step. (This would not include the payment of the garage's costs.)

■ *Theory:* The content of the records will deal with the condition of the car. The condition is material to negligence in that it will support or refute the allegation that Mr Slater properly maintained the car. There is no reason why the records should not be revealed.

■ *Outcome:* B is confident that he or she can persuade the court of the need for the records. The costs that may well be awarded against Daniel would be limited to that hearing and the ancillary expense of producing the records. B could make representations that the garage pay the costs in any event. If a report can be obtained by court order why should it not be revealed voluntarily? (See *Hall v Wandsworth Health Authority* (1985) 82 LSG 1329.)

When addressing the court B would give the reasons for the application, the legal authority giving the court the power to make the order and arguments against the order for costs being made.

Pre-trial advocacy in civil cases can arise in many other situations. What if B decided to raise interrogatories asking about the way Mr Slater maintained his vehicle? An application for an order to strike out for failure to answer interrogatories could be made (Order 14, rule 12). What if the particulars of claim need to be amended in the light of new evidence, such as negligence in maintaining the car's brakes? Leave to amend may be required in which case B would have to apply to the court (CCR Order 7, rule 17). What if there was a payment into court by Mr Slater's insurers and B was instructed to accept? An application for a payment out would have to be made because Daniel is a minor (CCR Order 11).

In each case B must identify the purpose for the hearing, the legal framework applicable, the theory behind the application and the outcome sought. The advocate must always have the 'Green Book' and 'White Book' available to check the exact legal requirements.

The skill of the advocate is therefore relevant throughout the pre-trial procedure from the writing of the letter before action to the day of the trial itself.

Trial

We have now reached the point that most people, including students, might understandably think of as advocacy. What are the skills relevant to the trial of cases?

We use trial in a very broad sense here to include not only a contest of prosecutor against defence, or plaintiff against defendant, but also other hearings where guilt or liability are not at issue. We are looking at the final disposal of a case (short of a re-trial or an appeal).

The skills of the advocate are underpinned by thorough and careful preparation of the case and compliance with the various procedural requirements. There is little virtue in Mrs Evans's solicitor or Daniel's barrister being the most impressive advocates in the business, if the lead-up to the trial is in some way tarnished or defective. At best, a trial advocate will have a much harder job to do, and at worst, the case will be fatally flawed.

It is worth summarising in the form of a checklist what must be done in broad terms where a case goes to trial. So far as our criminal case is concerned this list is a relatively short one:

1   Court date obtained for trial.

2   Client and witnesses advised of hearing date.

3   Client's and witness' proofs finalised and where relevant disclosed.

4   Legal aid obtained or extended to cover trial and any disbursements.

5   Witness statements received from CPS and in order.

6   Antecedents received from police. Is client in breach of any court order?

7   Counsel briefed if appropriate. Counsel's opinion sought if relevant.

8   Witness summonses issued if appropriate.

9   Trial plan drafted based on best theory and strategy for conducting trial.

It is the construction of the trial plan that is the foundation for the criminal case. The formation of the plan started in Chapter 4 (Research skills). It must now be continued by focusing on the specific elements of the trial: the opening speech (where relevant), the examination-in-chief, cross-examination, and the closing speech. The plan must be supported by the theory of the case. The preparation must target all aspects of the trial within the context of that theory.

The strategy to be adopted will depend on a variety of factors. The skills of the advocate are concerned not only with careful preparation and in-depth knowledge but also an assessment of the tactics needed for the presentation of the case.

How far should the defence in Mrs Evans's case attempt to discredit Mr O'Connor, one of the main prosecution witnesses? Will such an approach achieve the desired effect when the theory of the case centres on Mrs Evans's lack of *mens rea*? Attacking the credibility of Mr O'Connor (on the basis of the existence of previous convictions for dishonesty) may be of little value unless it has direct relevance for Mrs Evans (for example the till was 'light' owing to Mr O'Connor's intermeddling rather than Mrs Evans's actions). Careful thought must be given to this issue, for the court is likely to be unimpressed by the impugning of a witness for the sake of it as well as triggering the loss of the 'shield' against cross-examination of Mrs Evans on her record.

The checklist in a civil case might read as follows:

1   Are the pleadings in order and up to date (including the medical report and special damages calculation)?

2   Is discovery complete? Have reports and witness statements been exchanged?

3   Has a bundle of documents been agreed by the respective sides and paginated and submitted to the court?

4   Have all court orders and automatic directions been complied with?

5   Has counsel been briefed and is a conference necessary?

6   Have witness summonses or subpoenas been issued and served?

7   If legal aid has been granted are there any limitations on the certificate and if so have these been removed?

8   Has the client and have the witnesses been advised of, and prepared for, the trial?

9   Are any further negotiations possible or desirable?

10   Are there sufficient copies of all documents on file for counsel, the other solicitors, the court and witnesses?

11 Are any draft orders that may be made prepared on file in readiness for judgment or possible settlement?

12 Are special and general damage calculations complete? (Can they be agreed?)

13 Are authorities (case and statute) available?

14 Is the trial plan, based on best theory and coupled with trial strategy, in place?

We will presume that both solicitor A for Mrs Evans, and solicitor B for Daniel McAuley, are ready to go to trial. What advocacy skills come into play at the trial itself? The same four guiding principles apply: purpose, framework, theory and outcome.

We concentrate in this section on the criminal trial. Other than for some procedural and evidential differences the same process can be followed in the civil case if that were to reach the trial stage.

■ *Purpose:* This time we will presume that the criminal trial is taking place in the magistrates' court. The purpose of the hearing is to decide on the guilt or innocence of Mrs Evans. If found guilty, the court's purpose will be to sentence her.

■ *Framework:* The prosecution must prove beyond all reasonable doubt that the defendant is guilty (see Chapter 4 for an analysis of the elements of guilt here). In this case the proof would relate to the *actus reus* (the appropriation of property belonging to another) and the *mens rea* (acting dishonestly with the intention to permanently deprive). The specific rules regulating the trial of cases before magistrates are contained principally in the Magistrates' Courts Act 1980. The rules governing the giving of evidence are laid down by both statute and case law. A familiarity with all of these provisions is essential in the preparation for and conduct of a trial.

■ *Theory:* We have already seen (Chapter 4) the theories that underpin Mrs Evans's case. The best theory is that she had no intention to take the three £1 coins (no *mens rea*) and that there is no sustainable prosecution evidence of the theft by Mrs Evans of any other property (no *actus reus*). The prosecution theory is presumably that the circumstantial evidence imputes intent in respect of the coins; and the opportunity to steal, coupled with the evidence of the missing money, is enough to establish guilt in respect of the £545. The preparation of the defence case must concentrate on casting maximum doubt on these theories.

■ *Outcome:* If the theory holds up Mrs Evans must be acquitted. B may need to readjust the theory as the case unfolds and the evidence is given. Were Mrs Evans to be successful an order for costs might be sought. (If on legal aid this will be application for costs equal to her contribution.)

Against this general plan we can look at each stage of the trial to identify the discrete advocacy tasks within it.

Remember that if you are the advocate, as a solicitor or barrister, your task is to unfold a story, one that the court can accept or one the court prefers, as against other versions. This story must be related by the advocate in four stages. First, the scene is set through the opening speech. As mentioned before, the purpose of the opening speech is to lay out for the court what is to be proven and by whom. It is usually only the prosecution or plaintiff's lawyer who gets this important opportunity.

Secondly, facts are then adduced in the form of evidence, that is, testimony from witnesses, documentary evidence and real evidence. This provides a story presented from the point of view of one of the parties, be it the prosecution or defence or the plaintiff or defendant. The most important element of this is the examination-in-chief. This is the examination by the lawyers of their own witnesses.

The third stage is the challenging of this evidence by the opposing side. This is conducted through cross-examination. The purpose here is to undermine, discredit and otherwise challenge the version of events that has been presented by the opponent.

Finally, the fourth stage is to present arguments, in favour of the defence theory, based on the evidence and the applicable law in the form of a closing address. The last word is usually left to the party defending the proceedings.

Let us look in detail at these elements of story building, the examination-in-chief and the cross-examination, and at the opening and closing speeches. In the case of the examination-in-chief and cross-examination a suggested likely dialogue is included to show how the task might be presented.

The opening speech

The prosecution normally address the court at the start of a criminal prosecution. What should this speech contain?

■ *Purpose:* To give an outline of the case to the court. This will include the facts that are alleged and the evidence that the prosecution intend to rely upon. The prosecution should explain the elements of the offence to be proven and the law that governs the offence(s).

■ *Framework:* The opening speech is largely governed by convention and, in the case of proceedings before magistrates, the Magistrates' Courts Rules 1981 (S1 1981/552).

■ *Theory:* The opening speech should support the prosecution theory of the case. In other words it is a scene-setter and the evidence that follows should expand upon it and complement it. Emphasis can be made in the opening speech on the importance of particular evidence but excluding evidence where admissibility is contested.

■ *Outcome:* The prosecution want to focus the court's mind on what is to be proved and on the strength of their case.

The opening speech should therefore be planned to accomplish these objectives. It should contain all of the relevant points that the advocate wishes to make, in particular, the order and nature of the evidence and what the prosecution must prove to establish guilt.

The rules in the Crown Court differ slightly but the need for and shape of the advocacy plan are the same. In this case the target of the speech is the jury.

Adducing the evidence

The next stage in the trial process is the giving of evidence. Remember that the court is not being asked to find the truth. Rather, the court has to adjudicate on whose version of 'the facts' is the most credible. Whose theory is best? The skill of the advocate in trial is to present a believable version of what has happened and an acceptable version of what the law is and how it should apply. Examination-in-chief and cross-examination are the methods by which each side, in a court or tribunal, presents its own account of fact, and challenges the account given by the opposition.

A valuable preparatory task is to write out the exact questions you intend to put to the witnesses – both yours and your opponent's – together with the responses you expect to get. This can give you confidence that you know what to ask, as well as result in a very ordered presentation. If the answers do not come out as planned, especially from cross-examination, you can move on to the next set of questions or remould the questions to suit. Such a process is admittedly time consuming but is a great way of getting to grips with the questioning to come.

Examination-in-chief

This involves the giving of evidence by witnesses for each side in response to questions posed by their representative. It is the initial process in building the story and is full of challenges and obstacles for the advocate. It should be noted, however, that as a result of the requirement to exchange witness statements in most civil actions advocates are likely to know in advance of the trial what each witness will say and except in the case of civil actions triable by jury the court may direct that the exchanged statement shall be taken as the witness's evidence in chief. See in particular RSC Order 38, rule 2A(7)(a) and Practice Direction (Civil Litigation: Case Management) [1995] 1 WLR 262.

How does this translate in terms of our four-point plan?

- *Purpose:* To elicit evidence from the witnesses called by that side, in this case, the defence. It is important to understand that the purpose is also to present evidence to the court that supports the theory of the case both in the individual testimony and in the context of the defence case as a whole (witnesses giving an account that is consistent with other evidence heard). In our case study, therefore, Mrs Evans will (hopefully) give evidence of the lack of intention even presuposing that she did place the coins in her apron pocket (which she cannot remember doing). She should also be able to give evidence of the unsystematic method of money handling in the shop as might other witnesses.

- *Framework:* To adduce the evidence within the permitted rules, in particular the Criminal Evidence Act 1898 and the Police and Criminal Evidence Act 1984.

- *Theory:* To adduce evidence that supports the theory of the case, in this instance, for example, lack of *mens rea* on the first charge and *actus reus* on the second.

- *Outcome:* To convince the court of the content of the evidence and the credibility of the witness.

Consider the nature of the difficulties faced by A here. Take charge 1. As Mrs Evans's solicitor you have prepared the case on the theory that she lacked *mens rea*. You know that Mr O'Connor has previous convictions for dishonesty and that this may undermine his own credibility as a witness. What about charge 2? You wish to show that the money missing from the till may have been taken by someone other than your client. In both charges you have the problem of the confession and circumstantial evidence.

We look at the process in the light of these issues. What must you put to your witness by way of examination-in-chief? Four principles apply:

1   the witness, not you, must give the evidence;

2   the witness must only provide evidence of what he or she did, heard, saw or, if relevant, believed;

3   what the witness says should be succinct, relevant and comprehensive;

4   the witness must be credible.

These principles enshrine a number of the basic rules concerning an examination-in-chief. They are:

1   the rule against leading questions;

2   the rule against hearsay;

3   the requirement to 'put your case'.

What do these mean? Solicitor A must get his or her client to explain, in her own words, the events leading up to her arrest and charge. To do this effectively, and within the permitted rules of evidence, A should have a plan for eliciting this evidence. It might run something like this:

Prepare the witness   Instruct the witness to be polite and courteous in his or her manner and language. Tell the witness to give short, simple answers to questions and to address all answers to the bench and not to the questioner. Advise the witness to watch the bench to see, for example, whether they are writing down answers and keeping up with the evidence. (There is nothing improper, and indeed it is good practice, to direct a witness in these matters even as he or she is giving evidence, providing you do not interrupt the flow of evidence unduly.)

Introduce the client to the court and put the client at ease   Ask simple questions to reveal the client's identity, address, occupation, family status and possibly age.

The client can, through her own words, be established as an otherwise respectable member of society with a stable family home. The client is introduced gently to the task ahead. There is generally no need to worry about leading questions (questions that provide the answer within the question) in such matters, as the evidence is unlikely to be in dispute. Allowing the client to provide her own answers, rather than simply giving a yes or a no is, however, likely to make her feel more confident and at ease.

The questions therefore might be:

A: Can you please give the court your full name?

Mrs E: Winifred Edith Evans.

A: And where do you live, Mrs Evans?

Mrs E: At 6 Manor Close, Sheffield.

A: How long have you lived at that address, Mrs Evans?

Mrs E: About five years.

A: Do you have a family?

Mrs E: Yes, I live with my husband and two children, aged 13 and 9.

Question the client about her employment The testimony must now turn to the general circumstances of her employment with Mr O'Connor. A can either ask an open question, for example:

A: Since having your children, Mrs Evans, have you been in paid employment?

Or A could ask a closed question or even a leading question (as the matter is not in dispute):

A: Can you confirm that you were, until recently, employed on a part time basis by Mr O'Connor at 'Tasty's Bakery' on Granville Road, Sheffield. Is that right?

Mrs E: Yes.

A: When did you start working there?

Mrs E: About two years ago.

A: What were the terms of your employment?

This story is growing. The court now knows who Mrs Evans is, brief details about her personal circumstances and something about her employment with Mr O'Connor. The way in which the questions now unfold will depend on what you have got out of Mr O'Connor in cross-examination.

Discredit Mr O'Connor Remembering that part of the theory of the case is to discredit Mr O'Connor, A must, at some point during Mrs Evans's evidence, raise the issue of the unsatisfactory and unreliable way in which the shop's money handling system operated.

Directing questions on this specific issue involves a balance of the open and closed questioning techniques. Open questions introduce a general issue and allow the client to talk around the topic. For example:

A: Did Mr O'Connor have a system for handling the shop's takings?

Mrs E: Yes.

A: What was that system?

Open questions lead easily into the desired area but if not controlled (by intervention, follow-up questions, and perhaps closed questions) can encourage unstructured testimony. Closed questions here might include:

A: Who had access to the shop till?

Mrs E: Mr O'Connor, me and the other part time worker, Sharon.

A: Did the till have a paper roll on which all of the transactions were recorded? (*This would be a leading question unless it had already been established in her evidence, or previous witness testimony, that the till did have a till roll.*)

Mrs E: Yes.

The credibility of the witness may be enhanced by the use of open questions (in the sense that the answers are being given without the witness being obviously directed to them). The advocate, however, must be sure to retain control over the direction that the testimony is taking, and may need to intercede with further questions, to keep the testimony on track.

There is nothing wrong in principle in the advocate interrupting the witness. Indeed he or she should do so to ensure that answers are kept as simple and as relevant as possible. It is a part of the advocate's function to do so, not only in the story building exercise, but also to demonstrate to the court the clarity and relevance of the testimony. Care must however be taken, particularly with your own witness, not to interrupt or appear to be preventing the witness from giving his or her own account. If you keep checking the witness it may harm credibility.

Through the use of such questioning it is intended to show that Mr O'Connor's system of accounting was poorly organised and incapable of the requisite precision to show that anyone (including Mrs Evans) had been taking money from the till.

Describe Mrs Evans's own behaviour on the day of the arrest Here, A must be very careful not to use leading questions. A must allow Mrs Evans, in her own words, to explain that she had no intention to steal. Intention in this context involves two aspects: the intention to permanently deprive Mr O'Connor and the intention to act dishonestly. The circumstantial evidence against her is strong. There can, by the very nature of the evidence, be no corroborative evidence to back up her assertions about criminal intent. The credibility of the witness is all important. Very specific questions need to be asked that address the legal meaning of intent. These might be:

A: Where were the coins found?

Mrs E: In my apron pocket.

A: How did the coins get into your apron pocket?

Mrs E: I don't know, I suppose I must have put them there.

A: Why do you suppose that?

Mrs E: Because the coins were found there when the police asked me to turn out my pockets.

A: Do you actually remember putting them there?

Mrs E: No.

A: How do you think they got there then?

Mrs E: I must have put them in my pocket as I was busy serving.

A: If you did do that, what was your intention?

Mrs E: I suppose I must have meant to put them there, meaning to put them in the till later.

A: So the placing in the apron was a temporary move on your part? (*This appears to be a leading question but it is acceptable as it summarises what the client has already said.*)

Mrs E: Yes, I am certain that this is what I meant to do.

A: Can you remember having ever done this before?

Mrs E: Yes, when I was very busy.

A: (*If the issue has been explored with Mrs Evans and the other witnesses in preparing the case*) Is this something other staff do to your knowledge?

Mrs E: Oh yes, it was quite usual when the shop was full.

Did Mrs Evans mean to deprive Mr O'Connor of the coins. Was she acting dishonestly? The issue has now been raised in open court.

Refer to the weaknesses in the case before these are brought out in cross-examination Mrs Evans did say to the police in interview that she must have taken the coins. This would seem to be a confession. A needs to raise the issue and deal with it. This issue was raised in Chapter 4 (Research). A has decided that this evidence cannot be excluded under the Police and Criminal Evidence Act 1984, sections 76 and 78. A has therefore not requested a *voir dire* (a mini trial just on the issue of admissibility). The evidence of confession will have been presented by the prosecution witnesses. Examination-in-chief might continue as follows:

A: We have already heard (in the prosecution evidence) that you were interviewed by the police after your arrest. Was a solicitor present at that interview?

Mrs E: No.

A: Why not?

Mrs E: I didn't think I needed one. I was offered a solicitor but I felt very upset and just wanted it over and done with. I didn't think I needed a solicitor as I hadn't done anything wrong.

A: What did you tell the police?

Mrs E: The truth. That I had probably put the coins in my pocket.

A: Did you say whether you intended to take the coins?

Mrs E: Yes, but I didn't understand the meaning of intention, I was very confused.

A: We have heard that you gave a statement at the police station. Did you tell the police this during your interview there?

Mrs E: Yes.

A: Do you understand what intention now means for the purposes of theft?

Mrs E: Yes. I didn't mean to act dishonestly or take property from Mr O'Connor.

No doubt, the prosecution in cross-examination will suggest otherwise, but at least A has dealt with the confession and the weakness revealed in it.

Conclude by bolstering the client's credibility and reducing any inference of motive

A: How would you describe your personal financial position?

Mrs E: My husband works as an engineer and earns good money. I worked part-time in the bakery until I was sacked after my arrest. We are not in debt and although we don't have much money to spare, we get by.

A: Do you have any experience of handling money in situations other than at the bakery?

Mrs E: Yes. I used to be the treasurer of my son's football team. I handled cash for the club on a regular basis.

A: How long for?

Mrs E: Oh, about 5 years.

A: What sort of sums of money are we talking about?

Mrs E: Around £1,000 a year in subs and grants – it was a small club.

A: Have there ever been any problems in this respect?

Mrs E: No.

You will no doubt appreciate that the examples of questioning here are somewhat truncated. The questions are simply examples of how progress is to be made during an examination-in-chief.

Two further elements need to be mentioned. First, the court can at any time interject with questions or points of its own. The court will almost certainly do this, especially where it is uncertain what the witness is actually saying. Encourage the witness to speak clearly and slowly. One way to ensure that this is done is to ask simple questions that attract straightforward answers. Delay your next question until you see that the court is ready for it. Watch the bench and the clerk to see whether they are ready for the next question. Your plan would have included the point of telling the witness how the court takes evidence and you should have forewarned the witness accordingly. The witness should therefore be aware of not, for example, speaking to fill in spaces whilst the court takes notes. Direct the witness to answer at a speed and in a way that the court can follow and record what is said. You will attract the court's approval for controlling the witness, which can only add to the witness's credibility.

Secondly, remember that you have a limited right to ask further questions after the cross-examination. This is known as re-examination. Re-examination should be used to clarify issues which have been clouded or raised for the first time by the cross-examination. Careful re-examination can emphasise the strengths in your client's case. It may not be used as a means of raising issues that were omitted in the examination-in-chief, unless these further issues were brought out in the cross-examination. If you have nothing useful to add move on to the next witness or the closing speech. Ensure that you have raised all issues consistent with your theory of the case.

Cross-examination

How do you prepare for cross-examination?

Let us list the outline plan for Mr O'Connor's cross-examination. We are assuming the charge of taking the £545 is the relevant one. We prepare on the assumption that his evidence will follow his statement:

■ *Purpose:* To establish and highlight inconsistencies in the evidence of the opposition witness and/or to discredit the witness.

■ *Framework:* Questions must be relevant and not offend ethical practice rules. Our version of facts must be put to the opposing witness.

■ *Theory:* As for examination-in-chief, cross-examination should be designed to support the case theory. In our example, this should be to show the unreliable accounting system or to discredit the general credibility of Mr O'Connor. It should plant a seed of doubt in the magistrates' minds to suggest that Mr O'Connor himself may have removed money.

■ *Outcome:* To cast sufficient doubt on the reliability of the prosecution evidence (in this case of Mr O'Connor) and to lead to an acquittal.

Many of the principles and rules referred to in the context of the examination-in-chief also relate to cross-examination. The main difference is that the rule against leading questions does not apply. The leading question is the cross-examiner's stock in trade. It enables him or her to retain control over the witness, preventing the witness from repeating and re-emphasising the evidence-in-chief and enabling the advocate to keep the evidence focused on the theory of the case. Although responses to questions put in a leading form understandably carry less weight than answers that volunteer the information, leading questions should keep the cross-examiner in the driving seat. Remember that a leading question is one that contains (or implies) the answer.

Two additional principles apply to cross-examination:

1 Be polite but firm in your dealings with the other side's witnesses.

2 Ensure that every aspect of the witness' evidence-in-chief which is at variance with your theory of events is challenged. If it is not, this is likely to be noted by the court and accepted as the account of what happened. This means putting matters to a witness that are part of the evidence you will adduce.

The purpose of cross-examination is to allow you to question the opponent's witnesses and to get them to agree, wherever possible, with your theory of the case, or discredit theirs. This can be done by extracting their admission that your client's points are correct and/or by showing that their own account is unsustainable.

The acutely adversarial nature of this encounter is fraught with difficulty. Your questioning must be precise (to hit upon the inconsistencies or conflicts in the evidence), it must be insistent (to attempt to extract the response that supports your theory of the case) and it must be conducted in a professional and courteous way. This means that questioning can quite properly be protracted so as to pursue any weaknesses in the evidence or the answers given, but once the point has been reached where all relevant questions have been put, the cross-examination should move on or cease. There is nothing to gain, but much to lose, by allowing the cross-examination to develop into an unstructured argument.

There is also supposed to be a 'golden rule' of advocacy. This is, that you never ask a question to which you do not know the answer. The sense of this is important, for to pursue cross-examination (or examination-in-chief for that matter), with no certain direction in mind, is dangerous. It shows a lack of planning and structure. Questions should only be asked if there is a purpose in them. This is particularly true of cross-examination where the objective is very specific – to challenge a particular piece of testimony. We do not feel, however, that questions should never be put unless you know what the answer is going to be. Sometimes you need to ask questions, where you hope for and can reasonably predict an answer, even though it may not materialise.

There are of course dangers implicit in this. In our case, A asks Mr O'Connor questions about the shop and its accounting system. The only information that A has is what Mrs Evans has said and what is described in Mr O'Connor's statement disclosed by the prosecution. A needs to show that the system is at best unreliable. A can open the questioning gently to probe Mr O'Connor about the matter. The questioning must proceed carefully and if Mr O'Connor sounds as if he is describing a foolproof accounting method then questioning should stop or be modified. What A does not want to happen is for Mr O'Connor to describe the system fully including the fact that everything is recorded in a day book. If necessary A will have to put it to Mr O'Connor that he did take money, unrecorded from the till (to support the theory), but the opportunity must not be carelessly given to Mr O'Connor to bolster his own credibility.

Always, therefore, be aware of why a question is asked and the risks involved, even if you are not completely certain of what the response is likely to be. Also be prepared to change the direction of questioning if necessary. Do not jump in with both feet. Ask a preparatory question, with a supplementary killer prepared for use if the preparatory question elicits a response that suggests the follow up will work. The following court room cross-examination demonstrates this.

Let us return to Mrs Evans and the trial. Mr O'Connor has given evidence for the prosecution. He has said in his evidence that he has suspected for some time that money has been missing from the shop till. He describes his accounting system and the events on the day when Mrs Evans was arrested. It is now time for A to cross-examine him. A has prepared for this task by working out what is the goal of the cross-examination and what issues are to be concentrated on. In the extract given below A is questioning Mr O'Connor on his accounting system with a view to showing that Mr O'Connor did use money from the till for buying supplies for the shop and for his own personal use. A's theory is that these withdrawals were not always recorded and it is not possible to say accurately, therefore, what moneys should have been in the till at any one time. This supports the theory in Mrs Evans's case that others could have taken money from the till, particularly Mr O'Connor.

The cross-examination may go as follows:

A: You have said in your evidence that you check the till twice a day and bank the proceeds. Is that right?

Mr O'C: Yes.

A: And you alone do this?

Mr O'C: Yes, that's right.

A: Now I think that I am right in saying that Mrs Evans has been given training by you on the handling of money in the shop?

Mr O'C: I have told her and the other staff to ring in sales and put the money in the till.

A: You serve in the shop sometimes, don't you?

Mr O'C: Yes, sometimes.

A: You do this when the shop is busy?

Mr S: Yes, perhaps once or twice a week.

A: The shop is often busy, isn't it?

Mr O'C: I suppose so

A: So you may serve in the shop more than once or twice a week, isn't that right?

Mr O'C: It's possible.

A: Perhaps several times a day?

Mr O'C: Perhaps.

A: On these occasions, you follow the same procedures as the shop assistants, that's correct isn't it?

Mr O'C: Yes.

A: When you buy supplies for the shop, how are these paid for?

Note: a non-leading, or at least more open question, is used here. It is safe to do so as A can predict the answer and this is likely to support the theory of the case. It also breaks up the style of questioning, relieving monotony and focusing the court's attention.

Mr O'C: I normally write a cheque.

A: Now some of your supplies are delivered direct to the shop, aren't they?

Mr O'C: Yes, bread and cakes are delivered most days.

A: And how are these are paid for?

Note: this is again a non-leading or open question that prepares the way for the killer question

Mr O'C: Like I have said, by cheque.

A: But you do sometimes pay by cash don't you?

Mr O'C: Well, sometimes.

Note: if Mr O'Connor had denied this A would have attacked his credibility by challenging the assertion that a man who owns a business never uses (his) money in the till to pay for supplies or anything else for that matter. A knows that his witnesses will support the allegation that Mr O'Connor took money out of the till. In the event Mr O'Connor tells the truth. A can now use non-leading questions to identify the origin of the cash knowing that a leading question can be put at any time to pin Mr O'Connor down.

A: And where does this cash come from?

Mr O'C: I use my money.

A: Where do you take that money from?

Mr O'C: Usually my pocket.

A: Do you ever take money from the till?

Note: the killer question!

Mr O'C: I don't think so.

A: You don't think so. Now what does that mean? There are surely occasions when you use your money from the till to pay for deliveries. That has to make sense, doesn't it?

Mr O'C: I suppose I do sometimes, yes.

A: Yes. Thank you.

Note: A has made an important point and has extracted the response from Mr O'Connor that is necessary to show that the sales rung up on the till cannot be relied upon to match the amount of money in it.

A: Now presumably you keep a record of the money you take from the till, don't you?

Note: A knows from the defence witnesses that Mr O'Connor does have a day book and uses it erratically. A wants to test Mr O'Connor on the use of the book – calling into doubt his reliability as a book keeper.

Mr O'C: Yes, I write it down in the day book.

A: When do you write it down?

Note: non-leading or open question can be used to good effect here leading up to strong leading questions to finish with.

Mr O'C: As soon as I can.

A: Not necessarily immediately after paying the money over?

Mr O'C: No, not always. I often make up the books at the end of the day.

A: Let me just recap. Sometimes you pay for supplies out of the till and you keep a record of money paid in a day book which you make up either at the time or later in the day. Am I right in saying that you are a busy man?

Mr O'C: Certainly.

A: Do you accept that it is highly probable that not all money paid out of the till is in fact recorded in the day book?

Mr O'C: No, I don't think so.

A: Surely if you are busy and do not make up your records until later in the day, you may forget to include all of the items for which you have paid.

Mr O'C: I suppose it is possible.

A: Do you make any other payments out of the till?

Note: this is another preparatory question and is non-leading for A is confident of the response and his tactics if there is a negative one.

Mr O'C: No.

A: Are you sure?

Mr O'C: Yes.

A: The money in the till is yours, isn't it?

Mr O'C: Of course.

A: You are entitled to take this money at any time, aren't you?

Mr O'C: I suppose so.

A: If the money is yours and you are entitled to take it, you can do with the money as you feel fit?

Mr O'C: Well, yes.

A: Therefore there would be nothing wrong in you taking money from your till if you thought fit?

Mr O'C: No.

A: Mr O'Connor, I put it to you that you take money from the till on a regular basis for your own purposes and to give to your son Daniel.

Mr O'C: There is nothing wrong with that.

A: I am not suggesting there is. What I am suggesting is that because you do take money from the till you cannot say with any certainty whether the money in the till at any one time is the amount that has been paid into it by your shop staff.

Mr O'C: I don't think so.

A: But you have just told the court that you make payments from the till, some of which may not be recorded and that you sometimes use money from the till for your own purposes.

Mr O'C: I didn't say that.

A: Yes, thank you, Mr O'Connor.

The point has been made. Mr O'Connor, without necessarily acting unlawfully (although there could be a question of tax evasion involved) has been shown to have a less than reliable form of accounting. A will hope that the court takes note of this fact and takes this into account when deciding whether Mrs Evans was responsible for the missing money.

Skilful cross-examination is a mixture of art and science. The science involves the systematic questioning and methodical application of the advocacy plan. The art is the craft of the advocate, the use of language and the skilful construction of questions. This aspect of the advocate's skill is perhaps the most difficult to acquire and is something developed over a long period. Experience will greatly assist but our message is that you can do a good job if you understand the nature of the task and prepare properly for it. Careful planning and structure provide a platform for cross-examination. Both of us have seen law degree students effectively cross-examine witnesses and win cases, against qualified lawyers too, using this strategy.

In our example A could have continued questioning Mr O'Connor emphasising the inconsistencies and admissions that bolster Mrs Evans's contention that the accounting system was defective. However, having made the point, and having emphasised it, there is little to be gained by questioning the witness further. Indeed there is the danger of asking one question too many. Advocates must persuade the bench or jury, not the witness.

An apocryphal account of over-enthusiastic cross-examination is often related in this context. It runs something like this:

The lawyer for the defendant is cross-examining a prosecution witness. The allegation is one of assault causing grievous bodily harm. The defendant is said to have bitten off the victim's ear! The witness has been cross-examined effectively in that he (she) has said that there were many people present at the scene of the crime, it was dark and the defendant was standing over 30 yards away. Enough you might think to sow seeds of doubt in the court's mind as to the accuracy of what the witness says and the ability of the witness to identify the defendant as the perpetrator of the crime. The lawyer then asks one question too many:

'So how can you say that it was my client who bit off the victim's ear?'

to which the reply was:

'Because as he walked past me I saw him spit it out.'

In real life the examination-in-chief should have established this. If it did not then the danger of asking one question too many in cross-examination is apparent!

The end result in cross-examination should be either to show that the evidence-in-chief given by the witness does not stand up (either because it is contradictory or imprecise), or if it does, and it is in conflict with your own case, then the witness him or herself can be discredited.

Remember also that the opportunity for cross-examination is reciprocal. Prepare your own witness for the likely questions to be posed by the opponent. Ensure that your witnesses are aware of the right of the opponent to question them and of their need to stay calm and to answer questions as simply and as briefly as possible. It is perhaps a natural reaction for a person being questioned to become defensive. If that questioning is targeted at weaknesses in a case and is probing, the defensiveness can increase to such a point that the witness becomes annoyed and agitated. In such a condition the witness is likely to be less in control than he or she should be, and will add nothing to their credibility if they enter into a slanging match with the other lawyer. If you prepare your client and witnesses for the possibility of rigorous cross-examination they are perhaps less likely to fall into the trap of losing their temper and giving unhelpful answers. As a bottom line, a witness should be told, if repeatedly questioned on the same point, to emphasise that what they have said is the truth, and that there is nothing more they can add to it. Tell the witness in advance not to speculate and to stick to the facts. Speculation can create inconsistencies. If necessary intervene to prevent unfair or oppressive questioning. Object to the court if need be. Remember, though, that if the witness handles the cross-examination effectively it will carry more weight than you jumping up and down. An advocate who is cross-examining a witness is allowed to ask a question or series of questions on a particular point but should not continue with this line of questioning once a definitive answer has been given. The answer may not be what the advocate wants to extract, but he or she must try a different tack if the question is not answered in a way that helps the client's case.

It is beyond the scope of this book to consider the detailed rules of evidence. Can you, for example, impeach a witness if he or she has criminal convictions? What if your own witness fails to come up to proof or turns hostile to your case? What is the rule against hearsay? All of these questions might be legitimate research tasks. Some of them were addressed in Chapter 4 (Research skills). You will certainly encounter these rules on your litigation courses.

In terms of advocacy skill, be constantly aware of the need to build a story and of the fact that this is done through the testimony of witnesses. The court will eventually have to decide in the event of a conflict whose evidence it prefers and accepts. Your job is to persuade the court of the strength of your case.

This brings us to the advocate's skill in presenting his or her submissions at the conclusion of the case, or if necessary at a particular point in it when a ruling is required (for example, a submission after the prosecution evidence that there is no case to answer).

Submissions

As was seen at the beginning of this chapter, there is an order which is usually followed in proceedings before courts and tribunals. Sometimes this is a formal requirement and on other occasions proceedings develop at the direction of the adjudicator (particularly in tribunals).

Unless you are prosecuting there should be an opportunity in all cases for you to make submissions at the conclusion of the case. This is of great importance. It gives the advocate a chance to address the court or tribunal personally, without having to rely on witnesses.

It allows the advocate to focus attention on both fact and law. It provides a platform from which the advocate can draw together the strands of argument into a highly persuasive form which provides the court or tribunal with reasons, through which it can justify its conclusions.

There are three types of submission that need to be identified, each with a particular significance in terms of advocacy:

■ the closing speech pulling fact and law together;

■ the legal submissions which can occur at any point, such as a submission on admissibility of evidence:

■ representations on what the court should do, such as a plea in mitigation before sentencing or an application for an adjournment.

The closing speech

We have already seen when constructing the advocacy plan how your anticipation of the closing speech dictated your whole preparation process. If all has gone well, the closing speech that you prepared at the outset will now suit your purpose at the conclusion of the case. This is because the theory that you so carefully researched has been borne out by both the evidence and law. It is the speech that confirms the story you have been relating to the court during the trial. If it has to be adapted, because of unforeseen evidence at trial, ask for a short adjournment in order to prepare it.

As an exercise in advocacy how is this prepared? Again the same formula as before can be used:

■ *Purpose:* To summarise, in a persuasive manner, for the court, the facts and law which the defence (or, where permitted, the prosecution or equivalent parties in civil proceedings) say are applicable.

■ *Framework:* Proceedings in the Crown Court differ slightly from those in the magistrates' court in that, in the latter, only the defence has the right of address unless the court otherwise decides. The defence will have no such right if it exercises the right to have an opening speech (Magistrates' Court Rules 1981). Both sides have the right to make closing speeches in a civil case, with the last word going to the defendant.

■ *Theory:* To support the theory of the case by emphasising the credibility of evidence upon which that theory is based and by undermining the evidence supporting the theory of the other side. For example, in the criminal case, A will remind the court that the evidence of the poor accounting system in the shop supports Mrs Evans's assertions that she did not steal the money. Others, apart from Mrs Evans, could have taken the money. The fact that Mr O'Connor said under cross-examination that he did take money from the till should be stressed. Any weaknesses in Daniel's answers can be emphasised.

■ *Outcome:* The court is to be persuaded that the case put forward by the advocate is credible and that the law supports the conclusions that the court is invited to reach – in this case an acquittal.

A closing speech must, as for any other task in persuasion and communication, be properly targeted at its audience. More consideration might be given to an explanation of the law, say, when addressing a lay bench than if appearing before the stipendiary magistrate.

Legal submissions

It may be necessary at several stages in the trial process for you to address the court on the law. The most common will be at the beginning and the conclusion of the case. We have already seen that in opening a case the advocate may address the court on the law. In the closing submission the lawyer for the defendant should make submissions on what the law is on the relevant points. In Mrs Evans's case A would explain to the court the constituent elements of the offence of theft and what tests the court is bound to apply, before outlining why parts of those tests are not met by the prosecution evidence. The prosecution (or plaintiff in a civil case) may respond on the interpretation of the law.

Submissions can also be made on the law in other instances. Again both parties have the right to address the court. We will mention two more. The first is where you do not feel that the prosecution has made out a case. How does our formula read in this instance?

- *Purpose:* For the court to decide whether on the evidence heard so far the prosecution has failed to prove one or more elements of the case and could therefore not properly convict.

- *Framework:* The submission of no case to answer applies to both trial and committal proceedings. The legal principles are set out in *R v Galbraith* [1981] 1 WLR 1039.

- *Theory:* The original theory of your case prepared for trial may not have taken this into account, for one of the prosecution witnesses may, for example, have failed to come up to proof. The theory would have to be modified to include the point that the prosecution case did not satisfy the legal test. You may on the other hand already have incorporated this in your plan based on the theory of absence of credible evidence – A's theory on the second of Mrs Evans's charges is already based on this theory. If it were, however, that obvious, perhaps the prosecution would not have proceeded with the case, so it is rare that a submission of no case can be anticipated with confidence.

- *Outcome:* If the submission is accepted (as a point of law) the defendant must be acquitted.

A second example might arise in Mrs Evans's case if, say, there was a dispute as to the admissibility of evidence. Could A object to Mrs Evans's 'confession'? This was explored in Chapter 4. Preparation for this advocacy task should be on the same basis as before with the purpose, legal framework, theory and outcome clearly understood.

Representations – the plea in mitigation

One of the most important functions performed by defence lawyers, and often required of students as an advocacy exercise, is presenting pleas in mitigation. This advocacy task arises when a defendant pleads guilty. If the defendant has been found guilty, it is no longer properly called a plea, but similar factors arise. It is a damage limitation exercise.

This exercise is prepared on the assumption that Mrs Evans has pleaded guilty to one of the charges, the other having been dropped. We suggest A should prepare the plea in mitigation on the following basis, having first identified:

- *Purpose:* To influence the court on sentencing, by providing the court with details of the circumstances surrounding the commission of the offence, and the personal circumstances of the defendant.

- *Framework:* The law on the principles of sentencing is now mainly governed by the Criminal Justice Act 1991 (CJA 1991). Case law sets out guidelines for sentencing in certain cases (for example *R v Barrick* (1985) 7 Cr App R (S) 142, custody is to be considered where a breach of trust is involved, such as theft from an employer). The 1991 Act indicates for all sentencing decisions that seriousness is the key factor; the Magistrates' Association publishes guidelines giving seriousness indicators for a large range of offences – for example, theft in a position of trust, large amounts taken, involving preplanning, compared with an impulsive act, carried out alone, where little value is involved and all items are recovered. A very helpful book on sentencing, which includes the Magistrates' Association guidelines, is *Emmins on Sentencing* (Martin Wasik).

The Act also makes clear that a person's record is relevant to seriousness, as is the fact that an offence has been committed while on bail. If more than one offence is before the court (including offences taken into consideration) this can aggravate the court's view of seriousness.

The Act goes on to list the criteria that must be satisfied if the court is to impose a particular sentence, for example imprisonment. A pre-sentence report should be obtained if a custodial sentence is being considered. A must be able to use this framework in order to mitigate effectively. In particular section 28 of the Act states that the court may take into account any matters raised that are relevant in mitigation.

■   *Theory:* The offence was not serious because of the low value involved, the recovery of the property and the plea of guilty. The defendant has relevant mitigation that should affect the sentence to be imposed – loss of job, impact on family and lack of relevant previous offences.

■   *Outcome:* To obtain the best possible sentence for the client. (Best means best as agreed with the client in the light of A's advice.) The offence may be too serious to go for a discharge, or a small fine. A realistic best is a community sentence, so A looks up the powers of the court to impose such a sentence, the seriousness required (CJA 1991, section 6) and the exact nature of each sentence. A finds that section 2(1) of the Powers of Criminal Courts Act 1973 requires that probation be imposed where this is necessary to protect the public or reform the offender.

With an understanding of the nature of the advocacy task A must now exercise considerable skill in persuading the court of the appropriate sentence to be passed. What should A bear in mind in the construction and delivery of an effective plea in mitigation? We suggest this should contain the following:

1   *An acknowledgment of the seriousness of the case*: A realistic view of the crime: theft from an employer is a breach of trust and viewed with some seriousness by the courts. If A is to persuade the court of anything, the submissions must be credible.

   The CJA specifically mentions seriousness, as we have seen. This includes the determination of the length of a custodial sentence (section 2(2)). (If she has a record, or there are any associated offences, A will have to address the court on the extent that these do not make the offence more serious.)

2   *The remorsefulness and humility of the defendant*: Under section 28 of the 1991 Act these factors allow the court to reduce the sentence which the seriousness of the offence otherwise indicates is appropriate. Mrs Evans has pleaded guilty and this is an indication of her remorse. She is prepared to accept responsibility for what happened. She should be given credit for a guilty plea (historically allowed and now formalised by Criminal Justice and Public Order Act 1996, section 48). Case law suggests that the sentence for a person pleading guilty should be lighter than for a convicted person in the same circumstances (*R v Cain* [1976] QB 496). How much lighter is debatable (*R v Hollyman* [1980] Crim LR 60 and *R v Tonks* [1980] Crim LR 59).

3   *Co-operation with the police*: Rather like pleading guilty, a defendant should be given credit for admitting guilt at the early stage of initial arrest and interview (*R v Lowe*

(1977) 66 Cr App R 122), although the impact of this may be limited. This may not be relevant if Mrs Evans denied liability at the outset.

4   *The circumstances of the commission of the offence*: The seriousness of the crime is tempered by the circumstances surrounding its commission. It might be said that this was a one-off opportunistic theft and a foolish but isolated incident. It was not part of a history of dishonesty. It affects the view that the court will have of the seriousness of the crime.

5   *The situation of the defendant*: She is now unemployed. Mrs Evans was dismissed from her employment following her arrest. She is now suffering not only the humility and embarrassment of having committed the offence, but has lost her source of income. In addition, A must tell the court of her financial situation in terms of her income and outgoings and those of her family. This information is required to enable the court to decide upon an appropriate sentence, especially if it wishes to fine her. CJA 1991, section 28 specifically gives the court the power to take into account relevant mitigation such as her previous good character or the fact that she is needed by her family. The courts have long recognised such factors as relevant (*R v Ward* (1981) 3 Cr App R (S) 350).

6   *Her history*: Is there anything in her past that the court must hear about? Previous convictions are relevant here for the court is entitled to know what convictions, if any, Mrs Evans has. If there are other convictions this may well influence the court in determining sentence. CJA 1991, section 29 deals with previous convictions and states that the existence of a criminal record can be taken into account if it casts light on the seriousness of the present offence. A mere tendency to commit different kinds of offences can, A will argue, be of no such relevance. Also under section 29 the court can take into account how the defendant has responded to previous penalties in choosing the appropriate sentence in the present case.

7   *The appropriate sentence*: Can A suggest what sentence should be imposed? A plea in mitigation can properly include reference to the range of sentences that might be imposed in the case and make comments upon the applicability of that sentence. In our criminal case study theft from an employer is viewed as a breach of trust of a serious nature, so much so, that a custodial sentence is likely to be considered. Given this, A would need to address the effect such a sentence would have and might try to persuade the court that such a sentence would be extremely harsh in the circumstances. He or she might argue that there is little likelihood of further offences being committed and that a period spent in prison would have no value as a deterrent.

The alternatives to a custodial sentence might be raised (a suspended prison sentence is a custodial sentence – so never argue for this unless custody is inevitable, for you are conceding the very point that you should be arguing, that custody is inappropriate!). Proper alternatives for Mrs Evans could include: an order of supervision (probation or community service or a combination of the two) or a financial penalty. The latter would take into account the client's means.

A should be mindful of the requirements of the CJA with reference to particular sentences. Some of the restrictions on imprisonment have already been mentioned (CJA 1991, sections 1–3). Criteria must also be satisfied in relation to suspended sentences (Powers of Criminal Courts Act 1973, section 22), community sentences, for example probation or community service (section 6) and fines (section 18 as amended).

8   *Conclusions and recommendations*: Giving the court some options. A might ask the court to adjourn the case so that a report can be prepared by the probation service. This would be a concession by A that things are bad enough for at least a community sentence. Indeed, if a custodial (or community) sentence is to be imposed, as we have seen, a pre-sentence report (PSR) is normally required. If a report is already to hand, A might take up the recommendations in it if they are in Mrs Evans's best interests.

A has outlined the mitigation and only at the very end used the PSR. This is not because such reports are not helpful, on the contrary, but nothing annoys courts (and probation officers) more than solicitors who mitigate by merely regurgitating the pre-sentence report. That report, by and large, only addresses issues relevant to personal circumstances (CJA 1991, section 28 makes these relevant) and appropriate sentencing outcome. It does not address the key issue of seriousness, at least, that is not a function expected of it, except insofar as it mentions the offender's attitude to the offending behaviour.

You only need to refer to the PSR after you have decided on issues of seriousness and circumstances, in order to use material contained in the report to back up an argument you have already decided on in pursuit of the goal.

Try drafting a plea in mitigation for Mrs Evans. What might this look and sound like? This is an assessment task of a type you may well get on the LPC.

We suggest something along the the following lines:

> *Chair of magistrates (this time a man: Mrs Evans having pleaded guilty to the charge of theft of three £1 coins and the court having heard an outline of the case from the prosecution, including the fact that Mrs Evans has previous convictions):* Yes, Mr (Ms) A.

> *A:* Sir, I appear in this matter on behalf of Mrs Evans. My client is 46 years old and lives in Sheffield with her husband and two children.

> I would like to preface my remarks this afternoon by acknowledging at the outset the seriousness of this matter. Theft by a person in a position of trust, such as an employee, is never to be treated lightly, even if the amount involved may be small, as in this case. Having said that, there are in my respectful submission significant mitigating factors in this case that can be properly raised on Mrs Evans's behalf.

> I wish to address Your Worships on three issues: first, the circumstances surrounding the commission of the offence, secondly, the personal circumstances of my client and thirdly, the matter of the appropriate sentence in this case.

> So far as the offence itself is concerned this occurred on 1st September last. Mrs Evans had worked in the bakery shop for over five years. There was never any complaint made about her standard of work or her general behaviour. In fact the contrary was the case. Mrs Evans was a well liked employee who carried out her duties efficiently. She was popular with the customers. The shop gets very busy, especially at lunch time. On the day of her arrest Mrs Evans had served many customers and at about 1 pm she sold some sandwiches to a woman, who unknown to her was a police officer. On receiving the money for the goods, in her haste, she placed the coins, three £1 coins, into her apron pocket.

> *Magistrate (interrupting):* Tell me, Mr (Ms) A, did your client give any change to this customer?

A: So far as my client can recall, no, Sir. She did tell the police at her interview in the police station that she cannot actually remember putting the coins in her pocket, but she thinks she must have done so. She does not remember going to the till or giving change.

The important point I believe is this: Mrs Evans had no intention of stealing the money at the moment she received it. After the officer had left the shop and things were less hectic, Mrs Evans heard the coins jingling in her pocket and at that moment she remembered that she had to make a telephone call and needed change. (*These instructions were given by the client to A when she was going through her statement before the hearing. She had previously forgotten this important matter.*) She then foolishly and wrongly decided to keep the coins and use them for the call. Before she could do so the police officers came back into the shop and she was searched and then arrested. She made no attempt to hide the coins and fully co-operated with the police at her interview. She has pleaded guilty to the offence at the first opportunity and is in my respectful submission entitled to be given credit for this.

Sir, I would ask you and your colleagues to accept that this was one isolated incident of theft. It was an opportunistic theft that arose in very particular circumstances. Mrs Evans accepts that it is no less serious as a result. My submission to this court today is that the offence, although involving a breach of trust, is relatively low on the scale of seriousness in view of the circumstances that I have just outlined. There is no implication that this formed part of any history of stealing nor that it was planned or premeditated. It is true to say that Mrs Evans was initially charged with two offences, the one she has pleaded guilty to and the matter that the prosecution have offered no evidence on this afternoon. That would have been defended rigorously. My client's plea to this matter accorded exactly with the evidence or lack of it.

Perhaps I can now turn to my client's personal circumstances? I have already said that Mrs Evans had worked at the bakery for some five years or more. She has, as a result of this sad incident, been dismissed from her employment. This was perhaps the inevitable consequence of one isolated act of foolishness. The loss of her job is punishment in itself. She has no personal income as a result and has suffered the acute embarrassment of job loss. She is well known as well as liked in the community and she has had to face up to the consequences of her actions.

My client has two children aged thirteen and nine. She was able to combine her part-time work with their care. The family have had to carry the burden of this incident which still causes considerable tension in the home. Mr Evans has been supportive of his wife but is, understandably, also upset by the matter. The family now have to rely on his income alone. He works as a fitter for a local engineering company and after deductions he brings home some £200 per week. Mrs Evans receives child benefit of £20.75 per week. Out of this the family spend £70 per week on the mortgage on their home and their other expenses include gas, electricity and telephone charges, which total £40 per week. The rest of their income is taken up with food, clothing and other related expenses. As you can see, Sir, there is little left at the end of each week. Mrs Evans and her husband do have modest savings totalling £300.

You have heard, Sir, from the prosecution, that Mrs Evans has been before the courts on two previous ocassions. One offence was for dishonesty. This was when she was a juvenile and many years ago. I presume, Sir, that the court will not take this into account when considering sentence today?

Magistrate: No, the court is not concerned with offences that took place so long ago.

A: Thank you, Sir. The other offence is a totally unrelated matter of criminal damage. This incident was only last year but arose out of a matrimonial dispute and resulted in a broken window. Mrs Evans has paid the fine imposed and compensated the owner of the window.

Perhaps I can now address the question of the appropriate sentence? This matter is clearly a matter for Your Worships alone to decide upon. On Mrs Evans's behalf, however, I feel that it is proper for me to deal with the range of sentences and their respective appropriateness in the particular circumstances of this case.

I said in the preface to my remarks that theft from an employer is a serious matter. Indeed there is authority that I am sure the court is aware of that suggests that a custodial sentence can be appropriate in such cases. I wonder at this stage, Sir, to save the court's time, can I ask whether the court is considering a custodial sentence?

Chairperson of magistrates: At present, Mr (Ms) A, the court has an open mind on the matter.

A (disappointed): Thank you, Sir, for that indication. I would not want to address Your Worships on custody had it not been relevant to do so. If I may continue?

In my respectful submission a prison sentence, whether suspended or not, is not warranted here. As Your Worships will know, statute dictates that a custodial sentence can only be imposed if the offence is so serious that only custody is appropriate. Your Worships must be satisfied that no other punishment is appropriate for this offence. Without making light of the theft I must emphasise that it was a one-off incident, it was for a very small amount and there were no aggravating features in relation to it, other than the breach of trust for which Mrs Evans is deeply ashamed, and for which she has lost her job. Were Your Worships to be considering such a sentence I would respectfully remind you of the statutory requirement for a pre-sentence report.

Other means of disposal are open to you and are in my respectful submission more suitable in this case. Sir, the court may consider a community sentence. Again the need for a report arises. It may be of interest, Sir, for you and your colleagues to know that Mrs Evans is already an active member of her son's football club and is in fact the club treasurer. I should add there have been no problems in this respect. Mrs Evans is normally a thoroughly honest and reliable person.

I would urge you, Sir, to take an unusual course of action in this matter and either deal with this case by way of a financial penalty, although as you have heard there are limited funds available, or impose a discharge in this matter. Although at first sight this may seem overly lenient, in my respectful submission Mrs Evans and her family have been and continue to be punished for this incident in terms of job loss and humiliation. If a discharge was imposed conditional upon her good behaviour in the future this would, I have little doubt, act as the only necessary threat that Mrs Evans needs to ensure that she never comes before this court again.

Your worships, unless I can assist you further, those are my submissions.

If you were Their Worships what would your decision be?

One final point should be mentioned. It is one that applies to all advocacy performances but is of particular relevance to pleas in mitigation. Without compromising your duty to the client or the court, try to sound different. There is no virtue perhaps doing this for the sake of it. Remember we advise against egotism. Rather, if you are to attract and keep the court's attention you must find a means of doing so. The court has to listen to many pleas in mitigation on a daily basis and unless you can captivate the court the danger is that they will simply allow you to go through the motions. We are not suggesting that the court does this in any conscious way but as a body made up of other human beings it is inevitable that repetitive tasks such as pleas take on almost a routine appearance. Couple this with the magistrates' own sentencing tariff for offences and you will probably get the going rate in terms of sentence unless you can convince the court otherwise. Attempt therefore to adopt a style and approach that engages the court's attention and, we hope, sympathy.

(Actually, it may be enough of a difference to hear someone well prepared on the law and the facts!)

Post-trial

Once the final addresses have been given to the court, the role of the advocate is not over. What further issues may arise? In the criminal case, Mrs Evans may need to be advised as to the meaning and consequences of the court's findings. The question of an appeal, say on conviction or sentence, may be relevant. In the civil case the advocate may need to consider the enforcement of the judgment, the costs in the case or an appeal against the decision of the court. They may of course throw up additional research tasks in the continuation of the case. Should, for example, an appeal be considered, then the theory of the case and the objectives sought would have to be re-designed.

With a view to these ends, take a careful note of the outcome of proceedings. Where possible, record the decision of the court or tribunal in full, with reasons and outcomes. This may be used later for drafting an appeal, for advising the client, for briefing counsel or for your own education. In civil cases, it may be necessary for you to draft the order of the court and therefore you must know exactly what order the court made. Remember also that your client is the subject of all this. You owe a continuing professional duty to look after your client and this includes talking with the client about the outcome whether the client won or lost the case.

The overall message is the need to plan for all contingencies from the initial taking of instructions to the final disposal of the case.

7   The technique of persuasion

You should by now be aware that advocacy skill involves many aspects. It is imperative to understand both law and procedure and to prepare. The skills of the advocate have been referred to as 'the technique of persuasion' (Napley *The Technique of Persuasion*).

It is necessary, within this framework, to persuade the court, tribunal or other side of the worth of your arguments. To do so you must gain and keep their attention. You should behave in a manner expected of you professionally, that is, with courtesy but with direction. You will be judged, and so will your client, both by how you appear and on what you say. Be civil to the opposition, to the court and to the witnesses, but do not allow over-familiarity to come between you and your client or the court. Engage the court in a dialogue even if you are the one doing most of the talking. Allow a response wherever possible. For example, ask the court pointedly whether there is anything else with which you can assist them. Be as concise as the circumstances allow. Don't overuse repetition or time. Be aware that you are dealing with other human beings who may have their own prejudices and preferences. These should not be allowed to interfere with the judicial process but nonetheless must be recognised as being present. Take hints and be aware of feedback. Shape your responses and act accordingly.

Be aware of your style and manner of address. Modulate your voice to keep the court's interest and to stress the important parts of your address. Avoid the train announcer monotones. Maintain eye contact with the person or people you are trying to convince. Use examples to illustrate your points and watch for signs of the court's approval or otherwise. Above all talk to the court with respect but with the clear impression that you mean what you say. Confidence in public speaking may take some time to acquire but with solid preparation and intimate case knowledge you have a foundation from which to build successfully.

You are more likely to succeed on behalf of your client if you can keep the attention of the court and project the accurate impression that you are well organised and in control. You must convince the court that you are able to deliver what is necessary to prove your case. You must persuade the court that your story and your theory is the preferred one.

Speak far slower than your feeling of panic dictates. Most people speak faster than they realise, particularly under pressure. It helps you feel and appear in control if you slow right down, and pause frequently. Do not give the impression that you are in a hurry. Do not read word for word from the prepared text. Record yourself practising some of the advocacy tasks referred to in this chapter or on your course. Watch yourself on video. Use our checklist to think through and prepare for advocacy.

One final point. Although this chapter has concentrated on advocacy in a courtroom setting, you should be aware that advocacy skills do arise outside of the courts and in non-contested areas. The same requirement for planning and organisation will apply to a formal application for, say, a consent order for a child settlement such as Daniel's. With the increased role of alternative dispute resolution, advocacy skills will continue to be of vital importance in the negotiation and mediation settings. This is the case even if the strict rules of evidence and courtroom battles are not relevant.

Conclusion

For those who have found the material in this chapter interesting – and even more importantly, those of you who didn't – or for those who wish to read about this complex area in more detail, several publications can be recommended. *Fundamentals of Trial Techniques* (Mauet) and *Trial Advocacy in a Nutshell* (Bergman) are both highly instructive. They relate to proceedings in the United States but are equally applicable, at least in theory, to advocacy under our judicial system. *Fact Investigation, from Hypothesis to Proof* (Binder and Bergman) develops some of these concepts further and is also highly recommended. Another gem is an Australian book entitled *An Introduction to Advocacy* (Stuesser). You can't say we don't try to make things cosmopolitan!

OK, students who are pressed for time and money are hardly going to order expensive overseas textbooks. These, however, really are worth it – remember you can act on it when you have more time or money. For now, our advice will take you through any course assessment with ease (if you practise what we preach).

Chapter 8

CONCLUSION

So much for lawyering skills. Are you any wiser for ploughing through this book ? Perhaps not. We nevertheless hope you will be better informed. (Our thanks to Jonathan Brayshaw for this gem which was directed at a pompous tribunal chairperson, of course out of earshot – just!)

We have in the course of this book followed the four case studies and watched them develop. We suspect that you are just a little curious as to what happened to the clients and the other characters concerned. Any good documentary gives you a summary of where the participants have subsequently found themselves. Given that much of the case detail has been taken, and adapted, from real life, we wish to leave you with such an overview.

Mrs Evans eventually pleaded not guilty to the charges she faced. In her trial before the magistrates' court the facts and law, so carefully tested in the research chapter, held up. The theft of £545 was eventually not proven. However, Mrs Evans was convicted of the theft of three £1 coins. The court felt unable to accept her evidence that she did not have the requisite criminal intent. Perhaps in recognition of the worth of her argument, or in view of the excellent plea in mitigation delivered by her solicitor, she was treated relatively leniently and fined £250. A custodial sentence, even for a first offence, is not unusual for cases of theft from an employer. Mr O'Connor is ruing the fact that his takings have plummeted. 'Where is that nice lady that used to serve here?', he is often asked.

Daniel McAuley has recovered from his injuries. He seems to have suffered little lasting effect although he has been left with one leg very slightly shorter than the other. He received £10,000 in settlement – enough to buy a new bike and a few other comforts. Mr Slater, having had to reimburse his insurance company because he was in breach of the terms of his contract of insurance (having been convicted of drunk driving), is now teetotal.

Ms Kennedy and Mr Bennett are happily installed in Paradise Road. The super-tram runs smoothly and quietly by, even though no-one can afford the fares. House prices have held up and they plan to marry next year.

Mr Kader and Mr Khan have traded as a limited company for two years. Times are however hard in manufacturing, and the company is in some financial difficulty. Both are relieved to have the protection of limited liability although their bankers do have personal guarantees in respect of the overdraft. Mr Kader has from time to time thought about going it alone again but is aware of his responsibilities as a company director. Mrs Shearsby is hoping that the rent review will produce a substantial increase in the rent; the letting of the factory is bringing her a useful income, but things are no better with her step-daughter.

At a time when solicitors are competing furiously for clients, and reporting falling profits, our A, B, C and D – and the counsel they instruct – continue to attract and keep clients by following the principles of the Legal Skills Book. For them business is booming.

BIBLIOGRAPHY

Adair *The Effective Communicator* (The Industrial Society, 1988).

Adler *Clarity for Lawyers* (The Law Society, 1990).

Anderson and Twining *Analysis of Evidence* (Weidenfeld, 1991).

Archbold *Criminal Pleading Evidence and Practice* (Sweet & Maxwell, 1998).

Atkin's *Encyclopaedia of Court Forms in Civil Proceedings* (Butterworths, 1998).

Axelrod *The Evolution of Co-operation* (Penguin, 1990).

Barnard *The Criminal Court in Action* (Butterworths, 1988).

Barnard and Houghton *The New Civil Court in Action* (Butterworths, 1993).

Bellow and Moulton *The Lawyering Process* (Foundation Press, 1978).

Bergman *Trial Advocacy in a Nutshell* (West Publishing Co, 1979).

Binder and Bergman *Fact Investigation, from Hypothesis to Proof* (West Publishing Co, 1984).

Blackford *Specimen Letters for Solicitors* (Longman, 1989).

Blackstone's Criminal Practice (Blackstone Press, 1998).

Blake *A Practical Approach to Legal Advice and Drafting* (Blackstone Press, 1997).

Butterworths Company Law Handbook (Butterworths, 1997).

Butterworths Company Law Service (Butterworths, 1998).

Butterworths UK Tax Guide 1997–98 (Butterworths, 1997–98).

Cane *Atiyah's Accidents Compensation and the Law* (Weidenfeld and Nicolson, 1993).

Carter *Cases and Statutes on Evidence* (Sweet & Maxwell, 1990).

Child *Drafting Legal Documents* (West Publishing Co, 1992).

Clerk and Lindsell on Tort (1995).

Code of Conduct of the Bar of England and Wales (General Council of the Bar London, 1990, amended 1991).

Cordery on Solicitors (Butterworths, 1998).

Cowsill and Clegg *Evidence Law and Practice* (Longman, 1990).

Cross and Tapper on Evidence (Butterworths, 1995).

Thomas *How to Use a Law Library: An Introduction to Legal Skills* (Sweet & Maxwell, 1987).

Dawkin *The Selfish Gene* (OUP, 1989).

Encyclopaedia of Forms and Precedents (Butterworths, 1994).

Exley Publications *A Feast of After Dinner Jokes* (Exley Publications, 1992).

Evans *Advocacy at the Bar* (Blackstone Press, 1992).

Fairbairn and Winch *Reading, Writing and Reasoning: A Guide for Students* (OUP, 1992).

Farrand *Emmett on Title* (Longman, 1993).

Fisher and Ury *Getting to Yes* (Business Books, 1989).

Garner *Elements of Legal Style* (OUP, 1991).

Gold, Mackie and Twining *Learning Lawyers' Skills* (Butterworths, 1989).

Gower *Fowler's Modern English Usage* (OUP, 1965).

Greenbaum and Whitcut *Gowers, The Complete Plain Words* (Penguin, 1987).

Gregory R (ed) *The County Court Practice* (Butterworths, 1998).

Harvey et al *Business Law and Practice* (Jordans, 1997).

Holland and Webb *Learning Legal Rules* (Blackstone Press, 1996).

Hyam *Advocacy Skills* (Blackstone Press, 1995).

Inns of Court *Advocacy, Conference Skills, Negotiation, Opinion Writing and Professional Conduct* (Blackstone Press, 1997).

Jacob et al *Supreme Court Practice 1998* (Sweet & Maxwell, 1998).

Jones *Lawyers' Skills* (Blackstone Press, 1997).

Jowitt's Dictionary of English Law (Sweet & Maxwell, 1977).

Judicial Studies Board Guidelines for the Assessment of Damages in Personal Injury Cases (Blackstone Press, 1994).

Kemp *Kemp and Kemp on the Quantum of Damages* (Sweet & Maxwell, 1998).

Kenny and Hewitson *Conveyancing* (Jordans, 1997).

Law Society *Guide to the Professional Conduct of Solicitors* (1996).

Lee and Fox *Learning Legal Skills* (Blackstone Press, 1994).

Legal Aid Board *The Legal Aid Handbook 1997* (Sweet & Maxwell, 1997).

Levi *The Periodic Table* (Abacus Books, 1991).

Maslow *Towards a Psychology of Being* (D van Nostrand, 1968).

Mauet *Fundamentals of Trial Techniques* (West Publishing Co, 1989).

Mayson *Personal Management Skills* (Blackstone Press, 1992).

Mayson, French and Ryan *Company Law* (Blackstone Press, 1997).

Melville *The Draftsman's Handbook* (Oyez Longman, 1991).

Munkman *The Technique of Advocacy* (Butterworths, 1991).

Murphy *A Practical Approach to Evidence* (Blackstone Press, 1992).

Murphy and Barnard *Evidence and Advocacy* (Blackstone Press, 1994).

Napley *The Technique of Persuasion* (Sweet & Maxwell, 1991).

National Consumer Council *Plain English for Lawyers* (NCC, 1990).

Neighbour *The Inner Consultation* (MTP Press, 1988).

O'Hare and Hill *Civil Litigation* (Longman, 1991).

Osbornes Concise Law Dictionary (Sweet & Maxwell, 1993).

Pannett *Managing the Law Firm* (Blackstone Press, 1992).

Peck *The Road Less Travelled* (Simon and Schuster, 1978).

Pennington *Pennington's Company Law* (Butterworths, 1990).

Ramage *Kelly's Draftsman* (Butterworths, 1993).

Richman et al *Stone's Justices' Manual* (Butterworths, 1998).

Robins *Personal Power* (Robins Research International, 1989).

Rogers and Freiberg *Freedom to Learn* (Merrill, New York, 1994).

Rose *Pleadings Without Tears* (Blackstone Press, 1997).

Ross *Drafting and Negotiating Commercial Leases* (Butterworths, 1994).

Sprack *Emmins on Criminal Procedure* (Blackstone Press, 1997).

Sherr *Advocacy* (Blackstone Press, 1993).

    Client Interviewing for Lawyers (Sweet & Maxwell, 1986).

Silverman *Conveyancing* (Jordans, 1997).

Conveyancing Handbook (Law Society, 1997).

Handbook of Professional Conduct for Solicitors (Butterworths, 1992).

Sime *A Practical Approach to Civil Procedure* (Blackstone Press, 1997).

Steiner *Textbook on EEC Law* (Blackstone Press, 1996).

Steusser *An Introduction to Advocacy* (Law Book Company, 1993).

Storey *Conveyancing* (Butterworths, 1992).

Taylor *Parker's Modern Conveyancing Precedents* (Butterworths, 1989).

Taylor *Parker's Modern Wills Precedents* (Butterworths, 1987).

Thompson *Chagin Universities: From Evolution to Revolution,* chapter I in Armstrong Brown and Thompson *Facing up to radical changes in universities and colleges* (Kogan Page, 1997).

Tunkel *Legal Research* (Blackstone Press, 1992).

Vallins *Better English* (Pan, 1963).

Wasik *Emmins on Sentencing* (Blackstone Press, 1993).

Whitehouse *Revenue Law* (Butterworths, 1995).

INDEX